CW01655525

EXPANDED & UPDATED GRANDE MARQUE EDITION

A COMPREHENSIVE FAN GUIDE TO THE GREATEST SPY SHOW OF THE 1960s

QUITE QUITE FANTASTIC!

THE AVENGERS FOR MODERN VIEWERS

MICHAEL SCOTT PHILLIPS

**"The Avengers are indestructible. You are not. Remember this.
Do not try to imitate them."**

Cover Design, Graphic Design & Layout by Michael Scott Phillips

First Printing—2018
Ebook Edition/Second Printing—2019
Grande Marque Edition—2024

HARDCOVER ISBN 979-8-9913100-0-0
PAPERBACK ISBN 979-8-9913100-1-7

GR|OWL
BOOKS

Published by GR|OWL BOOKS
a division of Torc Books
Atlanta, GA

CONTENTS

ACKNOWLEDGEMENTS

Thank you to **Chad Moore** and **Keith Phillips**
for providing the first feedback on my work and encouraging me to continue.

And a very big thank you to fellow *Avengers* enthusiast and writer **Alan Hayes**
for all your support, feedback, and the wealth of information that you provided
while I was researching and writing this book.

FOREWORD TO THE GRANDE MARQUE EDITION

The truth be told about what happens in the heart and mind of a writer when he finishes a book is that he almost immediately begins to think of what he could have done better. Such thoughts are not easily suppressed even when they seem absurd on their face; we're always in two minds about whether we're finished or not, even while we bask in the warm embrace of accomplishment. It's just that the satisfaction of the work done—for the moment, anyway—exceeds the feelings of incompletion. Otherwise, we would never stop editing. The process would simply go on and on until we'd exhausted ourselves trying to make the book become the end-all and be-all of its genre.

It is true that I'd had ideas for the original edition of *Quite Quite Fantastic!* that never quite came off. I'd originally planned for the book to be in an 8 ½ x 11 trim size because I wanted full-page original artwork to be part of the final version. That artwork didn't happen for several reasons, and, stuck with a layout in that size, I was forced to satisfy myself by saying that the larger hardcover book would harken back to the good ol' days of the 1980s when cult TV as a concept was still relatively new. But still there was way more lacking than empty pages where illustrations should have gone.

Some have assumed that prior updates to *Quite Quite Fantastic!* were new editions, but they were never intended that way at all. The idea was to adapt the book into a Kindle to broaden my sales reach and move over to Amazon KDP, with only a few minor updates to the Appendices and the transmission dates added. At best, I would consider it to be a Version 1.1.

No, this, my friends— what you hold in your hands now— is the ***true*** new edition.

Therefore, I could not confuse people by calling it a Second or Third Edition. Instead, I had to come up with something much more significant. The clue was in what the prior edition had lacked. I'd always felt that not including much, if any, information about ***The Avengers*** class factor was an oversight. Champagne, cars, clothes, and canines were indeed sorely lacking in Version 1.1.

This new version was begun over a year ago and is the culmination of months of research and many re-watches of the show with a notepad and a clipboard. I've obsessed over which leather fighting suit Honor Blackman wore in the graveyard scene in "Mandrake" more times than I can count. What is the secret of Steed's favorite champagne label Meudon & Heim? Why does Steed drive Tara's AC 428 in "Invasion of the Earthmen"? Why did he give up his dogs? All the answers are within these pages.

In the end, I added more than 70,000 words to this book—which perhaps will be enough to overcome any remaining writer's inadequacy. This new tome is so ponderous that I was forced to compromise between a more compact size and a larger format book, eventually settling on a 7" x 10" trim size with over 500 pages, making it a hefty little book indeed!

So hefty that it needed a truly grand name. And the moment of revelation came when I was re-watching one of my favorite episodes. Steed nabbed a bottle of champagne from the rack and proclaimed it "grande marque." It was as though he'd handed the bottle directly to me. Thusly, just as superior brands of champagne are indeed called "grande marque," this new edition of *Quite Quite Fantastic!* is also the best version of itself that it can be. The Grande Marque Edition!

I hope you will find it as satisfying as a glass of sparkling champagne while sat in a charmingly appointed Westminster Mews flat with John Steed and Mrs. Peel themselves.

—Michael Scott Phillips

PREFACE

This book began life online over twenty years ago. In those days, the internet was almost brand new, and websites were springing up everywhere. Everyone wanted to have their own personal forum for propagating their opinions. This was long before Facebook or the Twitter-verse started. For my part, I had long been a fan of ***The Avengers,*** having first seen the fourth season on PBS in the early to mid-eighties, and the cable network A&E had been airing episodes of the series since the early nineties. Around that time, there was also an effort to collate and re-telecine all the Honor Blackman episodes by the rights holders, and this culminated in re-airings on many networks across the globe. The second and third seasons of the series had never been aired in the United States until the A&E network did so.

This was followed later in the decade by the releases of the various episodes of the series on VHS and DVD by A&E. With the release of a new feature film and the first new comprehensive book on the show in 1998, there was something of a mini-***Avengers*** renaissance going on. With all of this to inspire me, I found myself viewing and reviewing the episodes, some of them for the first time, and in the style of early internet blogs, uploading my opinions and ideas about the series on my own website. Enlisting the aid of a friend, we reviewed over three-quarters of the episodes and provided many production background details.

The website, entitled ***The Quite Quite Fantastic Avengers Website Ltd.***, was for a time quite popular, but eventually the enthusiasm wound down. My fellow reviewer and I had a serious falling out, and the website went without updates for several years. Later, around 2006, health issues forced me to scale back many things in my life, and the website was taken down as I didn't have the time or resources to maintain it.

After completing my first novel in late 2017 and experiencing frustration in the effort to find an agent or publisher, I sought other material that could be easily collated into a book and self-published for simplicity's sake. Digging up the old HTML files for ***The Quite Quite Fantastic Avengers Website Ltd,*** with thousands of words presumably already available for publication, I decided I could air out the material and create a new comprehensive book on ***The Avengers.***

As it stood, my standards for writing have since raised, and it was immediately obvious that the material wasn't suitable for publication. In addition, I couldn't use a single word that my friend had written, and not every episode had been reviewed in any case. I decided to completely revise everything. Subsequently, every episode of ***The Avengers*** and ***The New Avengers*** was re-watched and re-reviewed. Though many reviews say much the same as the website, as in many cases my opinion has not changed very much, every single line has been updated. All production information has also been reworked based on new research in the past twenty years. Additionally, though the first season of the series was very poorly represented on the website, I have added complete synopses and episode notes for each episode. These new notes are based on production photographs and John Cura Tele-snaps that were recovered in the last decade—and there are two full episodes that have been recovered since the late nineties.

A brand-new reverse lookup for the actors, directors, and writers has been added in a section called Co-conspirators. Many prominent guest stars in ***The Avengers*** are briefly profiled.

Quite Quite Fantastic!—The Avengers for Modern Viewers is a labor of love that has taken nearly two decades in the making. I hope you'll enjoy it.

HOW TO USE THIS BOOK

The purpose behind this book is largely fun. Since the core of the book is the episode reviews that were originally written as part of ***The Quite Quite Fantastic Avengers Website Ltd*** twenty years ago, this book explores mainly what we see on screen in the television episodes. I do provide some background information on the production of the program, but I do not consider myself a researcher, nor do I want this book to be perceived as academic. *The Avengers* was a fun show, and hopefully this book will be fun too. The point of the reviews is largely to amuse the reader and to provide the modern viewer with some context illustrating why the program is still enjoyable and relevant today. At the same time, I can assure you that the book will function admirably as a proper resource for any fan, or would-be fan. One fun way of exploring this resource could be to simply read about one episode a day. This book can be used as a resource on the series or as an entertaining read that can be picked up at any time.

For each episode entry I list the episode number, followed by (in parentheses) the season number, the production order, and the transmission order—format: ### (s#.p#.t#)—followed by the title. Underneath that, the writer and the director are listed, and the remainder is organized as follows:

GUEST CAST

This includes all credited guest actors for the given episode. In some cases, where known, any uncredited actors are also included. In every case, barring missing Season One episodes (see that section), the credits are taken off screen from the actual episode as broadcast. In a handful of cases, the name of the actor has been corrected when spelled incorrectly on the actual episode credits.

PRE-TITLE/TEASER

A brief vignette which provides an encapsulation of what the episode is about and hooks the audience, followed by the episode title which often emphasizes what we've just seen, sometimes also called a "teaser." By my personal definition, "pre-title" refers to the fact that it occurs before the episode title actually appears onscreen, whether after the title sequence and before the title, or before both. All episodes of *The Avengers* and *The New Avengers* can therefore be considered to have pre-titles, although in *The New Avengers*, these take place before the title sequence. These scenes are so distinctive and engaging that I think it's important to give them special recognition regardless of where they occur.

"MRS. PEEL–WE'RE NEEDED"

Another type of vignette occurring only in Season Five—"From Venus with Love" through "Who's Who???"—in which John Steed employs various unconventional means of bringing Mrs. Peel onto a case. In prior seasons, there was usually a much longer scene in which he had to persuade either Cathy or Emma's cooperation, especially with Cathy, but Clemens and Fennell decided Steed could employ quirkier and more charming methods, procuring Mrs. Peel's involvement in less than a minute and then get on with the story proper.

SYNOPSIS

The primary purpose of the synopsis is to provide a very brief summary of what happens in the episode. This section is largely spoiler free—if for some reason you still haven't seen a program that has been off the air for five decades! If you wish, you can read the synopses, decide which episodes you want to watch, and then come back and read the review afterwards. The exception is Season One. In that section, since there are many missing episodes that are impossible to view, I have provided as long a synopsis as possible, and the length varies depending on whether a script is available or not. Several episodes have only historical synopses that have survived. In these cases, only a condensed paragraph is provided.

REVIEW

This section is a full review from approximately 400 to 1800 words. Length of the reviews varies enormously depending on what I have to say. *The Avengers* is a wonderful show, but no television show is perfect, some episodes are blander than others, and therefore provoke fewer thoughts. The intent is to provide thoughts about the quality of the episode and insight as to how it fits into the bigger picture of the whole series. Periodically, I provide contextual insights into how a given episode relates to modern viewers. The reviews are essays and give away many plot details. If you don't want spoilers, then do not read the reviews until you've watched the show.

I had fun when I was writing these reviews, and quite often my tongue was firmly in cheek. I love *The Avengers*, which is why I chose the show as the subject for this book. But, as with anything, the program had peaks and valleys. It's all at least palatable, but some are below par. You may not agree with me on many of my reviews, but hopefully they will at least put a smile on your face while you're disagreeing.

My review style is largely relativistic, humorous, and narrative in tone. I mostly commentate on what actually happens on screen, and the eras of the show and their respective tones dictate the tone of my reviews. How I review the fourth season, you will note, is entirely different (and much lengthier) from the second. As an example, because of the limited nature of the production in its first three seasons, which in the videotaped era was largely a writer's medium not a director's, comments on the directorial style and visuals of the show are limited. Therefore, I spend comparatively little time remarking on them and more on story and narrative, my primary concern being whether the narrative works and whether the dialogue is engaging. The fourth season is something of a hybrid between two eras, so my comments tend to be more narrative in tone while simultaneously having much more to mention about the visuals. During the Tara King era, the direction and visual flare are some of the best in the entire series, while the production was troubled behind the scenes, and resultingly, I spend more time commenting on direction and production issues than I would elsewhere. Likewise, the quality of production during *The New Avengers* goes down considerably when compared to standard productions of the day; it becomes the lower end of average, especially during the second season. And this fact often becomes the target of my reviews.

Finally, my voice is necessarily that of an American writer; obviously, I can have no other perspective. However, I do write in a somewhat mid-Atlantic style, and I'm prone to use to British vernacular when it seems appropriate—which is quite frequently given the nature of the program.

Missing episodes are not reviewed.

EPISODE NOTES

In the case of extant episodes, these notes are comments about the production or behind-the-scenes activities by the regular cast or crew—or possibly any comments I have that do not fit into the context of the review. In the case of missing episodes, however, I use this space to provide as much commentary as I can based on what I can glean from the production photos, Tele-snaps, scripts, and/or synopses.

CHAMPAGNE, CARS, CLOTHES, AND CANINES

Obviously, *The Avengers* is known for its luxuriousness. Steed, Mrs. Gale, Mrs. Peel, Tara King, Gambit, and Purdey wore fabulous clothes, drove stylish cars, and drank the very best of champagne. Steed also had several special canine friends during his time working for the Ministry. All of the best of the four Cs are covered in this section under most episode entries to as reasonably a comprehensive level as space allows. I'll also have an overall cars and fashion section for each season. Typically, I'm only going to write about the cars driven and the clothes worn by the regular cast, but occasionally other automobiles and fashion will be discussed. Also, since I love vintage film cameras, I'll periodically identify those cameras used by the Avengers and people around them.

The emphasis of this section will change as the series progresses, depending on the era of the show. For example, there are precious few cars and very little champagne during the Honor Blackman years, but there's still plenty of fashion and the highest concentration of canines. On the other hand, during the Diana Rigg years, the cars and champagne come very much to the forefront along with the fashion, and dogs practically vanish. Plus, access to extensive production photographs for the Honor Blackman era made for a more comprehensive take on the fashions worn in that season than would otherwise be possible with rather fuzzy 405-line video.

TAG SCENE

Another short vignette that served as a humorous epilogue. These scenes usually took place in one of the main character's apartments and involved humor and more casual activities such as going out to dinner or driving in one of Steed's cars.

In Season Four, they usually involved Steed and Mrs. Peel returning home in an unconventional vehicle, such as a canoe, go-kart, or Mini Moke. In later seasons, they typically took place back at one of their flats. Only rarely did they even reference the narrative of the episode proper, and even then did so only indirectly, such as Mrs. Peel's 'invisibility experiment' in "The See-Through Man" or the fog in Tara's apartment in "Fog."

Perhaps a few readers will be annoyed by no entries for Seasons One through Three. In this writer's opinion, only Seasons Four through Seven of *The Avengers* have formal tag scenes. Sometimes, Seasons One through Three would have a 'wrapping up' scene which might be considered a semi-formal tag scene, but these scenes were in fact closer to the function of a denouement and lacked the standalone distinction of their filmed counterparts. The distinction is that the narrative of the episode could easily survive their loss. As for episodes of *The New Avengers,* they tended to end abruptly with no denouement or epilogue at all.

QUOTES

Under this heading, I list a series of quotes that I feel are the funniest, the wittiest, the most groan-worthy, or the most intriguing or memorable. They are presented without context to encourage you to hunt for them on your own. It's well-worth the trip, and you may find your own favorites along the way.

CLEARANCE LEVEL

The quality of the episode is rated by a 'clearance level' icon. The 'Red Card' (from "The Positive Negative Man") represents the highest grade of episode—Class A (John Steed), a must see. The other icons are Class B (Junior Agent), Class C (Talented Amateur), Class D (Trainee), and Class F (Unskilled Assistant), representing very good, good, mediocre, and poor respectively. Missing episodes are not graded.

The following headings are only relevant to Season One:

SURVIVING FOOTAGE AND MATERIALS

Under this heading, I will list what survives in the archives for a given episode: scripts; production photographs; Tele-snaps; and synopses.

ADAPTATIONS AND RECONSTRUCTIONS

Big Finish audio has reconstructed all of the missing episodes as audio plays. Also, the various StudioCanal DVDs and Blu-rays have reconstructions using the scripts, synopses, Tele-snaps, production photographs, and new narration. Under this heading, I have listed what reconstructions exist and where to find them.

TRANSMISSION ORDER VERSUS PRODUCTION ORDER

The controversy over non-networked television programs being listed in either transmission order or production order is practically as old as television fandom. ITV television in Britain in the sixties (and for decades thereafter) was not networked—meaning that the programs were not shown in the same order on the same days and times from one region of the United Kingdom to the other. Although *The Avengers* was typically shown on Saturdays at 10 pm, the specific episode aired was inconsistent from region to region and the time and date would vary based on the individual schedules of each broadcaster. Thus, the episode that was shown in the Midlands one week might have been different from what was shown in London or from what was shown in Scotland.

This has created some amount of controversy about the order of episodes in any episode guide, not just for *The Avengers*, but every ITV show from this period. And not only has it created controversy about the order of the episodes but even what constitutes a season of the program. The standard course that ITV television fandom has chosen today is to simply evade the issue altogether and use production order. This is fine for the most part. The StudioCanal DVDs and Blu-rays did this. And there is some merit in watching the episodes in this order as it gives one an opportunity to observe the changes in the program's production as it evolved. While using production dates might be necessary in some cases where the earliest transmission date is not known, in the case of *The Avengers*, we have all the necessary earliest transmission dates, and an episode guide ordered by transmission dates can be assembled. Personally, I feel it's worth the effort. Transmission order is frequently an indication of the vision of the broadcaster and/or producers. In most cases, there is a measure of continuity that is being conveyed.

I am well-aware of the fact that some episodes were transmitted in the United States before they were transmitted in the United Kingdom. I am also sympathetic to the fact that other countries, such as France or Germany, had completely different transmission dates and may be used to seeing the episodes in a certain order inconsistent with the initial UK transmissions. It is for all these reasons that production dates have generally become the default. Nevertheless, I have decided to go against the grain and use transmission dates for this guide.

However, even if one resolves the issue of transmission or production dates, there is another issue related to this, that of six or seven seasons. It has been argued that using production dates resolves this issue and necessarily forces the convention of six seasons with all the color Diana Rigg episodes being one group. While it is entirely possible that this was the intention of Associated British Corporation when they filmed those episodes, it is also true that there was a six-week filming break in between the two batches of episodes as well as a five-month gap in transmission dates. Additionally, there were minor stylistic changes in the tone of the episodes after the filming break, likely in response to ITV executives asking Brian Clemens and Albert Fennell to tone down the fantasy elements.

It should be said that none of this "proves" anything. The decision of how to represent episodes of *The Avengers* can be decided arbitrarily if need be, and it seems that the fandom has by-and-large done this. (For an example involving another program, the official fan club for the 1967 ITV show *The Prisoner* has an officially sanctioned production-based viewing order.) And thus, other products associated with *The Avengers* and other ITV programs will likely ignore what is printed here and continue with the established convention.

Nevertheless, I feel that there is considerable merit in establishing a viable transmission-order episode guide, and by exploring the background behind how the episodes were produced and transmitted we are provided an intriguing look inside the history of the program. For more on the issue of six or seven seasons, please see the relevant chapter, ***Are There Six or Seven Seasons?***

A NOTE ABOUT TRANSMISSION DATES

For many of the reasons noted above, it has been very difficult to pin down UK transmission dates—even within a given region the broadcast day of the week was often inconsistent—and, over the past several decades, much research has been undertaken to discover the earliest transmission dates. Recently, researchers have reconstructed the complete dates for the earliest ITV broadcasters in the UK. Mostly, that broadcaster was the London area, although, for Season One, it was Granada, and, in some rare instances, the Midlands was indeed the earliest transmitter, such as "Hostage" and "The Gladiators." The UK transmission dates for these three regions are the ones used in this volume as appropriate. For the US, I have used the New York City transmission dates, although, in the vast majority of cases, *The Avengers* was networked throughout the country.

It has to be said that currently every single printed resource of which I'm personally aware is incorrect on this subject, including previous editions of this book! Most print books on *The Avengers*, going back to the Dave Rogers books printed in the eighties, used dates from the Midlands, which usually ran a day or two behind London. I, too, used those dates by referencing those prior resources. I was very surprised to find that the dates I had were incorrect, and, since then, I have personally verified as much of the new data as I could by utilizing online digitized versions of the London edition of the TV Times. Therefore, do not be surprised if you find transmission dates in this volume that are a few days earlier than you recall. Mostly, however, this is only the case for seasons four, five, and six of *The Avengers*, and both seasons of *The New Avengers*. None of the changed dates affected the ordering of *The Avengers*; however, it did cause "The Gladiators" (from the second season of *The New Avengers*) to shift.

Rest assured, for now, that you have the lastest research on transmission data at your fingertips in this book. If there are further developments in this regard, I plan to update the information in subsequent editions.

WHY ARE SO MANY EPISODES MISSING?

The reasons for this are somewhat shrouded in mystery, and no one is one-hundred-percent certain how many episodes were archivally telerecorded to film in the first place. It should be noted that missing episodes are not at all uncommon for sixties British television. Huge swaths of British television history—mostly from prior to 1970—have been lost from both the BBC and ITV. The reasons for this are multitudinous but can be summarized as follows:

- Television was considered an ephemeral medium, much like a stage play, especially when the programs were live or 'live-to-tape.'
- The laws in the UK were such that repeats were considered very expensive as nearly everyone involved in production (actors, writers, etc.) required a royalty for subsequent re-airings. Therefore, the programs were not generally prepared with repeats in mind.
- Videotapes were so expensive that the only way to justify their cost was their reusability. Such tapes in the early sixties cost £100 each (approx. £2,200 or $3000 in today's money). Most such tapes were eventually reused for other programs once the episode had aired.
- Television broadcasters, specifically the BBC, ironically did not consider 16mm kinescopes/telerecordings (the other way to preserve programs) to be broadcast quality, despite their being the main recording media used for overseas sales.
- Constant drives for more archival space meant that television shows were prioritized for continued storage very judiciously, often resulting in more films being scrapped than preserved.
- In the early seventies, with all British channels broadcasting in color, black and white programming was considered undesirable and of less value.

- The revolution of home video was still well over a decade away, and in the era before VCRs, overseas sales drove the archive selection process. As soon as sales dried up, any films not producing money and taking up space were at risk.

Taking all of this under consideration, fans should probably consider themselves lucky that all of Honor Blackman's era survives—"The Golden Fleece" being the only episode that momentarily evaded re-discovery sometime in the early 1990s. The first season of *The Avengers* was never sold to any other countries, and it was likely that making telerecordings of this season was thus not considered a priority. On a positive note, the recent return of "Tunnel of Fear" provides fans of *The Avengers* with some small hope that other Season One episodes might reappear at some point in the future.

Thankfully, the success of subsequent seasons prompted scrupulous preservation of all material from the program, the money made from overseas sales being a significant driver. This change in priorities was apparently too late to preserve the bulk of episodes from the first season but ensured that the episodes of Cathy Gale, Venus Smith, Dr. King, and the entirety of the filmed era lived on.

Many episodes of other great 1960s British television have also been lost, including episodes of ***Adam Adamant Lives!*, *Doctor Who*, *Up Pompeii*, *Z Cars*, *Dixon of Dock Green*, *Not Only... But Also*, *Steptoe and Son*, *No Hiding Place*,** and ***Out of the Unknown***. The trend continued into the seventies with some programs like ***Doomwatch*** and ***Ace of Wands***. By the late seventies, the devastation was largely over, but the losses were massive. Fans of ***Doctor Who*** (Sydney Newman's other brainchild) have long been aware of the sad fact of that program's archival status, and no other British television program has received more attention in that regard, mainly due to its mass cult appeal (as well as the number of losses). For those seeking clarification on this subject in general (and specifically with regard to ***Doctor Who***), there is a definitive book on the subject of missing ***Doctor Who*** episodes, ***Wiped! Doctor Who's Missing Episodes*** by Richard Molesworth. While this is of course a different program (and the BBC as opposed to ITV), the production processes for television in the era were largely the same, and this book will likely provide some answers.

It also has to be said that American television was not immune to missing episodes. Many episodes of talk shows, soap operas, game shows, and other videotaped programs no longer exist for very similar reasons—the videotapes were regularly reused by such programs right through the 1970s. And going back to the earliest days of American television, there is, of course, much missing before the techniques of making permanent recordings became possible, i.e. the first video tape recorders and kinescope methods. What saved the bulk of post-1950s American television from a similar fate to British programming was the fact that commercial television allowed for the high cost of regularly filming on 35mm film, a medium which produced shows simply too expensive to be thrown out casually. And, of course, film couldn't be recorded over like videotape.

WHERE SHOULD NEW VIEWERS BEGIN?

In any other series, the answer would be obvious—at the beginning. Unfortunately, with *The Avengers*, this is a vexed question, one that is compounded by two factors: a. most of the first season is missing, and b. the first three seasons are multi-camera videotaped productions, which might feel ancient to newer viewers. You literally can't start from the beginning, and you may not want to start with Season Two because you'll find viewing the production quality difficult.

My advice is to ask yourself— 'Would watching something with roughly the same production values as William Hartnell-era ***Doctor Who*** make it hard for me to enjoy the show?'

If yes, then perhaps start with the filmed era and Season Four. "The Town of No Return" is a fan favorite and a great place to start. It introduces the delectable Mrs. Peel and sells the chemistry between the regular characters and the general concept of the show perfectly. Once you've enjoyed that episode, you're more than likely to find yourself binging the remainder of the season and the entire filmed era. Then you can go back and explore selected samples of the videotaped era, or the whole thing if you like. Some viewers might need to be a fan already before they can find the will to watch very early television.

If no, lower production values aren't your problem, then start with Season Two in transmission order. "Mr. Teddy Bear" is a fantastic episode to start out with. Cathy Gale is a revelation and the script is near perfect. It also has much of the general weirdness that would come to be associated with the show more heavily in the future.

If on the other hand, none of that matters to you and you're a real completist and a veteran of multi-camera 405-line videotaped productions, you could start with Act 1 of "Hot Snow" and take them in order, even listening to the Big Finish audio recreations of Season One as you go.

The important thing is that you start watching somewhere, because you don't want to miss one of television's all-time classics.

POLICE SURGEON

The Origin of *The Avengers*

The roots of ***The Avengers*** are planted in the 1960 drama series ***Police Surgeon***. While there is no direct continuity narratively or otherwise, ***Police Surgeon*** was a series that was specifically invented as a vehicle for Associated British Corporation's newest star—Ian Hendry. Like ***The Avengers***, the show was shepherded into being under Sydney Newman's reign as Drama Supervisor, and it was he that commissioned the program from writer Julian Bond, who initially served as producer.

The show was much more centered in the British kitchen sink realist movement than would be ***The Avengers***, and primarily focused on the plights of 'social misfits' with Hendry as Dr. Geoffrey Brent, a sympathetic doctor working for the London Metropolitan Police.

When Julian Bond tired of his role of producer, Newman then assigned Leonard White to the job. Though the first episode, "Easy Money," did not receive good reviews and the show never made it into the top ten, ***Police Surgeon*** was steady in the ratings throughout its short run. Unfortunately, Bond had secured a consultation deal with a real-life police surgeon. Though half of everything Bond earned was being shared with this consultant, the real life "Dr. Brent" nevertheless started to create trouble. Frustrated and not able to work out a deal with the consultant, Newman then pulled the plug on the show after only thirteen episodes. Nevertheless, he insisted that Hendry be showcased in another program.

Within weeks, a new concept had emerged with Hendry as its star and White as the producer—this became ***The Avengers***. Though qualities of realism would persist in proportions throughout the first few seasons of ***The Avengers***, they would ultimately diminish as elements of the bizarre took over, morphing into the hyperreal, and then into the surreal. This process began as early as the first season, as we can now see from the surviving footage, with a carnival hypnotist producing somnolent thieves straight out of ***The Cabinet of Dr. Caligari***. In the end, ***The Avengers*** would go against trend, finally becoming the fantasy program that it needed to be in order to capture the hearts of generations of television viewers.

As for the one surviving example of ***Police Surgeon***, "Easy Money" is a slow-moving and dialogue-heavy story revolving around an anti-social boy who needs a good talking to, which Dr. Brent ably provides. There is not a lot to see here, and it's difficult to imagine the concept going on for very long. So, in the end, it would seem that the demise of ***Police Surgeon*** was appropriate and allowed for the birth of a program that was orders of magnitude more entertaining.

SPYING THROUGH A LONG LENS

The Avengers on Videotape

The early episodes of *The Avengers* are typical of the era, production-wise. The cameras were massive, the lenses long, and the sets cramped. Hot and smoky, the studios were miniscule, and actors had to perform on hard, unforgiving flooring, necessary to enable the hulking cameras to easily glide from shot-to-shot, dragging their octopian collections of cables behind them. The sets were carefully plotted out, not for the ease of the actors but to enable those cameras to move into position swiftly. It was a dance to be performed live for the tape, which captured everything, warts and all.

Unlike film production, television in this era used the multi-camera method of shooting, always at least three cameras, often four. Scenes required that the shots be switched live via a vision mixer at a control desk. The director and his assistant would sit in the control room, watching the action on their monitors, and manually determine when to change the shot. This was an imprecise art which required a great deal of practice. Improperly done, the changes in shots could look slow or sloppy, cutting into the middle of an actor's lines. Vision mixer experts were highly valued as a result.

Additionally, actors had to be precisely on cue. Their marks were exact and unforgiving. Improvisation was deeply frowned upon. Because of the production limitations of the era, actors were required to rehearse for days before the actual recording began. Knowing their lines and their character perfectly was expected, and any acting nuances would be worked out ahead of time in multiple rehearsals in the days leading up to recording. The director needed the timing and positioning to be perfect in order to line up with his cameras at exactly the right time. Though many actors claimed that this stifled their performances, having been over-rehearsed in advance of the recording, the immediacy of the production, sometimes going out live—and always being at least live for the tapes with minimal breathing room in between scenes—prompted a kind of electric urgency that many believe enlivened the performances.

Videotape was the primary means of recording, and such tapes were remarkably expensive. Edits were rare, as they required that the tape be physically spliced, which could create complications when the tape was reused downstream. As a result, minor gaffes in the production were generally let pass, and second takes were almost unheard of anyway because they would require that the entire scene from the last recording break be restarted from the beginning. Some exterior footage was shot on film ahead of time and played into the studio recording at predetermined points via telecine equipment, and this also required exact timing, while serving as a mini-break that allowed cameras and actors to move into new positions or actors to change costumes.

From a creative perspective, there is some appeal to how these episodes were shot. Because the sets were so parsimonious and the lenses so long, there is a peering, searching, claustrophobic quality to this era of television. Wide angle shots were the province of the cinema, a luxury denied by the equipment (and sets) available. Instead, the view is intimate and personal. The viewers are flies-on-the-wall, privy to the personal dramas of the characters placed before them, drawn willingly into their lives and their turmoil. By thrusting the viewer into the middle of the action, it gives the production a visceral feel that was perfect for the hard-edged realism of the first few seasons of the show.

Due to the limitations of the studio, photographic artistry was almost entirely out, being confined to whatever the director could squeeze out of the occasional intriguing camera placements. Though direction was basic, the program did manage to be artistic often enough when pushed by an ambitious director. For example, the missing episode "Dragonsfield"—judging based on the surviving Tele-snaps—contained challenging shots and intriguing sets and scientific instruments. The Cathy Gale episode "The Golden Eggs" featured one particularly convincing scene set on a dingy street in a snow shower. Despite the move to film in 1964, which no doubt greatly enhanced the visual quality of the series, this early era of videotaped television was perfectly suited to a new concept—***The Avengers***. Gritty, dark and immersive, ***The Avengers*** combined the street-wise realism of early 1960s London with humor, wit, and espionage intrigue—hyperreal with an immediacy that hasn't been duplicated since.

SEASON ONE

26 episodes (405-line monochrome videotape, ~52 min. ea.)

Regular Cast
Ian Hendry—Dr. David Keel (episodes 1-25) *
Patrick Macnee—John Steed (episodes 1-5, 7-20, 22-26) *
Ingrid Hafner—Carol Wilson (episodes 2-4, 6-13, 15, 16, 18, 20, 22-25)
Douglas Muir—One-Ten (episode 7, 9, 14, 17, 18, 20, 22, and 24)

Produced by Leonard White
Story Editor: John Bryce, Reed de Rouen
Music: Johnny Dankworth

* although Patrick Macnee is absent from "Girl on the Trapeze" and "The Far Distant Dead" and Ian Hendry from "Dragonsfield," they are both credited in the end credits regardless.

1. **Hot Snow—w.** Ray Rigby (story by Patrick Brawn); **dir.** Don Leaver; UK tx. 7 Jan 1961; **rec.** 30 Dec 1960
2. **Brought to Book—w.** Brian Clemens (story by Patrick Brawn); **dir.** Peter Hammond; **UK tx.** 14 Jan 1961; **rec.** 12 Jan 1961
3. **Square Root of Evil—w.** Richard Harris (story by John Bryce); **dir.** Don Leaver; **UK tx.** 21 Jan 1961; **rec.** 21 Jan 1961
4. **Nightmare—w.** Terence Feeley; **dir.** Peter Hammond; **UK tx.** 28 Jan 1961; **rec.** 28 Jan 1961
5. **Crescent Moon—w.** Geoffrey Bellman & John Whitney (story by Patrick Brawn); **dir.** John Knight; **UK tx.** 4 Feb 1961; **rec.** 4 Feb 1961
6. **Girl on the Trapeze—w.** Dennis Spooner; **dir.** Don Leaver; **UK tx.** 11 Feb 1961; **rec.** 11 Feb 1961
7. **Diamond Cut Diamond—w.** Max Marquis; **dir.** Peter Hammond; **UK tx.** 18 Feb 1961; **rec.** 18 Feb 1961
8. **The Radioactive Man—w.** Fred Edge (adapted by Patrick Brawn); **dir.** Robert Tronson; **UK tx.** 25 Feb 1961; **rec.** 25 Feb 1961
9. **Ashes of Roses—w.** Peter Ling & Sheilah Ward; **dir.** Don Leaver; **UK tx.** 4 Mar 1961; **rec.** 4 Mar 1961
10. **Hunt the Man Down—w.** Richard Harris; **dir.** Peter Hammond; **UK tx.** 18 Mar 1961; **rec.** 12 Mar 1961
11. **Please Don't Feed the Animals—w.** Dennis Spooner; **dir.** Dennis Vance; **UK tx.** 1 Apr 1961; **rec.** 30 Mar 1961
12. **Dance with Death—w.** Peter Ling & Sheilah Ward; **dir.** Don Leaver; **UK tx.** 15 Apr 1961; **rec.** 13 Apr 1961
13. **One for the Mortuary—w.** Brian Clemens; **dir.** Peter Hammond; **UK tx.** 29 Apr 1961; **rec.** 26 Apr 1961
14. **The Springers—w.** John Whitney & Geoffrey Bellman; **dir.** Don Leaver; **UK tx.** 13 May

1961; **rec.** 11 May 1961

15. **The Frighteners**—**w.** Berkeley Mather; **dir.** Peter Hammond; **UK tx.** 27 May 1961; **rec.** 25 May 1961
16. **The Yellow Needle**—**w.** Patrick Campbell (adapted by Reed de Rouen); **dir.** Don Leaver; **UK tx.** 10 Jun 1961; **rec.** 8 Jun 1961
17. **Death on the Slipway**—**w.** James Mitchell; **dir.** Peter Hammond; **UK tx.** 24 Jun 1961; **rec.** 22 Jun 1961
18. **Double Danger**—**w.** Gerald Verner (adapted by John Lucarotti); **dir.** Roger Jenkins; **UK tx.** 8 Jul 1961; **rec.** 6 Jul 1961
19. **Toy Trap**—**w.** Bill Strutton; **dir.** Don Leaver; **UK tx.** 22 Jul 1961; **rec.** 20 Jul 1961
20. **Tunnel of Fear**—**w.** John Kruse; **dir.** Guy Verney; **UK tx.** 5 Aug 1961; **rec.** 3 Aug 1961
21. **The Far Distant Dead**—**w.** John Lucarotti; **dir.** Peter Hammond; **UK tx.** 19 Aug 1961; **rec.** 14 Aug 1961
22. **Kill the King**—**w.** James Mitchell; **dir.** Roger Jenkins; **UK tx.** 2 Sep 1961; **rec.** 30 Aug 1961
23. **Dead of Winter**—**w.** Eric Paice, **dir.** Don Leaver; **UK tx.** 9 Dec 1961; **rec.** 18 Oct 1961
24. **The Deadly Air**—**w.** Lester Powell, **dir.** John Knight; **UK tx.** 16 Dec 1961; **rec.** 7 Sep 1961
25. **A Change of Bait**—**w.** Lewis Davidson, **dir.** Don Leaver; **UK tx.** 23 Dec 1961; **rec.** 20 Sep 1961
26. **Dragonsfield**—**w.** Terence Feeley, **dir.** Peter Hammond; **UK tx.** 30 Dec 1961; **rec.** 27 Sep 1961

SEASON NOTES

The Avengers had its beginnings in the demise of *Police Surgeon,* having been quickly cobbled together by Leonard White and Sydney Newman to provide a similar role for their star Ian Hendry after the earlier series failed. Newman liked the name "the avengers" because he thought it implied revenge or vigilante action of some type, and indeed, the initial storyline does start out that way—the basis of "Hot Snow" being Dr. Keel's attempt to bring his fiancée's killer to justice. And, though it is a snappy and provocative title, right from the beginning the program seemed to be about so much more than that.

To large degree, *The Avengers* managed to maintain the realism that was such a big part of *Police Surgeon*. However, *The Avengers* switched gears, moving away from *Police Surgeon*'s real-life timbre involving 'social misfits'—a concept created as an attempt to show viewers a slice of life in Britain that was seldom seen otherwise—and into the area of the increasingly improbable. While it's likely that this switch in tone was initially to evade any connections to *Police Surgeon* that might cause complications for its creator Julian Bond (who was trying to avoid a contractual dispute with a paid consultant), it is equally likely that producer Leonard White and Drama Supervisor Sydney Newman wanted to continue the connection to the bizarre while giving the show more of an action-oriented adventure style. Eager to keep the unusual within the series, they turned the concept about ninety-degrees counterclockwise. In deference to the kitchen sink realism that made viewers flies-on-a-wall looking in on lives that were more freakish than their own, they were instead exploring the fantasy adventures of two people who were having enormously fun adventures. Swept along with the action, the audience lived the adventures by proxy.

The first season of *The Avengers* shied away from general policework and veered in the direction of relatively small-scale (for the time being) espionage. Indeed, *The Avengers* in its early days was more MI5 than MI6, dealing primarily with larceny, racketeering, prostitution, drug smuggling and blackmail, but, even in the first season's opening half, there were already provocative elements that hinted of the hyperreal and surreal far beyond that of everyday life, and soon after the plots began to move beyond Britain's borders.

Escapist fun, mystery and elements of the fantastic steadily crept in as the series progressed. Previously, it had been thought that these aspects were introduced later as the show became more popular and then later went to film, but a thorough examination of the available scripts and the recent recovery of "Tunnel of Fear" seem to indicate otherwise. That story involved a case of organized larceny by hypnotism, which is pretty bizarre by even Season Two or Three standards, and we know that other episodes dealt with radioactive contamination, secret neo-Nazi plots, deadly viruses, and space exploration research—all subjects that wouldn't be out of place in later years. And then, there's "Please Don't Feed the Animals," a quirky humorous turn for the series that seems to have fun with things like crocodile pit death traps and salacious strip clubs.

How much of this was inspired by the growing popularity of the James Bond novels is uncertain, but certainly the UK (and indeed the Western world) was about to engage in an all-out spy craze that would dominate television for the next decade. ***The Avengers*** was almost first out of the box, even if it wasn't the first to fully ripen. ***Danger Man*** had already been an international hit for ITC Entertainment the prior year. ***The Saint*** would be another hit for that production company the following year, and this would be followed by a plethora of similar concepts on both sides of the Atlantic, including ***The Baron, Man From U.N.C.L.E., Callan, Department S, I Spy, Mission Impossible, Get Smart, The Girl from U.N.C.L.E., The Prisoner,*** and ***The Persuaders!***

Unfortunately, we can't see very much of these early spy efforts of John Steed and Dr. Keel. Barring three complete episodes, we can only examine the surviving evidence in the form of scripts, John Cura Tele-snaps, and production photos. Most of the episodes were lost, and unlike Newman's other cult creation, ***Doctor Who,*** none of the episodes were recorded on audiotape. However, based on the surviving material, we have tantalizing hints that this season was just as creatively successful as seasons two or three, and possibly a good deal more.

One factor that is apparent from the surviving evidence is that in the first half of the season Steed and Keel seldom worked directly together throughout the entire narrative of a given episode. They would alternate, sharing the spotlight, but by midseason this would appear to have been resolved, and the format would resemble later seasons much more closely, with both leads working together much more extensively. While Dr. Keel's nurse Carol Wilson was not at all a talented spy, merely plucky and brave, she did occasionally assist either Steed or Keel in their adventures, and this pointed the way towards the female partners of the future, and it helps to make the exploration of Venus Smith's character, another *untalented* amateur, a lot more understandable.

Many of the writers working on this season will be familiar to fans of the filmed era—Brian Clemens, Dennis Spooner, and Richard Harris all make noteworthy contributions—and directors Don Leaver and Peter Hammond would direct the bulk of the episodes for the next three seasons. Together, these men, along with Ian Hendry and Patrick Macnee, were the talent that set ***The Avengers*** on its established course, one that would endure for almost the entirety of the 1960s.

INTRODUCING DR. DAVID KEEL

The story of Dr. Keel is one that is integral to the history of ***The Avengers,*** given that the series was initially focused squarely upon him, and it was he who first met John Steed and discovered an entire underground network of spy activities within the streets of London.

Dr. Keel was initially portrayed as an ordinary general practitioner sharing a practice in the Chelsea-Victoria district of North London with an older doctor named Dr. Tredding. The small surgery was somewhere north of the Westminster Bridge. His fiancée Peggy was initially his office assistant, and his nurse was Carol Wilson. Dr. Keel was tall, dark-haired, and wore conservative clothing. Well noted for a strong moral streak, he was often the guiding ethical force for John Steed during their brief association.

His involvement in the criminal underground began with Peggy's death at the hands of heroin smugglers after she inadvertently received a parcel of heroin accidentally delivered to Dr. Keel's partner. Keel was intent on solving Peggy's murder and through his ham-fisted efforts met John Steed, who was able to help him track down the killers and eventually break up the heroin racket. From there, they frequently worked together to bring other criminals to justice.

Dr. Keel appeared to have a thrill-seeking side brought out by the events surrounding his fiancée's death, one that was constantly stoked by his association with Steed. He frequently bristled at many of Steed's tactics, and they periodically had rows, one of which involved Keel threatening to beat "the living daylights" out of Steed. Regardless, they appeared to work very well together for the most part, each offering skills and knowledge that the other lacked.

Dr. Keel lacked most traditional crime-fighting skills, though he did possess a set of skeleton keys and appeared to speak fluent German. He also traveled internationally and had a few friends of relatively high status, including Sir Wilberforce Lungi, the prime minister of an African nation. His contributions were usually medical in nature, but he was capable of a strong arm when necessary, having played rugby when he was younger. He was stronger than most men of his size and could put up a good fight. He also was capable of astonishing bluffs based on his medical knowledge. In one incident, he was able to convince a criminal that his neck was broken.

He enjoyed sports, cigarettes, and the occasional glass of scotch. *The Avengers* novel, *Too Many Targets*, indicated that Dr. Keel had eventually left his practice and joined the World Health Organization, thus explaining why he was no longer able to work with Steed. Little more can be said about the character because the surviving material is limited to three (and one third) extant episodes, Telesnaps for the second half of the season, production photos, and eighteen extant scripts.

INTRODUCING JOHN STEED

John Steed was one of the most complex characters of 1960s television, exhibiting a multi-faceted persona with tremendous depth. Born into minor nobility, Steed attended Eton from where he was eventually expelled. He later fought in World War II, becoming a decorated veteran. He first trained with the Coldstream Guards and later transferred to Intelligence. He was then posted at RAF Camp 472 Hamelin, from where he would have been periodically dispatched to the continent for spy missions. During his participation in the war, he earned the Military Cross and the rank of Major before leaving the British Army to join the Ministry in 1945.

When first appearing in *The Avengers*, Steed was grittier and more streetwise, darker and more mysterious, a figure that would often disappear and reappear periodically to involve his uncertain cohorts within his schemes of espionage. Viewers of the later seasons of the series would scarcely recognize that Steed was a great manipulator, capable of positioning his helpers at the right place and time within a carefully constructed web designed to expose the criminals of the underworld.

However, even by the second half of the first season, he began to show signs of a fun-loving, good-humored man with a devil-may-care boyish streak. He was exceedingly charming when necessary, and capable of extraordinarily casual bluffs and feints to prompt the criminals to expose their motives. With women, he could be caddish and womanizing. However, as the series progressed and the grittiness of the early seasons diminished, replaced by much more fantastic situations, his own rough edges seemed to smooth away. His cad behavior vanished, and he cultivated the air of a perfect gentleman.

Though, early on, his wardrobe had occasionally consisted of slightly more casual garments, sometimes with a disheveled trench coat (as seen in the initial promotional photographs), he quickly transformed into a notable clotheshorse. Rakishly-dressed in sharp suits (sometimes pinstriped), a bowler hat and umbrella, he became a bon vivant, a connoisseur of the finer things in life—food, clothes, champagne.

His appreciation also extended to the women in his life, who were, like everything else Steed appreciated, the crème de la crème. The women with whom he associated were highly skilled and intelligent, academically gifted and witty, and usually possessed a greater sense of morality and fair play than he did. In their companionship, his sense of humor and boyish glee increased, and his long associations with his female partners frequently entailed rapid-fire exchanges of acid wit and humorous teasing. This reached a peak as their experiences became increasingly surreal. What else could they do, faced with situations of ever-escalating absurdity?

As far as languages, Steed understood spoken Greek. He also appeared to have a smattering of Russian and a moderate facility in French and Latin. He spoke Italian and Neapolitan fluently. He was also adept at disguise and was an expert at picking locks. Stealthy, despite his relatively large size, he was easily capable of skulking about without being observed. Though he was highly intelligent and crafty, his knowledge did not seem to spread much beyond espionage and the finer things in life. He seemed to know precisely as much as he needed in order to get the job done, and when required, he generally found partners who possessed the knowledge and skills he lacked.

Early on, little emphasis was placed on the cars he drove, but starting during his time with Cathy Gale, he was shown driving Bentley and Rolls Royce cars. He maintained well-appointed but modest residences in the mews throughout *The Avengers* but moved to a country estate with stables and horses in *The New Avengers*. By that time, he had also moved on to driving Jaguars. The decor of his homes betrayed a great love of the traditional old-world British empire days, and his persona and appearance were part of a stylized representation of the then fading British gentry.

In the early days, he seemed to manipulate circumstances so that he did not directly endanger himself. However, after becoming involved with partners who were extremely adept at martial arts, fights became more common and his fighting style was revealed to be highly eclectic, and though he was familiar with martial arts techniques such as judo, mostly he used a mixture of fisticuffs and unconventional strikes with his umbrella or steel-lined bowler hat. Typically, he eschewed guns, preferring to use them only occasionally. He would instead frequently use various props or improvised weapons nearby, such as a pot of hot oil in a kitchen or a ping-pong ball gun in the toy section in a department store.

His umbrella hid within a rapier-like sword that was nevertheless not used for violence onscreen, possibly because of a production team edict against visible blood (infrequently broken). His umbrella also contained spy devices such as hidden cameras and an audio recording device. And, every once and a while, he would produce some odd spy invention such as exploding cigarettes. Thus, he was a very nimble opponent who seldom met his match, most often being only temporarily defeated by either surprise or overwhelming opposition.

Early on, he reported mostly to an even more mysterious man than himself called One-Ten, who was later revealed to be part of a network of similarly named agents—One-Six, One-Seven, One-Twelve, and One-Fifteen. He was observed reporting in with the code name 'Delta' in "Tunnel of Fear." There was also another official overseer named Charles who would lose his position when he mistakenly accused Steed of being a traitor. However, by the time Steed began working with Emma

Peel, his bosses disappeared; perhaps by then, he had earned the right to be self-directing. This would later change once more as he began reporting to another high-level Ministry official, code-named 'Mother,' though this might have been for Tara King's benefit and education.

In his later years, he became more detached from everyday field espionage and primarily took on a supervisory role, guiding his partners with his superior knowledge and experience. This was no doubt due to a higher position within the Ministry, and in many ways, this brought out a more clinical, serious side of John Steed that harkened back to his darker roots. Throughout it all, however, he maintained his core persona and dignity, even when thrust into a setting such as 1977 Ontario where his old-world style was as masterful a demonstration of casual incongruency as conceivable.

ICONIC TITLES

In this season, the titles were composed of ink drawings that were based on photographs taken during the first publicity photo session in the winter of 1961. Taken in various locations, including the Berwick Street Market, Bourchier Street, Moroni's Newsagent at 68 Old Compton Street, and St. Anne's Car Park on Dean Street, these photographs featured Hendry and Macnee wearing trenchcoats wrapped tightly around them against the cold, and this image would dominate thoughts about how they dressed throughout the history of *Avengers* fandom despite the fact that they seldom dressed this way again (judging by the remainder of the production photographs). British jazz musician Johnny Dankworth provided the memorable theme music.

CHAMPAGNE, CARS, CLOTHES, AND CANINES

Quite naturally it's hard to provide a full accounting with regard to this season given that so many episodes are missing. Nevertheless, it is possible to glean a fair amount from the surviving production photographs, Tele-snaps, and some of the scripts. That said, it appears that John Steed started out nearly from the beginning with an impeccable sense of haute couture. Generally speaking, he would wear three-piece suits of finer cloth, and his umbrella and bowler show up well before the end of the season. Dr. Keel, on the other hand, dressed in a much simpler fashion, usually with two-piece suits in darker colors and common-or-garden striped ties. For Steed, there are far fewer outfit changes than there would be in subsequent seasons, perhaps two outfits per episode generally, and Dr. Keel tends to wear the same thing throughout the entire runtime.

Please note that it is particularly difficult to identify individual clothing pieces because of the blurry nature of Tele-snaps and telerecorded material. The production photos are usually of much higher resolution, but these do not exist for all episodes, and not all of them depict every outfit worn. Therefore, it may be impossible to determine precisely which outfits reappear and when, particularly when one takes into consideration the mixing and matching of clothes.

Steed has a dog named Puppy throughout much of the season, though it can be difficult to tell how long he's had her. Most of her appearances are in missing episodes, though we are fortunate to be able to see her in the recovered episode, "Tunnel of Fear." There is nothing notable in the way of champagne, and Steed is only seen with one car, the one which Harry Black steals in the same episode.

A NOTE ON SEASON ONE

Since this book is primarily about what we actually see on screen, there is comparatively little I can do with the first season. There are three (and one third) extant episodes to review here, so those are fully covered in this volume based on the available videos. The remaining episodes are missing from the archives of Studio Canal (the current rights holder) and have been missing since the days of

Associated British Corporation in the 1960s.

However, episodes 13 through 26 all have Tele-snaps taken by John Cura upon broadcast (in the Thames region), and all of these episodes, barring episode 17, "Toy Trap," have brief reconstructions on the available DVDs and Blu-rays from Studio Canal. Unlike some other television series with missing episodes, there are no known audio recordings of the original broadcasts. On the other hand, Big Finish has recorded audio adaptations of all twenty-six episodes, despite the fact that scripts exist for only fifteen missing episodes. The remainder—"Nightmare," "Crescent Moon," "Diamond Cut Diamond," "Hunt the Man Down," "Death on the Slipway," "The Far Distant Dead," "The Deadly Air," and "Dragonsfield"—have only synopses available, and this makes the audio adaptations for these episodes mostly guesswork or fresh re-imaginings. I do not consider the Big Finish audios of these episodes to be definitive for this reason, entertaining though they are, and most everything written in this volume is based on the surviving production materials; this book is primarily about the series upon original broadcast.

Since a proper review cannot be written using such inconsistent information, the section on season one will be handled differently from the other seasons in this book. For the missing episodes, I will provide as long a synopsis as is possible (this varies based on whether a script exists or not), a cast list which has been extensively crossed-checked against all available sources, and episode notes, which provide some thoughts and background details based on the spotty materials available. Obviously, camera scripts and Tele-snaps provide the most information, production photos are also helpful, but for some episodes, literally nothing exists other than synopses, so data for these episodes will necessarily be light.

> Readers who wish a more comprehensive guide to Season One should look no further than *Two Against the Underworld: The Collected Unauthorised Guide to The Avengers Series 1* by Richard McGinlay, Alan Hayes and Alys Hayes. The research within that book is exhaustive and thorough, and there is precious little sense in my repeating all of it here. Note that in the case of discrepancies between *Two Against the Underworld* and any other publications with regard to Season One, I have deferred to McGinlay, Hayes, and Hayes, since their volume is obviously the better organized resource. Thus, all guest cast lists, transmission dates, and other data herein have been checked against that volume for accuracy. Nevertheless, *Quite Quite Fantastic!* provides a reasonably complete reconstruction of Season One with *Two Against the Underworld* being the next step for the ardent fan.

JOHN CURA'S TELE-SNAPS

There will be many references to Tele-snaps inside this section on Season One of *The Avengers*. So, what are they? In brief, John Cura was an enterprising photographer in the 1940s, 50s, and 60s, who, in search of a means of making money from his passion, began taking photographs of television programs from the screen of his television receiver, which he then sold back to the rights-holders (and other interested parties) in the form of prints as a permanent record of the original transmission. This may seem strange today, but in the era before video recording technologies and the permanent preservation of television programs this was literally the only way that the original broadcast could be retained in any form.

As programs began to be recorded permanently on videotape and film kinescopes, Tele-snaps were still valued by the show's producers, directors and designers as a means of personally maintaining a record of the programs they had worked on. Accessing the original videotapes or films for these programs was not easy even for those that worked in television, and Tele-snaps were more convenient for quick access. Due to the reuse of videotapes and the mass junking of film telerecordings in the 1960s and 70s, in many cases, these Tele-snaps remain the only surviving visual record of thousands of British television episodes. For thirteen episodes of *The Avengers*, discounting publicity photographs taken during rehearsal, Cura's work remains the only surviving visual record of the original broadcasts.

Cura maintained something of a photographic empire through this business endeavor for almost three decades, and his service was regularly included in budgets for British programs in the 1960s; he was even periodically referred to in BBC memorandums. Cura used specialized equipment, and as far as anyone knows no one else did this kind of work. The original negatives for his Tele-snaps have been lost, and only contact prints survive.

In the 1950s, Cura co-wrote three volumes designed to help television viewers get better reception from their receivers—***Television Picture Faults, Correcting Television Picture Faults,*** and ***Improve Your TV Reception***—which sold into the tens of thousands of copies. He passed away in 1969 from colon cancer.

THE MOST MISSED MISSING EPISODES OF THE SEASON

1. "Toy Trap"
2. "Dead of Winter"
3. "Dragonsfield"
4. "Hot Snow" (Acts 2 and 3)
5. "Brought to Book"
6. "Square Root of Evil"
7. "The Radioactive Man"
8. "Dance with Death"
9. "Please Don't Feed the Animals"
10. "Double Danger"

1 (1.1.1) HOT SNOW

Written by Ray Rigby (based on a story by Patrick Brawn)
Directed by Don Leaver

MINISTRY RECORDS ARE INCOMPLETE

GUEST CAST

Philip Stone (Dr. Richard Tredding), Catherine Woodville (Peggy Stevens), Godfrey Quigley (Spicer), Murray Melvin (Charlie), Charles Wade (Johnson), Alister Williamson (Detective Superintendent Wilson), Moira Redmond (Stella), Astor Sklair (Detective Sergeant Rogers), June Monkhouse (Mrs. Simpson), Robert James (The Big Man)

PRE-TITLE/TEASER

None, the title appears almost immediately onscreen after the title sequence. There is no "set-up" for the episode that requires the emphasis of the title appearing.

SYNOPSIS

Part 1—Due to a mistake, heroin traffickers deliver a shipment of heroin to Dr. Keel's partner, Dr. Tredding, and their assistant Peggy receives it. Subsequently, the criminals send Spicer to retrieve the package before anyone opens it. Spicer, creeping from a side street and slipping into the interior of the office, is unable to do so without being seen. Dr. Tredding has the parcel now, and there is no chance of getting it back. Fearing that Peggy might recognize Johnson, the man who delivered it, the criminals decide to kill her in order to eliminate the only witness.

Dr. Keel and Peggy are engaged to be married in one week's time. As Keel and Peggy stand in front of Vinson's, the jeweler's, ready to select their wedding ring, a single shot from a rifle kills Peggy. Her body collapses in Keel's arms, and he is shocked to find blood on his hands.

Part 2—Three days later, still in shock, Dr. Keel visits the police station and speaks to Detective Superintendent Wilson and Sergeant Rogers. Wilson is convinced that Peggy's murder was a 'professional job,' meaning she was killed for a specific reason, but Keel can think of nothing that would implicate her—she hadn't an enemy in the world.

Nevertheless, when he returns to his surgery, Dr. Tredding reports that the package he received contains half a pound of heroin, worth a small fortune. Somehow, Tredding has been confused for another doctor, a Dr. Treading who was discredited a number of years ago. Looking up Treading's address, Keel goes there and has an odd experience. After a mysterious man opens the door and then disappears, he finds the body of Dr. Treading in the bedroom. Immediately, a woman named Stella rings the bell, and Keel answers. She is a heroin addict looking for a fix. After Stella provides a positive identification on Treading's body, Keel queries her about Peggy's murder. Stella denies all knowledge of the incident and dashes for the door, fleeing. Soon after, the police arrive, having been tipped off by Dr. Treading. Keel reports all of what he witnessed to Wilson and Rogers. They agree that he is not involved in the murder.

When he returns to his office, he is greeted by a mysterious figure, sitting casually in an armchair. It is the same man that opened the door at Dr. Treading's house. Keel threatens to call the police, but the man intrigues him with potential information about Peggy's murder, and Keel puts the phone down. John Steed refuses to reveal his name to Dr. Keel but insists that he is 'on the side of the angels.' He asks Keel to pretend to be a doctor with shady ambitions, that he is bored with his humdrum life. Keel will receive another parcel of heroin which he is to pass on as instructed. Steed explains that by Keel insinuating himself into the heroin smuggling gang, they can both find out who killed Peggy. Keel reluctantly agrees, not certain whether he can trust Steed or not.

Part 3—The next day, Keel sends Dr. Tredding away so he can be alone in his surgery and receives the package of heroin from Johnson and Stella. Johnson asks that Keel give Stella her 'fix,' but he refuses, insisting he must examine her first.

At the gang's base, Steed is playing cards with Charlie, who is uncertain about Steed's choice of Keel as a pusher. Steed replies that a practitioner of Keel's reputation is the best kind of pusher—no one will suspect him. They continue to argue until Charlie finally concedes the point. Keel completes his examination of Stella and provides her with a legal prescription of heroin, arguing that they shouldn't 'waste' the street heroin when a prescription is possible. Steed heads to Keel's office but is tailed by Spicer on Charlie's orders.

Steed and Keel discuss the next stage of plans. Keel is to pretend to want to get out of the deal and then refuse to cooperate. Spicer reports back to Charlie that Steed has visited Keel. Later, Johnson arrives at Keel's office, and Keel refuses to help him as instructed. Steed then phones Keel and instructs him to return to the jeweler's where Peggy was killed—he wants the gang to believe that Keel is reenacting the crime in order to find her murderer. Strangely however, the gang are listening to this conversation, and Steed seems to know it. "We'll pick him up at 12:15. By 1:15, he'll be floating out on the tide," he says to them.

Despite his concerns, Keel again does as instructed. Waiting for him is a car and Spicer. Two men, Charlie and Keel's mysterious ally, stand to the side with guns drawn. He is quickly bundled into the car, but, before Spicer can do anything else, a shot rings out, and Charlie falls dead. Steed is gone, having fled the scene, and Spicer is forced to retreat as Superintendent Wilson and Sergeant Rogers arrive. The police were tipped off anonymously. Wilson and Rogers assume that the shot that hit Charlie was intended for Keel, but Keel knows better. He is certain that his shadowy friend is looking out for him. Nevertheless, Peggy's killer is still at large.

REVIEW

Little can be said about this particular story as far as visuals, since so little survives on film. I've viewed the first 15 minutes (which are all that exist) many times. Visually, the production is very similar to other British television programs of the era. It has cramped studio sets and a close-up searching quality to the visuals. I am reminded of early Hartnell-era ***Doctor Who***, and in general, it is the look of 405-line videotape.

One potential surprise to fans of this era of television is the film location footage that opens the episode, displaying a dreary London street and Spicer creeping along until he surreptitiously enters the office of our main character. The story does not possess the needed time to unfold properly and ends with the rather awkward (and silent) death of Dr. Keel's fiancée. (The silence was apparently a deliberate decision not a mistake, as the gun was supposed to have a silencer. However, this detracts from the impact, in my opinion.)

What does stand out however is the tautness of the direction, despite the limitations of the studio equipment of the day, and the skill of the actors involved. Much can still be said for the merits of the rehearse-record format of early television. Since the production would have been recorded essentially live-to-tape, the actors had to be consistently on point, and the performances are highly realistic and convincing as a result.

John Steed never shows up in the available onscreen material since he arrives in the second part, which is no longer extant. However, the script is still available, and Steed first appears undercover within the criminal organization. He is a shadowy figure, about whom Dr. Keel is initially apprehensive.

CHAMPAGNE, CARS, CLOTHES, AND CANINES

As previously mentioned, Steed does not appear in the surviving footage. However, based on the photographic evidence, Steed wears a tan weatherproofed overcoat with flap pockets at the waist and a notch collar. The sleeves have heavy stitching around the cuffs in three rings. He wears it with a white shirt and a dark tie, and it's difficult to tell what sort of suit is underneath. Dr. Keel wears a simple two-piece suit in a dark tweed with a white shirt and dark tie. When his fiancée Peggy is shot, he is wearing a long, dark woolen overcoat. Not a trench coat in sight.

No dogs for Steed yet. The crooks do, however, have a Yorkie.

SURVIVING FOOTAGE AND MATERIALS

Synopses
The first 15 minutes ('Part 1') survive as a monochrome 16mm film telerecording.
Draft Script (entitled "The Avengers") & Camera Script
Production Photographs (4)

ADAPTATIONS AND RECONSTRUCTIONS

Big Finish Audio Adaptation

2 (1.2.2) BROUGHT TO BOOK

Written by Brian Clemens (from a story by Patrick Brawn)
Directed by Peter Hammond

MINISTRY RECORDS ARE UNAVAILABLE

GUEST CAST

Carol White (Jackie), Robert James (Ronnie Vance), Charles Morgan (Nick Mason), Philip Stone (Dr. Richard Tredding), Godfrey Quigley (Spicer), Alister Williamson (Detective Superintendent Wilson), Clifford Elkin (Pretty Boy), Joyce Wong Chong (Lila), Neil McCarthy (Bart), Lionel Burns (Prentice), Michael Collins (Detective Sergeant), Redmond Bailey (Lale), Anna Shan-Khoo (2nd Chinese Girl), Charles Bird (Peters), Lawrence Archer (Johns)

PRE-TITLE/TEASER

It's not clear from the available script if there was a pre-title or not, but the episode fades in with horse racetrack stock footage and then cuts to Prentice and Pretty Boy listening to the radio for the outcome to the race.

SYNOPSIS

Part 1—At his surgery, Dr. Keel is in a contemplative mood and sits staring at a photo of his deceased fiancée Peggy. Meanwhile, Steed is at the racecourse near the bookie's stand with two attractive women at his side. Inside the bookie's office, there is a seedy scene playing out. Two gangsters, Pretty Boy and Bart, are demanding protection money from Prentice and his two assistants. Prentice is reluctant to pay though clearly terrified. He has already paid someone, he finally admits. When Pretty Boy demands to know who, another man named Mason appears with several other men. Mason reveals that he is taking over the protection racket, and they quickly overcome Pretty Boy and Bart, deeply cutting Pretty Boy's face in the process.

Back at the surgery, Dr. Keel is introduced by Dr. Tredding to their new nurse, Carol Wilson. Keel remains pensive and appears to barely notice Carol. Then, he receives an unusual call from a woman with a Chinese accent bidding him to come to the House of the Rising Sun. Despite his reservations about the call, Keel quickly leaves with his medical bag, expecting an emergency of some kind. Dr. Keel arrives at a somewhat shady establishment—a smoke-filled tea room and club bar.

After being ushered by a Chinese girl, Lila, into a quiet alcove, Keel is shocked to find himself facing a very familiar figure who finally introduces himself as John Steed. Steed says that he trusts Keel and asks him to keep an open mind—perhaps one day he will learn to trust Steed. He explains the protection racket run by Nick Mason to Keel and reveals that he is undercover as a member of that gang. He also knows that a man named Spicer killed Peggy, but the police need proof. Keel offers his help to gather more evidence. Steed provides Keel with a packet of heroin that is to be used as bait in their quest. Keel places it in his medical bag, but before they can discuss the issue further, Ronnie Vance arrives in another room, and Detective Superintendent Wilson raids the bar. Thinking fast, Keel hides the packet of heroin in a nearby bowl of peanuts. Wilson demands to search Keel's bag but finds nothing there or on his person. Satisfied that Keel is clean, Wilson leaves Vance and Keel alone.

Vance is sharp-eyed however and immediately spots the heroin. Retrieving it, he offers Keel a chance to earn the drugs back, if he will work for them, starting with fixing up Pretty Boy's face. Steed is nowhere to be found, and Keel and Vance leave for the bar to talk things over. Then, Steed reemerges with the girl Lila. "The spider or the fly...?" he asks cryptically. It is all working precisely to plan; they have each infiltrated one of the gangs.

Part 2—Back at Vance's ornate flat, Keel is stitching up Pretty Boy's face, while Vance tangles with Pretty Boy's distraught girlfriend Jackie. Elsewhere, in Mason's gaming room, he and Steed play pool, discussing the downfall of their rival gang. Steed almost trips himself up when he implies he knows about Spicer's prior murder. Pretty Boy is bandaged up by now, his wound only likely to leave a slight scar. Vance is impressed and asks Keel to be his personal physician.

A week later, Keel hastens into his office, late for his daily schedule. Dr. Tredding expresses concern with his behavior but Keel brushes him off. Awaiting Keel is Steed, who pretends to be a patient. While Keel is pretending to examine him, Steed explains the plan. Spicer is going to be sent to kill the Vance brothers tomorrow afternoon, and Keel is to leave the door to the house unlocked. In order to guarantee that the brothers are alone, the Mason gang plans a takeover bid that will draw every Vance man out. Once the Vance brothers are alone, Keel is to call Steed, then the police will move in.

The next morning, the Mason assault begins, and a number of offices associated with the Vance racket are smashed. Steed calls Keel and sends him over to Vance's house. Carol expresses worry as he leaves, knowing that he might be in trouble.

Part 3—As soon as the trouble starts up, back at Vance's house, Ronnie Vance sends Bart out to round up their men, leaving only Ronnie, Pretty Boy, and Keel behind. Keel calls Steed to keep him up to date, revealing that he still has not had the opportunity to unlock the door without the others watching, but he agrees to risk it. Steed sends Wilson on his way, believing that the door will be open on time. Then, he calls Spicer to let him know that now is the time to strike. Spicer, still believing Steed to be part of their gang, does not question him.

Thankfully, Keel manages to unlock the door. Shockingly however, there is a twist in store for Keel. It is not Spicer that comes through the door, it is Mason himself, and he reveals that someone is playing both sides against the middle; Steed's plan is unraveling fast. Wilson soon barges in but can find no evidence of illegal activity. The plot having failed, Wilson is forced to withdraw. Mason reveals that Vance has an inside man as well—Keel! But the good doctor has legged it before they realize he is gone. Now, Mason orders Spicer to kill Steed at the House of the Rising Sun.

Fortunately, Keel arrives there first and gushes to Steed about a plot to murder him. Now frustrated by the need to rely on amateurs and stewing in the failure of his plans, Steed is skeptical.

Thinking fast, Keel punches Steed, knocking him out just before Spicer arrives. To Spicer's astonishment, Keel proclaims Steed dead from heart failure. However, Spicer recognizes Keel and a fight ensues. Steed awakens, and together they subdue Spicer with Lila's help. At first Spicer is reluctant to talk, but threatened by the prospect of a lethal injection, his tongue loosens and he quickly reveals all they need to know just as Wilson enters.

Spicer is led away, his gang due for a roundup. As for the injection, it was a harmless barbiturate—Keel was merely bluffing. Steed, impressed by Keel's resolve and ingenuity, suggests that they might work together in the future. Keel merely replies, "You know where to find me."

EPISODE NOTES

Though they are not officially connected by title, this episode is essentially part two of "Hot Snow." Though the events of "Hot Snow" do not result in a resolution of Peggy's murder as her killer is not yet brought to justice, with "Brought to Book" the cycle of events comes to a firm conclusion, and the Steed-Keel partnership is established. The events of the story are fairly complex for a single hour of television, but they synergize exceptionally well with the prior story, and the scripting is excellent, the dialogue assured. John Steed continues to be a somewhat mysterious character here, introduced for the first time last week as an 'avenging angel' but only named this week. It's a fascinating idea to imagine Steed as so inscrutable a character. We are used to him being a complex creation, one that was often forced to go undercover, but here, we are seeing it from an outsider's point of view. In subsequent adventures, the viewers are always in on the plot, already aware of how the game is played. In this case, the viewer is only slowly moved to insider status—something that would no doubt have provided considerable dramatic pull for the audience—and, as in "Hot Snow," Steed is granted a few cryptic lines that suggest he might not be as pure as he pretends to be. Is he setting up Keel for a fall? Is he ruthlessly willing to sacrifice Keel for his naïveté and relentless drive to ensnare Peggy's murderer? These are all issues that would arise in future episodes, with Keel frequently clashing with Steed over ethics and issues about how far it was acceptable for him to go. This would reach a dramatic climax in "Toy Trap," but the stage is set here.

Little however can be said about the episode's visuals, as precious few production photographs exist, several of these being scans from newsprint and one from a comic book!

One bit of trivia that might be of interest—this is the first episode to be designed by Robert Fuest, who would go on to design several more episodes of the series before leaving to direct television commercials. He returned to become one of the best directors working on the show during its final year. Fuest frequently credited Peter Hammond, who directed "Brought to Book," as being an inspiration for his becoming a director.

CHAMPAGNE, CARS, CLOTHES, AND CANINES

Steed has switched to a dark heavy woolen jacket and now wears a horizontally-striped white shirt (the stripes are a pale-blue) and a dark-gray tie with a tiepin. The shirt would feature throughout the season and into the next, as it is seen in several surviving promotional photos. The stripes are quite dark compared to the main color of the fabric and they come across as black or dark-gray on white. The stripes extend fully down the sleeves, but the cuffs and collar are unadorned. Dr. Keel switches to a slightly lighter two-piece suit with pleated trousers, a white shirt, and a light-colored tie with tricolored thick diagonal stripes.

SURVIVING FOOTAGE AND MATERIALS

Synopses
Rehearsal and Camera Scripts
Production Photographs (6)

ADAPTATIONS AND RECONSTRUCTIONS

Big Finish Audio Adaptation

3 (1.3.3) SQUARE ROOT OF EVIL

MINISTRY RECORDS ARE UNAVAILABLE

Written by Richard Harris
Directed by Don Leaver

GUEST CAST

Heron Carvic ('5'), Alex Scott (Jimmy Bishop—'The Cardinal'), Delphi Lawrence (Lisa), George Murcell (Charles Hooper), Vic Wise (Jackie Warren), John Woodvine (Steve Bloom), Cynthia Bizeray (The Secretary)

PRE-TITLE/TEASER

N/A, much like "Hot Snow," the episode title appears onscreen almost immediately after the title sequence ends (according to the available camera script).

SYNOPSIS

Part 1—A car drives along a quiet country lane. It stops in an isolated spot, and a dead body is unceremoniously dumped in a ditch before the car continues on its way.

Inside the office of his superior, '5,' Steed listens to a tape of a phone call between '5' and Tobert, a fellow agent. Tobert is expecting delivery of a special machine but remarks that it is difficult to find out anything else because his every move is being watched by 'the Cardinal.' '5' reveals that it was Tobert's body that was dumped in a ditch on that country lane. He had been infiltrating a forgery ring, and '5' shows Steed some of the remarkable forgeries being done on bank notes; Steed is unable to tell the difference between the forgery and the real one. The organization is huge, and its leader is a man called Hooper. Handing Steed a dossier, '5' gives him orders to impersonate an Irish man named Timothy James Riordan. Fortunately, according to '5,' none of Hooper's gang has seen Riordan, so it should be possible for Steed to slip in his place. Steed receives the rest of his briefing in the records room and flirts with the attractive young woman there while watching a film of the forgers: Steve Bloom, Jackie Warren, Hooper, and finally, Jimmy Bishop, the Cardinal himself.

Three weeks later, Steed emerges from Wandsworth Prison and is met by Bloom outside. Bloom immediately takes him for Riordan. Steed is taken to their secret operation, where he meets Hooper and is given a tour of the printing presses. The forgery operation is especially advanced, and Steed is impressed, but he is not told when shipping is to begin nor the locations of the buyers. However, the Cardinal is extremely suspicious of Steed and attempts to trip him up by introducing an old 'girlfriend' named Lisa. Fortunately, Steed is not fooled. He recognizes Lisa from the Ministry files; she is the Cardinal's wife.

Part 2—Later that evening, Warren explains how he doesn't like the Cardinal very much, claiming he is excessively paranoid and advising Steed to stay out of his way. Steed makes a phone call and reports in to '5.' Shortly thereafter, he breaks into the printing room safe and photographs all the records within. He is caught in the act however by Lisa, who reveals that she knows he isn't Riordan. Steed drops the act, but Lisa doesn't seem to be too eager to turn him in, explaining that the Cardinal is vicious and carries a gun now. She also knows he has committed a murder and hasn't reported it.

Steed points out how bad this would look before a jury.

At that moment, Hooper and the Cardinal arrive in the garage nearby, delivering a new order of paper for forged bank notes. Steed and Lisa hide under workbenches with the lights out. Steed hand is injured when Hooper and the Cardinal kick a pallet truck in his direction, but he manages to stay silent despite the pain, and he and Lisa are able to head for the garage once the coast is clear.

Just as they are ready to return to their own rooms, the Cardinal comes in, forcing Lisa to reveal herself in order to avoid exposing Steed, who remains in hiding. The Cardinal is convinced that she is snooping however, and he begins to beat her savagely. Steed can do nothing but continue to hide and watch this horrific scene of domestic violence.

Part 3—The next morning, Dr. Keel's nurse Carol Wilson is bandaging Steed's injured hand at the surgery. The wound is a nasty one, and Keel admonishes Steed for not coming earlier. Steed gives Dr. Keel the number for '5' and tells him to call the number only in an emergency. Agreeing to return at four o'clock for another injection, Steed leaves for the lion's den once more.

At four o'clock, Lisa serves afternoon tea to all the men. The bruises on her face are unmistakable. She and the Cardinal have another tiff in which she defends 'Riordan' as genuine. Hooper calls everyone to a meeting and announces that the money is being collected much earlier than expected—later that evening. Realizing that he needs to contact '5' immediately to update him about these plans, Steed feigns that he needs to phone his doctor about his hand. The Cardinal is skeptical but allows him to speak to Keel after Hooper makes the call and hears Carol's voice on the line. Despite not being recognized immediately due to the Irish accent he has affected, Steed manages to pass a coded message to Keel instructing him to contact '5.'

Having received the message, '5' instructs Keel to head to the address of the forgers, and Keel arrives there, insisting that Steed needs another injection for his hand. The Cardinal is unconvinced however, and when Keel is unable to explain how he got the address, the Cardinal tests Steed by throwing him a gun and ordering him to shoot Keel. Steed refuses and instead points the gun at the Cardinal. But the gun is not loaded, and the Cardinal leaps upon Steed in a rage. Keel and Steed join together to fight, and the criminals turn out to be relatively easy to overcome.

Knowing that his own Ministry men are due there any moment, Steed, grateful for Lisa's help, is content to allow her to escape. Knowing that he can replace the Cardinal, Hooper, Bloom, and Warren with his own people, Steed muses about possibly being able to discover the identity of the No. 1 within the organization.

EPISODE NOTES

This is a highly effective and gritty story with a rather sophisticated narrative. From the surviving evidence—a camera script—the program was already establishing itself as a seamless juxtaposition of hard-boiled spy drama and suave characters with witty dialogue. There are several wonderful lines in the script that demonstrate quite early on that John Steed was quite the card…and the cad. As such, this story is largely Steed's to bear, with Dr. Keel only appearing in the final third. Seemingly, this establishes that the program would alternate between storylines emphasizing one character or the other, as indeed appears to be the case based on the first half of the season, though the second half would feature scripts that integrated Steed and Keel much more seamlessly. After the premise-establishing first two episodes, in which Dr. Keel's involvement was driven by his desire to avenge his fiancée's murder, this story serves to assure that Dr. Keel will continue to join adventures with Steed on a regular basis, his appetite for crime-fighting having been whet by the earlier outing.

Intriguingly, we also are introduced to another of Steed's ongoing bosses—the first actually—a man called '5.' Soon after his first and only appearance, '5' would be replaced with One-Ten, who would provide Steed with regular instruction for almost the entire season. And apparently the viewers got to see the sets of the spy headquarters and a records room, thus so much more about the

Ministry is revealed at an early stage than thought previously.

Sadly, we have absolutely no idea what this episode would have looked like since there are no surviving tele-snaps or production photos of any kind. But, given the usual superior visuals managed by director Don Leaver, it is likely that it was engagingly shot.

CHAMPAGNE, CARS, CLOTHES, AND CANINES

It was following this episode that Patrick Macnee received feedback from Sydney Newman about the character of Steed. He was told by Newman that the character was simply too bland and uninteresting. It was shortly thereafter that Macnee decided to mold Steed's persona in a more dandyish direction, modeling him on people in his life, including his own father, Daniel 'Shrimp' Macnee, and from fiction. When he arrived at Teddington Studios for the next recording session wearing a three-piece suit with a bowler hat and umbrella, Newman remarked in his inimitable Canadian way, "Well, it's sure as hell different." Indeed, it was. And the new Steed was born.

SURVIVING FOOTAGE AND MATERIALS

Synopses
Camera Script

ADAPTATIONS AND RECONSTRUCTIONS

Big Finish Audio Adaptation

4 (1.4.4) NIGHTMARE

Written by Terence Feely
Directed by Peter Hammond

MINISTRY RECORDS ARE UNAVAILABLE

GUEST CAST

Gordon Boyd (Williams), Helen Lindsay (Faith Braintree), Michael Logan (Commander Reece), Robert Bruce (Dr. Brown), Redmond Bailey (Dr. Jones), Robert Sansom (Dr. Miller)

PRE-TITLE/TEASER

Unknown. There is no available script.

SYNOPSIS

Dr. Keel receives a phone call from a patient named Faith Braintree and assumes the identity of her husband, an eminent scientist working on top secret material, in order to investigate his disappearance. The disguise works, and the enemy tries to kidnap Dr. Keel, having mistaken him for Professor Braintree. In the ensuing battle, Keel is shot in the chest and requires minor surgery. Unfortunately, Keel's anaesthetist, acting on orders from the enemy, tampers with the doctor's oxygen, very nearly killing him.

EPISODE NOTES

Virtually nothing survives for this episode, not even a script or a single production photograph, just synopses, so there is no way to judge the quality of the production. It also appears as though the guest cast list is incomplete; there is no credit for Professor Braintree. In this episode, it is Dr. Keel's turn to dominate the story, and the fact that he ends up needing surgery and is almost murdered by his anaesthetist is likely the titular nightmare that he is facing.

SURVIVING FOOTAGE AND MATERIALS

Synopses

ADAPTATIONS AND RECONSTRUCTIONS

Big Finish Audio Adaptation

5 (1.5.5) CRESCENT MOON

Written by Geoffrey Bellman and John Whitney
Directed by John Knight

MINISTRY RECORDS ARE UNAVAILABLE

GUEST CAST

Patience Collier (Señora Mendoza), Harold Kasket (Bartello), Bandana Das Gupta (Carmelita Mendoza), Nicholas Amer (Luis Alvarez), Eric Thompson (Paul), Jack Rodney (Fernandez), Roger Delgado (Vasco), George Roderick (P.C. Carlos)

PRE-TITLE/TEASER

Unknown. There is no available script.

SYNOPSIS

Carmelita Mendoza is kidnapped from her home in the Caribbean. Suspecting political motivations, Steed and Dr. Keel investigate the family and their retainer Vasco, who later kills the kidnapper and abducts the girl himself. Steed finds and questions Vasco and finds out where the girl is located. Attempting to rescue her, he is attacked by Paul, the man behind the abduction. Steed then discovers that although Paul did coordinate the original kidnapping, he was acting on the instructions of the girl's father, General Mendoza, who was faking his own death in order to flee his power-hungry wife and Vasco.

EPISODE NOTES

This is another episode about which precious little can be said. Only various synopses have been printed over the years, and no production photos or other visual evidence survives. Nevertheless, it is doubtful that the production could have entirely lived up to its premise, given the restrictions to studio sets and videotaping. Thus, there was no Caribbean travel in the cast's itinerary. Stock footage might have been used to provide the illusion of a Caribbean island, such as Puerto Rico or Cuba. To find out what this episode might have looked like in general, watch the Season Two episode "Death Dispatch," which was set in Jamaica.

The episode also swung back to featuring Steed primarily, whereas Dr. Keel was limited to a few scenes.

SURVIVING FOOTAGE AND MATERIALS

Synopses

ADAPTATIONS AND RECONSTRUCTIONS

Big Finish Audio Adaptation

6 (1.6.6) GIRL ON THE TRAPEZE

Written by Dennis Spooner
Directed by Don Leaver

GUEST CAST

Kenneth J. Warren (Zibbo), Delena Kidd (Vera), Howard Goorney (Superintendent Lewis), Edwin Richfield (Stefan), Mia Karam (Anna Danilov), Ivor Salter (Police Sergeant), David Grey (Dr. Sterret), Dorothy Blythe (Box Office Clerk), Ian Gardiner (Policeman), Andy Alston (Turek)
Uncredited: Patricia Haines (Katrina Sandor)

PRE-TITLE/TEASER

Backstage, at a circus, a woman arrives and asks to see a friend, but when the woman steps into the dressing room to wait, she is quickly attacked by a clown.

SYNOPSIS

Dr. Keel rescues a young woman after she has dived into the Thames. He is unable to prevent her death, but before she dies, she whispers to him a name—Danilov. Suspecting foul play, he follows the lead to the Radeck State Circus. There, he meets Vera, a trapeze artist who is ostensibly guarding an 'injured' performer whose face is heavily bandaged. Before Dr. Keel can question the girl, he is trapped by Zibbo the clown, who informs him that the bandaged girl is Anna, the daughter of the defecting scientist Professor Danilov, who will be smuggled back to Radeck to blackmail the Professor into returning to the other side of the iron curtain...

REVIEW

Don Leaver's usual taut and tense direction allows this episode to shine despite the absence of John Steed. Although there is sadly little in the way of the wit and fights that would dominate later episodes of the series, even later in *this* season, Dr. Keel manages to hold his own well enough without Steed's professional and stalwart presence.

Nevertheless, there is something curiously lacking in "Girl on the Trapeze," perhaps a sense of camaraderie between the two leads. Although Dr. Keel's nurse, semi-regular Carol Wilson, does provide assistance, including a dangerous core twist at the episode's end that allows them to defeat the villains and wrap up this particular adventure, there is no real sense of the equality that would arise when Cathy Gale (and later, Emma Peel) would fulfill this role.

The irony of Steed's absence is magnified by the missing second and third acts of "Hot Snow," which omit his presence from that episode as well. Given the tortured history of this first season's archival status and the resulting lack of extant material, we are left wanting for more of Steed and the team quality that the series is so well known for.

One pleasant surprise is the extensive location shooting early in the story. Film location footage in this era of television was very rare, and night-shooting was even rarer, making it clear that Associated British Corporation was eager to project a special look of high-quality for their fledgling series.

CHAMPAGNE, CARS, CLOTHES, AND CANINES

Both Steed and Dr. Keel are shown wearing light-colored trench coats in the opening titles and in the title cards between acts. In the episode proper, Dr. Keel wears a dark two-piece suit with the same striped tie as in "Brought to Book."

QUOTES

"Well, that's very good. I should take a couple every two hours, if I were you. It's better than the powder." "Powder?" "Yes, I wouldn't take a powder, if I were you."

SURVIVING FOOTAGE AND MATERIALS

Complete monochrome 16mm film telerecording
Synopses
Camera Script

ADAPTATIONS AND RECONSTRUCTIONS

Big Finish Audio Adaptation

7 (1.7.7) DIAMOND CUT DIAMOND

Written by Max Marquis
Directed by Peter Hammond

MINISTRY RECORDS ARE UNAVAILABLE

GUEST CAST

Douglas Muir (One-Ten), Sandra Dorne (Fiona Charles), Hamlyn Benson (Dr. Collard), Joy Webster (Stella Creighton)

PRE-TITLE/TEASER

Unknown. There is no available script.

SYNOPSIS

Attempting to snare a criminal organization specializing in diamond smuggling, Steed is living in a home near Heathrow that was once owned by a suicidal air steward named Harcourt. One-Ten suspects that Harcourt was once a member of the diamond gang and sends Steed undercover as air steward Jack Ryan.

After meeting Fiona Charles, a nurse with connections to Globe Airlines, and spending a night drinking, Steed awakens to read the morning papers and finds that a maniacal intoxicated hit-and-run driver killed a 25-year old woman the night before.

Tipped off by a mysterious phone call, Steed checks his own car and finds the fender damaged and covered in dried blood. After blood and urine tests conducted by Dr. Keel reveal that Steed was drugged, he is absolved of any wrongdoing, and at the request of Fiona he heads to New York to deliver a package.

Returning home, Steed is confronted by Fiona and her employer Dr. Collard and discovers that they are in fact the smugglers. Deciding that his usefulness is over, they intend to kill him and make it look like a suicide, just like they had done for Harcourt. The twist here is that they will make it look like he killed Fiona first. Fortunately, Dr. Keel arrives, and he and Steed overpower Collard, who is sent to jail.

EPISODE NOTES

With only a single production photo and several synopses to pore over, this episode is almost as enshrouded in mystery as "Nightmare" and "Crescent Moon." After John Steed's complete absence in the prior episode, he once again returns to the fore, and the story seems to primarily revolve around his mission for One-Ten.

CHAMPAGNE, CARS, CLOTHES, AND CANINES

In the one surviving production photo, Steed wears a jacket with a very heavy weave in rows like corduroy. I do not recognize the fabric or the style. He also wears a light-gray shirt and a dark tie.

SURVIVING FOOTAGE AND MATERIALS

Synopses
Production Photographs (1)

ADAPTATIONS AND RECONSTRUCTIONS

Big Finish Audio Adaptation

8 (1.8.8) THE RADIOACTIVE MAN

Written by Fred Edge (adapted by Patrick Brawn)
Directed by Robert Tronson

MINISTRY RECORDS ARE UNAVAILABLE

GUEST CAST

Arthur Lawrence (Dr. Graham), George Pravda (Marko Ogrin), Blaise Windham (Campbell), Christine Pollon (Mary Somers), Barry Shawzin (Milan Radosevick), Mira Tomek (Frane), Madeline Kasket (Inica), Marie Devereux (Dora Radosevick), Dane Howell (Peter Somers), Basil Beale (Inspector Tudor), John Gayford (1st Police Constable), Paul (2nd Police Constable), John Kelland (3rd Police Constable)

PRE-TITLE/TEASER

Unknown. Unfortunately, there is no notation of the episode title appearing onscreen anywhere in the available script. It's highly likely that it did appear, but unfortunately we don't know when it did. It was likely just unscripted.

SYNOPSIS

Part 1—Four Eastern European immigrants—Frane, Inica, and Milan Radosevick and his daughter Dora—meet inside a radio shop to discuss plans for an act of terrorism that will bring attention to their communist cause. They are expecting their friend Marko Ogrin, but he is late, so they begin without him. Frane is concerned that someone might get hurt, but Milan counters that the bomb will be placed on a freight train with no passengers, far away from the engine. No one will be harmed, he explains. The others agree, but Frane insists on waiting for Marko's opinion.

At the Whitman Research Laboratory, Marko is finishing his shift as a cleaner. He runs into a scientist named Dr. Graham, who invites him for a cup of coffee. After a brief conversation regarding Graham's concern about his wife's pregnancy and Marko's lost ambitions to be a scientist, Graham is distracted by a telephone call from Dr. Keel with the latest update about his wife's condition. When he returns, Marko is gone and an especially important piece of scientific equipment has disappeared with him. Graham tries to stop Marko but misses him by mere moments.

Marko arrives home, where he lodges with landlady Mary Somers and her son Peter; he is very fond of both of them. He tells Mary that he must go out for a meeting with his friends but has a present for Peter that he will give him when he returns. It is only a fishing line with a lead weight he tells her, but the boy might like it.

Back at the laboratory, Dr. Graham is growing desperate. Finally, out of options, he instructs the receptionist, Campbell, to call the Ministry. Meanwhile, at the surgery, a fatigued Dr. Keel and Carol are discussing their evening appointments. They are interrupted by a telephone call from Steed, who asks Keel to meet him on the Embankment of the River Thames. Once there, Steed explains the situation. Marko Ogrin has stolen a radioactive pellet from the laboratory. The situation is very serious; the radiation could kill Marko or anyone he comes into contact with. Keel is to be as discreet as possible, but, since this is a national emergency, if Marko is not located by 9 pm, they may have to change their plans.

At the radio shop, Marko's friends await his arrival and discuss his recent change in attitude. They are worried that he isn't as serious about their plans as he used to be. Finally, Marko arrives, apologizing for his lateness. Milan explains that he will soon get his opportunity to prove that he is a true patriot.

At the laboratory, it is now 8 pm, and Dr. Graham is wracked with guilt about allowing Marko into a secured area. He explains to Keel that the pellet is a radium capsule, and Marko or anyone he comes into contact with will only have ten hours to live. But the point of no return will occur much earlier than that, perhaps in only five hours, which places their deadline for finding Marko at 1 am. Fortunately, Campbell has since been successful in finding Marko's address, and Keel and Graham leave immediately. They arrive at Mary Somers' house and ring the bell. Mary admits them to Marko's room, but they are unable to find the radium capsule. They're worried they've reached a dead end until Peter remarks that Marko promised him a fishing line. Though they explain nothing to Mary, they leave her with Steed's number, giving her instructions to call if Marko should return.

Back at the radio shop, Marko refuses to work with his friends on their new plot. Milan is furious with him and threatens to reveal that Marko is in the UK on a forged passport. Marko in turn threatens to kill Milan if he does this.

Later, at 9 pm, as Dora walks passed Marko's home, she sees policemen outside. Covertly observing them, she realizes that Marko is in trouble, but the reason is not what she thinks. A police announcement comes in over the radio—it's not a forged passport, it's radium!

Part 2—Marko calls Mary, telling her that he will not be able to come home because he's in trouble with the police. He explains to her about the fake passport under the assumption that this is the reason the police are pursuing him. Mary agrees to help him by giving him money. She meets him at Allen's Café, and they discuss his plans. Marko explains that he was stateless after fleeing to Italy from his home country and needed the forged passport to emigrate from there. Mary is steadfastly loyal to Marko but suggests that he might fare better if he gives himself up. He adamantly decides to run. Upon standing, he feels woozy and stumbles but dismisses it as a flu coming on.

Keel and Graham return to Mary Somers' house while she is still away and find a faint trace of radiation with a Geiger counter. Her son Peter does not know where she went. Dr. Graham explains that she and Peter are in great danger due to radiation. Peter is removed to the laboratory for radioactive decontamination, and the house is sealed for a decontamination crew.

Back at the radio shop, Dora tells her father about the police outside Marko's home. After Dora leaves to bring the others from downstairs, Marko enters and threatens Milan with a knife, assuming that he has made good on his threat about the fake passport. Milan denies this, and eventually Marko backs down. All of his friends agree that they must help Marko get out of the country, deciding that he must flee to Belfast and escape from there into Eire, where they have other allies.

Having cleaned Peter and themselves of radiation, Keel and Graham allow Peter to stay at Dr. Graham's house since he can't return home. In the midst of this, they receive the good news that Dr. Graham's wife has given birth to a baby girl. Graham manages to mobilize six technicians with

Geiger counters and radiosensitive film to scour the area for signs of radiation. Mary has also been picked up upon returning to her house, but she still does not assist the police.

Back at the radio shop, final plans are being made to get Marko out of the country. Unfortunately, he is now seriously flagging, and he falls to the floor. The radiation is steadily killing him.

Part 3—After extensively interviewing Mary Somers, the police find a connection to Allen's Café, which they then find to be contaminated along with six customers. They interview everyone including the owner, Flynn, but the trail is a dead end. However, in the process, Flynn is found to be in the possession of a large quantity of stolen watches with radium dials—found by happenstance with the Geiger counter.

At the radio shop, Marko is feeling somewhat better but is hardly ready for travel, despite Milan's insistence that he leave right away.

Outside, the police finally get a lead—a sheet of radiosensitive film has come back severely fogged. Retracing their steps, they quickly head for the building with the radio shop.

Inside the shop, Marko is making his farewells to his friends and leaves the radium pellet for Peter. Just in time, the police, Keel, Graham, Tudor, and Mary Somers arrive. Keel and Graham go in the front as the police circle to the back door, and Graham's Geiger counter goes off the scale. Despite attempts by Marko's friends to deter Keel and Graham, they find Marko, who points a gun at them. Carefully, as Marko's resolve fades, they talk him down, slowly convincing him that they are there to help.

Finally, Mary is brought inside to help convince Marko, now seriously disorientated by radiation sickness, and with Graham's Geiger counter turned on as proof, Marko gives in and is taken to the hospital with Mary and Dr. Graham. Outside, Keel is congratulated by Steed on his successful mission.

EPISODE NOTES

For such a sensational title, this episode is comparatively ordinary in tone, being not at all science-fiction but science-fact. The subject matter is also right up Dr. Keel's alley, being medical in nature and yet slightly fantastic for everyday life. The script reads as an exceptionally tense story, with the focal character evading capture for a surprising amount of time due to several believable contrivances. The radium pellet is the narrative's MacGuffin with its trail of radiation slowly guiding Keel and Graham towards their target by Geiger counter. However, it is unlikely that a radium pellet would be deadly that quickly. Possibly it was a particularly strong isotope such as radium-226, but it seems improbable that Dr. Graham would just happen to have such a powerful isotope lying around on his desk while he drinks coffee, giving Marko a chance to simply snatch it up and walk off. It would be interesting to see how this was staged on-camera. Was the pellet in a sealed container? If so, how did Marko spot it? Would he really have been so stupid as to go through that much effort to steal it if it were sealed away somewhere? Steed takes more of a backseat this week, with Dr. Graham essentially filling in as an assistant, and it would be interesting to see how effective a substitute he was. The unspoken ironic twist is that a terrorist plot is indirectly stopped by happenstance, and the *Avengers* appear to never actually hear of it.

SURVIVING FOOTAGE AND MATERIALS

Synopses
Camera Script

ADAPTATIONS AND RECONSTRUCTIONS

Big Finish Audio Adaptation

9 (1.9.9) ASHES OF ROSES

MINISTRY RECORDS ARE UNAVAILABLE

Written by Peter Ling and Sheilagh Ward
Directed by Don Leaver

GUEST CAST

Mark Eden (Jacques Beronne), Olga Lowe (Olive Beronne), Hedi Erich (Denise), Edward Dentith (Maurice Roffey), Peter Zander (Johnny Mendelssohn), Barbara Evans (Linda Chapman), Maureen Beck (Jean Lewis), Nina Marriott (Avril), Gordon Rollings (Sleeping Car Attendant), Douglas Muir (Voice of One-Ten), Juno (Puppy)

PRE-TITLE/TEASER

A night watchman at the timber yard sits down on his break to eat a sandwich and drink a cup of coffee. Startled by a sound, he goes to investigate, and this allows an intruder ("JOE - A BURLY TOUGH IN A RAINCOAT" according to the script) to slip in behind him. When the watchman returns he's knocked out by the intruder who then covers his body with wood shavings and kerosene and sets him alight. The sequence ends with stock footage of fire trucks rushing to the scene.

SYNOPSIS

Part 1—After arsonists burn the corpse of timber yard night watchman Pritchard in order to disguise the man's murder, Steed goes undercover as an insurance adjuster and interviews Maurice Roffey, the owner of the timber yard where the blazing inferno took place. Roffey seems agitated and becomes defensive when Steed reminds him that he tripled the fire insurance on the premises recently. Roffey answers that the verdict in court was Pritchard's carelessness with cigarettes, but Steed fires back that Pritchard gave up smoking two years earlier.

When Roffey receives a call, he writes down the number on a pad, tearing off the sheet and stuffing it in his pocket. Steed, reading Roffey's nervousness during the brief call, makes an excuse to use the notepad also, writing down the date and time of the train connection Roffey is claiming as an alibi, but his real goal is to take that next sheet of paper. Later, sharpening a pencil over the sheet, he is able to read the indentations of the phone number Roffey jotted down—the number dials a prominent beauty salon run by Frenchman Jacques Beronne, but the receptionist has never heard of Roffey.

At the salon, one of the assistants, Jean, is looking for an available hair dryer; she needs her hair done for her date with Jacques. Linda, the receptionist, gently admonishes her, reminding her that Olive Beronne is a forbidding woman and Denise is also interested in Jacques. Olive Beronne arrives and sends Linda into the meeting with Jacques and Mendelssohn. Linda mentions the call she received about Roffey, and Jacques appears to not know the name but Mendelssohn reacts nervously.

Back at Dr. Keel's surgery, Steed, convinced that the salon isn't a dead end, manipulates nurse Carol Wilson into taking part in the investigation by pretending to be a customer at the salon. Keel is at first suspicious and concerned about Carol's safety but finally allows it after Steed promises to buy her lunch.

Arranging for an emergency appointment, the salon gives Carol the dryer intended for Jean. Carol drops the name Roffey quite a bit, but no one, including Jacques, seems to know who he is. However, shortly thereafter, Carol's hairdryer explodes in a flash, and she slumps forward in her chair.

Part 2—Thankfully, Carol was just harmlessly knocked out, but it quickly becomes clear that the device was rigged to kill Jean. Steed decides to find out more about Jean by taking Denise out to dinner. After their meal, they end up back at Steed's flat, and Denise has a rude awakening about Steed's true intentions as he begins grilling her about Jean. Finally, Denise admits that Madame Beronne wants Jean out of the way due to jealousy over Jacques. Having answered his questions truthfully, Denise huffily rises to leave for being so caddishly treated, but Steed once again turns on the charm, and they end up in an embrace instead.

The next morning, Steed and Carol talk about what he has learned. Carol offers to help more, but Steed refuses to allow it; he is convinced that he has all the assistance he needs from Carol. Nevertheless, Carol has been bitten by the spy bug and decides to go back to the salon on her own. When Steed arrives at the salon later, he is surprised to find Carol there but cannot say anything without revealing that they know each other.

Carol receives a free massage from Jean as compensation for her earlier incident with the hairdryer. They begin talking, and Carol slowly reveals what she knows about the potential murder. Jean is incredulous about the idea that someone might want to murder her. Just as they are wrapping up, Olive Beronne comes in and blocks Jean's path.

Part 3—That evening, Steed and Carol arrive at Jean's apartment and discover that she has been strangled. Carol calls the police, and Steed finds Jacques' number in Jean's address book. He calls the number and finds out from the housemaid that the Beronnes are on their way to the train station, fleeing the country.

While Steed rushes to the train station to cut them off, Carol remains behind and encounters Denise, who enters Jean's flat on her own. They discuss Jean's murder and realize that the Beronnes may have set fire to the salon. Carol goes there to find out.

On the train, Steed intercepts Jacques and reveals that Mendelssohn is a professional arsonist; he knew Roffey and is the connection to the timber yard fire. Jacques admits that Olive has murdered Jean, and now, they are fleeing the country and burning the salon, but not before they removed all the expensive equipment and cash from it. The porter brings the left luggage ticket for the valuables, and Steed intercepts it and then knocks Jacques out.

Olive flees the train station with Mendelssohn, returning to the salon. Ahead of them, Joe, one of the arsonists, has already found Carol snooping around. Olive orders them to bind and gag Carol in the massage room and continue with the plan to burn down the salon, hoping to still salvage her scheme and collect the insurance money.

However, Steed arrives just in time. In the ensuing struggle, Steed's gun goes off and starts the fire prematurely. Steed knocks both Joe and Mendelssohn out and escapes with Carol just in time. Back at Keel's surgery, Steed's hands are bandaged from burns, but Carol has escaped unscathed. Olive Beronne was also saved and will soon be ready for trial when she gets out of the hospital. Mendelssohn is back in prison where he belongs. Steed rescued them all, and the only thing left for Dr. Keel to do is walk Steed's dog Puppy.

EPISODE NOTES

This is an unusual and likely humorous story revolving around murder, insurance fraud and arson in a beauty parlor. This is the second episode to heavily involve nurse Carol Wilson in the action. Previously, she had joined up with Dr. Keel in "Girl on the Trapeze," a story in which John Steed was totally absent. Here, she mostly appears alongside Steed in a story in which Dr. Keel features comparatively little—totally in keeping with the alternation between the two regular stars up to now. Carol shows considerable pluck during the events, despite her relative inexperience with crime-fighting, and it's easy to see how this might have translated to later characters like Venus Smith. *The Avengers* was already sticking its toe in the water with regard to female emancipation.

I'm inferring the humor based on a script which involves potential murder by an explosive hairdryer. This is a tantalizing hint that the series was already exploring bizarre and over-the-top means of murder even this early. Later one could easily imagine poisoned peroxide dye jobs, explosive curling irons, knock-out drugs in the shampoo, and drownings in the sink during a good rinse, but here it is kept relatively lowkey by comparison.

Unfortunately, the single extant production photo offers little indication as to the visuals in this story, but we can guess that it was almost entirely set-based, with only a couple of scenes filmed in the streets surrounding a few of the locations. In a line of recent episodes with titles that don't appear to have much to do with their plots, this one sounds much like a 1990s indie rock band. The phrase sometimes refers to a pinkish grey color, but it's hard to say what this has to do with the narrative—eye shadow? Lipstick? Hair color?

This was also the final episode of the series to be recorded live.

CHAMPAGNE, CARS, CLOTHES, AND CANINES

Steed's Great Dane, Puppy, makes her first appearance in the series.

SURVIVING FOOTAGE AND MATERIALS

Synopses
Camera Script
Production Photographs (1)

ADAPTATIONS AND RECONSTRUCTIONS

Big Finish Audio Adaptation

10 (1.10.10) HUNT THE MAN DOWN

Written by Richard Harris
Directed by Peter Hammond

MINISTRY RECORDS ARE UNAVAILABLE

GUEST CAST

Nicholas Selby (Frank Preston), Maurice Good (Paul Stacey), Gerry Duggan (Rocky), Melissa Stribling (Stella Preston), Susan Castle (Nurse Wyatt)

PRE-TITLE/TEASER

Unknown. There is no available script.

SYNOPSIS

Frank Preston is now a free man after serving his sentence for grand larceny, but the money stolen as part of his crime has never been discovered. Steed trails Preston unseen in the shadows as he leaves prison in search of the loot, but his quarry is set upon by thugs also eager for the money. Steed comes to Preston's rescue but not before he receives severe injuries. Steed takes him to Dr. Keel's surgery, where Preston remains only semi-conscious, and when his wife Stella arrives, the two of them soon depart in an ambulance for the hospital.

Shortly thereafter, Carol is abducted by two thugs under the employ of Stella; she intends to betray her husband for the loot. The thugs, Paul Stacey and Rocky, are the same two men that beat up Preston. Stella believes that Preston might have told Dr. Keel the money's location during his semi-conscious ramblings, and now she holds Carol hostage in order to force the information from Keel.

Preston escapes the hospital, returning home, and is surprised to find his wife kissing Stacey. Unseen by them, he returns to Dr. Keel's surgery where he elicits Keel's help in retrieving the loot in exchange for his helping free Carol. They travel to the money's hiding place but are tailed by Stella, Stacey, and Rocky, who bring Carol with them. Preston and Keel manage to retrieve the money from a sewer but a fight ensues with the thugs. Fortunately, Steed has been tailing all of them and arrives with the police to clean up the mess and seize the 'filthy lucre.'

EPISODE NOTES

Like Richard Harris' prior episode "Square Root of Evil," "Hunt the Man Down" appears to be a rather hard-boiled thriller. The surviving production photos, mainly shot during location filming for the loot retrieval sequence, have a wonderful artistic and film noir quality to them. Despite this, we know comparatively little about the story as there is no script.

Nevertheless, Ian Hendry recalled this episode in interviews, describing an extensive fight scene on an elaborate sewer set. He explained that he was required to jump right from the wet sewer to Dr. Keel's surgery, swapping out for a dry coat on the way. The low-resolution cameras of the day hid his dampness, and he carried on in his soggy pants and shoes.

Notably, this appears to be one of the better stories at narratively integrating the activities of both Steed and Keel, and their contributions appear to be roughly equal as a result. Carol Wilson is also extensively involved.

This is probably the result of a 27 Feb 1961 memo sent by Leonard White, which stated the following:

> As our episodes are fortnightly we have no need to split our 'leads' into alternative episodes. Now, (although perhaps still giving the 'edge' to one or other of them and continuing to think of stories as either predominantly 'Keel' or 'Steed') we must integrate the two characters into EACH episode. This should provide more opportunity for the 'relationship' between 'Keel' and Steed'.

This did not resolve immediately, of course, as the latest scripts needed to be developed over the coming weeks, and indeed there were episodes that still emphasized one regular over the other (sometimes quite heavily) right up until the final broadcast episode of the season—"The Yellow Needle," "The Far-Distant Dead," and "Dragonsfield." In general, however, this advice seems to have been taken on board by the production team, and steadily the two leads would develop a relationship that would nearly lead to a split in the missing episode "Toy Trap." Of course, "Dragonsfield" is the exception anyway since the lack of Dr. Keel was due to Ian Hendry's early departure and not a creative decision on the part of the production team.

CHAMPAGNE, CARS, CLOTHES, AND CANINES

This is the first episode with extensive production photos, and it's one in which the pale trench coat actually features. Dr. Keel wears one along with light tweed trousers and dark shoes. In other photos, he is wearing the same diagonally-striped tie as in "Brought to Book." Steed also wears the trench coat in one scene, and though the outfit underneath is not visible, Patrick Macnee is seen in a few of the photos taken after filming (several of which are at a bar or pub) wearing a dark three-piece suit with a white shirt and dark tie. It is difficult to pin down any further details, but this is presumably the outfit he wore for filming.

SURVIVING FOOTAGE AND MATERIALS

Synopses
Production Photographs (37)

ADAPTATIONS AND RECONSTRUCTIONS

Big Finish Audio Adaptation

11 (1.11.11) PLEASE DON'T FEED THE ANIMALS

Written by Dennis Spooner
Directed by Dennis Vance

MINISTRY RECORDS ARE UNAVAILABLE

GUEST CAST

Tenniel Evans (Felgate), Harry Ross (Kollakis), Alastair Hunter (Renton-Stephens), Carole Boyer (Christine), Genevieve Lyons (Sarah), Catherine Ellison (Yvonne), Mark Baker (Barman), Richard Neller (Evans), Charles Bird (Harrigan)

PRE-TITLE/TEASER

In a filmed sequence (in the script, on "t/c" or telecine), one man skulks through the empty and closed zoo, followed by another stealthy man whom the first does not see. The first man stops at the crocodile pit and looks over the parapet, searching for something. The second man reaches him and pushes him over the edge into the water with the crocs. (This really emphasizes the title when it appears, something of a darkly humorous quality.)

SYNOPSIS

Part 1—Late at night at the Brinkley House Zoo, a privately-owned zoo just outside of London, a man is fatally toppled into a crocodile pit. A month later, Steed meets with a ciphers clerk named Felgate. Unknown to Felgate, he is under suspicion, and Steed delays him long enough for Dr. Keel to arrive, so Keel can tail him. Keel follows Felgate to the Bromango Strip Club in Soho. There, Felgate asks for Mr. Kollakis as Keel listens closely at the bar nearby. While Felgate waits, he offers to sign Keel in as a guest so he can buy drinks; the club only serves members.

Once Felgate meets Kollakis, he asks for leniency on the money he owes. He's broke and can no longer meet his payments. Kollakis responds with thinly-veiled threats, and Felgate agrees to pay what little money he has—£22. He tries to hand the cash to Kollakis but is refused; Kollakis insists that it be delivered in "the usual way" as he hands him a sheet of festive Christmas wrap. As Felgate leaves, Keel follows. Meanwhile, back in Kollakis' office, he makes a phone call to Renton-Stephens, announcing that Felgate is ready for the next stage of extraction.

Outside in Steed's car, he and Keel continue to trail Felgate as they discuss the situation. Coming on the heels of the death of another ciphers clerk in the crocodile pit at the zoo, Felgate, not very well paid, is now under surveillance after regularly withdrawing large amounts of money from his account. Felgate is now heavily in debt, and Steed needs to find out why. He has been ordered to go undercover as another clerk and share an office with Felgate.

The civil servant gets on a bus and soon arrives at the Brinkley House Zoo; Steed and Keel follow in the car. Keel and Steed observe the man drop the crocodile a Christmas present, a small parcel wrapped in holiday wrap. Steed decides to see what happens to the present, and Keel distracts Sarah, the girl working the peanut stand nearby, while Steed gets into position. Sarah closes up her stand and joins the zookeeper Evans. The zoo is closing, and Keel must leave, but Steed stays hidden.

After a short time however, to his great surprise, after Steed briefly looks away and then back, the packet is suddenly gone. He moves closer to investigate and is grabbed from behind, and a violent struggle ensues.

Part 2—Shortly afterwards, Steed, Evans, Christine, and her father, the zoo owner Major Renton-Stephens, are in the zoo office talking. Evans apologizes. As he explains, worried about the earlier death in the crocodile pit, he made a snap decision to nab Steed. Steed—who has chosen the undercover name of Archibald—is gracious and accepts Evans' apology. Over a drink, they discuss Renton-Stephens' military career in India, and Steed meets Jimmy—a clever little monkey that the Major has taught a number of tricks. Christine mentions that only her father can get Jimmy to perform.

The next morning, Steed overhears part of a phone conversation between Felgate and Kollakis. His ears perk up when Felgate says "there isn't any more." Later, at the Keel surgery, Steed and Keel discuss what they know as Steed enjoys his lunch of pâté de foie gras! There is nothing to do but continue to surveil Felgate at the Bromango strip club.

At the club, Steed loudly makes it clear that he is a friend of Felgate's, hoping to be sucked into the same blackmail plot by Kollakis. Inside the office, Kollakis horrifies Felgate by revealing that this time he wants cipher information not money. When Felgate starts to refuse, Kollakis reminds him of the tapes they have of his infidelities and how ruinous it would be to his reputation and family.

Meanwhile, Steed meets a young stripper named Yvonne in her dressing room. Confirming that the room is bugged by a microphone, Steed knows he is halfway to being on the inside of the cipher plot. Dropping a lot of nonsense about a fictional family and his problems with his wife, Steed enjoys his 'adulterous' dalliance with Yvonne.

Back in the office, Kollakis is disappointed with Felgate's decision. He isn't willing to go that far; money was one thing, but top-secret information is too much. A burly bruiser named Harrigan enters and escorts Felgate away. Fearing for his life, Felgate gratefully accepts Keel's offer of a drink on the way out, but Harrigan insists on leaving. Sensing that Felgate is in trouble, Keel pretends to be drunk and starts a fight. He is punched by Harrigan just as Steed rushes out of the dressing room.

Part 3—The next morning, Carol greets the two men at the surgery. Steed has a black eye and Keel a bruised jaw. Keel saved Felgate's life, and in so doing, they received a full confession. Unfortunately, this produced no more information than they already had. Leaving for work at Felgate's office, Steed is surprised by a phone call from Kollakis, who insists that they meet at the club at lunchtime.

At the club office, Kollakis cuts to the chase and immediately starts to blackmail Steed, producing the tape recording of his infidelity with Yvonne the night before. Kollakis wants the 'Salamander file,' and though Steed initially makes a good show of uncertainty, he finally agrees. Kollakis present him with a sheet of Christmas wrap, instructing him to throw the cipher codes into the crocodile pit as the zoo closes that night.

Later, at his surgery, Keel receives a call from Steed instructing him to stake out the crocodile pit and find out if there is any other way in or out. That night at the zoo, Keel buys a chocolate from Sarah's stand and notices that she has Jimmy the monkey on a leash. She remarks that the monkey has the run of the place when the zoo is closed. Keel and Steed meet at the crocodile pit, and Steed reveals that he has dosed the parcel with a generous amount of dye that will expose anyone who touches it as 'green-handed.'

Taking daffodils he picked earlier, Steed proceeds to the Renton-Stephens house and offers Christine the flowers, while Keel remains hidden watching the pit. Keel is surprised to see the packet vanish among the vicious crocs—only a glimpse of movement amidst the shadows precedes its disappearance.

Back at the house, Christine complains that Jimmy has gotten something green on his paws, and, outside, Keel notices that the packet is now on the counter at the kiosk. Wearing gloves, Keel retrieves the packet, but Kollakis arrives, demanding it, and the two men fight. Keel emerges victorious and leads Kollakis into the house at gunpoint. There, the villains are shocked that neither Steed nor Keel are who they thought. A brief standoff occurs as Renton-Stephens pulls a gun on Keel, but Steed reveals that policemen are due to arrive at any moment, and the Major finally relents; his daughter is innocent, and he is concerned about her safety.

EPISODE NOTES

Like "Ashes of Roses" before it, this episode seems to play with slightly more absurdist and bizarre elements. This trend towards absurdity is underscored by the plot possibilities of a small London zoo, where trained monkeys swipe top-secret information packaged in Christmas wrap, and assassination by crocodile is a serious possibility. Add to this a seedy strip club where cipher agents are blackmailed into revealing classified information, and you have all the elements of a typical later *Avengers* episode, albeit in a somewhat grittier style. It is highly likely that this story was played in a more comedic and witty manner. (Various cast members, including Ian Hendry, have retrospectively commented on the show's humorous qualities in this season.) This script would also set a tone for the majority of Dennis Spooner's contributions to *The Avengers* and its successor series, almost all of them involving humorous sendups.

One concern I had from reading the script is that it is a little too obvious that the monkey has been trained to retrieve the cheerily-wrapped parcels of cipher codes. It is stated early on that only the elder zoo owner, Major Renton-Stephens, can get the monkey to perform its tricks, so the culprit is immediately obvious. As such, it's surprising that Steed and Keel don't figure it out earlier. Given that Kollakis almost immediately calls Renton-Stephens in Part 1, it appears that the script wasn't making the identity of the villains a secret to the audience at all.

One interesting tidbit is that Steed reveals a more casual 'runabout' than his usual Rolls-Royce, and this is an intriguing parallel with *The New Avengers*, in which he is seen occasionally driving much more modest vehicles. (I refer you to the second season *New Avengers* episode "Hostage.") Steed also has ample opportunity to philander with a young stripper named Yvonne, and their dialogue is surprisingly salacious for the era. Though this is all in an effort to convince the blackmailers of his corruptibility, one can easily imagine him reveling in this aspect of his work!

SURVIVING FOOTAGE AND MATERIALS

Synopses
Camera Script

ADAPTATIONS AND RECONSTRUCTIONS

Big Finish Audio Adaptation

12 (1.12.12) DANCE WITH DEATH

Written by Peter Ling and Sheilagh Ward
Directed by Don Leaver

MINISTRY RECORDS ARE UNAVAILABLE

GUEST CAST

Diana King (Mrs. Marne), Geoffrey Palmer (Philip Anthony), Ewan Roberts (Major Caswell), David Sutton (Trevor Price), Caroline Blakiston (Elaine Bateman), Angela Douglas (Beth Wilkinson), Pauline Shepherd (Valerie Marne), Norman Chappell (Porter), Neil Wilson (Police Sergeant), Raymond Hodge (Plain-clothes man), Graeme Spurway (Hotel Receptionist), Alan Barry (Ginger, the Barman), Ian Hobbs (Teenage Boy), Alan Clare (Pianist at Bar) and The Ken Bateman Formation Dance Team

PRE-TITLE/TEASER

Unknown. The available script is heavily annotated with indecipherable notations after the title sequence. The episode title is not explicitly noted anywhere in the script.

SYNOPSIS

Part 1—Dr. Keel is enjoying a rare evening out when he is called to attend to dance instructor Elaine Bateman at the local dance academy. Elaine had been asleep at her desk when someone turned on the gas fire without igniting it. Despite having been overcome by gas fumes, she is recovering swiftly but not yet awake. Keel speaks to her boyfriend Trevor Price and reveals that the police will arrive soon. Trevor seems annoyed by this, but Keel insists that it is routine. Elaine and Trevor explain to Keel that Trevor had left for a meal, and when he returned he found Elaine behind a locked door with the gas on. She had fallen asleep over the books after drinking a cup of tea. Keel notes that the used teacup is mysteriously missing. When the police sergeant and constable arrive on the scene, they aren't surprised to hear of the apparent attempt on Elaine's life, revealing that they have investigated many alleged murder attempts on Elaine and suggest that she might be mentally ill or suicidal. Since Elaine does not have a regular doctor, Dr. Keel suggests that she follow up with him at his surgery at eleven the following morning.

The next day, Keel discusses the incident with his nurse Carol; he believes that she might have been drugged when she drank the tea, and he wants to test her for any residual evidence. Elaine arrives promptly for her appointment and reveals that she hasn't been to a doctor in years because they all think she's hysterical. She insists that someone is trying to kill her and has a feeling that Dr. Keel might believe her.

Later, at the dance academy, Keel meets with Major Caswell to talk about Elaine's accident—Elaine is a partner in the business with Caswell. The Major reacts strangely, behaving as though he believes Elaine has already died. In fact, everyone seems to believe this, including Mrs. Marne and her daughter Valerie, who is also an instructor. Keel sets them all straight and finds out that the false news was started by the dance academy's pianist Philip Anthony.

Later, Elaine is back at work with a new pupil. In the corridor, Caswell expresses annoyance that she is taking on someone new, but his concern may be more motivated by jealousy than concern about her health. During Elaine's lesson, Trevor arrives and becomes jealous about her pupil, a teenage boy, insinuating that she has cheated on him before. Keel arrives and tries to calm Trevor down, finally resorting to force in removing him. He does not notice that he dropped his scarf in the struggle. Only when back at his surgery does he realize that his scarf is missing.

That evening, Beth, Valerie, and Elaine are planning a performance. When Beth and Valerie leave for the night, the lights suddenly go out and Elaine finds herself with Keel's scarf wrapped tightly around her neck, slowly strangling her.

Part 2—With Keel now a suspect in Elaine's murder, Steed agrees to help him but admits he can do little for now—he holds no sway over police investigations. Nevertheless, Steed quickly arranges to be a new client at the dance academy and goes undercover as 'Mr. Rogers.' Caswell and Mrs. Marne agree to show him around the school. Steed is escorted away by Caswell as Mrs. Marne and Valerie excitedly discuss an article being written by a journalist about the academy, complete with photographs of all the staff. Valerie is excited to borrow her mother's diamond necklace for the photograph and goes to tell Philip, who is practicing a new piece that he has written in her honor.

Later, in Keel's office, Steed flicks through the dance academy's prospectus, which includes photographs of all the staff. Keel shows him Elaine's photo, but Steed is more interested in another person, one that he recognizes from the Ministry's 'C.N. catalogue'—a book of people who have changed their names after committing a serious crime. They are people that they lack evidence to convict.

At the academy, Valerie has an argument with her mother over her independence and flees with the borrowed diamond necklace into Philip's arms.

Later, Steed and Keel meet in a cocktail bar, and Steed confirms that the man in the photograph at the dance academy is Clifford Gardiner, who murdered his own wife seven years ago but wasn't convicted due to lack of evidence. They have met in the bar because the barman there, Ginger, used to work with Gardiner. Steed sent a message to the academy to bring Gardiner there in five minutes, and Ginger is to identify Gardiner once he arrives but has to remain out of sight so that Gardiner won't spot him and flee. Ginger and Steed quickly duck out of sight, and the police take over while Keel sits and drinks. He is surprised to see Major Caswell walk in, and Caswell reports that he couldn't give the message as instructed; Gardiner (Philip) is nowhere to be found.

Part 3—Back at the academy office, Valerie is missing. She didn't show up for the photo shoot, and Mrs. Marne is inconsolable as Caswell tries to calm her down. Meanwhile, in a nearby cubicle, Beth is giving Steed another lesson. Nonchalantly, he manages to turn the conversation to the subject of Philip Anthony, and Beth naively reveals a secret—Philip and Valerie have eloped! Steed quickly reports this information to the Ministry.

At the reception desk of a hotel, Valerie and Philip have checked in as 'Mr. and Mrs. Phillips.' Philip wants to go out to eat, but Valerie has a headache and wants to stay in, so they return to their room, planning to order sandwiches later. The clerk assumes however that they have left as originally planned. In their hotel room, Philip seems anxious about the safety of the necklace.

At the dance academy, Keel treats Mrs. Marne and then asks about Elaine's boyfriend Trevor, who turns out to be there already. In the storeroom, Trevor is looking for a film that he claims shows he and Elaine in a compromising way. He says that Philip was trying to blackmail them and is searching through Philip's possessions for the film now that he is gone. There are many films with Elaine in them—she was blackmailed a lot! Steed phones asking Keel to meet him at the hotel. There, Steed and Beth are checking in as a couple in order to find Philip and Valerie, drawing an uncomfortable conclusion from the porter.

In their hotel room, Valerie is preparing for a bath while Philip continues to agitate about the necklace, insisting that they place it in the hotel safe. Philip orders his sandwiches. Steed finds out from Beth that Elaine knew Philip quite well, and they head to the room next to Philip and Valerie's. Steed is trying to bore a hole in the door in order to spy on them when the porter brings the sandwiches. The porter struggles to remove Steed, who he assumes is a peeping Tom. While Steed wrangles with the porter, Valerie is in her bath, and Philip is plugging in a gas heater. Steed fights off the porter and grabs his keys. Opening the door, Philip is caught red-handed by Steed, who knocks him out in a brief fight, while Keel bursts in through the hall doorway to block his escape. Later, Beth consoles Valerie over her loss, and Keel gives her a sedative to calm her down.

EPISODE NOTES

Much in the vein of "Ashes of Roses," this is a curious story interspersed with humor. Involving a serial murderer preying on a dance studio, this episode could be considered a precursor to the Season Four episode "Quick-Quick Slow Death." Nevertheless, based on the surviving script, the narrative suffers from unevenness throughout. Steed doesn't show up until the second part and then takes over. There is a comic scene with a porter who believes Steed is drilling a hole to see into the bathroom of an adjacent hotel room. Steed must fight him off as he tries to rescue the would-be murder victim, insisting that "there's a girl in that bathroom!" It's difficult to tell if this episode would have worked based on the script, but there's little doubt it would have required careful handling, its success dependent on the quality of the performances and the cast's comic timing. Fortunately, it does have a good cast featuring a young Geoffrey Palmer and Caroline Blakiston, who would both return in later episodes of the series. Unfortunately, there are no Tele-snaps, nor any surviving production photographs, so we haven't any idea what the episode would have looked like. Nevertheless, given the credit to 'The Ken Bateman Formation Dance Team,' it's likely that there was a dance sequence or two.

In a 17 May 1961 memo, Leonard White suggests again using Angela Douglas as a foil for Steed, saying that "she had a very good sense of comedy." This would seem to confirm that the episode was intended to be comedic.

SURVIVING FOOTAGE AND MATERIALS

Synopses
Camera Script

ADAPTATIONS AND RECONSTRUCTIONS

Big Finish Audio Adaptation

13 (1.13.13) ONE FOR THE MORTUARY

Written by Brian Clemens
Directed by Peter Hammond

MINISTRY RECORDS ARE UNAVAILABLE

GUEST CAST

Peter Madden (Benson), Ronald Wilson (Scott), Dennis Edwards (Pallaine), Malou Pantera (Yvette Declair), Steve Scott (Borsh, a Concierge of the Hotel Alsace), Frank Gatliff (Dubois, a Swiss Detective), Irene Bradshaw (Maid), Toke Townley (Bernard Bourg)

PRE-TITLE/TEASER

Unknown. Unfortunately, only a rehearsal script is available rather than a camera script, and the episode title is not explicitly noted anywhere.

SYNOPSIS

Part 1—After a brutal attack on Steed and a fellow agent named Wilson, Steed is left badly injured and his partner dead. The assailants—a well-dressed one-eyed gentleman named Benson and another thug—were searching for a secret formula for a medicine called Morgantol, which Wilson managed to burn just before dying.

After the fight, Steed asks Dr. Keel to meet him at a health club, where he has been laying low and recovering from his injuries. While he receives a massage, a wearied and humbled Steed explains that since the original courier is dead they now need someone else to carry the formula for Morgantol to their contact at the World Health Organization, preferably someone who is already going to the conference. Dr. Keel agrees to deliver the formula to the World Health Organization in secret, and Steed explains that they'll need special arrangements to carry it.

Meanwhile, the one-eyed villain contacts his boss, a mysterious man whose face is never seen and whose voice is disguised over the line. As the leader ponders a chess game, he listens as Benson gives his report, finally telling him that he'll call back later with instructions. Back at the surgery, Carol helps Dr. Keel pack his case. He is tense, clearly not enjoying the idea of this mission.

Still in the massage room at the health club, Steed briefs a young agent named Scott. He is to transfer some items to Keel's case—an admission ticket which contains the formula in microdots and an empty but conspicuous envelope. The hope is that the villains will seize the envelope and ignore the ticket. Steed then calls his contact at the W.H.O., a doctor named Pallaine. Pallaine panics when hearing of the recent assault on the courier, claiming that he's only a doctor and not used to this kind of dangerous espionage. Steed assures Pallaine that the situation is well in hand.

Scott performs as instructed, but when he reaches the doctor's surgery, Keel has been called away by a patient. He manages to surreptitiously place the envelope and ticket into Dr. Keel's case, but, before Keel returns to receive instructions from Scott, Scott is attacked from behind by Benson, who throttles him nearly to death with his sword-stick. Benson then steals the envelope; and pretending to be the messenger from the World Health Organization, he tells Keel that the entire mission has been called off. Keel is relieved. Now, he can just enjoy his trip without the added pressure.

On the plane, Keel meets a nervous young woman named Yvette Declair, who appears to be extremely afraid of flying. She is relieved to have someone to talk to, and they quickly hit it off. Benson again calls his boss; the envelope is empty and useless. Dr. Keel must have the formula somewhere else on his person, but where?

Back at the surgery, Carol has discovered Scott, who is barely clinging to life. Steed arrives and discovers what happened. When he speaks to Scott, he explains that while he delivered the information to Keel's case, he never saw Keel and passed on the instructions. Dr. Keel is oblivious to the fact that he is carrying the formula while the enemy agents continue to try and retrieve it. Steed reports the situation to Pallaine and asks him to take action on his end. Keel must be told what he is carrying.

When Keel arrives in Geneva, Yvette is seriously ill, having had an attack of panic while flying. He rushes her off the plane and ignores Borsh, the contact sent for him by Pallaine. Borsh calls Pallaine to report back about missing Keel, and Pallaine orders him to follow Keel at all costs. But, by the time Borsh finishes his call, the doctor is nowhere to be found.

Part 2—At Yvette's apartment, Dr. Keel can find nothing physically wrong with her. He eventually concludes that she is suffering from an acute attack of nerves caused by her prior traumas; several of her family members were killed in a plane crash. He gives her a sedative. Clearly fond of Yvette, Dr. Keel invites her to lunch the next day and hands her one of his admission tickets. He tells her he will be staying in room 27 at the Hotel Alsace.

As he arrives at his room, he is met by Borsh, who demands to speak to him. Keel agrees begrudgingly, and the two enter the room to find Benson sitting in the dark, waiting for them with a gun. A brief fight ensues, and Borsh also draws a gun. Keel assumes that both men are his enemy and grabs Borsh's gun, shoving him aside. Benson fires, hitting Borsh, and then clubs Keel with his pistol.

When Keel awakens, he finds Benson's gun in his hand. Policemen are gathered around him, and Borsh's body lies nearby covered in a sheet. Keel's luggage has been ransacked, no doubt by Benson looking for the formula. One policeman, Dubois, interviews Keel as they try to reconstruct what happened. Keel struggles to explain the rather implausible scenario that he himself does not entirely understand, all with a sizable bump on the head! He stops short of explaining about Steed and the formula however. Happily, Steed shows up just at that moment and asks that Dubois release Keel into his custody. However, Dubois is reluctant, forcing Steed to use emergency means of persuasion—he pulls a gun on the policeman! Steed and Keel escape and meet with Pallaine.

Quickly, they figure out that the man Keel saw at his surgery was not Steed's fellow agent Scott, and Keel realizes that he has given Yvette the admission ticket with the microdots. Swiftly, they try to clean up this mess. Keel provides Yvette's address, and he and Steed rush over to her apartment. Meanwhile, Pallaine stays behind to make a phone call.

When Steed and Keel arrive at Yvette's home, and Keel knocks at the door. She does not answer, but on the other side of the door, Benson is searching her apartment. Hearing the knocks at the door, he quickly wraps up and flees via the fire escape. Noting that the door has been forced, Steed and Keel enter and find no sign of either Yvette or Benson. The place is a mess, and it is easy to imagine what happened. Steed wonders if Yvette could somehow be involved with the enemy, but

Keel doubts this, pointing out that they wouldn't need to search her apartment if she was in on the scheme. Steed is still doubtful but leaves to try and pull some strings to keep the police at bay.

Left alone in Yvette's apartment, Keel tries to tidy up a bit but is surprised by the appearance of Yvette's maid. After a brief moment of confusion, Keel manages to explain his presence there, and something the maid says sparks his memory. Yvette had mentioned her uncle's name—Bernard Bourg—and he realizes that's where she is! Looking up his name in a directory, he finds the address—37 Rue Viennes.

Part 3—Arriving at a sinister-appearing building, Keel rings the bell. After several rings and no answer, Keel steps inside. He looks around the cathedral-like room and spots a stuffed owl perched nearby. On a lighted dais in the middle of the room, there is a large figure covered in a sheet. Removing the sheet, Keel is startled by a massive stuffed ape underneath.

He is then startled again by the appearance of a pallid, odd man—Bourg. Bourg is distinctly lugubrious and speaks cryptically about all the animals he has prepared, trying to guess what kind of animal Keel might be. Keel is half convinced that the man is insane before Bourg finally explains that he is a taxidermist specializing in preparing pet animals after death—this is a funerary emporium. Nevertheless, Bourg denies all knowledge of Yvette, and even that he has a niece at all. However, the eccentric taxidermist speculates that Yvette might have meant Bern Aldbourg, a nearby German-speaking village, but he charges Keel fifteen francs to use his telephone!

Back at his office, Pallaine is fretting, worried about Keel being at large while fiddling absently with a chess piece, but Steed reassures him. Keel manages to ring Yvette, who is surprised to hear from him. Noting that neither his hotel room nor her apartment is safe, Keel arranges to meet Yvette at the taxidermist's shop. But he quickly calls Pallaine to inform him of the progress being made, providing the address of the taxidermist. Pallaine does not however reveal this information to Steed, claiming that the phone call was merely related to conference business.

Yvette arrives at the taxidermy shop and gives Keel the admission ticket. Shortly thereafter, Pallaine arrives and asks for the ticket as well. However, his behavior appears odd, and Keel insists on giving the ticket directly to Steed. Pallaine opens the door to allow Benson and two more thugs inside. They search the shop, looking for others, and return with Bourg bound and gagged. Pallaine then orders them to dispose of the witnesses, but Keel plays for time, inquiring about Pallaine's motives.

Becoming increasingly unhinged by the minute, Pallaine reveals that he regrets having accepted only a meager pay for his work on the formula; it is worth millions, and now he wants it all for himself. Brooking no further delay, he orders his men into action. Taking advantage of the momentary distraction created by Yvette's scream, Keel topples a display case on top of two of the thugs and then frees Yvette just as Steed and the police burst inside. The villains are quickly apprehended, and poor Mr. Bourg is released from his bonds. Steed is then introduced to Yvette, and she, Steed and Keel exit together arm in arm.

EPISODE NOTES

Mostly, "One for the Mortuary" seems to be standard spy stuff and fairly typical of the earlier episodes of the season. The program still very much seems to be Ian Hendry's show and the bulk of the action is Dr. Keel's. His compassion is very much on display. He meets a sick woman on the plane to Geneva and finds himself unable to resist helping her, despite the distraction it entails. This becomes the central twist as she unwittingly receives the admission ticket with the microdots, adding another complication to an otherwise straightforward plot.

One interesting aspect of this story, that stands out based on the surviving Tele-snaps, is the introduction of a mirror universe version (not literally) of John Steed—Benson, who is a bowler-hatted, sword stick-wielding blackguard with one lens of his glasses blacked out. He carries the superficial qualities of the English gentry just like the Steed of later years but is much more sinister. He reports to a man whose identity is not at first revealed, his voice is distorted over the telephone. I am slightly reminded of SPECTRE with Blofeld (whose face remains unseen throughout several films) and his eyepatch-wearing henchman Largo, except in this case it is a chess board that is 'stroked' instead of a Persian cat! It turns out that Steed's contact Dr. Pallaine is the mastermind behind the chess game being played, and he is finally stopped by the police and Steed in a taxidermy shop with a stuffed crocodile prominently on display, according to one particular Tele-snap. (It's those little touches that count.) And the shop owner is a true *Avengers* eccentric, much in the style of those that would more frequently appear in the filmed era.

CHAMPAGNE, CARS, CLOTHES, AND CANINES

Although Dr. Keel is wearing some kind of dark suit, no further details can be discerned from the one surviving production photograph. Fortunately, we have complete Tele-snaps for this episode, and I can confirm that Dr. Keel wears a dark two-piece suit, probably navy, with a white shirt and a dark tie with thin horizontal stripes. He later pairs this with a rather silly-looking fedora; its band has a very ostentatious Southwest Native American geometric pattern. I can also confirm that Steed starts out wearing a trench coat! (Okay, so not totally a myth.) Shortly thereafter, he is wearing only a towel as he receives a massage. He then wears a dark-gray (or possibly navy-blue) three-piece suit with a double-breasted waistcoat. (I believe this same waistcoat shows up in "Kill the King.")

SURVIVING FOOTAGE AND MATERIALS

Synopses
Rehearsal Script
John Cura Tele-snaps (76)
Production Photographs (1)

ADAPTATIONS AND RECONSTRUCTIONS

Big Finish Audio Adaptation
Reconstruction—Studio Canal Blu-ray Release, Season Five, Disc Five

14 (1.14.14) THE SPRINGERS

Written by John Whitney and Geoffrey Bellman
Directed by Don Leaver

MINISTRY RECORDS ARE UNAVAILABLE

GUEST CAST

Arthur Howard (Mr. Groves), Donald Morley (Neame), Charles Farrell (Straker), David Webb (Pheeney), Douglas Muir (One-Ten), Ann Sake (Melanie), Barbara Evans (Lisa), Brian Murphy (Haslam), Michael Forrest (Elton), Ian Ainsley (Prison Governor), Margo Andrew (Caroline Evans), Max Miradin (Arthur), Charles Saynor (Skewer), Tom Payne (Jessup)

PRE-TITLE/TEASER

Unknown. Intriguingly, the available camera script indicates a telecined film sequence "`KEEL ARRIVING AT PRISON`" after the title sequence, followed by a caption with the episode title. However, both are crossed out in pen, and the sequence is handwritten just after the ABC logo and before the title sequence, making it potentially the first episode to feature a scene before the title sequence. However, the available Tele-snaps indicate neither a scene before or after the title sequence, and the total Tele-snaps prior to the episode title number only three, so it is very difficult to decipher what may have actually happened upon broadcast. The safe assumption would be that there was no sequence before the opening titles.

SYNOPSIS

Part 1—In an effort to discover how convicts have been escaping from Dartmoor prison, Steed sends Keel undercover as inmate Dr. Fenton, while he poses as a guard. The prison governor is an old friend of Steed's and is aware of the plan. Steed briefs Keel on their mission, remarking that the fake facial scar that Keel wears as part of his disguise adds character. Steed and Keel believe that information is being passed to potential escapees via seemingly innocuous encoded conversations.

The escapees use canals leading to a coastal town named Belport, traveling from there to Scandinavia. Steed shows Keel a photograph of Fenton, and Keel is dismayed by the fact that there is little similarity between them. Steed reassures him that it's unlikely that anyone along the escapee pipeline has seen Fenton. Keel also indicates that he is being harassed by one of the guards named Haslam, and he is eager to leave as soon as possible. Promising to break him out shortly, Steed leaves and meets with One-Ten, who confirms Steed's suspicions about the escape route.

Part 2—Steed goes undercover as Commander Kenilworthy at the Belport College for Young Ladies; he has brought Melanie with him, who poses as his eighteen-year-old daughter. The corruption there is extensive and involves the principal, Groves, the school matron, Lisa, and Neame, a parent who seems very attached to Lisa.

It turns out that Haslam's apparent dislike for Keel is a put on to throw off suspicion, and, still believing him to be Dr. Fenton, he helps him escape from Dartmoor. Making his way through the locks to Belport, Keel finds it more difficult than expected to convince the other gang members of his identity but is ultimately successful.

Steed plants a tape recorder at the school but is caught and temporarily disappears from view as Keel arrives.

Part 3—Steed is held at the school, handcuffed to a chair. Groves is worried that Neame will kill Steed. Keel and Lisa arrive. Lisa is left guarding Steed, and Neame holds Keel at gunpoint until his identity can be verified. They show him to his living quarters in the meantime. Worried, Melanie phones One-Ten, who refuses to perform any further action without more information.

Elsewhere, a new visitor named Arthur arrives at the college; he's the man who will identify Fenton. Groves supervises moving Steed up to the storeroom. Meanwhile, Lisa expresses her worries that Groves is a risk to Neame, but he dismisses her concerns; Groves can be trusted, he's too concerned about his school. Groves visits Keel in his attic room and assures him that everything is going to plan. Melanie decides to act on her own and calls on the college, but she meets her friend and fellow student Caroline at the gate, and they decide to go out riding.

Keel calls for Skewer (another of the villains at the school), who arrives at the locked door to the attic room. Keel tricks him into opening the door and then attacks him, dispatching him and taking his gun. Locating Steed in the storeroom, Keel uses Skewer's keys to unlock the door. Before he can enter, Lisa interrupts him. Concerned that he has left his room and Skewer is nowhere to be found, she escorts Keel downstairs but not before he can surreptitiously slide the handcuff key under the door for Steed.

Neame is ready to leave and wants Arthur to identify Fenton first, but they are interrupted by the girls Melanie and Caroline arriving. Groves arrives to take the girls to the stables. After they leave, Keel pulls his gun on Neame and relieves him of his firearm. Caroline and Melanie quickly run upstairs while Groves finds his hat. There, they discover Steed having just escaped his bonds. Arthur reveals that Keel is not Fenton, but Keel manages to hold them both at gunpoint until Steed comes to his aid. Together, they round up everyone, and Steed calls One-Ten to send backup.

EPISODE NOTES

This is a slightly complicated prison escape story that is oddly difficult to summarize. Part 1 also seems suspiciously short. Despite that, the script exists, and it's easy to see how this story, properly executed, could have been a rather thrilling one. Intriguingly, it's a basic narrative that would be repeated in Season Two as "Intercrime," with Cathy Gale pretending to be a German convict in order to infiltrate an international criminal organization, and another variation on this theme would occur in "The Gilded Cage," one of the best stories from the third season.

Like those later stories, and judging from the available Tele-snaps, "The Springers" appears to be visually ordinary and largely set-based—hardly surprising, since the main sets are a prison and a school. Don Leaver no doubt however utilized his typical well-paced direction to give the story some excitement.

It is interesting to see how the writers were steadily improving at integrating the activities of the two leads. Here, their activities synergize well as they leapfrog over each other several times.

CHAMPAGNE, CARS, CLOTHES, AND CANINES

This episode begins with Steed dressed as a prison guard and Dr. Keel as an inmate. The Tele-snaps are rather blurry and this makes it hard to work out any details, but Dr. Keel is wearing a fake scar on his left cheek, and his outfit consists of a dark jacket, with snapped pockets, matching trousers, and a white shirt and dark tie. (Prisoners certainly dressed well back then!) He later wears a plaid shirt. Steed's guard outfit appears to be a dark suit with a white shirt but little else can be discerned. The tan overcoat returns at one point, and throughout many of the later scenes, he can be spied wearing a naval commander's uniform in his disguise as Commander Kenilworthy. (Even through the Tele-snaps it's clear that Macnee enjoyed playing this role.)

Though one outfit appears only in one of the production photos, this might be a historic occasion, as Steed wears a gray Prince of Wales blazer and a black waistcoat with silver buttons for possibly the first time. The blazer has a single flap pocket at the left breast and two at the hips. While it's difficult to tell whether the subsequent seasons would feature the exact same clothes, some form of gray Prince of Wales blazer and black waistcoat with silver buttons would be a major outfit for Steed for the entirety of the monochrome era. Clearly, it was a favorite outfit for Macnee. Here, he pairs them with a white shirt, tan trousers, and a pale-gray knit tie.

SURVIVING FOOTAGE AND MATERIALS

Synopses
Camera Script
John Cura Tele-snaps (81)

ADAPTATIONS AND RECONSTRUCTIONS

Big Finish Audio Adaptation
Reconstruction—Studio Canal Blu-ray Release, Season Six, Disc Six

15 (1.15.15) THE FRIGHTENERS

Written by Berkeley Mather
Directed by Peter Hammond

GUEST CAST

Willoughby Goddard (The Deacon), Philip Gilbert (Jeremy de Willoughby), Philip Locke (Moxon), Doris Hare (Mrs. Briggs), Stratford Johns (Sir Thomas Waller), Dawn Beret (Marylin Weller), David Andrews (Nigel), Godfrey James (Nature Boy), Neil Wilson (Beppi), Eric Elliot (Butler), Ann Taylor (Secretary), Ralph Tovey (Waiter), Benn Simons (Inspector Foster), with Eleanor Darling (Flower Seller), Benny Nightingale (Grekio), Victor Charrington (Fred the Cabbie), Frank Peters (Street Sweeper), and Charles Wood (Plain-clothes Officer)

PRE-TITLE/TEASER

In an office building, a businessman receives a telephone call and orders his men to get on with their job, "I want him frightened good and hard… don't overdo it, just make sure he doesn't forget it!"

SYNOPSIS

After discovering an organization of thugs who beat up people for a living, Steed and Dr. Keel follow the trail to a young man named Jeremy de Willoughby. Sir Thomas Waller has paid a man named The Deacon to beat-up Mr. Willoughby in order to keep him away from his daughter Marilyn. Dr. Keel tricks one of Deacon's thugs into revealing their secret hideout, and after arranging to have the whole gang arrested, they discover that de Willoughby is in fact a "professional marrier." However, they have no evidence without a confession. Can they trick him into revealing the truth…?

REVIEW

As a gritty, highly enjoyable hour of television, "The Frighteners" holds up remarkably well for its age. Despite its more mundane approach, the story remains strongly engaging. Particularly striking is one scene in which Mr. Willoughby is beat up by The Deacon and his men wearing stockings over their faces. Steed and Dr. Keel arrive just in time to rescue him.

In a characteristic line of continuity, this episode proves that the wit and humor the show has become so well known for was evident even in the first season. One of the most humorous moments involves Dr. Keel forcing a thug to reveal his secret base by convincing him that his neck is broken using medical sleight-of-hand. Once reaching the criminal hideout, Dr. Keel threatens to kill the kingpin with a syringe filled with hydrochloric acid. The resulting spray into the crime boss's eyes provides a wonderful moment of comedy, and we can see it all happening in the poor man's mind—the melting flesh and agony before he suddenly realizes he's okay. The syringe was merely filled with witch hazel, a pleasant facial toner and astringent.

All of this provides intriguing hints into Dr. Keel's character. Contrasting this kind of deception with his compassion for his patients and his gentle admonishment of Steed for his strong-arm tactics (and the occasional threat of mild torture for extraction of information), we have a picture of a man of contradictions, much like Steed himself. And this may be an indication of what connects the two men. They both use bluffs and subterfuge in order to get what they need, and, in true film noir style, walk a fine line between light and dark, and yet have a strong sense of justice. They are ruthless to the bad guys and equally compassionate to people in need; hard men when needed and gentle enough to stroke a cat's head when called for. This is likely the key to the success of this series and the formula for the chemistry between its stars. And yet, we also have Steed counseling Dr. Keel after his brazen bluff at the criminals' lair, reminding him to not be so impulsive. And this is another indication of Keel's unbridled passion for the cause.

Later, this relationship would morph after Keel left and become more of a unified quasi-romantic partnership between Steed and his female helpers, but here it is a constant push-and-pull between two very similar men with great respect for each other. It's too bad there is only the two extant episodes of them together.

As in some of the Honor Blackman episodes, in this episode Steed comes across as something of a bounder. This is highly enjoyable to watch. We know him in later episodes as a kindly and gentlemanly creation, but here, he is allowed to portray a freer, more cad-like character.

The production is typical of the era, sporting a live-in-studio 'warts-and-all' feel. On the other hand, the episode features no glaring mistakes or production errors, which is indeed a strong credit to the production staff and the actors, who perform exemplarily throughout. This is also a major testament to the power of the rehearse-record production standard of the day, something that has been abandoned in recent decades.

On the down side, the filmed street scenes in London interspersed with the videotaped segments stick out like a sore thumb and looks a trifle forced; it may or may not be stock film but it certainly feels like it. It does partially relieve the claustrophobia of the tight sets however, which was surely the intention.

Berkeley Mather is a pseudonym for John Evan Weston Davies, a writer born in Gloucester 25th February 1909. This is his only contribution to *The Avengers*.

CHAMPAGNE, CARS, CLOTHES, AND CANINES

Again, both Steed and Dr. Keel are shown wearing trench coats in the title sequence and in the title cards between acts. In the episode proper, Steed wears a gray three-piece suit with a white shirt with thin vertical stripes (barely visible and only in some shots) and a dark-gray silk tie. He also wears a black fedora with a silk band and carries a black umbrella with a whangee handle. The outfit is topped off with a white carnation in his lapel. In one scene, he smokes a cigarette with a holder. Later, he wears a dark wool overcoat with a felt collar, a light-colored floral scarf, and a black bowler with the whangee umbrella (so this may be the first verified appearance of both a bowler and a brolly). In the third act, he dons a black tuxedo and black tie with a white silk scarf. Dr. Keel wears a gray two-piece suit with a white shirt and a dark tie.

There are no dogs, but both Dr. Keel and Steed briefly stroke a friendly cat.

QUOTES

"At least you can do is to be frank with us. These people should be dealt with properly." (They hear a shout.) "Sounds as if somebody *is* being dealt with properly."

"Oh, just giving him a little gentle psychology. Hey—you don't really think I was going to shiv his blithering ear off with that slasher, do you?"

"So, Keels rush in where Steeds and angels fear to tread?"

SURVIVING FOOTAGE AND MATERIALS

Complete monochrome 16mm telerecording
Synopses
Dialogue Script
John Cura Tele-snaps (79)

ADAPTATIONS AND RECONSTRUCTIONS

Big Finish Audio Adaptation

16 (1.16.16) THE YELLOW NEEDLE

MINISTRY RECORDS ARE UNAVAILABLE

Written by Patrick Campbell
Directed by Don Leaver

GUEST CAST

Margaret Whiting (Jacquetta Brown), Andre Dakar (Sir Wilberforce Lungi), Bari Johnson (Chief Bai Shebro), Wolfe Morris (Ali), Dolores Mantez (Judith), Eric Dodson (Inspector Anthony), Christian Holder (Asiedu), Michael Barrington (Head Waiter), Humphrey Heathcote (Police Sergeant), Harold Holness (Porter), Juno (Puppy)

PRE-TITLE/TEASER

There is a short sequence preceding the onscreen title, but the actual details are uncertain, except that they depict Sir Wilberforce walking along the streets in London, presumably coming to visit Dr. Keel. (There are only two Tele-snaps of this scene.) The available camera script describes the following at the bottom of page 1. "Grams; Seque[ence] Big Ben 10.00" and "Traffic noises shot (S.O.F.) Tom-toms under seque[ence] to theme" followed by "FADE TO BLACK." On page 2, it indicates that there should be a title caption ("SUPER T/C | SLIDE: "THE YELLOW NEEDLE") superimposed over a shot, but this entire page is crossed out. This scene merely had a few lines with Carol greeting Sir Wilberforce and the latter asking to see Dr. Keel. It was probably deleted because it's non-essential. Page 3 begins with Carol coming in and announcing Sir Wilberforce's arrival. Judging from the Tele-snaps, the onscreen title appeared directly after the filmed sequence and a fade to black, but before the scene with Carol announcing Sir Wilberforce's arrival. The bottom line is that there was a pre-title sequence, but we don't know exactly what it was.

SYNOPSIS

Part 1—On the streets of London, a boy is shot dead at the feet of Sir Wilberforce Lungi, the prime minister of Tenebra. This failed assassination attempt had been intended for Sir Wilberforce, who is shepherding his country towards independence.

Back in Tenebra, this is a process that is met with opposition from Chief Bai Shebro, who will stop at nothing to prevent Sir Wilberforce's plans from succeeding. Dr. Keel then hosts Sir Wilberforce, who is an old friend and mentor of his, and his assistant Jacquetta Brown, an expert on African politics and sociology. He also administers regular insulin injections to Wilberforce who suffers from diabetes.

Part 2—Steed heads to Tenebra to meet Bai Shebro, undercover as journalist James Sanderson. He is surprised by the hospitality provided by Shebro, which includes air-conditioning and iced drinks. However, Shebro soon discovers that Steed is a fraud—the real James Sanderson is in Tokyo—and Steed is confined to his room under guard, his host unwilling to kill him due to an aversion to violence. Shebro's Syrian chemist Ali has also developed a toxin that will kill Sir Wilberforce, and he hints at Steed about something called 'the Kondor Society.'

Part 3—Shebro's fourth wife, Judith, frees Steed with the help of a servant named Asiedu, and he escapes to Tangiers where he phones Dr. Keel to warn him of an imminent attack against Sir Wilberforce. Jacquetta, however, is revealed to be a traitor. She palms a knockout drug into Dr. Keel's drink.

When Steed arrives back in London, he finds Dr. Keel unconscious and Sir Wilberforce infected with a fast-acting variant of yellow fever, introduced deliberately to his regular insulin injection by Jacquetta. With Sir Wilberforce near to death, Jacquetta is revealed to be a member of the Kondor

Society and is escorted away, while Dr. Keel fights to save his old friend's life.

EPISODE NOTES

This is an intriguing story, one that deals with international politics. Despite the expected condescension towards Africa and African characters that would have been common in the era, the narrative manages to provide two black characters with some notable depth. ***The Avengers*** was not at all known for featuring people of darker skin tones—something that would be formalized as an unspoken rule during the Clemens-Fennell era—and this meant that such characters were a rarity. Notable exceptions during the filmed era were "Small Game for Big Hunters" and "Have Guns—Will Haggle."

That Dr. Keel knew Sir Wilberforce and trained under him in tropical diseases was a fact that was likely a contrived convenience to the plot. Nevertheless, it adds an unusual international twist to the doctor's character, especially for a doctor with an otherwise modest practice—modest, except for the fact that he somehow manages to attract all the trouble in the London area!

Based on the available Tele-snaps, the visuals to this story appear to be ordinary, with the expected studio sets as a stand in for Africa.

CHAMPAGNE, CARS, CLOTHES, AND CANINES

Dr. Keel wears a gray two-piece suit with a white shirt and a gray knit tie. (This is almost certainly the same suit as in "The Frighteners" albeit with a different tie.) Later, he switches it out for a dark suit, probably the navy suit from "One for the Mortuary," a white shirt and the dark tie with thin diagonal stripes. Steed wears a completely new outfit, however, a dark (probably navy) jacket with a very pale (possibly cream or white) waistcoat with black buttons and matching trousers. (This is possibly the same waistcoat he is seen wearing in a publicity photo from "Build a Better Mousetrap" in which Macnee sits behind Honor Blackman on her motorcycle, though this would make the color a muted yellow.) The shirt underneath the waistcoat is white and the tie dark. The jacket has a notch collar. Once he goes undercover as a journalist, he effects a remarkable transformation: he wears an ill-fitting sports jacket over a loose white shirt with several of the buttons unbuttoned and thick glasses. Disheveled and sweaty, he also has dark circles under his eyes. (This is probably the most unkempt we will ever see Steed.) Later still, he is a bit more buttoned up when he wears a bowtie and a Panama hat, and his trusty umbrella is close at hand.

SURVIVING FOOTAGE AND MATERIALS

Synopses
Camera Script
John Cura Tele-snaps (80)

ADAPTATIONS AND RECONSTRUCTIONS

Big Finish Audio Adaptation
Reconstruction—Studio Canal Blu-ray Release, Season Six, Disc Six

17 (1.17.17) DEATH ON THE SLIPWAY

Written by James Mitchell
Directed by Peter Hammond

MINISTRY RECORDS ARE UNAVAILABLE

GUEST CAST

Peter Arne (Kolchek), Frank Thornton (Sir William Bonner), Nyree Dawn Porter (Liz Wells), Paul Dawkins (Sam Pearson), Sean Sullivan (Charles Fleming), Redmond Bailey (Geordie Wilson), Robert G. Bahey (Jack), Barry Keegan (Inspector Georgeson), Tom Adams (PC Butterworth), Douglas Muir (One-Ten), Gary Watson (Pardoe), Patrick Conner (PC Geary), Hamilton Dyce (Sergeant Brodie), Billy Milton (Chandler), Juno (Puppy)

PRE-TITLE/TEASER

Yes, definitely. This is described in the first two lines of the synopsis. There are seven Tele-snaps depicting this scene, so it must have been a fairly long sequence. There is no surviving script, however.

SYNOPSIS

Two men, Kolchek and Fleming, enter a top-secret government dockyard and attempt to break into a safe. Discovering that they are being watched, Kolchek strangles the man observing them and drops his body into the ocean. Posing as a metallurgist, Steed investigates the disappearance of a fellow agent, and the body of Kolchek's victim is discovered. Kolchek and Fleming are still on the premises, working by day as part of the company, and Fleming starts to get cold feet. Kolchek recognizes Steed and attempts to kill him but fails. It turns out that the criminals want to blow up a hidden nuclear submarine, but Steed manages to throw the bomb into the water where it harmlessly explodes.

EPISODE NOTES

Until "Dragonsfield," this and "Kill the King" are as close as it gets to a Steed solo adventure; Dr. Keel is only seen at the beginning and end of the story, and he declines to help Steed, preferring to remain with his practice. There were other Keel-lite episodes in the first half of the season, but, even in those, he featured rather more than here.

What ensues is a gripping cloak-and-dagger mystery with excellent visuals, judging from the available Tele-snaps which reveal a gritty industrial setting. Peter Hammond's decision to shoot many scenes through wire meshes gives the production a contrasted film noir look.

Admittedly, not much is known about this story since no script exists, and the accepted narrative is based upon Tele-snaps and prior synopses. The Big Finish audio adaptation seems to take enormous liberties with the storyline.

Steed's dog puppy is featured in this episode and appears to accompany Steed to the dockyard. Peter Arne also makes his first appearance in the series.

CHAMPAGNE, CARS, CLOTHES, AND CANINES

In one of the surviving production photographs, Steed is pictured wearing a gray three-piece suit while talking on the telephone. His dog Puppy is by his side. During the episode proper, he appears to be (possibly) in the same suit, though it is difficult to tell since there are no clear full-length Tele-snaps of him (the most prominent closeup is through a metal screen). However, it looks as though the waistcoat is double-breasted, which may make it the same suit that shows up later in "Kill the King." He later wears it with the tan overcoat, and still later he wears a black polo shirt both solo and with the tan overcoat. Dr. Keel, as previously mentioned, is barely in the episode, but he appears to be wearing the same navy suit from "One for the Mortuary" with the dark tie with thin diagonal stripes.

SURVIVING FOOTAGE AND MATERIALS

Synopses
John Cura Tele-snaps (87)
Production Photographs (2)

ADAPTATIONS AND RECONSTRUCTIONS

Big Finish Audio Adaptation
Reconstruction—Studio Canal Blu-ray Release, Season Five, Disc Five

18 (1.18.18) DOUBLE DANGER

MINISTRY RECORDS ARE UNAVAILABLE

Written by Gerald Verner, adapted by John Lucarotti
Directed by Roger Jenkins

GUEST CAST

Peter Reynolds (Al Brady), Vanda Hudson (Lola Carrington), Kevin Brennan (Leonard Bruton), Ronald Pember (Bert Mills), Charles Hodgson (Mark Crawford), Robert Mill (Harry Dew), Gordon Phillott (John Bartholomew), Blaise Wyndham (Taxi Driver), Howard Daley (Ted Mace), Uncredited: Douglas Muir (Voice of One-Ten)

PRE-TITLE/TEASER[1]

Harry Dew and Lew Sleater are waiting at a prison wall in their getaway car to help Ted Mace escape. Mace climbs over the wall in his convict clothes and they drive off together, but they are stopped by another car with Al Brady and Bert Mills inside, who then kidnap Mace and rush him away in their car. Lew jumps out and fires his handgun at the escaping vehicle and Mace is hit.

SYNOPSIS

Part 1—Dr. Keel is kidnapped by Al Brady and Bert Mills under false pretenses and taken to a houseboat where he is forced to treat recently escaped convict Ted Mace for a bullet wound. Insisting that he doesn't have what he needs to perform surgery, he requests equipment from his nurse Carol and manages to slip in a coded message asking her to call Steed.

But it turns out that Steed is who sprung Mace from prison in the first place. He was working undercover as a gang boss himself, only to have Mace snatched from his own men by Brady and Mills. The two gangs are looking for a stolen cache of diamonds and only Mace knows where it is. Steed is trying to recover them for the authorities but is caught in the middle of the activities of the rival gangs.

Keel is told by Brady and Mills that he must save Mace's life or he'll be killed himself. Unfortunately, lacking the ability to provide a much-needed blood transfusion, Dr. Keel is unable to help Mace, who finally dies.

---

1 Based on the surviving camera script, this sequence was shot on-location with 35mm film and was originally intended to be telecined into the broadcast prior to the title sequence (and just after the ABC logo). However, this appears to have been changed prior to broadcast as the available six Tele-snaps show this sequence occurring after the title sequence. The scene appears to have been shot during the daytime despite the original rehearsal script calling for it to be shot at night.

Part 2—Keel tries to escape but his attempt is thwarted. Nevertheless, the crooks spare him because they believe Mace may have told him something before he died. Steed finds the houseboat and deceives the gang into thinking that a large group of policemen have arrived to round them up. They scurry from the boat like rats, leaving Keel and Steed alone to discuss the situation.

At a different hideout, the gang leader Bruton talks to Brady and they decide there's still hope for the diamonds, providing that Keel heard some of Mace's semi-conscious ramblings. Acting on a hunch, Steed finds an old man who previously rented a home to Ted Mace and his girlfriend Lola. Steed is run off by Mills shortly afterwards, receiving a grazing bullet wound to the forehead, just managing to catch the old man's name as he does so—Bartholomew. Unfortunately, the name Bartholomew is unfamiliar to both Steed and One-Ten.

Soon after, Carol Wilson is abducted by the gang and held as a hostage at a Hart Street garage, and thus Keel is forced by phone to divulge what he knows. The information does not help the criminals however, as they do not recognize the name Bartholomew either.

Part 3—Gang member Lola is captured and questioned, finally being forced to reveal where Carol is being held. Steed and Keel head for the garage, but Carol escapes ahead of them with Bruton's help; he is double-crossing everyone.

When Steed and Keel arrive at the garage, Carol is already gone, and the two men and Lola are captured by Brady and Mills, who bind them all and leave them to die from carbon monoxide poisoning from the car engine they leave running. Steed and Keel manage to break free however and quickly recover from the fumes.

Meanwhile, Brady and Mills interrogate Bartholomew but get nothing out of him. He's too old to be afraid to die. Nevertheless, something he says cues Brady in, and they find the diamonds in Bartholomew's burial plot nearby. However, Steed and Keel show up, and Steed takes the diamonds and covers the crooks with a revolver just as it starts to rain.

EPISODE NOTES

This episode was originally written by Gerald Verner but was subsequently re-written by John Lucarotti. Verner detested the changes and felt vindicated when the episode received one of the worst reviews of the season in ***The Stage and Television Today***, which derided the episode as clichéd and lacking in thrills. Verner never wrote for ***The Avengers*** again, but Lucarotti contributed several more scripts over the next three years, none of which are particularly noteworthy.

Despite the controversy, I find quite a bit to appreciate here. The accusations of cliché-ridden dialogue and one-dimensional gangster type characters notwithstanding, the plot appears to be a rather exciting one with a lot going on—evidenced by the circuitous synopsis above. The careful interweaving of the activities of Steed and Dr. Keel also continued. On the other hand, the show seems to be continuing some of its own recently-established tropes—Carol Wilson is captured again and used as a hostage, and once more the criminals are searching for loot that was hidden by an unconscious or dying character (both are plot elements in "Hunt the Man Down"). The kidnapping of Dr. Keel is not new either—neither to the series nor to the common B-grade film noir.

None of this is inexcusable—indeed, the filmed era would positively thrive on its own tropes, repeated ad nauseum—but the first season is known more for its writing and carefully constructed plots than lightweight adventure stories, so it's easy to imagine that this story might have seemed run-of-the-mill for the era.

Nevertheless, the visuals appear to have been well-executed. The houseboat set was detailed and well-lit, and the episode began with an exciting prison escape under a hail of bullets. This opening scene was filmed on 35mm film on location, so it would have added considerably to the story's visual excitement, though it was filmed during the day rather than at night as scripted.

CHAMPAGNE, CARS, CLOTHES, AND CANINES

Dr. Keel wears a two-piece suit in a mid-tone with a subtle stripe. His shirt is white and his tie is again diagonally-striped albeit more thinly. Later, he's looking pretty disheveled and unshaven, his shirt unbuttoned, and no tie. Steed returns to his heavy tan overcoat with the heavily-stitched cuffs and a gray three-piece suit. This is later traded out for an even darker three-piece suit, possibly navy, with a black bowler, dark socks, and black shoes. The tie appears to be a floral pattern in silk. Again, he carries an umbrella with a whangee handle.

SURVIVING FOOTAGE AND MATERIALS

Synopses
Rehearsal & Camera Script
John Cura Tele-snaps (78)
Production Photographs (53)

ADAPTATIONS AND RECONSTRUCTIONS

Big Finish Audio Adaptation
Reconstruction—Studio Canal DVD Release, Season Three, Disc Four

19 (1.19.19) TOY TRAP

Written by Bill Strutton
Directed by Don Leaver

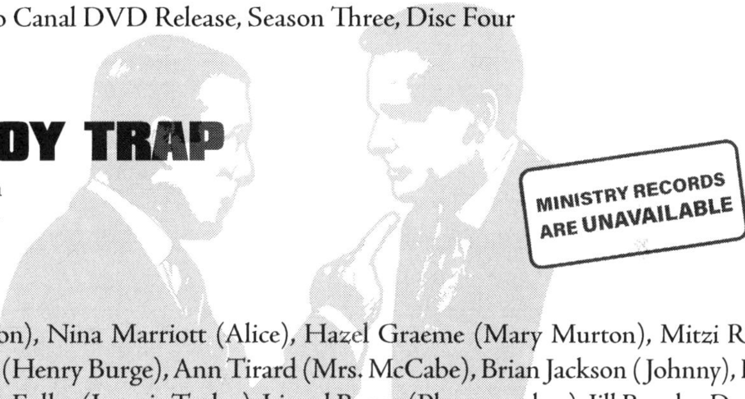

GUEST CAST

Sally Smith (Bunty Seton), Nina Marriott (Alice), Hazel Graeme (Mary Murton), Mitzi Rogers (Ann), Tony Van Bridge (Henry Burge), Ann Tirard (Mrs. McCabe), Brian Jackson (Johnny), Brandon Brady (Freddie), Tex Fuller (Lennie Taylor), Lionel Burns (Photographer), Jill Brooke, Dorothy Watson, George Betton, Felicity Peel, Peter Fenton (Speaking Extras)

PRE-TITLE/TEASER

A man searches a notice board for a listing that is to his liking. He finds one with a photo of a female model: May, a 20-year-old brunette with the measurements 36-14-35. He phones her and asks to see her. She immediately agrees and gives him her address. The camera focuses upon a buxom female doll and the title caption appears next to it.

SYNOPSIS

Part 1—Bunty and May meet after a day's work at a department store, but as they are changing out of their work clothes Bunty notices bruises on May's torso. May seems unhappy and distant and announces that she cannot make that evening's dinner plans due to another engagement.

Bunty instead meets Dr. Keel for a dinner date and confides her concerns about May's behavior to him. Keel agrees to check in on May at her home, and they stop by there on the way to dinner. Finding no sign of May, they instead discover compromising photos of both May and another girl—May is involved in pornography and prostitution. Unseen by either of them, Bunty and Keel are spied on by a mysterious man on crutches outside May's flat. They cancel their dinner reservations and instead eat a more modest meal at his home where Steed joins them. Steed agrees to investigate the girls' seedy and salacious lifestyles.

Meanwhile, Freddie, the man on crutches seen earlier, reports to an odd woman in heavy makeup named Meyer. She instructs Freddie to clear out May's flat.

The next morning, Steed and Keel visit a photographer's shop in Soho, and Steed recognizes the other girl in May's photos among the photographer's collection. Her name is Chrissie, and the photographer agrees to set her up with Steed. He phones the girl but receives no answer. She is dead upon the floor of her flat.

Part 2—Steed visits the department store where the girls work but is unable to find out any more about Chrissie. He is convinced that Chrissie was killed because she wanted to get out of prostitution and is concerned the same thing might happen to May.

Pretending to be a doctor, Steed speaks to the department store boss—a man named Burge—about May and receives the address of her parents' house. He also shows Burge a photo of Chrissie and finds out she used to work at the store over a year ago. He speaks to another employee named Alice also, and she turns out to be very familiar with Chrissie's lifestyle, providing many details. It is now clear that they have stumbled upon an extensive vice ring run from the continent. Steed suggests that Bunty be used to infiltrate the organization but Keel is horrified by the prospect.

Later, Dr. Keel is tricked by a caller who claims to be May, asking him to come to her flat. There, he is instead beat up by Freddie and two other men, who try to intimidate him into silence. Investigating the flat of a bouncer named Lennie Taylor, Steed and Dr. Keel find May Murton inside, clearly beaten and traumatized.

Part 3—Having fallen into the trap of prostitution, May has been held captive, her bruises the result of an attempt to escape. Steed and Keel take her back to Keel's surgery where she is treated. The prostitution ring preys upon young, single women who make little money and are eager to leave the hostel where they live, and all of it is run by the madam Meyer, assisted by Burge's endless supply of attractive women that pass through his employ.

After setting up an ambush in the toy department of the store with Bunty as bait, Steed fights Burge and Freddie, as well as Meyer, who underneath all her makeup turns out to be the woman running the hostel where the girls live. All the criminals are rounded up by Steed and his fellow agents, but Dr. Keel is furious at Steed for involving Bunty and threatens to beat the living daylights out of him if he ever does anything like that again. They part without a resolution to their argument with Keel telling Steed, "From now on, you're on your own."

EPISODE NOTES

This appears to have been an extraordinary story with a realism, bluntness, and salaciousness that would have been uncommon at the time. The only equivalent would be the Season Four episode "A Touch of Brimstone," which would possibly exceed the seediness of "Toy Trap," though it could hardly be called 'realistic.' The plot of "Toy Trap" appears to be especially well-structured, making it a shame that Bill Strutton did not write any further episodes. Judging by the ample number of production photographs and the Tele-snaps, the visuals appear to be very strong as well. In another interesting parallel to Season Four, there is a climactic fight scene in the toy department of the store, much like in "Death at Bargain Prices," with Steed popping out of a toy teepee and surprising his foes.

Nevertheless, the real show-stopper is the violent argument between Steed and Dr. Keel after the main fisticuffs are over. In a foreshadowing of future relationships between Steed and his assistants, Dr. Keel's moral indignation overflows, and he excoriates Steed for his amoral manipulations, threatening him with bodily harm should he try anything similar again. The episode ends with their apparent falling out; their argument is not settled, and Keel makes it clear that he doesn't want to work with Steed any longer. This makes the episode a perfect fit for transmission right before "Dragonsfield," in which Hendry was absent for entirely different reasons, thus providing an explanation for Hendry's departure from the series. However, such was the nature of episodic television that the reset button was pressed each week, returning the show to its formula under the assumption that last week's troubles had been resolved. At the time, no one involved in the production, including Hendry himself, had any idea that he would leave at season's end. Indeed, this episode was aired long before "Dragonsfield" was shot and the beginning of the Equity strike that resulted in Hendry's departure. Nevertheless, many fans have noted this dramatic development as a missed opportunity, one that looms almost as large as the fact that we can't see any of these episodes!

We'll just have to assume that Steed and Keel eventually cooled off and reconciled, with Steed perhaps accepting a measure of Keel's argument, evidenced by a tempering of his predilection for manipulation in future seasons. However, a few subsequent lines, including a more humorous one in "Tunnel of Fear," would suggest that the core disagreement was far from over.

CHAMPAGNE, CARS, CLOTHES, AND CANINES

Steed wears a dark-gray three-piece single-breasted suit with six round cloth buttons and a lapeled waistcoat, paired with a white shirt, a dark tie, and a black bowler with the whangee umbrella. The trousers are pleated, and the coat is double-vented and has three flap pockets—one at the left breast, two at the hips—and one ticket pocket. This is the first appearance of a major outfit for Steed, some variation of which would continue to appear until the final season of the series. Steed's Prince of Wales blazer and black waistcoat also appear, but since I cannot verify that he wore them in "The Springers" (or earlier) with absolute certainty, this also might be their first appearance in the series. Dr. Keel wears a dark two-piece suit with the same tie as in the previous episode.

SURVIVING FOOTAGE AND MATERIALS

Synopses
Camera Script
John Cura Tele-snaps (81)
Production Photographs (138)

ADAPTATIONS AND RECONSTRUCTIONS

Big Finish Audio Adaptation

20 (1.20.20) TUNNEL OF FEAR

Written by John Kruse
Directed by Guy Verney

GUEST CAST

Anthony Bate (Harry Black), Miranda Connell (Claire), Doris Rogers (Mrs. Black), John Salew (Jack Wickram), Douglas Muir (One-Ten), Douglas Rye (Billy Flowers), Stanley Platts (Maxie Lardner), Bill Maxam (George Milner), Hazel Coppen (Madame Zenobia), Morris Perry (Police Sergeant), Julie Samuel (Rosie) with Juno (Puppy)

PRE-TITLE/TEASER

At a coastal amusement park, a carnival barker invites a middle-aged man to take a ride through "the tunnel of fear," but when the car emerges at the other end, only his umbrella is still riding. The man is missing.

SYNOPSIS

As Dr. Keel is about to shut down his practice for the evening, a banging at the back door produces an injured man with cuts to his head and back. Though the man's story for how he received his injuries doesn't quite gel, Dr. Keel dresses his wounds. When the unidentified man passes out from pain, a quick search through his pockets reveals a letter to his mother that describes an escape from prison. His name revealed to be Harry Black, when confronted with the letter, he proclaims his innocence, and this leads Dr. Keel and Steed on an investigation through a funfair in which the local hypnotist might be using his abilities for more than just idle entertainment…

REVIEW

Originally found in the United States, the surviving film print of "Tunnel of Fear" was purchased in the 1990s in an unmarked can by an anonymous UK film collector. The film remained unidentified in his collection for years until 2016, when the collector decided to catalog his films and present some of them for sale. It was at this time that he discovered that the film was a highly desirable missing episode and posted online for help in placing it with a buyer. Rights holder StudioCanal were not initially interested in purchasing the film, only in making a copy, but the film was eventually purchased—along with seventy other film prints that included episodes of ***Z Cars, Dr. Findlay's Casebook,*** and ***Softly, Softly***—with the aid of the classic television organization Kaleidoscope. The announcement of the purchase was made by Kaleidoscope member Christopher Perry on 3 October 2016 via their Facebook page.

"Tunnel of Fear" was greeted with excitement by fans after it was screened twice that year, once at the Missing Believed Wiped event at Birmingham City University and three weeks later at BFI South Bank in London. Until it was found, there was little information available on "Tunnel of Fear." It was, in fact, one of a number of episodes for which no camera script survived, leaving one to speculate based on the John Cura Tele-snaps and surviving production photographs as to what it was actually about.

As it turns out, it is a near perfect complement to the other extant episodes. Sadly, the surviving first part of "Hot Snow" and the complete episode "Girl on the Trapeze" do not feature John Steed at all. While Steed is in "The Frighteners", Dr. Keel seems to have most of the action to himself. Steed is comparatively laid back and comes across as a much more mysterious character operating on the periphery. Thus, it could be said that we're truly seeing Steed for the very first time in this episode.

Much to my surprise, there is so much more to the character of Steed at this early stage than anyone ever thought. Every character facet that Steed ever exhibited comes through, and he is very much the same as he was during the second and third seasons. He is casual, insouciant, boyishly enthusiastic, and he even has a humorous turn as an eccentrically costumed funfair barker with a variable accent. He was often a bit of a cad in the second and third seasons, for which he was reproached by the substantially more moralistic Cathy Gale, and here he gives a few dancing girls a pinch on the bum. Far from making him seem like a soulless bounder, in retrospect, this projects Steed as a very complex and nuanced character, with multiple layers of personality hiding just beneath the surface. Here, it is all somewhat raw, but in later seasons Macnee would play Steed as if those many layers were all barely submerged beneath a suave, savagely-dressed exterior and about to burst through at any moment, whether it was when playing with toy soldiers in "Requiem" or inviting a secretary to sit on his lap in "How to Succeed….At Murder". But, here, he does burst out completely, and in full costume, and he seems delighted by the opportunity to ham it up. The boyish side also comes out when he displays apparent glee for the odd electronic cipher contraption in the criminals' hideout. Equally, Macnee seems to have a blast while under the influence of hypnotism, spouting seeming drivel while comically staring wild-eyed at the camera.

For Dr. Keel's part, Ian Hendry's lines do a great job of setting the tone for his morality and strong sense of justice. And, generally, his scenes and interactions with Steed set a tone for the series that was maintained throughout the next two seasons (with Honor Blackman as Cathy Gale becoming the other side of the coin after the departure of Ian Hendry). In this season, we're given a vision of Steed as a shadowy secret agent (with a fun side), someone that is almost a confidence man, willing to play it fast and loose with the rules in order to get the job done, someone who needs another more honest man to keep him on an even moral keel. Dr. Keel was that man.

Keel is a highly ethical man, a physician, willing to help people to the point of risking his own life in the process, but his sense of justice and obeisance to right-and-wrong don't allow him to entirely disobey the rule of law. For example, when presented with injured escaped convict Harry Black, he's willing to patch him up, but is also resigned to send him back to jail, (not without a good dose of sympathy), in hopes that the system he believes in will bring the innocent man justice. Predictably, Steed shows up and has other ideas—using Black as a means of stopping much more serious evil-doers. Despite his law-abiding tendencies, Dr. Keel is also a man with an innate sense of adventure, one that might never have been tapped if not for the tragic death of his fiancée Peggy, one that just needed the prompting of a more reckless man to engage his own riskier side. Thus, this ethical tug-of-war is the theme of this season and the reason why the two men work so well together. Together, the two of them pivot around a central theme of vigilante film noir-style justice—full of self-serving characters that are just barely on one side or the other of moral neutrality.

Having committed themselves to this obviously riskier action that once again takes Dr. Keel away from his practice, we see that it is John Steed's recklessness and confidence man bluffs that are needed to save the day—not to mention unexpected high-tech spy devices. When he presents the criminals with a lit cigarette, claiming it's actually a bomb, we're convinced he's bluffing, at least until such time as the tables have turned and Dr. Keel holds the criminals at bay with a gun. At this point, Steed carefully snips away the burning part of the cigarette and laments the cost of such high-priced and specialized equipment. He casually offers Keel one of the ciggies, who politely declines, once again demonstrating how far each character is willing to go. Dr. Keel cannot be tempted to use the same desperate measures that Steed is willing to employ; he will fight criminals, wield guns, engage in fisticuffs, and even use drugs to subdue them, but he will not resort to blowing them up with explosive cigarettes. Keel's line about "thinking of giving it up" could be a hint about giving up the whole spy business, which indeed, he ultimately does.

Starting out with a pre-title sequence reminiscent of a very similar scene in the film ***Brighton Rock***, "Tunnel of Fear" is an excellent example of an early ***Avengers*** episode, one that gives more insight into the characters and their relationship than I personally thought would have been possible, but, despite the fact that I greatly enjoyed it, I cannot quite give it top marks.

The episode is the only episode written for the series by John Kruse and is a well-crafted example of its era; in deference to many other episodes this season, each act leaves the audience hanging at key moments in the narrative, guaranteeing that they'll return after the commercial break. It is also ably directed by one-time ***Avengers*** director Guy Verney, who manages to pull creative camera work out of the show's largely studio bound videotaped production, but the episode's central idea of robbery through hypnotism doesn't quite fly; I'm just not convinced that anyone is that talented at hypnosis. ***The Avengers*** is largely grounded in a reality similar to our own, one where hypnosis simply doesn't have that much power to influence behavior. The hypnotism idea does however fit in with other episodes in which psychic abilities exist, such as "Warlock" and "Too Many Christmas Trees", and it is an interesting twist for what fans of ***The Avengers*** always thought was a much more mundane and grounded first season. (I note this concept borrows a page from the early German expressionist film ***The Cabinet of Dr. Caligari***, which also features a master hypnotist who uses his abilities to commit crimes.) Thus, I'll consider it another piece of that puzzle that says ***The Avengers*** has a little more of the mysterious and arcane in it than does our own world.

While "Tunnel of Fear" will likely be considered essential by diehard fans who want to know more about the origins of the series, it's unlikely to be as interesting to casual viewers and those who have never seen the show before. They will probably prefer to start out with one of the Honor Blackman and Diana Rigg seasons before treading back here to see John Steed's slightly more humble and mundane origins.

CHAMPAGNE, CARS, CLOTHES, AND CANINES

In this episode, Steed's most distinctive outfit is a long-sleeved traditional Chinese robe, possibly made of silk or satin with extensive brocading. He pairs it with a turban with strings of pearls and tall white feathers jutting from the top. Later, the black waistcoat with silver buttons shows up under a gray suit. When dressing more casually at the finale, he wears tan trousers with a thin belt and a white shirt with the sleeves rolled up above his elbows. Dr. Keel wears a dark-gray two-piece suit with the same thinly-striped tie as before.

Steed's Great Dane, Puppy (played by Juno), makes another appearance, the first in a surviving episode, having previously appeared in "Ashes of Roses," "The Yellow Needle," and "Death on the Slipway." Steed's Rolls-Royce Silver Cloud is also briefly seen before it is stolen by Harry Black during Puppy's attempt at escape.[2] Gee, thanks, Puppy! Steed seems eager to get rid of Puppy in this episode, even offering her to Dr. Keel "to keep the children quiet in the waiting room." Perhaps it was her lack of leash training that triggered him. We're left to assume that he succeeded in palming off Puppy to a new owner as she never appears again. Sadly, the canine actor Juno died from injuries received in a London Underground accident while on the way to shoot *Candid Camera* in the month following this episode's recording.

QUOTES

"Woman's intuition, doctor." Keel: "Men can have it too, you know!"

"Look, it's none of my business to judge you one way or the other. You came into my surgery, and I'm helping you. I might even go on helping you, but first you've got to help yourself. Now, breaking out of jail doesn't seem a very good way of doing that."

"Look at Puppy!" (Puppy takes to Harry Black immediately.) "Ah—she likes him. She never makes a mistake on character. She's very unpopular."

"I can tell you just one thing. Your future isn't worth this much."

(referring to Madame Zenobia) "She's been in the fortune-telling lark so long, she can't even order a pint without making a riddle of it." "She managed to tuck a pound note away pretty quickly."

"I know a fellow in the Post Office. It's a fascinating piece of bric-a-brac, you know. I should think two and a half thousand words a minute, eight cipher messages simultaneously."

"I must confess, I nearly frightened myself for a moment. I'm quite frightened now—they cost a fortune!"

SURVIVING FOOTAGE AND MATERIALS

Complete monochrome 16mm film telerecording
Synopses
John Cura Tele-snaps (75)
Production Photographs (67)

---

2 Harry was played by a double in this scene since Anthony Bate was unavailable, and the double wears a flat cap, though presumably to help disguise his face rather than as a fashion statement.

ADAPTATIONS AND RECONSTRUCTIONS

Big Finish Audio Adaptation
Reconstruction—Studio Canal Blu-ray Release, Season Five, Disc Six

21 (1.21.21) THE FAR DISTANT DEAD

Written by John Lucarotti
Directed by Peter Hammond

MINISTRY RECORDS ARE UNAVAILABLE

GUEST CAST

Katherine Blake (Dr. Ampara Alverez Sandoval), Reed de Rouen (Luis Garcia), Francis de Wolff (Hercule Zeebrugge), Guy Deghy (Inspector Gauvreau), Tom Adams (Rayner), Andreas Malandrinos (Godoy), Michael Mellinger (Mateos)

PRE-TITLE/TEASER

Yes, there is a pre-title sequence, but there is no surviving script and the Tele-snaps depict in only three frames a man tasting his soup and then collapsing in pain. This is presumably the fisherman who became sickened by the hydraulic fluid that was being sold as cooking oil.

SYNOPSIS

On his way back to England from Chile, Dr. Keel visits Mexico City in order to help out after a catastrophic cyclone. Realizing that his services as a doctor will be highly useful in the aftermath, he volunteers his assistance to the local police chief Luis Garcia.

There, he meets another doctor, Ampara Alvarez Sandoval, and she and Keel bond over their common passion for attending to the injured and the sick before traveling together to the devastated areas. Quickly, Dr. Keel comes across a case of food poisoning. The man became ill after using cooking oil that was donated by a local warehouse manager named Godoy.

After testing the oil, Keel finds out that it is actually highly toxic hydraulic fluid. After questioning Godoy, Dr. Keel finds out that he was unaware of the oil's deadly properties and had donated it under the assumption that it was truly cooking oil and that the owner would not mind donating it during the emergency. Meeting again with police chief Garcia, Dr. Keel and Ampara hear of a much earlier case of a fatal poisoning in the small coastal town of Vera Cruz months earlier.

They travel to Vera Cruz and investigate, asking the dead man's widow about the incident. She reveals that her husband died after stealing the cooking oil from a steamer ship. Research soon reveals that the shipment came from Marseilles. They travel there and meet with police inspector Gauvreau, but the process quickly comes to a dead end; Gauvreau knows nothing that can help them. Unknown to Keel and Ampara, a man named Raynor has noticed their presence and contacts his boss, the same mysterious merchant responsible for the hydraulic fluid fiasco. Later, Dr. Ampara's hotel room is invaded by a man named Caron, who is caught searching through Ampara's bag. After the tables are turned by Dr. Keel, Caron is forced under duress to reveal the name of his boss—Zeebrugge. Soon after, unknown to Dr. Keel, Ampara confronts Zeebrugge directly at gunpoint, threatening to kill him in revenge for all the suffering he has caused in her home country. Zeebrugge confesses that the fatal theft and donation were accidental and he only changed the labels to avoid higher import taxes, planning to issue corrected labels later. Unmoved by his paltry effort at contrition, Ampara destroys much of Zeebrugge's precious art collection in a rage. However, Dr. Keel arrives with the French police. He calms Ampara down as Zeebrugge is led away for his crimes, confident that justice is being done.

EPISODE NOTES

This episode was the second solo Keel adventure after "Girl on the Trapeze" earlier in the year. This was a surprising decision considering that the second half of the season had been much more successful at weaving plots that heavily involved both the leads. Thus, this story would have made a perfect adventure to air right after "Toy Trap"—an episode that featured an apparent falling out between the two men at the climax—but in between is "Tunnel of Fear," in which they are seen happily working together again as if nothing had happened, with only a good-natured double entendre from Keel to indicate that he was "thinking of giving it up."

Nevertheless, this story appears to have worked fairly well, pairing Dr. Keel with another passionate doctor like himself. Perhaps unsurprisingly however, Dr. Keel finds himself playing the same moral role with Ampara as he does with Steed. She also shows a willingness to be more ruthless than Keel, threatening to kill the criminal responsible for so many deaths. Zeebrugge is also a somewhat amoral villain. Not necessarily evil, though he does not seek to do harm deliberately, he is unconcerned with how his actions might affect others.

Though there were no on location shoots for this story, the episode once again featured foreign locations—Mexico and France—and judging from the available production photographs, the sets for the Mexican refugee camp and makeshift hospital are notably convincing. To add a touch of native realism, live chickens were used in the studio!

Despite especially fine sets, this is another one of those episodes where it's difficult to tell how successful it would have been based on the scraps of evidence. It likely would have depended on the quality of the performances and pacing. It is noteworthy however that Sydney Newman singled "The Far Distant Dead" out as being unsatisfactory, perhaps already expressing a desire for more fun and fantasy than the dark tone presented here.

CHAMPAGNE, CARS, CLOTHES, AND CANINES

Dr. Keel wears a slightly ill-fitting light-gray two-piece suit with a white shirt and matching handkerchief and the same dark horizontally-striped tie as in "One for the Mortuary." Mostly though, he goes very casual, not wearing the jacket and with his sleeves rolled up above his elbows. He wears a signet ring on his left little finger.

SURVIVING FOOTAGE AND MATERIALS

Synopses
John Cura Tele-snaps (76)
Production Photographs (56)

ADAPTATIONS AND RECONSTRUCTIONS

Big Finish Audio Adaptation
Reconstruction—Studio Canal Blu-ray Release, Season Six, Disc Nine

22 (1.22.22) KILL THE KING

MINISTRY RECORDS ARE UNAVAILABLE

Written by James Mitchell
Directed by Roger Jenkins

GUEST CAST

Burt Kwouk (King Tenuphon), Patrick Allen (General Tuke), Lisa Peake (Mei Li), Moira Redmond (Zoe Carter), Carole Shelley (Ingrid Storm), Peter Barkworth (Crichton-Bull), James Goei (Prince Serrakit), Ian Colin (Major Harrington), Andy Ho (U Meng), Eric Young (Suchong), Myo Toon (Ta Pai), Victor Charrington (Detective), Douglas Muir (Voice of One-Ten), Unity Bevis (Concubine), Sarmukh Singh (Steward Assassin), Jerry Lee Yen (Servant), Jean Woo Sam (Servant), Eugene Che (Male Extra)

PRE-TITLE/TEASER

This sequence is described in the first paragraph of the synopsis. It is quite a long sequence, spanning two and a half pages of the script. More than any other episode so far, this encapsulates how pre-title sequences would work in the near future.

SYNOPSIS

Part 1—King Tenuphon of the far eastern nation of Shanpore travels to London aboard a jet with Prince Serrakit and his granddaughter Mei Li. A steward attempts to shoot the King but misses and strikes Prince Serrakit instead, wounding him superficially. Quickly, the would-be assassin is restrained by the King's head of security General Tuke and thrown from the plane as it nears London.

The King has traveled to England to sign a treaty for oil concessions, and there are those in his country who are willing to kill to prevent it. Steed has been assigned to protect the King while he is in London and has been told that his job depends upon his success, but the King's casualness and indiscretions seem likely to make his job very difficult. Meanwhile, he meets with a Foreign Office man, Crichton-Bull, who stresses the need for their success. Carol Wilson arrives to treat Prince Serrakit's wound, which is very minor; Dr. Keel is not available.

Meanwhile, Major Harrington calls at the house of Zoe Carter, bringing news of her husband, presumed dead over a year ago. Harrington says he believes Carter is alive and the prisoner of Shanpore rebels. He proposes that if he is allowed to stay at her home, posing as a friend of her husbands, he will arrange to free her husband. When asked about his plans, Harrington suggests that he is planning an assassination. The likely target is King Tenuphon, and Mrs. Carter's windows line up perfectly with the King's suite. He aims his rifle, lining up his sights on Steed who surveys the surroundings.

Back in the King's suite, not surprisingly, Steed immediately finds the security arrangements to be suspiciously lacking, despite assurances from Crichton-Bull; the windows offer too clear a shot for a potential assassin. Steed also questions General Tuke's decision to throw the assassin from the plane without a thorough interrogation.

Feeling guilty about the way she treated her husband, Zoe Carter agrees to Harrington's proposal and vouches for him when Crichton-Bull comes to investigate the house.

Elsewhere, at a bookshop, three Shanpore nationals—U Meng, Suchong, and Ta Pai—discuss their opposition to King Tenuphon's plans, deciding to stop him at any cost; they decide that Suchong is their man. Hearing of Harrington, Steed is wary despite reassurance from Crichton-Bull.

Part 2—The King visits a London nightclub and brings an attractive woman named Ingrid Storm back with him, making Steed's job even harder. Ms. Storm reveals that she was bribed with an expensive ring to ingratiate herself to the King and report back with information to U Meng.

At Zoe Carter's home, Harrington is evasive about how he might help her husband. As they are talking, Steed arrives to investigate Harrington personally, having not been convinced by Crichton-Bull's efforts. Harrington claims he runs a rubber plantation in Malaya and is in town to visit relatives in the North of England. Steed questions Zoe about Harrington alone, but worried for her husband's life, she lies to Steed and continues to corroborate Harrington's story.

A student demonstration in the streets draws King Tenuphon to his window, and a shot rings out; Suchong made his attempt but missed. Steed rushes back to the King's suite and admonishes him not to enter the balcony without his permission. Ingrid reports to U Meng in the dressing room of the nightclub and reveals the security arrangements but warns him of Steed. U Meng takes her warning seriously and decides to lure him there.

Part 3—Zoe Carter confronts Harrington about her husband again and demands the truth. Harrington finally concedes that her husband is dead, but now threatens Zoe with death in order to keep her silent.

Crichton-Bull arrives in Ingrid's dressing room instead of Steed, having agreed to deputize for him. She apparently agrees to work with them against U Meng and provides the man's address. Later, Steed stops another assassination attempt by U Meng at the King's suite. The address given by Ingrid turns out to be a deception.

Steed returns to Mrs. Carter's flat but is sent away by her—Harrington, she says, has left town. Steed is not convinced however and returns to warn the King of another imminent attack that he believes will happen when the King makes his appearance on the balcony. He convinces the King to cancel the appearance.

The next day, Harrington prepares to shoot the Tenuphon. Having arranged to have a helicopter fly overhead at that precise moment, Harrington draws the King to the balcony. Despite warnings from Crichton-Bull, the King goes to observe the helicopter anyway and is bundled to the ground by Steed. Harrington's shot misses the King and strikes Prince Serrakit instead, killing him. Harrington tries to escape but General Tuke barges in and shoots him dead. Steed sees through the plot however. It was all arranged by Tenuphon to have the Prince killed. But Steed cannot do anything; the King has diplomatic immunity.

EPISODE NOTES

This episode seems like an exceptionally well-written example of the series, one that would have looked extraordinary on screen. James Mitchell had previously written "Death on the Slipway," and he would go on to write several more for the series, but this one seems like it could have been his best work on *The Avengers*.

The story was an entirely set-based production; there were no location shoots. This is just as well as the sets are excellent and fairly elaborate, and the production required nothing else to make it work. To me, this was likely *The Avengers'* attempt at BBC-style costume drama. No doubt the production team were well-aware of this fact given the sheer quantity of production photographs that were taken during rehearsals—more than any other Season One episode, 303. However, it's uncertain whether this is due to more photographs being taken or more surviving.

The cast was made up of a large number of Asian actors, a real rarity in the 1960s. Burt Kwouk made his first of several appearances in the show, so it's easy to imagine how his performance might have gone. Peter Barkworth also appeared for the first time in the series. He would later return in episodes such as "The Correct Way to Kill" and "The Morning After." Ian Hendry was seen only briefly at the very end, pondering why he spends so much time fighting crime.

CHAMPAGNE, CARS, CLOTHES, AND CANINES

Steed wears the dark-gray three-piece single-breasted suit with the lapeled waistcoat, a white shirt with a gray silk tie, and brown leather Chelsea boots. In one shot, he can be seen wearing a white shirt with subtle horizontal stripes under his jacket from the same suit, although this could have been before he donned the full outfit. Briefly, near the end, there is a navy-blue three-piece, single-breasted suit with a double-breasted waistcoat, worn with the white shirt with the horizontal stripes, and a blue tie. An unusual and challenging suit for the day; double-breasted waistcoats were practically unheard of, as were horizontally-striped shirts. Dr. Keel doesn't show up until nearly the end, but he wears a dark-gray two-piece suit in what might be serge, with a white shirt and the same tie with thin diagonal stripes. The jacket has a notch collar and it looks like he might be trying to dress up a little more than usual, given it's a diplomatic situation.

There is also a lot of traditional Chinese-style clothing worn by the guest actors.

SURVIVING FOOTAGE AND MATERIALS

Synopses
Camera Script
Designer's Floorplans
John Cura Tele-snaps (70)
Production Photographs (303)

ADAPTATIONS AND RECONSTRUCTIONS

Big Finish Audio Adaptation
Reconstruction—Studio Canal Blu-ray Release, Season Four, Disc Four

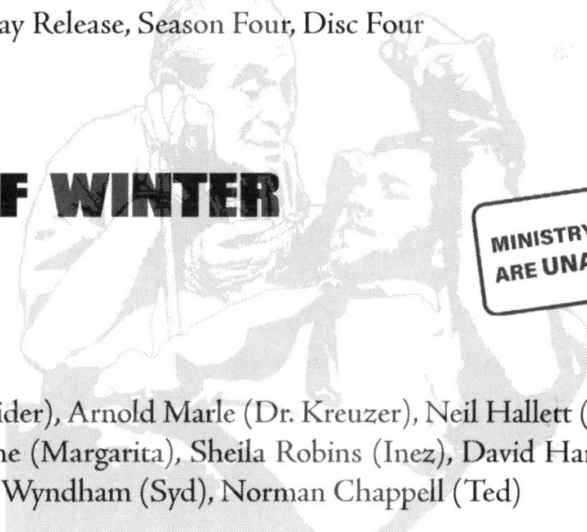

23 (1.26.23) DEAD OF WINTER

MINISTRY RECORDS ARE UNAVAILABLE

Written by Eric Paice
Directed by Don Leaver

GUEST CAST

Carl Duering (Hans Gerhardt Schneider), Arnold Marle (Dr. Kreuzer), Neil Hallett (Weber), Michael Sarne (Willi), Zorenah Osborne (Margarita), Sheila Robins (Inez), David Hart (Dr. Brennan), John Woodvine (Harry), Blaise Wyndham (Syd), Norman Chappell (Ted)

PRE-TITLE/TEASER[3]

The refrigerator ship, the San Parma, arrives from Buenos Aires. Typically, the cargo contains frozen prime beef, but once at the frozen storage sheds, one worker finds something strange about one of the sacks. He calls his supervisor over who then orders him to open it. Inside the sack, they find a human corpse, frozen solid.

SYNOPSIS

Part 1—The San Parma refrigerator ship containing frozen beef arrives from Buenos Aires with one sack containing a dead man's body, frozen solid. Steed investigates this bizarre seeming murder and invites Dr. Keel to examine the man's body. They meet with police surgeon Dr. Brennan who is wait-

3 John Cura must have been a little late to this episode. His Tele-snaps do not capture any frames of the title sequence and he only took five shots of the teaser scene.

ing for them at the morgue. The autopsy cannot be performed as yet because the body is still well below freezing, but Steed speculates that the man has been dead since the ship left Argentina—two weeks and five days ago—and kept frozen ever since.

Back at Keel's surgery, Steed questions Inez, an Argentinian agent that was in Buenos Aires, and she immediately recognizes the dead man's photo—he is Hans Gerhardt Schneider, a Nazi war criminal that was living in exile. Knowing that he was trying to escape to Europe somehow, she had surveilled him closely but lost track of him about four weeks ago. Schneider is a member of an organization called Phoenix that wants to reestablish Nazism. Steed knows that the beef importer, Webster (real name Weber), is likely involved in this plot, but he also suspects that someone else in England is connected—a Dr. King. King's real name is Dr. Kreuzer, he reveals. Dr. Keel knows the name; he was responsible for a series of ground-breaking medical books, ***Neurology and Cell Structures***, disappearing after joining the Nazi party.

Later, Steed goes undercover as a customs man at the dockyard and questions Weber and a dockworker named Harry, but Weber is very suspicious of Steed's credentials, and Harry isn't particularly helpful either. Weber asks his henchman Willi to report to Dr. Kreuzer. Later that evening, Dr. Brennan calls Keel to inform him that the corpse of Schneider has thawed sufficiently to begin an autopsy. Keel rushes over with Steed, but they are both shocked to find Dr. Brennan dead under the sheet in Schneider's place.

Part 2—Later, Steed meets Keel and reveals that another Phoenix member is thought to be arriving in London on the S.S. Whitney soon. He has also managed to have yet another Phoenix member, Dr. Fischer, detained on smuggling charges, and he wants Dr. Keel to impersonate him, giving him two weeks to learn how to do so.

Two weeks later, Willi is talking to Weber's secretary Margarita, and they both worry that they are getting too deeply involved in Weber's schemes. Keel arrives posing as Dr. Fischer and manages to convince Weber of his identity.

Later, as they discuss Keel's successful disguise, Steed reveals that he leaked Dr. Fischer's cover story to Weber, and Keel is not pleased, feeling that this almost tripped him up. Willi arrives to bring Dr. Keel to see Dr. Kreuzer. Steed heads to the docks for the arrival of the S.S. Whitney and is surprised to find another dead body among the cargo—that of Inez!

At Kreuzer's surgery, Keel is shown Schneider's body lying on a table. He proclaims him the future leader of their order, and, to Keel's utter astonishment, Schneider opens his eyes and sits up.

Part 3—Steed confronts Weber on the fact that two bodies have been found in his shipments. Weber deflects this criticism and suggests that there must be a gang of some kind operating on the Argentinian side. Steed is unconvinced. When Weber suggests that he might shut down his business, claiming lack of profit, Steed points out the matter of a surprisingly large number of Deutschmarks being transferred into Weber's account. The conversation then turns sinister as Weber suggests that the murders might have been committed to keep nosey people like Steed quiet. After Steed leaves, Weber calls Dr. Kreuzer, who demands that Steed be dealt with. Kreuzer reveals to Keel that he has mastered suspended animation. Unfortunately, he also informs Keel that he has seen through his disguise.

Back at Dr. Keel's surgery, Steed is worried about Keel but has no idea where to go. Suddenly, Margarita arrives at the surgery, looking for help. She and Willi want out of Weber's insidious plot. She reveals to Steed that Dr. Keel will be taken to the docks later that evening.

There, Dr. Kreuzer restrains Keel on an operating table. Revealing to him their plot to freeze all their members and then start a nuclear war that will wipe everyone else out, he threatens to experiment on Keel in order to test his procedure's effectiveness in protecting against radiation. Keel is to be subjected to every known radiation hazard over a period of one month! The freezing solution is then administered to Keel, who loses consciousness.

Steed confronts Weber who holds him at gunpoint, bringing him to Dr. Kreuzer's lab. However, a group of dockworkers appear and subdue the neo-Nazis as Willi shoots Schneider in order to free himself from his influence. Dr. Kreuzer reveals however that Willi will die within six months due to the earlier and more primitive experiments that were conducted on him. Steed grabs Willi's gun and holds Kreuzer at gunpoint as the dockworkers round up the villains. Thankfully, Keel recovers quickly back at his surgery with no ill effects.

EPISODE NOTES

This seems to have been an astonishingly good story with many similar features to later seasons, even to the filmed era. There is a diabolical mastermind, a slew of neo-Nazis, the science-fiction idea of suspended animation, and the threat of a global apocalypse by nuclear war. The writing is superior, and each part of the story ends with an especially shocking moment. Visually, the story looks strong as well, although it was entirely studio bound with only a few feet of stock film used to provide transition to the dock scenes.

The scientific ideas in this episode might be intentionally erroneous. Dr. Kreuzer's theories are questionable; it is unlikely that being frozen would protect anyone from radiation. Thus, there is more than a whiff of medical quackery about Dr. Kreuzer, and this recalls the infamous Nazi doctor Josef Mengele, which makes Kreuzer even creepier. The fact that Dr. Keel was going to undergo a dangerous and scientifically implausible series of tests against his will is a particularly ugly reminder of concentration camp experimentation, one of the darkest chapters in World War II and indeed in all of human history.

This was the final story to be recorded for Season One, and though it was not transmitted as the finale, it seems likely that the production team intended to finish on a strong note. However, they were quickly thrown for a loop by an Equity strike and an agreement with a fellow ITV broadcaster to alternate with another similar series called ***Deadline Midnight***. This would mean that the final four episodes of *The Avengers* would be broadcasts months apart from the rest of the season. In the interim, they would lose Ian Hendry to a film contract.

CHAMPAGNE, CARS, CLOTHES, AND CANINES[4]

Steed wears the dark-gray three-piece suit with the lapeled waistcoat (first seen in "Toy Trap") with Chelsea boots, and he periodically pairs it with a black bowler, and the tan overcoat first seen in "Hot Snow." Later, he wears the gray Prince of Wales blazer and black waistcoat, with tan trousers, the horizontally-striped white shirt, and a light-gray knit tie. He also wears the black fedora from "The Frighteners." All in all, it's quite the dashing look!

Dr. Keel wears a light-gray two-piece suit with the striped tie with thin horizontal stripes. For an overcoat, he wears the tan trench coat. In some surviving shots, Ian Hendry can be seen wearing eyeglasses, though, as these photographs were taken during rehearsal, it's not clear if he ever wore them on camera.

SURVIVING FOOTAGE AND MATERIALS

Synopses

---

4 In a famous promotional photo of Patrick Macnee smoking during a break, he is wearing the white shirt with horizontal stripes and what looks like a dark two-piece suit, probably navy, and a dark paisley tie. Given some of the other photographs on the same roll, this appears to be part of an actual scene over a glass of wine and a pot of tea with Ian Hendry, but he is clearly posing for the camera, so it is difficult to know if this was the final outfit worn for the episode, especially since it doesn't match any of the other photographs.

Rehearsal Scripts
John Cura Tele-snaps (79)
Production Photographs (116)

ADAPTATIONS AND RECONSTRUCTIONS

Big Finish Audio Adaptation
Reconstruction—Studio Canal Blu-ray Release, Season Four, Disc Five

24 (1.23.24) THE DEADLY AIR

Written by Lester Powell
Directed by John Knight

MINISTRY RECORDS ARE UNAVAILABLE

GUEST CAST

Ann Bell (Barbara Anthony), Michael Hawkins (Dr. Philip Karswood), Keith Anderson (Heneager), Richard Butler (Herbert Truscott), Allan Cuthbertson (Dr. Hugh Chalk), John Stratton (Dr. Owen Craxton), Douglas Muir (One-Ten), Cyril Renison (Dr. Harvey), Anthony Cundell (Keo Armstrong), Geoffrey Bayldon (Professor Kilbride)

PRE-TITLE

There is a sequence before the onscreen title caption appears, but it is difficult to tell what it was about. Taking place at Truscott Research Laboratories, this is presumably the scene in which Heneager is knocked out. There are only three Tele-snap frames capturing this scene.

SYNOPSIS

Two of the staff at a research center specializing in vaccines—Dr. Philip Karswood and his assistant Barbara Anthony—are working on a new vaccine that is needed urgently. After an incident of sabotage, in which an assistant named Heneager is knocked out and batch of vaccines is destroyed, Steed is asked to investigate, bringing Dr. Keel for his much-needed medical expertise.

While Dr. Hugh Chalk is preparing to set up a final test, Steed speaks with Barbara to try and discover any potentially suspicious behavior. Drs. Chalk, Karswood, and Craxton set up the next vaccine test with Karswood volunteering to be the test subject. Karswood becomes seriously ill during the test and is hospitalized in the facility. Quickly, they discover that the vaccine isn't the problem; in a guinea pig test, it proves effective. Something else caused Karswood's collapse.

Steed investigates with the center's engineer, Armstrong, and finds signs of sabotage near an intake fan in the air supply system for the isolation room. A broken glass phial is found, apparently set to break open when the circulation fan started up, releasing its contents into the Karswood's air supply. Bravely, Steed and Dr. Keel then decide to become the next test subjects. Unfortunately, signs of sabotage are immediately apparent. Suspicious, Armstrong checks the air intake again and finds the saboteur at large, ready to release another phial of a deadly substance into the air. It's Heneager! He stabs Armstrong and escapes, but Armstrong hangs on just long enough to stop the air intake before collapsing dead.

Saved by Armstrong's selfless act, Steed and Keel then find an *unbroken* phial upon the intake fan, giving them an opportunity to test the contents. An old friend of Keel's, Professor Kilbride, performs the necessary tests and discovers that the phial contains an especially strong concentration of the vaccine itself—one-hundred times as strong as needed—enough to cause potentially fatal reactions.

Later, Barbara is knocked out by an unknown assailant, and the final batch of vaccine is stolen.

Upon awakening, she can remember nothing of what happened. Realizing that Kilbride is under threat as the only person with a clue of what is happening, Keel races to save his friend, arriving just in time to stop another fatal stabbing by Heneager, who is revealed to be working for Dr. Craxton. Dr. Craxton wants to discredit the vaccine and then leave the center and 'invent' it himself.

Before Keel can return to warn Steed, Craxton tricks Steed into the sealed isolation room and turns on the intake, a fresh vial of vaccine on the fan. Keel and Dr. Chalk try to rescue Steed but Steed is convinced he is now infected and will not leave the decontamination room. This turns out to be a deception, as, unknown to Craxton, the head of the center, Truscott, has had all fatal forms of the vaccine removed and replaced with harmless water. Steed is just fine, and Craxton is escorted away by security.

EPISODE NOTES

Despite having something of a science-fiction (or science-fact) flair, "The Deadly Air" appears to be a rather common-or-garden episode. The plot is straightforward with a saboteur operating within the research center, brazenly attacking people in order to sabotage progress on a much-needed vaccine. While I certainly understand the need for expediency in an hour-long television episode, the events move too quickly and openly to be reasonable. It's highly unlikely that this scheme could have succeeded whether Steed and Keel intervened or not. It's just too obvious that the saboteur is an insider that knows about the research center operations. I also find it highly improbable that vaccines would work as presented. Since a vaccine is simply a weakened or dead form of a virus or other pathogen, a vaccine for a virus that is one-hundred times as strong as needed would simply be a lot of live viruses or an especially virulent strain of the virus. And if the phial breaks open on a fan, then it seems like anyone who goes near the fan would also be contaminated and most certainly Steed who touches the broken phial. I'm by no means a virologist, but the story seems to play fast and loose with medical knowledge.

Intriguingly, this basic narrative is something that would be repeated in the season finale "Dragonsfield," and indeed, the plots are very similar, the difference being vaccines versus radiation shielding, and both are being sabotaged by a traitorous scientist. On the other hand, "Dragonsfield" has far more going for it due to being of stronger visual interest. Observing the available Tele-snaps and production photos reveals that the sets on "The Deadly Air" are rather pedestrian and the lighting dullish. The likely highlights were in Geoffrey Bayldon's scenes, though there's no way to be certain.

Two other facts of note present themselves: "The Deadly Air" was the highest rated episode of the season, bringing in possibly as many as 11 million viewers and reaching the national top ten chart as the number 10 show of the week; and there was a similar science-fiction story in 1957 that was written for the Canadian network CBC by Lester Powell. It was called *Night of the Plague*, and that production coincidentally starred Patrick Macnee and was produced while Sydney Newman was Head of Drama at CBC. It's a small world.

CHAMPAGNE, CARS, CLOTHES, AND CANINES

Dr. Keel wears the same dark-gray two-piece suit and dark tie with thin diagonal stripes. Steed wears the same navy-blue three-piece suit seen in two prior episodes with the double-breasted waistcoat. They both wear light gray lab coats at one point.

SURVIVING FOOTAGE AND MATERIALS

Synopses
John Cura Tele-snaps (76)
Production Photographs (110)

ADAPTATIONS AND RECONSTRUCTIONS

Big Finish Audio Adaptation

Reconstruction—Studio Canal Blu-ray Release, Season Six, Disc Nine

25 (1.24.25) A CHANGE OF BAIT

Written by Lewis Davidson

Directed by Don Leaver

MINISTRY RECORDS ARE UNAVAILABLE

GUEST CAST

John Bailey (Lemuel Potts), Victor Platt (Archie Duncan), Robert Desmond (Herb Thompson), Gary Hope (Barker), Henry Soskin (Peter Sampson), Arthur Barrett (Andre), Graham Rigby (Nat Fletcher), Norman Pitt (Bryan Stubbs), Harry Shacklock (Charlie), Gillian McCutcheon (Ivy), Michael Hunt (Steed's Helper)

PRE-TITLE/TEASER

The available camera script indicates that there is no pre-title scene per se. After the main title sequence, there is only a brief shot outside Potts' office before the episode title appears.[5] This shot is captured in only one Tele-snap, confirming that the scene was very short indeed. It seems that the familiar format was not fully established in the first season.

SYNOPSIS

Part 1—Archie Duncan has speculated on a shipment of bananas, paying £7000 for them and expecting to sell them for £12,000. However, he was required to take out a loan of £5000 from Mr. Barker at the Finance Loan Corporation. Unfortunately, the shipment is twenty-four hours from docking, his loan is overdue, and he has yet to find a buyer. Not only this but the bananas are becoming overripe. Archie appears to have found his savior in Mr. Potts, who has a buyer for Archie's bananas; Potts' agrees to act as his agent in return for a seven percent take on the sale. After Archie leaves Potts' office, Potts telephones his contact at the docks, Peter Sampson, and tells him unequivocally to declare Archie's bananas 'black' and not to unload them. Later, Steed telephones Archie anonymously to inform him that his bananas will not be unloaded. Archie is so shocked by the news that he suffers a mild cardiac episode and collapses.

Back in his office, Potts is speaking to his right-hand man Herb; he tells him to organize the dock strike that will prevent Archie's bananas from being unloaded. He then telephones his buyer, Fletcher, asking him to set up a proper contract for the fruit, assuring him that the sale will never actually go through.

Dr. Keel turns out to be Archie's general practitioner and arrives at his patient's house to give him a thorough examination. Determining that he has had a mild stroke, he orders Archie to take total bedrest for two days. Archie promises to follow Dr. Keel's orders, but, after he leaves, Archie immediately prepares to go out.

Back at Keel's surgery, Steed explains everything about Archie and the oncoming dock strike. Potts is fully insured against loss in instances like this, and according to the contract has full possession of the produce until Archie pays him. It's a racket—Potts never intended to deliver the fruit. He wants a lot more than the seven percent; he wants the entire £12,000 that the insurance will pay when the bananas rot on the dock. However, Steed doesn't quite understand Barker's role and needs

---

5 In the script, `HALL OUTSIDE POTTS' OFFICE/INT - DAY | 1A NO BOOM | M.S. Hall (Blacked off). By f/gd. As man goes, follow. Pick up Archie. PAN him R.`

more information in order to put the fraudsters away.

At Barker's office, Barker explains to Archie what has happened and what it means to him. The loan for £5000 is fully insured so Archie will owe them nothing. However, Archie still frets over the loss of his own personal investment of £2000. Compassionate to Archie's plight and eager to put the scammers away, Steed decides to make sure that the strike ends and the shipment of fruit is unloaded. Going undercover as a union man, he blackmails Sampson to end the strike, and Sampson bends. Steed also arranges to have Potts' switchboard operator route his call to a phone box. When Potts asks to speak to Fletcher, Steed answers the phone instead and accepts Potts message not to receive the fruit. Of course, that message will never be delivered, and Archie will deliver his bananas as planned.

Part 2—The deception is quickly spotted when the bananas are delivered and an angry Fletcher demands an explanation and refuses to pay. Potts knows someone is manipulating them behind the scenes. Quickly, they move on to the next scam at an antiques dealer. Potts arranges to burn out the shop and collect on the insurance. They set a time for 3 am the next morning. Steed and Keel scout out the antiques shop. Meanwhile, it looks as though Archie will get his money, but Steed isn't convinced. He suspects that the check won't be any good.

Part 3—Steed and Keel return to the antiques shop and hide inside a Victorian wardrobe with an infrared stills camera. When Herb and his accomplice Charlie arrive and prepare to burn down the building, a click from Steed's camera alerts them. Quickly, Herb slams the wardrobe shut and turns the key to lock them inside. He and Charlie then set a one-hour fuse and scurry away, leaving Steed and Keel to die in the coming conflagration. Steed and Keel struggle against the door of the wardrobe, but it is made too well; they cannot escape.

Back at Potts' office, his conscience twinges, and he demands that Herb return to release the trapped men in the wardrobe, but Herb refuses. Thankfully, the owner Andre arrives at his shop by mere chance and releases Steed and Keel. Quickly, they stop the fuse. Andre calls Potts to complain that the incendiary hasn't worked, prompting Potts to return with Herb and Charlie to make sure that the job is done right this time. Upon arriving however, they discover that it is Andre who is in the wardrobe, bound and gagged. Steed and Keel suddenly appear and hold the criminals at gunpoint until the police arrive.

The game is up, or almost. Steed takes Potts with him back to his office. There, he tricks Potts into making a phone call that implicates Barker as well. The phone lines have been tapped, and everything that Potts and Barker said was recorded.

EPISODE NOTES

This episode deals with a fairly typical racketeering plot that is nevertheless told with great precision. Though the scam is rather circuitous, it is easy to understand. The plight of the victim, who is suffering from heart troubles exacerbated by stress, works to engage the viewers' sympathy, providing greater satisfaction when the criminals have been put away. The minor downside of this story is its mundanity, which involves an unusually high degree of telephone use (something that has been pointed out in other volumes on the series). There's not anything wrong with that per se—the show often dealt with more ordinary subjects such as this—but, surrounded by episodes involving far-out science-fiction concepts and international intrigue, this story sticks out like a sore thumb, signaling a script far more similar to the first half of the season rather than the second. Nevertheless, the show would continue to alternate between the mundane and extraordinary for the next two years before becoming firmly rooted in the fantastic with the first filmed season.

Visually, this episode is rather ordinary as well; it was primarily studio bound with only a couple of mute film recordings and a jumbled antiques shop to provide some visual interest. However, in one amusing anecdote, the sturdy antique wardrobe that was intended to be inescapable was anything but sturdy according to Ian Hendry. He was quoted in the *TV Times Souvenir Extra—The New Avengers* as saying, "The wardrobe, made of fragile plywood, couldn't have withstood an assault by a placid four-year-old girl, much less the combined physical might of two magnificent *Avengers*."

One possible factor that is hard to judge based on the script alone is Steed's apparent playfulness and humor, indicating that the story was intended to be lighthearted. There are several good quips by Macnee, including one about waiting for the Hampstead bus while stuck in the wardrobe. Though the subject might seem to hardly allow for it, *The Avengers* had and *would* frequently play with a mixture of violence, crime, and humor, and this would become something of a signature during the filmed era. Nevertheless, while I'm sure that this was a solid episode and would have entertained contemporary viewers, it is unlikely to have stood out very much at the time.

CHAMPAGNE, CARS, CLOTHES, AND CANINES

Dr. Keel appears to primarily wear the same suit as in the prior episode. Steed wears a navy three-piece suit with flap pockets and one ticket pocket, the horizontally-striped white shirt, black Chelsea boots, and the black bowler, which, in an out-of-character moment, appears too big for him. The tan overcoat with heavily-stitched cuffs and whangee umbrella also appear. In the third act, he also wears his Prince of Wales blazer and black waistcoat.

SURVIVING FOOTAGE AND MATERIALS

Synopses
Camera Script
John Cura Tele-snaps (78)
Production Photographs (78)

ADAPTATIONS AND RECONSTRUCTIONS

Big Finish Audio Adaptation
Reconstruction—Studio Canal DVD Release, Season Three, Disc Five

26 (1.25.26) DRAGONSFIELD

Written by Terence Feely
Directed by Peter Hammond

MINISTRY RECORDS ARE UNAVAILABLE

GUEST CAST

Sylva Langová (Lisa Strauss), Alfred Burke (Saunders), Ronald Leigh-Hunt (Redington), Barbara Shelley (Susan Summers), Thomas Kyffin (Dr. Jack Alford), Keith Barron (Technician), Amanda Reeves (Secretary), Eric Dodson (One-Fifteen), Steven Scott (Boris), Michael Robbins (Landlord), Herbert Nelson (Peters), Morris Perry (Second Technician)

PRE-TITLE/TEASER[6]

A young technician tests out the readings on his panel, and then, satisfied that they're safe, he un-

6 This would have been quite an engaging scene, in my opinion. There are only five Tele-snaps capturing it, but I can easily imagine Johnny Dankworth's 'mysterious' musical cue being played over it. There is one frame of an impressive facility with pipes, and valves, and stairways crossing everywhere.

locks and enters the radiation chamber. Once he is inside, an intruder wearing a radiation hazard suit spies on him through the observation window. Finally, the technician is shocked to find that the intruder has closed and locked the door and flooded the chamber with radiation.

SYNOPSIS

At a space science research center, scientists are testing new methods of protecting astronauts from radiation in a joint British-American effort. Unfortunately, there is a saboteur at large, and after one man is mortally affected by radiation in a murderous act, Steed is sent by One-Fifteen to investigate. Immediately, it is evident that there is suspicious activity among some of the technicians, and a security man named Saunders doesn't seem to trust any of them. Dr. Alford and Susan Summers have a troubled romantic relationship, and Saunders takes exception to their dalliances.

Soon, the still unidentified saboteur nearly strangles Dr. Alford with mechanical grab arms normally used for handling radioactive materials. Fortunately, Alford survives and is discovered semi-conscious by Steed in the radiation chamber. Expressing frustration with their lack of success so far, Saunders and Steed agree to work separately in the hopes that individual paths will improve their chances of finding the murderer. In order to tempt the guilty out of the shadows, Steed volunteers for an experiment. True to his expectations, Steed is nearly killed when the equipment is sabotaged. But the equipment was sabotaged before the experiment even began, and the saboteur remains hidden.

Saunders moves his investigation outside the center where he discovers two taciturn men in a pub, one of whom is named Boris. Boris is heavyset, and his unnamed accomplice is a thin man. They both speak with heavy Eastern European accents. Saunders tries to infiltrate their company and convince them that he shares their ambitions, but they are skeptical. Boris and his friend force Saunders to drive them to an abandoned mill where they hold him at gunpoint. Boris makes a call to his superior, who asks him to keep Saunders prisoner.

Though Steed is severely weakened, he follows Saunders' trail outside of the center. Noting that Saunders' car is still in the parking lot of the pub, he inquires after him to the landlord. Discovering that 'two foreign fellows' spoke of going to the mill, Steed goes after Saunders. Catching the two men by surprise, he overpowers them and then forces Boris to reveal the name of the saboteur by threatening to place his hand between two grinding cogwheels. Boris screams out the name of Susan Summers. Steed and Saunders then bind the men to the mill workings and rush to the center.

There, Lisa and Susan are setting up the next experiment, and Susan, wearing her space suit, begins to strangle Lisa. Steed and Saunders race in just in time to pull Susan off her. Summers had been working with a foreign organization behind the Iron Curtain, with a goal to slow progress at the center, allowing them to beat the Americans in the space race.

EPISODE NOTES

This episode, like a few before it, such as "The Radioactive Man," begins to curve towards scientific subjects, highly suggestive of later seasons. Though not necessarily science-fiction, it does have elements of the bizarre. The ordinary but high-tech situation is taken to an extreme, something that *The Avengers* would do repeatedly throughout its run. As such, it feels more like an episode from much later in the series and features a plot that wouldn't have been entirely out of place in an episode of *Doctor Who* or *Doomwatch*.

The plot is fairly straightforward and linear. The research center is plagued by a saboteur who seems to completely lack any subtlety or finesse. The unidentified attacker strikes quite brazenly and murderously, seemingly without fear of being caught merely by way of wearing a radiation suit. While this provided for some wonderful visuals—based on the surviving Tele-snaps and production photographs—it defies narrative credulity. After all, one merely has to be wary of anyone wearing a suit, and the obvious technical knowledge of the assailant narrows the field of suspects down to just the technicians, who number around four. Not to mention the fact that Susan Summers is the one that is frequently seen wearing the suit. Perhaps it was directed in such a manner as to make the tension about whether Steed and Saunders will discover what the audience already saw from a mile off. Or maybe the production team thought that making the saboteur a woman would be as much of a twist in 1961 as was needed.

The fact of a female villain does provide some amount of salaciousness. Hearing that the two female technicians, Lisa and Susan, are headed to a shower—a standard precaution when dealing with radioactive materials—Steed decides to follow and spy them out, getting an earful of their conversation and perhaps an eyeful of much more. This shower scene, with Barbara Shelley showering nude behind a skimpy translucent glass screen, is documented extensively in both Tele-snaps and production photographs, and it is highly likely that the production knew exactly what they were doing. Shelley was already a notable and attractive film actor and would star in ***Village of the Damned*** with George Sanders later that year. To have her showering down on display could well have been a ratings-grab. While an obvious example of early ***Avengers*** kinkiness, it could have also been a minor indication of the program's intention to move towards female agents, as indeed Summers turns out to be.

Steed once again demonstrates that without Dr. Keel's moral guidance he can be quite ruthless. Repeatedly throughout this season, he had been willing to utilize torture in order to extract information, something that was frowned upon by Dr. Keel. Here, he extracts the name of the saboteur from one of the enemy agents by threatening to place his hand between two steel cogwheels in an old mill.

This is the only episode from the first season that does not star Ian Hendry as Dr. Keel, even though his medical expertise would have been entirely appropriate for the story. As a result, the character of Saunders becomes a temporary partner for Steed. Hendry was taking time off to prepare for a role in a production of ***Armchair Theatre***. This break would end up being permanent as an Equity strike would hit shortly thereafter. In the imposed interim of the strike, Hendry, eager for work, would pursue and receive a film contract that would prevent his return to the series. "Dragonsfield" aired last in the season, and because of this there is a seeming direct line of continuity to the second season in which Steed has moved on to other partners, and we are left to assume that Dr. Keel was subsequently unable to aid Steed any further due to other commitments. The episode also contains the first and last appearance of One-Fifteen as a temporary replacement for One-Ten.

CHAMPAGNE, CARS, CLOTHES, AND CANINES

Steed wears a navy-blue three-piece suit with a ticket pocket (the same cut as the gray suit with ticket pocket), a double-breasted waistcoat with two rows of three cloth-covered buttons, a white shirt with a subtle stripe, and a paisley tie. During the scene in the windmill, he switches to the Prince of Wales blazer with the black waistcoat with silver buttons. And, finally, Steed is shirtless for the second verified time in the series. (Unfortunately, he's being tortured.)

SURVIVING FOOTAGE AND MATERIALS

Synopses
John Cura Tele-snaps (79)
Production Photographs (149)

ADAPTATIONS AND RECONSTRUCTIONS

Big Finish Audio Adaptation
Reconstruction—Studio Canal Blu-ray Release, Season Five, Disc Six

SEASON TWO

26 episodes (405-line monochrome videotape, ~52 min. ea.)

Regular Cast
Patrick Macnee—John Steed
Honor Blackman—Catherine Gale (episodes 27, 28, 30, 33, 34, 36-39, 41, 42, 44, 45, 47, 49, 51 and 52)
Julie Stevens—Venus Smith (episodes 29, 32, 43, 46, 48, and 50)
Jon Rollason—Dr. Martin King (episodes 31, 35, and 40)
Douglas Muir—One-Ten (episodes 27, 32, 39, 42, and 44)

Produced by Leonard White (episodes 27-40)
Produced by John Bryce (episodes 41-52)
Story Editor: John Bryce (episodes 27-40, 44)
Story Editor: Richard Bates (episodes 41-43 and 45-52)
Music: Johnny Dankworth

27. **Mr. Teddy Bear—w.** Martin Woodhouse; **dir.** Richmond Harding; **UK tx.** 29 Sep 1962; **rec.** 4 Aug 1962
28. **Propellant 23—w.** Jon Manchip White; **dir.** Jonathan Alwyn; **UK tx.** 6 Oct 1962; **rec.** 21 Jul 1962
29. **The Decapod—w.** Eric Paice; **dir.** Don Leaver; **UK tx.** 13 Oct 1962; **rec.** 12 Aug 1962
30. **Bullseye—w.** Eric Paice; **dir.** Peter Hammond; **UK tx.** 20 Oct 1962; **rec.** 20 Sep 1962
31. **Mission to Montreal—w.** Lester Powell; **dir.** Don Leaver; **UK tx.** 27 Oct 1962; **rec.** 12 May 1962
32. **The Removal Men—w.** Roger Marshall & Jeremy Scott; **dir.** Don Leaver; **UK tx.** 3 Nov 1962; **rec.** 4 Oct 1962
33. **The Mauritius Penny—w.** Malcolm Hulke & Terrance Dicks; **dir.** Richmond Harding; **UK tx.** 10 Nov 1962; **rec.** 18 Oct 1962
34. **Death of a Great Dane—w.** Roger Marshall & Jeremy Scott; **dir.** Peter Hammond; **UK tx.** 17 Nov 1962; **rec.** 1 Nov 1962
35. **The Sell-Out—w.** Anthony Terpiloff & Brandon Brady; **dir.** Don Leaver; **UK tx.** 24 Nov 1962; **rec.** 9 Jun 1962
36. **Death on the Rocks—w.** Eric Paice; **dir.** Jonathan Alwyn; **UK tx.** 1 Dec 1962; **rec.** 9 Jan 1962
37. **Traitor in Zebra—w.** John Gilbert; **dir.** Richmond Harding; **UK tx.** 8 Dec 1962; **rec.** 29 Nov 1962
38. **The Big Thinker—w.** Martin Woodhouse; **dir.** Kim Mills; **UK tx.** 15 Dec 1962; **rec.** 13 Dec 1962
39. **Death Dispatch—w.** Leonard Fincham; **dir.** Jonathan Alwyn; **UK tx.** 22 Dec 1962; **rec.** 23 Jun 1962
40. **Dead on Course—w.** Eric Paice; **dir.** Richmond Harding; **UK tx.** 29 Dec 1962; **rec.** 9 May 1962
41. **Intercrime—w.** Terrance Dicks & Malcolm Hulke; **dir.** Jonathan Alwyn; **UK tx.** 5 Jan

1963; **rec.** 29 Dec 1962

42. **Immortal Clay—w.** James Mitchell; **dir.** Richmond Harding; **UK tx.** 12 Jan 1963; **rec.** 10 Jan 1963
43. **Box of Tricks—w.** Peter Ling & Edward Rhodes; **dir.** Kim Mills; **UK tx.** 19 Jan 1963; **rec.** 17 Jan 1963
44. **Warlock—w.** Doreen Montgomery; **dir.** Peter Hammond; **UK tx.** 26 Jan 1963; **rec.** 7 Jul 1962
45. **The Golden Eggs—w.** Martin Woodhouse; **dir.** Peter Hammond; **UK tx.** 2 Feb 1963; **rec.** 31 Jan 1963
46. **School for Traitors—w.** James Mitchell; **dir.** Jonathan Alwyn; **UK tx.** 9 Feb 1963; **rec.** 9 Feb 1963
47. **The White Dwarf—w.** Malcolm Hulke; **dir.** Richmond Harding; **UK tx.** 16 Feb 1963; **rec.** 16 Feb 1963
48. **Man in the Mirror—w.** Geoffrey Orme & Anthony Terpiloff; **dir.** Kim Mills; **UK tx.** 23 Feb 1963; **rec.** 22 Feb 1963
49. **Conspiracy of Silence—w.** Roger Marshall; **dir.** Peter Hammond; **UK tx.** 2 Mar 1963; **rec.** 1 Mar 1963
50. **A Chorus of Frogs—w.** Martin Woodhouse; **dir.** Raymond Menmuir; **UK tx.** 9 Mar 1963; **rec.** 8 Mar 1963
51. **Six Hands Across a Table—w.** Reed R. de Rouen; **dir.** Richmond Harding; **UK tx.** 16 Mar 1963; **rec.** 15 Mar 1963
52. **Killer Whale—w.** John Lucarotti; **dir.** Kim Mills; **UK tx.** 23 Mar 1963; **rec.** 22 Mar 1963

SEASON NOTES

There are two seasons of *The Avengers* that are well-worth watching in production order. This is one of them—the other is Season Seven with Tara King. The reason for this is the uncertainty about the series that was going on behind the scenes that becomes well-evident to the viewer when viewed in this manner. The series was in flux, and though the production chaos that plagued the final season did not beset Season Two, this season takes several episodes to settle down. Producer Leonard White was eager to move on, and ultimately did so about two-thirds of the way through the series, with John Bryce taking his place. But, more importantly, the creative improvisation that had originally started the series was being employed once again.

During the Equity strike in late 1961 and early 1962, Ian Hendry had left the series to pursue a film career, with hopes of Hollywood eventually knocking on his door (or at least sending him a letter), and the production team for *The Avengers* was searching for potential replacements. This left Patrick Macnee to be the obvious star of the program, and his character John Steed had likely been stealing the show for some time, if the episode "Tunnel of Fear" is to be considered typical of the era. Having bumped Macnee up to first billing, their next logical thought was to replace Hendry's Dr. Keel with a similar type of character as Steed's *new* assistant. To this end, Jon Rollason was cast as the prophetically named Dr. Martin King.

Dr. King was possibly proof positive that direct imitations often become pale ones. While Rollason was certainly a talented actor, with quasi-Matinee idol looks to boot, he never quite managed to capture the same chemistry as Hendry with his costar, nor did he manage to distinguish himself in any notable fashion as a unique character creation. Much of Rollason's failings may be the result of the scripts written for him—although the medical qualifications required for Steed's helper were integral to the story, John Bryce, the script editor, was overwhelmed with commissioning new scripts for the season and likely didn't have the time to provide an over-arching viewpoint for Dr. King. Nevertheless, three episodes in, it was obvious that the character was not working.

This was fine because the production team had already decided to explore more radical options. Two *female* helpers were slated to take over from Dr. King—Venus Smith and Cathy Gale. Though this was not entirely without precedent—Ingrid Hafner as Carol Wilson had frequently joined in the adventures in Season One—the new characters were to be permanent replacements for the male lead. Before them for consideration, the production team had two female characters with very different backgrounds. Venus Smith was a nightclub singer who would be periodically roped into the dangerous underground world of espionage by Steed's manipulations, a strategy hinted at in the few extant episodes during Season One. On the other hand, Cathy Gale was a widowed anthropologist, formerly based in Kenya, and she would have all the skills needed to be fully employed in secret agent work. But which one would earn the position?

Venus Smith, played by Julie Stevens, was an idea that clearly had limited staying power. In her debut episode, "The Decapod," she was the saucy singer who resented the deception needed to garner her help, but nevertheless rose to the challenge with considerable spunk. This continued to work for a brief time, due to Steed's increasingly inventive cajoling, but ultimately became improbable as the contrivances needed for her involvement ran out. This was compounded by John Bryce's decision to give her a makeover by season's end. Stripped of her bravery, her working class zeal (and accent), and her bouffant hair, the character lost all credibility for involvement in the spy game, becoming little more than a temporary companion for Steed, one to operate on the periphery or need rescuing while he did most of the work.

This left the season to be all about Honor Blackman as Cathy Gale. And it was her appearance that fired the imaginations of the viewers and began to project ***The Avengers*** into the top ten in the TAM ratings on a regular basis. The character was a revelation. This was the first time anywhere that viewers would have seen a woman in a regular television series throwing men over her shoulder and fighting alongside her male costar. She was strong, independent, highly intelligent and educated. She was frequently shown to possess more knowledge than Steed on almost every subject, barring the traditions of the gentry and general spy work. She was high-minded and ethical. She wore the attire of a strong and liberated woman of the 1960s, which included top hats and capes as often as it did leather fighting suits, and yet Steed still managed to manipulate her into action in virtually every episode.

Their relationship was quasi-romantic and yet sibling-like, with the two quarreling frequently. Their relationship was based in (productive) tension, mitigated by several dollops of mutual respect. It worked, and this balanced but tense relationship became the new chemistry for the series, with Blackman as the other half of the baton.

By season's end, it was obvious. Cathy Gale was the only viable replacement for Hendry's Dr. Keel. The viewers (and the ratings) had spoken. Venus Smith was allowed to continue with her singing in peace, and when the series returned for Season Three, it was all Honor Blackman. ***The Avengers*** was to be fully liberated, and John Steed and Cathy Gale became television's oddest and hottest couple, the first set of unstoppable and fabulous superspies, stylishly fighting all diabolical masterminds.

This season starts (and ends) uneven but is very strong at key moments, with Leonard White having guided the series mostly along the same lines as the previous year—rooted in realism and spy drama with surrealistic and bizarre moments peppered throughout. Many of these early episodes seem very like the filmed seasons, but it oddly comes screeching to a halt with the John Bryce switchover. Just as the series is solidifying with Steed and Cathy Gale, the holdover of Venus Smith just barely lingering on, the bizarreness falls away and the series veers in a more conventional direction. The quality of the scripts also sinks near the end—the last six episodes being of highly questionable quality—and this does not bode well for Bryce's continuation. However, we can be thankful that the next season would turn out to be one of the strongest and most consistent in quality in the entire program.

INTRODUCING CATHY GALE

Born on 5 October 1930, Mrs. Gale was a talented, well-educated woman, with skills in hunting, fighting and self-reliance that she learned while living with her husband on their farm in Kenya. When her husband was killed, she returned to London where she received her Ph.D. in anthropology. When she first met John Steed, she was working as a curator for a museum, a job that often involved her expertise in ceramics and pottery.

Fiercely independent, her fighting skills involved a variety of judo techniques, including complicated throws that would send most men reeling, and she was a crack shot with firearms. Her academic knowledge seemed to cover most subjects, from science to computers to black magic to wildlife. She was often called upon to go undercover for long periods of time and displayed great skill at subterfuge. On several occasions, she demonstrated fluent Spanish and German, and in one instance, affected a highly convincing German accent and persona.

A highly ethical woman, she often took exception to Steed's manipulations and ruthless methods while working with him in the spy underworld, often becoming the voice of charity and compassion, prompting frequent disagreements. This compassion for the disenfranchised was underscored by her regular work for charitable organizations. Despite her passion for helping others and her many skills, she appeared to have made very little money with her endeavors. By the final third of the second season, she was staying in Steed's apartment until she could get her own place. Though initially she seemed to show little interest in helping Steed, doing so only begrudgingly, her relationship with him was somewhat cozy and domestic by this point—though little more than mere sexual tension seemed to be happening. It was made clear that Steed was staying somewhere else while she was using his apartment, and they were never seen to be involved in an obvious romance.

By the third season, Mrs. Gale once again had her own flat, which was fully modernized with a security system and automatic door. Though she and Steed seemed to be more relaxed with one another by this time, some amount of tension remained a theme of their partnership until the very end. By the end of the third season, it seemed that her patience was finally exhausted. Refusing to submit to any more of his cajoling, she left Steed to depart on a holiday trip, requiring him to pick up his little black book and call the next potential female helper.

DR. MARTIN KING

Very little is known about Dr. King except that he was a regular physician. He was originally introduced in episodes written for Dr. Keel in the first season. He was tallish, dark-haired, square-jawed, and handsome with a prominent boot toe chin. He professed a love for football and was very athletic, capable of charging in for a tackle in a fight. He spoke in a bright, somewhat high voice, had an easygoing demeaner, and seemed more casual about the goings-on than Dr. Keel had been. Regardless, Dr. King's personality was otherwise very similar to Dr. Keel, and his behavior suggested that he and Steed had worked together for a long time, though there were only three onscreen adventures.

VENUS SMITH

Venus was a blond nightclub singer in her early twenties who lacked any professional skills in espionage and crime-fighting. It is unknown why Steed wanted her to participate in his spy adventures, but he was clearly attracted to her, and she betrayed some attraction to him as well. Though it is difficult to say whether this was a romantic interest, it is likely that Venus was drawn to Steed's mysterious and glamorous lifestyle. Venus was initially reluctant to be involved in the dark underworld that Steed inhabited but later showed excitement at the prospect. In the beginning, she was portrayed with some edge and a working-class fire, but halfway through her six-episode run, Venus underwent a transformation into a younger appearance and persona—wearing fab clothing associated with the youth culture of the time. With this, her strength of character seemed to fade, and paradoxically she appeared even less capable at crime-fighting while becoming even more willing to engage in it. Her adventures with John Steed were punctuated with musical interludes by a jazz group—either the Dave Lee Trio or the Kenny Powell Trio—usually performing at the nightclub where she worked.

ICONIC TITLES

The titles used in this season are very similar to those of the first season, except there are new ink drawings that also include Honor Blackman, Julie Stevens, and Jon Rollason as needed.

CHAMPAGNE, CARS, CLOTHES, AND CANINES

Fashion gets more serious with this season with a mix of original designs, outfits "off the peg," and customized pieces bought and then modified by the wardrobe department. Patrick Macnee would begin working with wardrobe supervisor, Audrey Liddle, and Head of Wardrobe Department at ABC, Ambren Garland. They would work out details with Macnee and then pass them along to Macnee's tailor, Bailey and Weatherill of Regent Street, with Mr. James acting as his cutter. This association would continue even after Pierre Cardin was brought on as the designer in Season Five.

Honor Blackman's clothes would be even more elaborate, often with several clothing changes per episode, but would focus more and more on leatherwear as the series progressed. Blackman took to it well and her athletic appearance made her an impressive foe whenever she donned her fighting leathers. Nevertheless, this was frequently broken up by beautiful and elaborate garments, sometimes from British fashion designers like (then up-and-coming) Mary Quant.

The production also seemed to take the possibility of a full line of clothing for Blackman seriously. In May of 1962, fashion designer Michael Whittaker was approached to design a full wardrobe for her, but in the end his contributions appeared in only seven episodes, and costume designer Ambren Garland later claimed that Whittaker didn't actually design anything and that all outfits chosen for Blackman were off the rack. Most frequently, the designers selected the clothing from outside retailers and then it was modified as necessary in the costume department.

Honor Blackman's first leather fighting suit was designed by Audrey Liddle. It wasn't black, but a muted dark-green, as black didn't read as well on 405-line videotape. Patrick Macnee's suits were often navy-blue or dark-charcoal which read as black onscreen but did not create the anomalies associated with pure black on videotape, though he did wear a black suit in Season Three. In any case, in this section, I may periodically refer to such clothing items as 'black' simply because the precise color is unknown (due to the lack of color production photos) and because they appear that way onscreen. I may also refer to clothes as being 'dark-gray' or 'light-gray' because, again, the exact color is unknown.

Champagne and cars still did not have much of an association with the show during this era. As for cars, in studio videotaping was the norm and on-location filming was relatively rare, making the inclusion of cars difficult. Nevertheless, a few of the *Avengers* cars show up during this season.
On the other hand, this is the strongest season for canines (at least of the seasons that still exist), and Steed has two dogs who make several appearances: Freckles, the Dalmatian, and Sheba, a Whippet mix.

Best Dressed: "Bullseye"
Worst Dressed: (tied) "The Removal Men" and "Death Dispatch"

AVENGERS CARS

JOHN STEED

AC Greyhound (880 OPA) in "The Sell-Out."
1935 Alvis Speed 25 (CPT 75) in "Traitor in Zebra."
Triumph Herald (7061 MK) in "Warlock."

CATHY GALE

MGA (RVB 115) in "Mr. Teddy Bear," "Propellant 23" (mocked-up version), and "Warlock."

THE MOST FANTASTIC EPISODES OF THE SEASON

1. "Mr. Teddy Bear"
2. "Intercrime"
3. "The Golden Eggs"
4. "Death of a Great Dane"
5. "Warlock"
6. "Bullseye"
7. "The Decapod"
8. "Death Dispatch"
9. "The Removal Men"
10. "Death on the Rocks"

27 (2.6.1) MR TEDDY BEAR

Written by Martin Woodhouse
Directed by Richmond Harding

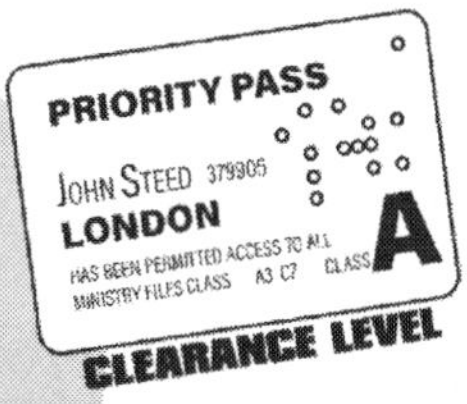

GUEST CAST

Douglas Muir (One-Ten), Bernard Goldman (Mr Teddy Bear), Tim Brinton (Interviewer), Kenneth Keeling (Colonel Wayne-Gilley), John Horsley (Dr Gilmore), John Ruddock (Dr James Howell), Michael Robbins (Henry), Michael Collins (Technician), Sarah Maxwell (Cafe Girl)

PRE-TITLE/TEASER

A live episode of the television talk show "The Man and the Place" begins with the host introducing Colonel Wayne-Gilley, but the Colonel collapses and dies almost immediately.

SYNOPSIS

After a man drops dead from cyanide poisoning on live television, One-Ten wants Steed to find a professional assassin—code-named 'Mr. Teddy Bear.' As part of Steed's plan, Mrs. Gale helps find the crook and negotiates a deal with him to murder Steed. An attempt is made on Steed's life and narrowly fails, but Mr. Teddy Bear becomes suspicious and tricks Cathy into returning to him. Her cover blown, she may have no choice but to do what he says, even if it means taking a 'sleeping pill' to keep her quiet...

REVIEW

From the first few minutes, one can immediately observe that this episode is exceptional—the dialogue stands out, the ideas more engaging. This was the sixth episode to be filmed, and the season was clearly throwing off the languidness of the prior episodes and the uncertainty about the show's timbre. Remarkably, this episode is way ahead of its time. It's too bad that this episode's quality was not consistently maintained throughout the season. Quite often, it seems more like a fourth season episode than the second. I say this not to impugn the production staff and actors of the day but merely in reference to the higher standard of production in the later seasons of the series. Often, the budget will greatly limit the action by way of cramped sets and dull lighting, and cramped sets mean dialogue-driven scripts. This script is probably the best story that Martin Woodhouse produced for the series, but the episode exceeds the expectations of merely good story and strong dialogue and ups the ante with surrealism, eccentrics, humor, original spy ideas, and a diabolical mastermind.

From the live television assassination in the pre-title, to Steed plonking out *The Blue Danube* on a piano in Mrs. Gale's apartment, to Steed getting fresh with Mrs. Gale while practicing judo, to his near-death by nerve gas on his telephone, and to the final confrontation with Mr. Teddy Bear in his own lair, there really is so much here that suggests a more evolved episode of the series, a harkening of the future. Mr. Teddy Bear shows a tremendous amount of dimension for an *Avengers* villain this early on—a character with as much wit and personality as the series regulars, just like the diabolical masterminds of the later seasons.

The thread of humor and surrealism that the show is known for is strongly in evidence throughout. The mood of the scene in which Mrs. Gale and Mr. Teddy Bear meet for the first time is deadly serious—the actors play the scene totally straight—but one can't watch without at least chuckling at the absurdity of it; Mrs. Gale is talking to a teddy bear!

Patrick Macnee is spectacular in this story, coming across as suave, confident and slightly caddish throughout. Not quite the John Steed of later years, still in his early phase of the undercover spy confidence man that lives in the Mews and has a predilection for Dalmatians instead of champagne.

The dog would all but disappear after the third season, only briefly re-emerging in a new incarnation for a ridiculous cameo at the end of "Take Me to Your Leader" during the Tara King era, but here, Freckles' spots are regularly on display.

On the downside, the relationship between Steed and Cathy is still underdeveloped at this stage. Steed mostly treats her like a paid lackey, giving her orders; and though she does push back slightly here, she would later require much more coercion and even outright deception to involve her in Steed's plots. The only other complaint might be the lack of scope for the sets, beyond even what was usual for the show at this time. Mr. Teddy Bear's office looks like one of Associated British Corporation's back office file rooms.

Nevertheless, this is how the whole season should have gone. If every episode had been like this, we'd be talking about this season as much as anything from Diana Rigg's era. Why they instead frequently wasted time on mundane spy drivel, questionable gimmicks like unbreakable pottery, and spunky blond nightclub crooners before accepting the inevitable is beyond me.

CHAMPAGNE, CARS, CLOTHES, AND CANINES

Steed starts out straight away in a dark-gray (possibly navy) three-piece single-breasted suit with a white shirt, a dark tie with a diamond tiepin, and a matching bowler hat and umbrella. He's later seen in plain trousers and a white shirt with subtle wide horizontal stripes. He also wears his gray Prince of Wales blazer with the black waistcoat with silver buttons and gray checked trousers with his horizontally-striped white shirt and a dark tie. Later with the black fedora (seen in "The Frighteners" and "Dead of Winter"). This outfit was established in the prior season, appearing in several episodes, and it would continue to be a favorite of Macnee until Season Four. (Back at headquarters, he strips down and is once again seen shirtless and then with a terry cloth bathrobe.) Just before he is temporarily disabled by poison on the telephone, he wears a tan overcoat with wide lapels and a white cravat with dark spots. And finally, he wears the dark-gray three-piece single-breasted suit with the lapeled waistcoat (last seen in this incarnation in "Dead of Winter") with a white shirt and a dark floral-patterned tie, plus a bandage on his left hand. This suit will appear several more times over this season and the next.

Mrs. Gale wears a light-gray worsted wool suit with a collarless blouse, safari jacket, and a matching mid-calf length split skirt, designed by Michael Whittaker. The jacket is trimmed with oversized black stitching like a heavy dashed line that crosses at the waist where it is cinched and buttoned with a single button. Later, she dons a dark jacket with pale-gray lining and cuffs over a pale collarless short-sleeved blouse, with a matching skirt and black belt. She also briefly dons thick eyeglasses. She later removes the jacket. She also wears long-sleeved dark-gray jersey blouse. Her main fighting suit is a V-neck leather tunic that zips up the back with matching leather trousers—this is the one designed by Audrey Liddle—worn with a cheetah-print blouse. (This would be the leather fighting suit for this season, though several more would be added as the series progressed.) She also wears a beautiful Mandarin-style jacket in a vibrant print. The colors are unknown, but my guess is that it is primarily a bright crimson, though it could be a rich cerulean (there are no color photos of this outfit).

Mrs. Gale briefly drives an MGA (RVB 115) in a bit of nighttime on-location filming in which she is followed by a man on a motorcycle.[1] The bike is a 1955 Ariel Huntmaster 650, and she later disables it.

Mr. Teddy Bear has champagne prominently placed but no one drinks it.

Finally, Steed's Dalmatian, Freckles, makes an appearance, and Patrick Macnee's line, "Hey, you're

---

1 Interestingly, it looks like part of the interior to Mr. Teddy Bear's hideout is shot on film, as it continues straight on from the exterior night sequence. This would make it a rare case of an interior 'set' being shot on film prior to Season Four.

molting, aren't you, old girl?" sounds improvised. Freckles seems to be a very nervous girl indeed; in both production photos depicting her, the poor little thing has her tail between her legs. Perhaps the cameras, lights, and noise frightened her, and perhaps this is why she was ultimately replaced with Sheba, a Whippet mix who belonged to Macnee's then girlfriend (and future wife), Kate Woodhouse.

QUOTES

"It's not often a man falls dead in front of television cameras. The viewers got good value last night."
"Better value than you think. He was murdered." "You've made my day."
"You must forgive my sense of humor. It sometimes runs away with me."
(Gasps) "Why aren't you dead!" "Oh, looks as though I am. Hey—that's a very good photo. I had a passport photograph taken once that looked as though I had a perpetual hangover, but *that* is very good."
"What do you want?" "£198,000 in industrial diamonds would do for a start!" "Anything you say. Be a good little girl, will you? Put it in your little safe."
"Oh, by the way, do you leave your bathroom window open deliberately?"
"I killed my first man when I was sixteen years old. There was no doubt about him. He died and he deserved to die. The issues were clear. These days, there is getting to be more and more doubt."

28 (2.5.2) PROPELLANT 23

Written by Jon Manchip White
Directed Jonathan Alwyn

GUEST CAST

Justine Lord (Jeanette), Catherine Woodville (Laure), Geoffrey Palmer (Paul Manning), Ralph Nossek (Roland), Barry Wilsher (Pierre), John Crocker (Lieutenant "Curly" Leclerc), Trader Faulkner (Jacques Tissot), John Dearth (Siebel), Frederick Schiller (Jules Meyer), Nicholas Courtney (Captain Legros), Michael Beint (Co-Pilot), John Gill (Baker), Graham Ashley (Gendarme), Deanna Shenderey (Shop Assistant)

PRE-TITLE/TEASER

A middle-aged plane passenger is alarmed when he receives a message reading "Unable meet you Marseilles. Join you Paris. Love. S." and demands to speak to the captain, finally breaking into the cockpit. The pilot agrees to talk to him, and the passenger stammers in terror, announcing that someone is going to kill him.

SYNOPSIS

Steed is on the hunt for a new rocket fuel, brought to Marseilles for him by a contact. The contact dies as he arrives at the airport with the rocket fuel nowhere in sight. Believing it to be in the man's case, Steed breaks into the airport security office. He is attacked by another agent after the same fuel. Meanwhile, someone has mistaken the top-secret concoction for a hair restorer...

REVIEW

This is a curious artifact of an episode. It's full of perhaps unintentional surrealism—or at least incongruity. The whole story takes place in Marseilles, and yet, all of the actors (except Justine Lord) carry on in English with an English accent. Apparently, the production team felt that if all the characters said "Oui, Madame" enough times everyone would be convinced that the story was in France. Personally, I had to keep reminding myself. The best I can assume is that this was a failed attempt at a French farce or a parody thereof. Sadly, it doesn't work; the humor consistently falls flat. Sometimes it's vaguely funny, most times not. Nor is it very exciting, moving at a rather languid pace.

Cathy Gale doesn't have much to do in the first act, except for sitting around smoking while Steed makes repeated attempts to retrieve Meyers' briefcase, and once the case is found, she is charged with the task of squeezing tubes of toothpaste and shaving cream in search of the missing propellant. She is still playing some vague version of an assistant with the superficial appearance of a femme fatale. Steed gives her a gun so she can defend herself, and it gets stowed in her garter belt. Later, Mrs. Gale demonstrates her martial arts skills—the first hints of what was to come. In another hint of the future, there is a good scene with Steed and Cathy in a lingerie shop—part of the show's kinky side. This wouldn't be the last time lingerie featured in the show.

In production order, this episode is number five, just the second with Honor Blackman (after the initial three Dr. King episodes were recorded). In light of that, I'm going to go out on a limb here and make the observation that the show was in a transition period and didn't quite know what to do with itself. The attempt to restart the series with a new actor playing a physician assistant to Steed—replacing Ian Hendry—had failed. For whatever reasons, the show was unhappy with the status quo but wasn't quite ready to let it go either. The *Police Surgeon* concept that had inspired the whole series was dead. It had started with Ian Hendry, and it didn't work with anyone else in that type of role. Jon Rollason would not be back, but a chirpy nightclub singer would pop in from time to time, as the production team was still uncertain about what kind of assistant they wanted—and perhaps whether they wanted the character to be a woman at all.

It is now part of fan lore that Sydney Newman was against hiring Honor Blackman. (She was in fact signed into a contract while Newman was on vacation.) The shift was on, but the production had not yet found its footing. That would only come when they finally saw the obvious—that Blackman was the perfect new *Avenger*.

CHAMPAGNE, CARS, CLOTHES, AND CANINES

Mrs. Gale's dark jacket with pale-gray lining returns. Steed wears the same dark-gray three-piece single-breasted suit (with the lapeled waistcoat) with a white shirt and a dark silk tie, along with his black fedora. Later, he changes to a new navy-blue single-breasted three-piece suit worn with the horizontally-striped white shirt, a dark-blue tie with diamond tiepin, and a matching bowler. Mrs. Gale's Whittaker safari jacket and matching skirt return, this time worn with a dark-gray collared blouse with cuffs and black leather boots. This outfit is worn in this episode with a garter holster for her pistol, though this was abandoned when it proved impractical. She does however use it when bluffing Manning (very effectively too).

Steed admires some black lingerie in a French department store, and Mrs. Gale's line, delivered with a penetrating gaze by Honor, is priceless. "Black's so obvious!"

Mrs. Gale's MGA also returns—although this is a mocked-up version inside the scene dock at Teddington Studios—and she and Steed sit inside several times over the course of the episode to talk over their case (presumably with it meant to be parked in the airport parking lot).

QUOTES

"Do you always arrange to take your calls in a lingerie department?" "If humanly possible."

29 (2.7.3) THE DECAPOD

Written by Eric Paice
Directed by Don Leaver

GUEST CAST

Paul Stassino (Yakob Borb), Philip Madoc (Stepan), Wolfe Morris (Ito), Lynne Furlong (Edna Ramsden), Raymond Adamson (Harry Ramsden), with Harvey Ashby (Guards Officer), Pamela Conway (Girl in Shower), Stanley M. Ayers, Douglas Robinson & Valentino Musetti (as 'Valentine Musetti') (Bodyguards), Valerie Stanton (Cigarette Girl) and The Dave Lee Trio

PRE-TITLE/TEASER

A woman steps out of the shower and, still wrapped in a towel, takes a phone call. She tells the caller she has found out what they wanted to know and promises to meet with them the next day. However, as soon as she hangs up, she's knocked out by a man wearing a black hood and cape.

SYNOPSIS

The president of the Balkan Republic, Yakob Borb, is visiting London to negotiate a military deal. After his private secretary is killed mysteriously, Steed is assigned to investigate. Coercing Venus Smith, a nightclub singer, into posing as Borb's secretary, Steed witnesses another murder in a wrestling match, involving Borb's bodyguard, a wrestling champion himself. The murderer is apparently a famous masked wrestler known as The Decapod. After another bodyguard is killed, Steed suspects that all is not what it seems, and Venus may be caught in the middle...

REVIEW

The Avengers meets pro wrestling? Despite the lack of Honor Blackman, "The Decapod" stands out as one of the finer second season stories. Here, we are instead introduced to Venus Smith—the saucy but endearing nightclub singer—and thus the story takes a different approach with regard to the relationship between Steed and his cohort. Venus performs regularly with a group called the Dave Lee Trio, and Steed pops 'round and somehow manages to talk her into a mission, usually by promising her something that doesn't end up happening.

This approach actually works quite well, at least for the one occasion, but how many times could Steed realistically con Venus into working for him without making her look stupid? And why would he bother when he has a much more capable assistant available—with all the needed skills? Venus' relevance declined and her personality became less saucy and more vacuous in future episodes. Thus, despite the relative success of this episode's novel approach, it's a wonder that they decided that Cathy Gale should be supplanted for more of it—five episodes more, in fact. The remainder of her episodes were nowhere near as promising, and Venus Smith likely should have remained a one-off experiment.

Because of the shift in character style for the female lead, there is a lot less fighting going on. In fact, the only fight scenes are the two pro-style wrestling matches. What an odd thing to see—Steed getting tossed about by a costumed character in the squared circle! Perhaps he deserved it after manipulating Venus so callously.

This is a very nicely scripted episode with a surprise plot twist at the end. Sometimes shot with the look of a fourth season episode, the direction is also often rather workman-like, including a mistake by the cameraman, but at least there are no boom mics visible.

Philip Madoc makes his first of several appearances in the program.

CHAMPAGNE, CARS, CLOTHES, AND CANINES

Steed wears his navy-blue three-piece, single-breasted suit with a double-breasted waistcoat (first seen in "Kill the King"), the white horizontally-striped shirt and gray tie with the diamond tiepin. In the third act, Steed appears in a charcoal jacket with a flap breast pocket, worn with the black waistcoat with silver buttons (which is usually worn with his Prince of Wales blazer), a white shirt, and a gray knit tie. Later, with the black fedora. We get a good look at the black waistcoat when he is forced to wrestle in the ring. He's lucky to have not lost any buttons.

Venus wears a glittering sequined knee-length evening gown in an oversized herringbone pattern with dark shoulder straps that cross under the bust. She later wears a darker outfit with a knee-length skirt, again cut across the front in a bodice with slightly pleated shoulder straps, and a brooch in the center. She later adds a fur coat. Later, she wears another sparkling knee-length dress, darker this time, with a single shoulder strap over the left shoulder. Her final outfit is a simple cotton short-sleeved knee-length dress in a dark gray, worn with a white print scarf tied about her neck. Later, it's worn with a long black leather (or possibly vinyl) coat.

In an episode involving lots of shirtless wrestlers, you weren't expecting too much fashion, were you? Speaking of which, the wrestling matches were choreographed by judo expert, wrestler, and bodybuilder, Douglas Robinson, who also trained Honor Blackman in judo. He appears as one of the bodyguards alongside Valentino Musetti.

QUOTES

"Just how many bodyguards do you get through in a week?"
"This is what we call a nerve spot. There are a dozen others on your body I can reach in less than a second. With any one of them, I could render you senseless before you could even cry out."
"I'm sorry it didn't work out." "Why are you? You knew from the start that it would never work out. There was going to be no tour, no contracts. You left me alone with this man that was a…" "I said 'I'm sorry'!" "Alright, but don't do it again." "As if I would!"

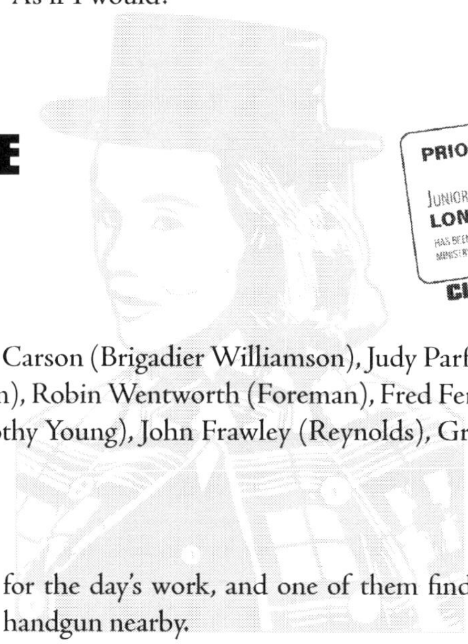

30 (2.8.4) BULLSEYE

Written by Eric Paice
Directed by Peter Hammond

GUEST CAST

Ronald Radd (Henry Cade), Charles Carson (Brigadier Williamson), Judy Parfitt (Miss Ellis), Felix Deebank (Young), Mitzi Rogers (Jean), Robin Wentworth (Foreman), Fred Ferris (Inspector), Bernard Kay (Karl), Laurie Leigh (Dorothy Young), John Frawley (Reynolds), Graham Bruce (Shareholder)

PRE-TITLE/TEASER

Two secretaries arrive at their office for the day's work, and one of them finds that the boss, Mr. Anderson, is dead in his office with a handgun nearby.

SYNOPSIS

Guns are being smuggled into Africa. They may be coming from a small arms manufacturer called Anderson's. Steed gets Cathy involved as a twenty-percent stock shareholder in order to investigate. As shrewd and crude businessman Henry Cade threatens to buy the company out, one by one the shareholders are mysteriously killed, leaving the company vulnerable for a take-over. When Cathy ends up holding the largest remaining share that will give Cade a majority, she becomes the next logical target...

REVIEW

Eric Paice's strength as a writer is to take a mundane theme and make it extremely engaging. Proving that rule, this is another strong script from his pen. The only writing flaw is that Paice makes it a little too obvious that Henry Cade is the murderer, what with his obvious "lack of morality" and vested interest in the company. Cathy being a suspect at one point is also an obvious red herring, which we, the viewer, cannot possibly believe in. Despite these flaws, Cade makes for an interesting character (as played by Ronald Radd); his office is designed to look and feel like his holiday home in the Bahamas.

"Bullseye" simultaneously supports and deflates the female liberation movement of the day by revealing Cade's murderous henchman to be a woman (and an excellent shot) but then qualifies it by showing that she was manipulated by a man. Mrs. Gale remains the only superwoman in this show. The look on Karl's face when he realizes that he's dealing with no ordinary woman in the form of Mrs. Gale is priceless.

This is the first appearance of one of Mrs. Gale's most iconic ensembles (see ***Champagne, Cars, Clothes, and Canines below***), taking her statuesque beauty to the next level. She certainly does smoke a lot in this episode however.

Steed does not feature heavily, but shows up to deliver some wonderful lines, much to Cathy's irritation and invasion of privacy. Limited though their interactions are, they already have the familiar quality that would dominate the remainder of this season and the next.

CHAMPAGNE, CARS, CLOTHES, AND CANINES

This is the first appearance (in transmission order) of two major clothing items for Mrs. Gale—she wears the tartan plaid cloak with the black fur stole. Although there are no color photos of this cloak, the available evidence is that it was a scarlet red. Its design was credited to Frederick Starke, though this is disputed. The second clothing debut is her black porkpie hat[2], still with the cloak, but she ditches the stole. Underneath is a black knee-length dress with long-sleeves, collared neckline with lapels, and three bright buttons down the front. With her reversible tartan cloak and black vest with chain links, this is her statement piece for the season and it gives her a powerful, dominant aesthetic with far more gravitas than any leather garment.

Later, she appears at the shooting range wearing a simple black stretch jersey long-sleeved shirt, and this is followed by another simple black blouse with a dark coat with pale-gray lining, which appears to be similar to the jacket worn in "Propellant 23," but longer like an overcoat, with an integrated belt in the collar, presumably to fasten the collar closed against the weather, and a tied cloth belt at the waist. She follows this up with a dark-gray knee-length dress in a fitted stretch jersey fabric; it is zipped up the back with a boat neck, and worn with a glittering floral jeweled brooch over her left breast. The tartan cloak is worn over it, albeit reversed with the tartan print as the lining and the plain crimson side on top. The slits in the sides hint that this cloak was either a Mary Quant design or was inspired by her design work since her outfit worn by Honor Blackman has this same feature.

---

2 There may be some disagreement about whether this hat is considered a porkpie or not. I've heard it called a 'top hat,' a 'squat top hat,' and a 'Billy Budd hat' in other sources, and I've called it the former myself on occasion, including in earlier editions of this book, but this hat conforms with all the traits of a modern porkpie, which are: an upturned brim all the way around, a low flat circular crown, not pinched, sometimes called a 'telescope crown,' and a crown that is generally shorter than a fedora.

This is followed by another dark outfit, this time in separates: a buttoned and collared long-sleeved blouse with a matching knee-length skirt, and worn with a black belt. Finally, her V-neck leather tunic and matching trousers return with the cheetah print blouse underneath.

Steed returns to the dark-gray three-piece suit with the lapeled waistcoat, white shirt, pale-gray tie with diamond tiepin, and the black fedora. His Prince of Wales blazer, black waistcoat, and horizontally-striped shirt also return with the black fedora, and he would stay in this ensemble for the remainder of the episode. (This has been a successful outfit ever since "Dead of Winter.")

QUOTES

"Did you conduct anymore of my private business while I was out?" "Yeah, a fellow called Young. He called you up and said he'd missed you at the office, but would you come and have drinks with him tonight at eight o'clock. I think it's in a houseboat."

"You're really trying to impress me with your lack of morality, aren't you?"

"To get back to my offer, Cathy, how do you feel?" "I feel that if I can hold on a little longer, someone's going to go up to £3." "If you hold on too long, someone's going to put a bullet through your head."

"Hey—that's £6000! Oh, it's nice to have money coming in."

31 (2.1.5) MISSION TO MONTREAL

Written by Lester Powell
Directed by Don Leaver

GUEST CAST

Patricia English (Carla Berotti), Iris Russell (Sheila Dowson), Mark Eden (Nicholson), Gillian Muir (Judy), Harold Berens (Film Director), Alan Curtis (Brand), John Bennett (Marson), Gerald Sim (Budge) with Eric McCaine (Pearson), Allan Casley (Barman), John Frawley (Passenger), Malcolm Taylor, Terence Woodfield, Leslie Pitt (Reporters), Pamela Ann Day (Peggy), William Back (Photographer), Angela Thorne (Secretary), Peter Mackriel, William Swan (Stewards)

PRE-TITLE/TEASER

A woman looks around fearfully in a darkened house lit only by candlelight. A man sneaks up behind her and she gasps as he puts his hand over her mouth.

SYNOPSIS

Steed's new assistant Dr. King is assigned to be the personal physician of the neurotically unstable but adored film star Carla Berotti as she makes her way to Montreal on a ship. Steed simultaneously goes undercover as a steward, and he and Dr. King attempt to recover a stolen film containing details of the North American early warning system that Berotti may have inadvertently come across. Unfortunately, in her unstable pill-popping state, she is hardly forthcoming with any information, and her secret lover isn't helping matters...

REVIEW

"Mission to Montreal" is a slow-moving story—as slow as an ocean liner on a leisurely cruise—that is only partially saved by the characterization of the unbalanced Berotti. This episode fails to hold viewer attention for the most part, sailing nonchalantly to nowhere interesting.

Jon Rollason provides a reasonably good performance as Dr. King, what with his superman-like jawline and boot toe chin, but he never manages the same screen presence as Ian Hendry. He delivers his lines with a sharp thin voice that is mitigated by a tendency to mumble and an almost preternatural ability to avoid the strategically placed microphones on set. In his defense, I often suspect that there was only one. Though intended as a replacement for Dr. Keel, it's easy to see why this plan was abandoned after a mere three episodes.

Patricia English deserves some praise for her portrayal of the sexy but mentally destitute film star. Perhaps wisely, the story thus centers around Carla and her problems, and conversely the spy issue seems almost trivial. It's appropriate for two reasons: she is the 'star' and part of the point is that everything revolves around her, much to her chagrin; and, due to the fact that the production was severely limited to cramped sets, it makes sense to explore characterization and writing, which would indeed become the raison d'être for most of the next two seasons. Thus, her performance dominates the episode with all its scene-chewing glory. It is too bad that this wise decision was insufficient to produce a truly gripping hour of television.

CHAMPAGNE, CARS, CLOTHES, AND CANINES

Not a lot of fashion here from the regulars. Dr. King wears a basic charcoal two-piece single-breasted suit, and later black tie with a black waistcoat and velvet lapels. Steed spends the bulk of the episode in a steward's outfit on a cruise ship. He does however bring three bottles of Moët to a party in Carla Berotti's room, though he doesn't actually drink any himself. Carla herself wears the most glamorous (and saucy) outfits, including one gray party piece with a structured brassiere top, shoulder straps, white piping along the corset, and a skirt that is split into two sections: the front is a micro-skirt which threatens to reveal all should she... uh, move; and the back is a very elaborate multi-layered affair with pleating along the sides that reveals the lining. The whole ensemble is decorated with white ball-shaped tassels hanging from every layer of trim, including underneath the cups of the brassiere and the shoulder straps. It's worn with black pumps.

QUOTES

"Who could suspect a temperamental film star? Well, now, she's in the way. I'm ordering you to remove her."

32 (2.9.6) THE REMOVAL MEN

Written by Roger Marshall and Jeremy Scott
Directed by Don Leaver

GUEST CAST

Edwin Richfield (Bug Siegel), Reed de Rouen (Jack Dragna), Patricia Denys (Cecile Dragna), George Roderick (Binaggio), Douglas Muir (One-Ten), Hira Talfrey (Charlie), Edina Ronay (Nicole Cauvin), Donald Tandy (Godard), Ivor Dean (Harbour Officer), Hugo de Vernier (Jailer), George Little (Waiter) and The Dave Lee Trio

PRE-TITLE/TEASER

In a hip London jazz club, two men sit at a table and argue about the price for a job—100,000 francs—with each initially refusing to budge. Finally, the buyer agrees to the steep price and is promised that the target will be dead by Sunday.

SYNOPSIS

Steed is hot on the trail of an organization that commits high-profile assassinations for a very high price. Steed dupes Venus into doing some snooping for him, then he goes undercover as a new assassin for hire. After Venus sees Steed leave with his first victim, his faked murder job is accidentally exposed, leaving him in hot water with Venus quite possibly singing her last number...

REVIEW

"The Removal Man" is a flawed gem with a solid plot that unfolds neatly over the course of the episode. Sustained mainly by Roger Marshall and Jeremy Scott's superlative writing, and a terrific performance from Patrick Macnee, it is among the most film noir of *The Avengers* episodes, albeit in a slightly over lit set, with shady criminals, basement nightclubs, jazz music, twenty-somethings doing the Twist (it was 1962), a haze of cigarette smoke likely futzing with the camera's electronics. As one of those actors smoking those cigarettes, Macnee practically carries the show without an equally strong female lead. While efforts were made to make Venus Smith spicy and fiery initially, this faded with time and she became much more of a naïve debby with questionable singing skills instead. Oh, she could carry a tune, but could she belt? No, never. Limited range too. Speaking of a limited range, it bears repeating that Venus didn't possess the spy skills of Cathy Gale and subsequent female accomplices, and this played into the events of this episode's narrative notably.

Though the story is gritty and realistic—some real caddish behavior from Steed as he's practically playing a villain when undercover—there's a strange moment at the end when Dragna and Siegel have Steed defenseless with a gun to his back at the nightclub. And do they kill him? No! They ask Venus to sing them a nice song and have a few more drinks. Then, somehow Steed miraculously manages to get the better of the crooks and quickly dispatches them. Did Marshall and Scott write themselves into a corner? It would seem so. Can you see the need for a helper with martial arts skills in this situation? It's almost as if they thought they had Cathy Gale until the last few minutes, then realized Venus couldn't fight. Thus, she instead distracts the villains with a song—a true bard. Julie Stevens remarked in interviews that she is actually playing the piano on set, and while her playing is convincing enough, the situation is not.

Generally, I enjoy the musical numbers, though occasionally of shaky quality, as I feel they gave the show more dimension in a way that was never duplicated again. This time, there is an extended musical interlude from The Dave Lee Trio, which frankly didn't require the vocal stylings of Venus in the least. This is also the only episode of *The Avengers* to mention Miles Davis, which can only serve to delight me. Nevertheless, this musical formula had its obvious limitations and the program thankfully succumbed to the inevitable and embraced Honor Blackman on a permanent basis.

There is some particularly strong location filming in the second act, which greatly enhances the artistic look of the story. Sadly, the episode is marred by some horrible accents. Donald Tandy as Godard affects a particularly bad Inspector Clouseau-type French accent. And I honestly don't know what accent Edwin Richfield is attempting. Australian? Then, there's Steed in a bathing suit!

CHAMPAGNE, CARS, CLOTHES, AND CANINES

As Steed is trying to infiltrate an assassin's organization, this is one of the least well-dressed episode of the season for him. He starts out in a baggy white V-neck short-sleeved collared shirt (which has the look of a traditional Indian shirt, although a ribbed knit fabric rather than linen) with matching trousers and a dark ribbed cardigan. At the club when recruiting Venus, he ditches the cardigan, which somehow makes it worse. It's simply too casual for Steed. Speaking of casual, he's later shirtless and in swimming trunks with One-Ten at the Les Centaurs Plâge beach set. (Not very convincing.) Eventually, the black ribbed cardigan is paired with a white suit shirt and a pale-gray silk tie, which classes it up slightly. He does, however, follow this up with a gray two-piece suit with a white shirt with subtle horizontal stripes (last seen in "Mr. Teddy Bear"), a dark-gray tie, a pale-gray cummerbund, and a flattish white straw fedora with a dark band. It's kind of a half-step up towards the Steed we know. He comes back down again with a similar shirt to the first one, albeit in a smoother light-gray material; it's worn with dark slacks.

Venus wears a simple pale-gray button-down shirt (its structure and stitching has a hint of western shirt about it) with black slacks. She wears the sleeves rolled up to her elbows. For her singing performance, she wears a sheer, sequined cropped black top and black hip-hugging pants cut off just above the ankles and worn with black pumps. It isn't as classy as it might sound.

Steed calls for champagne in the nightclub and the crooks bring it. They drink a few glasses before Steed spills the bottle to create a distraction. The rogue!

QUOTES

"But why kill a pretty little film star? What's the point?" "Every profession has its ethics. It's a code of behavior. In our business, Steed, we don't ask questions, as you well know."

"I thought there was someone on my tail, so I lost him. It wasn't particularly difficult."

"The piano is introspective, reminiscent of Bill Evans when he was playing with Miles Davis."

"We've got a choice. Either we lose her or you. Which is it to be, Steed?"

"Why'd you let the band go! Little Venus and I could have had a little twisting session." "Well, she could always sing for ya."

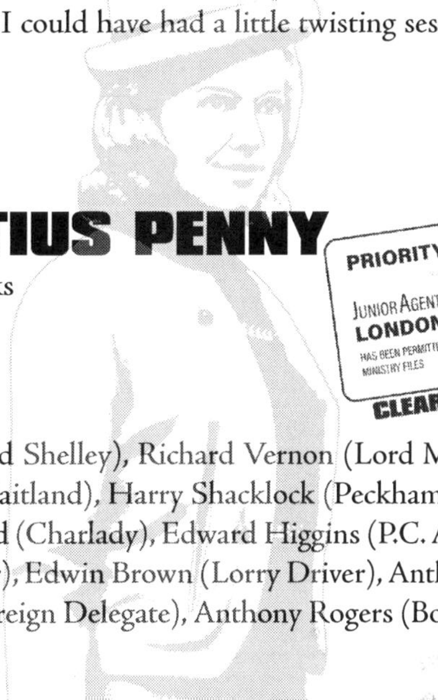

33 (2.10.7) THE MAURITIUS PENNY

Written by Malcolm Hulke and Terrance Dicks
Directed by Richmond Harding

GUEST CAST

Alfred Burke (Brown), David Langton (Gerald Shelley), Richard Vernon (Lord Matterley), Sylva Langova (Sheila Gray), Edward Jewesbury (Maitland), Harry Shacklock (Peckham), Philip Guard (Goodchild), Alan Rolfe (Burke), Grace Arnold (Charlady), Edward Higgins (P.C. Andrews), Delia Corrie (Miss Power), Raymond Hodge (Porter), Edwin Brown (Lorry Driver), Anthony Blackshaw (Lorry Driver's Mate), Theodore Wilhelm (Foreign Delegate), Anthony Rogers (Boy)

PRE-TITLE/TEASER

An intruder stealthily breaks into a stamp collecting shop and begins searching, but when he hears the voice of the owner in the inner office, he draws a gun. The intruder enters the office to find the owner on the phone very excited about "a Mauritius penny." Despite the fact that the owner appears to know him, he shoots him dead and leaves him collapsed over the desk with the phone ringing.

SYNOPSIS

Investigating the death of a stamp-collecting shop owner, Steed and Cathy trace the murder to a philatelic auction, at which another man is murdered. Cathy ends up working as an assistant in the shop and discovers the cadaver of the first murdered man. Steed meets a ruthless dentist who is also a member of a neo-Nazi organization called the New Rule. The New Rule organization is intent on taking over the country with a surprising government representative...

REVIEW

"The Mauritius Penny" is an enjoyable but unbalanced episode. It can be admired for its scope but not the overall execution of its central premise. Somehow it manages to go from stamp-collecting to a neo-Nazi organization with government-toppling ambitions. This is well within the usual outline of *The Avengers*, so fair enough. However, it oddly runs out of time, and the whole affair is literally wrapped up within seconds. A bit more editing might have solved this problem by progressing more rapidly to the point rather than wasting so much time on philatelic distractions. The connection turns out to be that the name of the stamp is also the code name of the fascist leader, the most tenuous of connections possible.

On the plus side, there are some very enjoyable superficial scenes that help move things along, but to be certain they are merely set pieces without sufficient depth to fully engage the viewer. Steed's interaction with his housekeeper is amusing, inviting a working-class element into the picture that wouldn't normally be permitted in later seasons under producers Fennell and Clemens. There is one humorous scene—one of the funniest of the Cathy Gale era—in which a lorry driver comes to retrieve his crowbar just as the villain Brown is brandishing it as a weapon against Mrs. Gale. He meekly hands it over to preserve his cover, but as soon as the driver leaves, both the crook and Mrs. Gale scramble to start their violent tête-à-tête. Needless to say, now weaponless, Brown proves no match for Mrs. Gale, and we see another man in shock as he realizes he isn't capable of countering her training with raw masculine strength alone. In another twist of expectations involving women physically overpowering a man, Steed's visit to the dentist swiftly turns into every dentophobe's nightmare. He is threatened by the German-accented Miss Gray with a drill—shrieking in his ear so loud that it drowns out the dialogue—and then is suffocated with the anesthetic mask.

Foreshadowing the quirky eccentric characters that would dominate later seasons, the stamp shop owner is gunned down crying "Good shot!" as he falls. This specific scene (the pre-title) contains an egregiously bad continuity error however. Mrs. Gale refers to the philatelic phone conversation having been tapped after they listen to the recording together, and yet the recording appears to continue well past the point when the telephone was hung up.

In any case, the quirkiness (intentional or otherwise), while fun, is all so much fluff really, as the central premise isn't revealed until the last few minutes, with the connections to stamps and dentistry being more than a little confusing. I understand the need to have an intellectually-stimulating circuitous path for *The Avengers* to follow in their quest to vanquish the evildoers—normally this would provide more interest and spice to the story—but it shouldn't happen at the expense of clarity.

Because of the rushed ending, one could speculate that the narrative might have unfolded better over a longer serial of some kind. Perhaps this is why Malcolm Hulke and Terrance Dicks' writing styles were ultimately considered less than ideal for the show during the production and writing team shakedown of season four. They would both later spend a great deal of time working on another show possibly more suited to their talents—*Doctor Who*—producing many classics for that series.

Still, the story is superficially entertaining, endowed as it is with much prescience of the current political environment.

CHAMPAGNE, CARS, CLOTHES, AND CANINES

Mrs. Gale wears a black rollneck jumper with a scarlet wool cape closed by two linked chains (very Chanel), a matching split knee-length flared skirt with inverted pleats, and a 'trilby' hat[3], all designed by Mary Quant. It's worn with black gloves, a black belt, and black leather calf-length boots. Later, the reversible scarlet tartan cloak (from "Bullseye") returns, with the tartan on the outside, worn with the same Quant outfit, but without the cape, of course. At the finale in the third act, her Whittaker

---

3 Though called a 'trilby,' the hat is virtually uncategorizable, having a mix of styles. Its brim is turned up like a porkpie but so sharply that it forms a bowl shape. The crown is round and slightly bulbous but has a slight pinch at the peak. There is a black ribbon but it's almost hidden by the turned-up brim.

safari jacket and skirt reappear.

Steed wears his navy-blue three-piece single-breasted suit with a white subtly-checked shirt and a dark tie with diamond tiepin. He later wears this outfit with a matching bowler, brolly, and eyeglasses. The second act brings his horizontally-striped white shirt back with gray tweed trousers and a sleeveless V-neck cardigan, zipped up on the left side. Later, he wears his Prince of Wales blazer over this same outfit, but somehow the blazer is gone when he wakes up on the floor after being attacked and knocked out. Perhaps his housekeeper cared just enough for him to take it off to make him more comfortable. Even later, the black waistcoat with the silver buttons replaces the cardigan for his trip to the dentist. Once again, when he wakes up after being knocked out, his blazer is gone. Perhaps the psychopathic dentist cared just enough for him to take it off to make him more comfortable. And his tie changes to a diagonally striped black one that I can't imagine Steed ever wearing. More like something Dr. Keel would wear. Fortunately, the complete ensemble comes together by the end when Steed opens his new stamp collection.

The rest of the clothing is Neo-Nazi stuff designed by Fascistwear Ltd—boring brownshirt stuff. I have to say that their logo design is rather poor. It looks like a muddled version of the British Rail logo. Ah—Nazis! What do they know about design? Probably not a gay man among them.

Freckles makes several brief appearances throughout the episode, even taking care of poor Steed when he's unconscious on the floor. In fact, she shows far more concern for him than the housekeeper does. We get to see Steed's wine rack, but no champagne.

QUOTES

"No, you're mad! Good shot!"

"I mean, have you finished your sleep?" "I might as well have finished my sleep. I had a rather wild party."

"Compulsory dental inspection! Any decent government would insist on that sort of thing!"

"You didn't really think you could take over this country with a few fanatics in fancy dress, did you?"

"We intend to provide this country with the strong leadership it needs. You may call that fanaticism, but to me it is political inevitability." "I seem to have heard that somewhere before."

"The basis of our movement is a return to the traditions that have made this country great."

"The day of the New Rule must be postponed."

34 (2.11.8) DEATH OF A GREAT DANE

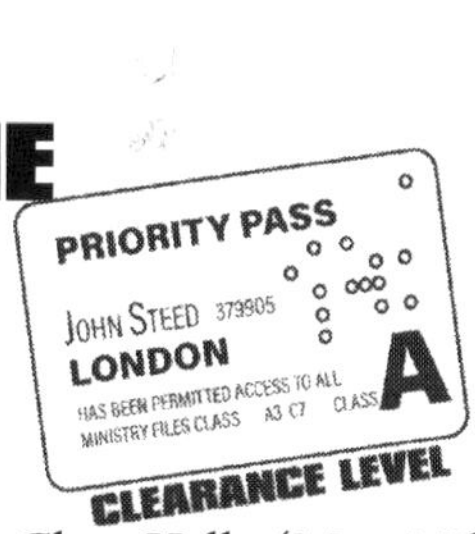

Written by Roger Marshall and Jeremy Scott
Directed by Peter Hammond

GUEST CAST

Frederick Jaeger (Getz), Leslie French (Gregory), John Laurie (Sir James), Clare Kelly (Mrs. Miller), Dennis Edwards (1st Assistant), Anthony Baird (2nd Assistant), Billy Milton (Minister), Eric Elliott and Roger Maxwell (Winetasters), Herbert Nelson (Gravedigger), Michael Moyer (Policeman), Frank Peters (George Miller), Kevin Barry (Kennels Man), Junia (Dancer), Heidi (Bellhound)

PRE-TITLE/TEASER

A sad funeral in the rain. Only the priest, the gravediggers, and one man with his dog attend. As the man leaves, he is consoled by the priest, but the twist is that it's a pet cemetery called The Happy Hunting Grounds and the recently departed is the man's other dog.

SYNOPSIS

After a man named George Miller is taken to a hospital for injuries suffered in a car crash, £50,000 in diamonds is found in his stomach, and Steed and Mrs. Gale investigate Miller's practical jokes shop Big Laugh and then the owner of the diamonds Mr. Litoff. Mr. Litoff is ostensibly very ill, but no one except his assistant Mr. Getz and his doctor have seen him recently. When Steed's attempt to return the diamonds provokes little interest, and the body of Mr. Litoff is found in the grave of his own Great Dane, it becomes clear that a lot more than £50,000 is at stake...

REVIEW

Cathy shows off her woodpeckers, Steed ponders her photographic skill. Cathy asks if a man always travels with diamonds in his stomach, Steed puts on a conjuring show—to demonstrate the profession of the man with the indigestible breakfast. This is about as good as the second season gets. "Death of a Great Dane" is one of the strongest scripts in the season, one that effortlessly combines humor and wit with the usual spy flair.

Frederick Jaeger as Getz is exceptional, his cool response to being blackmailed with Steed's delivery of the diamonds, fresh from Mr. Miller's digestive tract, and his sociopathic cavalier attitude in general foreshadow the aristocratic villains that would feature so prominently in subsequent seasons. Apparently suffering from continuous sick headaches, judging by Jaeger's tendency to rub the sides of his head frequently (conscience bothering him?), Getz however turns out to be more than just a shrewd businessman; he possesses a willingness to kill. Villains in *The Avengers* are not—despite popular opinion—at all similar to James Bond villains. They are in fact similarly over-the-top and extreme but inevitably more complex and often absurd—seldom wanting to rule the world so much as transmute it into some (usually) bizarre vision of how they believe it should be. Though this season and the next would largely stick to the more mundane plots, mostly street criminals, drug smuggling, and embezzlement or grand larceny—as in this episode—many later episodes would feature masterminds that have bigger and more comical ambitions, generally based on their quirks and eccentric visions of the world. These villains seem to bridge the gap more than others this early in the series.

John Laurie, an actor known for eccentric comedy roles, is something of an *Avengers* regular guest star and would appear in three more episodes over the next few years. Leslie French appears as Gregory the butler, another early eccentric. Both of them are a joy to watch. It appears that Steed baits Gregory to find his motivation for desiring so much money, and the answer from the seeming genteel man is repulsive, and perhaps Steed allows him to sink for this reason, and yet Gregory's behavior is all too human. Such is the sympathy one might feel for his human weakness that it's sad to witness his inevitable arrest, Steed tolerating but ultimately ignoring his sycophantic efforts at ingratiation.

My only complaint would be that the script is perhaps a little too dry. There's not all that much action either; what little there is occurs at the very end, accompanied by Johnny Dankworth's ubiquitous swing jazz theme, abruptly terminated by Mrs. Gale firing her pistol. (Perhaps she startled the grams operator?) This might be why the story was chosen to be re-filmed during the sixth season, using a production process that would ultimately allow the story to breathe in a way that cramped studio sets could never allow. Nevertheless, you won't find me grousing too harshly about any of Roger Marshall's work, and this script really is first rate.

EPISODE NOTES

This is the episode when Honor Blackman's judo training went into high-gear. She received a five-week course from the Robinson brothers, Douglas and Joe, Douglas having appeared previously in "The Decapod." Patrick Macnee also received some judo training from the Robinsons.

CHAMPAGNE, CARS, CLOTHES, AND CANINES

Mrs. Gale starts out in the darkroom developing her bird-watching photos in a black-and-white short-sleeved collarless print t-shirt with a Holstein cow pattern (or perhaps a Rorschach pattern) and a black leather pencil skirt. When Steed shows her slides, she wears a sparkly sleeveless silk dress with black leggings and with her hair up. She later wears a deep-cerulean full-length flowing sleeveless gown with a scooped neck and straps gathered with slight pleats and an integrated cape. (It's only seen briefly when she's lying down.) Her tartan cloak also returns with the tartan inwards over her dark-gray long-sleeved, knee-length dress (as in "Bullseye") with the jeweled brooch, as does her dark windbreaker coat with the belted collar. This is replaced at the finale with a shiny pale mackintosh over her leather fighting tunic and trousers with a black rollneck jumper underneath.

Steed wears his dark-gray three-piece suit with the lapeled waistcoat and cloth-covered buttons, and the white shirt with subtle horizontal stripe and a gray silk tie. Later, over the same suit, he wears a new tan overcoat, with a black plaid lining, ribbed collar, and heavy stitching over the sleeves, and the black fedora and umbrella. Later, the fedora is replaced with a black bowler, and then the navy-blue three-piece with the horizontally-striped shirt. In the slide-viewing scene, we get a good look at the white shirt with the subtle stripes; it looks as though the change in value is accomplished by altering the weave rather than using a different color, but it's hard to be certain.

Lots of dogs in this one, Great Danes (Dancer and Bellhound), and even ceramic dogs on a shelf, but, alas, none are Steed's. At Litoff's office, Steed mentions that he once had a dog like Dancer, named Racer "by Martyr out of Satyr." (Referring to the dog's lineage.) In fact, Bellhound was played by Macnee's own dog, Heidi.

Lots of wine testing, but no champagne.

QUOTES

"But you've been away a fortnight, and three birds to show for it?" "They don't stand still and pose for you, Steed." "They do for *me*."

"Did he always travel on a full stomach?"

"I prefer to settle now. You do realize that in blackmail an immediate cash settlement is normal?"

"It's the power that excites me, sir! I want to be rude and ill-mannered and order people about. And then, I look forward to an association with a considerable number of good-looking women."

"Men of principle need handling with infinite care, but in the final analysis everybody's corruptible. It's just a question of price."

35 (2.3.9) THE SELL-OUT

Written by Anthony Terpiloff and Brandon Brady
Directed by Don Leaver

GUEST CAST

Frank Gatliff (Harvey), Carleton Hobbs (M'sieur Roland), Arthur Hewlett (One-Twelve), Gillian Muir (Judy), Anne Godley (Lilian), Michael Mellinger (Fraser), Richard Klee (Workman), Storm Durr (Gunman), Cyril Renison (Customer), Anthony Blackshaw (Policeman), Ray Browne (Price)

PRE-TITLE/TEASER

Steed and Dr. King are at a hotel when a man is shot. Dr. King rushes to the rescue along with Steed, but the man has already died.

SYNOPSIS

Under the instructions of One-Twelve, Steed is protecting Roland, a U.N. negotiator who is in London for important talks. After they fail to prevent one assassination attempt, several of Steed's colleagues and even Steed himself come under suspicion, but Dr. King proves to be the key to discovering the traitor's identity...

REVIEW

"The Sell-Out" is a fairly well-scripted straight-forward affair of spies and counter-spies and features a generous amount of location footage for an early episode. It even includes a rather unusual attempt to carry out a phone conversation between Steed on a car phone and Dr. King's secretary in a studio set. Jon Rollason mumbles his way through the production as usual, but there's a very good scene in which Steed passively convinces Dr. King to help despite King's vow to remain nothing but a doctor. Presumably, this persuasion lasted only for the remainder of the episode since the doctor vanishes, never to return—this was the final Dr. King episode to be recorded—displaced as he was by a perky blond nightclub singer and a former Kenyan landowner with the best judo chops in the business.

The story's punchline is the nonchalance of Frenchman Roland, who at the end has no idea how much trouble Steed and Dr. King went through to protect him. One-Twelve makes his one and only appearance in the series. This is probably the strongest of the three Dr. King episodes, none of which are anything close to spectacular.

CHAMPAGNE, CARS, CLOTHES, AND CANINES

In the opening scene at the hotel, Steed wears a gray tweed overcoat with a breast pocket and a black bowler, while Dr. King wears a pale mackintosh with up-turned collar over a navy-blue two-piece suit with a white shirt and dark tie. When Steed takes off the (rather baggy) overcoat, he reveals the suit with the lapeled waistcoat and cloth-covered buttons, clearly becoming a favorite for Macnee. Later, he switches out the baggy overcoat for a brand-new dark-charcoal double-breasted overcoat with a felt collar, in a rare callback to his dark-gray suit that first appeared in "Kill the King." (Very rarely were any of Steed's suits double-breasted, but even more rarely the waistcoat as well.) However, double-breasted may be an overstatement as the overlap is rather slight. In keeping with Dr. Keel in Season One, Dr. King's outfit does not change throughout the episode.

There are a total of five filmed sequences[4] in this episode, one of which is set at night. In three of these sequences, Steed drives an AC Greyhound (880 OPA)—one of only a few car appearances in this season, as the budget and recording methods didn't allow for much exterior filming. He also goes undercover with a limp and a cane (and a carnation in his lapel), riding in a chauffeured 1953 Rolls-Royce Phantom IV Touring Limousine and followed by a 1962 Sunbeam Alpine Series II (238 VC) in yet another filmed sequence. He uses a car phone for what appears to be the first time. There is a fourth sequence as the Sunbeam escapes. This makes "The Sell-Out" the car-heaviest episode so far and probably for the entire season, as well as a very big episode for exterior filming.

---

4 As usual, the film is foggy and smeary with poor contrast, a potential consequence of several stages of processing—negative development, print processing, or the final telecine process in which the projection of the film is fed into the videotape through a mixing board (usually live during the in-studio recording), of which I suspect the latter is to blame since the film development just a couple of years later was generally excellent.

QUOTES

"It's a question of who's to guard the guards themselves, eh, Steed? A problem that's bound to arise in our line of business from time to time."

"Ah, Monsieur Steed! Well, you see, I'm still very much alive. I told you there was nothing to worry about."

36 (2.12.10) DEATH ON THE ROCKS

Written by Eric Paice
Directed by Jonathan Alwyn

GUEST CAST

Meier Tzelniker (Samual Ross), Gerald Cross (Fenton), Ellen McIntosh (Liza Denham), Naomi Chance (Mrs. Daniels), Hamilton Dyce (Max Daniels), David Sumner (Nicky), Richard Clarke (Van Berg), Toni Gilpin (Jackie Ross), Douglas Robinson (Sid), Annette Kerr (Mrs. Ross), Haydn Ward (Painter), Jack Grossman and Vincent Charles (Diamond dealers)

PRE-TITLE/TEASER

A woman receives a beauty treatment at the salon. Assured by the beautician that the facial beauty pack hardens almost instantly, her face is covered completely and the beautician unexpectedly proceeds to smother her.

SYNOPSIS

After the wife of a diamond merchant is killed, Steed and Mrs. Gale go undercover as a married couple to stop the sale of illegal diamonds and discover how the illicit rough stones are being smuggled into England…

REVIEW

"Death on the Rocks" is an intensely serious episode, rooted in the mundane style that features so heavily in the first three seasons; it is produced in a style that would be repeated even more pleasingly in "Intercrime," one involving international criminals, an interesting death by beauty products (something of a throwback to "Ashes of Roses"), plenty of diamond merchant talk, and several thrilling action scenes.

Cathy and Steed continue to increase their domestic involvement, this time posing as a married couple. With Mrs. Gale, it's never that easy, and proper negotiations are necessary before she agrees to become "Mrs. Steed." Later, you can feel the barriers coming down as Steed gives Cathy a ride on his shoulders. This brief moment of gaiety provides perhaps the lightest moment in an otherwise very serious episode about diamond smugglers. And it does have a classic line at the end with the lion's head turning over just as Steed has fixed it into place.

Mainly, this episode is a very good example of the series falling back on its bedrock of classic domestic spy work, employing sharp dialogue and a gritty plot to make its point. It makes its point very well, even if a little conventionally and with a largely unremarkable guest cast—only Hamilton Dyce and Meier Tzelniker truly distinguish themselves, the latter with a sympathetic performance as Mr. Ross, an honest man blackmailed into joining the illicit diamond trade.

EPISODE NOTES

Douglas Robinson appears in the series again (as Sid), as he was stepping up Blackman's judo instruction, resulting in some truly exciting and realistic fight scenes. In the famous fight between Blackman and Robinson in this episode, Blackman can be seen afterwards visibly wincing and rubbing her back. The judo rolls she was doing were quite difficult on her spine, but she nevertheless insisted that the guys really go after her to make the rolls look as convincing as possible.

CHAMPAGNE, CARS, CLOTHES, AND CANINES

Steed opens the episode wearing his dark-charcoal double-breasted overcoat with a felt collar (last seen in "The Sell-Out"). His shirt is white and he wears a dark patterned silk tie and a black bowler with a matching brolly. Later, he goes black tie at a party and he dances with Mrs. Daniels. Then, his dark-gray three-piece suit with the lapeled waistcoat and cloth-covered buttons returns, continuing to get good mileage since its debut towards the end of Season One. (In one scene, we can see the waistcoat without the jacket, and the back is black satin.) Later, he wears a dark button-up cardigan over the subtle stripe white shirt. Nice cufflinks. They look like gold with a dark gem, possibly garnet, quite the honkers. Finally, the gray Prince of Wales blazer reappears with only a white shirt with subtle wide stripes underneath.

Mrs. Gale begins the episode by wearing her charcoal-gray separates (from "Bullseye"), the buttoned long-sleeved blouse and matching skirt. Later, she goes casual by returning to her Holstein black-and-white print shirt with tight black leather pants. At the party, she debuts a sparkly, fitted, long-sleeved evening gown. The gown is zipped up the back, and the skirt is split on the sides. Afterwards, she wears a black rollneck jumper (zipped up the back) with high-waisted tweed trousers and the Starke cloak with the tartan on the inside. Later, the cloak is replaced with the dark windbreaker coat with the belted collar. And, in the third act, the crimson Mary Quant ensemble returns.

Lots of drinks at the party, but no champagne. And plenty of liquor bottles get shot up in Mrs. Gale's new flat.

QUOTES

"Oh, don't misunderstand me. It's just that I need a wife for a couple of weeks." "So long?"
"I'll let you know as soon as you can move in, Mrs. Steed."
"Did you enjoy it, my love?" "Not much."
"How can one have an accident with a face pack?" "It was made of a sort of plaster of Paris compound, and it hardened rather quickly. The coroner gave accidental death. I don't think so though. I have doubts."
"My dear, for better, for worse."

37 (2.13.11) TRAITOR IN ZEBRA

Written by John Gilbert
Directed by Richmond Harding

GUEST CAST

John Sharp (Rankin), Richard Leech (Franks), Noel Coleman (Nash), Jack Stewart (Thorne), Ian Shand (Mellors), William Gaunt (Graham), June Murphy (Maggie), Katy Wild (Linda), Danvers Walker (Crane), Richard Pescud (Escorting Officer), Michael Browning (Wardroom Stewart)

PRE-TITLE/TEASER

In a British naval office, Sub-Lieutenant Greene is informed by Admiral Nash that he is to be placed under arrest to await his court martial for espionage.

SYNOPSIS

Steed and Mrs. Gale investigate reports that an officer on HMS Zebra is passing secret information to the enemy. They discover that the information is in fact being passed by someone else on notes disguised as darts scores. Eventually the real traitor is revealed, and he plants a bomb, but Steed forces him to diffuse it with a display of iron nerves...

REVIEW

"Traitor in Zebra" is run-of-the-mill and mundane, even by second season standards; it isn't bad, just a terribly ordinary bit of spy melodrama. Like most of the earlier episodes, the budget made directorial extravagance cost-prohibitive, but in this particular instance the characters spend a more than usual amount of time standing around engaged in dialogue, most of which centers around a pub and multiple games of darts. Very little of the character interaction is interesting with the exception of Cathy's half-hearted romance with Franks, which occurs in a few blink-and-you-miss-them moments. The implication is that she genuinely likes him but cannot commit herself to anything while she is on assignment. Other than this, there isn't a lot going on even with the main cast, who spend most of their time on the periphery.

The best character is probably the villain Rankin, who comes across as a lay-about pensioner, virtually living in the pub, sending classified information—passed to him by darts scores—through the spy network. The neat twist is that the spy information is hitched to his pet dog's collar. Together, Rankin and his pooch leave the pub and walk along a suburban lane in front of a row of shops, the streets slick with water, the air hanging heavy with moisture and the sky bleached out in white—or is it the foggy telecined 35mm film?—and the duplicitous dog, freed from his leash, darts into the Pond House shop to drop off his top secret payload in a studio set. It's a jarring transition back to videotaped doldrums after a bit of artistic location filming. When the best you can claim about an episode is it has a canine courier in a misty landscape, you know you're on shaky ground! Sadly, Rankin faces a rather ignominious end, stabbed in the kidney by Franks while he hides from the *Avengers*.

Or perhaps the dog-in-the-fog moment is second best. The most exciting moment comes at the end when Steed, showing tremendous resolve and ruthlessness, forces Franks to diffuse a bomb by locking him in the room with it. However, this brief burst of excitement is too little, too late for a rather languid episode.

CHAMPAGNE, CARS, CLOTHES, AND CANINES

Steed dresses as a naval officer for most of the episode, including the cap and the double-breasted greatcoat with decorated epaulettes and underneath he wears the double-breasted peacoat with eight round brass buttons. Later, he switches to his black ribbed cardigan over a white shirt, gray vest, and dark tie. His pale bulky weatherproof overcoat with the black plaid lining also returns with the black fedora. His final outfit is a black button-down shirt with a zippered pale-gray jacket (probably suede) and pale tweed trousers.

Mrs. Gale wears a leopard-print vest over a pale-gray jersey cardigan. (This is possibly the same leopard print worn under the leather tunic, though it is typically seen bunched up around her neckline in that case.) She later wears the pale mac over the black jumper (last seen in "Death of a Great Dane") sometimes with her eyeglasses (from "Mr. Teddy Bear"), and this is followed by a much warmer heavy black shearling coat with a white lining, and then the crimson tartan cloak (with the tartan on display) over her black jersey jumper and trousers. She finally debuts a completely new outfit: a black-and-white jumper with pale-gray panels flowing vertically along the lower torso to a flare at the bottom with a black hem, but the rest all black from the shoulders to the arms, and worn with pale-gray slacks and black calf-high boots.

Steed drives a 1935 Alvis Speed 25 (CPT 75) to the naval base and, at the end, to confront the spies at their hideout with Mrs. Gale. There's also a 1957 Morris Minor 1000 (UJY 292). Plenty of drinking throughout, but no champers. Technically, one of the criminals is a canine, an adorable shaggy little spy who appears both on film and in the studio.

QUOTES

"They're very fine things, those bombs, you know. May not kill you, just mess you up a bit."
"Are you quite sure I'm not wasting my time here?"
"I see. Well, you want your head blown off?"

38 (2.14.12) THE BIG THINKER

Written by Martin Woodhouse
Directed by Kim Mills

GUEST CAST

Anthony Booth (Dr. Kearns), Walter Hudd (Dr. Clemens), David Garth (Dr. Farrow), Tenniel Evans (Dr. Hurst), Allan McClelland (Broster), Penelope Lee (Clarissa), Marina Martin (Janet), Ray Browne (Blakelock), Clive Baxter (Nino)

PRE-TITLE/TEASER

In a vast 1960s computer room with many circuits clicking and humming away, one computer technician spots gas escaping from a leaking pipe. He tries to stop it but accidentally knocks the pipe completely free and quickly passes out from the fumes.

SYNOPSIS

Using her anthropologist background as a cover, Cathy Gale investigates some sabotage on the most advanced computer in the world, Plato, which the government is interested in using for military missiles. Cathy is encouraged to find out more by getting to know the project's boy wonder mathematician, Dr. Kearns. After more sabotage and another murder, suspicion falls on the somewhat immature Kearns, but after the real saboteur locks both he and Mrs. Gale into the refrigerated section of Plato, it's up to Steed to rescue them and help find the real traitor…

REVIEW

The best that can be said about this story is that it's the first extant episode dealing with future science issues, essentially science-fiction, in what would become a tradition of *The Avengers*—one that would become increasingly more absurd as the series progressed, starting with mere computerization and progressing to killer robots and electrified men as shocking assassins or insta-mold that rots wood in a split second. Here, the story deals with the then novel idea of a building-sized computer, one that pretends to be on the cutting edge of technology. Writer Martin Woodhouse (a real-life computer designer!) doesn't dwell on the technical aspects of the subject but spends a great deal of time focusing on characterization, including that of the computer, who, perhaps predictably for this era, has a perceived personality of sorts, indicated by its operators with the old clichéd line of "you talk about it as if it's a person."

I was pleased that this story didn't turn out to be another "mad computer" story as one would expect. Though not a cliché at the time, the idea of a giant super-computer that runs everything—which *The Avengers* does here, in 1962, before most anybody else including *2001: A Space Odyssey*—is cliché enough now without the added insanity twist. The insane computer plotline is so overdone by now (and virtually dispensed with as a tool in the science-fiction writers' toolkit) that it would be at best quaint in the 21st century. The reversal is refreshing. Plato is just a very large and smart computer with no megalomaniacal ambitions at all. Thank you, Mr. Woodhouse.

The other good points are that there is a lot of clever dialogue and some lovely interplay between Cathy and Steed, who keeps threatening to go to the Middle East but somehow never does, much to Cathy's chagrin and eventual relief. The episodes most charming moment occurs when Steed and Mrs. Gale meet in the Doctor Death Parlour pinball arcade. Equally, Mrs. Gale's scenes with the mildly immature Dr. Kearns are a highlight.

The best moment of direction comes with the murder of Dr. Clemens, recorded by video camera inside a ventilation shaft—something I imagine was hard to do with the massive equipment of the era. Indeed, this is a rare artistic moment from the otherwise frequently conventional Kim Mills. Nevertheless, Mills is smart enough to make the biggest star of the show the Plato set itself, which truly is one of the most impressive of the era.

Nevertheless, I have little else to recommend other than the superficial aspects already listed, as Plato is otherwise the centerpiece of a schizophrenic episode that tries too hard to cover too many bases. The main downside is the rather ill-conceived plot and the lack of focus on the villain Dr. Farrow. We never actually find out the full story of what he was up to (something to do with a game of cards) as the story flits from one about sabotaging the computer to something else and then back again.

CHAMPAGNE, CARS, CLOTHES, AND CANINES

Mrs. Gale wears a stunning black fur stole over another pale cape in a similar style to the Mary Quant cape, albeit without the chains but buttons instead, and a black jumper. Later, the same cape is worn over her leopard print blouse and a black knee-length skirt. Later, for the party, she wears a magnificent pale full-length sleeveless watered-silk dress with a scooped neckline and pleating in the sides of the skirt and a ruched waistline. It's so long it practically sweeps the floor and the fabric produces a moiré pattern as the light plays on it. She tops it with a short black fur coat. At the computer center, the pale mac returns. The Mary Quant chain-linked cape and skirt also make an appearance with the black porkpie hat, also with just the black jumper and skirt and no cape or hat, followed by a collarless print jacket in a Mandarin cut with three-quarters sleeves, and then, her leather tunic and trousers, though at first without anything visible under the tunic, and then later with a new print blouse underneath. Finally, she wears fuzzy striped pajamas (or perhaps a dressing gown) as she's relaxing at home after her ordeal.

Steed's bulky tan overcoat returns, the one with the heavy stitching over the sleeves and cuffs, as first appeared early in Season One. Also, his gray Prince of Wales blazer with the black waistcoat returns, along with a white shirt, a dark-gray tie, and pale tan trousers (the first of many appearances of this precise combination).

This is also the first appearance by Steed's dog, Sheba, a blond, short-haired Whippet mix, and a real cutie. When Mrs. Gale is instructed on how to take care of Sheba, she is told to feed her with "half a pound of raw meat... and a few biscuits daily." Sheba belonged to Macnee's then girlfriend (and future wife), Kate Woodville, and the sweet dog clearly loved him very much.

Lots of drinking and gambling but no champagne.

QUOTES

"Plato is this building, Mrs. Gale, the whole building."

"You talk about it as though it were a person, not a machine."

"You better keep an eye on young Kearns. He's an ideal target for subversion."
"I should never have left you alone. A few more moments and you'd have been vacuum-packed, along with your boyfriend."

39 (2.4.13) DEATH DISPATCH

Written by Leonard Fincham
Directed by Jonathan Alwyn

GUEST CAST

Richard Warner (Miguel Rosas), David Cargill (Monroe), Valerie Sarruf (Anna Rosas), Douglas Muir (One-Ten), Gerald Harper (Travers), Hedger Wallace (Baxter), Michael Forrest (Rico), Maria Andipa (Singer), Alan Mason (Pasco), Geoff L'Cise, Arthur Griffiths (Thugs), Bernice Rassin (Chambermaid), Jerry Jardin (Customer)

PRE-TITLE/TEASER

At a hotel room in Jamaica, Alan Baxter, a British courier, settles in and places a call to the governor's secretary, claiming that he has an intuition that something is amiss. After retreating to the bathroom to take a shower, an intruder breaks in and briefly searches the room before hiding. Emerging from his shower in a dressing gown, the hotel guest intuits that someone has broken in and tries to phone the police but is quickly dispatched by a knife in the back.

SYNOPSIS

A British courier in Jamaica is killed for the papers he is carrying, but the papers are of a completely mundane nature. Why is a foreign power so interested in apparently mundane government dispatches? Steed and Mrs. Gale investigate in Jamaica, Bogota, and Santiago, and they trace the problem to a very wealthy man named Miguel Rosas...

REVIEW

This episode opens with very unconvincing stock footage of Jamaica and a lazy jazz theme. The story is very straightforward and deals with the more banal variety of spy work, but it is nevertheless entertaining. In essence, "Death Dispatch" is about introducing Cathy Gale—though *The Avengers* rarely introduced characters properly. This is the first recorded episode starring Honor Blackman. And it shows. Cathy gets a lot of activity, coming across as flirtier with Steed than she would later be. Steed even gets to kiss her (the first of two times). Has he wined and dined her to this point, gently leading her to an epiphany of spy work? We'll never quite know. She is great however in her undercover job as a hotel maid. She demonstrates perfect Spanish, and ruthlessly uses Anna Rosas as a shield in the final confrontation with her father. By whatever means she entered the spy trade, she was clearly cut out for it. The chemistry between the two leads is immediately obvious, and it would only strengthen as they continued to work together.

In one bizarre scene, Cathy gets serenaded by a female singer-guitarist while in Santiago. I'm not quite sure what they were trying to convey with this—perhaps mocking her for having a doll called Juanita? The script is perhaps a little too ambitious for its own good with studio sets masquerading as countries in Central and South America. It's more than a little obvious in its fakeness, though this was not at all unusual for the time. Gerald Harper gets a small role as a humorous British diplomat. Four years later, he would star in his own *Avengers*-style series—***Adam Adamant Lives!***

CHAMPAGNE, CARS, CLOTHES, AND CANINES

Steed relaxes in Jamaica wearing plain tweed trousers, his baggy white casual shirt with a V-neck (from "The Removal Men"), and a dark striped jacket. Arriving in Bogota, Steed wears an ill-fitting pale-gray two-piece suit with his straw hat (again, from "The Removal Men"). Sadly, Steed continues to dress casually, wearing dark knee-length shorts and a hideous white shirt with an integrated candy-striped cummerbund and a plunging V-neck. Thank goodness it's hidden under a fluffy white bathrobe.

Mrs. Gale wears a long shiny white coat over a short-sleeved dress in an abstract black-and-gray pattern with a belt. (In production order, this is her first episode, and she wears her hair much shorter than she would later.) She's later seen wearing only a black brassiere while dressing. She puts on a dark-gray sleeveless collarless blouse with a matching pencil skirt. The fabric has pale flecks or spots and is lustrous and shiny. She later disguises herself in a maid's white uniform (over the previous outfit) and speaks fluent Spanish. When being serenaded, she wears a simple pale short-sleeved knee-length dress with the white coat over it.

Steed and Mrs. Gale split a bottle of champagne in a hotel room in Jamaica.

QUOTES

"She's dark, very pretty, Latin American. I bought her specifically for you."
"She's wrong, you know. I wouldn't have hung that in the rear window of my car."

40 (2.2.14) DEAD ON COURSE

Written by Eric Paice
Directed by Richmond Harding

GUEST CAST

John McLaren (Freedman), Liam Gaffney (Michael Joyce), Donal Donnelly (Vincent O'Brien), Peggy Marshall (Mother Superior), Elisabeth Murray (Deidre O'Conner), Janet Hargreaves (Sister Isobel), Nigel Arkwright (Hughes), Bruce Boa (Bob Slade), Margo Jenkins (Margot), Trevor Reid (Pilot) and Edward Kelsey, Mollie Maureen, Denis Cleary, Wilfred Grove

PRE-TITLE/TEASER

Inside the cockpit of a commercial plane, the pilots prepare for touchdown, but after warnings from air traffic control that they are still flying too high, it is revealed that the control tower's instructions were incorrect; they are in fact flying too low and crash into a power line. The plane explodes instantly.

SYNOPSIS

Investigating a mysterious plane crash in Ireland, Steed and Dr. King discover that the site of the crash and the convent where the bodies and survivors have been taken are no accident. Furthermore, the nuns and their newfound Mother Superior are surprisingly less than innocent...

REVIEW

This is the second episode to be filmed for the second season. Reluctant to give up the popular formula of pairing Steed with a doctor, the program's producers tried essentially re-casting the role of

Dr. Keel. Jon Rollason was chosen to play the new role of the prophetically-named Dr. Martin King (nothing to do with civil rights). He does a good job, but ultimately, he is doomed to unsuccessfully repeat what had gone before.

This is not surprising really. The whole point was that Dr. Keel was accidentally drawn into spy work due to his fiancée's death being coincidentally connected to heroin dealers. Thus, it makes little sense that Steed (or Steed's superiors) would specifically recruit another doctor. Is there some particular reason why Steed would need to work with a physician? Clearly, with the absence of Ian Hendry, the original star of the show, Patrick Macnee, was being asked to step up, and he does so admirably, appearing confident and capable on his own.

The story itself is largely engaging television, though heavily flawed. The finale in particular is incredibly rushed, full of several dramatic revelations in rapid succession that come across as confusing. The parade of bad Irish accents is also rather disconcerting. The plane crash at the beginning was done well for the era, even if it was only a model shot and some stock footage. And the sets are rather good this week.

CHAMPAGNE, CARS, CLOTHES, AND CANINES

Steed starts out right away in a much better outfit than in the previous episode—his Prince of Wales blazer, black waistcoat, and the horizontally-striped white shirt and a dark knit tie (which later turns into a pale knit tie). Later, at the nunnery, he adds his tan overcoat with the heavy stitching and the black fedora and umbrella. Dr. King wears his navy-blue suit and pale mackintosh (from "The Sell-Out"). And, believe it or not, these are their only outfits for the entire episode. Otherwise, lots of nuns with guns. (They have bad habits.) Still, the Prince of Wales blazer is probably the best outfit to be stuck in if you have to be stuck in a convent with trigger-happy nuns. But no champagne, no cars, no canines.

QUOTES

"She was after all on a mission of mercy. The girl asked for water and she left for a few moments to fetch some." "In those few moments, somebody was murdered." "She will remember that all her life."
"I take it we're not flying back?"

41 (2.15.15) INTERCRIME

Written by Terrance Dicks & Malcolm Hulke
Directed by Jonathan Alwyn

GUEST CAST

Kenneth J. Warren (Felder), Julia Arnall (Hilda Stern), Angela Browne (Pamela Johnson), Patrick Holt (Manning), Alan Browning (Moss), Jerome Willis (Lobb), Paul Hansard (Kressler), Donald Webster (Palmer), Rory MacDermot (Sewell), Bettine Milne (Prison Officer Sharpe), Charlotte Selwyn, Jean Gregory (Trusties)

PRE-TITLE/TEASER

In a quiet suburban home, two thieves ransack a room stealing jewels, but a third man shows up brandishing a gun and demanding to know who authorized them to perform the job. Unsatisfied by their answers, he shoots both of the thieves.

SYNOPSIS

Cathy takes the identity of a German criminal named Hilda Stern to infiltrate Intercrime, an international cartel of criminals and murderers and finds herself forced to defend a foreigner accused of stealing from the group. Acting as executioner and forced to kill several threats to Intercrime's London operation, Mrs. Gale has no warning when the real Hilda Stern murders a guard and escapes from Holloway...

REVIEW

"Intercrime" is an excellent gritty crime drama with hard-edged realism and a genuine pall of danger hanging over it. Though somewhat dated—the world no longer fears jewel thieves—this story is easily one of the great highlights of the second season and is Terrance Dicks and Malcolm Hulke's best and most beautifully-plotted script for the series. The organization of Intercrime is something of a homage to SPECTRE of James Bond fame, perhaps inspired by Ian Fleming's novel ***Thunderball,*** which was published the previous year.

Honor Blackman is wonderful once again, going undercover as the aptly-named Hilda Stern, portraying the fräulein's chill perfectly. In subtle embellishments, adeptly executed by Blackman, Mrs. Gale allows her conscience to betray her twice, once during the trial of Kressler when she becomes too emotional about the outcome, and again when she fails to 'execute' him while being tested by Felder.

Given that this thriller has an airtight script and is played almost totally straight, it is extremely unfortunate that the production lets it down so often. In one scene, a stray camera strolls by when Julia Arnall fails to close a door upon entering. In another, the supposedly dead prison matron blinks quite noticeably in shot. There are also curious pauses in the actors' motions during the climactic confrontation at the shooting gallery. The camera cuts to the action before the actors receive their cues, demonstrating the standard production method of the day—shooting virtually live-to-tape with a vision mixer cutting back and forth between cameras on cue from the director. A vision mixer operator was likely off his or her game that day. In this case, it might have been worth it to go for the second take or propose an edit or two for the fight scene. It certainly would have helped to raise this fine example of the series to the perfection that it deserves. Unfortunately, the limitations of television production of the day mean that Intercrime is something of a down-market SPECTRE that hangs out in a bland shooting gallery with a storeroom/office combo. Thus, the episode excels almost entirely with acting and dialogue, rising above those studio limitations to a degree that was seldom the case in television productions of the day.

The organization of Intercrime is notably one of two recurring ***Avengers*** foes—the other being the Cybernauts. Dicks and Hulke would later resurrect Intercrime in an episode called "The Great Great Britain Crime," filmed and then scrapped in 1967. That story was part of the now notorious first block of the Tara King series. During that tumultuous period, the script was reworked, given new framing material and turned into the lamentable "Homicide and Old Lace." Sadly, that eye-abrasive epitaph is a completely unworthy sequel to this immensely enjoyable hour of classic television.

CHAMPAGNE, CARS, CLOTHES, AND CANINES

Mrs. Gale starts right out in her Mary Quant scarlet ensemble, though again the hat is missing (she seems to have abandoned it). Mostly prison clothes (simple dark sweater and knee-length pale skirt) and fräulein-wear (her big pale mackintosh, rollneck jumper, and black gloves) for Mrs. Gale this episode, but she does end the episode in her tartan cape, black fur stole, and porkpie hat.

Steed begins the episode in a white button-down shirt, a gray vest (as in "Traitor in Zebra"), and black trousers. At Holloway, when acting as Mrs. Gale's advocate, he wears his navy-blue three-piece single-breasted suit, a white shirt, and a dark tie, with a black bowler and umbrella, plus his eyeglasses. At the rifle range, he wears his tan overcoat with the black plaid lining (from "Death of a Great Dane") and a houndstooth flat cap. But when he visits Pamela Johnson, he wears a dark charcoal suit with a very foppish sparkling waistcoat underneath his suit jacket; it has a dark color with flashy metallic threads and bright buttons and its own lapels. Finally, he appears again at Johnson's house in the tan overcoat with heavy stitching, the black fedora and umbrella, and a patterned ascot, and later completely reverses course by wearing black trousers, a black shirt, and the suede zippered jacket (from "Traitor in Zebra").

QUOTES

"Think over what I've said, Mrs. Gale, I think you'll see there's no other way out."
"Here's to Intercrime—system, organization and continental good will."
"A few weeks ago, I came across a file of yours which told me quite enough of what was really going on. At first, I couldn't believe it! I loved you, and I wanted to help you, but I didn't know what to do. I suppose I should have gone to the police at once."
"In an expansive mood, I made a rather large order from Rifle Ranges International Limited. Unfortunately, I forgot to cancel it."
"Mind you, of course, they might ask some pretty searching questions. People have been sent to jail for less, haven't they?"

42 (2.17.16) IMMORTAL CLAY

Written by James Mitchell
Directed by Richmond Harding

GUEST CAST

Paul Eddington (Richard Marling), James Bree (Miller), Bert Palmer (Josh Machen), Gary Watson (Allen Marling), Steve Plytas (De Groot), Rowena Gregory (Anne), Didi Sullivan (Mara Little), Douglas Muir (One-Ten), Frank Olegario (Blomberg)

PRE-TITLE/TEASER

Cathy Gale visits a ceramics studio where one designer tells her about his attempts to perfect his secret formula, a ceramic material that is unbreakable. She is then led to another room to see how the ceramics are made, but they are both surprised to find a corpse in the vat of mud.

SYNOPSIS

Allen Marling is on the verge of discovering an unbreakable ceramic. Unfortunately, someone is willing to kill for it. Cathy Gale, who happens to be writing a book about ceramics, goes undercover as a potential buyer in order to find out which crook is doing the killing...

REVIEW

I joyfully dub this episode "*The Avengers* Discover Corelle Ware!" This is an unusual story, a quasi-science-fiction piece from first-time *Avengers* writer James Mitchell with some interesting characterizations that underpin the central plot. De Groot is an interesting villain, and some of the other characters, like the kooky Mara and the passionate Allen, are fairly engaging, though I find myself with little else to recommend explicitly. The central problem seems to be that the plot and subject matter are as dull as the mud bath into which they dropped the dead man in the pre-title. No number of eccentrics seem to be able to save it completely.

Unbreakable china tied into the spy game? People killing over the secret of the formula? Given the reality of unbreakable faux ceramic in this day and age, we know that such a product is unlikely to allow anyone to corner the market. Though I'm sure the makers of such unbreakable 'ceramics' (actually a tempered glass product) today secure a fine profit in kitchen wares, people who wish to collect actual ceramic dishware are not going to be fooled by such inferior products and are far more likely to go to a potter instead. Corelle Ware has a plasticky texture quite unlike real bone china or stoneware. We know this, and it places "Immortal Clay" at a unique disadvantage for the modern viewer.

It would indeed be science-fiction to transcend the laws of physics and make genuine china impervious to breakage, and it seems likely that the story failed to convince even the viewers of the early 1960s that unbreakable ceramics would carry enough weight to involve master spies in the protection of their formulae. Steed's comment at the end indicates that he questions the value of the newfound material himself.

Despite the failure to convince us of the subject's urgency, we have an interesting villain to amuse us—one that has the odd habit of receiving backrubs from a three-hundred-pound bald man whilst playing chess and eating from a box of chocolates within the privacy of his own home. Suggestive at the least, this was an early sign of ***The Avengers*** pushing the envelope.

Nevertheless, the humdrum nature of the central premise prohibits any real excitement, and the climactic fight scene is incredibly poorly staged—the telephoto lenses are used on the cameras, tight on the subjects in their cramped set so that it looks like everyone is just falling over each other. But there is that interesting bit of prescience to consider; Corelle Ware did after all happen. So, while "Immortal Clay" gets the Nostradamus award of the week, it's still nothing more than an average second season outing, and possibly quite a bit less.

CHAMPAGNE, CARS, CLOTHES, AND CANINES

The episode opens with Mrs. Gale wearing her Frederick Starke cloak with the tartan inwards, over a dark knee-length dress, with the Mary Quant scarlet hat. When working later, she reverses this mixture of outfits and wears the Mary Quant linked-chain scarlet cape with the black porkpie. (I'd love to see a color photo of this ensemble.) She works in a white long-sleeved blouse, a black calf-length pencil skirt, and another leopard print vest (although this one seems to be a reverse of the prior one, with a greater emphasis on the dark spots). Mrs. Gale then wears a heavy black wool coat with wide lapels and a light-gray long-sleeved blouse with bright buttons and a chevroned placket, paired with a knee-length skirt.

Steed starts out straight away shirtless in a sauna (once again with One-Ten just like at Les Centaur Plâge). Then, the dark-gray three-piece suit with the lapeled waistcoat returns, worn with a black bowler and umbrella, white shirt, dark tie, diamond tiepin. Then, the tan overcoat with the heavy stitching returns, followed by a light-gray jacket over a dark sweater vest, white shirt, dark tie; the fit of the jacket is a bit off, slightly baggy and longer than his usual jackets, and worn with a patterned handkerchief prominently placed in the breast pocket; looks to be worsted wool. Then, in a slightly odd continuity break, it's the same jacket but with the black waistcoat with silver buttons instead of the sweater vest, as if we're not supposed to notice the difference. Finally, the Prince of Wales blazer returns with the black waistcoat, and the transformation is complete, as if he was experimenting and finally realized the old favorites are best. Then, the gray worsted jacket inexplicably returns for an encore.

QUOTES

"I just like him, that's all. I think he's wonderful. And as for the other one, he's dreamy!"

"Look—there it is. The only one there is, and it's worth five or six million! Isn't it likely someone

would kill for that."
"All that fuss over a little piece of mud."
"It'll be great not to break a cup every time I wash up but I don't see what that's got to do with security."

43 (2.18.17) BOX OF TRICKS

Written by Peter Ling and Andrew Rhodes
Directed by Kim Mills

GUEST CAST

Jane Barratt (Kathleen Sutherland), Maurice Hedley (General Sutherland), Edgar Wreford (Dr. Gallam), Ian Curry (Gerry Weston), April Olrich (Denise), Dallas Cavell (Manager), Jacqueline Jones (Henriette), with Robert Hartley, Royston Tickner, Gail Starforth, Lynn Taylor, Gregory Scott and The Dave Lee Trio

PRE-TITLE/TEASER

At a London club, a stage magician performs his 'disappearing woman' trick in a vanishing cabinet. However, when he brings her back, she does indeed reappear, but immediately falls to the floor, dead.

SYNOPSIS

Steed's investigation into a leak of classified NATO secrets leads him to the nightclub where Venus is employed. He then learns that Venus is an old friend of the daughter of General Sutherland, the man he's investigating. At the nightclub, two magician's assistants have been murdered in a disappearing cabinet, and the general is being 'cured' by a faith healer and his magic boxes. Is there a connection between these seeming disparate events...?

REVIEW

This quite ordinary episode proves without a doubt that the program only truly works with Dr. Keel or one of Steed's liberated female companions—in other words, a strong, competent person with notable skills that translate well into spy activities. In an odd twist after the change of producer, the character of Venus Smith was altered to become far more vacuous and lightweight than before. Gone is her spice and fire and the massive permed beehive hairdo, and in their place a chirpy demeanor and a pixie haircut. It's not a change for the better. Though there's nothing wrong with what Julie Stevens is doing here—her acting and singing are at least passable—she's not given anything truly engaging to do. Indeed, neither is anyone else.

The whole plodding script is dependent on the stupidity of the guest stars, all of whom must be so gullible as to believe in magic healing boxes and to not draw the conclusion that they might have some more nefarious quality. Kathleen is so absorbed in trying to help her father that she still can't quite believe that the healing boxes are a hoax even when tape recorders are discovered within. I also find it very improbable that the magician would eagerly continue to perform his vanishing cabinet act and think nothing of it as more and more assistants die in the process. This alone should be enough of a cue to the audience that the magician's act is somehow tied to the spying. This is the type of transparent plotting necessary to make this script function.

The best moment comes when Steed is playing the role of a wealthy eccentric and hypochondriac in need of the spying 'quack' doctor's assistance. Most of the witty lines, few as there are despite otherwise sharp dialogue, are concentrated in this brief scene. On another positive note, there is quite a tense confrontation at the end with Steed by himself defending the dense and gullible Kathleen against the spies. Overall, this is a mixed bag at best, probably better skipped in favor of a Cathy Gale second season episode. We're just marking time until the team is finally and permanently together.

CHAMPAGNE, CARS, CLOTHES, AND CANINES

Steed starts out in his navy-blue three-piece single-breasted suit with the double-breasted waistcoat (first seen in "Kill the King"), worn with a white shirt, dark-gray tie and his diamond tiepin. The heavily-stitched tan overcoat returns briefly, followed by a pale dental tunic, buttoned up at the right shoulder with a high collar and a left breast pocket, worn with black trousers. He later deliberately overdresses as part of a disguise as a hypochondriac: swamped in a black wool shearling overcoat with black lining, lapels, and cuffs, and a generous patterned ascot (as seen in "Intercrime") and gray gloves, as if he's always cold, and a cane. It's possibly the best scene in the episode. Otherwise, I think this is a missed opportunity to have Steed dressed in traditional magician's garb.

Venus wears a white sequined sleeveless dress with a pleated knee-length skirt and matching pumps with bows (a youthful touch perhaps to remind us of the ruby slippers from ***The Wizard of Oz***). Later, she wears a woolly white dress with a Peter Pan collar, buttoned down the front like a coat. This is followed by a dark-gray rollneck jumper and matching knee-length skirt, and a plaid jacket with linked chains at the waist, and black pumps, then by a black-and-gray striped jumper and a dark coat with a frilled placket, very shiny brass buttons, and (again) a Peter Pan collar. (They were trying to bring out a more youthful image, and what could be more youthful than Peter Pan?) Then, another jumper, this time knitted and lumpier with an abstract pattern in black-and-white stripes, followed by a very sparkly buttoned long-sleeved dress with an integrated bow tied in front, worn with matching pumps. And, finally, a knee-length dark-gray line dress with a pleated skirt and an open neck and back. It's layered with a sheer outer fabric over an inner one. This is the first episode in which she wears her new pixie haircut, having bleached her hair after wearing wigs for the first few episodes. Her makeup is also softer and more youthful.

QUOTES

"Each box contains a complicated and finely balanced arrangement of minerals. Each works in conjunction with its neighbor, together producing radiant vibrations of such a nature and intensity as to override completely any physical dispiriting."

"And this is the best treatment for me? It doesn't involve exercise or diet or anything nauseating like that?

44 (2.16.18) WARLOCK

Written by Doreen Montgomery
Directed by Peter Hammond

GUEST CAST

Peter Arne (Cosmo Gallion), John Hollis (Markel), Pat Spencer (Julia), Douglas Muir (One-Ten), Olive Milbourne (Mrs. Dunning), Alban Blakelock (Peter Neville), Brian Vaughan (Doctor), Gordon Gardner (Pathologist), Philip Mosca (Mogom), Susan Franklin (Barmaid), Herbert Nelson (Pasco), Christina Ferdinando (Miss Timson) and Bill Haydn, Anna Sharkey, Roy Gunson, Maggie Lee, Fred Evans, Gillian Bowden

PRE-TITLE/TEASER

A cabal of magicians in black robes dance to a tribal beat around a pentacle, with candles burning and a photo of their black magic victim to one side. As their leader raises his fist, the glass of the victim's photograph cracks.

SYNOPSIS

Steed is assigned to courier the plans for a propellant, but finds the inventor, Neville, in a coma. After Neville's death, the malevolent Markel comes looking for the same plans, under the pretense of looking for research notes. Markel has contracted a black magic coven to put a spell on Neville, putting Steed and Mrs. Gale in conflict with both himself and Cosmo, the money-grubbing warlock of the coven...

REVIEW

An unusual episode and an experiment that would not be truly repeated for two years when a similar psychic theme was explored for "Too Many Christmas Trees." Sometimes I think that this might have been a mistake and perhaps the alternate trope of having the 'magic' accomplished by fakery would fit in better with *The Avengers* universe. Despite the improbable mix of supernatural powers and *The Avengers*—a show which has mainly adhered to science as the means for its miracles—this story is surprisingly successful and engaging.

Cathy Gale has a chance to show that she's an expert on black magic cults, as well as practically everything else, and is forced to go undercover as a potential disciple of Cosmo the Warlock. This is the episode in which she reveals her birthdate—5 October 1930—assuming that this is not a ruse.

Peter Arne and John Hollis are both doing great jobs in their respective roles. Arne seems to be channeling Dr. Karswell from the excellent Jacques Tourneur film ***Night of the Demon***. The series regulars really gel also, with Mrs. Gale's acidic Chelsea wit in evidence during her interactions with Steed. This is a sign of the series being on track when John Steed and Cathy Gale were allowed to work together without the otherwise unwelcome interruptions by temporary assistants.

I also found the direction to be of a higher quality than most second season episodes with some particularly good nighttime location footage. However, so tiny is the set for the pre-title black magic ceremony that it looks like it is being conducted in a cupboard. I also find the 'creepy' witchcraft-in-operation music to be rather irritating.

EPISODE NOTES

The black magic sequences were especially coordinated by dance instructor Pat Kirshner, as seen in the production photographs from the day, in which Peter Hammond and Patrick Macnee appear as well. Macnee was included because he was required to pretend to be one of the coven in the episode's climax. The scene appears to have been meticulously rehearsed under Hammond's direction with Peter Arne also standing at the lectern and rehearsing the Dr. Cosmo Gallion role.

CHAMPAGNE, CARS, CLOTHES, AND CANINES

Steed's navy-blue three-piece suit with the double-breasted waistcoat (last seen in "Box of Tricks") returns with his horizontally striped shirt, a navy-blue tie, and a black bowler and brolly. Later, he changes to the Prince of Wales blazer, the black waistcoat, cream trousers, and the black fedora, but with the same shirt, though it's hard to see the horizontal stripes during the on-location film sequence—in which he drives the Triumph Herald and climbs over a barbed wire fence and gets attacked by a guard dog—so it might be a plain white shirt in that scene. The right sleeves of the Prince of Wales blazer and shirt appear to get torn by the dog attack. (It would take a magical spell to mend that invisibly!) Finally, he wears the same black robes as the black magic practitioners, courtesy of Satanwear Ltd.

Mrs. Gale's wears a tricolor striped blouse for the first time, and later episodes next season would feature a similar blouse. It's worn with a gray tweed knee-length skirt. Later, it's worn with her Whittaker safari jacket. She visits the bookshop wearing her dark windbreaker coat with the collar closed with the belt so that the pale lining doesn't show. It's worn with matching leather gloves. Lastly, she wears a charming dark nightgown, followed by a dark-gray long-sleeved stretch jersey blouse with what looks like the Mary Quant split skirt. This is paired with the windbreaker coat later at the pub.

Steed drives a Triumph Herald (7061 MK), and Mrs. Gale drives her MGA (RVB 115). I have to say I wonder why they bothered to do a mockup of her car for "Propellant 23," as the scene in this episode is on videotape and yet the MGA is started up and driven off set.[5]

And, of course, the canine-of-the-week is the German Shepherd guard dog behind Dr. Gallion's bookshop.

QUOTES

"Black magicians have real power, at least over people who believe in them."

"Mr. Markel, you're really a very stupid man. Like all your kind, you only believe what you can see and what you can touch."

"Neville's your side of the problem. Work *something* out for yourself."

"You come here often?" "My first visit. I don't think I'll be asked again."

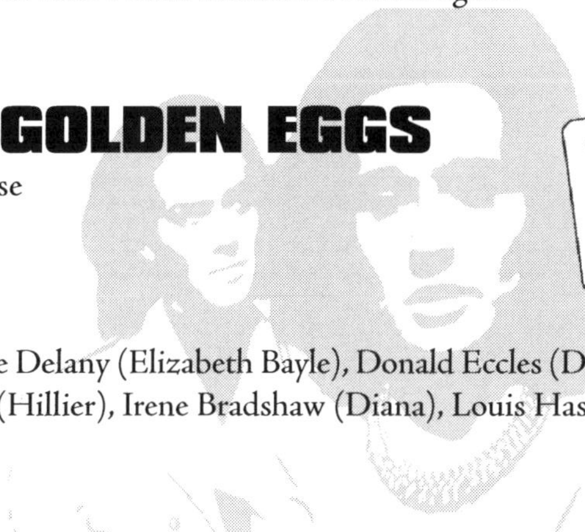

45 (2.19.19) THE GOLDEN EGGS

Written by Martin Woodhouse
Directed by Peter Hammond

GUEST CAST

Peter Arne (Redfern)[6], Pauline Delany (Elizabeth Bayle), Donald Eccles (Dr. Ashe), Gordon Whiting (DeLeon), Robert Bernal (Hillier), Irene Bradshaw (Diana), Louis Haslar (Campbell), Charles Bird (Hall)

PRE-TITLE/TEASER

In a luxurious study, an elderly scientist leans over a microscope. Saying he plans to work late, he dismisses his assistant. However, once she leaves, another man enters to find the scientist reaching into a safe. There is a fight, the older man is knocked out, and the intruder steals the safe's contents: two golden eggs.

SYNOPSIS

A pair of gold-plated eggs are stolen from Dr. Ashe's laboratory, but Dr. Ashe isn't talking about it. After the thief becomes ill with a deadly virus, it becomes apparent that Dr. Ashe's experiment with biological warfare has attracted the interest of a certain diabolical mastermind who wants to sell the plague to the highest bidder...

---

5 Apparently, this was accomplished by parking the car directly outside the scenery door to Studio 2 and the cameras were simply trolleyed outside. The scene was recorded on Friday, 6 July 1962 at 8:45 pm in a brief 15-minute session.

6 Peter Arne returns immediately after "Warlock" while playing a completely different role. A very unusual move. Usually, for obvious reasons, a major guest star would not come back within the same season.

REVIEW

The pre-title opens with a theft in progress, taking place to a Johnny Dankworth swing jazz action number. The prize? Eggs. Two golden ones. But these eggs are definitely not the kind to be cracked, let alone boiled, poached, or fried sunny side up; it would be the last breakfast you ate. Over a different sort of breakfast, Steed reminds Mrs. Gale that he's allowing her to use his flat as long as she provides groceries and cooks his meals. For the remainder of this season she appears to do neither. Nevertheless, their relationship appears to grow more domestic in this season. By the next, Mrs. Gale would once again have her own apartment, updated to space-age standards, replete with electronics such as an intercom and automatic door. For now, she is itinerant and tolerating domesticity with Steed.

Honor Blackman appears to be corpsing in one scene with Steed while repairing broken pottery; this scene predictably ends with Steed clumsily re-smashing the vase just as it is nearing complete restoration. The pottery theme follows up on a thread started with "Immortal Clay," in which Cathy was writing a book on ceramics.

The first act terminates with a very well-staged ambulance accident, taking place at night on a lonely, snowy country road. The winter theme continues later in a back alley set with falling snow[7]—Cathy easily fending off a gun-toting crook with judo. Blackman is terrific throughout, not just in this scene. To top that, she outwits the diabolical mastermind without any help from Steed, who absconds to the market to pick up food sundries that were neglected by Cathy. Yes, there's a certifiable diabolical mastermind in this episode, the first since "Mr. Teddy Bear," and Redfern's little bit of eccentricity is that he likes music boxes—he constantly works on their repair and maintenance while engaged in dialogue. (A variation on this would be explored in season four's "Dial a Deadly Number" in which the villain would repair clocks.) Appropriately, the villain is defeated to the chimes of his own music boxes rather than a jazz action number. (That track was already used in the pre-title.)

This is an excellently scripted and well-directed episode that has a gritty, somber mood—punctuated by humorous scenes involving Steed and Mrs. Gale's continued cohabitation crisis—and it is one of a few during this early era to deal with the possibility of worldwide destruction. One of the stronger stories of the era, it harkens forward to a formula that would dominate during the fourth season.

CHAMPAGNE, CARS, CLOTHES, AND CANINES

Steed wears a pale-gray shirt and a black ribbed velour vest while cutting out the toy on the back of a box of Wild West Cornflakes and spilling the cereal everywhere. (That's why we love you, Steed, you're just a big kid!) Later, he wears the same outfit with the Prince of Wales blazer (its right sleeve having been repaired from the dog attack). At the climax, the tan overcoat with the black plaid lining returns with the black bowler and umbrella.

Mrs. Gale has quite the run of fashion in this episode. She wears a quilted patterned jacket with a black pencil skirt for breakfast before dressing with her Starke crimson tartan cloak (tartan turned inwards) and black porkpie hat. Underneath the cloak, is a knee-length skirt, a buttoned blouse (probably from "Propellant 23"), and a fitted wool jacket, all in a deep cobalt and navy and worn with her eyeglasses; further on down the road, the hat disappears and is replaced by the black fur stole. This is then followed by a brown rollneck with the Mary Quant scarlet skirt (while repairing pottery); then, the pale mackintosh; the black wool shearling coat with a white lining, cream trousers, and black leather boots for the fight scene in the snow; and finally, the leather fighting V-neck tunic and trousers with the same black rollneck.

---

7 The fight scene was shot on an interior set using fake snow. However, in the filmed exterior scene involving the ambulance crash, it was in fact quite snowy outside (this episode having been filmed in January 1963).

QUOTES

"I couldn't find any butter..." "...I don't suppose we've got any left. You'll have to get some more. And that was part of the bargain. You have this flat until you get a new one. In return, you provide me with slap-up bumper meals. Keeps my mind off my ice-cold hotel."
"Do you know what's so fascinating about clockwork? It's predictable. It works. You wind it up, send it on, and it gets results. If it doesn't, it's of no more use."
"What do I care who has it? People are all the same." "Not Julius Redfern. He's something quite exceptional." "He is. Once you're in, you're in. Or dead." "Do you think we'll be offered the same choice?"
"Are you in the market for a handful of death?"

46 (2.20.20) SCHOOL FOR TRAITORS

Written by James Mitchell
Directed by Jonathan Alwyn

GUEST CAST

Melissa Stribling (Claire Summers), Anthony Nicholls (Dr. Shanklin), John Standing (East), Richard Thorp (Roberts), Reginald Marsh (Higby), Frank Shelley (Professor Aubyn), Frederick Farley (One-Seven), Terence Woodfield (Green), Ronald Mayer (Proctor), Janet Butlin (Barmaid), and The Kenny Powell Trio

PRE-TITLE/TEASER

At her jazz club, Venus Smith sings for a pajama party. After completing her number, she finds her friend Richard dead in his office with a revolver in his hand.

SYNOPSIS

After a university tutor and acquaintance of Venus apparently commits suicide, Steed investigates and soon finds that a criminal organization is operating at the university. Various tutors are being tricked into forging checks and then blackmailed into committing crimes for the organization...

REVIEW

In an episode that begins with Julie Stevens singing "The Varsity Drag" and dancing in an impossibly bubbly fashion while wearing a mortarboard cap, a flapper-era waist-length bead necklace and striped pajamas, I cannot have expected anything good to emerge from the approaching onslaught of narrative. Despite this highly suspect start, I found "School for Traitors" to include at least one relatively smart twist involving Venus—in this case, Venus actually calls Steed and alerts him to the crime. Nevertheless, the fact that they were already jumping-the-shark with the character, having turned her into a crooning debby instead of a fiery and strong-willed singer on the cusp of stardom and needed creative twists to make the character work, should be clue enough that the situation was not tenable. But some TV executives need more time than others. Thus, put on a happy face, as we must endure only another two of these all-singing, all-dancing experiments before the undeniable brilliance of Cathy Gale is allowed to reign unchallenged.

Perhaps the best aspect of this episode, which is otherwise unexceptional, is that it has a major female villain. She's an astonishingly unsuccessful artist and a master manipulator, tricking her various would-be lovers into forging checks and then blackmailing them into working for her. The character is essentially another female role-reversal, playing the flirtatious philanderer to the hilt, a sociopathic liar juggling suitors. Thus, Melissa Stribling secures a place in the history of ***The Avengers***, in an archetype that was rare even for a show that was already challenging traditional female roles—that of the femme fatale vamp. She also gifts Venus with an acid-based face cream. (Yikes!)

Apparently, this episode was shot on the same day it was broadcast, and it does show. The sets are a bit Spartan and the direction rather pedestrian. The challenges of the tight schedule do however result in some great ad-libbing by Patrick Macnee when Julie Stevens fluffs a line. Macnee was always so generous with his fellow actors.

Interestingly, John Standing was considered as a possible replacement for either Honor Blackman or Julie Stevens or both, and his role here is notably significant for a typical guest star. The reason for this incomprehensible consideration—Honor Blackman was obviously perfect—is that the sexist television executives of the day were concerned that the show was becoming 'hag-ridden.' Shocking but true!

All in all, this is in the upper half of the Venus Smith stories, though this is not really saying that much. "The Decapod" is still far better.

CHAMPAGNE, CARS, CLOTHES, AND CANINES

This time it's pajamas and clown suits for the opening scene. Venus sings while wearing vertically-striped pajamas and a black mortarboard while twirling a massive strand of white Mardi Gras beads. Later, her black-and-white jumper with abstract patterns returns and then her horizontally-striped jumper (both from "Box of Tricks"). She later adds a black jacket with a plaid lining and a pale-gray railroad engineer's cap (probably blue in actuality). Next is a black rollneck with a black-and-white striped wool tunic dress with a V-shaped front, a pleated skirt, and a faux integrated belt. Next, as she sings, she wears a frill-fronted long-sleeved white blouse and bowtie in silk (sort of a mock tuxedo shirt for women) with a matching knitted wool dress which is designed to be worn like overalls with buttoned on straps that cross in the back. Finally, a tricolor vertically-striped long-sleeved knitted wool jumper with a large black patch in the front with faux knitted buttons and black trousers; she later wears them with a black jacket and the railroad engineer's cap.

Steed wears a white rollneck jumper, pale tweed trousers, a black jacket with bright silvery buttons (this jacket would become a semi-regular through Season Three) and brown Chelsea boots, only changing to his dark-gray three-piece suit with the lapeled waistcoat and cloth-covered buttons about twenty-five minutes in. He later adds his tan overcoat with the heavily-stitched cuffs and the black bowler.

QUOTES

"Your cover usually has a large element of wishful thinking."

(When Stevens fluffs her line, Macnee adjusts his lines accordingly.) "Jack Steed, this is…anyway. Marvelous! Call me Burt. Thank you. How do you do?"

"He's raving mad! What do you want me to do—kill someone?" "That's exactly what we want you to do."

47 (2.21.21) THE WHITE DWARF

Written by Malcolm Hulke
Directed by Richmond Harding

GUEST CAST

George A. Cooper (Maxwell Barker), Philip Latham (Professor Cartright), Peter Copley (Henry Barker), Bill Nagy (Johnson), Vivienne Drummond (Elizabeth Fuller), Daniel Thorndike (Minister), Constance Chapman (Miss Tregarth), George Roubicek (Luke), Keith Pyott (Professor Richter), Paul Anil (Rahim), John Falconer (Butler)

PRE-TITLE/TEASER

At an advanced observatory, the elderly astronomer tracks a mysterious and very large object in the nighttime sky while recording his notes on a reel-to-reel tape recorder. Comparing his observations to a previous photograph, he determines that the object has moved, but an intruder slips up from behind and murders him.

SYNOPSIS

Astronomer Professor Richter has made a startling observation. He believes that the solar system will be obliterated by the return of the sun's stellar twin. Unfortunately, before his theory can be verified, he is murdered. Cathy goes undercover to find the truth, and she and Steed soon realize that certain people could benefit from the promotion of a fake solar calamity...

REVIEW

This episode's main selling point is having had the courage to attempt a pure science-fiction story in *The Avengers*. I commend Malcolm Hulke for taking this course, but he would be far more successful in future attempts in that sphere, mostly outside of this series. Frankly, even though it's well-written, the whole experiment doesn't wear well. *The Avengers* would ultimately have a somewhat mixed history with attempts at science-fiction, seldom would the genre come off as completely successful, either seeming slightly off-kilter ("The Man-Eater of Surrey Green") or coming across as completely absurdist ("Who's Who???"). It would be the latter that would secure the love of fandom in the end—remote-controlled killer robots, laser beams, mind-swapping and shrink rays would all feature in the series, and many might argue that they were far better executed than any of the more serious speculative science-based narratives. "The Big Thinker," "Immortal Clay," and "Build a Better Mousetrap" could all be considered to have elements of science-fiction, the latter of which pointed towards a fantasy aspect that would later dominate, but this episode sticks resoundingly to scientific plausibility in a way that none of the others did.

The idea of a twin sun was likely original (or at least very forward-thinking at the time) for television. The theory of Nemesis—a red or brown dwarf star playing hide-and-seek beyond the Oort cloud—was proposed in 1984 by two teams of astronomers working independently as a potential explanation for periodic mass extinction on Earth, albeit in cycles of millions of years. Within a few years of this theory's emergence, astronomers failed to find any evidence of the twin star's existence. This is all very interesting. Astronomers gathering around the old cathode ray tube watching *The Avengers* for their hypotheses? Or was this just a coincidence?

In any case, besides a bit of philosophizing about what the end of the world would mean, there really isn't much here to carry the story through a full hour of television. Either the world is going to end or it isn't, and keeping that mystery unknown until the climax isn't enough to hold the viewer's attention, because we all know that Steed and Cathy are going to return to fight another day. (The alternative is that the arrival of the white dwarf would become one hell of a series finale!) This leaves the script to get on with page after page of nothing but dialogue with no chance of payoff and a built-in anti-climax. I will award bonus points for solid scientific speculation however, and the final nighttime gunfight has some all-too brief zing. On another plus side, we find out that the astronomy book Steed refers to is the *Boys Books of Astronomy*, giving us an idea of the level of sophistication of his knowledge on scientific subjects.

Another stab at science-fiction would be attempted two seasons later in the form of an alien invasion, and that script would be enough to convince the production crew (and perhaps many viewers) that *The Avengers* and straight science-fiction just don't mix particularly well. Killer robots were instead on the rise. (Hurrah!)

CHAMPAGNE, CARS, CLOTHES, AND CANINES

Steed starts out in a dark silk dressing gown with white concentric patterns, and this is his only clothing debut of the episode. Later, the dark-gray three-piece suit with the lapeled waistcoat returns; then, the cream rollneck jumper and black jacket (from "School for Traitors"), worn with dark-gray tweed trousers. His tan overcoat with the black plaid lining also makes a showing.

Mrs. Gale reprises her pale mackintosh with black leather boots, her charcoal jacket and skirt (from "The Golden Eggs") with a lovely brocaded silk blouse with a bow at the neck, her dark leopard print vest and white blouse and black leather trews, and a pale stretch jersey jumper with the same pants, later worn with the black shearling coat with white lining and wide lapels. She finishes off in her only clothing debut: a red long-sleeved blouse with white vertical stripes and a white collar.

Sheba makes a return appearance hanging around on the settee while Steed lounges in his dressing gown and pajamas drinking coffee.

QUOTES

"Who would stand to gain out of a widespread scare about something that isn't going to happen?"
"Well, politically, the social order would come to a grinding halt the moment the news got out. No one would care anymore." "Exactly. There'd be chaos, and everybody'd have a feeling that nothing mattered. The country that knew it was a fake scare would just walk in."
"Don't you think you ought to talk this over with Mary before you do this big boy scout act and ruin your career?"
"It won't be the end of the world."

48 (2.22.22) MAN IN THE MIRROR

Written by Geoffrey Orme and Anthony Terpiloff
Directed by Kim Mills

GUEST CAST

Daphne Anderson (Betty), Ray Barrett (Strong), Julian Somers (Brown), Rhoda Lewis (Jean), Haydn Jones (Trevelyan), Michael Gover (One-Six), David Graham (Producer), Frieda Knorr (Iris) and The Kenny Powell Trio

PRE-TITLE/TEASER

Inside an amusement park haunted house, completely with recorded screams and dangling skeletons, a murdered man is left on the floor.

SYNOPSIS

Venus takes some pictures at a fun fair, and when one of the rolls of film is developed, it shows the face of a cypher clerk who has been dead for a week. Steed soon discovers that the clerk faked his own death so he could sell secrets to the other side...

REVIEW

Another week and another contrivance to bring a nightclub singer into the spy game. Dependent on coincidence by his writers, John Bryce, the new producer of ***The Avengers***, had to have seen it by now. Honor Blackman had fourteen episodes under her belt and was igniting the public's imagination as she terrorized male performers with her judo throws, Jon Rollason's pale imitation of Dr. Keel was long over, and Venus Smith, transformed into a waiflike, pixie haircut-endowed party girl and part time spy mistress, wasn't gelling at all. (Sigh) I apologize to Julie Stevens. Sometimes I feel I'm too hard on her. Again, there's nothing wrong with her performances; there's just no justifying the character, who consistently and increasingly feels shoehorned into a show that doesn't have a fit for her. She had the pipes, but Mrs. Gale had the chops, and music doesn't make enemy agents fall down.

"Man in the Mirror" is a reasonable effort despite the odds, and again proves to be one of the better Venus Smith stories—by comparison. Normally, the combination of Venus Smith, Kim Mills and a new pair of writers should have spelt disaster for the episode, but the writers were fairly inventive in the way they brought Venus and Steed together. Venus has an unusual record recording session in studio—maybe her career is looking up—but the visits to the funfair (where they apparently play the same record in a continuous rotation) are about the most fun in the story. Steed wins Venus a teddy bear, and she watches Parisian dancing girls through a mutoscope. The same funfair, with its ubiquitous beat music, naturally becomes the setting for the final fight between Steed and the villains, allowing for an unconventional and moody atmosphere.

The plot, on the other hand, is very conventional; it wasn't the first time, nor would it be the last, that an enemy agent pretended to be dead in order to hide from pursuit. Not exactly a scintillating idea, barely spruced up with originality by the inclusion of the arcade setting and a perky but useless nightclub singer, the latter of which allows for more threat as Steed is captured without a capable agent to rescue him. Incidentally, Venus gets even more youthful here, and her relationship with Steed is sometimes a tad creepy in retrospect. She comes across more like a teenager than the fiery working-class jazz singer, and now he's taking her around the fairground winning teddy bears for her.

I can't help but think, in the end, that this episode might have worked far better with a slight rewriting to accommodate Cathy Gale instead.

CHAMPAGNE, CARS, CLOTHES, CANINES, AND... CAMERAS!

Steed starts out straight away in his heavily-stitched tan overcoat, black bowler and umbrella for a meeting with One-Six. Later, he's wearing the dark-gray three-piece with the lapeled waistcoat. The tan overcoat with the black plaid lining returns along with his black fedora. It turns out that the navy-blue three-piece suit with the double-breasted waistcoat is underneath this one (also with a white shirt and navy tie with diamond tiepin).

Sheba reappears briefly—as Venus is taking care of her as a favor (a typical Steed move)—and for once we get both canines and cameras. Venus borrows Steed's Rolleiflex[8] twin lens reflex camera for photographing the fairground, taking several photos including some self-portraits in a distorting

8 This is probably the same camera model that the photographers used for the production photographs, or at least some kind of 6 x 6 TLR. You can tell because the camera is held at waist level while looking directly down through a viewfinder. The result is that the photos have a distinctive upwards angle, looking slightly up at the subject, as if shot by a much shorter person. And, indeed, most the production photos from this era have this look, as well as being a square ratio.

mirror and some of Sheba. Sadly, the camera gets stolen.

Venus dresses very fashionably for the 1960s in a pale oversized mac, a tricolor jumper, black pants, and the railroad engineer's cap (from "School for Traitors"). Not exactly classy so much as hipster. Later, she sings (rather flatly for the first half of the song until she warms up) wearing a long-sleeved t-shirt in a cream color with a V-shaped patch in front with tricolor stripes. It's worn with black pants. She also wears a cameo brooch that is later stolen along with Steed's camera. (She gets a replacement for it as a gift from Steed, a jeweled representation of the planet Venus.) Next, the dark-gray rollneck jumper, matching knee-length skirt, and plaid jacket (from "Box of Tricks") return for her next singing performance.

QUOTES

"Have we got a choice of records?"
"That wasn't very clever of you, young girl, was it? Now, what are we going to do about you?"

49 (2.23.23) CONSPIRACY OF SILENCE

Written by Roger Marshall
Directed by Peter Hammond

GUEST CAST

Robert Rietty (Carlo), Sandra Dorne (Rickie), Alec Mango (Sica), Roy Purcell (Gutman), Tommy Godfrey (Arturo), John Church (Terry), Artro Morris (James), Willie Shearer (Professor), Ian Wilson (Rant) and Elizabeth & Collins
Uncredited: Leggo as himself

PRE-TITLE/TEASER

At the office of a fun fair, two men argue over who will kill their victim. Threatened by the memory of the name "Roberta" by his colleague, one of the men agrees and is handed a gun and a photo of John Steed.

SYNOPSIS

In an attempt to quell some Mafia-oriented drug smuggling, the mob calls on a reluctant circus clown named Carlo to assassinate Steed. He makes the attempt but loses his nerve at the last minute and deliberately misses. Cathy goes undercover as a reporter and photographer at the circus in order to find Carlo, but supposedly no one has seen him since the assassination attempt. Eventually, they flush him out just as the mob leader arrives to force Carlo to complete the job...

REVIEW

After the establishing pre-title sequence, in an unusual type of location filming, we find Steed playing with his dog in the park. This footage, being shot on film, is among the best footage shot during this era, due to the artistic flexibility possible with single-camera. Sadly, telecine equipment at ITV in 1963 must have been extremely poor quality—never once does any location shooting in this season or the next look anywhere near decent, and this footage is blurry and fogged out with poor contrast. If the original films still existed, then they could be freshly scanned on high-end equipment in high-definition. Sadly, they were probably chucked out the minute the telecine was completed.

Steed doesn't show up much in this one, which is slightly rude considering he's the target of a

Mafia assassination. Instead, Honor Blackman ends up carrying the show for the most part, and though normally there would be no complaints with that, it's too bad she doesn't have much else to do besides walking around taking pictures of the circus members while undercover as a reporter doing a piece on the performers. This leaves the circus to provide all the interesting characters and dialogue, allowing for some reasonably good direction in the process.

Given that this circus is possibly the most cramped in history, owing to the limitations of television production in the day, we don't get much spectacle; even properly presented, a circus can only be so interesting, and without the massive three ring vista and wide-angle lenses necessary for shooting it, you've got very little to work with other than characters in clown outfits and the tiny Professor. Thus, while there are a few witty moments, and generally it's well scripted, the story takes a very long while to get going and is short on thrills.

Perhaps the most interesting part is the tension evident between Steed and Cathy in one superb scene. They have quite the blowup, in which Steed calls Cathy out for her idealism. Never one to allow a verbal jab to slide, Cathy snaps back with equal intensity at Steed's cynicism. It's hard to find a more serious disagreement between the two characters over ethics and idealism, and this would set the tone for their relationship over the following season. I certainly can't blame Cathy for being a bit irritated after Steed's naughty, caddish comment to her over the phone.

The narrative suffers from some rather sad Italian stereotyping and subtle prejudice. There seems to be an assumption that anyone of Italian descent in England is somehow tied in with either the Mafia or tomato sauce. I'm sure that in the years that followed, Britain learned that there was more to Italian culture than pasta and la cosa nostra.

CHAMPAGNE, CARS, CLOTHES, CANINES, AND... CAMERAS!

In a fun filmed location sequence, Steed plays with Sheba in the park, and she looks quite fashionable in her black doggie coat. He looks equally fashionable in his tan overcoat, a pale scarf, cream trousers, Chelsea boots, and black bowler and umbrella. When he meets with Mrs. Gale, the dark-gray three-piece suit with lapeled waistcoat returns. His final outfit is the navy-blue three-piece suit with the double-breasted waistcoat.

Mrs. Gale's scarlet Starke cloak and porkpie hat return but the cloak and hat are later replaced with the pale mackintosh and a brown leather newsboy cap. (She must have been influenced by Venus!) At the circus, she mostly wears her black stretch jersey jumper with cream pants. She later adds the black shearling coat with white lining. Then she transitions to her black leather trousers, to which she eventually adds the leather V-neck tunic.

To photograph the circus, Mrs. Gale uses a Leica III 35mm rangefinder camera (most likely the IIIf since the viewfinder is still quite small and the IIIf was manufactured during the 1950s). This definitely would have been the hallmark of a professional in that era.

QUOTES

"First, there's the matter of protecting my neck. Of course, that's incidental."

"Would you like to bring up your kids in this horse manure and sawdust?"

"Oh, you'll have to wait for that—I'll scrub your back for you!"

"Either he'll give us that information, or I'll have him deported. By Monday, he'll be canning tomatoes in Naples!" "You're fighting fire with fire."

"May I remind you, Mrs. Gale—we are dealing with the Mafia not the Boy Scouts!" "You offer him a satisfactory alternative to the Mafia and he'll help you." "So, you're an idealist!" "And you're a cynic!"

50 (2.24.24) A CHORUS OF FROGS

Written by Martin Woodhouse
Directed by Raymond Menmuir

GUEST CAST

Eric Pohlman (Mason), Yvonne Shima (Anna), Colette Wilde (Helena), John Carson (Ariston), Frank Gatliff (Pitt-Norton), Michael Gover (One-Six), Alan Haywood (Jackson), Stephanopoulus (Makki Marseilles), Norman Johns (Ship's Officer), Steve Cory (Stewart), Colin Fry (Man) and The Kenny Powell Trio

PRE-TITLE/TEASER

Deep under the water in a submersible, a Greek diver suddenly cries that he cannot breathe and quickly dies.

SYNOPSIS

After a diver mysteriously dies of the bends, Steed must investigate the death on an ocean liner in Greece. There, he meets up with Venus Smith. Eventually, he runs into the brother of the dead man who is also trying to solve the fatal mystery. They soon discover that the death was the result of a bathyscaphe experiment. Unfortunately, the perpetrators are quite desperate to guard their secret...

REVIEW

This is the sixth and final installment in the Venus Smith saga, and frankly, the whole singing series can be looked upon as very much a mixed bag. Ranging from good stories like "The Decapod" and the promising but flawed "The Removal Men" to the appallingly bad "Box of Tricks," the 'serenading spy' experiment went right across the range in quality. For the record, this one's dull—*very* dull—dealing with a subject as tedious as diving experiments, which is about as fast-paced as watching aquarium cleaners at work and perhaps just a step up from ***The Avengers*** stopping a vicious gang of fruit stand robbers. Come to think of it, the latter might prove a better opportunity for character development.

The less said about the contrived nature of Venus' appearances the better. She becomes involved in the events by working as a crooner on a cruise ship, although in this case it appears that Steed arranged for the job. And again, we're forced to ask why he would pull strings to get her a job so that they could work together on a spy mission. Surely, it would be more efficient to get Mrs. Gale to work with him, since she has all the necessary skills for espionage work. Nevertheless, the scene in which Steed and Venus meet in her cabin on the ship is charming enough, suggesting again that Steed has an attraction to her, thus explaining a motivation for continuing to employ her questionable services. They appear to share the cabin for the remainder of the episode.

We're working our way to the end of the season, and since John Bryce took over the program as producer, not much, including everything in this story, manages the bizarre quality of the season premiere, the superb "Mr. Teddy Bear," which could have been and should have been the model for the entire season. Had this story been given a few absurd deaths, an eccentric or a criminal mastermind, it might have succeeded. Instead, we're subjected to "A Chorus of Frogs" that croaks upon arrival. The season was winding down rather than racing to a climax.

One-Six reappears, with the total of 'Ones' at five—One-Six, One-Seven, One-Ten, One-Twelve, and One-Fifteen, sometimes hyphenated, sometimes not. He fails to make much of an impact.

CHAMPAGNE, CARS, CLOTHES, AND CANINES

Steed goes very casual, wearing a black-and-white striped jumper (that looks like either a prison uniform or a sailor's shirt) with a black wool cardigan. Later, a pale-gray button-down shirt with the sleeves rolled up, cream trousers, and a patterned neckscarf. His white ribbed shirt with the V-neck (from all the way back in "The Removal Men") returns. He ends up in a black long-sleeved polo shirt and finally his black jacket with silver buttons.

Venus wears a simple cream-colored sleeveless sundress in a satin fabric, buttoned up the front, with subtle pinstriping. This is later exchanged for an even simpler sundress in the same color, with no buttons. Her pale jumper with the tricolor triangular patch in the front returns as do her striped pajamas. She finishes off in an oversized, very fluffy tricolor jumper. She also sits in her cabin trying to learn Cantonese. (Good luck with that one, darlin'!)

Otherwise, it's mostly frogmen-wear, wetsuits, and submarines. Perhaps the low classiness level is due to Mrs. Gale's absence.

QUOTES

"You see, I just had to get to America." "We're going the wrong way!"
"What have I got in my pocket?" "Oh, I see. A small gold frog."
"I'll be out all night." "Too right, you will!"
"You can come out. It stopped raining."
"Oh, the singing, yes…and I've got to sing again in half an hour, so you hang onto your eardrums, eh."

51 (2.25.25) SIX HANDS ACROSS A TABLE

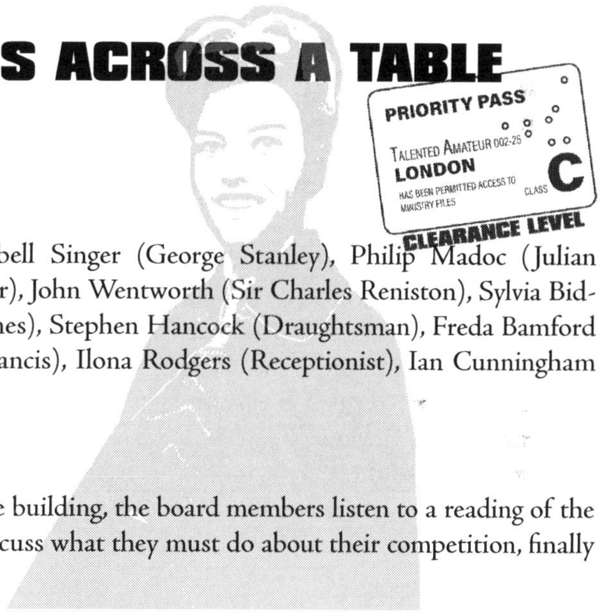

Written by Reed R. de Rouen
Directed by Richmond Harding

GUEST CAST

Guy Doleman (Oliver Waldner), Campbell Singer (George Stanley), Philip Madoc (Julian Seabrook), Edward de Souza (Brian Collier), John Wentworth (Sir Charles Reniston), Sylvia Bidmead (Rosalind), Frank Sieman (Bert Barnes), Stephen Hancock (Draughtsman), Freda Bamford (Lady Reniston), Gillian Barclay (Miss Francis), Ilona Rodgers (Receptionist), Ian Cunningham (Butler)

PRE-TITLE/TEASER

At a luxurious boardroom in a stately office building, the board members listen to a reading of the current fiscal year's accounts. They then discuss what they must do about their competition, finally deciding that he must be killed.

SYNOPSIS

Cathy goes undercover at the house of wealthy shipbuilder Oliver Waldner. As a genuine romance heats up between the two, she reveals a darker side to her would-be lover involving ruthless, murderous business practices, unresolved 'accidents,' and self-delusional jingoism…

REVIEW

It's a hard sell, being more soap opera—*Coronation Street?* —than *The Avengers*, but "Six Hands Across a Table" manages to be slightly engaging television anyway. Full of grim men being deadly serious about the shipwright business and coupled with the rivalry between two feuding shipbuilding families, one can expect little humor and a lot of dry dialogue from this script. What is most interesting however is the fact that Oliver and Cathy are clearly very interested in each other; they engage in a romance that becomes the closest Mrs. Gale comes to a serious relationship in the show. Genuinely upset about Oliver being taken to jail in the end, when asked about her feelings for him, Cathy responds with uncertainty, showing a conflict between her loyalty to Oliver and her job. In an interesting moment of dualism, she looks very stunning and elegant in her formal wear, but this is also the debut of her leather fighting gear, which appears for the first time in the third act at the moment of her greatest vulnerability. Often erroneously referred to as a "catsuit," it is actually separates, a matching tailored leather jacket and pants. Furthermore, Cathy's new high-tech apartment flat debuts.

Patrick Macnee is starting to look especially like the Steed of later years, having fully morphed away from the street clothes and raincoats of the early Ian Hendry era. The sharp suits, bowler hats and umbrellas are now solidified as his persona. Though there would be some fluctuation in the quality of his outfits from week-to-week, this is basically the Steed we know and love.

Other than that, there are only a few well-choreographed action scenes, which may be this week's only other typical *Avengers* aspect in this otherwise rather bland, straight-forward affair. Kudos to the show for trying to create a genuine romance (and the resulting conflict) for one of the regulars, but romance isn't what the show is about, and experimenting with such this close to season's end mostly manages only to drain even more momentum from the closing passages of the season's oeuvre.

Philip Madoc makes a second appearance in the series, and Guy Doleman's rich voice manages to cut through much of the dialogue doldrums.

CHAMPAGNE, CARS, CLOTHES, AND... CAMERAS!

Unusually, the episode starts right out with Mrs. Gale wearing her leather V-neck tunic and trousers, and these double as riding gear. Her hair is up throughout this episode, way up. Almost immediately, however, she changes to a fabulous sequined black evening gown, long black gloves and black cloak with a red lining, her hair still up. The gown is low-cut and sleeveless, and everywhere is sequined (or possibly sewn with Swarovski crystals) in rows almost like icicles on a Christmas tree. The cloak is fastened at the throat with a short chain. This ensemble is so striking that it's almost a comedown to see her return to her black stretch jersey jumper. Later, she wears a fitted silk ankle-length nightgown with an elaborate quilted collar—it's so fancy it's more like an evening gown!

The pale mackintosh returns, followed by a brand-new outfit combination—a tricolor striped silk blouse under her fitted deep-cobalt-blue jacket and skirt (from "The Golden Eggs"). Though the blouse's stripes are mostly vertical, the jacket is cropped at the bottom much like a riding jacket to expose the waist where the stripes are instead horizontal, suggesting that the blouse is worn with a cummerbund of some kind since the stripes aren't aligned this way when she takes the jacket off. The blouse also has a bow that is tied at the neck and two tassels that hang down at the waist. This outfit would become a semi-regular in the following season, and it's one of her best, especially when paired with the porkpie hat. The leather V-neck tunic, black jumper, and leather trousers return for the climax.

Steed wears the navy-blue three-piece with the double-breasted waistcoat again. In an interesting fashion twist, Steed switches to his dark-gray suit jacket with ticket pocket—from the three-piece suit usually worn with the lapeled waistcoat—instead in combination with the black waistcoat with silver buttons usually worn with the Prince of Wales blazer, now worn together with a white shirt with French cuffs, a pale-gray knit tie, and the gem cufflinks. Later, with the black bowler and umbrella. Even later, with a black trilby. Not the same as the black fedora, as it has a much smaller crown, so this is probably a new hat. Finally, he changes the waistcoat out for the lapeled one that normally goes with the jacket, now wearing the full suit.

Mrs. Gale's car reappears, although when it was mocked up for the video recording on set, it was given a roof, so this could not be the MGA, which was an open-roofed vehicle (not a convertible).

QUOTES

"He's in love with you." "I know." "And you?" "Why do you ask?" "You'll be better out of it."
"Your interest is touching, Mr. Seabrook. You really don't care what impression you make on people, do you?"
"Well, I think I'd better be going. Unless, of course, you'd like to give me a lift. There doesn't seem to be a horse in sight."

52 (2.26.26) KILLER WHALE

Written by John Lucarotti
Directed by Kim Mills

GUEST CAST

Patrick Magee (Pancho), John Bailey (Fernand), Kenneth Farrington (Joey), Morris Perry (Harry), John Tate (Willie), Julie Paulle (Angela), Christopher Coll (Laboratory Assistant), Robert Mill (Brown), Fredric Abbot (Sailor), Lyndall Goodman (Receptionist), Brian Mason (Tiger), Models from the Kenneth Sweet Collection (June Hodgson, Diane Keys and Elaine Little)

PRE-TITLE/TEASER

Ringside at a boxing match in a private gym, Steed intently observes two boxers, and when the fighter he bet on loses, he is advised to take up boxing management himself.

SYNOPSIS

Steed has been trying unsuccessfully for a month to uncover what he suspects is an ambergris smuggling operation at Pancho Driver's gym. Fortunately, his luck turns when Mrs. Gale's young judo student, Joey, turns out to be an amateur boxer looking to turn pro. Steed agrees to sponsor him as a means of breaking into the business. However, Joey quickly stumbles unwittingly on to some smuggled ambergris and is threatened as a result...

REVIEW

The Avengers is perhaps uncommon in that its seasons tend to run out of gas rather than reaching a crescendo. The exceptions to this are probably the Emma Peel season finales—"Honey from the Prince," which remains one of my personal favorites, and both "Who's Who???" and "Mission... Highly Improbable" have considerable merit. While I cannot speak for "Dragonsfield," the missing episode from the first season, the remainder are mediocre at best, with "Bizarre" and "Emily" being mostly terrible.

While "Killer Whale" doesn't do much to allay this season-ending sag, John Lucarotti has at least done a fine job of creating a bizarre juxtaposition of boxing, high fashion and ambergris smuggling. On the other hand, the direction's not up to par, and the action scenes are appallingly bad, with Kenneth Farrington delivering the most unconvincing punch from a supposed boxer that I've ever seen, a flailing stab that was unlikely to dent a barrier of Bacofoil but magically fells his opponent. In general, he is barely convincing as a boxer—the other men in the gym stand a head taller than he—and the first act of the episode is spent unfolding the drama of the hungry would-be professional pugilist getting his first shot in the ring. Farrington at best survives on his chirpy youthful enthusiasm rather than his affected fighting skills. The most interesting aspect of this character is that he's the pupil of

Mrs. Gale, who is his judo instructor. Steed being absent for long stretches of the episode, Cathy and Joey work together for the most part in the third act—something of a throwback to the Ian Hendry era.

Patrick Magee, who made a career out of playing crazed curmudgeons with a voice like a rusty buzzsaw, was perhaps tailormade to play the role of a crusty boxing coach. His return next season would only magnify his reputation for playing abrasive characters.

Thankfully, there are some bizarre moments which sharpen up this conventional story. Dead sailors keep turning up in the oddest of places. Steed puts one corpse into Fernand's closet to scare him into talking! He easily subdues both Fernand and Pancho by himself, slyly smiling all the while. He then gives Mrs. Gale some perfume as a "mark of our appreciation."

This episode also manages one of the most (unintentionally) condescending credits I've seen: "Models from the Kenneth Sweet Collection." Kenneth Sweet has a collection of models? And you thought *The Avengers* wasn't a sexist show!

CHAMPAGNE, CARS, CLOTHES, AND CANINES

Steed's Prince of Wales blazer returns with the black waistcoat with silver buttons, worn with a white shirt, a pale-gray knit tie, and the new black trilby (from "Six Hands Across a Table"). His tan overcoat returns, the one without the heavy-stitching, nor the black plaid lining, but with a left breast slit pocket and shiny buttons (last seen in "The Sell-Out"), with his black bowler and brolly. At the private fashion show, he wears the dark-gray suit jacket and trousers from the three-piece suit with the lapeled waistcoat and ticket pocket, but instead pairs it with the sparkly waistcoat (from "Intercrime"). The complete suit finally reappears in the third act.

Mrs. Gale wears the black shearling coat with white lining over a black jumper (first seen in "Traitor in Zebra"), then the pale mackintosh and the brown leather newsboy cap, and later a brand-new outfit: a black-and-white vertically-striped skirt with another tricolor striped long-sleeved blouse, black pumps, and the black shearling coat. In the second act, her Starke tartan cloak reappears with the tartan outwards for the first time in a long while, with the black porkpie hat. Later, she relaxes at home reading while wearing a white stretch jersey jumper and matching slacks, with a lovely sparkling charm bracelet on her left wrist. The leather V-neck tunic and trousers return for the climax, and the leopard-print vest is seen in the final moments when Steed gifts her some new perfume.

Otherwise, lots of boxing shorts (on the boxers). No complaints from me.

QUOTES

"I'm sorry. We are closed." "But open to suggestion."

"It's a small present. A mark of our appreciation." "Our appreciation?" "Hmm, myself and the Treasury. Of course, the Treasury don't know about you. I'm afraid it's the last of the line."

SEASON THREE

26 episodes (405-line monochrome videotape, ~52 min. ea.)

Regular Cast
Patrick Macnee—John Steed
Honor Blackman—Catherine Gale

Produced by John Bryce
Story Editor: Richard Bates
Music: Johnny Dankworth

53. **Brief for Murder**—**w.** Brian Clemens; **dir.** Peter Hammond; **UK tx.** 28 Sep 1963; **rec.** 1 May 1963
54. **The Undertakers**—**w.** Malcolm Hulke; **dir.** Bill Bain; **UK tx.** 5 Oct 1963; **rec.** 2 Aug 1963
55. **Man with Two Shadows**—**w.** James Mitchell; **dir.** Don Leaver; **UK tx.** 12 Oct 1963; **rec.** 21 Jun 1963
56. **The Nutshell**—**w.** Philip Chambers; **dir.** Raymond Menmuir; **UK tx.** 19 Oct 1963; **rec.** 10 May 1963
57. **Death of a Batman**—**w.** Roger Marshall; **dir.** Kim Mills; **UK tx.** 26 Oct 1963; **rec.** 14 Aug 1963
58. **November Five**—**w.** Eric Paice; **dir.** Bill Bain; **UK tx.** 2 Nov 1963; **rec.** 27 Sep 1963
59. **The Gilded Cage**—**w.** Roger Marshall; **dir.** Bill Bain; **UK tx.** 9 Nov 1963; **rec.** 25 Oct 1963
60. **Second Sight**—**w.** Martin Woodhouse; **dir.** Peter Hammond; **UK tx.** 16 Nov 1963; **rec.** 11 Oct 1963
61. **The Medicine Men**—**w.** Malcolm Hulke; **dir.** Kim Mills; **UK tx.** 23 Nov 1963; **rec.** 8 Nov 1963
62. **The Grandeur That Was Rome**—**w.** Rex Edwards; **dir.** Kim Mills; **UK tx.** 30 Nov 1963; **rec.** 30 Nov 1963
63. **The Golden Fleece**—**w.** Roger Marshall & Phyllis Norman; **dir.** Peter Hammond; **UK tx.** 7 Dec 1963; **rec.** 24 May 1963
64. **Don't Look Behind You**—**w.** Brian Clemens; **dir.** Peter Hammond; **UK tx.** 14 Dec 1963; **rec.** 5 Jul 1963
65. **Death a la Carte**—**w.** John Lucarotti; **dir.** Kim Mills; **UK tx.** 21 Dec 1963; **rec.** 14 Jun 1963
66. **Dressed to Kill**—**w.** Brian Clemens; **dir.** Bill Bain; **UK tx.** 28 Dec 1963; **rec.** 6 Dec 1963
67. **The White Elephant**—**w.** John Lucarotti; **dir.** Laurence Bourne; **UK tx.** 4 Jan 1964; **rec.** 22 Nov 1963
68. **The Little Wonders**—**w.** Eric Paice; **dir.** Laurence Bourne; **UK tx.** 11 Jan 1964; **rec.** 3 Jan 1964
69. **The Wringer**—**w.** Martin Woodhouse; **dir.** Don Leaver; **UK tx.** 18 Jan 1964; **rec.** 20 Dec 1963
70. **Mandrake**—**w.** Roger Marshall; **dir.** Bill Bain; **UK tx.** 25 Jan 1964; **rec.** 16 Jan 1964

71. **The Secrets Broker**—**w.** Ludovic Peters; **dir.** Jonathan Alwyn; **UK tx.** 1 Feb 1964; **rec.** 19 Oct 1963
72. **Trojan Horse**—**w.** Malcolm Hulke; **dir.** Laurence Bourne; **UK tx.** 8 Feb 1964; **rec.** 30 Jan 1964
73. **Build a Better Mousetrap**—**w.** Brian Clemens; **dir.** Peter Hammond; **UK tx.** 15 Feb 1964; **rec.** 28 Aug 1963
74. **The Outside-In Man**—**w.** Philip Chambers; **dir.** Jonathan Alwyn; **UK tx.** 22 Feb 1964; **rec.** 12 Feb 1964
75. **The Charmers**—**w.** Brian Clemens; **dir.** Bill Bain; **UK tx.** 29 Feb 1964; **rec.** 27 Feb 1964
76. **Concerto**—**w.** Terrance Dicks & Malcolm Hulke; **dir.** Kim Mills; **UK tx.** 7 Mar 1964; **rec.** 26 Apr 1963
77. **Esprit de Corps**—**w.** Eric Paice; **dir.** Don Leaver; **UK tx.** 14 Mar 1964; **rec.** 11 Mar 1964
78. **Lobster Quadrille**—**w.** Richard Lucas; **dir.** Kim Mills; **UK tx.** 21 Mar 1964; **rec.** 20 Mar 1964

SEASON NOTES

This season was the one in which *The Avengers* truly became a hot property for Associated British Corporation. Cathy Gale was a leather-clad sensation, and the series took off in ratings and overseas sales. The prior season had possessed an uncertainty that had not been fully resolved until nearly the end. John Bryce, who had previously been the show's script editor from the very first episode, became the producer in the final third of Season Two, and the issue of whether to retain Cathy Gale or Venus Smith had been prolonged until very late. The season had not necessarily ended strong either. All of this uncertainty was wiped away by a fresh series in the autumn of 1963 with a relationship between the regular cast that was challenging and unusual, and most importantly fun.

Season Three reached a new height in popularity that not only thrilled television viewers but inspired fashion…and even music. In 1964, Patrick Macnee and Honor Blackman would record "Kinky Boots," a novelty track that poked fun at the show's own image, that of being sensationalistic and fetishistic.

This was the first season in which the *Avengers* were superspies, heroes that were untouchable and hyperreal. Realism was out; fantasy was in. And Cathy Gale had to be above it all. As Honor Blackman said in the Daily Mirror in 1964, Cathy Gale "cannot be seen brushing her teeth. She must not be touched by a man. She cannot be seen to have a lover." This is an image that would be maintained (and indeed amplified) by her successors as well. Starting now, the *Avengers* had lives that appeared to be centered around leisure until interrupted by their work, a paradigm that would reach epic proportions in the following year.

John Bryce, who had seemingly fumbled the later third of Season Two, would bring the show together along slightly more conventional lines that nevertheless set the stage for the future. The whole of the season is rooted in quality writing, more grounded but laced with bizarreness throughout. Adding Brian Clemens back to the writer's cadre became Bryce's best decision. It is Clemens' contributions that bring the most spark to the series, and it should be no surprise that four out of five of these episodes made the top ten list. Rounding out these episodes are many contributions from a reliable trio of writers consisting of Eric Paice, Martin Woodhouse, and Roger Marshall, as well as several scripts from Malcolm Hulke and Terrance Dicks, either writing together or apart.

The bulk of the direction would come from Bill Bain, Peter Hammond, Kim Mills, and Don Leaver. True to the videotape era of the show, as a writer's medium, the program would be mainly about quality scripts, but these directors would still manage to periodically pull off challenging visuals.

As popular as the show had become, it could still not be sold to the United States due to the inability to convert 405-line video to 525-line, but the executives at Associated British Corporation had plans to remedy that. Following in the footsteps of ITC Entertainment and their successes with such programs as ***Danger Man*** and ***The Saint***, they made the decision to shoot the next series on 35mm film. The problem was that their star of the moment was not coming along for the ride. Having her own 35mm film to shoot, Honor Blackman had decided to leave at the end of her contract for the latest and most exciting James Bond film to date, ***Goldfinger***.

ICONIC TITLES

This season produced two entirely new title sequences using simple animation. In the first version, the title of the program, 'The Avengers,' appears in block letters with a silhouetted agent balanced atop the loop of the letter 'G.' With each advancing frame, the title comes closer, and the silhouetted figure changes position as if the man is running towards the camera. Finally, the figure fills the frame with black and the names of our main cast are revealed.

In production order starting with "Death á la Carte," there is a variation in which the title text constructs itself from a jagged white line that begins out of the top left corner of the screen. The silhouetted figure seems to be forging ahead in the path of this white line which steadily expands, and when the program title is fully formed he repeatedly teleports about among the letters in various poses until settling above the 'G' once more. Finally, as the camera tracks in, the silhouetted figure endures a spontaneous attack of vertigo that causes him to spin until he fills the frame with black as before. The same Johnny Dankworth theme music as the previous two seasons is used, although it is a minor variation with a slightly brassier sound and additional percussion.

CHAMPAGNE, CARS, CLOTHES, AND CANINES

The fashion situation is largely the same as the previous season, although Frederick Starke is generally credited as the designer for Honor Blackman's clothing in the end credits, and both the regulars get even more clothing changes than before. However, both cars and canines diminish quite a bit, with only two car appearances. And Steed's latest Great Dane never gets a name. There is a camera or two to be spotted.

Best Dressed: "November 5"
Worst Dressed: "Man with Two Shadows"

AVENGERS CARS

JOHN STEED

1930 Lagonda 3 Litre (GK 3295) in "Don't Look Behind You."

CATHY GALE

Triumph Twin motorcycle (987 CAA) in "Build a Better Mousetrap."

THE MOST FANTASTIC EPISODES OF THE SEASON

1. "The Gilded Cage"
2. "Brief for Murder"
3. "Don't Look Behind You"
4. "The Charmers"
5. "Dressed to Kill"
6. "Esprit de Corps"
7. "The Wringer"
8. "Concerto"
9. "The Golden Fleece"
10. "The Undertakers"

53 (3.2.1) BRIEF FOR MURDER

Steed is tried at the Old Bailey for the murder of Catherine Gale
Written by Brian Clemens
Directed by Peter Hammond

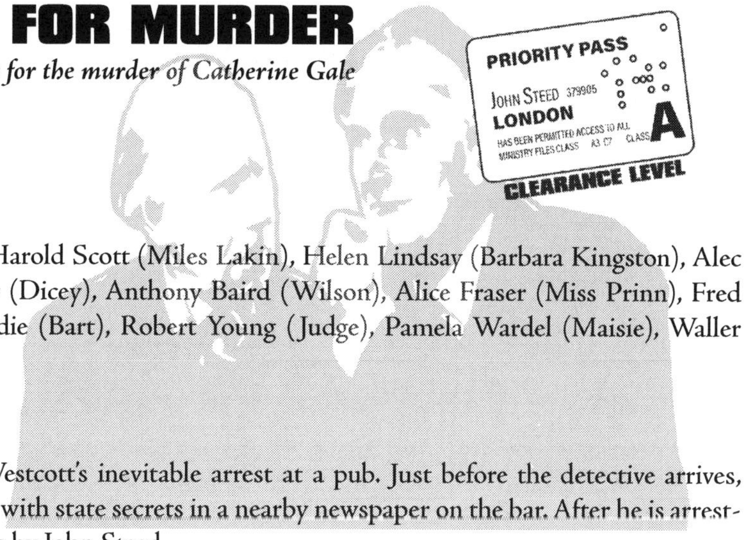

GUEST CAST

John Laurie (Jasper Lakin), Harold Scott (Miles Lakin), Helen Lindsay (Barbara Kingston), Alec Ross (Westcott), June Thody (Dicey), Anthony Baird (Wilson), Alice Fraser (Miss Prinn), Fred Ferris (Marsh), Michael Goldie (Bart), Robert Young (Judge), Pamela Wardel (Maisie), Waller Swash (Foreman of the Jury)

PRE-TITLE/TEASER

Westcott and Darcy await Westcott's inevitable arrest at a pub. Just before the detective arrives, Westcott hides a slip of paper with state secrets in a nearby newspaper on the bar. After he is arrested, the newspaper is picked up by John Steed.

SYNOPSIS

Steed and Mrs. Gale go undercover to crack the case of a couple of eccentric attorneys, Miles and Jasper Lakin, who guarantee acquittal for criminals by arranging the crime and manipulating the evidence. When Steed is implicated in the murder of Cathy Gale, the Lakin brothers arrange for his acquittal, but is Mrs. Gale really dead…?

REVIEW

This plot, which involves Steed and Mrs. Gale ostensibly working against each other, is an inventive and engaging one. Since the episode starts out without a hint to the audience as to what is going on, it's great fun in the first half-hour trying to figure it out. We're left to believe that Steed and Mrs. Gale must have had a sudden and severe falling-out in between seasons. Of course, there is no other conclusion than they're undercover, though this is never explicitly stated. A lesser script would have had some kind of exposition that gives the viewer insight into the ploy, or perhaps a pre-title sequence that involves a planning session, but not in this show. Swiftly, the narrative moves into exciting territory when the murder of Cathy Gale is apparently arranged and executed. Steed and Mrs. Gale never break character, even to the audience, and this allows Steed to work his way into the confidence of the sleazy Lakin brothers, who otherwise sit in comfy chairs 'round a fire with cigars and snifters of brandy, laughing about their legal conquests and contemplating their skillful subversion of the law. These are some of the most amusing scenes involving early *Avengers* eccentrics, but the frightening and gritty realism of this story is that one has little doubt that the legal system could be manipulated like this.

While I'm not a fan of courtroom drama, this remains one of the exceptions. The court scenes are engaging throughout. They even do a reverse of the O.J. Simpson trick—the bowler hat dropped at the scene of the crime swallows Steed's head. After Steed is acquitted, the twists really begin as Steed and Mrs. Gale hook the greedy little fish with an even more complicated criminal plot that succeeds in downing the crooks despite Mrs. Gale's cover being blown. Without a doubt one of the best Honor Blackman stories, the script involved a return to the series by writer Brian Clemens, who would become the guiding light for the series for the remainder of its run, and this episode is something of a harbinger for future efforts.

CHAMPAGNE, CARS, CLOTHES, AND CANINES

Mrs. Gale begins the episode wearing her cropped riding jacket and skirt with the tricolor striped blouse (from "Six Hands Across a Table") and the black porkpie hat, making this the first time these clothes are paired this way in transmission order. This is remarkably stylish and suitable ensemble for her and makes her look about ten feet tall and yet exceedingly graceful. However, the jacket seems to have an added black trim around the lapels, perhaps a modification made by Ambren Garland and Audrey Liddle in between seasons. At the yoga studio, she wears the pale mackintosh over a black stretch jersey jumper and black sheer tights. In the scene when she takes a dip in the lake[1], she is wearing more casual boating clothes, a buff-colored stretch jersey pullover with a dark cardigan and jeans. Once undercover, she disguises herself with a new black leather overcoat with a dark wig and sunglasses.

Steed wears a three-piece, single-breasted, chalk-striped[2] wool suit—and though it reads as black onscreen, based on the few color photos from this era it's actually a dark navy-blue. It gives him something of a roguish quality (due to its association with 1930s gangsters), which is appropriate for an episode where he's supposed to be the villain. This is the first appearance of the chalk-stripe this season (in transmission order), but it would come to define Steed's look for this season. During the faux assassination scene, there's also an important holdover from the previous two seasons: his gray Prince of Wales blazer paired with his dark waistcoat with silver buttons, cream tweed trousers, and a black bowler. He also wears brown Chelsea boots and black gloves. Unusually, he makes his escape on a bicycle, one of the few times Steed is seen riding one. Surprisingly, especially for a season debut, this is his only clothing change.

QUOTES

"Well built, known as 'Johnno,' speaks and dresses well. Holds a position of trust. I think it fits you very well."

"I take it you believe in absolute purity, Mr. Steed?" "Couple bars a day, good soap."

"Now, Mr. Steed, we need to know the name of the deceased-to-be." "Gale. Mrs. Catherine Gale."

"The law does not function in superstition, Mr. Steed. There's no luck involved, only facts."

54 (3.9.2) THE UNDERTAKERS

Steed meets an undertaker — Cathy joins the millionaires

Written by Malcolm Hulke

Directed by Bill Bain

GUEST CAST

Lee Patterson (Lomax), Jan Holden (Paula), Lally Bowers (Mrs. Renter), Patrick Holt (Madden), Mandy Miller (Daphne), Howard Goorney (Green), Marcella Markham (Mrs. Lomax), Ronald Russell (Wilkinson), Helena McCarthy (Mrs. Baker), Denis Forsyth (Reeve)

PRE-TITLE/TEASER

Undertakers exit a lift bearing a casket into a luxurious office. One undertaker shoots the businessman inside and the others remove their hats in a sign of respect and reveal that the casket is empty and ready to receive the corpse.

---

1 Though she was replaced by a stuntperson for the shot, she still had to get her clothes (and herself) wet for a shot in which she escaped the water. It was cut for transmission however.

2 Some may call this suit a "pinstripe suit," but it is not; pinstripes form much tighter, more precise lines, whereas chalk-stripe is a softer, wider line.

SYNOPSIS

After Steed fails to contact a friend with whom he plans to market an invention, he and Mrs. Gale go undercover to expose a plot by the families of millionaires to evade death taxes. The family arranges to have the money transferred to the surviving spouse, then quietly hushes up the death and replaces the deceased with a double, who will represent that person for the legally required waiting period of five years. But are these millionaires dying of natural causes, and what happens to the double when the five years are up...?

REVIEW

This episode starts right out with a bit of *Avengers* bizarreness—a man being shot and placed directly into a coffin, complete with pallbearers. In a scene much later, Madden steps out of a coffin to grab some tea and sugar cubes and then steps back in as if everything were normal. Of course, it's all part of the plot by the villains, who this time pre-arrange inheritances—and the required deaths. It is proof positive that these quirky twists existed long before the Emma Peel era though it was still comparatively understated at this time. As I often do, this is an opportunity to ponder what this episode might have been like if filmed in the Fennell-Clemens era. Likely, they would have spent a lot more time with pseudo-sepulchral scenes in the high-spoof style of *The Avengers*.

From this bizarre pre-title, the story heads right into a classic example of Steed trying to convince Mrs. Gale to help him on yet another case—this time with pathetically-obvious reverse psychology, prompting a cool and unconcerned reaction by Mrs. Gale and several witty lines. Patrick Macnee is really at the top of his game in this episode, playing the usual overly pushy yet intensely polite character that enables him to get his foot in the door—with whatever situation that requires it. This time, he's a salesman, dealing in mechanical graders, plastic flowers, and music, all for funeral homes. It's absurd that anyone would sell such a diverse lot of products, but he hawks it on pure chirpy enthusiasm.

This is immediately followed by a meeting with the lovably kooky Mrs. Renter, who seems cheerily unbothered by everything (barring estate taxes). And that is quickly followed by a casual conversation with Daphne, who lives next door and has crossed their shared balcony to help herself to a drink from Mrs. Renter's cupboard. The whole episode is like that—a parade of interesting characters that emerge and then disappear as naturally as conceivable. Such is the depth of the acting and the skill with which their performances are interwoven by director Bill Bain. This is both the episode's strength and weakness. While it keeps the narrative flowing almost entirely on dialogue alone, it does require considerable attention to follow; this might overwhelm modern, more pampered, audiences. Nevertheless, it is worth noting that this kind of story would be the type to be spiced up with more surrealism, eccentrics, and action scenes in the future when production standards were raised and they could at last leave the cramped studio floor.

Having said that, this episode does reach its climax with a lengthy and tense gun fight in palatial gardens on an estate[3]. Imagine the possibility of episodes like this being shot on 35mm film all the way through. That is precisely what ABC was imagining at the time—a dream that was only a year away from being realized.

CHAMPAGNE, CARS, CLOTHES, AND CANINES

Mrs. Gale wears a deep-blue full-length satin dress (inspired by Napoleonic military uniforms) with a wide skirt and silver stud buttons in a black facing with a quasi-militaristic feel. It makes for quite the dramatic look, especially when she's reassembling her L1A1 rifle! This is followed by her newest leather fighting outfit, a leather vest with silver buttons and a chevroned button, worn over a black

---

3 This is a very long sequence— a four-minute shootout that was filmed at York House and in the adjacent gardens, only two miles from Teddington Studios.

rollneck jumper and matching pants. Then, the pale mackintosh and the brown leather newsboy cap return (last seen in "Killer Whale"), followed by a dark-blue stretch jersey dress (zipped up the back), followed by the leather V-neck tunic and trousers with a black rollneck jumper underneath. Finally, the debut of a frill-fronted pale-blue silk blouse with a gold satin vest and charcoal hip-hugging pants with the black leather boots, sort of an 18th century riding outfit.

At the start, Steed wears his navy-blue chalk-striped three-piece suit with a navy bowtie with white spots, later with the black bowler and umbrella and a white carnation. This is followed by the dark-gray three-piece suit with the lapeled waistcoat, worn with a white shirt with French cuffs and a pale silk tie with diamond tiepin. Once again, the Prince of Wales blazer appears, though this time without the black waistcoat, just a white shirt, pale tweed trousers, dark tie, and Chelsea boots.

Briefly, Steed stops to admire a black 1928 Rolls-Royce Phantom I Hearse (XV 8015) parked outside the Adelphi Park estate. He later takes cover behind it when chasing the villains.

They drink champagne with Mrs. Renter at the end.

QUOTES

"Send you a postcard?" "Put a stamp on it this time."
"There's a man been here, looking for Renter. Thought you'd want to know. *Do* you want to know?"
"So, she's threatening us again." "She's going to give me until tomorrow morning to think about it."
"Darling, what are we going to do?" "Call the undertakers."
"But I already have a million." "I'm sure another one wouldn't be in the way." "Well, I'm not so sure, what with death duties, being rich hardly seems worthwhile."
"There's always national assistance."

55 (3.6.3) MAN WITH TWO SHADOWS

Steed hides from himself — Cathy is ordered to kill him
Written by James Mitchell
Directed by Don Leaver

GUEST CAST

Daniel Moynihan (Gordon), Paul Whitsun-Jones (Charles), Philip Anthony (Cummings), Gwendolyn Watts (Julie), Geoffrey Palmer (Dr. Terence), Anne Godfrey (Miss Quist), George Little (Sigi), Douglas Robinson (Rudi), Terence Lodge (Borowski), Robert Lankesheer (Holiday Camp Official)

PRE-TITLE/TEASER

In a room at Baxter's holiday camp, a young man sits on his bed smoking a cigarette while reading a book. He relaxes and strips down to his shorts. Going to the armoire, he opens it to find his exact double hiding inside with a gun. The double shoots him dead and then signals with a torch to someone outside. He dresses in the dead man's clothes and walks out, leaving the gun behind with the corpse.

SYNOPSIS

Interrogating a man called Borowski who has been given split personalities by a foreign power, Steed and his superior, Charles, discover that someone is creating perfect doubles of various agents, and Steed may be one of them. Investigating the first man to be replaced in a holiday camp, complications develop when Cathy fears that Steed may have already been replaced. She is ordered to eliminate

Steed's doppelgänger, but is he really the double...?

REVIEW

This is the first of several doppelgänger stories for *The Avengers*. Although later episodes would involve twists of various kinds, here, the doubles are rather straight-forward and used for straight-forward purposes as one might expect for an episode during this era. The result, however, is one of the better episodes of the season.

Steed takes the place of his own double, and this confuses Mrs. Gale while going undercover in the villains' organization. After Steed cannot convince Mrs. Gale of his authenticity, Cathy gets the authorization to kill Steed if she can't positively identify him. The switch apparently occurs in a bizarre resort location with chimes and intercoms calling people 'to the chalet,' after which they are replaced. This setting allows for an incongruent final fight scene to the music of *The Blue Danube*—a quasi-surreal juxtaposition of elements that is so typical of the series, even this early. Mrs. Gale wins of course.

The idea that perfect doubles can be made using a medical file is never really explained. This is a wise decision; it's too far-fetched for a technical explanation that wouldn't extend into the territory of science-fiction. *The New Avengers* story "Faces" would later largely remake this episode, and the half-baked attempts to explain the methods used did them no favors.

Terence Lodge is particularly memorable as the insane Borowski, flying through several characters, accents, and languages in a span of mere moments. The show rarely dealt with insanity so directly, at least the non-comic kind. (Other examples would be "The House That Jack Built," "How to Succeed....At Murder" and "The Joker.") The idea that they made a Jewish man think he is a Nazi is particularly sadistic.

The casual fan of *The Avengers* will very likely remember Mother (Patrick Newell), the Ministry boss for Steed and his partners. The more serious fan may also remember One-Ten (Douglas Muir), but few will remember Charles (Paul Whitsun-Jones). This is unsurprising considering he was only in two episodes. His next appearance would lead to an ignominious end.

CHAMPAGNE, CARS, CLOTHES, AND CANINES

Steed starts out straight away with his navy-blue chalk-striped suit, this time with a navy necktie, and his gray three-piece, single-breasted suit with the lapeled waistcoat returns. Here, he wears it with a gray tie and his black bowler and brolly. He takes a step down with his ill-fitting light-gray two-piece suit made of a cheap fabric and paired with the pale straw hat (both from "Death Dispatch"). He tends to wear this outfit whenever he's trying to appear less sophisticated or while undercover. It's followed by a simple black shirt with a V-neck, and then another similar ribbed shirt in white with thin vertical stripes, before finally returning to the classic dark-gray suit.

Mrs. Gale starts out in a black-and-white vertical-striped blouse with long sleeves and a white sailor collar, her hair up and slightly bouffant. Possibly the least successful outfit this season; it comes across as a bit schoolmarmish. But she makes up for it with sizzling navy underwear, worn like a bikini with a black belt, and then the frill-fronted pale-blue silk blouse with the gold satin vest (last seen in "The Undertakers") returns, though this time with a black pencil skirt and black pumps. She also debuts a new simple dark cobalt-blue sleeveless collarless knee-length dress with prominent white stitching along the shoulders and along its square neckline. Next is her debut of a gold lamé dress—boat neck, long-sleeved and knee-length, with pale slacks. She dons her leather vest with studded buttons and no blouse underneath, followed by a short-sleeved knit wool ribbed pullover with metallic threads and her leather trews in which she fights off a crook to a shopping music version of *The Blue Danube* by Strauss.

QUOTES

"Can't take any chances, Mrs. Gale—If it isn't Steed, you must kill him."
"What's for breakfast?" "Cook it and see."

56 (3.3.4) THE NUTSHELL

Steed hunts a traitor, and finds himself fighting Cathy
Written by Philip Chambers
Directed by Raymond Menmuir

GUEST CAST

Charles Tingwell (Venner), John Cater (Disco), Patricia Haines (Laura), Christine Shaw (Susan), Edina Ronay (Elin), Ian Clark (Anderson), Ray Browne (Alex), Jan Conrad (Jason), Edwin Brown (Military Policeman)

PRE-TITLE/TEASER

An intruder in scuba gear slips into a top-secret facility. Crossing several corridors and dodging electric eyes and cameras, she finds the control center where she takes several photos, but when a camera finally spots her, the alarms sound and she flees.

SYNOPSIS

Someone has stolen 'Big Ben'—a secret microfilm containing information on all the British and American agents working on the other side. Thus, it is revealed that there is a traitor in the midst at the maximum-security building called The Nutshell. Could Steed be the one...?

REVIEW

This is another episode that attempts to be on the cutting edge of automation and computing in the early sixties and will, unfortunately, appear to be very dated to modern viewers. Too many scenes take place in a computer room with wall-to-wall tape drives and settee-sized printers going clickety-clack. However, I'd advise everyone to overlook this because they'd otherwise be missing out on a fine story. And this is true of every episode this season—as production quality is a challenge even in the best of stories when shooting on 1960s videotape.

The wonderful witty repartee between Steed and Mrs Gale forms the better part of this episode, as the latter remains confused on Steed's behavior and even questions his loyalty at one point. She is completely left out of his plan for the first half. As an outsider to Steed's Ministry (this still being *The Avengers* era of the 'talented amateur'), she quite rightly asks him at one point how she can be certain he isn't working for a foreign government. The story is very strong on Honor Blackman, who expresses almost motherly concern throughout and great tension and stress as she remains worried about Steed's apparent betrayal. Nevertheless, her concern is unwarranted and only plays into his plan in the end. Thus, paranoia is the name of the game and it carries the bulk of the story. Nevertheless, all things yield to the great Steed and his schemes.

The direction by Menmuir flows as seamlessly as possible for the technological limitations of the era, and he uses the many monitors in the control room to good effect. At one point, Menmuir places Steed's face in close-up on a screen as he paces in his cell, while Mrs. Gale discusses his inevitable interrogation. It's about as classy a production as one could do on videotape in that day. There are, however, a few unexpected klutzy errors by actors, in which objects are knocked over, but no retakes were possible, and the accidents stand in the final tape.

CHAMPAGNE, CARS, CLOTHES, AND... CAMERAS!

Steed starts out in his dark-gray three-piece suit with the lapeled waistcoat. Next, he switches to the Prince of Wales blazer and the black waistcoat with a white shirt and a pale-gray knit tie, before going into the Nutshell where he mostly just has the trousers and the white shirt. He does manage to hold onto the blazer for the coming episodes, however. The whole fuss turns out to be over a photo of Steed nude on the beach.

Mrs. Gale wears her cobalt-blue cropped riding jacket and skirt (first seen in "The Golden Eggs") with a black stretch jersey jumper underneath and black pumps; she soon adds her black porkpie hat; later, she ditches both the hat and the jacket. Finally, her leather fighting V-neck tunic and trousers return.

Not much of a camera episode and not much chance of identifying the spy camera used by the scuba diver in the pre-title—a Minox of some kind.

QUOTES

"The thought processes of the hunter and hunted can be so related, almost interchangeable. Only their motives distinguish them."
"It is a document which lists all known double agents on both sides in the Cold War. In hostile hands, it can deal a death blow to every allied agent working on the wrong side of the Iron Curtain."
"You might be doing a great service to the nation." "I might be helping to sell the nation down the river for all I know."
"Now, that's a very interesting question, and for the moment, it'll have to remain academic!"
"Nothing like overdoing it to make one feel younger." "Well, you don't look any younger."

57 (3.10.5) DEATH OF A BATMAN

Steed is named in a will — Cathy goes into Big Business
Written by Roger Marshall
Directed by Kim Mills

GUEST CAST

André Morell (Lord Teale), Philip Madoc (Van Doren), Katy Greenwood (Lady Cynthia), David Burke (John Wrightson), Geoffrey Alexander (Gibbs), Kitty Attwood (Edith Wrightson), Ray Browne (Cooper)

PRE-TITLE/TEASER

In a bedroom, an elderly man lies dead as a woman grieves over him. A younger man stops an alarm clock at the time of death: ten till nine. He then removes the dead man's military service medals and places them in a drawer. The camera then pans across a photo of the dead man in his uniform before settling on a photo of John Steed dressed as an army officer.

SYNOPSIS

At the reading of Wrightson's will (Steed's former batman), Steed discovers that his deceased friend possessed £180,000, despite his £20 a week salary. Steed and Mrs. Gale begin investigating the man's estate to make sure the money was obtained legally. Of course, it wasn't, but they are surprised to find out who was responsible...

REVIEW

As soon as I saw André Morell walk onto the screen, I knew I was in for a treat. It's no surprise that he would be chosen for this role as his regal demeanor is perfectly suited to playing a character with the stature of Lord Teale. Despite Morell's considerable gravitas, it is Katy Greenwood as the eccentric Lady Cynthia who steals the show. Her kinky and flirtatious dialogue with Steed is the highlight of the episode. In a humorous twist, she seems to become Steed's temporary girlfriend and inexplicably buys him a pith helmet for a gift. Philip Madoc also appears in this episode and similarly distinguishes himself as always, playing the usual dark malevolency for which he is known.

Cathy Gale is given another good episode. In one scene, she breaks into the deceased batman's home to covertly take photographs. She is ambushed by another lurker and easily dispatches him, casually going back to taking her pictures. In another scene, she is again heard speaking fluent Spanish (as in "Death Dispatch").

On the writing side, though it lacks any science-fiction elements, this story could be considered almost a trial run for Roger Marshall's fourth season classic, "Dial a Deadly Number." It's similarly talkative and deals with some area of finance, but it lacks the somewhat more fantastic nature of the latter script, and this underscores the subtle difference between the third and fourth seasons. Mostly, that difference is built upon surrealism, eccentrics and wit, and although all of that exists in the third season, the volume is turned up the following year. Kim Mills doesn't provide any directorial flourish but he gets the job done. In any case, this is an enjoyable story with witty and engaging dialogue. Much of that engaging dialogue is Morell's, some of which comes across as still highly relevant today on the political scene.

It should be said, for American audiences, that the term "batman" does not refer to the superhero type. There are no Robins in this story. A batman is a soldier assigned as a valet or servant to a commissioned officer in the British army or Royal Air Force. But you probably already knew that. You're an *Avengers* fan.

CHAMPAGNE, CARS, CLOTHES, AND CANINES

Steed brings out the navy chalk-striped suit for the opening, at first worn without the jacket, then the dark-gray three-piece with the lapeled waistcoat, white shirt with subtle pinstripes, dark tie, diamond tiepin, black bowler and brolly. We also get an eyeful of Steed in his dressing gown (last seen in "The White Dwarf"). He soon dons the black jacket with silver buttons (first seen in "School for Traitors") and a gray tie. Finally, the Prince of Wales blazer, black waistcoat, white shirt, and gray knit tie, with the black bowler and brolly.

Mrs. Gale debuts a new pale-gray fedora with her pale mackintosh. Underneath is the leather vest with a charcoal blouse, matching pants, and black leather boots. Later, her tricolor blouse returns under the same mac. She then wears the dark-blue stretch jersey long-sleeved dress (from "The Undertakers"), with her hair up. Her second tricolor blouse returns (last seen in "Killer Whale," you can tell the difference because the colors are less contrasted and there isn't a bow at the neck), before the cobalt-blue cropped riding jacket and skirt return.

Steed's new unnamed dog makes an appearance, a pale blond Great Dane, but he shoos her away from the settee and later asks her to "get the phone book, A to D." Though her name is never given onscreen, she is played by Katie.

QUOTES

"I'm sending the Lady Cynthia's portfolio. You can start selling every shareholding. Everything. The lot."

"That's what comes from biting your fingernails."

"What about Mrs. Gale?" "Ooh, she's my old nanny. It's her 69th birthday. Tootle-pip!"
"Kill him?" "Yes." "You can't be serious." "Oh, yes, I am. We have a unique role to fulfill, Harry. Never forget that. We can help make this country great again and save the world. That's a reasonable life's achievement."
"What, kill him?" "Execute him, would have been my word, but that's what I want. Ten thousand a year is a lot of money. Take him in that room there."
"Please do as she says! She'll break my arm!"

58 (3.12.6) NOVEMBER FIVE

Steed buys a firework — Cathy stands for parliament
Written by Eric Paice
Directed by Bill Bain

GUEST CAST

Ruth Dunning (Mrs. Dove), David Davies (Arthur Dove), Ric Hutton (Mark St. John), David Langton (Major Swinburne), Iris Russell (Fiona), Gary Hope (Dyter), Joe Robinson (Max), Aimée Delamain (1st Lady), John Murray Scott (Returning Officer), Frank Maher (Farmer)

PRE-TITLE/TEASER

Outside City Hall in Southeast Anglia, the results of the recent election are announced: Michael Osbourne Dyter is declared elected and is immediately shot by an assassin hiding in the bushes nearby.

SYNOPSIS

After a shocking political assassination of a recently elected candidate, Mrs. Gale runs for the now vacant seat in parliament in order to find out who was responsible for the death. However, a nuclear missile has been stolen from a government convoy, and Steed believes that the political assassins are going to use it to blackmail the government…

REVIEW

This might be considered either an early example of bizarre violence or a shocking political thriller. Either way, the pre-title depicts the shortest political career in history—the elected politician being assassinated less than five seconds after the final vote tally.

In years past, I'd have said that I'd rather explore the murky depths of Loch Ness without an aqualung than plumb the impenetrable mysteries of British politics. Now, I'm not only a lot more astute about politics in other countries, including the United Kingdom, but in any case it seems infinitely preferable to today's goings-on in the United States! I imagine there could have been some controversy at the time over what was then considered to be sensationalist television. Although it seems tame now, at the time it was somewhat prophetic, preceding the Kennedy assassination by three weeks.

The direction is average at best. There is some small amount of wit which somewhat makes up for it, and the relationship between Arthur Dove and his wife is amusing as both confess their boredom with their partner to Mrs. Gale. This is a decent story from Eric Paice, who weaves a political tale while avoiding getting overly specific about the British political system. The problem is that it is overall rather dull and lacks sufficient tension and pace, never really rising to a ***Manchurian Candi-***

date level of suspense and intrigue. Surely, that is the sort of political drama they would have wanted, but the limitations of the television studio technology of the day prevented it. For example, in the final action scene, Steed engages in a stealthy gun fight with the villain on a set about ten feet across, with each of them in plain view of one another. They seem to be hidden from each other only by the murky grey tones of the 405-line video.

Strangely, Steed makes an uncharacteristically stupid mistake, conspicuously leaving his umbrella on Mark St. John's desk while sneaking around and then retrieving it in full view of him when he leaves. Or maybe he was just being daring? Speaking of daring, those villains are awfully brave to confront Mrs. Gale in the open to find out how much she knows, especially when she didn't know of their involvement until then. I suppose you need nerve like that if you're planning to blow up the government.

CHAMPAGNE, CARS, CLOTHES, AND CANINES

Lots of clothing debuts in this episode! Steed starts out right away in his navy-blue chalk-striped suit with a white shirt, a pale-blue silk tie, a diamond tiepin, and black bowler and umbrella. In the same scene in which Mrs. Gale debuts her new leather tunic dress, he then debuts a completely new black three-piece single-breasted suit with cloth-covered buttons, worn with a white shirt with a red-and-blue paisley tie and dark-gray bowler hat. The dark-gray three-piece with the lapeled waistcoat then returns. In the third act, the black three-piece suit returns worn with a Guy Fawkes mask as he calls at Mrs. Gale's flat.

Mrs. Gale starts out in her black stretch jersey jumper, with leather shorts over black stockings, and then she puts on her leather boots. The shorts and stockings are later replaced with charcoal-gray slacks for her skiing lessons, but she soon debuts a couple of leather fighting suits designed by Frederick Starke that would dominate this season: first, a leather tunic dress with a scooped boatneck, worn over a black rollneck jumper with black boots; then, her double-fronted leather jacket that buttons up the right side with oversized stud buttons and matching trousers, black boots, and a dark jumper. She debuts a sparkling gold lamé tunic dress (the same fabric as previously seen in her "Man with Two Shadows" lamé dress), worn with a black rollneck jumper, and it serves as a softer parallel to the prior leather tunic. She also debuts one more Frederick Stark-designed leather item this episode—a beautiful leather coat with a black-and-white fur lining and collar. The latter would feature several more times this season. Next, she debuts a pale-gray long-sleeved silk dress with blue and white dots and a high collar, over which she adds a tailored buttoned-up collarless jacket in a charcoal-gray and a black leather toque (or mini-turban). She ends the episode with a new dark-green tailored jacket and knee-length skirt with a red wool flowerpot hat with a dark band, one of several this season in different materials.

QUOTES

"But I'm not a traitor. I didn't agree to blackmail." "It's too late now!" "If necessary, I'll go to the police. I'll resign the House."

"For Queen and Country?" "Yes, that's something you wouldn't know." "I wouldn't even like to try."

"I suppose you know it's an offense to fire those things within fifty yards of the street?"

"Guy Fawkes himself couldn't have wished for more."

59 (3.15.7) THE GILDED CAGE

Steed masterminds a robbery — Cathy is framed for murder
Written by Roger Marshall
Directed by Bill Bain

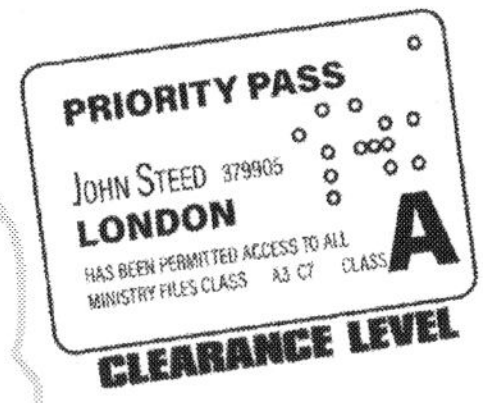

GUEST CAST

Patrick Magee (J. P. Spagge), Edric Connor (Abe Benham), Norman Chappell (Fleming), Margo Cunningham (Wardress), Fredric Abbott (Manley), Alan Haywood (Westwood), Martin Friend (Hammond), Terence Soall (Peterson), Geoff L'Cise (Gruber), Douglas Cummings (Barker), Neil Wilson (Groves)

PRE-TITLE/TEASER

Steed and Mrs Gale tour a gold depository with Mrs. Gale acting as tour guide. Entering a secure room with over three million in gold bars, Steed asks how many men it would take to remove it all. Mrs. Gale replies that it would take six, saying, "I've got it all planned."

SYNOPSIS

Steed has set Cathy Gale up as the employee of Britain's largest gold repository in order to hatch a plot to capture a millionaire criminal mastermind, J. P. Spagge. However, after he tempts Spagge with the bait, Cathy is arrested for the murder of the millionaire, and Steed's plan begins to unravel...

REVIEW

This is another brilliant script from Roger Marshall, who is quite my favorite ***Avengers*** writer, certainly for this season. The story starts out with the curmudgeonly Mr. Spagge—curmudgeonly might be too gentle a word here, but I'm going to keep this review clean. Played by Patrick Magee, who would later be better known for films like ***A Clockwork Orange***, in which he plays a very similar character, Spagge is a highly dimensional old rotter. The story is full of dimensional characters like him, delivering sharp and sparkling dialogue all the way through. Though I'm not familiar with the rest of the guest cast, they all perform well and keep a great script on track. (Few gangs of thieves have been so jolly since Robin Hood and his Merry Men.)

The script is highly believable—a quality viewers may have come to expect from Marshall—and the similarities between this story and ***Goldfinger*** (in which Honor Blackman would later star) are striking, though one can only assume that they are largely coincidental. (Perhaps Marshall was inspired by the Bond novel.) That said, the real star of this episode is again Honor Blackman, who is spectacular throughout, playing the cool detachment of Mrs. Gale to the hilt. But even her icy demeanor is momentarily cracked when she is accused of having murdered Mr. Spagge. After she has been captured, drugged by the gang, and left disoriented by her apparent imprisonment at Holloway, she quickly recovers her composure. Without skipping a beat, she flows so effortlessly and subtly from being ignorant of her situation to understanding it that one could almost miss the transition.

This episode ably demonstrates why Honor Blackman was chosen for Steed's permanent assistant, making one wonder why it took so long to come to the conclusion, instead of forcing us to endure the pretty but shallow Venus Smith and the languid Dr. Martin King for nine episodes last season. Blackman can easily carry an entire episode without batting an eye. And, in this case, she manages to nearly single-handedly save the situation when Steed's plan has fallen apart. The mild irony of showcasing Mrs. Gale in this way is that it actually makes Patrick Macnee appear stronger as well. Macnee is one of those wonderful actors that benefits enormously from a strong partner with whom to work. The stronger they are, the stronger *he* is. In this case, his concern for Mrs. Gale, as he realizes his plan has fallen apart and brought about Mrs. Gale's disappearance, boils his ruthless spy traits to the surface, and his intimidation of Spagge's butler is one moment in which his genteel persona (the one that casual viewers are most aware of) fractures violently. "The Gilded Cage" is one of the highlights of this remarkably good season.

CHAMPAGNE, CARS, CLOTHES, AND CANINES

Mrs. Gale wears her leather boatneck tunic dress and black jumper as she gives Steed a tour through the gold depository, but she tones it down later with a pale buff cardigan, trousers, and black leather boots when relaxing at Steed's apartment. Later, her pale mackintosh and brown leather newsboy cap lie in a rocking chair while she debuts her V-neck pinafore dress with a black jumper underneath. She would wear this often throughout the season as it made for a more comfortable version of the similarly-cut leather V-neck tunic dress. A large portion of the episode features her in prison garb. She also wears her leather double-fronted jacket with stud buttons and matching trousers when providing her instructions to the robbers and during the theft, briefly paired with a gas mask.

Steed wears the dark-gray three-piece with the lapeled waistcoat, followed by the black three-piece with a white shirt and gray knit tie, and later, a simple black button-down shirt, and still later, a return of his dressing gown (debuted in "The White Dwarf"). Finally, his Prince of Wales blazer and black waistcoat return with the red paisley silk tie.

Steed's Great Dane makes another appearance. In production order, this is the last appearance by one of Steed's dogs for a very long time.

QUOTES

"I find other people's illnesses a bore."
"When I don't say anything, it means go on!"
"How could I go through a whole trial and not remember anything!"
"Mrs. Gale, when someone puts you onto three million, it *is* dramatic! Very dramatic."

60 (3.13.8) SECOND SIGHT

Steed fights in the dark — Cathy exposes a millionaire's precious light
Written by Martin Woodhouse
Directed by Peter Hammond

GUEST CAST

John Carson (Marten Halvarssen), Judy Bruce (Eve Hawn), Peter Bowles (Neil Anstice), Ronald Adam (Dr. Spender), Steven Scott (Dr. Vilner), Terry Brewer (Steiner)

PRE-TITLE/TEASER

Dr. Vilner, Neil Anstice, and Eve Hawn demonstrate the means of preserving and transporting replacement corneas to John Steed.

SYNOPSIS

Investigating a cornea transplant for a blind millionaire and a mysterious death, Steed sends Cathy undercover as a biochemist to the home of Martin Halvarssen in Switzerland to observe the operation. However, the revelation that the corneas are from a live donor startles them, and soon the donor is found dead, causing suspicion to fall on one of Halvarssen's party…

REVIEW

"Second Sight" is about as well-shot as 405-line monochrome video can be; Hammond finds all kinds of intriguing places to put the camera. Peter Bowles delivers an excellent performance as the show's villain, laughing maniacally at Halvarssen as he rants passionately about his desire for restored sight. Equally, John Carson is engaging as Halvarssen, looking much like a tall and regal Max von Sydow.

Otherwise, there isn't a significant amount to recommend in this relatively static presentation. This is a decent if ultimately disappointing mystery. Woodhouse's script is respectable, but one cannot help but feel let down by the mundane nature of the mystery. Not to mention the fact that it seems like very small potatoes for *The Avengers*. It doesn't help that Steed and Mrs. Gale don't really seem to have very much to do.

A breath of fresh air in the form of new music actually graces the episode, which mitigates the relentlessness of Johnny Dankworth's repeated themes being played ad nauseum for two seasons.

CHAMPAGNE, CARS, CLOTHES, AND... CAMERAS!

Steed starts out right away in his black three-piece suit with a white shirt with French cuffs, and a gray tie. He later debuts a black cardigan with large round buttons, and then relaxes in a black long-sleeved polo shirt. Steed eventually gets tired of all the rain and breaks out the tan weatherproofed overcoat with a navy and white spotted ascot. The black jacket with silver buttons also makes an appearance.

Mrs. Gale starts right out in wet leather pants, her black stretch jersey jumper, and a very bad mood! How's that for an episode opener? It rains quite a lot in this episode and Mrs. Gale gets her fedora (from "Death of a Batman") wet several times, which might explain why she switches to a new charcoal-gray blazer suit with skirt; followed by the charcoal-gray collarless jacket and skirt with the gray spotted silk blouse and the black leather toque, and eventually, she fights the cold rain by bringing out her fur-lined leather coat (all from "November 5"). Later, her V-neck pinafore dress returns (from "The Gilded Cage"). The pale mackintosh and fedora also return. Finally, her double-fronted leather fighting suit returns.

Mrs. Gale uses a Minox Wetzlar III-S Subminiature 'spy' camera. The 'S' stands for flash synch, and you can clearly see the flash synch connector on top of the camera.

QUOTES

"...it just struck me, it's like taking pennies from a blind man."
"They are a token for me. They're a symbol, that I have won again, in a world full of men that can see what is going on in front of them!"

61 (3.16.9) THE MEDICINE MEN

Cathy takes a Turkish bath to help Steed prove the value of good soap.
Written by Malcolm Hulke
Directed by Kim Mills

GUEST CAST

Peter Barkworth (Geoffrey Willis), Newton Blick (John Willis), Harold Innocent (Frank Leeson), Joy Wood (Miss Dowell), Monica Stevenson (Fay), John Crocker (Taylor), Peter Hughes (Edwards), Brenda Cowling (Masseuse)

PRE-TITLE/TEASER

At a Turkish bath, a woman eases comfortably into a sauna chair. Carefully zipped inside by an attendant, she is then suffocated with a bath towel.

SYNOPSIS

Steed and Mrs. Gale investigate the sale of cheap imitations in the foreign markets of pharmaceutical products produced by Willis-Sopwith. A mysterious death amongst the staff of the company leads to an avant-garde artist and a plot to poison the consumers...

REVIEW

This is a good script, though it again deals with a plot that is very low-key and exceptionally mundane—criminals attempting to pass off imitations in the cosmetics market which covers a mass murder racket. Shades of "Immortal Clay." Despite setting itself up for the doldrums, this episode features a skilled guest cast. Peter Barkworth does a fine job; it's nice to see an actor put so many subtle and eccentric movements into his character. The regulars similarly get in on the game. Patrick Macnee gets a chance to put on a silly costume and a bizarre accent as he plays an eccentric Icelandic art buyer, possibly his most outrageous disguise since "Tunnel of Fear."

Although not nearly as kinky as it sounds, Cathy has several shower scenes at a Turkish bath house. And this is the episode where she passes herself off as an efficiency expert as a means of working undercover for Lilt cosmetics. Now, this is an odd profession for the twenty-first century. Does such a thing exist? When I first saw this episode about twenty years ago, I was perplexed by it. The internet was a nascent creation, and subjects such as this weren't easily Googled. Now, they are, and I can confirm that business efficiency experts do still exist, though as a niche field for people with MBAs. Such an emboldened profession was it in the sixties that it apparently landed Mrs. Gale with an eye injury. She ends up wearing an eyepatch throughout the last third of the episode, making her look very much like a pirate. Add the top hat and it would have really made her look intimidating!

This episode is something of a mixed bag, which may be considered the season sagging in the middle as it survives on good writing, characterization and the strength of the regular cast—the bread-and-butter of television shot on videotape—even if the core concept is rather dull by comparison to the rest of the season. Ideas do indeed tend to run thin around this time in a twenty-six-episode series.

Interestingly, this episode aired on the same date as the premier of another prominent series created by Sydney Newman, ***Doctor Who***. I guess it's just a coincidence that this episode is about medicine, is written by a soon-to-be ***Doctor Who*** writer (Malcolm Hulke), and features a guest star that would appear in both series (Peter Barkworth). You can't fool me. I know there's a connection. Okay, maybe not.

CHAMPAGNE, CARS, CLOTHES, AND CANINES

A heavy fashion episode for Mrs. Gale with many clothing changes. She debuts straight away another leather fighting suit, a jacket with black studded buttons in columns on either side, reminiscent of an Edwardian chauffeur's uniform, and matching trousers. Steed practices his putting by placing his bowler on her leather boots. This is the episode for Mrs. Gale to get a bit risqué. Due to an injury sustained in the fight scene at the end of the second act, she wears an eyepatch over her right eye. Combined with her leather boatneck tunic dress and boots, it's a severe look, even more kinky than Mrs. Peel's outfit in "A Touch of Brimstone." She also appears nude in the shower at the spa—naughty bits not revealed, of course! Which, naturally, gives Blackman the opportunity to do some ecstatic shower acting. This is followed by her charcoal-gray blazer suit (from "Second Sight"), combined with a new black-and-white straw flowerpot hat and long black gloves, when posing as an efficiency expert. Then, she wears her dark-blue stretch jersey dress (from "The Undertakers"); followed by a new collarless satin dress with six satin-covered buttons, a boat neck, and a cloth belt; followed by a new leather jacket with a ribbed wool collar, with the leather fighting suit and the blazer suit interspersed throughout. The pale mackintosh also makes an appearance.

Steed starts out in his black three-piece suit—which is quickly becoming a favorite for the season despite the way it soaks up the light—worn with a pinstriped white shirt and a gray knit tie. He later adds the tan overcoat with the heavy stitching, and the Prince of Wales blazer and black waistcoat return. He also hams it up an outrageous long fur coat and fur cap over his navy chalk-striped suit while posing as an Icelandic art dealer. He also briefly slums it (by his standards) in a cream ribbed cardigan.

And a little pug-nosed Shih Tzu dog named Samson makes an appearance, having been a temporary guest at Steed's home while Fay is there, so I guess that counts as an *Avengers* dog.

QUOTES

"She's a very elegant little young lady, a sartorial little avant garde."
"You did very well with your hands tied behind your back and an eyepatch on one eye."

62 (3.8.10) THE GRANDEUR THAT WAS ROME

Steed attends a Roman orgy — Cathy is offered as a human sacrifice
Written by Rex Edwards
Directed by Kim Mills

GUEST CAST

Hugh Burden (Bruno), Colette Wilde (Octavia), John Flint (Marcus), Ian Shand (Eastow), Raymond Adamson (Lucius), Kenneth Keeling (Appleton), Colin Rix (Barnes)

PRE-TITLE/TEASER

In an Italianate home with a Roman atrium and ancient statues, Sir Bruno greets Marcus at his front door and they exchange encoded messages while drinking wine. Sir Bruno then throws earthworms into a pan of dirt, promising that they shall soon serve "simple naked fear."

SYNOPSIS

Steed and Mrs. Gale encounter a scheme by an insane self-appointed Caesar to poison the world with a new strain of bubonic plague, while he and his associates are safely inoculated with an antidote. Cathy is captured while investigating, and the plan is to make her the guinea pig for the first inoculation...

REVIEW

The mid-season sag continues as *The Avengers* investigate desolate soil, disappearing earthworms, and pigs that walk backwards—and, believe me, that makes it sound far more interesting than it is. These seemingly innocent agricultural endeavors lead to a secret cabal of closeted Roman wannabes in England who are intent on taking over the world and installing their dreary Nero-like leader as emperor. For heaven's sake, why? I could hardly bear to be in the same room with him as obnoxious and pompous as he is. He reminds me of a certain current American political figure.

Oddly revealing the plot of the villains in the first third, this episode turns into a tired and lifeless attempt to bring Roman intrigue into the modern era. Full of tedious acting and wearisome quotes in Latin (as if this somehow makes it more authentic), the characters come across as merely delusional Britons engaging in a faux-Roman toga party. I can only assume that all the villains are slightly camp and enjoy a bit of dress-up when in private. To be fair though, they were ahead of their time on cosplay. Never once was I engaged by these goings-on and not for one moment is there any believability as to their plan actually succeeding. Thus, no tension.

Hugh Burden is flailing throughout, peering through beady eyes, barely an ounce of emotion registers on his face, and he spends almost the entire episode in a Frankenstein haircut and toga plotting his scheme out loud to his cronies and making dull speeches. He does however occasionally manage a twisted sociopathic malevolency. I imagine the idea was to create a modern Nero, but seldom does he come close. More of a second-rate Claudius really.

Kim Mills' direction is not much better. Cameras bump into things, and the action scenes are very poorly choreographed. And frankly, we didn't need Mrs. Gale to get captured and need rescuing again. She's not that sort of character. On the upside, she again looks splendid in her top hat. Then again, Steed looks ridiculous in his glasses.

The episode concludes with an orgy-on-the-cheap, meaning no one takes their clothes off and instead mill about acting vaguely libertine. Not that I'd advocate something racier, but it probably wouldn't have hurt in bumping up the ratings on this snoozer.

CHAMPAGNE, CARS, CLOTHES, AND CANINES

Mrs. Gale starts out with a real stunner, a new scarlet jacket (very much in the style of Mary Quant), open like a cape but clasped with a black leather tie, and worn with a black rollneck and the black porkpie hat. This is later replaced by the brown striped blouse (from "Man with Two Shadows") and then with the pale mackintosh, black jumper, brown leather newsboy cap, and boots. Her fighting suit of the week is the leather vest with the silver buttons, plus a black rollneck jumper, leather trousers, and boots.

Steed wears his black jacket with silver buttons over a buff-colored fisherman's jumper, and later, he dons his heavy dark cardigan (from "Second Sight"). Three suits appear: his black three-piece; his dark-gray three-piece with the lapeled waistcoat (worn with a pinstriped white shirt in the darkroom and no jacket and sometimes with his thick eyeglasses); and his navy chalk-stripe with a navy bowtie with white spots, a black bowler, umbrella, and the eyeglasses, but he soon forgoes them all for a cream-yellow Roman toga with mauve stripes so he can join the party. In fact, lots of togas for everyone. Lots of wine too, but the only champagne is the glass that Steed drinks while Mrs. Gale works at her microscope.

QUOTES

"You know, one chap told me that whole species of birds have been wiped out, simply because of absorbed poisons from chemical-sprayed fields."

"It's a terrific idea. I salute you, excellency. The world will be ours!" "Not ours, Marcus. Mine."

"I've had about enough of this Roman gimmick!" *(me too!)*

"...and what's cooking with Mrs. Gale, eh? You told us a couple of fibs. That's naughty."

"Oh, those Bacchanalia—such outrageous orgies!"

63 (3.4.11) THE GOLDEN FLEECE

Steed hunts a modern Robin Hood — Cathy joins the Army
Written by Roger Marshall and Phyllis Norman
Directed by Peter Hammond

GUEST CAST

Warren Mitchell (Captain Jason), Tenniel Evans (Major Ruse), Barry Lineham (Sergeant Major White), Robert Lee (Mr. Lo), Yu Ling (Mrs. Kwan), Lisa Peake (Esther), Ronald Wilson (Private Holmes), Michael Hawkins (Jones)

PRE-TITLE/TEASER

At the Blore Camp Southern Command post in Aldershot, British army officers enjoy their coffee at a meeting. One of them smokes right in front of a No Smoking sign. An officer reads the minutes from the last meeting, and the treasurer reveals that their total financial holdings amount to £56, 19 shillings, and 7 pence.

SYNOPSIS

Steed accidentally claims the wrong coat from a Chinese restaurant and finds a check for £5,000. Thus, Steed and Mrs. Gale find themselves on the trail of gold smugglers within the army and a sociopathic killer. Then again, Steed never does anything by accident...

REVIEW

This episode was once the only post-Ian Hendry story that was not available for viewing in North America, until a print was found in the Thames Television archive. The modern viewer is fortunate that this episode is now available because it's an especially fine one from the pen of Roger Marshall and his writing partner Phyllis Norman.

The whole of the Steed and Mrs. Gale relationship could be summed up as one of tension—tension that is mitigated by mutual affection and subtle flirtation. Far from being like that between Steed and Mrs. Peel, whose relationship was much more suggestive of romance, whether prior or current, Steed and Mrs. Gale were more like that of employer and employee, manipulator and manipulated. Their relationship could be cold or warm from episode to episode but was always mutually one of respect. Thus, the highlights of "The Golden Fleece" are the delightful character interactions between Steed and Mrs. Gale, the episode being full of classic moments of manipulation by Steed as he deftly maneuvers Mrs. Gale into the right place at the right time to help him in his cause. The best moment comes when Mrs. Gale thinks she has a new job helping the army sort out their museum, which, of course, turns out to be planned by Steed.

There are some truly sadistic incidents that would have been considered especially violent in the 1960s. Mr. Lo runs down Jones with the car parked in his garage. Steed shoots Captain Jason in the hand in order to subdue him.

The script's only flaw is dated writing for Chinese characters that would have been perceived as normal for television of the era. It's not exactly racist in tone, just mildly condescending. At least we can say that actual Asian actors were cast for the guest parts, which is a great deal more than can be said for *The New Avengers* episode "Trap," which would, fourteen years later, inexplicably feature an actor of clear European descent in the major role of a Chinese villain.

It's also notable that Warren Mitchell (in the role of Captain Jason) would completely reverse personalities when cast as Keller in "The Charmers." He would later become even more over-the-top as Brodny in "Two's a Crowd" and "The See-Through Man."

CHAMPAGNE, CARS, CLOTHES, AND CANINES

Steed's navy chalk-stripe suit returns, this time with the white pinstriped shirt, dark silk tie, diamond tiepin, and, of course, the black bowler hat and umbrella. This is followed by the dark-gray three-piece with the lapeled waistcoat and brown Chelsea boots. Later, he wears just his suit trousers and a white shirt with French cuffs and cufflinks while he smokes a cigar; then, the Prince of Wales blazer with the black waistcoat, the same white shirt and cufflinks, the cream tweed trousers, and the black trilby.

At the restaurant, Mrs. Gale wears a loose diaphanous gown in chiffon, with a pleated skirt and the gold satin vest (from "The Undertakers"). This is the only appearance of this outfit. This is followed by the leather vest with silver buttons over a pale silk blouse, worn with charcoal pants, black pumps, and the pale mackintosh. (This is the outfit she wears when she rants at Steed in his flat.) She also wears her cobalt-blue cropped riding jacket and skirt with a black jumper and the black porkpie hat. She briefly wears a hooded coat lined with black fur, which Steed sniffs before he hangs it up. The leather V-neck tunic and trousers also return.

QUOTES

"I've learned from experience that whenever you've wined and dined me as well as this, it's always been the prelude to some hideous adventure."

"Can't you just tell me in plain straightforward language that you're after gold smugglers? Instead, we have to go through this ridiculous rigmarole of candlelight and wine and old Chinese proverbs. Well, here's another old Chinese proverb. He who does not tell truth gets cushion in eye."

"You make parting so much easier."

64 (3.7.12) DON'T LOOK BEHIND YOU

Steed takes a country drive — Cathy endures a night of terror

Written by Brian Clemens

Directed by Peter Hammond

GUEST CAST

Maurice Good (Man), Kenneth Colley (Young Man), Janine Gray (Girl)

PRE-TITLE/TEASER

In a stately home, a man opens a magazine to a photo of Mrs. Cathy Gale. Bit by bit, he dissects the photo into pieces with a pair of scissors and rearranges them into grotesque patterns.

SYNOPSIS

Cathy Gale is invited to spend the weekend at the home of Sir Cavalier Resagne, an expert in mediaeval clothing. Once there, she is greeted by the eccentric Ola, who tells her that Sir Cavalier is away for the evening. Soon, Cathy is besieged by bizarre incidents and an encounter with a very strange young man. Eventually, an old enemy is revealed to be behind the disturbing activity, and now, he is stalking her with murderous intentions...

REVIEW

This episode is proof that a good script can't be held down, even by poor production quality. Now, I say that with full acknowledgment that virtually every episode in this season is like that, but with the added caveat that this story was later remade almost line-for-line as "The Joker" with Diana Rigg as Mrs. Peel and with much higher production values—in color and on 35mm film. Thus, we are able to simultaneously judge how much of a difference film makes versus videotape and yet understand that the narrative is the real strength in any production.

The opening pre-title would be repeated closely for "The Joker," and in that version it is a very powerful opening statement that sets the tone for the entire episode—the scissors lovingly caress the photo before they begin to cut, suggesting that the mind behind the hands is confused about its emotions, expressing love (or at least the appreciation of beauty) as well as hate and the desire for revenge. Here, the hands and scissors move too slowly and awkwardly, only getting halfway to revealing the emotional drive behind their activity before time seemingly runs out and the title has to appear on screen.

On a similar note, in this version, Steed drives Mrs. Gale to Sir Resagne's estate, and this is a delightful scene that is alas almost ruined by some of the worst telecined film I've ever seen. In those days, on-location footage was always shot on film and then telecined to videotape and played in live to the recording of the videotaped footage shot in studio. The completed program was then either aired from the master videotape or from a film copy thereof. In either case, the final product would be telerecorded to 16mm film for storage and overseas sales—which is what we're now viewing, albeit with the minor improvements made possible with digital restoration techniques. Thus, the location footage is burned in as is, being a copy of a copy, and it looks terrible, like it was shot on 8mm rather than some larger film format.

Aside from this, the sets are by definition more cramped, but Peter Hammond makes the most of them to create a claustrophobic atmosphere. My only other complaint is that there was no new music written for this episode, and this mitigates how much suspense the production can generate (using the same old cues from the past two seasons). And thus, we can see why ***The Avengers*** production team were eager to move to film production. They were probably looking at other ITV material like ***Danger Man*** and ***The Saint*** and asking themselves why they couldn't shoot on film and sell to America. ***The Avengers*** certainly had the goods. Therefore, by comparing these two episodes—"Don't Look Behind You" and "The Joker"—their goals and the reasons for film production become evident.

I must admit it's very hard to assess this episode fairly. I'm sure it sounds like I'm judging it harshly by making comparisons. To redress the balance, I will say that the reality is that "Don't Look Behind You" is undoubtedly one of the better Cathy Gale stories, and probably the best reason for watching it is the chance to see Honor Blackman have almost an entire episode to herself. The villain doesn't turn up in any form until the end, so there's none of the creepy spying going on, but when he does appear, the scene with his voice seemingly coming from all directions is much longer—perhaps too long.

After arriving at the castle, they find it occupied only by musty old furniture and weird girls who like to quote Italian poetry[4] and gab about teeth and pirates. Initially not bothered by this rampant display of eccentricity, Cathy submits herself to staying without Steed's company, fearless as always. But this resolve slowly melts as the mystery deepens, eventually forcing her to don her leathers almost as if armoring herself, and yet leaving her much more fractured than Emma Peel would be in the remake.

The final confrontation with Martin is both bizarre and intriguing, with Cathy, a woman rarely shaken by anything, being clearly disturbed by the reappearance of the man she helped put away.[5] She seems frightened even though it is she that holds the Beretta 950 automatic, and when she

---

4 The Italian quote by Ola is "La notte é pieno di mistero. La notte é la mi'amica."—meaning "The night is full of mystery. The night is my friend." Gray's pronunciation is actually pretty good.

5 Honor Blackman reportedly struggled with her emotions during this scene and found it impossible not to cry despite director Peter Hammond urging her to play it more tough.

shoots him it appears to be an accident. Clearly, she had feelings for Martin—a genuine romantic relationship. Her fear briefly turns to rage when she momentarily thinks that Steed knew what she was in for all along, once again a victim of his manipulations. As the periodic manipulation from Steed was absent from his relationship with Mrs. Peel, therein might lie the most critical difference between these two episodes, episodes which otherwise are only separated by production values.

The villain is credited on-screen as simply "Man," played by Maurice Good, although both Cathy and Steed clearly refer to him as Martin Goodman several times in the episode. Similarly, Ola Monsey-Chamberlain, played by Janine Gray, is credited only as "Girl."

CHAMPAGNE, CARS, CLOTHES, AND CANINES

Steed's Prince of Wales blazer with the black waistcoat and cream tweed trousers returns. He adds his tan weatherproofed overcoat, black bowler, and leather gloves for the ride through the countryside. Mrs. Gale mostly wears her tricolor striped long-sleeved blouse and tailored cobalt-blue cropped riding jacket and skirt (first seen in this combination in "Six Hands Across a Table"). During the car ride, she adds a military-inspired overcoat with epaulettes and a headscarf. In the final act, she switches to her leather V-neck tunic and leather trousers.

Finally, one of Steed's cars appears—a 1930 Lagonda 3 Litre (GK 3295). He gives Mrs. Gale a lift through the countryside to the Resagne estate, with Cathy clearly enjoying the ride and some locals thrilling at the sight of his old-fashioned charm, and he gallantly stops to pick her some flowers. Possibly the most perfect filmed sequence in the Honor Blackman era.

QUOTES

"I think you're onto something, Mrs. Gale, as long as you're not thinking of reintroducing the chastity belt."

"A few insignificant refugees." "Nobody's insignificant! Not those refugees, nor that poor boy upstairs."

65 (3.5.13) DEATH À LA CARTE

Steed turns Chef — Cathy tries to prevent a murder
Written by John Lucarotti
Directed by Kim Mills

GUEST CAST

Robert James (Mellor), Henry Soskin (Emir Abdulla Akaba), Paul Dawkins (Dr. Spender), Ken Parry (Arbuthnot), Gordon Rollings (Lucien), David Nettheim (Umberto), Coral Atkins (Josie), Valentino Musetti (Ali)

PRE-TITLE/TEASER

Deep in a jungle, a British army officer breaks into a small potting shed and steals mushrooms, placing them into a briefcase marked with the emblem of the Emir Abdullah Akaba.

SYNOPSIS

Emir Abdulla Akaba is visiting London for his annual medical examination by Dr. Spender. Unfortunately, Steed is expecting an assassination attempt, and he and Mrs. Gale go undercover at the hotel where the Emir is staying. Steed poses as a chef and eventually discovers that poisoned mushrooms may be part of the plot. Then, the Emir dies of natural causes before the villains can hatch their plans, forcing them to violently reveal themselves to Steed and Mrs. Gale...

REVIEW

From the truly weird to the rather mundane. Perhaps "Death à la Carte" should have been called "*The Avengers* Cook for the Sheikh"! Far more like a second season episode than one of the more evolved third, the plot is basic, the direction pedestrian, and the camera work rather poor—for example, several shots reveal the top of the set wall. Then again, one shouldn't expect too much from Kim Mills, direction-wise.

There are however some nice comedic touches involving the two chefs and Steed—particularly when Steed is attempting to explain his recipe. Let's face it. Just the idea of Steed as a chef is rather amusing, and he comes across as a culinary confidence man. The Emir has humorous nuances to his character as well; he is quite the gourmand, and everything centers around making sure he is well fed.

When the death of the Emir smokes the villains out of hiding, there's also a climactic fight scene involving Steed and Ali which shows promise for future episodes. At one point it seems like it will evolve into a food fight, and this is something that actually occurred during the fifth season. It ends with Steed splashing boiling water (or sauce?) in Ali's face. Very nasty. Moments like these add a bit of interest to a dull-as-dishwater plot. It's something like compensating for a bland meal by over spicing, just as Steed might have done as he faked his way through his emergency masterspy culinary crash course. Regardless, this is a very run-of-the-mill offering.

CHAMPAGNE, CARS, CLOTHES, AND CANINES

Mrs. Gale sports her tricolor striped long-sleeved blouse with the cropped riding jacket and skirt again (last seen in "Don't Look Behind You"). She also debuts a quasi-military uniform with a black shirt with slightly blousy sleeves, a thin leather baldric, a wide belt, and charcoal-gray trousers. This is its only appearance. Finally, her long-sleeved gold lamé dress with the boat neck reappears (last seen in "Man with Two Shadows").

Steed spends the vast majority of the episode in a full traditional chef's uniform with a maximally-sized toque and worn with his cream tweed trousers.

There is champagne for the guests, though none for the *Avengers*, but they end up with wine and fish and chips at the end.

QUOTES

"Do you suffer from vertigo?"
"...with a tidgen of bay leaves and a smurse of tyme."

66 (3.18.14) DRESSED TO KILL

Steed is quick on the draw — Cathy becomes a highway woman
Written by Brian Clemens
Directed by Bill Bain

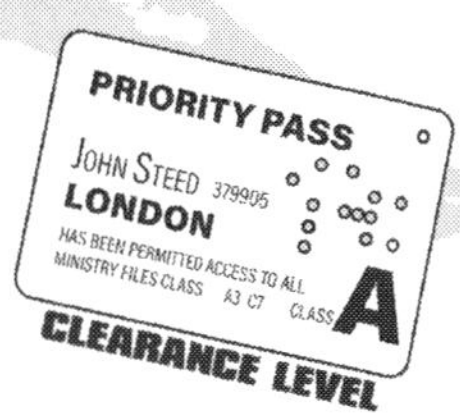

GUEST CAST

Leonard Rossiter (Robin Hood), Alexander Davion (Napoleon), Richard Leech (Policeman), John Junkin (Sheriff), Anneke Wills (Pussy Cat), Anthea Windham (Highwaywoman), Leon Eagles (Newman), Frank Maher (Barman), Peter Fontaine (1st Officer)

PRE-TITLE/TEASER

A man stalks through hedges carrying heavy radio equipment. Through binoculars, he spies a sign reading: "War Department. No Admittance." Inside the facility, radar operators detect a blip on their screens and sound the alarm. Hearing the sirens, the man outside signals a compatriot on his radio and announces that their plan is working, wishing him, "A Merry Christmas."

SYNOPSIS

A missile attack that is detected by all but one early warning station turns out to be a false alarm. When property nearby is put up for sale, all the potential buyers, including Steed, are invited to a New Year's party on a train. One by one, the guests are being killed, and Steed and Cathy must find the culprits...

REVIEW

This episode was later loosely remade into "The Superlative Seven" and is the only occasion where the original is superior to its clone—at least story-wise. One of the reasons for this is the *lack of* cookie cutter fabricated cartoon characters creating a show for hidden agents by displaying quaintly obsolete skills. The characters here are (mostly) ordinary people in fancy dress at a New Year's party who just happen to want to buy a piece of property, rather than a motley crew of gunslingers and strongmen who are selected for their highly questionable and outmoded combat skills. The result is a more realistic approach involving ordinary party-goers who are given permission to act incongruously by way of their various outfits. For example, the 'sheriff' has a gun and the 'policeman' has handcuffs, both of which are put to use.

This episode and its remake could be considered something of illustration of the differences between the Mrs. Gale and Mrs. Peel eras. In the color era of the show, common sense is often thrown out in favor of the surreal, which either works or it doesn't. Most of the time it does, or we just let it slide because it's fun, but sometimes it intrudes so much on one's reasoning centers that it impinges on that enjoyment. This happens rarely, true, but "The Superlative Seven" is one occasion where I'd argue that it does. Thus, this story is far more well-suited to the Cathy Gale era. Realism rules the day and real-life people put real-life objects to use in order to get out of a sticky situation, quite what you'd expect in this more down-to-earth period in the show's history.

Patrick Macnee is great as always, being largely the locus of the action as Honor Blackman takes a mini-vacation, though the whole of the episode proper starts with Mrs. Gale visiting in the aftermath of a wild Christmas party at his place. Steed sifts through the debris as he informs Mrs. Gale of the missile crisis. Later, in a rare musical break from Johnny Dankworth's relentless jazz themes modulated into various keys (which you're bound to be bored with after two seasons), anthemic Western music is played as Steed enters the train station dressed in western gear. This does wonders in selling Steed's boyish side, but it is Anneke Wills who steals the show as Miss Wentworth the pussy cat with her superbly saucy interchanges with Steed. Fans of Mrs. Gale won't be entirely disappointed when she assumes the place of the original highwaywoman and uses an old handgun that came with the costume. The mystery is set up nicely, and the train environment is used to good claustrophobic effect. Generally, this is a highly enjoyable episode that puts the season back on track after brief flirtations with mediocrity.

CHAMPAGNE, CARS, CLOTHES, AND CANINES

This is sort of this season's Christmas and New Year's episode, and cutting-edge fashion takes a break for festive wear. Steed's apartment is a mess but festive after a wild party. He starts out, however, in his dark V-neck knit cardigan and a striped white shirt. On the train, he dresses as a gambler from the deep south with a frill-fronted shirt, black string tie, and a western hat, but—who are we kidding?—the real showstopper is Mrs. Gale's highwaywoman outfit with her pale-blue frill-fronted shirt (from "The Undertakers"), velvet vest and matching trousers, black boots, tricorn hat, and a black eyemask. Her smoking a cigar in that number could stop traffic! She also briefly wears a monk's cloak to sneak into the party. Plenty of champagne at the New Year's party too, before all the trouble begins that is. More champagne at the end, this time the '45. "The liberation of France. Great year!" (after all that WWII trouble ended.)

Mrs. Gale also briefly wears a dark, collarless, knee-length dress, trimmed in satin with large cloth-covered buttons; she wears the leather baldric (from "Death à la Carte") over it. This is its only appearance in the series. Steed's black jacket with silver buttons reappears at the end.

QUOTES

"So much for the homme fatale. I could see she was just crazy about you."
"Beneath the wooing words hangs the evil deed."
"Committing a world to an atomic war—you call that a mission?" "There will be destruction, yes. But there will also be the defeated and the victors. I intend to be among the latter."
"Talking of 'years,' a happy new one to you. I didn't get a chance before." "And to you, my dear, and many of them, very, very many of them!" "Let's not push our luck, Steed, we only just got through this one."

67 (3.17.15) THE WHITE ELEPHANT

Steed tracks a white elephant — Cathy hunts big game
Written by John Lucarotti
Directed by Laurence Bourne

GUEST CAST

Godfrey Quigley (Noah Marshall), Edwin Richfield (Lawrence), Scott Forbes (Conniston), Bruno Barnabe (Fitch), Judy Parfitt (Brenda Paterson), Rowena Gregory (Madge Jordan), Toke Townley (Joseph), Martin Friend (George)

PRE-TITLE/TEASER

At a zoo, the keeper discovers that Snowy the elephant has somehow escaped her cage.

SYNOPSIS

An albino elephant at Noah's Ark (a zoo) goes missing, and Steed coerces Mrs. Gale into posing as a former big game hunter in order to apply for a position as chief zoologist. Unfortunately, Steed uncovers a lot more than just a missing elephant, and Cathy ends up in the tiger cage...

REVIEW

This episode starts with an intriguing role-reversal between the leads that turns into another manipulation by Steed to place Mrs. Gale into a strategically important position for his latest spy scheme. Steed engages in Trāṭaka yoga by staring at daffodils. It's odd because this seems so much more like something Mrs. Gale would do. She was after all the one that attended the yoga club in "Brief for Murder" not too long ago. Or perhaps that was merely a cover for their scheme? Later, this goes in a much more unexpected direction, in which Steed and Cathy end up practicing various forms of concentration—Steed balancing champagne glasses on his head and Cathy standing on hers.

The story turns into an ecological story well ahead of its time. It's remarkable to hear them talking about the same issues as today—the poaching of elephants for their ivory in 1964. In this case, the situation centers around a small white elephant called Snowy. Poor Snowy is wandering the countryside, lost, hungry and alone—or is she? Turns out she has been kidnapped for more nefarious purposes. Somehow, I don't think an albino elephant could slip unnoticed into Berkeley Square or Hampstead Heath. *The Avengers* never works that way anyway.

One scene that stands out is Steed's visit to a gunsmith's shop where he inquires about purchasing an elephant gun. He does his usual trick of blatantly—and with seeming innocence—announcing his intentions (however bizarre) purely in order to provoke a reaction. Steed also has a highly suggestive and kinky encounter with a woman at a manacle manufacturer, whose clientele seem to include zoos and possibly sadomasochistic customers. For Cathy Gale's part, in a brilliant moment she challenges Lawrence's manliness and then quickly dispatches him after he relinquishes his gun. This scene is a highlight of the season and essentially sums her character up. Edwin Richfield also puts in his best performance of the series as Mrs. Gale's unfortunate victim.

Despite the fact that the episode is slightly marred by a few production gaffes, including a sudden drop-out of the ambient sounds during a scene at Noah's Ark, it's par for the course in this era and certainly not enough to hold back a good script like this. In "The White Elephant," John Lucarotti delivered another clever and engaging script with good characterization and sharp witty dialogue. Its only flaw is one that periodically occurs during this season and the prior one—a mundane theme. But this story is about as good as the mundane gets.

CHAMPAGNE, CARS, CLOTHES, AND CANINES

Fashion is kept fairly simple and more casual in this one, except for Steed's tan overcoat and polka dot ascot and his black jacket with silver buttons. The dark-gray three-piece with the lapeled waistcoat also returns, and he debuts a new heavy black shearling overcoat with black lining and lapels. The Prince of Wales blazer with the black waistcoat also returns.

Mrs. Gale's pinafore dress and pale mackintosh both return (separately), along with her charcoal-gray blazer jacket and skirt (first seen in "Second Sight") and the leather fighting suit with the double-fronted jacket with stud buttons. Finally, she wears the high-collared gray silk blouse with spots and the collarless charcoal-gray jacket (first seen in "November 5").

Otherwise, there's a lot of metal kinkwear at the shop, and a distinct lack of clothes in one shot in which a very muscular man stands shirtless while forging new irons to bind someone or something. Steed is very unbothered by either. Though he does subsequently beat up the muscleman despite his superior strength.

QUOTES

"Yoga—it's a very good method of improving concentration."

"Poor little creature. I hate to think of her wandering around the countryside, unrecognized, lost, hungry." "Your sudden concern for our four-footed friends is touching but not very convincing."

"I'm going after an albino—the white elephant." "Oh really, how very interesting. I understand they're very rare. Where would you be going? India? Burma?" "I thought I might try the home counties."

"Do you really need a gun to deal with a woman?"

"Inlaid eyeballs—are they pretty valuable?"

68 (3.20.16) THE LITTLE WONDERS

Steed joins the clergy — Cathy follows a headless doll
Written by Eric Paice
Directed by Laurence Bourne

GUEST CAST

Kenneth J. Warren (Fingers), David Bauer (Bishop), Lois Maxwell (Sister Johnson), Tony Steedman (Beardmore), Harry Landis (Harry), John Cowley (Big Sid), Rosemarie Dunham (Gerda), Frank Maher (Hasek), Alex MacDonald (Porter), Mark Heath (Coalman), Christopher Robbie and Rick Jones (Thugs)

PRE-TITLE/TEASER

In a stately office, Right Reverend, the Lord Bishop of Winnipeg and his assistant Sister Johnson are warmly greeted by Mr. Beardmore. They discuss the bishop's health and Mr. Beardmore offers to examine him. With Sister Johnson's aid, he undresses, revealing that he wears a holster with a pistol about his person.

SYNOPSIS

Bibliotek, a criminal organization fronted as an international church, is planning a conference for their major members. When one of their members falls dead before arriving, Steed quickly assumes his place, leaving him open to assassination as the various 'clergymen' turn upon one another...

REVIEW

This episode contains an Anglican religious clan that's really an international summer camp for gun-toting crooks disguised as vicars. Now, *that* is a bizarre twist. In fact, "The Little Wonders" is a genuinely strong stab at some of the best surrealism attempted in the series. They all hang out in a school room, occupying children's desks. There's a 'collection period' when all the vicars remove their guns and place them on a silver platter. The organization is Bibliotek, an international crime syndicate in a crisis because their leader is dying. The result is a shakedown in which several vicars die, allowing Steed to slip into place disguised as one of them. The problem of winnowing down the field of applicants is subsequently solved by Sister Johnson (played by Bond star Lois Maxwell), who blasts away with a machine gun, killing several vicars and wounding Steed.

The subplot involves top secrets on microfilm being smuggled to buyers via china dolls for £20,000 each—the process is organized by a 'doll hospital.' (Shades of *North by Northwest*.) And in a reveal to the audience, the crooks immediately smash the head of a valuable doll after promising Cathy that they'll take care of it. It turns out that they want to replace the head in order to put the microfilm inside.

This is another great episode for Cathy Gale, who easily dispatches a thug at the doll hospital with judo and later Sister Johnson by pistol but also has to endure a smooch from Steed while pretending to be his girlfriend.

What this episode lacks is a good diabolical mastermind, but it does have a very unusual femme fatale in the form of Sister Johnson, who turns out to be a threat to virtually everyone. It's very entertaining, perhaps all the more notable as something of a template for the construction of future episodes once the series moved to film the following year.

CHAMPAGNE, CARS, CLOTHES, AND CANINES

Steed wears his black three-piece suit, then the dark-gray three-piece with the lapeled waistcoat, and then a vicar's outfit with dog collar, which he subsequently combines with the dark-gray suit, black bowler and umbrella.

Mrs. Gale wears her charcoal-gray blazer jacket and skirt, and later, the pale mackintosh, and then, a magnificent tailored black leather coat that flares at the hips. Also, her charcoal-gray collarless suit with the high-collared gray dotted silk blouse returns. Her leather fighting suit of the week is the Edwardian chauffeur-inspired jacket with two columns of black stud buttons and matching leather trousers.

QUOTES

"I said, go in peace, Reverend, and I mean it."

"The settling of internal differences is both traditional and honorable, but I will not tolerate massacre from another gang."

"I'm afraid not, Bishop. You're due for defrocking anyway."

"You and your lady friend could live like kings for the rest of your life." "Thank you, but I prefer the simpler life."

"Whoops!—mind the vicar of Towamba."

69 (3.19.17) THE WRINGER

Steed is sentenced as a traitor — Cathy helps to brainwash him

Written by Martin Woodhouse

Directed by Don Leaver

GUEST CAST

Peter Sallis (Hal Anderson), Paul Whitsun-Jones (Charles), Barry Letts (Oliver), Gerald Sim (Lovell), Terence Lodge (The Wringer), Neil Robinson (Bethune), Douglas Cummings (Murdo)

PRE-TITLE/TEASER

A man sleeps on a train on a rainy night. As he sleeps, he hears a mysterious voice, perhaps in his dreams, speaking Italian.[6] Suddenly, he is startled awake and a photo of John Steed falls from the folder in his lap.

SYNOPSIS

After six agents have died in an espionage "pipeline" on the Austro-Hungarian border, Charles assigns Steed to investigate fellow agent and friend Hal Anderson, who vanished six weeks ago on the same assignment. Steed tracks Anderson to Scotland. Unexpectedly, Anderson presents Charles with overwhelming evidence that it was Steed who murdered the agents. Charles sends Steed to an

---

6 This is very hard to make out because of all the train noise, but he says: "Ciao, aspetta momento. Non dice niente. Credevo che ho ascoltato. No c'e niente. Niente." Translation: "Hi, wait a minute. Don't say anything. I thought that I heard. No, it's nothing. Nothing." And then the train noise becomes so great that nothing is clearly audible, but the script continues: "Nessuno. Ma cinque giorni. Sono venuto qui la sera. Io lo so. Anche, so come tu sia trattata da lui. Ma adesso sono venuto per accompagnarti a Milano. Va bene? Is okay? Okay? Sst! Guardi—" describing a possible clandestine meeting in Milan.

interrogation camp run by a man called the Wringer, who is willing to use any means necessary to find the truth...

REVIEW

A remarkably good episode with a hardboiled spy feel that exceeds even that which is typical for *The Avengers* during this period, not a surprise given Don Leaver's direction. In deference to later seasons, the producers in this era were not averse to diversity, exploring a broad number of subjects and styles—in this case, the subject is the (suspected) traitorous spy being grilled for information. Steed and Mrs. Gale are split up, with one on the inside being tortured and the other outside trying to convince Steed's superiors that he's innocent.

The Wringer is an interesting character, albeit somewhat miscast with the wiry, weedy Terence Lodge. His obvious self-absorption is worsened by his quoting the works of Ludwig Wittgenstein and other philosophers, whose wisdom he deftly distorts into untruth in order to suit his purposes. He is this episode's attempt at O'Brien, plucked straight from Orwell's ***Nineteen Eighty-Four***. In spite of this, he seldom manages to seem truly threatening amid his inane grins and hipster beatnik speak.

Despite a next-to-nothing budget, resulting in several sets wobbling noticeably, the library of projected film clips—designed to psychologically wear Steed down in his cell—are effectively used on the cramped interiors, creating an atmosphere that conveys the claustrophobia and isolation quite well. It's also yet another great example of John Steed's resilience and ingenuity under fire, resulting in the humiliation and deposing of his own boss. Silly Charles! He should have known better than to go against the hero of this story.

CHAMPAGNE, CARS, CLOTHES, AND CANINES

Mrs. Gale's collarless black suit returns, this time with a white scarf and a tricolor striped leather flowerpot hat (white at the brim, gray in the middle, and darkest at the top), worn with the collarless charcoal-gray suit, and later, the charcoal-gray blazer jacket and skirt with the sleeveless gray silk, spotted blouse. But the real stunner this episode is her black leather ball gown with a full-length cloak with green satin lining.

Steed starts out in his navy-blue chalk-striped suit, and he is fitted for a new suit while wearing the waistcoat—not something you'd be likely to see in the filmed era of the series. He then wears hunting gear, with a diagonal leather belt over his right shoulder, a thickly-knit woolen jumper, and a fur-lined leather hat, getting terribly wet in the process. Upon return to headquarters, he wears the black three-piece suit until he's forced to go through the 'Wringer' mostly wearing a gray shirt with epaulettes and the sleeves rolled up. With everything wrapped up, he returns to his dark-gray three-piece suit with the lapeled waistcoat.

Both he and Mrs. Gale get horribly muddy in their escape, her in her pale mackintosh. Lucky her! But she also injures her arm which requires that she wear a sling (which, of course, is also black leather)—over which she wears her leather coat (from "The Little Wonders").

QUOTES

"They're our rules. We make them and occasionally we break them. That's our privilege, Mrs. Gale."

"The picture Anderson's file draws of Steed doesn't sound like the Steed I know. That means either you're wrong or I've been very stupid." "We are not wrong." "Then, I better know just how stupid I've been, hadn't I?"

70 (3.21.18) MANDRAKE

Steed pulls crackers to help Cathy unearth a grisly racket
Written by Roger Marshall
Directed by Bill Bain

GUEST CAST

John Le Mesurier (Dr. Macombie), George Benson (Reverend Wyper), Madge Ryan (Eve Turner), Philip Locke (Roy Hopkins), Annette André (Judy), Robert Morris (Benson), Jackie Pallo (Sexton)

PRE-TITLE/TEASER

John Steed attends a funeral at a very rainy St. Alban's Tinbey Parish Church cemetery. The ceremony ends and the other attendees depart, but Steed stays and places a wreath of flowers on the casket.

SYNOPSIS

Steed attends the funeral, in Cornwall, of a retired agent and notices a surprising number of recent burials. Steed and Mrs. Gale investigate a murder-for-hire scheme by "Mandrake Investments," who arrange for poisoned corpses to be buried in a churchyard where the heavy arsenic levels of the soil hide the nefarious truth of the victims' deaths...

REVIEW

A strong episode typical of this season with some of the best writing and dialogue so far but production-quality that is frequently a letdown, what with wobbly sets and muffled audio. Roger Marshall frequently wrote some of the best episodes of the series in this early videotaped era, and in this case, he does not disappoint. The scheme to use soil poisoned by industry to cover up a murder racket is ingenious and fits *The Avengers* proforma very well.

This particular episode was also famous in its day for Honor Blackman accidentally knocking out the wrestler (and stuntman) Jackie Pallo during a live-to-tape fight scene. The episode also contains one of the earliest and most notable examples of Steed fighting with an umbrella, disarming one of the crooks and parting him from his gun—a foreshadowing of things to come.

CHAMPAGNE, CARS, CLOTHES, AND... CAMERAS!

Steed opens the episode wearing a trench coat at a funeral in the rain—he's almost unrecognizable! Then, he's quickly on to his tan heavy overcoat and spotted gray ascot, with the old reliable dark-gray three-piece with the lapeled waistcoat underneath, black bowler and umbrella. His gray Prince of Wales blazer reappears with the dark waistcoat. He also wears the navy chalk-stripe suit with a white shirt, a gray floral tie and silver tiepin, and a black bowler.

Mrs. Gale begins the episode wearing her charcoal-gray stretch jersey jumper, leather trousers and boots; the trousers are later switched out for a leather skirt. She also debuts a new black leather mackintosh with the leather newsboy cap and leather boots in the graveyard where she takes photographs, and even her camera is a stylish Zeiss Ikon Contax IIa (or maybe the II) 35mm rangefinder which comes in its own leather case—so apparently she'd abandoned her Leica III for the competitor.[7]

She switches out for her charcoal-gray wool blazer suit with oversized buttons and leather boots in the second act. During the famous fight scene with Jackie Pallo in the church cemetery she wears

---

7 Indeed, the Contax II and IIa had a number of improvements, such as a faster shutter speed and a single viewfinder for both composing and focusing.

her double-fronted leather jacket with the stud buttons up the right side and matching trousers. Mysteriously, by the time she's in the church speaking with the vicar, her outfit has changed to the Edwardian chauffeur-inspired leather fighting suit. I can only presume the fight scene necessitated a garment change, and the two suits do look very similar. She again wears her black leather mac with a print blouse or scarf to the funeral at the end.

In the first act, Robert Morris performs his entire scene shirtless, certainly not something that you'd see in later seasons.

QUOTES

"They do a rattling good trade for a ghost village!"
"As far as I'm concerned, Mr. Hopkins, you're just another tradesman."
"Ah, that's better. The world's too harsh unless you see it through tobacco smoke."
"Of course not. We have the most discreet crackers in the business."

71 (3.14.19) THE SECRETS BROKER

Written by Ludovic Peters
Directed by Jonathan Alwyn

GUEST CAST

Avice Landon (Mrs. Wilson), Jack May (Waller), Ronald Allen (Allan Paignton), John Stone (Frederick Paignton), Patricia English (Marion Howard), John Ringham (Cliff Howard), Brian Hankins (Jim Carey), Jennifer Wood (Julia Wilson), Valentino Musetti (as 'Valentino Mussetti') (Bruno)

PRE-TITLE/TEASER

At a séance with a small group of people in an audience, a woman speaks to spirits and reveals messages from the "other side." During the course of the séance, a man retrieves a small box and leaves; once outside, he reveals that it contains a pistol.

SYNOPSIS

The Paignton brothers are involved in a conspiracy that implicates them. The schemers include a fake spiritualist, her violent mother and a wine merchant. Steed and Mrs. Gale are on the case, but it's not going anywhere…

REVIEW

This story has some highly palatable aspects to it, despite the usual low-grade production quality of the era. The drawbacks of videotaped 405-line visuals on cramped sets will no doubt challenge modern viewers more in this particular episode than in others—the sets are largely limited to a wine cellar and a small meeting room. This limitation is due mainly to an overly complex plot and a series of set pieces that never truly hang together by the end, though they are individually entertaining.

Ronald Allen and Patricia English are doing a fine job as the two lovers, and they form one of the more believable aspects of the story. Avice Landone as Mrs. Wilson is as slick a blackmailer as ever depicted on television, and she will instantly create antipathy with the viewer as she uses Luciferic-inspired emotionally-manipulative speech throughout. Thusly, unlike in the earlier episode "Warlock," the clairvoyance and séance used by this episode's practitioners are of course fake and part of a scam, with the antagonist relying instead on conman tactics to get the job done.

Waller uses a swordstick in his climatic fight with Steed (as did Benson in "One for the Mortuary"), which may have inspired the production crew to include a sword in Steed's umbrella in later seasons. (Another example of stylistic foreshadowing. Steed himself would later use a swordstick in "Small Game for Big Hunters.") This season was after all building the format that is typically recognized as *The Avengers* today, and throughout it we see all the elements, usually piecemeal from one episode to the next. However, for the moment, this episode largely tends to fall more in the category of the mundane, albeit with skillfully executed writing, direction and acting.

CHAMPAGNE, CARS, CLOTHES, AND CANINES

Mrs. Gale starts out in a sleeveless dot dress with a matching cravat (it's the same fabric as the dress that first appeared in "November 5"). She later adds the charcoal-gray blazer suit and skirt (from "Second Sight"), the spotted gray silk blouse from earlier, and the red wool flowerpot hat (from "November 5"). She soon retrieves her Starke leather overcoat with black-and-white fur lining (first seen in "November 5"), and her Edwardian chauffeur-inspired leather jacket with two columns of buttons and trousers (from "The Medicine Men") also appear. Her leather boatneck tunic, her charcoal-gray collarless suit and gray silk spotted blouse (not sure if it's the sleeveless one or not), and her double-fronted leather tunic with stud buttons all return.

Steed starts the episode and ends it in his black three-piece suit, with white shirt, dark-gray tie, black bowler and brolly. Arriving for a private wine-tasting, he wears his heavy tan overcoat with a dark scarf with white spots. He arrives for his wine order wearing the black shearling coat with black lining and lapels (from "The White Elephant"). His navy-blue chalk-stripe suit surfaces in the second act.

No champagne but lots of burgundy wine, so much that Steed falls down, and a whole case of Château-Grillet '53 at the end, "discreet, yet richly bodied, perhaps a little young, but of noble lineage."

QUOTES

"I thought you were supposed to be going to bed early." (as Mrs. Gale has Steed prone on the floor)
"Mind the burgundy, Mr. Waller!"
"Now, all we need is money!"

72 (3.22.20) TROJAN HORSE

Steed goes horse racing — Cathy becomes the favourite for murder
Written by Malcolm Hulke
Directed by Laurence Bourne

GUEST CAST

Basil Dignam (Major Ronald Pantling), T.P. McKenna (Tony Heuston), Derek Newark (Johnson), Arthur Pentelow (George Meadows), Geoffrey Whitehead (Rt. Hon. Lucien ffordsham), Lucinda Curtis (Ann Meadows), John Lowe (Lynton Smith), James Donnelly (Kirby), Marjorie Keys (Tote Girl)

PRE-TITLE/TEASER

Outside a horse racetrack, two bookies, little more than petty thugs, wait for George Meadows to emerge, and when he does they demand the money he owes them. When he cannot pay at once, they beat him with brass knuckles. But when he drops to the ground, apparently dead, they flee. Meadows has been feigning death, however, and smiles as he slips away.

SYNOPSIS

When Steed is assigned to ensure the security of a shah's horse, currently in the country for a season of races, he uncovers a gang of blackmailers and killers using the facilities for nefarious purposes. As George Meadows owes a high-priced bookie a large gambling debt for betting on his own horses, he cannot speak without implicating himself, so Steed sends Mrs. Gale to get an executive position within the business…

REVIEW

As is often the case during these early episodes, the scripts used have perhaps more in common with early British cop shows like *No Hiding Place* than with the version of *The Avengers* that most viewers find familiar. On the other hand, it could equally be argued that the only significant difference between the third and the fourth season is the quality of the production, greatly enhanced in one year by the celebrated decision to move to film instead of videotape. Each viewpoint has merit, suggesting that we're in a transition point just before the production values took off and about a year before the surrealism and fantasy elements went off the charts. Personally, for these reasons, my favorite season remains the fourth, simply because it has the same script quality of the third season but with the added production quality of film. Nevertheless, this says a lot about the writing in the third season, which reaches something of a zenith with many superb writers like Bian Clemens, Roger Marshall, Eric Paice, Terrance Dicks and Malcolm Hulke contributing smart and concisely-written scripts that manage to stay anchored in the real world and yet adding many of the humorous and surrealistic touches that would come to dominate in future seasons.

That said, there are some moments which might have gone over the heads of the average viewers, including one lengthy sequence in which Mrs. Gale impresses Mr. Heuston with her extensive knowledge of horserace book-making and mathematics in a quest for an undercover job in his office. She succeeds, but the viewers—unless of course horse racing fans themselves—are left dazzled by how she did it, which might have been the point. It's an incredibly stylish bluff, especially considering that we know she had just lost her race, far from winning over £9000. It's the kind of bluff that only Honor Blackman could have pulled off actually. Diana Rigg could have probably done it too, but this kind of brainy, cool and detached approach was Blackman's bread-and-butter. Later, she quickly and easily dispatches Heuston in a magnificent headlock and then coolly tells Ann to call the police. This is Blackman at her best.

This episode gives Steed a chance to show his equestrian affinity, which would not resurface until "Silent Dust," and then again in *The New Avengers* when he moves to his country estate and is frequently seen giving a fine filly a brush-down with his girlfriend-of-the-week. His responsibility for a horse named Sebastian is merely part of an undercover mission, but he must have decided to become more serious about equines in later life. Here, in a flash of the high *Avengers* style and Steed's bon vivant tendencies, he casually sits in the stables and eats a spread of caviar during a break. Politely, he offers to share with the stable hand before he knocks him out in order to receive a balcony view of the 'dope gang' meeting.

The guest cast is excellent in this story. Everyone is playing a strong character with depth. Derek Newark is good as the Cockney dope gang leader, and he has a typical Newark meltdown as he rages about being treated like a serf. T.P. McKenna makes for an appropriately slick and dimensional villain.

This is the kind of sharp and engaging early sixties drama that Britain was known for in its golden age of television—gritty and rough around the edges but smart and realist. It isn't for what *The Avengers* is best known, but it possibly should be.

CHAMPAGNE, CARS, CLOTHES, AND CANINES

Despite being around horses and stables for the bulk of the episode, Steed remains his usual dapper self. The tan overcoat with the heavily-stitched cuffs and the dark polka-dot ascot return briefly, with either the black or the navy-blue chalk-striped suit underneath. Very hard to tell. Otherwise, his dark cardigan, white shirt, and cream tweed trousers, and lots of jumpers. The tan overcoat is later replaced with the heavy weatherproofed version with padded collar but with the same ascot.

Mrs. Gale sports her gray silk sleeveless dot dress again, this time with her charcoal-gray wool blazer suit. Her collarless satin dress (from "The Medicine Men") also returns, along with her leather tunic dress worn with a black jumper (last seen in "The Secrets Broker"). Her leather flying suit of the week is the double-fronted one with stud buttons.

QUOTES

"Winnings don't last forever. You should know that."
"Oh, you could call those the dead files in there. Dead, or about to be dead."
"We train killers—highly professional murderers—and you're part of the organization whether you like it or not."
"I'm sick and tired of being treated like a serf!"

73 (3.11.21) BUILD A BETTER MOUSETRAP

Steed visits two witches — Cathy rides a motorbike to do the ton plus ten
Written by Brian Clemens
Directed by Peter Hammond

GUEST CAST

Athene Seyler (Cynthia), Nora Nicholson (Ermyntrude), Harold Goodwin (Harris), John Tate (Colonel Wesker), Alison Seebohm (Caroline), Donald Webster (Dave), Marian Diamond (Jessy), Allan McClelland (Stigant), David Anderson (Gordon)

PRE-TITLE/TEASER

Cathy Gale rides a motorcycle through the countryside with a group of motorcyclist friends. They stop at an old barn where two women live to ask for directions. The elderly women provide the directions but are not particularly hospitable. When they find out that Cathy and her friends have permission to use the area for their cycling, one of the old women threatens to put a spell on them.

SYNOPSIS

Steed and Cathy are investigating the mysterious stoppings of mechanical devices around the vicinity of an atomic research station. The station's own clocks are stopping, and cars that are in perfect working order also cease to function. Cathy joins a local motorcycle gang whose motorcycles have also been affected. Everything seems to point to an old mill where two elderly sisters live in total solitude. Soon, the two old ladies are suspected to possess an advanced electronic device, but some crooks also have their eyes on it...

REVIEW

In one peculiarly anti-prescient line, eccentrics are referred to as "a dying breed." How ironic that such a statement would be made in the Brian Clemens story that many will regard as the most striking example of *Avengers* eccentric behavior from this era. Celebrated rather than endangered, eccentrics are not a dying breed in this episode—or in this series, for that matter. They were in fact being spotlighted by Clemens in this new template for the series that would dominate in the following season when he took creative control.

Generally, this story is a real treat. Two crackpot old ladies have somehow managed to build an electronic device capable of shutting down the modern world. In my middle-aged years, suffering from tinnitus and a vestibular disorder that drove me to writing in the first place, I can sympathize with their need for total quiet. In fact, I wouldn't mind having one of their devices. The world is now a *lot* noisier than in 1964.

The motorcycle gang is possibly an attempt for *The Avengers* to do their own tamer version of *The Wild One*, and if you ever hear references to Cathy Gale riding a motorcycle, then this is the episode. Many people today, on both sides of the Atlantic, may not realize that there was a fairly extensive motorcycle culture in London (and throughout England) during this time period, one that was ultimately mitigated by the eventual enforcement of speed limits within the City.[8] The flipside of this historical footnote is that the series is, of course, playing with the image of the stereotypical old lady as they fight to end the noise pollution of this horrid new trend of motorcycling—tilting against the windmills of the modern world. It's a humorous sight to see Cynthia, face covered in soot from a prior mishap, as she tinkers away on a mechanical box with spinning cogs and flashing lights. The image is that of a modern witch—albeit with modern mechanics not spells—and this perception is conjured up on several occasions, including the opening scene in which the sisters threaten to put a spell on the motorcycle enthusiasts. Basically, these are among the first real *Avengers* eccentrics.

Unfortunately, the prohibitive cost of extensive location filming at this point in the series' history prevents the episode from utilizing the motorcycles to much advantage. Consequently, the scenes involving them are generally the most uninteresting in the episode. Far too many scenes begin with the sound of a motorcycle dubbed in before someone walks onto a cramped set that is mostly filled with the bikers and their girlfriends dancing to early sixties beat music. This was a limitation of the technology of the era and a common problem that would be solved in less than a year.

One engaging factor however is Caroline's apparent interest in Steed, which ultimately turns out to be a ruse in order to drug him. The plot is something of a muddle and the jamming device a bust, but it's fun. And Steed's line at the finale is one of the best of the series, referring to the effectiveness of Cynthia's mousetrap after it explodes on the would-be thief—a cute final touch to a charming but flawed episode.

CHAMPAGNE, CARS, CLOTHES, AND CANINES

This episode is all about Mrs. Gale's biker outfit. She fits right in with the rest of the ton-ten gang wearing her leather vest with studded buttons, a black jumper, black trousers, and black boots, plus the biker helmet (with an S lightning bolt logo) and gloves. Perhaps trying to stay slightly more casual in order to better relate to the gang, Steed spends most of his time in his gray Prince of Wales blazer over a cardigan with hard leather buttons and a dark patterned tie. It almost works. It's also worn without the cardigan. He later gets some wine at their secret club. No champagne though, just lots of soda pop. He also wears a quite unusual brown-and-black checked blazer (reads as almost

---

8 I'm a major fan of the work of British neurologist and author Oliver Sacks, who recounted his involvement in the motorcycle cultures of both the United States and the United Kingdom, as well as the various motorcycles he owned and rode during the 1950s and 1960s. His memoir *On the Move: A Life* is highly recommended.

entirely black onscreen) over a taupe jumper with a white shirt and a coppery-yellow knit tie. This is the only appearance of this outfit in the series.

Motorcycles seen in the episode include: a BSA A7, a 1958 BSA A-Series (possibly the same motorcycle), 1960 BSA A10 Super Rocket, 1958 Triumph Speed Twin, and an unknown year and model of Royal Enfield. Cathy's motorcycle is a 1961 Triumph Speed Twin (987 CAA) with a windscreen. The filming for the motorcycle scenes was done at dusk or nighttime[9], so it can be very difficult to identify the bikes. Some more of the registration numbers seen during the episode are 643 TPK and (the slightly humorous) 304 JNK. These latter two appear to be more Triumph Speed Twins with their characteristic side-facing front fender plates.

QUOTES

"Genuine eccentrics are a dying breed...could be amusing."
"Booby prize for our Mrs. Gale. You're the last in. I suspect you could use this. Long walk back across the field, eh? Pretty muddy."
"My cause is for the world, for its betterment. That's why I feel a sense of purpose. That's why I cannot brook any interruptions. None whatever."
"It seems to be equally effective with the larger rodents."

74 (3.23.22) THE OUTSIDE-IN MAN

Steed plots murder — Cathy tries to stop him
Written by Philip Chambers
Directed by Jonathon Alwyn

GUEST CAST

Ronald Radd (Quilpie), James Maxwell (Mark Charter), William Devlin (Ambassador), Basil Hoskins (Major Zulficar), Beryl Baxter (Helen Rayner), Arthur Lovegrove (Michael Lynden), Virginia Stride (Alice), Philip Anthony (Sharp), Anthony Dawes (Edwards), Ronald Mansell (Jenkins), Valentino Musetti, Eddie Powell (Guards), Paul Blomley (Butcher)

PRE-TITLE/TEASER

John Steed appears at the butcher's asking for venison. He and the butcher, who turns out to be Quilpie, Steed's new superior, banter for a few moments as Steed is taken to a secret office at the back of the shop and is given his next mission.

SYNOPSIS

A former Briton named Sharp is a traitor and a revolutionary who is negotiating arms talks in England. Steed is assigned to protect him. In an amazing moment of coincidence, Mark Charter, an agent originally assigned to kill Sharp five years ago and thought to have died in the attempt, arrives on the scene. Fearing that Charter, after five years in prison, may wish to continue his failed mission,

---

9 In a famous dusk photoshoot taken during on-location filming, Patrick Macnee is seen with Honor Blackman on a Royal Enfield motorcycle (not the one she rides in the episode). He is wearing a white shirt, a mustard-yellow cardigan, and a long dark blazer, with the black bowler and umbrella. Presumably, this was Macnee visiting during the filming since he wasn't required for these scenes in the episode. He does however ride on the back of a motorcycle with Donald Webster (as Dave) in the studio recording.

Steed and Cathy must find and stop Charter before he ruins the arms talks...

REVIEW

Slow-paced but entertaining, "The Outside-In Man" features mundane spy issues with very minor touches of the bizarre interspersed throughout. I will say that it certainly manages to set an even pace. Never once was I in danger of having my neck snapped by a violent acceleration of plot exposition. Speaking of violence, there is precious little action as well.

Another of Steed's mysterious leaders is introduced: Quilpie, the first since One-Ten and Charles disappeared. His office is hidden behind the cold room in a butcher shop. As Quilpie, Ronald Radd makes another fine appearance and brings the character suitably to life. Mrs. Gale is once again apparently left out of Steed's scheme, forcing her to operate as something of a free radical. This is likely Steed's idea, using her to stir things up. She has a typical Mrs. Gale moral indignation scene when confronting Helen Raynor, and her courage is astonishing as she stands right in front of the would-be assassin's gun.

All in all, a decent script but not one that stands out in particular from the remainder of the season. Although it fails to have anything of what many fans will expect from *The Avengers*, it does manage to be reasonably engaging.

CHAMPAGNE, CARS, CLOTHES, AND CANINES

Mrs. Gale starts out in full leather fighting suit, the Edwardian chauffeur-inspired leather one with the two columns of buttons, as she lounges about in Steed's flat. Steed is in his magnificent black three-piece suit with a pinstriped white shirt and gray knit tie; then, he wears the weatherproofed tan overcoat with padded collar while Mrs. Gale brings out her leather fur-lined overcoat and later the double-fronted leather suit with stud buttons. Steed's navy chalk-stripe suit makes an appearance, and Mrs. Gale wears her pinafore dress with a pleated blouse. She also debuts a new pale-gray twill top with a white cotton collar (or possibly a blouse underneath) and flared-back cuffs, worn with charcoal-gray slacks. Steed's black jacket with silver buttons also makes for an appearance as he reads the Tintin book *The Secret of the Unicorn*.

QUOTES

"You don't know what it's like to be made a widow." "Yes, I do."
"I had to let Mrs. Gale do the donkey work in case either of us were being followed."
"They know my face from a little blood-bath on the border about four years ago."

75 (3.24.23) THE CHARMERS

Steed goes to charm school — Cathy joins forces with the opposition
Written by Brian Clemens
Directed by Bill Bain

GUEST CAST

Fenella Fielding (Kim Lawrence), Warren Mitchell (Keller), Brian Oulton (Mr. Edgar), Vivian Pickles (Betty Smythe), John Barcroft (Martin), Malcolm Russell (Horace Cleeves), Frank Mills (Harrap), John Greenwood (Sam), Peter Porteous (Vinkel)

PRE-TITLE/TEASER

At a fencing studio, two men agree to spar for practice, but after a brief few rounds of sparring, one man stabs the other fatally.

SYNOPSIS

An enemy agent from behind the iron curtain is killed, and Steed gets the blame. When Steed is exonerated, he and Mrs. Gale split up to work with the other side and discover the real murderer. With Mrs. Gale working with a Soviet agent and Steed receiving a 'partner' in return, the two teams find that all clues lead to a charm school that is producing assassins disguised as perfect gentleman...

REVIEW

This is a wonderfully well-scripted episode with first-class comedy in the classic style of *The Avengers*. With its strong emphasis on bowler hats, sword-umbrellas, and the old-world gentry, "The Charmers" is a kind of trial run for the fourth and fifth seasons. And again, Brian Clemens is leading the charge. I can imagine Steed picking up one of those sword-umbrellas on his way out and using it in the title sequence two seasons later.

Sporting great lines and subtle Shakespearean references, this is one of the best Cathy Gale stories and one of Brian Clemens' better scripts. It's no wonder it was chosen to be remade in color as "The Correct Way to Kill."[10] I say this frequently enough—and I admit it's not always very fair—but this is such a good story that it deserves much better than the rather lackluster production it is afforded here. Nevertheless, the lowly production standards, so typical of the era, are worth ignoring for such a superb story.

Many of the characters are enormous fun, especially Fenella Fielding as Kim Lawrence, the aspiring actress and knife-thrower extraordinaire, and Warren Mitchell as Keller the nasal inhaler-addicted double agent. In another example of the show's bizarre mastermind locations, Keller operates out of a basement armory adorned with nude mannequins—nude, that is, except for bullet belts draped like baldrics across their chests.

We also have one of our earliest appearances of the classic eccentric in Horace Cleeves at the executive tie shop. Mr. Edgar at the Academy of Charm is also a wonderful character, and the Academy itself is a classically wacky *Avengers* organization, taking something that should be so natural and turning it into a military maneuver. Steed and Mrs. Gale have another blowup over his manipulations which produces Steed's usual great cheer and Cathy's resentment. Perhaps this is building up to her inevitable departure? Nevertheless, she agrees for the time being to work with the enemy agent Martin.

In many ways, all of this story's breakthroughs would be amped up for the remake during the fifth season—by which time the eccentrics, humor, bizarreness and whimsy would all be crystallized for color film—but this version works great merely on story, dialogue, humor and great characterization, which is what the third season does so well.

CHAMPAGNE, CARS, CLOTHES, AND CANINES

Steed starts right out where he left off in the prior episode—in his black jacket with silver buttons, this time with a white shirt and an Eton tie. I've so warmed to this jacket over the season I wouldn't mind one myself. The tan weatherproofed overcoat with padded collar returns. Later also his dark-gray three-piece with the lapeled waistcoat, with the return of the dark diagonally-striped tie. And yet his navy chalk-striped suit becomes the suit of the day before yielding to the black three-piece

---

10 Instead of a photo of Mrs. Peel with the words "Very dangerous, do not handle at all" on the back we have a reference to Mrs. Gale being #2 on their most-wanted listed after 'J.B.' Now, I wonder who that could be?

suit with the white pinstriped shirt and gray knit tie.

Mrs. Gale returns to her pale-gray twill top with white collar (from "The Outside-In Man"). Her boatneck leather tunic dress also makes an appearance. She wears her black leather mackintosh even to the dentist! Then, the charcoal-gray collarless suit with a pale silk scarf, followed by the pale mackintosh, and finally, of course, she wears a white fencing uniform.

QUOTES

"Alas, poor George." "You knew him?" "I knew him well. Georgie Brinkel, he's one of their top agents. He's funny. He's the second one they've bumped off this month."
"Very well, Colonel, very well. We will infiltrate the horse guards. Perhaps with a horse."
"I thought you'd jump at the chance, working cheek by jowl with Martin." "My cheek is going nowhere near his jowl!"
"But you're a sly, cunning, devious, scheming—" "Splendid. I'll let them in. Happy smiles. I want them to like you."
"She was a sweet old lady. Terribly good with a knife. And stamina. Did you know she went on working until she was eighty-nine?"
"Half-a-loaf is better than low bred."
"It would do you little use, Miss Lawrence. The bonds of the old school tie are well-nigh impossible to break."

76 (3.1.24) CONCERTO

Steed spars with an old opponent — Cathy protects a young pianist
Written by Terrance Dicks and Malcolm Hulke
Directed by Kim Mills

GUEST CAST

Nigel Stock (Zalenko), Sandor Eles (Stefan Veliko), Dorinda Stevens (Darleen), Bernard Brown (Peterson), Geoffrey Colvile (Burns), Carole Ward (Receptionist), Valerie Bell (Polly White), Leslie Glazer (Robbins) and Junia

PRE-TITLE/TEASER

As Cathy Gale departs having visited Veliko at his apartment, another woman arrives claiming to have an appointment to interview the famous concert pianist. Cathy explains that Veliko is practicing at the moment but suggests that she wait. Once the woman is alone, however, she immediately tears her own blouse and dishevels her hair before calling reception claiming she was sexually assaulted. When the hotel manager arrives and hears her story, he says he'll "deal with the matter straight away" and then immediately strangles her.

SYNOPSIS

A young woman is found dead inside the apartment of a visiting Soviet concert pianist—Stefan Veliko. Clues lead Steed to a strip club and Mrs. Gale to the British Cultural Council. Eventually, the death is revealed to be part of a plot to blackmail Veliko into committing a murder that will end British-Soviet trade talks. But the revelation puts Cathy into an unpleasant situation involving a gun and only one bullet…

REVIEW

This is another fine story, this time from the highly competent pens of Terrance Dicks and Malcolm Hulke, two screenwriters who frequently collaborated during this era. "Concerto" is nicely scripted with some particularly nasty violence, including Mrs. Gale being interrogated via a harrowing game of one-sided Russian roulette and Steed bashing in a man's brains with a telephone. There are also some seedy elements that you wouldn't find in the fourth or fifth season, such as Steed visiting a strip club called Le Stud Club, as well as some rather unsavory strippers and blackmailers, both professional and amateur. Those who might feel inclined to dismiss the Cathy Gale series as not being classic *Avengers* will be missing out on a much more gritty and realistic series.

There are wonderful performances all around, especially from Honor Blackman in a terrifying interrogation situation. Steed sympathetically gives her a brandy afterwards. And she drinks it! Despite the fact that this episode was held back in the transmission order for almost a year, the writers seem to be setting up Mrs. Gale's imminent departure, in which she, fatigued by Steed's manipulations and stressed by events like her torture session, finally refuses to do any further work for him. This might be the reason for the broadcast delay. Steed's suit also matches the previous episode, and this is the second time in a row that an agent from the other side—Zalenko—is a friend of Steed's. Zalenko makes an astonishing breaking-the-fourth-wall reference to the show itself when he claims he has learned his martial arts moves from watching British television. Effectively, Cathy Gale is his instructor!

As it approached its finale, the third season was on a roll and yet setting up for major changes, the hints for which had already been dispersed over the previous few episodes.

CHAMPAGNE, CARS, CLOTHES, CANINES, AND... CAMERAS!

Mrs. Gale starts out right away with her tricolor vertical-striped blouse and tailored jacket and skirt (first seen in "The Golden Eggs" and first paired this way in "Six Hands Across a Table") with the black porkpie hat, so this would have been the debut of this complete ensemble in production order. However, in transmission order, this is the last appearance of the porkpie, which had been part of her signature look throughout Season Two and the early part of Season Three, and it appears this late in the season because "Concerto" was the first episode recorded. Later the same outfit is paired with the Starke cloak with the tartan on the inside, and no hat or jacket. Soon this is replaced by a new cream-colored coat much in the same style as the Mary Quant cape with enormous cloth-covered buttons and arm slits instead of sleeves. She wears her white frill-fronted blouse with the gold satin vest and charcoal knee-length skirt (first seen in "Man with Two Shadows") and then the deep-blue satin dress with Napoleonic facings.

Steed wears his navy chalk-striped suit (which would be its first appearance in production order), and this is his ensemble until he wears his tan overcoat with heavy-stitching on the sleeves (from Season One), with the patterned ascot (from "Intercrime" and "Box of Tricks"). Given the subject matter, naturally he finishes off in black tie, which he was apparently wearing under the overcoat and ascot all along. The black fedora also returns.

Steed's Great Dane makes a guest appearance and remains unnamed. In transmission order, this is the last appearance of any of Steed's dogs for a very long time. During the filmed era, it seems the production team decided to simplify things, and perhaps canines on set didn't fit in with their quirky vision for Steed.

Veliko is photographed with a 35mm rangefinder camera of some type, but the shadows are too deep and the video quality too low to properly identify the model. If I were to guess it would be a Zorki 1, given that the agents are supposed to be Soviet.

QUOTES

"I have been a member of the British Cultural Council ever since I came back from Africa, and this is the first time they've asked me to do anything on this scale." "They've finally recognized your potential!"

"And where did you learn that particular piece of nastiness?" "Saturday afternoons, British television, last time I was here...you should watch."

"I'm a newly pledged member. Paid my twenty-five quid, and I want to see that little little girl undo that little ole golden chain." "She's not here tonight. Now, you go along home. You'll wake the neighbors." "No, I'm going to come inside."

77 (3.25.25) ESPRIT DE CORPS

Steed faces the firing squad — Cathy becomes pretender to the throne

Written by Eric Paice

Directed by Don Leaver

GUEST CAST

Duncan MacRae (Brigadier General Sir Ian Stuart-Bollinger), Joyce Heron (Lady Dorothy Stuart-Bollinger), Roy Kinnear (Private Jessop), John Thaw (Captain Trench), Pearl Catlin (Mrs. Craig), Douglas Robinson (Sergeant Marsh), Hugh Morton (Admiral), Anthony Blackshaw (Private Asquith), James Falkland (Signaller), George Alexander (Piper), Tony Lambden (Drummer), George MacRae (Highland Dancer)

PRE-TITLE/TEASER

At an inspection of the Highland Guards, Private Jessop is put on report for dandruff, and then the soldiers execute a man by firing squad before marching off to bagpipe music.

SYNOPSIS

Corporal Craig of the Highland Guards has apparently been murdered, and the bullets that killed him came from three different rifles. Steed and Cathy investigate and discover that the death was an execution for treason. Soon, a plot to take over the government and replace the Windsors with a descendent of the Stuart royal line is revealed, and, as a result, Cathy may soon be crowned as Queen Anne II...

REVIEW

This is a lovely story that manages to be surprisingly funny through a façade of macabre qualities. It's another fine script from Eric Paice and works amazingly well. Sadly, Paice would be one of the writers that would be dropped from the roster by producers Fennell and Clemens for future seasons.

It's an amusingly absurd idea that the Scots could in 1964 still be harboring a grudge against the British royal family for the deliberate bypassing of the Stuart line and the snubbing of Bonnie Prince Charles in 1745. It's so absurd that it's probably true. At least, I'm almost convinced by this episode.

It all begins with a surprising pre-title scene in which an apparent Steed lookalike is shot by firing squad in a Scottish regiment. Foreshadowing? This particular regiment does indeed seem to have almost a firing squad fetish. They love a good ceremonial shooting. With a significant dose of historical drama mixed in with dark humor and the additional location footage, the clear arc towards the future of *The Avengers* continues as this episode sets the stage for the fourth season. And it's easy to see this story could have been done on film with Diana Rigg instead of Honor Blackman as part of the following year's complement, although Blackman's regality is probably better suited for the impersonation of a queen.

Honor Blackman continues to be an exceptionally strong performer right up to the finish line in this sterling season, and for the time being, it must have seemed impossible for viewers to imagine anyone else alongside Steed. Indeed, Cathy throwing her 'royal' weight around, both in the martial arts classes and the throne room, is well worth the price of admission.

This marks Roy Kinnear's first of four guest-starring roles for *The Avengers*, and the scenes between Private Jessup and Steed are wonderful; the two actors display an abundance of chemistry, and it's no wonder Kinnear was invited back so many times.

CHAMPAGNE, CARS, CLOTHES, AND CANINES

Steed appears at the launderette in a full overcoat and seems completely befuddled by a coin-operated washing machine. Later, he's back in his Prince of Wales blazer with a dark waistcoat. The navy chalk-stripe also makes a return appearance. Steed also dons a tuxedo in this episode at a party, and Mrs. Gale joins him in the charcoal-gray collarless boat-neck satin dress (first seen in "The Medicine Men"). In the second act, leopard print returns to Mrs. Gale's wardrobe for the first time since Season Two, but this time in a full fur coat instead of a vest. As "queen," she wears her gold lamé dress with the green satin-lined cape, and she indeed looks very royal. The pale-gray twill top with white collar (from "The Outside-In Man") makes its final appearance in the first act. The leather fighting suit of the week is the double-fronted with the stud buttons.

QUOTES

"Oh, so, I'm related to your adopted son?" "More than that. It means you're second-in-line of succession to the Scottish throne."

"If you're going to open that, you'd better be quick—I'm going to be shot in half an hour."

"He thinks I'm Queen Anne II. If you'd been around, you'd have gotten an invitation to my coronation."

"If I'd known I would go in front of a firing squad, I would have applied to you for a royal pardon."

"Those lineage charts were fake, General. I arranged it with the curator."

78 (3.26.26) LOBSTER QUADRILLE

Steed goes fishing — Cathy hunts a knight
Written by Richard Lucas
Directed by Kim Mills

GUEST CAST

Leslie Sands (Captain Slim), Burt Kwouk (Mason), Gary Watson (Bush), Jennie Linden (Katie), Norman Scace (Dr. Stannage), Corin Redgrave (Quentin Slim), Valentino Musetti (as 'Valentino Musseti') (Jackson)

PRE-TITLE/TEASER

Two fishermen in a quiet fishing shack somewhere on the coast discuss whether a journalist will show up or not. One of them reveals that he did indeed turn up earlier and apparently had considerable knowledge of their plans. The journalist, with a bowler hat and umbrella, now lies dead on the floor. The fishermen decide to destroy the evidence and throw a lit oil lantern into a nearby pile of straw, setting the shack on fire.

SYNOPSIS

An agent is killed while investigating an increased level of radioactivity in seafood. This attracts Steed and Cathy to the scene, and they uncover a plot by a man named Quentin Slim, who was thought to be dead and is now smuggling drugs. Will Cathy survive the revelation when the pyromaniacal Quentin sets fire to the hut where she is held captive...?

REVIEW

The story starts with a pre-title of two men setting fire to a cabin, destroying the evidence of their crime, a third man lying dead on the floor. This is about as exciting as it gets in this awkward season finale. Such as it is, this is a slow-moving story with only a reasonable script and relatively lackluster direction. "Lobster Quadrille" is only really significant for one reason, the fact that it is Honor Blackman's final episode as Cathy Gale. Fans of Cato from the ***Pink Panther*** films may take exception to that last statement, and I will admit that the episode's other minor plus is the appearance of Burt Kwouk, who does indeed distinguish himself as an authentic and interesting Asian character. But that really is about it.

Incidentally, barring Diana Rigg's disappointing departure episode, this is the closest to a write-out of a major character that the series received. Granted, that's not saying a lot. Dr. Keel, Venus Smith, Dr. Martin King, Tara King, Gambit and Purdey all came and went and never even came close to a departure scene, unless you count Tara and Steed engaging in a backyard space program and blasting off into orbit (and television limbo). I suppose it's more realistic to not contrive a departure scene. Spies should come and go as needed. One of the problems of "The Forget-Me-Knot" was that it was contrived in its burning need to make it clear that Mrs. Peel was leaving and Ms. King was taking over. Here, we get a subtle hint and off Mrs. Gale goes, never to return, leaving Steed to pick up that little black book and call another female helper. Personally, I think I prefer it that way. No messy mushiness, no marry-offs, no forced melodramatic deaths, just away you go, out with the old and in with the new. How very nice and tidy!

It is disappointing however that they decided to send Cathy off with such a banal story, written by a one-time writer for the show and directed by the show's least skillful director. Even the famous but ubiquitous Dankworth music largely seems to disappear, replaced mostly with stock music and long periods sans music, particularly in the first half. As much as I have tired of Dankworth's music by this time, fragments of Béla Bartók are no substitute for the swing jazz that drives most of the series. "Lobster Quadrille" is no feast of a finale, more like a bland digestif at the end of one. Fortunately, looking back, the third season was indeed the rich meal.

CHAMPAGNE, CARS, CLOTHES, AND CANINES

Fashion-wise, like the rest of it, this episode is rather unremarkable. Mrs. Gale's leather mackintosh, charcoal-gray collarless suit and gray silk dotted blouse, pale mackintosh, and pinafore dress all re-appear. Steed's navy chalk-stripe, gray three-piece with lapeled waistcoat, and black single-breasted suits all return, and he wears his heavy pale overcoat. No dogs or champagne, but there is a lobster sniffing moment from Steed.

QUOTES

"Not Confucius, please. What was wisdom to my ancestors is now mere pomposity in this enlightened age. Today we need new rules."

"You see, I'm not going to be pussy-footing along those sun-soaked shores—I'm going to be lying on them."

"Not pussy-footing? I must have been misinformed."

SEASON FOUR

26 episodes (35mm black & white film, ~52 min. ea.)

Regular Cast
Patrick Macnee—John Steed
Diana Rigg—Emma Peel

Produced by Julian Wintle
In Charge of Production: Albert Fennell
Associate Producer: Brian Clemens
Script Editor: Brian Clemens (uncredited)
Music: Laurie Johnson

79. **The Town of No Return—w.** Brian Clemens; **dir.** Roy Baker; **UK tx.** 28 Sep 1965; **US tx.** 1 Sep 1966; **filmed** Oct-Nov 1964 & Jul-Aug 1965
80. **The Grave-Diggers—w.** Malcolm Hulke; **dir.** Quentin Lawrence; **UK tx.** 7 Oct 1965; **US tx.** 4 Aug 1966; **filmed** Mar-Apr 1965
81. **The Cybernauts—w.** Philip Levene; **dir.** Sidney Hayers; **UK tx.** 14 Oct 1965; **US tx.** 28 Mar 1966; **filmed** Mar 1965
82. **Death at Bargain Prices—w.** Brian Clemens; **dir.** Charles Crichton; **UK tx.** 21 Oct 1965; **US tx.** 11 Apr 1966; **filmed** Jan-Feb 1965
83. **Castle De'ath—w.** John Lucarotti; **dir.** James Hill; **UK tx.** 28 Oct 1965; **US tx.** 2 May 1966; **filmed** Aug 1965
84. **The Master Minds—w.** Robert Banks Stewart; **dir.** Peter Graham Scott; **UK tx.** 4 Nov 1965; **US tx.** 11 Jul 1966; **filmed** Dec 1964-Jan 1965
85. **The Murder Market—w.** Tony Williamson; **dir.** Peter Graham Scott; **UK tx.** 12 Nov 1965; **US tx.** 30 May 1966; **filmed** Nov-Dec 1964
86. **A Surfeit of H_2O—w.** Colin Finbow; **dir.** Sidney Hayers; **UK tx.** 19 Nov 1965; **US tx.** —; **filmed** Apr-May 1965
87. **The Hour That Never Was—w.** Roger Marshall; **dir.** Gerry O'Hara; **UK tx.** 26 Nov 1965; **US tx.** 25 Apr 1966; **filmed** Jul 1965
88. **Dial A Deadly Number—w.** Roger Marshall; **dir.** Don Leaver; **UK tx.** 3 Dec 1965; **US tx.** 24 Jul 1966; **filmed** Jan 1965
89. **Man-Eater of Surrey Green—w.** Philip Levene; **dir.** Sidney Hayers; **UK tx.** 10 Dec 1965; **US tx.** 25 Aug 1966; **filmed** Jun 1965
90. **Two's a Crowd—w.** Philip Levene; **dir.** Roy Baker; **UK tx.** 17 Dec 1965; **US tx.** 9 May 1966; **filmed** May 1965
91. **Too Many Christmas Trees—w.** Tony Williamson; **dir.** Roy Baker; **UK tx.** 23 Dec 1965; **US tx.** 11 Aug 1966; **filmed** Feb-Mar 1965
92. **Silent Dust—w.** Roger Marshall; **dir.** Roy Baker; **UK tx.** 31 Dec 1965; **US tx.** —; **filmed** Jun-Jul 1965
93. **Room Without a View—w.** Roger Marshall; **dir.** Roy Baker; **UK tx.** 8 Jan 1966; **US tx.** 27 Jun 1966; **filmed** Apr 1965

94. **Small Game for Big Hunters**—**w.** Philip Levene; **dir.** Gerry O'Hara; **UK tx.** 15 Jan 1966; **US tx.** 4 Apr 1966; **filmed** Sep-Oct 1965
95. **The Girl from Auntie**—**w.** Roger Marshall; **dir.** Roy Baker; **UK tx.** 21 Jan 1966; **US tx.** 6 Jun 1966; **filmed** Oct 1965
96. **The Thirteenth Hole**—**w.** Tony Williamson; **dir.** Roy Baker; **UK tx.** 28 Jan 1966; **US tx.** 18 Aug 1966; **filmed** Sep 1965
97. **Quick-Quick Slow Death**—**w.** Robert Banks Stewart; **dir.** James Hill; **UK tx.** 4 Feb 1966; **US tx.** —; **filmed** Oct-Nov 1965
98. **The Danger Makers**—**w.** Roger Marshall; **dir.** Charles Crichton; **UK tx.** 11 Feb 1966; **US tx.** 4 Jul 1966; **filmed** Nov-Dec 1965
99. **A Touch of Brimstone**—**w.** Brian Clemens; **dir.** James Hill; **UK tx.** 18 Feb 1966; **US tx.** —; **filmed** Dec 1965
100. **What the Butler Saw**—**w.** Brian Clemens; **dir.** Bill Bain; **UK tx.** 25 Feb 1966; **US tx.** 28 Jul 1966; **filmed** Dec 1965-Jan 1966
101. **The House That Jack Built**—**w.** Brian Clemens; **dir.** Don Leaver; **UK tx.** 4 Mar 1966; **US tx.** 16 May 1966; **filmed** Jan 1966
102. **A Sense of History**—**w.** Martin Woodhouse; **dir.** Peter Graham Scott; **UK tx.** 11 Mar 1966; **US tx.** 20 Jun 1966; **filmed** Jan-Feb 1966
103. **How to Succeed....at Murder**—**w.** Brian Clemens; **dir.** Don Leaver; **UK tx.** 18 Mar 1966; **US tx.** 13 Jun 1966; **filmed** Feb 1966
104. **Honey for the Prince**—**w.** Brian Clemens; **dir.** James Hill; **UK tx.** 25 Mar 1966; **US tx.** —; **filmed** Feb-Mar 1966

SEASON NOTES

By videotaped standards, the first three seasons of *The Avengers* had been a smash hit. Cathy Gale, the first female superhero on television, caused a sensation, titillating viewers as she casually tossed men over her shoulder week after week. The show was an overseas sales success as well—many other countries in Europe were thrilling to the adventures of John Steed and Mrs. Gale. And the series would have been popular in the Commonwealth countries such as Canada, New Zealand, and Australia. This was all very exciting to ITV executives and Associated British Corporation. However, there was one country to which they could not sell the program—The United States. The program was shot on 405-line videotape, whereas America used the 525-line NTSC broadcast format. At that time, there was no means of converting one broadcast standard to another—the computations necessary could not be accomplished in real-time. This meant that the only way to capture the potential millions available through the American market was to shoot the entire series on film.

Aside from the technical reasons, from the American perspective, shooting on film was essential. All American television drama from the 1950s (and the time of the West coast television revolution) had been shot on 35mm film. Aside from a seventies trend of videotaping some sit-coms in multi-camera before a live studio audience that continues to this day, only soap operas, game shows, and television news were regularly shot on videotape. Thus, for the next four decades, Americans would largely cringe at any drama recorded on video, declaring that it "looks like a soap opera," which was synonymous with 'cheap' and 'low budget' both thematically and quality-wise. Although there were occasional exceptions to this rule, mostly cult hits like ***Upstairs, Downstairs,*** film was necessary in order to open up programs like *The Avengers* to the American market. This was the new mid-1960s zeitgeist for independent television in Britain and another way of competing with the BBC—film their programs and export them to America. ITC Entertainment had already established this practice with notable success—***Danger Man*** and *The Saint* were both shot on 35mm film from the outset—and now, it was *The Avengers*' turn for the luxury treatment.

Ironically, the show had begun as a mere fill-in for the failure of ***Police Surgeon***, and no one had ever imagined that the show that had been dreamt up in a few afternoon meetings by Sydney Newman and company would become this big. But would it work? ***Danger Man*** and ***The Saint*** had been deliberately given a mid-Atlantic appeal to soften the blow, but ***The Avengers*** was as British as Steed's bowler hat and Bentley.

To guide the series into the new bold era, new producers were chosen. Julian Wintle was considered a man that was strong on film, and he was there to ease the transition. Brian Clemens had been writing for the series since the first season, and few knew more about ***The Avengers*** than he did. His responsibility was for the creative side and the scripts; unofficially, he was also the script editor. Meanwhile, Albert Fennell handled the behind the scenes production tasks, keeping the production on an even keel.

Artistically, the success of the fourth season can be found in its tremendous ease and simplicity. Tensions between Steed and his former assistant would vanish, replaced by a flawless and completely relaxed relationship. Bosses and regular working hours would also dematerialize, and the players would move into action when the events they encountered mobilized them. Otherwise, they were engaged in relaxed social situations, and one is left with the perception that they were unbothered by the interruption because they secretly enjoyed their work just as much as their downtime. Nowhere else in the series is their camaraderie so in evidence than in this season. In the color series, the connection between Steed and Mrs. Peel would often be overwhelmed by the absurdity of their situations, but, here, it is front and center.

Nevertheless, the production was unlikely to have been as smooth behind the scenes as it appears on screen. There was at least one hiccup that sent the show scrambling briefly, and this centered around the character of Mrs. Peel. Eleanor Bron was originally offered the role, and when she turned it down, it was then offered to Elizabeth Shepherd, who accepted. Filming commenced in November of 1964 on the episode "The Town of No Return," on location in Wighton and Holkham, two small villages in Norfolk, England. When this episode was completed, the production moved on to "The Murder Market." It was then that producers Julian Wintle, Brian Clemens, and Albert Fennell decided something wasn't quite working. For reasons that are not entirely understood, due to the footage featuring her being lost, perceived issues with Elizabeth Shepherd's performance meant that she was dismissed from the program. From the producers' side, the point-of-view was that Shepherd wasn't capturing their intended vision of Mrs. Peel. From Shepherd's side, she was contributing ideas and engaging with them in a forthright manner that wasn't appreciated for reasons that may or may not have been (ironically) sexist in origin. Regardless of the precise reasons, Shepherd and her production team weren't gelling, and a new casting call went out.

Eleven actresses were then auditioned for the part over a period of three days before Diana Rigg was cast in a decision that Brian Clemens famously called "fait accompli." And it's easy to see why in this series. Diana Rigg steps into the part as if it was written for her and immediately establishes a brilliant and beautiful companion for John Steed, their characters melding effortlessly on screen.

The production itself would also come across as beautifully shot, frequently brilliantly scripted, and almost flawlessly executed. The ideas were simpler, filled out by the grace, humor and bizarreness so often exhibited by the eccentrics and situations that the two lead characters would encounter on a regular basis. It was said quite often in the videotaped era of television that it was a writer's medium first and foremost. Indeed, the writing on the third season was some of the best the series has ever seen with clever plots, fresh ideas and punchy dialogue. (Casual viewers of the program may not realize that the famous *Avengers* wit was there long before Diana Rigg appeared on the scene.) And this adage was true even after filming began on *The Avengers* in late 1964; the show was still primarily about writing, and many of the show's best scripts were unveiled during this season with Roger Marshall's contributions becoming the cream at the top of a very strong season.

For this season, most of the prior writers would disappear, with only Roger Marshall, Brian

Clemens, Malcolm Hulke, Martin Woodhouse, and John Lucarotti being retained, the latter three contributing only one story each. Frequent contributors Terrance Dicks and Eric Paice would not return despite having written some of the strongest stories in recent years. The reasons for this shift in screenwriters are rather obscure but may have something to do with royalty complaints for newfound sales to the American market. Nevertheless, several intriguing new writers would join in. Philip Levene, Tony Williamson, Robert Banks Stewart, and Colin Finbow would all contribute solid scripts, with Levene and Williamson ultimately sticking around for the next few seasons.

And yet, the superb writing would be sweetened by the addition of crisp, startling black and white filming, and the show would blossom into a parade of exciting visuals as well. The lighting was usually film noir in influence, and the directors working on this season, culled from Associated British Corporation's film department (and elsewhere as the British film industry shrank), would shine just as much as the writers.

On the director's side, the shakedown was even more profound. Director Don Leaver (who had been in the control booth for the lion's share of episodes during the videotaped era) and Bill Bain were the only two directors invited back from the prior season, and their contributions to this season would be their last. Leaver has gone on record as saying that the film department looked down on them and their skills despite their contributions to this season showing them to be just as capable when working on film as with videotape. (Don Leaver's "Dial a Deadly Number" in fact deserves something of a 'best of show' award.) Nevertheless, the territorial nature of the artistic world was the likely culprit, and Leaver and Bain would disappear when the series moved to color.

New directors to the series, which was being shot on 35mm monochrome film for the first time, would be Roy Baker, Peter Graham Scott, James Hill, Charles Crichton, Gerry O'Hara, Sidney Hayers, and Quentin Lawrence. Charles Crichton and Roy Baker were both distinguished directors in the British film industry. Peter Graham Scott had originally worked as an editor and had been more recently employed on ***Danger Man***. James Hill and Sidney Hayers would consistently turn in solid work over the next few seasons, with both of them even returning to work on ***The New Avengers***.

History has shown that the move to film worked. They had been able to make the show ten times better on film just as Julian Wintle had announced. Though not without the occasional minor misstep, in the end, this season would solidify into arguably the best season of ***The Avengers***, with writing, directing and production combining with wonderful chemistry between the regular cast members to produce something of a creative peak for the series.

The American network ABC purchased twenty-one episodes of this first series for £2 million, a completely unprecedented sum for the day, and even at a budget considered high for British television—£56,000 per episode—this meant substantial profits. The response in Britain was enthusiastic, and after a Nielsen-stumbling start, the show was a summer replacement hit in America, and Associated British Corporation were hopeful of a full season of twenty-six episodes as the next order from ABC. This was not to be the case, and rather ironically, the startling success of the series would drive it down a path that would ultimately become a rocky one.

INTRODUCING EMMA PEEL

Of all of John Steed's partners, we know the most about Emma Peel (née Emma Knight). Prior to both her marriage and her spy work, she had made her fortune running her deceased father's business—Knight Industries. Resultingly, she appeared to have plenty of time to indulge in her many interests, hobbies, and academic studies as well as espionage. Similar to Cathy Gale, she was highly intelligent and demonstrated great knowledge on a wide variety of subjects. Dark haired, tall and lean, Emma was exceptionally beautiful and elegant. She was fun-loving with a keen sense of humor and considerable wit, but she also possessed a vaguely aristocratic air that might have kept some men at bay. Her apparent wealth allowed her to maintain a stylish and modern apartment and a glamor-

ous wardrobe with cutting edge fashion clothing.

She was seen to have no obvious romances while working with Steed, and her relationship with Steed has long been a subject of great debate. Though their friendship was laced with humorous byplay, gentle teasing, and great affection, it was never certain whether she and Steed had any romantic involvement or not. However, multiple hints throughout her time with Steed indicated a possible past romance that had since cooled.

Completely unflappable under threat, Emma was exceptionally talented at martial arts, especially judo and kung-fu, and she seldom came up against a foe she could not defeat. She often came to Steed's rescue. Initially, she wore black leather suits, just as her predecessor had done, but later she changed to more comfortable, flexible, and colorful garments specifically tailored for action. She also proved herself very capable at fencing and an expert with firearms.

Though Emma did go undercover many times during her adventures with Steed, she did not necessarily show the same capability at acting and subterfuge as her predecessor. It is possible that her predilection for bluntness and boldness negated her ability to bluff, and many of her undercover attempts were rather bludgeoning (much like Steed), charging into the enemy's territory and daring them to expose themselves with a reaction. Nevertheless, she frequently posed as a magazine reporter in order to penetrate the criminal organizations to which she was assigned. Regardless, when her cover was blown, she was more than capable of fighting her way out. Linguistically, she displayed considerable familiarity with French, Russian, and Latin, though it is difficult to say whether this extended beyond merely an academic understanding and fully into fluency.

Emma was married to Peter Peel, a pilot and adventurer who had gone missing in the Amazon years earlier, leaving her ostensibly a widow for the bulk of her time as Steed's partner. However, when her husband unexpectedly reappeared, Emma quickly abandoned the spy trade to return to his side. In a humorous twist, it turned out that Mr. Peel was something of a Steed lookalike, who dressed in a similar fashion with bowler hat and umbrella and drove a modern Bentley. Ironically, when she briefly appeared in *The New Avengers* many years later, Emma revealed that she was no longer called Mrs. Peel. She was the third and final 'talented amateur' to be partnered with Steed. All subsequent partners would be full agents within the Ministry.

ICONIC TITLES

These titles start much in the same style as the previous season but are much more sophisticated in their execution. As before, the name of the program appears in tall bold letters filling the screen. The letters start as a negative, thus in white with a black background, and then flip to a positive. From here, a procession of still photographic blowups of Patrick Macnee and Diana Rigg in character are shown in a series of cuts that progress to the rhythm of the music. John Steed is depicted in his usual suit, bowler hat and umbrella. He hands a carnation to Emma Peel, who appears in both her black leather fighting suit and a diaphanous evening gown. The names of the actors and those of the screenwriter, director, and producer are shown in the sequence, finally settling on producer Julian Wintle, but the episode title is withheld until after the opening sequence (or 'pre-title'). Laurie Johnson composed the music, which is still jazzy in tone much like previous seasons but more upbeat and triumphant. There is also a proper end title sequence, which depicts in the same style Steed and Emma fetching their hat and boots respectively from a hatstand and then riding in Steed's Bentley.

For the American airings of this season in 1966, the official title sequence was preceded by a special segment designed to introduce the characters to American audiences. This sequence featured Steed and Emma on a giant chessboard toasting each other with champagne retrieved from a fallen fencing dummy. An announcer with an American accent (or perhaps a British announcer putting on a mid-Atlantic accent) boldly declares, "Extraordinary crimes against the people and the state must be avenged by agents extraordinary. Two such people are John Steed, top professional, and his partner Emma Peel, talented amateur. Otherwise known as 'the Avengers.'" This line is the only point in which the term 'talented amateur' is mentioned in the series, having been an unspoken intention by the producers for all of Steed's assistants up to this point. This short sequence was generally used on all syndicated reruns of the program in America and has been included on all video releases in America as well as on European DVDs and Blu-rays as an extra. It almost certainly inspired the similar champagne-toasting title sequence used during the color Diana Rigg era.

CHAMPAGNE, CARS, CLOTHES, AND CANINES

Given the bigger budget, more effort was put into developing the fashion aspect of the series, and the production team began to look for outside designers. Patrick Macnee would continue to have his clothes made by his Regent Street tailors, relying on ABC staff designers for consultation, while designer Jan Rowell would begin Season Four exclusively responsible for Diana Rigg's wardrobe. However, partway in, a decision was made to ensure that all of Rigg's clothes were custom designed by a fashion designer. Initially, this was Jean Muir of Susan Small Limited, and the plan was that she would start an *Avengers* line of clothing. However, while Muir provided outfits for four episodes, her efforts to produce a clothing line for whatever reason came to nothing, and John Bates was approached to take her place. Fortunately, Bates was very keen and enthusiastically took on the project. The result was the Jean Varon Avengers Collection, which was officially launched on 24 August 1965 with a fashion show at Courtaulds Fashion Theatre at Celanese House in Hanover Square, London. The show was a tremendous success and produced advance orders amounting to over £10,000.

Initially, the word was that Diana Rigg's wardrobe would head in an even kinkier direction with Brian Clemens once saying "she's going to wear a studded dog collar, and we are experimenting with shiny jet-black polythene materials," but this was intimidating to Rigg and ultimately vetoed, resulting in altogether less kink rather than more. Even when Mrs. Peel wears leather, it tends to be integrated into woven fabrics. She has more of a pop-art fashion sense than Cathy Gale, with many softer, more feminine, and more elegant outfits, such as her 'TV' outfit with a mini-skirt and pumps.

As far as Patrick Macnee's wardrobe is concerned, many new clothes are added, with only the few old favorites staying on, such as the Prince of Wales blazer and black waistcoat with silver buttons, the navy chalk-stripe three-piece, and the old reliable dark-gray three-piece with the lapeled waistcoat and cloth-covered buttons (the latter having been worn in all three of the prior seasons).

In general, however, Steed's fashion starts to take more of a backseat to Emma's, having fewer clothing changes in each episode, but both his cars and Emma's are featured much more prominently than before. The dogs are gone for now, but the champagne really takes off during this era, appearing in many episodes for the remainder of the series and in the American title sequence.

Diana Rigg's fashions were provided by the following—

Jan Rowell in "The Murder Market," "The Master Minds," "Dial a Deadly Number," "Death at Bargain Prices," "The Cybernauts," and "Too Many Christmas Trees."

Jean Muir in "The Gravediggers," "A Surfeit of H2O," Two's a Crowd," and "Silent Dust."

John Bates in the remainder of the season, plus one outfit in "Silent Dust."

Edward Rayne supplied all of Rigg's shoes and boots for most of the season and was credited for this on the final thirteen episodes (in production order).

Best Dressed: "The Town of No Return"
Worst Dressed: "Two's a Crowd" (only because of all those bad outfits Macnee has to wear)

AVENGERS CARS

JOHN STEED

1924 Vauxhall 30-98 (XT 2076) in "The Gravediggers" and "The Thirteenth Hole."
1927 Bentley 4 ½ Litre (UW 4887) in "The Master Minds" and "Too Many Christmas Trees."
1937 Bentley 3 Litre (YT 3942/UW 4887[1]) in "Small Game for Big Hunters," "The Danger Makers," "A Touch of Brimstone," "The House That Jack Built," "How to Succeed.... At Murder."
1924 Bentley 3 Litre (XR 6056) in "The Hour That Never Was" and "The Man-Eater of Surrey Green."
Land Rover (VX 897) in "A Sense of History."

EMMA PEEL

1965 Lotus Elan S2 Convertible (HNK 999C)—white—in "The Cybernauts," "Castle De'Ath," "Two's a Crowd," "Man-Eater of Surrey Green," "Small Game for Big Hunters," "The Girl from Auntie," "What the Butler Saw," "The House That Jack Built," and "How to Succeed.... At Murder."

THE MOST FANTASTIC EPISODES OF THE SEASON

1. Dial a Deadly Number
2. Honey for the Prince
3. The House That Jack Built
4. The Girl from Auntie
5. Quick-Quick Slow Death
6. The Cybernauts
7. The Danger Makers
8. Silent Dust
9. Too Many Christmas Trees
10. The Town of No Return

1 At some point, the registration was moved from the 4 ½ Litre to the 3 Litre.

79 (4.1.1) THE TOWN OF NO RETURN

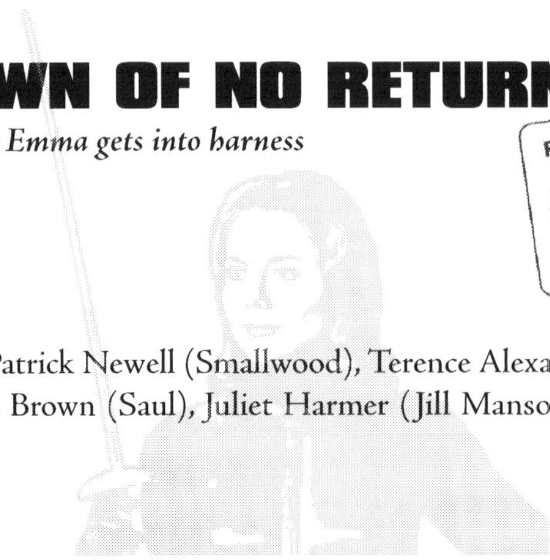

Steed finds a town full of ghosts — Emma gets into harness
Written by Brian Clemens
Directed by Roy Baker

GUEST CAST

Alan MacNaughtan (Brandon), Patrick Newell (Smallwood), Terence Alexander ('Piggy' Warren), Jeremy Burnham (Vicar), Robert Brown (Saul), Juliet Harmer (Jill Manson), Walter Horsbrugh (School Inspector)

PRE-TITLE/TEASER

In a small English village, a man climbs out of the ocean in a giant plastic bag and emerges completely dry wearing a sharp suit with hat and umbrella.

SYNOPSIS

Steed and Emma head to Little Bazeley by the Sea, a small seaside village where several agents have disappeared recently. Posing as a real estate prospector and a school teacher, they begin to investigate the villagers, quickly finding out that they are not the original inhabitants. Eventually, the whole scheme is revealed to be the prelude to an invasion by a foreign enemy, but the vicar and school inspector don't intend to allow Steed and Mrs. Peel to use that information...

REVIEW

As if Albert Fennell and Brian Clemens had it all worked out from the beginning, this season starts right out projecting exactly what they must have wanted. Deeply surefooted with a clear point of view, "The Town of No Return" is consistent with every other fourth season episode in overall style and content. We are left with no uncertainty as to what to expect for the next twenty-five episodes. This season increases the more bizarre qualities explored in earlier episodes such as "Build a Better Mousetrap" and "The Charmers," adding even more surrealism and eccentrics along the way, while retaining the superb writing that had been such an indelible part of the series since the beginning, all of it updated production-wise to 35mm black and white film with film noir lighting.

Immediately beginning with the bizarre—a man climbs out of what appears to be a giant plastic garbage bag, just after bobbing out of the ocean, and casually asks for directions from a lone fisherman—the setting is a stereotypically tiny English seaside village with suspicious townspeople, who are resistant to outsiders, their voices turning dour and expressionless when their suspicions kick in and they glance furtively at their fellow conspirators. These are the same suspicious townsfolks we've seen in dozens of films before and since, such as ***Plague of the Zombies, Doomwatch, The Wicker Man,*** and ***American Werewolf in London,*** the type of cliché that might curtail tourism to Britain if believed too enthusiastically.

Diana Rigg immediately establishes herself as cool and confident, the chemistry between her and Steed is instant and palpable. Despite public perception to the contrary, this was an entirely different relationship in tone and in practice from that of her predecessor. If one were to categorize the primary quality of Steed and Cathy's relationship, it would be built upon tension, tension of all kinds, including the much-vaunted romantic variety. They conflicted on so many levels, ethically and morally, with Mrs. Gale frequently calling out Steed for his callousness and bristling at his manipulations. Nevertheless, they genuinely enjoyed each other's company and the success that their association brought. Their relationship was, if anything, sibling-like—squabbles persisting amidst intense affection and mutual admiration.

Between Steed and Mrs. Peel, this tension melts away completely. If I were to describe their interactions with one word, it would be 'effortless'—effortless yet preserving the witty banter and occasional acidic barbs passed between them. They meld as if married, on multiple levels, with the requisite romantic suggestions leaving questions unanswered about the intensity of their involvement. Producer and writer Brian Clemens revealed his interpretation on their relationship, that they had recently had a 'mad affair,' which was now over, leaving the two former lovers brimming with affection for one another, their ardor now substantially cooled and yet accounting for their ease and intimacy in each other's presence. I find this explanation the most satisfactory, though there are many other viable theories.

No scene secures this interpretation better than their opening one, as Mrs. Peel practices fencing while Steed pursues a cup of coffee. Mrs. Peel's apartment is modern and automated—drawing a parallel with Cathy Gale—but it is more open and spacious, allowing for such activities as swordplay with plenty of settees to leap over. Friendly advice turns to friendly competition when Emma makes Steed fence his way to the cream. Mrs. Peel's wry bemused smiles, a gentle play of humor about her lips, visible even beyond a fencing mask, are those of a woman who is enjoying the presence of a man she is currently resisting, despite persistent affection on both sides. Perhaps for her it is over, and for him it is not? Diana Rigg is the master of such winsome expressions. She has a vast array in her arsenal. In one scene in a church, fleeing from the imposter of a vicar and confronted by stalwart men blocking her flight, does she shriek? Does she flee in the opposite direction? No, of course not. She flips on the charm, smirks and leans casually against the doorframe in an expression that is simultaneously sensual and unbothered, as if to say, "Oh, well, you got me, boys. Come on in."

On their way to Little Bazeley by the Sea, mildly surrealistic touches continue as Steed pulls a boiling kettle out of a carpet bag in order to make tea on the train. Mary Poppins-like magic or a secret spy device? We are never told, but this is the show's subtle wink to the audience, adding reality-twisting embellishments to our infinite delight. We're in a different world now where the rules are different. Dr. Keel's streetwise world of heroin dealers and jewel thieves has been replaced with subtle fantasy built upon superspies and their unstoppable panache. No trick, big or small, is too much for them to pull out of their magic bag in order to win the day.

Once arriving, their newfound environment is openly hostile, with shredded linens and pipes that gurgle and snort like greedy pigs snarfing mud while suffering from severe colds. And they're kept up all night by the sounds of marching feet upon the cobblestoned streets. All the agents preceding them have gone missing, presumably having succumbed to such horrible hotel service.

The pub owner, played by Terence Alexander with a mustache like hairy wings, ear-abrasively wheezes in greasy guffaws that are both humorous and sinister, suggesting darker motives. One wonders if the mustache might be better suited for twirling. Thus, in their undercover operation, no townsfolk can be trusted, and Steed and Emma are thrust close together as the only two people upon whom they can rely, their comradery being what pulls them through in the end, loyal as the best of friends. This is the magical new formula for the series.

This isn't the greatest episode of this season, but it is a fine story nonetheless with fun dialogue, a clever central premise, its tone-setting remarkable for a season debut. Even greater ideas, more fabulous spy hijinks, even more surrealistic fantasy fun were to come as this season reached something of a high-water mark for the program.

EPISODE NOTES

"The Town of No Return" was originally completed with Elizabeth Shepherd playing Emma Peel. Production then continued with "The Murder Market," which was partially completed before Shepherd's departure from the series. There are a few scenes from the original Shepherd production of "Town" still in the final version, but most of these do not involve Emma Peel, though one shot retains

Shepherd's hands. The editing for this changeover is generally excellent and invisible; this is no haphazard cut and paste job, as would later be the case in "Invasion of the Earthmen," which similarly dealt with a production shakeup partway through filming. The remount of "Town" with Diana Rigg in the role of Mrs. Peel was 14th in production order.

CHAMPAGNE, CARS, CLOTHES, AND CANINES

In her introduction scene, Emma wears a black cloth catsuit with built-in vinyl tunic that tapers to a bikini shape at the bottom, buttoned down the front, and black-striped white boots by Edward Rayne. She switches to 'Blackboard', a soft pale-colored outfit with a blouse with cloth buttons down the front and a slightly darker sleeveless tunic, designed by John Bates. On the train, it's worn with trousers and a beret with concentric circles in black and white like a target, but she switches to diamond-checked stockings the next morning in Little Bazeley. The hat returns later. She then pairs the hat with the catsuit and a black-and-white print headscarf. She also debuts a long white dress with long sleeves and black stitching. The shoulders are padded.

The return of Steed's gray Prince of Wales blazer with the black waistcoat with bright buttons, along with a tan overcoat, possibly the same as the one in Season Three. Good to see that some of the best of his outfits from the previous season are being retained, and the blazer and waistcoat would become one of his main pieces throughout the remainder of this season. You get a really good look at the black waistcoat several times in this episode when he takes off his jacket. Towards the end, he ditches the waistcoat and wears the blazer over a white shirt, and the dark gray steel-lined bowler makes its debut in a fight with the fake blacksmith.

The motorbike in the tag scene is a 1962 Piaggio Vespa GT 125, and since they take the train to Little Bazeley, this is the only vehicle you see them driving in the episode.

TAG SCENE

Steed and Emma skip the train and ride home through the countryside on a Vespa with Emma driving and Steed sitting in back.

QUOTES

"That was very, very dirty!" "You're quite right, but I didn't promise to fight fair."
"Milk or lemon?" "Lemon." "It'll have to be milk."
"We must be prepared to make concessions, my dear. Back to nature." "Well, you might have warned me. I'd have packed my pot of woad."
"What happened to pussy-footed pussy?" "Isn't it time you were in bed? You have to be up early for school tomorrow."
"We must be careful. We nearly mishandled that, like that ugly business on the beach last night."
"Would the wheeler come to the unsaddling enclosure?" "All this is supposed to go on a horse, you know."
"...the butcher, the baker, the candlestick maker—all imposters!"

80 (4.8.2) THE GRAVE-DIGGERS

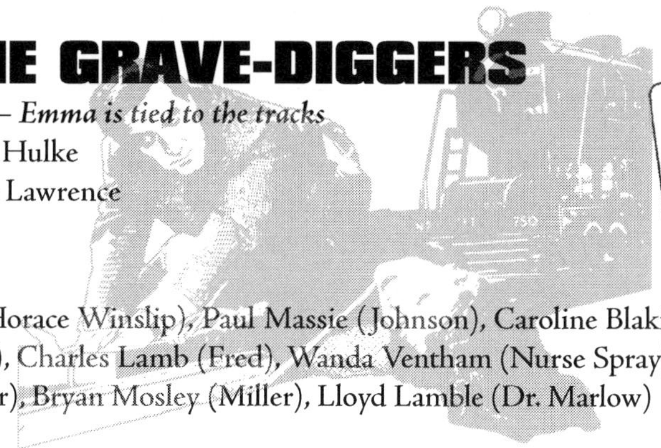

Steed drives a train — Emma is tied to the tracks
Written by Malcolm Hulke
Directed by Quentin Lawrence

PRIORITY PASS
TALENTED AMATEUR 002-25
LONDON
HAS BEEN PERMITTED ACCESS TO MINISTRY FILES
CLASS C
CLEARANCE LEVEL

GUEST CAST

Ronald Fraser (Sir Horace Winslip), Paul Massie (Johnson), Caroline Blakiston (Miss Thirlwell), Victor Platt (Sexton), Charles Lamb (Fred), Wanda Ventham (Nurse Spray), Ray Austin (Baron), Steven Berkoff (Sager), Bryan Mosley (Miller), Lloyd Lamble (Dr. Marlow)

PRE-TITLE/TEASER

An unusual funeral. The mourners leave silently, and the gravediggers begin their job of filling the grave in. The hearse pulls away with the grave finally filled, but a tiny telescopic aerial emerges from the dirt emitting a mysterious signal.

SYNOPSIS

Someone has momentarily jammed Britain's radar defense grid. The problem has been traced to a Dr. Marlow, whose entire life had been devoted to the improvement of radar, but Marlow died four weeks ago, and somehow his work lives on. Steed investigates the hospital where the man died, and Emma goes undercover as a nurse. Together, they discover that the hospital's 'patients' in the operating theatre are oddly electronic, and a rich eccentric railway fanatic is being duped. With Emma's cover blown, will she be railroaded as a result…?

REVIEW

An antenna rises from a grave in the opening pre-title, but it's not the dead tuning into heavenly broadcasts. Something far more terrestrial is going on. Coincidentally, it turns out that it's the same grave that is supposed to contain radar expert Dr. Marlow's body, but in *The Avengers* there are no coincidences, and Steed must investigate. Thus, somewhat unusually, we are thrust right into the action of an improbable story that contains undertakers, hospital operating rooms, disturbingly obtuse train enthusiasts running miniature railways, and radar jamming technology, all within apparent walking distance of one another, and from there, it ebbs and flows in spurts that are in equal parts drab and bizarre.

This particular story seems to cement the classic idea of an *Avengers* eccentric, and this time it's the loony train-obsessed Sir Horace Winslip, who, when he's not funding a hospital for "ailing railwaymen," insists upon taking lunch onboard a mockup of a train car in his own living room. His wearied servant runs desperately behind the scenes, shaking the train car to simulate motion as a painted backdrop cycles on a conveyor before the windows. He blows train whistles and plays sound effects on a gramophone record in order to keep up the illusion. (Wealth clearly has its privileges! This was virtual reality for the sixties generation.) Winslip is another example of a common eccentric in this era of *The Avengers*, one who is unhappy with the way that the traditions of the country are seemingly slipping away. He's an older version of Steed himself, one to draw his sympathies, a grandfather to Steed's fatherly persona. However, in this case, unlike in "Death at Bargain Prices," this eccentric is being used and is guilty of nothing but stupidity, his generous fortune going towards a plot to destroy the country.

The villains this week are a bland lot, almost interchangeable, their chief characteristic of villainy being their superpower of being condescending to Nurse Emma, provoking multiple instances of side-eye from the usually unflappable Mrs. Peel. Thus, it's fortunate that the most bizarre scenes involve their activities, for they are so dullish that we have little else with which to dress them up. They operate out of Sir Horace's hospital, in which a blowtorch is a primary tool in the operating theatre instead of the scalpel, instantly cluing us into the fact that the patients are not ordinary ones. Scores of undertakers parade in coffins on a regular basis (much like in last season's "The Undertakers"), the contents are 'operated' upon and then returned to their final resting places where they remain restless, thrusting small telescopic antennae into the air for the purpose of jamming all radar throughout the country. We never get this far, of course; in fact, the only appearance of an active antenna in the pre-title appears to be merely a test, which ironically draws the attention of our heroic agents. In fact, we never even get to a point where there appears to be any actual threat, which is a major disappointment.

The plot is lightweight, the villains unengaging, the eccentric Winslip, humorous though he is, remains entirely too dim to be believable. This leaves the episode to finish out with a miniature railway action scene with Emma tied to the tracks in black leather trousers and jacket, a moment of kinky fun for some of you. I've been assured that Pauline in her many perils was never actually tied to a train track, but the honkytonk piano added to Laurie Johnson's score leaves no doubt as to what was intended. That the villains chose this situation to kill Emma—or a train for anything at all—is questionable, except as a quasi-bizarre setting twist for the finale. And how stopping this train defeats the plot of the antagonists is anyone's best guess, but I suppose it makes about as much sense as everything else they do in this half-hearted, ill-coordinated effort—or in any other mustache-twirling melodrama with a damsel-in-distress.

Steed and Emma—who have surprisingly little screen time together in this episode—depart backwards on the mini-train, smiling radiantly at each other, and this is about the most charming moment in the whole hour.

CHAMPAGNE, CARS, CLOTHES, AND CANINES

Mrs. Peel wears a beautiful woolen jacket with embroidering and white court shoes and black leather gloves. She would later remove the jacket revealing a sleeveless blouse and pleated knee-length skirt. Sadly, this is this outfit's only appearance. This is also the episode in which she dons a nurse's uniform. For the finale, she wears a leather jumpsuit over a black jumper, with a matching leather jacket. Steed debuts a beautiful single-breasted suit in brown serge with a print silk tie. He tops the look off with a matching bowler, black Chelsea boots, and an umbrella with a whangee handle. This outfit would become a major ensemble for Steed as he would wear it in eleven more episodes. For a more casual look, he wears a suede-fronted cardigan.

Steed debuts his 1924 Vauxhall 30-98 (XT 2076), the first new vehicle (in transmission order) this season.

TAG SCENE

Steed and Emma ride backwards on the mini-train seen earlier in the episode. Steed pulls the whistle and grins like a little boy as Emma puts her hands over her ears.

QUOTES

"I'd like some grapes." "Desperate for them, I'd say."
"Forceps…scalpel…blowtorch."
"I'd better follow that coffin."
"I do so abhor violence, dear chap!"
"What is that young woman doing tied to the railway line? She'll break the engine!"

81 (4.7.3) THE CYBERNAUTS

Steed receives a deadly gift — Emma pockets it
Written by Philip Levene
Directed by Sidney Hayers

GUEST CAST

Michael Gough (Dr. Clement Armstrong), Frederick Jaeger (Benson), Bernard Horsfall (Jephcott), Burt Kwouk (Tusamo), John Hollis (Sensai), Ronald Leigh-Hunt (Lambert), Gordon Whiting (Hammond)

PRE-TITLE/TEASER

A man in a dressing gown runs from an intruder in his home. He locks himself into a study, blocking the door with a settee. He fires several shots at the intruder with both a pistol and a shotgun as the unstoppable assassin breaks down the door with terrifying ease. The bullets have no effect and the still unseen murderer breaks the man's neck with a single blow.

SYNOPSIS

On the case of several disturbing deaths involving broken necks, shattered doors, and bent shotgun barrels, Steed and Mrs. Peel trace the murders to an automations expert Dr. Armstrong. Armstrong, through the use of special homing devices attached to his victims, is destroying his competition in the electronics field with a mechanical automaton called a Cybernaut. As Steed begins to figure out the full extent of Armstrong's plans, he discovers that the pen he gave Mrs. Peel is drawing a deadly Cybernaut ever closer to her...

REVIEW

It's a treat to simply sit back and enjoy television as uniquely dated as "The Cybernauts." While the basic narrative is one that would set a template for a common plotline utilized by *The Avengers*, one that would be repeated many times over the next few years, with death after death occurring just before Steed and Emma reach the hapless victims, this particular story is nevertheless a precise rendering that could have only happened in its day. People are no longer obsessed with ideas of domination by electronics and computers. With its talk of electronics, automation, cutting-edge robotics, and frankly, very sexist ideas about what a woman can do, nothing could be more emblematic of sixties television. The strength of "The Cybernauts" is not really its florid brand of science-fiction—it's not particularly good science-fiction anyway—nor is it the spy drama, of which there is little, nor is it the speculative science, for it lacks the required intelligence and understanding. Instead, frequently, this kind of program is called 'telefantasy' in the United Kingdom—a term meant to be applied to television that is uncategorizable, juxtaposing elements of both fantasy and science-fiction in the context of a good adventure story. And that is squarely where this episode sits, *adventure* television. Taken in this vein, it is delightful, and is no doubt one of the most memorable episodes of the original series.

Most of this appeal is due to the iconic nature of the Cybernauts themselves, their star power threatening to eclipse that of Steed and Mrs. Peel, whose camaraderie and usual witty banter take a backseat this week. Indeed, the scenes featuring the massive automatons are thrilling and highly memorable as they smash through solid oak doors and deflect shotgun shells with ease, their arms swishing whip-like through the air. The Cybernauts leave each victim with either a broken neck or a fractured skull and render the defenders' shotguns hostile to chandeliers by introducing a seemingly impossible u-bend to their barrels. Despite this impressive display of murderous robotic prowess, modern audiences may nevertheless find the relentless talk of dated sixties technology hard to endure, or perhaps even laughable. It is worth considering, however, that in actuality we are (or perhaps should be) more concerned than ever with the threat of artificial intelligence. Thus, the subtext of "The Cybernauts" probably should instead be thought of as ahead of its time, having been interpreted in the only context available in the era in which it was made, that of bulky transistors and automatic doors powered by punch cards. It might be a hard sell but one worth considering.

Nevertheless, even allowing for this, the narrative suffers from a real doozy of a red herring, a rare one for Mrs. Peel. She's completely off track with her quest to find the assailant in an arrogant sensei's cadre of stoic karate enthusiasts. (Played by John Hollis in a particularly sexist manner, this sensei cannot even manage to pronounce his own title correctly.) Sadly, the intolerably condescending situation fails to produce the payoff. Emma's mark—a karate master named Jephcott (Bernard Horsfall), who can easily split a solid oak door when he's not running an electronics toy company—is quickly dispatched by the Cybernauts in a painfully ironic twist that leaves the team with no option but to see what the audience has known practically since the beginning. It's a robot. Their dawning realization is provoked by the sudden activity of a toy robot found in Jephcott's office, as if they needed a supernatural jolt in order to spark realization of the obvious.

John Steed is however on target, having been led to the offices of sixties authoritarian fruitcake Dr. Clement Armstrong, played by Michael Gough with an especially sour malignancy. Armstrong is obsessed with the idea of the world being ruled by automation, no doubt with the computers being personally programmed by himself. Naturally, the narrative never progresses that far because the episode can only be fifty-three minutes long, and the Avengers are usually on the ball. This leaves the climax to occur in Armstrong's sequestered fortress, guarded by another automaton wearing a flat cap and overalls, a machine that is equally capable of re-adjusting thermostats and human vertebrae in devastating knockout blows.

Though Steed escapes the wrath of this maintenance man-cum-assassin—it's funny how capacious ventilator shafts are in these programs!—it's Emma that's subjected to the real threat, having borrowed Steed's pen. The pen's a questionable gift from Armstrong and his loyal assistant Benson, one that brings Cybernauts flocking to her. (Not her usual admirers!) Happily, she is overcome by worry for Steed, who remains overlong on his mission into Armstrong's bastille, and she meets Steed for their final confrontation with the two mechanical madmen…as well as the Cybernauts themselves. And for the finale, the two automatons destroy each other in a flurry of flailing strikes that ultimately blow the maintenance man's mind—with lots of nice boxes to knock over in the process.

That Armstrong's death comes at the hands of his mechanical monstrosities is the type of irony that is in equal measures appropriate, satisfying, and obvious, the kind that a screenwriter would have found himself unable to resist, and thus, the narrative comes to a circular close, having delivered on all levels an adventure story that could have worked in virtually any television series, not necessarily *The Avengers*. But you'll likely be glad it was *The Avengers* and not some lesser vehicle.

CHAMPAGNE, CARS, CLOTHES, AND CANINES

Steed debuts a new gray three-piece single-breasted suit with matching bowler and knit tie. Mrs. Peel's first outfit is a woolen coat with a black fur trim. She pairs it with a black purse and gloves. The primary color of the coat is a deep crimson, but we won't see that until it shows up later in "The Hidden Tiger" worn by Gabrielle Drake. Later, Steed appears in a navy chalk stripe suit much like the prior one in Seasons Two and Three, though this one has slit pockets instead of flap pockets. He wears it with a matching waistcoat, white shirt, knit tie, gem tiepin, and black Chelsea boots. Mrs. Peel changes her outfit to a Chinese jacket with a knee-length skirt, and she shows up for the Cyber-fight in her leather jumper. Then, she finishes the episode off with a beautiful full-length woolen coat in black with two columns of bright brass buttons and a matching skirt. She tops it off with a black headscarf. Of course, this is also the episode where she wears a white karate gi.

Mrs. Peel's Lotus Elan S2 convertible (HNK 999C) debuts, and for the tag scene, Steed sits in a 1906 Humber Beeston veteran car. This was not his usual car, and it would not reappear.

TAG SCENE

Emma drives up in her Lotus while Steed sits in his car attempting to solve a crossword puzzle. The 9-letter word Steed is looking for is "Cybernaut." After attempting to loan him the same pen gifted by Armstrong earlier, which Steed refuses, Emma roars off again in her Lotus. "I don't hold with those new-fangled things," Steed says.

QUOTES

"It's unique, isn't it? Whichever way you aim it, you hit the chandelier."
"It's that casual air of elegance. It always betrays me."
"If I'm not back by 11:30, I've stayed for breakfast." "You don't eat breakfast."
"Oh, is that another one? Looks almost human."
"What's the end product, the perfect politician?" "Exactly. Government by automation." "Sounds like an electronic dictatorship."
"It's moves in the dark, it leaves no mark, it's as hard as steel. Now, what would that be, Mrs. Peel?"

82 (4.5.4) DEATH AT BARGAIN PRICES

Steed fights in Ladies Underwear — Emma tries 'feinting'
Written by Brian Clemens
Directed by Charles Crichton

GUEST CAST

André Morell (Horatio Kane), T.P. McKenna (Wentworth), Allan Cuthbertson (Farthingale), George Selway (Massey), Harvey Ashby (Marco), John Cater (Jarvis), Peter Howell (Professor Popple), Ronnie Stevens (Glynn), Diane Clare (Julie)

PRE-TITLE/TEASER

A secret agent covertly prowls after hours through a department store. He is surprised by an armed thug who shoots him through the scissor gate of an old-style push-button lift.

SYNOPSIS

After a top agent is found dead in an alleyway, Steed and Emma trace the murder back to a department store via a mysterious receipt, found in the dead man's pocket. As Emma works undercover as a store clerk, they unravel a plot for world domination with a hidden nuclear explosive…

REVIEW

This episode begins with an agent on a late-night shopping spree—the twist is that he's shopping for criminals. After emerging from behind a plastic animatronic elephant, he explores the now closed and empty department store. Abruptly, an assailant springs from behind an inflatable Yogi Bear and shoots the agent multiple times in the store's lift, its grill-like gate providing no protection. Yogi's face smirks a coy expression in a touch of irony typical of the series—combining humor with violence was to become a hallmark for *The Avengers*, escalated to an ever-higher crescendo as the series progressed. This pre-title scene is silent except for the screech of the early push button elevator and the thwip-thwip sound of the gun that kills the agent, with a silencer securely in place.

As Steed and Emma investigate, there are plenty of opportunities for the pair to engage in the humorous possibilities of a department store, violent or otherwise. Steed orders a dozen bowler hats to be put "on account." The two are mistaken for a married couple expecting a child when they locate the department listed on the dead agent's receipt—department 19, the baby department. Emma's expertise on china (shades of Cathy Gale) lands her an undercover job in the lingerie department, where practically everyone takes a fancy to her. Steed also has a charmingly flirtatious scene with the girl in the foods market. But this department store is far from just a paragon of kinky fun. It's the kind of store where you'll find house detectives dead in the camping department with gigantic pikes stuck in their backs. It even has Daleks hung upon the walls in the toy department, no doubt ready to exterminate—a rare intersection of two wildly popular sixties programs. The very fabric of the building is deadly—quite literally. In fact, it turns out that the whole building is a blast, and not in a good way.

The villains are an antiqued lot, operating in the most incongruous ways imaginable, with their leader, Horatio Kane—played with abandon by the great André Morell. Kane is a stereotypical invalid stuck in a wheelchair, whacking those that displease him with his cane and waxing lyrical about the good old days, complaining about how things keep changing. He's appropriately living in the Department of Discontinued Lines, half-buried among artifacts of diminishing relevance and eager to dig himself out. (Kane is quite likely a reference to Charles Foster Kane of ***Citizen Kane,*** the discontinued artifacts likely representing the possessions piled up at the end of the film.) Steed listens politely but impatiently to his diatribe, as we all must, an all too familiar part of the human condition. If Steed is slightly archaic—your father in sixties England—then Morell's Kane is your thoroughly antiquated grandfather (or possibly your mad great uncle) ready to blow up the world if he can't have his treasured traditions back. The current political situation seems to reflect this, so it is as relevant as anything on record.

Kane's henchmen are far more modern, only common crooks concealed underneath old-world gentility, probably merely using Kane's eccentricity and wealth for their own ends, piggybacking upon his insanity and ruthlessness. Polite, genteel, speaking in Received Pronunciation, one of them nevertheless decks Steed in the eye after politely escorting him to the door, having caught him among the Discontinued Old Men. (Who could blame Steed for visiting his dear old dad?) They appear to have much more practical ambitions, power and money, naturally, and one can only wonder how long they would have tolerated old curmudgeon Kane before dispatching him after their plans succeeded. Their outer charm conceals the sociopathy that Kane wears proudly and crustily on the outside, letting it slip out when given the more convenient opportunities.

Watching the subtle character revelations, the wit, the humor, the kinky lingerie, and Steed and Emma's banter is all great fun, but what started out as "let's write a story set in a department store"—let's face it, you can hear that popping out of a writer's mouth in a producers meeting, can't you?—turns into a take-over-the-world-with-a-bomb plot, with the villains' eagerness to explain their scheme slightly more than a trifle unbelievable. Simplified character motivation is something of a quality in this new version of ***The Avengers,*** often papered over in the best of stories with scads of superficial fun, and this leaves the story to make it on charm, sophistication, cheeky dialogue and acting. This it does quite well.

The climactic battle is a real nail-biter—the bomb is the store itself, set to detonate when the elevator reaches the basement—and this finale is full of some of the most bizarre and quirky violence in the series. Thus, the location's dividends do pay off in the end. Steed distracts the villains with a ping-pong ball gun and deflects a hunting knife with a cricket bat in the sporting goods department. Emma—wearing an outfit that might remind modern viewers of Janet Jackson's Rhythm Nation, a full black leather catsuit complete with studded baldric, gloves, and a belt buckle collar—introduces an entirely new form of martial arts called 'feinting,' which turns into one of the more bizarre fight scenes in the series as she brazenly psyches out her opponent.

While it's a shame that better motivations for the villains couldn't be found, this episode is well cemented in the new style of *The Avengers*, ticking off all the boxes needed. I'm certain you won't fail to be amused, and the inflatable Yogi Bear would no doubt smile in approval.

CHAMPAGNE, CARS, CLOTHES, AND CANINES

Steed starts out in his dashing navy three-piece single-breasted suit with a matching waistcoat, bowler, and umbrella. It reads as deep black, however, on b/w film. The suit will show up thirteen total times this season. Black tie with white spots. Mrs. Peel debuts a black woolen fitted jacket with fur collar and shiny black buttons. She briefly dons a matching bowler, and it suits her very well. Once employed at Pinter's, she wears a flounced silk blouse in a champagne color with a black knee-length pencil skirt and black belt. A black brassiere preserves her modesty. The woolen coat from the tag scene to "The Cybernauts" returns. So does Steed's chalk-stripe suit. Later, Mrs. Peel debuts her leather fighting catsuit with silver zips, the one that would dominate the season—in more ways than one. Once in Pinter's toy department, she adds silver gauntlets, boots, and a baldric, thus, all ready to work in the space age along with the toy Daleks on the wall. These accessories are discarded after she is captured by the criminals and never appear again. In the tag scene, she wears a ruffed-front blouse with a broad hat with her sheer headscarf wrapped over the top. Very Mary Poppins! Steed wears his tan weatherproofed overcoat with the padded collar and black bowler.

TAG SCENE

Steed and Emma ride down a country lane on matching bicycles they received as gifts from the department store they just saved from catastrophe.

QUOTES

"I wonder if you're buying a cot, if I might recommend this one, sir? Baby will be very happy in it." "I think baby's too big. Come along, my dear."

"What would he want with a pram?" "Perhaps his nanny had her license endorsed." "For reckless pushing?"

"I asked the chief predator where to find you, and he said 'Our Mrs. Peel is in ladies underwear.' I rattled up the stairs three at a time."

"Merry Quips department on the fifth floor, sir."

"A glorious age. Gracious, leisurely, ordered. A time…for many things. A machine was a thing of joy then. Built to last a man's lifetime. Now, it's out of date before it's left the assembly line."

"What on Earth's that?" "Hmm? Oh, it's an exploded molecular construction." "So, that's what hit me!"

"Came for my teddy bear, can't sleep without one!"

"Straight drive to mid-on. It's all in the grip, you know."

83 (4.15.5) CASTLE DE'ATH

Steed becomes a strapping jock — Emma lays a ghost
Written by John Lucarotti
Directed by James Hill

GUEST CAST

Gordon Jackson (Ian), Robert Urquhart (Angus), Jack Lambert (McNab), James Copeland (Roberton), Russell Waters (Controller)

PRE-TITLE/TEASER

In a Scottish castle, a man is tortured to the wailing of bagpipes in a medieval torture chamber.

SYNOPSIS

Investigating the disappearance of the fish along the English coastline and the death of a diver, who was put on the rack, Steed and Emma go undercover at Castle De'ath, the home of the 35th Scottish laird of clan De'ath. Emma is working as a representative of a promotional company that will open the castle to the public, and Steed is disguised as a writer, working on a book about the 13th laird, Black Jamie. With a mysterious bagpipe-playing ghost and a crushing experience for Steed in his bed, it all adds up to an underwater plot beyond the iron maiden...

REVIEW

I'm not sure anything in this season of ***The Avengers*** counts as a 'guilty pleasure.' For the next season, "Epic" would surely count as a guilty pleasure for many, for it cannot be any other type of pleasure. On the other hand, "Castle De'ath" is lightweight and fluffy on story but not without considerable visual artistry.

The opening pre-title is one of the most abstract in the series' history, an eerie vignette stylishly directed by James Hill. We are swept along the corridors of an old Scottish castle with bagpipes wailing distantly. The evocation of ancient Celtic times is palpable, and the sets are wonderfully realistic, suits of armor, candelabras, book cases everywhere, Claymores on the walls. The bagpipes swell in volume as the viewer is taken below into the dungeon, where a shirtless man lies on the rack, his face stretched in agony, soundless. The drone of the bagpipes reaches a blaring crescendo as if a surrogate for his screams. The camera finally settles on a sympathetic face painted upon an iron maiden, and the episode title appears.

That the name "Castle De'ath" was chosen for this particular episode and is so casually thrown about by the cast without comment is part of the cheeky humor of the series. Though the name is a real one—there is a former BBC producer named Wilfred De'Ath—the name for the castle and the clan in this situation, one that involves people being tortured in dungeons, is such a punishing play on words that it's hard to imagine it not provoking a wry smile from anyone who utters it. Nevertheless, the laird, played with grim dignity by Gordon Jackson, utters it freely and proudly.

Steed, posing as a historian, dons a kilt and takes on the ill-fitting name of Jock McSteed. His cover is that he's writing a book on Black Jamie, the 13th laird and a blackguard so infamous that his portrait is sequestered in the dungeon. Emma goes undercover as a consultant for a company with the most improbable acronym imaginable—ABORCASHAATA, the Advisory Bureau on Refurbishing Castles and Stately Homes as a Tourist Attraction, a name that only becomes completely self-explanatory once laboriously pronounced. They are thrust into an ongoing feud between two cousins—Ian and Angus—over control of Castle De'ath. Angus wants to modernize the property and turn it into a tourist attraction; Ian wishes to maintain the old traditions and prefers the castle be kept private. The trouble is that it's difficult to tell who is the more sincere. Ian is stuffy and curt but seems earnest at first glance. Angus is more fun-loving but also slightly immature, like a big kid who just wants to play in the castle.

Speaking of playing, my favorite scene is a confidential contretemps between Steed and Mrs. Peel that inexplicably becomes an impromptu miniature bagpipes performance by Emma and a sword dance by Steed (with a shillelagh and umbrella in place of weapons). They both carry on until they're out of puff. You'll be out of puff too, from laughter. It's an irresistible bit of silliness in an otherwise gloomy story.

The story takes a decidedly more serious turn in its final fifteen minutes as Steed is captured while taking a dive in the moat. When Emma is asked to leave by Ian, she does so but changes into her leather fighting gear and returns in secret, discovering a vast conspiratorial operation in effect underneath the castle. This is a plan to pass submarines through the nearby loch while covering the sounds by playing bagpipes. Inside dour men run a vast control board with lighted signs saying things like "Quayside Signal Stations" and "Action stations!" However, they inexplicably don't have one that says "Activate bagpipes!" or "Emergency bagpipes to full power!"

Much time is spent on keeping the viewer guessing about the identity of the villain. Is it Ian, the mean one, or Angus, the nice one? Turns out it's McNabb, which is a bit of an obvious but essential twist that should seep into the viewers consciousness a few minutes before it is revealed. The problem is that it's also Angus, a less obvious and much more contrived twist that raises all kinds of issues. Why would Angus deliberately invite both Steed and Mrs. Peel to the castle when a highly secret operation is going on there, and then spend the whole of the hour championing their presence while Ian objects to it? It reeks of trying to throw us off the scent. It's an even bigger mistake than Angus could possibly have calculated too, because they're both agents. This makes one wonder how it all got set up. How did Steed and Mrs. Peel get themselves invited? We also never get a full answer on what is going on with the submarines. They're rather improbably going back and forth in Castle De'ath's shallow moat, but why? Perhaps we are to assume that they are carrying secrets back and forth from behind the Iron Curtain? Perhaps frogmen are carrying the secrets to the submarines? The scheme is never really spelled out. It seems a little impractical whatever it is.

Steed and Angus have a fine battle with Claymores and shields, the expected leaping upon tables and flying crossbow bolts and etcetera on display. And Emma throws a piper over a balcony. No chandelier-swinging though. It's all a sort of mock-Scottish adventure, with Gordon Jackson putting in an especially good performance as a tragic romantic figure, but even the castle is fake—the exteriors were filmed at Allington Castle in Maidstone, Kent on the River Medway. Regardless of its Scottish inauthenticity, the main attraction for this episode is the castle's ambience, which makes for a beautiful location, providing just about everything one needs to make up for the failings of the plot. And thus, ABORCASHAATA and their representative were right after all. Silly Angus and Ian! One should always listen to Mrs. Peel. Turning your castle into a tourist attraction clearly pays better than the spy trade when *The Avengers* go Scottish on you.

CHAMPAGNE, CARS, CLOTHES, AND CANINES

MacSteed starts out in a V-neck pullover and MacGregor tartan kilt, and Mrs. Peel wears a sleeveless top and hip-hugging pants in contrasting tartan patterns (though the same colors) and she tops it off with a tailored collarless pale cardigan with epaulettes and pleated pockets. It reads as a jacket onscreen at first but it becomes clear that it's a soft cardigan in closeups. Nice contrast of cut and materials. Also, Edward Rayne's black-striped white ankle boots. At dinner, Mrs. Peel switches to a tailored silver-blue lamé pantsuit. Like many of Diana Rigg's clothes this season, it has a name—'Flash.' Steed dons traditional Scottish formal dress—black jacket with silver buttons and a ruffled white shirt with a dress kilt and knee-high Argyle socks. He also briefly explores the moat in Scuba gear. Late at night, Mrs. Peel prowls in the castle in a sheer silk nightie, very diaphanous and elegant and yet a bit racy. She pays the price by getting locked in the dungeon all night. She finishes off the episode in her black stretch cotton and vinyl catsuit.

Although Mrs. Peel arrives in her Lotus Elan S2 convertible, Steed drives her home in a 1965 Amphicar Model 770 (ELK 981C).

TAG SCENE

Steed and Emma return home in an amphibious car, puttering straight into a lake and motoring off.

QUOTES

"Did you also know that that frogman was four inches taller when he was dead than he was when he was alive? He'd been on the rack."

"Coffee, Mr. McSteed?" "Thank you. Good early morning coffee gives me that glad-to-be-alive feeling!"

(finding Mrs. Peel in the dungeon wearing her nightgown) "I'm extremely sorry to disturb you. Well, the door *was* closed. You *are* here on your own." "I was locked in. All night. And this thing wasn't designed for sleeping on."

"I'd enjoy very much putting a bullet in you, McSteed." "But the wee hole would show when they found my corpse in the loch."

84 (4.3.6) THE MASTER MINDS

Steed becomes a genius — Emma loses her mind

Written by Robert Banks Stewart

Directed by Peter Graham Scott

GUEST CAST

Laurence Hardy (Sir Clive Todd), Patricia Haines (Holly Trent), Bernard Archard (Desmond Leeming), Ian McNaughton (Dr. Fergus Campbell), John Wentworth (Sir Jeremy), Georgina Ward (Davinia Todd), Manning Wilson (Major Plessy)

PRE-TITLE/TEASER

Several men dressed in Royal Horse Guard[2] uniforms methodically extract files from a vault to photograph the top-secret contents. One of them fumbles and accidentally sets off the alarm, trapping himself behind a descending portcullis. The others shoot him and escape.

SYNOPSIS

After Sir Clive Todd is found near-mortally wounded and unconscious in a high security area that has just been raided, Steed and Emma begin an investigation that reveals a secret organization of people with high IQs, called Ransack. When Steed and Emma join the organization, Emma begins to fall under the influence of a mysterious hypnotic force and may end up practicing archery on Steed...

REVIEW

The pre-title sequence begins with the usual visual wit. As three men in Royal Horse Guard uni-

---

2 In 1969, the Royal Regiment of Horse Guards, also known as the Blues, were merged with the Royal Dragoons to form the Blues and Royals, a cavalry regiment of the British army.

forms photograph top secret files in a vault-like archive, the process ends awkwardly when one of the men trips and sets off the burglar alarm while rushing forth with more masses of paper for the camera. The audacious punishment for such clumsiness? —a bullet in the head. The penalty for failure in this criminal organization is apparently death. The fallen man survives, oddly enough—a plot continuity error that we'll ignore for the moment since it starts our heroes out on their mission—but he has amnesia and drifts in and out of consciousness, speaking incoherently, forcing Mrs. Peel to go undercover as his nurse so that she can slowly but steadily ply him for information while bringing him glasses of water and taking his pulse periodically. It turns into a red herring as soon as someone else within the mystery organization commits suicide, leaving a clue, paperwork with the name Ransack printed upon it. It turns out that Ransack is an organization of criminal masterminds, all of whom possess genius level intelligence.

The villains hang out at Dorrington Dean College For Young Ladies—"Defend Thy Honour"—where the school employees practice archery in Robin Hood outfits, their arrows thripping through the air and striking with an absurd sproing sound upon impact. Their instructor is Holly Trent, played by Patricia Haines in the second of three performances in the series. She's the most dimensional character of this mostly mono-dimensional bunch, and the twist at the end is all the more apparent due to the added focus given her. This added dimension isn't saying much, but it is much more than can be said for Professor Spencer, who is a loopy Einsteinian stereotype tragically beset with a cod German accent; he stands on his head to increase his intelligence by improving blood circulation, something he appears to need. He is not the mastermind behind this organization, though we're half-heartedly led to believe this for all of about two minutes.

Emma fits right in, but Steed isn't enjoying his stay despite the sign in his room that reads "If You Can't Sleep, Ring for a Mistress" (ooh, err!)[3]. He's left out of things; his intelligence isn't high enough—Mrs. Peel has to fake all his scores—and he keeps missing all the important messages. These messages are delivered by a brittle voice coming from speakers in everyone's bedrooms, naturally transmitting instruction on the next act of espionage under hypnosis, leaving the perpetrators with no memory of what happened. On this level, the story is supported mainly by the fact that Emma also falls under the hypnotic influence, and this misfortune temporarily fractures the unstoppable superspy team, leaving Steed on his own, isolated. Unfortunately, it's all too obvious what is happening, even obvious who is behind it. Most of the characters are too simplistic to be the leader. Other plot issues are equally problematic. How do the ostensibly awake characters in the show gets coerced into committing crimes? —Campbell killing Sir Todd, for instance? There was no voice instructing him then. Post-hypnotic suggestion perhaps?

The final scenes give Peter Graham Scott a chance to produce some fine visuals, the mysterious leader in silhouette behind a projection screen, the voice eerily distorted through speakers in the auditorium. This is carried to the next level during the climatic fight scene, executed in an experimental style, Royal Air Force stock footage projected onto the screen as our heroes fight in flickering light, klaxons sounding, no music. This gives the final moments style in abundance, but there's no substance to this story, which survives mostly on superficiality, both in characters and ideas.

The gimmick of this story is a quality one, the idea of using a mass intelligence of certified geniuses to solve highly complicated tasks for a criminal organization is noteworthy. "The Master Minds" unfortunately suffers from poor pacing, two-dimensional characterizations, and a transparent plot. Almost nothing in this season is unpalatable, given the majesty afforded the production, but much better still awaits the viewer.

CHAMPAGNE, CARS, CLOTHES, AND... CAMERAS!

The episode starts right out with one of Steed's vintage cars—a 1927 Bentley 4 1/2 litre (UW

---

3 The beefcake pinups in his armoire don't seem to be helping either. (ooh, er!)

4887)—with Mrs. Peel asleep in the passenger seat wearing a luxurious black-and-white brindled overcoat and handwarmer. Once inside, she takes it off to reveal a metallic catsuit with embroidered button holes and a ribbon belt tied in a bow. Steed wears his tan weatherproofed overcoat over his gray three-piece suit and white shirt and dark tie, and later over his Prince of Wales blazer with the dark waistcoat. After taking up another undercover position in the role of nurse, Mrs. Peel dons the traditional uniform and even having to give up her nail varnish. Her crimson woolen coat with black fur collar also returns, as does Steed's navy single-breasted suit with a dark spotted tie and tiepin, followed by the brown serge suit. But here is where one of the show's fashion disasters occurs—Steed dons a pale cardigan that looks like they just sheared the sheep and stuck it on. It's pretty bizarre and inelegant at the same time. Unfortunately, it shows up three more times this season. For the finale, Mrs. Peel's leather jacket and trousers are her fighting outfit, plus a black leather cap.

The camera used in the pre-title sequence is likely a Minox B Subminiature camera.

TAG SCENE

As Steed and Emma ride through the wintry countryside in Steed's Bentley, he remarks with pleasure that he came out of the whole affair with a genius-level IQ. Emma admits that he is a genius... "at cribbing."

QUOTES

"Has anyone ever remarked on the astonishing resemblance between yourself and Florence Nightingale?"
"Your facetiousness, Mr. Steed, covers an edgy temperature. In fact, I'd say your nerves mostly jangle like wires in the wind."
"Watch out. I lure the intelligentsia from their course whenever I get the chance."
"I've done some archery. Let me kill Steed."
"Still I came out of it with something—an IQ at genius level." "You *are* a genius—at cribbing."

85 (4.2.7) THE MURDER MARKET

Steed seeks a wife — Emma gets buried
Written by Tony Williamson
Directed by Peter Graham Scott

GUEST CAST

Patrick Cargill (Mr. Lovejoy), Suzanne Lloyd (Barbara Wakefield), Naomi Chance (Mrs. Stone), Peter Bayliss (Dinsford), John Woodvine (Robert Stone), Edward Underdown (Jonathan Stone), Barbara Roscoe (Receptionist), John Forgham (Beale)

PRE-TITLE/TEASER

An elderly man and a younger woman, both dressed very elegantly, meet for an apparent date. Silently, the woman draws a gun and shoots the man, both killing him and punching holes in an aquarium behind him, which sprouts numerous leaks.

SYNOPSIS

Steed, in surprising mathematical fashion, tracks a string of murders to a matchmaking firm called Togetherness. Joining as a client in search of love, his finances and "family inheritance" situation make him an ideal candidate for a scheme in which Togetherness will murder his cousin, and in return he will assassinate a spy named Emma Peel, but, in the process of "murdering" her, will the villains see through Steed's cover...?

REVIEW

In this episode, the opening pre-title again sells the Fennell-Clemens paradigm for the show. A glamorous dark-haired woman, drenched in white furs, meets a stately older gentleman on a blind date. The man is earnest in his desire to meet a peerless companion for the evening, but she has other ideas. Wordlessly, she pulls a gun equipped with a silencer from her purse and fires, sending him flailing into an aquarium, which springs a leak from the bullet holes. What—too old? I've heard of severe disappointment on these kinds of dates, but usually people just feign a headache and bail out early at dinner. In the worst cases, they climb out of bathroom windows to escape. But murder? The program is about stylish people engaging in bizarre over-the-top criminal acts in a hyper-idealized version of England in the 1960s, and it makes no apologies about it.

Even more sixties in tone is perhaps the fashion photographer, who in an unapologetically stereotypical manner engages in the most over-the-top vision of a sixties photographer imaginable, made legit by the inescapable fact that he surely wasn't a stereotype in the sixties. Truly, he would give David Hemmings a run for his money. (Antonioni, were you watching this?) With three cameras dangling on his neck and in between hipster speak and relentless shouts of "come on, baby!" and "animate!"—inspiration for Austin Powers?—he barely has time to speak to Steed. Nevertheless, in his usual good-natured fashion, Steed loans his bowler hat and umbrella to the obliging young female model, who in kinky *Avengers* fashion lacks pants. It's perfect! Turns out they're photographing a watch.

Patrick Cargill runs a murder racket—plucked straight from Hitchcock's *Strangers on a Train*—with a darkly genteel personality, a shadowed member of the gentry, a mirror image for Steed casually tossing out lines about how they keep the riff-raff out of their exclusive clientele. He is one of a series of classy villains that would dominate this season, usually navigating much better narratives.

A relatively slow-moving story that never quite gels, "The Murder Market" suffers under a vaguely banal plot. The murder swapping business gets a little more gas from the twist of Steed being ordered to kill Mrs. Peel, and the result is the tension of not knowing if the villains will see through the double-cross, as the viewers surely know that this murder has not and will never take place. This minor but smart twist, though essential, is not enough however to sustain an hour of television by itself. One the other hand, the surety of the production, the chemistry of the new regulars, Mrs. Peel's sonorous rendition of *Ride of the Valkyries* on a tuba (terminated by Steed's hole-in-one with a golf ball), and a receptionist whose name really should be Bambi do jazz up the episode considerably. However, it should be said that these are all elements that would be amplified much more significantly and to greater effect in later episodes. Here, they are essential in order to provide the story with its basic color and serve to dress up what isn't nearly as sure-footed as the season premiere nor the vast majority of this otherwise stellar season.

EPISODE NOTES

This is the second episode of this season to enter production, also with Elizabeth Shepherd initially playing Emma Peel. It was during this filming that producers Fennell and Clemens decided that Shepherd was not gelling with their vision. To be fair, Shepherd has her own ideas about why she was fired from the show, which involve the condescension of the producers towards her opinions and her strong-willed approach to the role, threatening the dominance of the mostly-male crew. Regardless of the exact reasons, Shepherd left during this production and the filming was remounted for both this episode and "The Town of No Return" in subsequent weeks. Again, the seams from this transition are virtually invisible. Despite a few mildly out-of-character moments—Emma gets a bit tipsy and dances around the morgue and has a rather Cathy Gale-like argument with Steed over ethics—Diana Rigg appears to drop right in with a very strong sense of her character.

CHAMPAGNE, CARS, CLOTHES, AND... CAMERAS!

Mrs. Peel wears a knee-length gray marle woolen dress with a boat collar; she tops it with a luxurious fur coat, possibly mink. Steed wears his black waistcoat with a white shirt and print tie and cufflinks. Later, he adds his Prince of Wales blazer.

Steed swaps out for his rawhide cardigan, previously seen in "The Master Minds" ('raw' is simply the only way to describe it). For his trip to Togetherness Inc., his navy three-piece suit returns with black bowler and brolly. Then, the tan overcoat, a black blazer with brass buttons over a pale pullover with a rollneck, and a return of both the gray three-piece and the navy chalk-stripe (later under a black overcoat). Mrs. Peel switches to another gray woolen dress with a black fur collar (she plays the tuba in this), then in turn, a black knee-length spaghetti-strap cocktail dress with a white mink fur stole, a white funerary dress, a black open-necked blouse with the black leather laced-up vest (as in "The Master Minds"), and finally she ends up in a chauffeur's hat over a white headscarf with a black woolen jacket in a floral pattern that doesn't seem to appear anywhere else in the season.

For the photography studio scene, the cameras are a Kodak Retinette 35mm rangefinder, an Asahiflex Ia (or IIa) 35mm SLR, possibly with the 58mm lens, and an all-black 1958 Canon VL2 35mm (the one he's shooting with), probably with the 50mm lens, and a rangefinder attachment on the hotshoe, probably the 50mm Lumi-Field.

TAG SCENE

Emma drives a 1934 Rolls-Royce Phantom II Hearse with Steed in the back (playing on the fact that he was to be assassinated by the villains earlier). Steed speaks but his voice isn't audible until he parts the window separating them.

QUOTES

"It needs something else. It's needs a bit of charm. A bit of elegance. A bit of savoir faire, as it were!"
"Tried working once, it didn't work out. Too much like work."
"Now, have you any particular preference for your marital partner?" "Well, broadly speaking, female."
"As long as she's got a good seat—on a horse—plays a fair game of bridge, mixes a dry martini, whips up a passable soufflé. You might say a good all-rounder."
"That must have set them a problem—" "Eh?" "—finding a match for you!" "I don't know, educated, charming, cultured—" "—ruthless, devious, scheming, have to be quite a girl. A mixture of Lucrezia Borgia and Joan of Arc."
"Well, he would have to be mature. A man of culture and intelligent..." "Mature, cultured, intelligent..." "...with stamina!"

86 (4.10.8) A SURFEIT OF H20

Steed plans a boat trip — Emma gets very wet
Written by Colin Finbow
Directed by Sidney Hayers

GUEST CAST

Noel Purcell (Jonah Barnard), Albert Lieven (Dr. Sturm), Sue Lloyd (Joyce Jason), Talfryn Thomas (Eli Barker), John Kidd (Sir Arnold Kelly), Geoffrey Palmer (Martin Smythe)

PRE-TITLE/TEASER

A poacher sets fresh traps in a grassy field. Sudden thunderclaps and dark clouds startle him, and before he can escape, a torrential rain begins and he quickly drowns in the downpour.

SYNOPSIS

A poacher drowns in the middle of a field, an absurd death which draws Steed and Mrs. Peel to investigate. In the surprisingly dry English countryside, all-too frequent torrential downpours occur, while a local carpenter named Jonah preaches of a Great Flood. And the local vegetable winery has a large cloud permanently parked above it that may be a harbinger that concurs with this gloomy prediction...

REVIEW

Playing upon the stereotype of English weather, "A Surfeit of H_2O" is an aptly-named story that begins with a man being drowned in a field by torrents of rain and continues from there in a parade of Flood metaphors and deaths by rain, mixed with dry dialogue (and occasional dry wit) that fails to soak up the damp. Thus, this is a relatively serious story, one that nevertheless manages to introduce several key eccentric characters that provide most of the interest for this week in a series of fits and starts.

Jonah is the main eccentric, a harbinger of watery death pulled from the streets of any major urban center, practically quoting delusions of doom and gloom right from the Bible. He really should have been called Noah, as he plays his role to the hilt, building a boat in his barn. (Perhaps writer Colin Finbow thought that name would be too obvious.) Jonah's doomed disciple is Eli Barker (Talfryn Thomas), a believer in Jonah's prophecy that lives in the leakiest house of all time—one has to wonder how much his own dampened dwelling has influenced his thinking in this matter. And he functions according to his name, a carnival barker calling everyone to Jonah's sideshow. When Emma Peel visits Eli, his home is so leaky that he is required to continually place containers about the house to catch drips as it pours outside—and soon inside. Giving up on pots and pans, he finally succumbs to using umbrellas, which by scene's end naturally prove inadequate as well, a shower falling upon Emma's head. But neither Jonah nor Eli are the cloud in this episode's storm. They are benign eccentrics, and, in an unusual twist, Steed and Emma make Jonah's barn their base, working with the eccentrics against the businesslike rainmaking vintners.

However, even the act of trying to make wine in England in the 1960s could be considered an eccentric act, and the villains at Grannie Gregson's Glorious Grogs Inc (their name is the funniest thing about them) are a dry and dour lot, just as you might imagine fictional deleterious English vegetable winemakers to be, sour and frustrated like tiny grapes, wanting for sunlight amid an endless downpour. Like their factory, they have permanent clouds hanging over them. This is especially true of the impossibly rude Dr. Sturm, who is perpetually pickled, like he's been left in vinegar too long. How he could not give Mrs. Peel more of his time when she appears in one of her most stunning outfits yet is beyond me.

Steed's visit to the winery goes far better, and far funnier, as he plays his usual gentility to absurd and idiotic proportions in multiple attempts to scope out a room emanating with the sound of continual rain. Initially provoked into a forced modicum of politeness, Dr. Sturm is eager for a sale but quickly tires of Steed's intrusions and retaliates by capturing Mrs. Peel and putting her under a wine press. (Possibly the first "whole-body" mammogram ever given.) This prompts Emma to exploit the show's own mythology when she proclaims Dr. Sturm a "diabolical mastermind."

Despite the drowning deaths and the diabolical masterminds, there's actually not much threat happening here, leaving the episode to function mainly on what little absurdity and action there is. This brings us to the story's core set piece, a sloppy slip-and-slide fight scene inside the chamber of perpetual rain, which continues until everyone is so wet that no one can keep their feet. The villains are finally piled up unconscious outside, and thus, the quest for a fruity little English vegetable wine comes to an end. In the end, their business model was a tad too ambitious to be believable…and the rainmaking idea is pretty crazy too! Steed and Emma then depart, finally dried out, in a stylish Mini Moke, the kind that would show up in abundance a few years later on ***The Prisoner***.

One factor that stands out is Emma's parade of high fashion. She takes tea under an umbrella in a simple black jumper and a wool coat, and then comes out for her appointment with Dr. Sturm in a fantastic cheetah print overcoat. In the next scene, she's in a shiny rubber suit complete with a black and white bathing cap. (Who needs a mac when this outfit is perfect for both those drippy English afternoons in the countryside and those drippy nights on the fashion catwalk?) Immediately thereafter, she's wearing a shirt that makes it look like she's ready for a hoedown. I can only assume she's having to change outfits frequently because the relentless rain has caused a garment-shrinking crisis. Speaking of which, peeling her out of her leather outfit after the soaking finale must have been quite the process—which I'm sure would have inspired many a salacious would-be male helper, eager to volunteer.

My main problem with this story is that Colin Finbow doesn't seem to know how to make a plot flow for ***The Avengers***. The whole of the narrative plays out without much of the Steed and Emma camaraderie and with precious little banter. Too much time is spent hanging around Jonah so that he can earnestly shout about the oncoming storms, interspersed with visits to the winery that produce little action each time. The whole of the story comes to an end when the villains improbably kidnap Mrs. Peel, forcing Steed into action, which prompts a cleanup that could have happened about forty minutes earlier if Steed could have just gotten through that door and found out what was making that rain sound—or something like that.

The villains' scheme is directionless and open-ended. Are they obsessed with making wine or making rain? They appear to already have the ability to do what they want to do, make torrential rain that is, and we never actually find out how they plan to use this ability because they are apparently completely distracted by trying to run an impractical business model as a front. Making good-tasting vegetable wine appears to be more challenging as far as diabolical mastermind plots go, and thus, one can only assume that they needed to have the final piece of their scheme in place before they could destroy the world—plenty of fresh vegetable wine with which to toast their victory. After all, all the other wineries would be rained out.

CHAMPAGNE, CARS, CLOTHES, AND CANINES

Steed wears a traditional riding outfit with a brown hunting jacket with brass buttons, a white shirt, a checked stuffed cravat, and riding boots. He carries his whangee umbrella and a shooting stick. He later switches the bowler out for a top hat, and the brown serge suit returns, followed by the Prince of Wales blazer and black waistcoat, which is the outfit that gets soaked. (No wonder he switched out of the brown serge!) Mrs. Peel wears a plethora of outfits, as mentioned above, but the most striking are the leopard-print overcoat with black handbag (her hair up) and the black shiny PVC catsuit with black-and-white bathing cap (her hair down) with a military-style khaki shirt with epaulettes underneath. She finally dons the black leather catsuit with silver zips for the final slip-and-slide scene with the villains, topped with a matching cap.

They drive a 1965 Austin Mini Moke (BOX 656C), possibly dark gray or red, throughout and in the tag scene.

TAG SCENE

Steed and Emma depart the country estate in a Mini Moke with Emma driving. Emma sneezes with an apparent oncoming cold.

QUOTES

"Mrs. Peel, it's you again. You should be preparing. The flood cometh!" "Yes, well, I put a down payment on a canoe."
"What is it?" "Old Bark." "Must have put the dog in it too!"
"Ah, Mrs. Peel, science cannot avert the approaching gloom!" "Perhaps not, but science can at least prepare us for it."
"My colleagues and I have just reached the end of a long hard road. We don't want to have that jeopardized, not now that we've finally succeeded." "Succeeded, in what?" "Succeeded in making rain, Mrs. Peel, rain such as the world has never seen before. Torrential driving rain, to order."
"You, diabolical mastermind, you!"
"It was over very quickly. I don't think it suffered."

87 (4.14.9) THE HOUR THAT NEVER WAS

Steed has to face the music — Emma disappears
Written by Roger Marshall
Directed by Gerry O'Hara

GUEST CAST

Gerald Harper (Geoffrey Ridsdale), Dudley Foster (Philip Leas), Roy Kinnear (Hickey), Roger Booth ('Porky' Purser), Daniel Moynihan (Corporal Barman), David Morrell (Wiggins), Fred Haggerty (Driver)

PRE-TITLE/TEASER

A stray dog runs through the English countryside as Steed and Emma ride in Steed's Bentley. The dog runs into the road causing Steed to crash. Both Steed and Emma are knocked unconscious with Steed's car clock stuck at one minute to eleven.

SYNOPSIS

As Steed and Emma are traveling to the Hamelin RAF base, Steed swerves to avoid a dog and crashes into a tree. They wake up sometime later to discover that the whole base is deserted, and all the clocks are stopped at eleven. When the base begins to vibrate with a piercing sound, Emma disappears, and Steed sees the base seemingly return to normal, but dead bodies keep turning up and the staff are acting more than a little strangely…

REVIEW

Starting out with Steed's canine-caused car crash, the episode begins a long period of Steed and Emma in isolation with little to comment upon as they search an abandoned RAF base—and Emma's initially in somewhat of a sour mood. The main issue with this episode is that the first third is just a recce of sorts for Steed and Mrs. Peel, and each time they actually see someone or hear something, this clue fails to produce any answers. Either the person is mysteriously killed or the noise remains a mystery, prompting yet more exploring with nothing in particular to report. Though these scenes are done with a hallucinatory quality, prompting confusion from our heroes (the sound of a milk float being heard repeatedly out of nowhere), continued any longer and it would have produced tedium. Fortunately, director Gary O'Hara knew when to quit and give the viewers some meat, and with sufficient time, the story blossoms nicely into a typically solid script from Roger Marshall.

The idea for the story came from Roger Marshall and Brian Clemens scouting out a deserted airbase in Norfolk for the episode "The Town of No Return," and it was there that shots on a playground and at an abandoned barracks were filmed for that story. Obviously, the location had a haunting appeal for the writer, who no doubt found the nostalgia and abandonment intriguing, and he wrote another story with the location in mind. However, for "The Hour That Never Was," the location ultimately chosen was Bovingdon Airfield outside London (now a Wendy Fair Market every Saturday). This proved to be an even better setting for the episode's eerie sense of isolation.

The location itself provides most of the interest in the first half, and it's easy to see why it was chosen, as the industrial buildings give O'Hara ample opportunity for directorial flourish and visual flare—plenty of texture and light to play with in the background. This reaches something of a peak with the sequence involving a piercing vertigo-inducing auditory attack, in which objects rattle and shake and the camera tilts violently back and forth. Quite my personal worst nightmare! And none too pleasant for Steed and Mrs. Peel either.

When a third body turns up, thankfully, it's still alive, and Roy Kinnear makes his second appearance in the program as the very much living Hickey, a derelict man hiding on the base and possibly the only person who knows what is going on. Kinnear does a marvelous job with this brief role. When the base's occupants reappear, we're meant to think the mysterious state of desertion was a concussion-induced hallucination by Steed, but in *The Avengers*, there is never a simple or mundane explanation. We know that Steed and Emma are always together, so when Emma disappears, this fragile theory starts to crumble. And then we are shocked by Hickey's disturbing death. From here, the mysterious fatalities keep piling up as the base's staff scramble to dispose of all the bodies behind the scenes, a milkman as ersatz undertaker, porting around corpses on his float. (Just the kind of thing to make you cancel your milk!)

While the explanation for the base's abandoned state is a bit mundane and hairbrained—the Broughton Suspension Bridge incident was real but how that translates into mind-control is more than a little tenuous—it's no more hairbrained than most of the villainous plots in *The Avengers*, and I can easily imagine people cringing at the sound of a dentist drill. (The first time this was used for threatening purposes was "The Mauritius Penny.") The mystery solved and the villains revealed, this leaves the story to skim over any further explanations and end on an action scene steeped in nitrous oxide-induced guffaws. Steed finds playing with the canisters impossible to resist despite Mrs. Peel's admonishment and disposes of his adversary amid laughing gas hysterics. Emma knocks out one man after dousing his eyes with sand from a fire bucket. Then, both heroes laugh themselves to a close and depart chasing after the milk float, sped up *Benny Hill* style, or as I prefer to imagine it, like the Beatles in *A Hard Day's Night*.[4]

It's not Roger Marshall's usual style to plot out a story this uneven and dialogue-light, eerie silence in the first half, followed by parties 'round a punch bowl and action scenes in the second, but it works well enough for this one example, and the two halves balance each other out in their extremes.

EPISODE NOTES

Gerald Harper seems doomed to criminally small roles in the series. He had a tiny comedic role in "Death Dispatch" in the second season and would return in "The Great Great Britain Crime," filmed as part of the first block of episodes starring Linda Thorson when John Bryce was briefly producer

---

4 Apparently, the sped up film created considerable controversy at the time. All the details can be found in *Bowler Hats and Kinky Boots: The Unofficial and Unauthorised Guide to The Avengers* by Michael Richardson, pgs. 149-150. Personally, I don't understand the controversy. In my opinion, it makes the scene more charming. Such was the power of *Benny Hill* at the time, I suppose. But it's not like they added a yakety-sax as well.

in late 1967. That last role was much more extensive, though we'll likely never see the bulk of it, as the episode was injudiciously cut up for inclusion in "Homicide and Old Lace," and the remainder was reportedly thrown away.

CHAMPAGNE, CARS, CLOTHES, AND CANINES

The vintage car that Steed crashes is a 1924 Bentley 3 Litre (XR 6056). This is its first appearance in transmission order, though in production order it is the last, possibly due to the crash or maybe the staged damage that is seen onscreen, including a shattered windscreen.[5] Hickey's dog, Rosie, the one that causes the accident, looks to be a French bulldog. Good thing she's not Steed's dog, otherwise she'd be a 'bad girl' and liable to get no treats for the remainder of the day. Steed had apparently given up on dogs; maybe he decided he was too busy to take care of them, after all he was always getting someone else to do it for him.

Mrs. Peel debuts a new outfit, pink hip-hugging pants with a black, sleeveless, collarless fitted top and matching black-striped jacket with tapered pocket closures, also called a trouser suit, designed by John Bates. Worn with Edward Rayne's black-striped, white ankle boots and a broad black belt. Her watch with a tartan band either has very bad time, or they've been at the base for over four hours by the time she loses it. Later, it's reset to twenty past twelve. Like Mrs. Peel, Steed wears the same outfit throughout—the navy single-breasted three-piece suit with black bowler and brolly. But there are two versions. If you look very closely, one is single-vented and the other double.

No champagne but lots of liquor at the party, including punch with "too much brandy," according to Steed.

Since they at least *try* to drive the milk float, I'll go ahead and identify it— a 1955 Wales & Edwards (594 EMX).

TAG SCENE

Steed and Emma depart on a milk float and suddenly realize no one is driving. They then jump off and chase after the float as the film speeds up.

QUOTES

"As our host isn't here to receive us, 'Do have a drink, Mrs. Peel, Mr. Steed. So glad you could come to our little shindig.'" "Shade too much brandy." "Your recipe, I suppose?"

"I've been living off dustbins all my working life, sir. From Biggin Hill, Mildenhall, Cardington, Hamelin here…" "All air bases?" "Oh, yes, sir. 'Cerpantly.' None of that Army or Navy rubbish for me. I'm loyal, I am. Loyal to the Air Force. Always have been. Best dustbins in the business."

"I'm a 'conscimentious subjector.' I detest war. Or violence. Or stamp collectors." "Stamp collectors?" "Filthy habit, collecting stamps. All that old saliva. More disease gets spread that way. Generations of old saliva. Foreign saliva, too."

"I suddenly felt dizzy and I must have passed out. Next thing I knew I was here, but how I got here…?" "Probably a milk float. They do a regular service, door-to-door every five minutes."

"Don't play around with that, Steed! It's nitrous oxide, laughing gas." "Ha, ha, ha!"

---

5 It was later exported to the United States. Current whereabouts unknown.

88 (4.4.10) DIAL A DEADLY NUMBER

Steed plays Bulls and Bears — Emma has no option
Written by Roger Marshall
Directed by Don Leaver

GUEST CAST

Clifford Evans (Henry Boardman), Jan Holden (Ruth Boardman), Anthony Newlands (Ben Jago), John Carson (Fitch), Peter Bowles (John Harvey), Gerald Sim (Frederick Yuill), Michael Trubshawe (The General), Norman Chappell (Macombie), John Bailey (Warner), Edward Cast (Waiter)

PRE-TITLE/TEASER

A group of business men sit at a table in a busy club. One businessman remarks about the new device he's acquired—"a bleeper"—which signals him whenever he has an important phone call. Another man sits alone at the bar counter, and after bumping into the departing businessman, he covertly exchanges the device with another identical one. Once the businessman has begun his meeting, the mysterious man dials a number on the telephone which causes the businessman to die suddenly of an apparent heart attack.

SYNOPSIS

Stock market investors are dropping dead one by one from mysterious causes. The only link is they all have a new business product called a 'bleep,' a small pen-shaped mechanical device, a precursor to an electronic pager. As a result, Steed investigates a merchant bank, and Emma investigates the company that makes the 'bleeps.' Unfortunately, Steed has been given a special device of his own, disguised as his watch, which may make a much louder sound…

REVIEW

This is as close as it gets to seeing how an episode of the third season might have looked if updated to single camera shooting on 35mm film. Roger Marshall was one of the finest writers working on the second and third seasons, and Don Leaver is a director that goes all the way back to the first. Known for his taut direction, Leaver was one of a handful of directors that was capable of squeezing out a modicum of artistry from multi-camera videotaped productions. Freed from the straightjacket of videotaping, here he delivers a film noir style that pays significant homage to the genre. No more bulky video cameras that dwarfed the actors on tiny sets, the lenses could now be wider angle, the sets larger, and the camera could move right up to an actor's face. And this latter technique is frequently used throughout to emphasize subtle reactions of the cast to the rampant subterfuge on display, usually the amusingly genteel confidence man bluffs of Patrick Macnee, who is at something of a peak for his portrayal of Steed. The tactic so often used by him was to blatantly lay his cards on the table, just to get a reaction, delivered with such congenial charm that the opposition didn't know what to think or how to react. "Is he serious?" they might wonder. This reaches a pinnacle with his ruse involving a watch that the villains believe has a bomb in it. Thankfully, Steed discovered its explosive qualities earlier, and, having secretly resubstituted the watch for a benign one, has a blast feigning ignorance about its perceived deadliness. Resultingly, he has the crooks on pins and needles as he swings the watch nonchalantly and carelessly taps it upon the table, sending them scurrying in terror.

This is how you make a story about boardroom politics, wine-tasting, stock tips, and "put options" interesting for television—wit, humor, artistic camerawork, and spy-oriented innuendo, subtly delivered through sparkling dialogue.

However, these are just the superficial dressings that typically elevate *The Avengers* to the next level. What makes this episode exceptional? As always, story, story, and story. The script is one of the finest to grace the program. Like a good Bond film, it pulls the viewer in through its characters, involves them in their motivations, adds risk to produce tension and then provides ample payoff, usually executed in the quirky *Avengers* high style—a champagne bottle cork produces the finishing coup de grace to our hapless villains in this situation, the end result of the unusual and original concept of a wine-tasting duel.

This episode crystalizes many aspects that would become part of the program for the next three years, aspects that would have been presented part and parcel in the previous three seasons but were now coming sharply into focus. These include avant-garde ideas on the cusp of science and technology, the typical upper-class interests, eccentrics, humor, and wit, and the deadly spy-oriented plots. All of it reaches a zenith here.

On the other hand, "Dial a Deadly Number" is strangely old-fashioned as well. (It even repeats a line from "Death of a Great Dane" almost verbatim.) The science involved is speculative but hardly ahead of its time—beepers were first developed in the late fifties—and, in fact, is nowhere near science-fiction, not really, just on the cutting edge, made all the more terrifying to audiences of the day by its novelty.

The motorcycle attack upon Steed in an underground parking lot must have surely been the kind of scene that John Bryce's crew would have loved to have presented in the third season—deep shadows and contrasting pools of light, the camera twirling to show Steed's disorientation as he fends off the cyclists, their headlamps blazing into his eyes. A mundane threat but brilliantly shot, just as Julian Wintle reportedly promised when he proclaimed that he'd be able to do the show ten times better on film. Indeed. This is *The Avengers* for the Hitchcock generation. And yet, when Steed disables a motorcyclist by throwing his coat over the man's eyes like a bullfighter, it is harkening to the future with its usual quirky charm.

The eccentric murderer Fitch is an old school type as well, having much more akin to Redfern in "The Golden Eggs" than to Professor Poole or Z. Z. Von Schnerk or Marcus Rugman. He is an obsessive clockmaker, an horologist that builds and then stops a clock for each of his victims. Reclusive, secretive, he's the de facto leader and secret weapon for the criminals, always working behind the scenes, preferring to keep to himself as the power behind the throne. Like Redfern, he is a craftsman mastermind, whose mental processes are clocklike and authoritarian, ranting about the ravages of time.

All of this may in fact be a holdover from the third season in both tone and style; *The Avengers* would move on to even more camp humor, to more fantasy, more eccentricity, more absurdity, until it reached a shrill crescendo that could no longer be sustained, much as Brian Clemens later remarked, but for this brief moment in time two eras of the series came together and produced a masterpiece—one perfect in its harmonious balance between the future and the past.

CHAMPAGNE, CARS, CLOTHES, AND CANINES

Steed begins the episode wearing his navy single-breasted suit with a white shirt, dark tie, and tiepin, whereas Mrs. Peel debuts a new outfit: a pale tailored jacket with fur trim descending from the collar to the hem, a pale knee-length skirt, and black high-heels. Steed wears his gray single-breasted, three-piece suit, then his pale blue overcoat with the bi-colored collar, with a striped shirt, gray tie, and matching bowler hat. Mrs. Peel briefly switches to a hooded coat tied with a drawstring about the neck. Steed wears black tie at the dinner party, but Mrs. Peel outdoes him in a knee-length embroidered evening dress in an orchid pattern with applique and sequins. She tops it with a gray fur coat, probably mink, cinched at the waist with an elegant rope-belt. Lots of wine. At the wine-tasting, Steed returns to his gray single-breasted, three-piece suit while Mrs. Peel debuts yet another dress in this fashion-heavy episode, a purple velvet dress with lace about the shoulders and the cuffs in a vine pattern. Very Victorian in tone. To finish off the episode, Steed wears his navy chalk-stripe, his gray Prince of Wales blazer and black waistcoat with silver buttons, and his brown serge suit in rapid succession; and Mrs. Peel in her leather catsuit with silver zips. Not a lot of champagne, but a champagne cork takes out the villain in the climax and they do toast their victory at the end, so I'm calling it a win for the sparkly stuff.[6]

At least one of the motorcycles is a Triumph Speed Twin (452 YMF), but they're hard to identify. One of the motorcyclists was played by stuntman Alan Chuntz, who was required to fall off the bike after running into wooden packing crates in the underground parking garage.

TAG SCENE

Steed and Emma ride in a cab surrounded by caskets of fine wine, presumably booty from their recent exploits, and Emma "guesses" the vintage they're drinking by covertly reading the label.

QUOTES

"Legacy of my uncle." "Pity it's dented." "Battle of the Somme, 1916." "German bullet?" "Canadian mule."
"Mr. Steed, I admire your attack, but even on the strength of these references, a loan of two million pounds…" "Loan? You misunderstand me! I haven't come here to borrow, I want to deposit."
"And her?" "Attractive, intelligent, and expensive." "Cold as ice." "And promiscuous." "Promiscuous?" "Beyond that, my lips are sealed. A true gentleman doesn't—" "—a true gentleman doesn't know of a woman's promiscuity."
"1908…would *not* be the year…1909, from the northern end of the vineyard."
"It's as much as I'd imagined it." "The fact that you imagined it at all intrigues me."
"Not tactful, optimistic. And I admire a woman with a past." "What's optimistic about that?" "The hope that history may repeat itself."
"First choose the pigeons…" "…then, put the cat amongst them."

89 (4.12.11) MAN-EATER OF SURREY GREEN

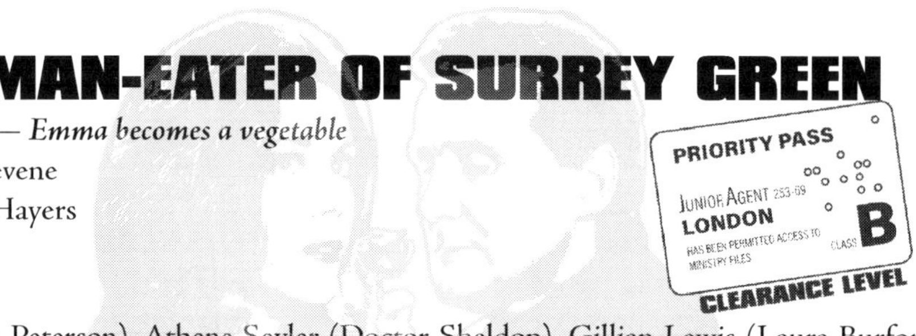

Steed kills a climber — Emma becomes a vegetable
Written by Philip Levene
Directed by Sidney Hayers

GUEST CAST

Derek Farr (Sir Lyle Peterson), Athene Seyler (Doctor Sheldon), Gillian Lewis (Laura Burford), William Job (Alan Carter), David Hutcheson (Wing Commander Davies), Joe Ritchie (Publican), Donald Oliver (Bob Pearson), Joby Blanshard (Joe Mercer), Uncredited: Edwin Finn (Professor Taylor), Harry Shacklock (Professor Knight), Ross Hutchinson (Dr. Connelly), John G. Heller (Lennon)

PRE-TITLE/TEASER

A scientist couple in a greenhouse remark on a new plant species they've created. The woman runs into the yard but suddenly stops when she hears an eerie sound. Inexplicably, she walks in a hypnotic

6 The champagne bottle that Steed pulls from the rack is referred to as 'Grande Marque' and that is where this edition gets its name.

daze to the road and enters a limousine driven by a chauffeur.

SYNOPSIS

When a newly-engaged botanist goes missing from her normal job, Steed finds out that she and three other missing botanists are suddenly in the employ of Sir Lyle Peterson, who is apparently developing a new flowering shrub. Investigating further, Steed and Mrs. Peel trace industrial deliveries to an abandoned farm, where a recently crashed British space capsule has brought back an alien seed pod from space. They at first believe Sir Lyle is attempting to cultivate the plant, but it soon becomes obvious that the plant is meat-eating, has a brain and mind-control powers, and is forcing the humans to assist in its plan to grow over the entire Earth...

REVIEW

You could scour the entire history of ***The Avengers*** and not find an episode so unique and out-of-character for the series as "The Man-Eater of Surrey Green." What, you say? What about "Warlock" with its mind-controlling wizard? What about "The White Dwarf" with its speculative science? What about killer robots in "The Cybernauts"? What about the alien invasion theme in "From Venus with Love"? The point is well-taken. Individually, those are all worthy examples of science-fiction or fantasy, though the final one is a red herring. (Spoiler: there are no aliens.) But consider this. Is there any other episode of the show that combines all of those elements, lays them bare without explanation so brazenly, and tells the story dead serious without any of the elements of the show so carefully cultivated during this period? The atmosphere, the feel of the story, is one that is unique in ***The Avengers***. It is something more akin to early sixties science-fiction films like ***Children of the Damned***—the eerie mind-control sound effects are very similar to what is used in that film—or the ***Quatermass*** serials from the early fifties. Those are fine concepts, worthy of exploration, though it's surprising to find them represented here. But ***The Avengers*** is a unique show and explored many varied topics over its many seasons, so open-mindedness is encouraged. Very well—mind-controlling spores from outer space it is.

For a bizarre moment of kinkiness, perhaps fitting for such an off-color story, Steed nearly sits on a spiny cactus placed precariously under a blanket on his car seat. Its phallic appearance is highly suspicious, and in the next scene, as Steed and Emma examine the deadly dildo, it is dropped and rolls under a settee. This scene, for all its humor value, is played totally straight, if that is the correct word. And the whole episode is like that, as if the humor and surrealism and everything else that the series has been building for three seasons has been drained right out of it in an attempt to make a pure science-fiction story. The frequent bizarreness, which is perceived as hyperreal or surrealistic in other episodes, is in this case played as if totally real instead. This is probably because, in science-fiction, whatever concept introduced becomes the reality, and the tone must always represent that. Thus, ***The Avengers***, for this week, is no longer a spoof of its genre.

This is not entirely a bad thing. Taken for what it is, "The Man-Eater of Surrey Green" is for the most part quite enjoyable. The direction in particular is really excellent, with Sidney Hayers making good use of back-lighting in several scenes. The scenes of characters under hypnosis are quite eerie at times. The writhing of germinating creepers is simulated by movement under a sheet, which hypnotized characters gaze over reverently like deluded cultists. Similarly, there is a tragic and disturbing death by electrocution for Alan Carter while his mesmerized fiancée looks on unbothered, and Sir Lyle's chauffeur kills a hypnotized lorry driver with a shotgun blast at close range. Very creepy stuff!

This episode's eccentric is Sir Lyle Peterson. The term 'plant enthusiast' would be selling this fellow short. His entire estate is swamped in thick vines and creepers, which he oddly drapes over nude female mannequins, strategically positioned throughout his home. (Apparently, they have real hair too.) His house also contains many Venus flytraps, which rather improbably snap suddenly closed when provided rare sweetmeats such as imported beetles. He treats the plants like pets and feeds them with disturbing glee. As a supporting act in eccentricity, Athene Seyler has a fun turn as a kooky botanist, having played a similarly eccentric character in last season's "Build a Better Mousetrap."

Steed and Emma remain close together throughout the story, which can never be a bad thing, and the final battle amidst a jungle of animated deadly plants is one of the more serious threats that their team has faced up until now, with one particularly harrowing moment in which Emma loses her protection against the plant's mental control, forcing a fight between the partners. The battle quickly becomes a dance to seize the herbicide necessary to destroy the menace. The special effects are quite good in this scene with a collapsing manor set and writhing plant tendrils.

"Man-Eater" is an unusual science-fiction break in the season's continuity, much like "Too Many Christmas Trees" is for psychic powers—though that example is far more successful at working within the show's proforma. Nevertheless, considering the rarity of space alien visitors, it makes sense that *The Avengers* would only have to worry about it every nine years or so; therefore, this concept seems fine for a one-off presentation.

EPISODE NOTES

This story has so many points of reference that are repeated in a *Doctor Who* story called "The Seeds of Doom" (the mad herbimaniac, the dotty old botany expert, the massive space plant-monster tearing up an old manor, the herbicide that ultimately kills it) that I'm surprised that writer Robert Banks Stewart wasn't sued for plagiarism. He was working on *The Avengers* during this season and surely would have been familiar with this story. Philip Levene passed away in 1973 and wasn't available to defend his intellectual property when the *Doctor Who* episodes aired several years later. Nevertheless, it should be noted that *Doctor Who* is perhaps a more appropriate vehicle for such a worthy science-fiction concept, and the core ideas were nicked from earlier examples anyway. Ultimately, in British science-fiction television, only Nigel Kneale has any legitimate call to complain about plagiarists.

CHAMPAGNE, CARS, CLOTHES, AND CANINES

Mrs. Peel wears a tailored corduroy jacket with pleated pockets and a knee-length skirt. Steed starts out casual in a black pullover and trousers, which would end up becoming one of his mainstays for casual dress; then he switches to his brown serge suit with a white shirt, dark tie, and the tan overcoat. Then, riding in Mrs. Peel's Lotus Elan S2 convertible, Steed wears his brown riding jacket, this time with dark buttons, checked cravat, and top hat (from "Surfeit of H2O"), and Mrs. Peel adds a black beret to her outfit. Steed's rawhide cardy blights the screen again before another overcoat appears with a bi-colored collar with felt in black; this one is pale blue in color rather than tan. Mrs. Peel finishes up in her leather jumpsuit over a black pullover, with matching black leather jacket, and Steed in his Prince of Wales blazer with the black waistcoat (both of which apparently survived the flooding in their last outing). In the tag scene, Steed's brown serge suit returns.

Otherwise, a lot of houndstooth in this episode. Ms. Sheldon wears a pantsuit in the material, and lots of the somnambulists wear houndstooth flat driving caps.

The 1925 Bentley 3 Litre appears for the second and final time.

TAG SCENE

Steed and Emma ride in a tractor-pulled haycart down a country lane.

QUOTES

"Morning Sunrise, a full-fledged bloom of delicate russet tints in a haunting bouquet—for you, Mrs. Peel."

"You have your own built-in early warning system, you know. A certain look in the eye, roses…"
"What pretty hair!" "Yes, real too."
"Imagine sitting on that. If my car had a roof, I'd have gone through it!"
"Where does that little beggar come from?" "Mars." "Mars!" "Mm, or even the moon. Recent photographs show whole areas of vegetation." *(??)*
"And think of the tendrils!" "I'd rather not." "Reaching out for miles. If it were allowed to seed, it would cover the Earth in, well, a matter of weeks!" "Well, there'd be no shortage of beans."
"I'm an herbicidal maniac, didn't you know?"

90 (4.11.12) TWO'S A CROWD

Steed is single-minded — Emma sees double
Written by Philip Levene
Directed by Roy Baker

GUEST CAST

Warren Mitchell (Brodny), Maria Machado (Alicia Elena), Alec Mango (Shvedloff), Wolfe Morris (Pudeshkin), Julian Glover (Vogel), John Bluthal (Ivenko), Eric Lander (Major Carson)

PRE-TITLE/TEASER

A model airplane cruises over London, including the Houses of Parliament, before it divebombs a man drinking punch on a stylish balcony. The model plane drops its 'bomb' which lands in the punchbowl with a "poing!" The message inside is from "Psev" proclaiming that he's arriving at 12 o'clock.

SYNOPSIS

Steed and Emma are in charge of security at a defense conference when the department learns that the master spy Colonel Psev has entered the country. Psev and his assistants force Ambassador Brodny to help them in their scheme to infiltrate the conference. All looks bleak for Brodny, who is sympathetic to British ways, until a chance meeting with model and unemployed actor Gordon Webster produces a dead ringer for Steed…

REVIEW

"Two's a Crowd" opens with terrible special effects of a prop plane. It looks just like a model, one of the worst models you've ever seen in any film or television show anywhere. But wait! It's *supposed* to be a model plane. It's the sound effects that are convincing, and that's throwing you off; it sounds just like a real dive-bombing plane, heading for a bombing run. This sequence concludes with the model plane ejecting a tiny plastic bomb, which sproings into Ambassador Brodny's punchbowl, flicking punch into his eye, a handy metaphor for the arrival of his boss. Colonel Psev (or Pzev, as is printed on Steed's dossiers), when he arrives, proceeds to verbally or physically slap Brodny on a regular basis, putting to an end his plush decadent life as an ambassador. This is most unfortunate for Brodny, who has become quite accustomed to life in the Western world (they don't have punchbowls in Russia), and by twists and turns over this season and the next, he would become an object of ridicule for both political sides. Poor Brodny!

This is a silly, fun story that focuses on character. Patrick Macnee is wonderful in two roles. As Gordon Webster, a seeming dark fantasy for Steed, he is an indulgent lush and a cad with an odious mustache. He slouches, constantly smokes cigars and displays total corruptibility. When Webster takes over as Steed, it becomes clear that acting as if you're acting like someone else, and acting well, is a subtle business, and Macnee is doing a great job. Emma gets pushed to the side somewhat with all the focus on Steed. She goes undercover as a prim clerk in a model airplane shop. (They probably don't have those in Russia either. Model airplane shops, that is. Not prim clerks.)

Aside from the doppelgänger angle, there is the mysterious Psev, a foreign agent who is never seen, his usual affairs run by his four assistants with the stoic and snide Vogel (Julian Glover) in apparent charge. Off-camera, Psev apparently spends all his time building model airplanes, drinking crème de violette, and smoking cigars, and he's very picky about his brands, but the British agents are dying to see him in the flesh, even to the point of bringing liqueurs as gifts to tempt him out into the open. The twist is that Psev doesn't really exist, the name made up from the initials of the four 'assistants.'

The four Psevs now have full run of their embassy and quickly adopt Brodny's idea to use Gordon Webster to infiltrate a major conference. They proceed to test his believability on Mrs. Peel. Initially, Emma sees right through the fake Steed, forcing the agents to take her hostage. From here, Webster fine-tunes his performance, leaving both Mrs. Peel and the audience confused as to who's who, and everything ends as it must in *The Avengers,* with the real Steed impersonating his impersonator. This clever twist of expectations results in one of Steed and Emma's best scenes together, when she still isn't sure if Steed is Steed and not Gordon Webster, and by now, neither is the audience.

In the style of the Cathy Gale era, the whole affair turns out to have been planned by Steed from practically the beginning, Emma's participation and ignorance of the true scheme once again necessary for the plan's success. As a result, the agents' ruse backfires on them, forcing them to reveal themselves to Steed, whom they believe is Gordon Webster. Clever ole Steed.

In another turn of the Wayback Machine to earlier seasons, Steed is given a bodyguard in the form of Major Carson, who becomes Steed's roommate at his flat, irritatingly squeezing his toothpaste from the middle of the tube. He dresses just like Dr. Keel and Steed in promotional photographs for the first season, a trench coat perpetually tied close about him, and this subtly suggests a spoof of that early secret agent persona.

One of the best aspects of this story is the clever and bizarre use of model airplanes and ships as methods of attack by the enemy agents. Aside from the opening pre-title in which Brodny has his punch turned into an eyewash by a wayward missile from one model plane, a would-be traitor on their side is killed by a submarine in a lake, and Steed and Emma face two attacks by model airplanes with machine guns installed, the latter of which is turned upon the villains by radio interference.

"Two's a Crowd" is spy story that manages to spoof its genre subtly without betraying this to the audience, never giving the viewer much time to think about the story's improbability. The Russians are stereotypes. (Though their country of origin is never mentioned, the accents give it away.) They are stiff and uptight, always talking about drinking vodka and complaining about lateness or lack of efficiency. Stereotypical too are the British. Even when Macnee is playing Webster as John Steed, he portrays a kind of indulgent British layabout with a faint Cockney accent, the flip side of the gentry when it goes dark.

The whole of the plot is patently absurd but nevertheless plays out as believable, and the victory over the villains is a relatively meager one; they tease out the true identity of mystery spy agents as they simultaneously destroy them, or so it seems, as the walls of their embassy fall in upon them from a crashing model airplane. This is the new template for *The Avengers,* and it only works when everyone is a fantasy or hyperreal version of themselves.

EPISODE NOTES

Warren Mitchell, who plays Brodny as an obtuse court jester within his own embassy, would return as the same character in "The See-Through Man" next season, where he would become even more of a buffoon and a source of slapstick humor.

CHAMPAGNE, CARS, CLOTHES, AND CANINES

This one gets a little complicated for Patrick Macnee, so I'll just stick with what we know the real Steed wears throughout. He starts in a black cardigan, and then the dark gray single-breasted, three-piece suit with the single breast pocket, then the navy chalk-stripe, and then the pale gray suit with a satin tie. Otherwise, Macnee gets to slum it up in a lot of houndstooth, Hawaiian shirts, and tweed, and other hideous outfits—we'll leave the rawhide cardigan out of it for this one time!

Mrs. Peel starts out in a black catsuit with a white PVC quilted vest or tabard. As a model shop assistant, she wears a tailored white long-sleeved blouse with a black knee-length pleated skirt, but she later swaps this out for an elegant black sleeveless top and trousers with black pumps. She tops this with a brindled black-and-white print coat. For the riding scene at the tag, she wears a fitted black jacket, checked gray trousers, and a broad-brimmed fedora, and he wears a soft, zipped cardigan and pale trousers.

TAG SCENE

On horseback, Steed and Emma meet at the bridge at Tyke's Water Lake in Elstree. Emma initially pretends to not recognize Steed (a play on his questionable identity earlier in the story) but then calls for him to follow her.

QUOTES

"Roguish—an ensemble that says 'man.' The chapeau-ist with the mostest and slacks built for action. Wear them when swinging the cha-cha-cha..."
"This is the outfit for you, cunningly cut to accentuate that male, male build, yet remains loose and easy for action wear. Gentlemen, really an outfit to go stag in!"
"Do you always squeeze the toothpaste from the middle?" "No, I never did until I got married."
"Come now, Mrs. Peel. If I had a twin, I'm sure Mother would have mentioned it!" *(Mother?)*
"Major Carson, make yourself at home...and feel free to take off that raincoat." "He can't do that!" "Oh!"
"You fool! Why don't you put a stick of celery in there as well!"
"A hostage in the hand is worth two in the tomb."

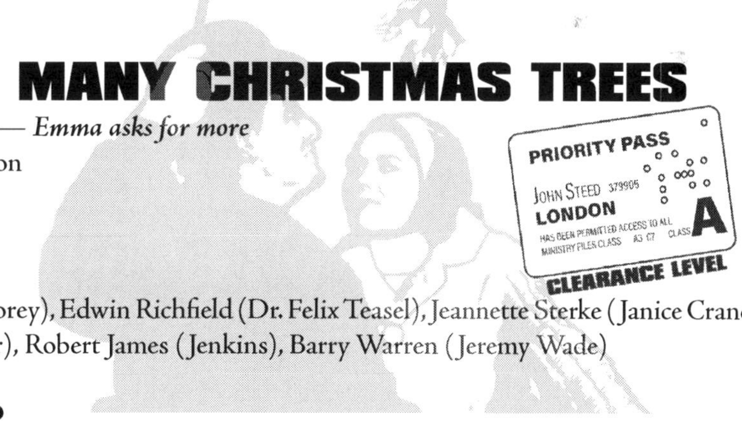

91 (4.6.13) TOO MANY CHRISTMAS TREES

Steed hangs up his stocking — Emma asks for more
Written by Tony Williamson
Directed by Roy Baker

GUEST CAST

Mervyn Johns (Brandon Storey), Edwin Richfield (Dr. Felix Teasel), Jeannette Sterke (Janice Crane), Alex Scott (Martin Trasker), Robert James (Jenkins), Barry Warren (Jeremy Wade)

PRE-TITLE/TEASER

Steed has a terrifying nightmare involving a disturbing, masked Santa Claus and he opens a Christmas present from Emma that turns out to be a photograph of himself. Santa then shows him the dead body of a friend and fellow agent and then laughs mockingly until Steed wakes.

SYNOPSIS

Steed is having nightmares about old St. Nick, and "he's a particularly nasty type!" His dreams predict the death of a fellow agent that is accused of selling secrets. To take his mind off the troubling dreams, Emma invites him to accompany her to the house of Dickens fanatic Brandon Storey, and there, he dreams of his own death by guillotine in ***A Tale of Two Cities*** theme. Soon, a group of telepaths are revealed to be the fiendish masterminds who are draining Steed's thoughts to learn his secrets...

REVIEW

The Avengers does ***Men Who Stare at Goats***! In the opening pre-title, Steed navigates a nightmare before Christmas that could have been directed by Salvador Dali, and this is simultaneously a chance to explore his boyish glee at receiving presents and his worst fears about spy work—the death of a close friend that he trained with. (His fears were justified, going by later episodes.) Once again, we're exploring the juxtaposition of humor and violence, a common theme in the program.

In Steed's strikingly surrealistic dream, the deliberately two-dimensional and stagey tree forest contains a massive barrel of Christmas gifts the size of a small swimming pool. Here he finds a photograph of himself and a terrifying St. Nick wearing a Santa fright mask, the kind that scared the hell out of young children in 1940s photographs. Being ***The Avengers***, naturally the dream ends with a murder, the corpse being transposed with a pair of Christmas stockings stuffed with candy and satsumas, and Steed is mocked by Santa's throaty maniacal laugh to the dream's conclusion. Thus, from the outset, we know we are not exactly going to get ***The Avengers*** equivalent of ***A Charlie Brown Christmas*** in this deeply bizarre experimental episode about psychic espionage.

One could quite rightly ask what any of this has to do with either Christmas or ***The Avengers***. The question would be well-taken as the episode is far from the usual paradigm employed by the series before (and rarely since), and the Christmas trappings are almost entirely incidental to the narrative. The answer to the question therefore is, quite rightly, nothing—or *almost* nothing—but fortunately that appears to not be a problem in this historically catastrophic Christmas for John Steed, whose torments engage both our sympathies and that of Mrs. Peel. Fortunately, the whole of the experiment is successful, even if almost unique in the history of the program, being not only the lone proper Christmas episode in nine seasons (broadcast on 25 December 1965), but one of a handful to deal with the subject of psychic powers or even psychic manipulation of the main characters, whether by drugs or other means. Even the most surreal or bizarre episodes in the future would not match the sheer psychic terror of this story, amplified by Roy Baker's superb film noir direction.

As such, we would not again see Steed this disabled by his enemies until "Stay Tuned," in which he is nearly turned into a ***Manchurian Candidate***-style assassin through mind-altering drugs. In this episode, however, his dreams don't end; in fact, they get worse, until he appears to be presciently seeing objects and events ahead of time, leaving him to become steadily worn down and sullen. Fortunately, Steed is far cleverer than he is often given credit for, and he has a great twist of expectations in store for his psychic assailants.

It all reaches a sort of peak mid-episode with Janice Crane's party trick, a 'mind-reading' ruse that is clearly going in the other direction, with Steed becoming an unwilling participant in a psychic attack rather than harmless telepathic yuletide fun and games—you know, the normal kind at all Dickensian-themed Christmas parties. In this frightening scene, Baker's dreamlike direction breaks through into reality for Steed, indicating his worsening condition, the cards held in his hand turning into bleary hallucinatory objects of terror. Well, it's far more interesting than playing The Minister's Cat!

Indeed, this theme of surrealistic hallucinations continues for the audience's benefit as well, through Baker's direction, as Jeremy Wade is killed in the Hall of Great Expectations, his corpse lying under a net of cobwebs lit only by flickering candlelight. And in the climactic Hall of Mirrors battle scene we're treated to a gun battle and a wrestling duel. And this is naturally a battle that is handily won by Mrs. Peel, who knees her assailant in the coccyx amid disorientating mirror-like distortions. Mrs. Peel seems angry at the end, having watched her companion being slowly tortured by the fiends, and shows a grim lack of remorse upon having shot one of them, like she's seriously put out and can't be bothered any longer. This is classic sustained tension and release for the audience as well as the heroes.

This fight scene is driven to a crescendo by Laurie Johnson's most exciting jazz music yet, the first use of such in an otherwise eerie musical score, as if to underscore the awakening of *The Avengers*, whose superhero expertise is finally allowed to cut through the dreamlike delusions, their victory close at hand. And yet, when Brandon Storey's St. Nick is nicked in the end, shot and sliding down, his reflection in the mirror is distorted just as in Steed's nightmares. It is a final blurring of dreams and reality.

As a couple, Steed and Emma have never betrayed so much irritation with each other's flirtatiousness in polite company, cementing the idea that they are former lovers, and yet, their companionship is closer than ever before. It's great fun to watch for all the subtle ways that their intimate friendship is depicted. The look upon Mrs. Peel's face as Steed holds mistletoe over her in the tag scene is one of adoration mixed with amusement, and her fretting over her beleaguered friend's condition in the first half of the story is a charming indication of their clear status as best friends, betraying a profound closeness seldom reached outside of fantasy.

The guest cast is really quite excellent this week—Edwin Richfield in particular, whose red herring of collusion with the villains and sour demeanor help distinguish his character—but none of them manages to drive a wedge between Patrick Macnee and Diana Rigg's partnership, as strong and central as it is, harmonizing both in song and otherwise.

My only problems with this script are the seeming incongruities in what the psychics are doing to Steed's mind. They project the images of Brandon Storey's Saint Nicholas, the Christmas tree, and the bucket of presents into Steed's mind ahead of time, providing the only hints for him as to what is happening. Lest you think that this was a mere accident, they also send him an unsigned Christmas card with similar iconography printed upon it, and I'm puzzled as to why they should do this except to provide the writer with an out for Steed, who works his way out of his dilemma built entirely upon these clues.

"Too Many Christmas Trees" may have nothing, or almost nothing, to do with what went before, barring a few minor exceptions like "Warlock" or "The Master Minds," which more indirectly dealt with the same subjects, but the script was in fact establishing a new and different template for future episodes that would occasionally be explored. Sadly, none of those future examples would reach the high-water mark established by this episode, which shines for its camaraderie between the regulars and its directorial brilliance.

CHAMPAGNE, CARS, CLOTHES, AND CANINES

You know it's an unusual episode when Steed starts out in white silk pajamas and a black dressing gown. Mrs. Peel joins him at his apartment in her tailored woolen suit (from "The Cybernauts"). Both change for their drive to Brandon Storey's house: he dons his Prince of Wales blazer and gray trousers with the pale blue overcoat with bi-colored collar. He also has a dark-colored cravat, a pale gray bowler, and black driving gloves. She wears a full-length mink in a champagne color with an integrated hoodie; underneath is a buff-colored rollneck jumper and ski pants. The second half of the episode is spent in historical Dickensian outfits: Mrs. Peel in an *Oliver Twist* costume, and Steed dressed as Sydney Carton from *A Tale of Two Cities*.

They finish out the tag scene with near matching garments in contrasting black and white. Steed wears a black ribbed rollneck with a black fur vest with a plush fur collar and oversized buttons. Mrs. Peel wears the same, only in white.

The vintage car of the week is the 1927 Bentley 4 ½ Litre (UW 4887).

No champagne, though Emma offers to cheer Steed up with some; he's disinterested because he's too obsessed with his nightmares. They must indeed have been doozies!

TAG SCENE

Steed and Emma ride in a horse-drawn carriage as Steed holds a sprig of mistletoe over Emma's head. She smiles charmingly as the theme tune plays to the closing credits.

QUOTES

"It must be your past catching up on you." "If it were that, that would be fun!"
"Well, it's a simple case of childhood regression, dating back to the time that you first discovered there really isn't a Father Christmas." "Oh, dear, isn't there?"
"Who...is... *Boofums*?"
"That's the fellow that deals in old prints and manuscripts. Is he still after your first edition?"
"The quality of a lady's performance is not measured by her years."
"You know, I've always rather fancied myself in one of these." "So have I. I mean, I have too."
"Out of your mind!" "What!" "They are."

92 (4.13.14) SILENT DUST

Steed watches birds — Emma goes hunting
Written by Roger Marshall
Directed by Roy Baker

GUEST CAST

William Franklyn (Omrod), Jack Watson (Juggins), Conrad Phillips (Mellors), Norman Bird (Croft), Hilary Wontner (Minister), Joanna Wake (Miss Snow), Isobel Black (Clare Prendergast), Charles Lloyd Pack (Sir Manfred Fellows), Aubrey Morris (Quince), Robert Dorning (Howard)

PRE-TITLE/TEASER

On a sunny day in a field, birds flock in the trees and nearby brush but then mysteriously begin to die and fall into a pile under the baleful gaze of a scarecrow.

SYNOPSIS

Investigating the disappearance of a bird called the Martlett in the English countryside, Steed and Emma discover that someone is using Silent Dust, a fertilizer that went wrong and is killing all the animals and vegetation, but they have no idea who. The deadly material hasn't been used since its creation, and the inventor was fired, shamed, and eventually died. When Steed and Emma discover that rich locals are using the faux fertilizer to blackmail the country into submission, Steed may end up getting his wings clipped by a shotgun, and Emma finds herself on the wrong side of a "fox hunt"...

REVIEW

Ah—the sounds of nature, the morning chorus! There's nothing quite like it. Birds, birds everywhere, singing brightly. The English countryside is warm and pleasant. It's another a beautiful day. Then, suddenly, without warning, a deathly stare from a scarecrow causes stuffed birds to fall to the ground in a pile beneath a single tree. Perplexing, isn't it? What could be causing those precariously-placed stuffed birds in that tree to die? No, this isn't an attack of mad taxidermists—though that might fit in with an episode of *The Avengers*—it's a story about a banned fertilizer that's killing off *real* birds, though you mightn't know that from the stiffness of our deceased avian friends. We'll just have to give this episode a pass and assume that Silent Dust causes severe avian paralysis followed by death.

And that's about the worst I'll say about this delightful hour of *The Avengers*—its being sorely lacking in the avian special effects department—for this is a particularly witty and stylish episode that manages to spoof the British aristocracy as much as it celebrates them. It seems that Roger Marshall never lets the series down, and this is another tightly constructed script that unfolds in an easy natural way with realistic villains and motivations.

The upper-class elements are moved to the foreground here, and Steed takes advantage of this by swapping out his bowler for a top hat and his umbrella for a stylish cane. His jacket has a cravat stuffed within. He looks quite a rake in haute couture—for Edwardian times anyway—and Macnee plays it to the hilt. His chatting up Joanna gives him a chance to display some of the equestrian interests that would surface again during *The New Avengers*.

The lone eccentric is Quince, a weaselly bird-watcher played by Aubrey Morris, who ends up dying in the first third, killed by Juggins. Emma later finds his body in a pile of potatoes in a cupboard—or possibly just his head, it's difficult to tell. Mellors the gamekeeper is not so much an eccentric as a sociopath, seemingly itching for an excuse to shoot someone. He ends up winging Steed, who also gets caught in a bear trap in one of the deadlier scenes to occur in the series.

Steed manages to slip away, and what follows is a scene like no other in the program, one of the more surrealistic moments in any era. (It is after all a dream.) Steed passes out from pain and blood loss and dreams that Mrs. Peel is an Old West doctor with a handlebar mustache that pulls the bullet from his wound using a monkey wrench and hunting knife sterilized by a candle flame. Appropriately, according to his sense of self-importance, he is wearing a sheriff's badge in this hallucination. That he seems to almost instantly recover from his pain and disorientation is emblematic of the show's new sense of hyperreality and invulnerability, as if Marshall's script could not resist having a moment of seriousness and Brian Clemens emended it to bring it forward into the future.

The main villain in this episode is an upper-class throwback to earlier seasons, not surprising coming from Roger Marshall, who wrote some of the best episodes from the prior two seasons. Omrod (William Franklyn) is charming, scheming, slick and nonchalantly violent, and surrounds himself with hired hands that are unapologetically brash and bloodthirsty. He's a blackguard, a nobleman gone rogue. He puts on a pretense of civility while his associates do not. The narrative utilizes most of the available stereotypes of the British aristocracy—country estates with its overzealous gamekeepers, sherry and biscuits, and foxhunting. And it is in this latter activity that the main action of the finale takes place.

In an extended fox hunt, which is picketed by people carrying signs reading "Be Kind to Animals" in a nod to modern times, Emma becomes the hunted prey while Steed faces down a stable hand wielding a scythe. Fortunately, Emma is wilier than a fox, and the stable hand only manages to harvest Steed's top hat. Emma easily evades capture and deals with Mellows and Omrod, but when Juggins attacks with a whip, he proves more of a challenge. Fortunately, Steed rides to the rescue and wallops Juggins with a protestor's placard reading "Down with Blood Sports." As if to top that, the tag scene features Steed and Emma, again in Edwardian garb, riding a hot air balloon. Mrs. Peel ever so slightly breaks the fourth wall, staring into the camera as the balloon takes off, her eyes widening in such a hysterical look of shock that I could watch it on a perpetual loop and never stop laughing.

Like "Dial a Deadly Number," this is another near perfect episode that manages to work within the new and more stylish format of the series—humor, wit, and close camaraderie on display in abundance—while holding on to the more grounded dialogue-driven scripts of the past, just what you'd expect from a reliable old hand like Roger Marshall and a wonderful director like Roy Baker.

CHAMPAGNE, CARS, CLOTHES, AND CANINES

After a slightly off week, this episode becomes quite the fashion show, with many new outfits debuting! Steed and Mrs. Peel start out in boating outfits; he wears a navy jacket with gold stripes, his school tie, white trousers, and boating shoes; she wears a navy t-shirt and hipster pants, and a boater straw hat. Her t-shirt has a large capital 'E' over the left breast, presumably for 'Emma.' Later, she adds a tailored tweed jacket in a houndstooth pattern with black buttons. Steed takes a ride in a 1963 Rolls-Royce Silver Cloud II (1 CBK), and he wears his dark gray single-breasted, three-piece suit, with a black bowler. He then swaps this out for the navy three-piece suit, which is later topped with his black overcoat. This is followed by Mrs. Peel's gray knee-length skirt and a black jumper with a tailored sleeveless jacket. She tops this with a black beret. She steps it up later with a tailored snakeskin (python) jacket with Mandarin collar and epaulettes, and hip-hugging pants, which she later pairs instead with a black long-sleeved shirt. Steed's riding gear (from "A Surfeit of H2O") returns, though this time, he later changes out for a fox-hunting gear with a red coat and knee-high riding boots. Mrs. Peel matches him in a black blazer and riding helmet, white blouse, khaki jodhpurs, and woolen gloves with a black bowler. She also wears a black-and-white honeycomb print scarf (a pattern that had already turned up in "A Surfeit of H2O"), first paired with a black cardigan and then with the snakeskin jacket. And, of course, she gets to dress up in both merely a sheet and an Old West doctor's costume, replete with handlebar mustache and spittoon. In the tag scene, her ruffed-front blouse and hat and veil (from "Death at Bargain Prices") returns.

TAG SCENE

Steed and Emma ascend in a hot-air balloon with Emma expressing concern about what happens when they run out of ballasts.

QUOTES

"I almost took you for a poacher just then. I have orders to shoot poachers."
"I'm sure you won't mind. I told your butler not to bother." "We haven't met, have we?" "My name's Steed." "Sorry, oil." "Sorry, buckshot."
"His mistook me for a partridge. Seriously ruffled my wing feathers." "I must speak to him, tell him to be more—" "—accurate?"
"Steed's become a problem. I've warned him, but I don't think it will do any good. Sherry?"
"Can't keep him away from the trough. Just seems to want to keep drinking all the time." "Oh dear, once had an auntie like that!"
"Normal hunting calls." "First one to her, gets the ears."

93 (4.9.15) ROOM WITHOUT A VIEW

Steed becomes a gourmet — Emma awakes in Manchuria
Written by Roger Marshall
Directed by Roy Baker

GUEST CAST

Philip Latham (Carter), Paul Whitsun-Jones (Chessman), Peter Jeffrey (Varnals), Richard Bebb (Dr. Cullen), Peter Arne (Pascold), Vernon Dobtcheff (Pushkin), Peter Madden (Dr. Wadkin), Jeanne Roland (Anna Wadkin)

PRE-TITLE/TEASER

The camera pans over a series of Budai on a shelf amid other Chinese artifacts. A man's hand caresses them before finally falling on the photo of a beautiful Asian woman. Elsewhere in the house, the same woman hosts a dinner party. She goes to close a window and finds the man at the curtains. She reacts in shock when she realizes that he is her husband.

SYNOPSIS

A scientist, missing for two years, reappears at his home, but he has cracked under torture and is now moronic and child-like. Steed and Mrs. Peel retrace his steps and deduce that he was abducted from London's Chessman Hotel and has spent the intervening years in an infamous Manchurian prison camp. Steed goes undercover as a food critic in order to meet Mr. Chessman, and Mrs. Peel takes a job as a reception clerk, but her snooping gets her sent to the mysterious Room 621 and—it seems—a trip to China...

REVIEW

It's fascinating how little the opening pre-title of this story has to do with the rest of the narrative, aside from merely setting a generally bizarre tone and providing a twist of expectations. In the wake of an attack on Mrs. Wadkin by her husband (physicist Dr. Wadkin just having reappeared after a long absence) in a creepy sequence set amidst wind chimes and rows of Budai upon a shelf, we find that the scientist disappeared from the Chessman Hotel in London and shows all the signs of severe torture. We've all experienced bad room service before, but this hotel was enough to drive him to wit's end! Wadkin isn't the first disappearance either, there have been seven such incidents over the previous year. Sensing something more serious at work than bad English cuisine and unwelcoming concierges, Steed and Emma naturally investigate.

Though there is little of the usual wit and banter between the regulars, Steed gives a remarkable speech, almost a soliloquy, on Nee San, as if he's been imprisoned there himself. It's a powerful and strikingly serious moment, atypical for the season but consistent with Roger Marshall's style of writing. (A similar imprisonment would be referenced in "Take-Over" during the Tara King era, in which Steed and his friend Bill would reference a prison in Nan King.) Steed also gives Carter a cat-ate-the-canary look when he pretends to be a famous gastronome, Monsieur Gourmet, and Emma has a rather Cathy Gale-like argument with Cullen over his lack of compassion.

Aside from these intriguing moments and the pre-title, I found my interest seldom piqued throughout this episode's first half, despite an attack by unconvincing Chinamen in a laundry truck. It is only when the hotel is reached and Peter Arne discovers the nature of Room 621—a room not only without a view but no exit either—that I found my ears perking up. Even the quasi-eccentric behavior of the hotel's gourmets and Steed and Emma going undercover don't quite sell the story in the way that other adventures in this era might.

By the time the episode garners some real threat—Emma being trapped in Room 621 herself—the story is almost over; until then, it's mostly a story about people working in a hotel. Thankfully, the final moments include a delightful revelatory twist that nearly saves the story for me. Having a communist Chinese torture prison for English spies underneath the London hotel is something of a masterstroke that would be achieved far less well in Season Five's "The Living Dead," albeit with an underground army training camp in that case. It's the kind of thing that immediately seems obvious once it happens, even though you might never have seen it coming.

The finale's fight scene amidst the blaring of a malfunctioning tape recorder is amusing. Emma spends most of it attempting to exit her cell with the guard's massive ring of keys, her hand stuck through the food slot. Nevertheless, neither of these late entries into the territory of typical ***Avengers*** danger and wit are adequate to overcome the mild-to-moderate doldrums of the first forty-nine minutes. Roger Marshall is quite my favorite ***Avengers*** writer, but everyone has their off days.

EPISODE NOTES

Peter Jeffrey makes his first appearance in the series as a character about 180 degrees away from his later villainous roles—that of a mild-mannered Ministry agent and psychologist. Paul Whitsun-Jones makes his first appearance since playing the quasi-villainous Charles in "The Wringer." Here, he plays Chessman, a hotelier with the bizarre (and easily exploitable) weakness of requiring high ambient temperatures. Quite the disadvantage in England.

CHAMPAGNE, CARS, CLOTHES, AND... ART!

Steed drives Mrs. Peel in his 1927 Bentley 4 ½ Litre. (The registration is barely visible as UW 4887.) This is its last appearance in the series, and its registration would be moved to the 3 Litre. Mrs. Peel debuts a new herringbone woolen coat in two-tone pink with scalloped hems with matching pink knee-length skirt, scarf, and blouse. Steed wears his pale-blue overcoat with the black collar with his brown serge suit, a white shirt, and a black bowler; later, the dark-gray suit with the same bowler; then, the navy suit; then, the navy chalk-stripe; then, black tie and tuxedo; then, the pale-gray suit; and, finally, he goes undercover in a white waiter's uniform (though still with black tie). Mrs. Peel wears a black vinyl jacket with synthetic fur collar over a gray marle dress with her hair done up. Working at the hotel, she switches to something more conservative: a white cotton blouse with black trousers and shoes.

The artwork in this episode requires a mention. Everywhere you look there are grotesque prints of medieval bishop statuary. Some of them look almost mummified, like a lich straight out of ***Dungeons & Dragons***. However, they are supposed to represent chess pieces, the type of artwork preferred by the chess-obsessed Max Chessman.

TAG SCENE

Steed gives Emma a ride down a country lane in a rickshaw.

QUOTES

"He seconded from the Ministry, eager beaver, everything in triplicate. I wonder what he'd think of you."

"Not to worry, I'll be responsible for Mata Hari."

"Rice husks, gruel, shavings of bad pork and water. Brackish water, tasting of dust."

"You take the one on the left." "What?" "His jacket will fit you better."

"You rang, madam?" "Yes, I want to change my room with the honeymoon couple next door."

94 (4.17.16) SMALL GAME FOR BIG HUNTERS

Steed joins the natives — Emma gets the evil eye
Written by Philip Levene
Directed by Gerry O'Hara

GUEST CAST

Bill Fraser (Colonel Rawlings), James Villiers (Simon Trent), Liam Redmond (Professor Swain), A.J. Brown (Dr. Gibson), Peter Burton (Fleming), Paul Danquah (Razafi), Tom Gill (Tropical Outfitter), Esther Anderson (Lala), Peter Thomas (Kendrick)

PRE-TITLE/TEASER

A man flees from a 'jungle' to the sounds of African drums and tribal calls. He is brought down by a poisoned arrow just before reaching a stone marker reading "London 23 miles."

SYNOPSIS

In darkest Hertfordshire, a local farmhand is found in a coma similar to the type tsetse flies induce. Mrs. Peel calls in an expert on African magic native to Kalaya (recently freed from Imperial rule) to diagnose the sleeping sickness, and Steed takes a trip 'down river' to a club of British ex-Colonial officers who plan to retake the 'dark continent' for Britain...

REVIEW

"Small Game for Big Hunters" starts off with a smashing pre-title sequence and then proceeds at a much slower pace than is comfortable. It does take a surprisingly long time to get to the point, apparently preferring to sustain the mystery while exploring the peculiar habits of that curious and rare animal called 'the *Avengers* eccentric.' For that, it may be forgiven, since it is one of the main reasons that the show is so enjoyable.

Colonel Rawlings is a true example of that unusual breed. If not completely out of his mind, he's damn close, still believing he's back in the jungle and unable to live anywhere else. In order to sustain this illusion, the villains have created their own simulation of the fictional African country of Kalaya in the middle of England, all of it to satisfy Rawlings' need to sleep under mosquito nets and slurp quinine-laced beverages to stave off malaria. This also provides the opportunity for Emma to be decked out in native costume, and Steed manages a fairly convincing Tarzan yell. Nevertheless, my addiction to that noble *Avengers* eccentric satisfied, I cannot help but imagine that a snappier pace would have moved this story from merely average to exceptional.

The red herring this week—a very common plot device in this season—is the fictional African black magic technique of Shirenzai. (It's pronounced like "Sharon's Eye," and every time I hear it spoken I cannot help but think of that Sharon Tate film *Eye of the Devil*, which also came out in 1966.) The idea of putting everyone to sleep with sleeping sickness prior to a takeover is fairly ingenious but overly complex, as it required re-creating a jungle realm in England. Surely, this is not nearly as efficient as conducting these experiments in Africa, where they would be much less likely to be found out by British secret agents—a possibility that is amplified by their regular African drumming sessions!

This suggests that the whole story started with the idea of the pre-title and a twist of expectations—a man emerging from a jungle to see a marker reading "London 23 miles"—and then the script was fleshed out to justify it. The sleeping sickness of two men is also left curiously unresolved. Local farm hands, no matter how attractive, are probably not considered very consequential by ***The***

Avengers. Some Ministry official was probably left to mop things up after the fact, but the program never bothers much with epilogues.

"Small Game" is humorous in places, has good dialogue, but remains largely inconsequential in this generally excellent season.

EPISODE NOTES

Paul Danquah appears as Razafi, one of a very few speaking roles for people-of-color in this Fennell-Clemens era of the program, and he provides an intriguing twist when he speaks English in perfect Received Pronunciation—he's also an undercover agent. Sadly, he gets called a "full-blown savage" by Steed. If that's what Steed thinks of handsome black men just because they have a little face paint on…well, my word! Later, Steed pulls a swordstick on him. Psev from "Two's a Crowd" also makes a brief appearance in this episode. The name (spelled "Pzev") is printed on one of Steed's files when Razafi attempts to pilfer it.

CHAMPAGNE, CARS, CLOTHES, AND CANINES

Mrs. Peel drives her Lotus Elan wearing a PVC jacket, matching pants with black trimmed hems, a black tailored sleeveless top, wide white belt, and the black-and-white 'target' beret. She also wears the Edward Rayne ankle boots. Though Steed doesn't drive a car this episode, his 1927 Bentley 3 Litre is seen parked outside. For once, Steed changes his outfit more than Mrs. Peel; he wears in succession: his navy suit, his navy chalk-striped suit, and finally a white safari suit with pith helmet. Mrs. Peel eventually changes however into a 'native' outfit, a floral-patterned sarong with a flower in her hair. This episode also introduces Steed's sword stick.

In the tag scene, Mrs. Peel adds a white jumper to her first outfit, and Steed changes into a navy coat with a peaked cap, as if he's playing at being a boat captain. No wonder he didn't think he had to "start the second engine." That's Mrs. Peel showing him who's really the boss!

TAG SCENE

Steed and Emma depart in a canoe, paddling down river, with Emma insisting that Steed start the "second engine."

QUOTES

"The gentleman in the bed is a latter-day Sleeping Beauty." *(He is rather cute.)*
"Had a spot of bother with the natives. A full-blown savage with a very unfriendly disposition."
"What's missing?" "Colonel Rawlings' file. Fortunately, he overlooked my cucumber sandwiches."
"I once shot a bull elephant myself." "Really! What did you use?" "f/8 at 500th of a second and a small roll of film." *(Steed is my kind of big game hunter!)*
"By Jove, the natives are restless tonight!"

95 (4.18.17) THE GIRL FROM AUNTIE

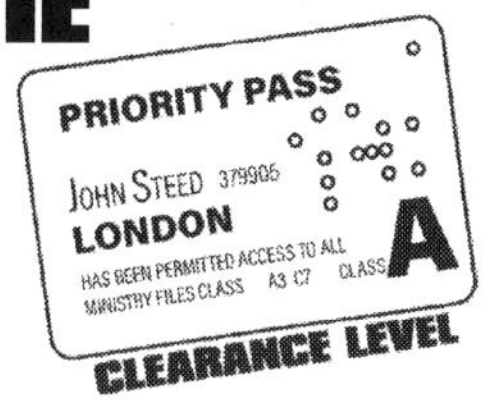

Steed almost outbids himself — Emma is a bird in a gilded cage
Written by Roger Marshall
Directed by Roy Baker

GUEST CAST

Liz Fraser (Georgie Price-Jones), Alfred Burke (Gregorie Auntie), Bernard Cribbins (Arkwright), David Bauer (Ivanoff), Mary Merrall (Old Lady), Sylvia Coleridge (Aunt Hetty), Yolande Turner (Receptionist), Ray Martine (Taxi Driver), Maurice Browning (Russian), John Rutland (Fred Jacques)

PRE-TITLE/TEASER

A woman in a bikini emerges from beyond a massive stone gate to be greeted by a man in a giant pig-head mask. They drive off together romantically. Mrs. Peel emerges from the gate shortly thereafter but is drugged and captured by an old woman on a bicycle.

SYNOPSIS

Emma is kidnapped and replaced by an unskilled actress named Georgie Price-Jones, and Steed must come to her rescue. Encountering a mysterious agency that "obtains the unobtainable" for a price, with Georgie's help, Steed eliminates Emma's original buyer, forcing an auction, in which Emma is sold to the highest bidder...

REVIEW

It could be successfully argued that *The Avengers* is the beginning of British TV surrealism, and this is the precise moment—if any such moment could possibly be pinned down—where *The Avengers* brand of surrealism crystalized into a formula that would dominate for the next three years. The second and third seasons started the gentle but inevitable march forward into the surrealistic spy-spoof subgenre. The fourth season crystalized the style, the fifth exploded it, and the following seasons tried to tamp it back down, trying in vain to put the genie back in the bottle while dealing with producer changes and the loss of their popular lead actress. It would then periodically burst out in fits, as if those in charge could no longer completely contain themselves.

The series had spoofed its genre before and it had used surrealism and/or hyperrealism at various points, but none had done so this strikingly, nor incorporated so many bizarre and incongruous elements. As if to announce this fact, the story starts off with a pre-title that could only be described as pushing the limits of incongruity. A woman emerges from beyond an ornate gate. Wearing only a skimpy bikini, she greets a man wearing an enormous carnival pig mask. They casually walk off arm in arm to their vehicle. It's as though we've suddenly stepped into the "I Am the Walrus" sequence from *Magical Mystery Tour*!

Mrs. Peel then emerges, similarly bikini-clad, though her swimming gear is even more striking (we'll get to that later), leaving us to wonder what on Earth goes on beyond this gate! Before we can contemplate this for very long, Emma is knocked out by a hypodermic needle administered by an old woman who falls from a bicycle. And for once we get an opening pre-title that doesn't give us a clue as to what is going on. In fact, it obscures it. Cue title. (Even casual fans of the sixties spy television genre will instantly realize that the title is a pun on *The Man From U.N.C.L.E.* television series that ran from 1964-1968 on NBC in the United States.)

The eponymous 'girl' referred to can only be presumed to be Georgie Price-Jones, played by Liz

Fraser, who spends most of the episode standing in for Mrs. Peel. This is a vacation episode for Diana Rigg, who likely desperately needed a day off. The schedule for filming twenty-six episodes a year was brutal. Patrick Macnee has been quoted as saying he didn't remember what the sixties were like while he was filming *The Avengers*; he got into his car at 5:30 in the morning and returned home at 9 at night. Thus, an Emma-lite episode allowed Rigg to film most of her scenes in only one day, freeing her up for the remainder of the week. It would be a Steed-lite episode for Macnee a few weeks later in "The House That Jack Built," but for now, he was obliged to work with a stand-in while Rigg no doubt sunned herself in that bikini for real.

Steed spends the episode somewhat displaced as well. Having just come back early from holiday, his Bentleys presumably still in cold storage, he travels around in a taxicab with his extremely divergent collection of souvenirs and a very tolerant taxi driver, who is encouraged to play with the toys while he waits and waits and waits.

It turns out that Georgie Price-Jones is a very unconvincing Mrs. Peel. Steed sees through the deception right away and proceeds to bewilder her with phony lobster deliveries and outrageous and perplexing phone calls until he finally calls her bluff. Almost immediately confessing her impersonation, they set off together to find the real Mrs. Peel. Along the way, the program begins to spoof its own myths, as with each new clue, they arrive just in time to find numerous fresh corpses impaled with knitting needles, the guilty old woman on a bicycle always a few turns of the pedals ahead of them. The last set of fatalities by 'double Os' is the four Jacques brothers, going by the names of John, Paul, George, and Fred, in a clear reference to another sixties British pop culture phenomenon. One of them has survived the assault—it's Fred, naturally—and he gasps out the only clue with his last breath. "It's Auntie. Auntie did it."

Liz Fraser has a lovely scene in which she is attacked by the knitting needle assassin while reading Mrs. Peel's judo instruction book (naturally written by *The Avengers* stunt arranger, Ray Austin). She manages to implement a few successful moves in her defense while reading from the book but is finally forced to improvise by slamming the tome atop the old woman's head, narrowly avoiding being stabbed by her attacker's knitting needles.

The eccentrics are many in this episode, most of them gender-bending in quality, but the primary example is Arkright, played by a young Bernard Cribbins. He seems remarkably obsessed with knitting for a man of his day, and he spends all of his time chanting tortured knitting adages like "Grab that skein, begin again" and presiding over old ladies that seem like they'd know more about the subject than he. It doesn't help that the instruction provided seems so useless and superficial that one is surprised many of them didn't simply tell him to buzz off so they could get on with that knitted bungalow. Frankly, it's so tedious as to make a peaceful lover of knit fabric want to stab someone, maybe with a nice fat double O close at hand.

The novel convention of death by poison knitting needle is one of the most strikingly funny and bizarre of the entire series. Here, it is an eccentric little old 'lady,' apparently going rogue, and she pins the noxious knitting implements on those who would dare to unravel the villains' carefully woven scheme. That the Arkright Knitting Circle is in close proximity to Auntie's offices seems to be purely a coincidence that is exploited by the assassin, who turns out to be a cross-dressing mustachioed man in disguise. Why this man should disguise himself as an old woman or use poisoned knitting needles as his favored weapon is anyone's guess! He appears to have an unhealthy old lady fetish that would have given Norman Bates a run for his money. I suppose everyone needs a hobby.

Another eccentric is the villain Gregorio Auntie, his name chosen presumably to make the pun of a title work. Far from the stereotypically slick Bond villain type, he's a goatish man who trades in anything and everything, promising to provide the unobtainable for the right price—including persons of high value. This turns out to include Mrs. Peel, who is held captive inside an enormous birdcage in the basement and is promised to a Russian agent willing to pay $140,000. (A disappointing price for the delectable Mrs. Peel!) Inside, she's still wearing the bikini from the pre-title, which turns out to be a string suit with only feathers over the private areas to preserve her modesty. The fine threads making up the suit are almost invisible on camera and so the whole ensemble reads as practically nude—about as racy as it got back in 1966! She casually sits on a swing covered in tinsel garland eating grapes and making acerbic remarks to her captor but occasionally casts a worried glance at the camera.

Thankfully, Steed goes undercover as Wayne Pennyfeather ffitch to get her back, giving Macnee plenty of opportunities to go full-on eccentric himself, pretending to be an art expert with a priceless Goya in his apartment (naturally, it's on loan from the National Gallery). When Steed eliminates Mrs. Peel's original buyer by forcing his assassination—an ignoble death in which director Roy Baker focuses entirely on his eyes—it prompts an auction that Steed must win. When this auction doesn't go quite as planned, it forces a fight by Steed and Georgie to spring Mrs. Peel from her cage. This bird having flown, Steed and Mrs. Peel are reunited and (in a bizarre and inexplicable tag scene) depart in a bubble car, while Georgie motors away in a vintage Bentley. Perhaps a reward for services rendered?

"The Girl from Auntie" isn't perfect. It has two remarkably forced red herrings that can't have possibly been expected to work. Aunt Hetty (played by the delightful Sylvia Coleridge) has to pull out a realistic-looking water pistol and speak lines that don't really make sense in casual conversation in order to throw us off the scent regarding the assassin's identity. Arkwright utters one angry line about the theft of knitting needles and makes a stabbing motion with one of the ubiquitous double Os that I imagine is supposed to make us suspect him... for all of about ten seconds. One wonders why they bothered with either of these unconvincing sleights of hand. Equally, Georgie Price-Jones is supposed to have been a replacement for Emma Peel, just as the villains provide for everything they steal and sell on their black market, but she looks nothing like and acts nothing like Emma, and blatantly lacks any of her skills and knowledge. These minor drawbacks are unlike Roger Marshall's usual sharp writing style and seem much more like the style of the script editor—that's you, Brian Clemens!—who probably modified the story prior to shooting. (Marshall would later take exception to the new style of the series and depart.) Still, these are very minor nitpicks that in no way impact one's enjoyment of this landmark episode.

People may wonder why I spent so much time, and so many words, on this particular outing. The reason is that it's seminal, regardless of its high quality. "The Girl from Auntie" marks as much of a dividing line in the series as "The Town of No Return" did when it demarcated the Cathy Gale era from that of her successor. This episode advances the series yet again, taking it from a more joyful, hyperreal version of the prior season to a frenzied celebration of the bizarre and surreal that would peak in about a year from now. This is a particularly good episode to show to anyone who is curious about the show because it incapsulates so much about the program during its zenith. They may not necessarily decide to watch more, but they're certain to be amused.

CHAMPAGNE, CARS, CLOTHES, AND... ART!

With this one, we'll start right out with the showstopper—Mrs. Peel's fishnet and feather bikini. The fishnet reads as practically nude on camera (at any distance further away than a closeup) and the bikini's pretty skimpy too. At least she keeps her decency with a black-and-white striped fur coat, design by John Bates and dubbed 'Chemin.' Ms. Price-Jones drives Mrs. Peel's Lotus (HNK 999C), but apparently she prefers the top up (a dead giveaway). Steed first appears in his pale-gray suit and a rather fuzzy gray bowler, with a white shirt, a gray silk tie and tiepin, and a gray umbrella with whangee handle. After borrowing a famous painting as bait, he wears a black rollneck jumper and slacks; then, a full tux and black tie with matching overcoat (as in "Room Without a View"); then, the brown serge suit. He ends up in a tan overcoat, probably over the previous outfit with a black bowler, and Mrs. Peel finally gets to put her 'Chemin' coat on again.

Steed doesn't drive a car in this episode, he instead spends the entire time riding around in a cab, played by a couple of different Austins (VGF 345 and BG 193B), but he does ride in a 1955 Messerschmitt KR 200 (905 TPU) driven by Emma, while Georgie Price-Jones drives a Bentley (ATL 431) not altogether unlike Steed's.

Two famous paintings are seen in this episode— ***The Portrait of Doña Isabel de Porcel*** by Francisco Goya, and the ***Mona Lisa*** by da Vinci. The original of the latter is smashed over Auntie's head, thus requiring that the Louvre be satisfied with "a very nice reproduction."

TAG SCENE

Steed and Emma depart in a tiny trike car—a 1955 Messerschmitt KR 200—while Georgie Price-Jones drives a Bentley. They wave to each other as they pass.

QUOTES

"Knitting is one of the neglected arts. It binds the family together, brings peace to the home. Listen… the sheer serene sound of clicking needles."
"Turning the force of the attacker to advantage, bringing the knee up into the ribcage of the opponent with a sickening…Hmm, she must have some very aggressive boyfriends!"
"Oh, Steed! I thought you were an old lady with a veil and knitting needles!" "They do say I take after Granny."
"Definitely yes! The air breathes well. My nerve ends are positively tingly!"
"She looks a bit broody. Can't you have her move about a bit?"
"And no cracks please about birds in gilded cages." "As if I would!"

96 (4.16.18) THE THIRTEENTH HOLE

Steed finds a bogey — Emma gets a birdie
Written by Tony Williamson
Directed by Roy Baker

GUEST CAST

Patrick Allen (Reed), Hugh Manning (Colonel Watson), Peter Jones (Dr. Adams), Victor Maddern (Jackson), Francis Matthews (Collins), Donald Hewlett (Waversham), Norman Wynne (Professor Minley), Richard Marner (Man on T.V. screen)

PRE-TITLE/TEASER

A man plays golf on a field. Spotting an agent spying on the greens nearby, he asks his caddy for his 303 rifle and shoots the agent.

SYNOPSIS

After an agent is killed on the thirteenth hole of the Craigleigh golf course, Steed and Emma join the club to investigate. Eventually, Collins, the club's acting secretary and club professional, is killed by a golf ball fired by the villains. Steed and Emma soon discover that Reed is always insistent on playing Dr. Adams, and he's willing to knock Steed out of the tournament to do it…

REVIEW

It's tee time instead of tea time for *The Avengers*, and Patrick Allen doesn't like golfers who play through. Instead, he kills anyone snooping around the thirteenth hole with a .303 Jungle Carbine stuffed into his caddy instead of a 4-iron. The gun even has its own head cover with a label. Such cheek! Thus, the pre-title sets up the story as it does in all good episodes of the series. Golf enthusiasts trade for spy secrets on the links.

"The Thirteenth Hole" is somewhat of a break for the fourth season. It gives Steed and Emma a chance to relax, play a few rounds of golf, have drinks, play a few games of pick-up sticks in the clubhouse, and put away a few diabolical masterminds on the side. And that is just how the story plays out. The stakes are not particularly high and there is a casual feel throughout.

This casualness is even betrayed in one nighttime fight scene between Emma and Collins, in which she almost becomes complacent, smirking at the ease with which she kicks him into a sand trap multiple times before he briefly gets the better of her and drags her in with him. Then, he is killed by a high-powered golf ball flying through. It leaves the imprint of its label on his head. Someone didn't bother to call "fore!" Except it's not a golfer with lousy aim, it's a tank, or at least a golf cart tricked out with a golf ball bazooka on the back. Yes, an armed golf cart is roving the golf course at night, killing club secretaries. Only in ***The Avengers***.

Patrick Macnee is especially good in this episode, and we need that because even Patrick Allen isn't stepping up in particular. Again, Steed pushes his luck as he always does. With a superhuman burst of gentility he blatantly gives away all he knows about the villains' scheme just to get a reaction, leaving them quite stunned and not knowing what to say. He also gets a chance to turn on the eccentric act at full force, incorporating all kinds of measurement devices into his golf game. He checks the wind and measures the incline on the vertical with a plumb line. You would think that Venus had to be in Leo before he could drive. However, it should be noted that he's a stellar golf player—especially with a little help from his adorable fairy godmother, Mrs. Peel.

The golf match is played for all its silly potential, with every humorous cliché involving a sand pit or soft patch being played out by the end. Finally, when the villains get tired of all the fun and games, out comes the golf ball bazooka again, and Steed is knocked out. He recovers in the clubhouse while Emma absently flicks shillings into a bowl. Despite this brief lay about, our heroes manage to put away the vicious golf ball-firing crooks in an exciting and surprisingly serious fight scene at the end—within an underground bunker underneath the thirteenth hole. It's serious, except for one thing—why do those scientists cringe when Steed throws a stick at the TV screen? They're scientists and yet they don't know that a stick can't be thrown at them through a television screen? Having saved the Vostic 2 satellite and terrified Russian scientists on television as a finishing move, how do Steed and Mrs. Peel leave...? On a golf cart drinking champagne, of course!

"The Thirteenth Hole" is a fun episode, if slightly slow-paced and inconsequential. It manages to make Steed and Emma look incredibly talented as they easily dispatch the enemy, but frankly, there's something all too effortless about it to make it really interesting or exciting. The production of this episode also lets it down somewhat in the form of screamingly obvious rear-screen projection or optical printing for some of the closeup shots in the golf course scenes. This seems to be an unusual lapse for Roy Baker, who planned exterior shots at Mill Hill Golf Club in North London but was for reasons unknown forced to do them in studio. On the flip side, the nighttime golf course set is quite convincing.

CHAMPAGNE, CARS, CLOTHES, AND CANINES

Mrs. Peel begins by wearing a new leather catsuit with a white rollneck blousy jumper, or jumpery blouse, whichever; the catsuit is fairly similar to the leather jumpsuit worn earlier in the season but is actually a different outfit. Steed dons a brand new double-breasted gray-blue overcoat with a black fur collar and two columns of black buttons. He tops the outfit with a short stovepipe hat like the one in "A Surfeit of H2O." He drives a 1924 Vauxhall 30-98 (XT 2276) for the second and last time in the series, by which time he has gone more casual with a suede military-style windbreaker, zipped up the front over a jumper with a dark collar and a speckled scarf, and trousers. Similarly casual, Mrs. Peel wears a military-style white shirt with epaulettes, a black-and-white checked scarf, and hip-hugger pants that look like they're made out of cozy wool. She keeps herself warm with 'Chemin' the black-and-white striped fur coat designed by John Bates. She also wears the same watch that she nearly lost in "The Hour That Never Was" (which matches her belt), and the Edward Rayne ankle boots.

During the golf tournament, Steed turns into a golfing eccentric, wearing checked plus fours pants, a dark jumper, and a soft-looking hat with something of the shape of a trilby that also happens to be "lined with chainmail." Mrs. Peel returns to her leather jumpsuit with white rollneck.

They leave on a golf cart while drinking champagne, with Steed returning to an overcoat and black bowler, and Mrs. Peel to 'Chemin.'

TAG SCENE

Steed and Emma depart on an electric golf cart while drinking champagne.

QUOTES

"Two…four…303."

"Should something go wrong tomorrow and this fellow Steed should win…?" "Then, he'll sign his own death warrant. If he wins…you'll have to kill him."

"Fear not, for 'ere this day is done, you shall have a hole in one! I am your fairy godmother."

"Guaranteed to knock a hole in one every time."

97 (4.19.19) QUICK-QUICK SLOW DEATH

Steed has two left feet — Emma dances with danger

Written by Robert Banks Stewart

Directed by James Hill

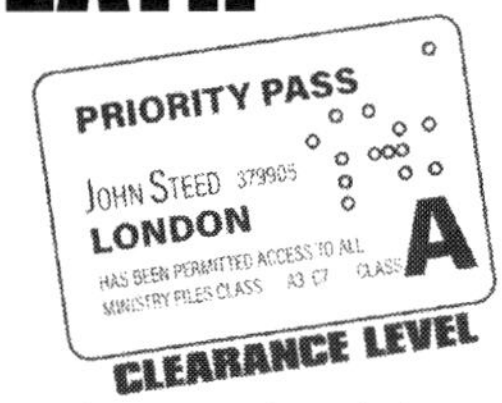

GUEST CAST

Eunice Gayson (Lucille Banks), Maurice Kaufmann (Ivor Bracewell), Carole Gray (Nicki), Larry Cross (Chester Read), James Belchamber (Peever), John Woodnutt (Captain Noble), Alan Gerrard (Fintry), David Kernan (Piedi), Colin Ellis (Bernard), Graham Armitage (Huggins), Charles Hodgson (Syder), Ronald Govey (Bank Manager), Michael Peake (Willi Fehr)

PRE-TITLE/TEASER

A crook pushes a pram down a street in London. When he goes to make a call in a phone booth, a faulty brake allows the pram to roll down the street and turn over, revealing a dead man inside wearing formal eveningwear.

SYNOPSIS

An enemy agent loses his pram in an accident, and it appears to be holding a dead man in evening wear. Steed and Emma trace the tuxedo the man was wearing and his tattoo and find that a dance studio called Terpsichorean Training Techniques is one of the last places he visited—his name is revealed to be Arthur Peever. However, a totally different Arthur Peever is currently studying at the studio, forcing Mrs. Peel to go undercover as his dancing instructor, and one of the agents is likely to step on her toes…

REVIEW

It's every secret agent's worst nightmare. He's pushing a pram containing the corpse from his latest hit job, safely hidden away from prying eyes by a baby blanket. Surely, no one will suspect that he's pushing it to the morgue rather than the nursery. He's almost there, but he's just got to phone in the kill to his diabolical mastermind. (Just one more murder and he can claim that toaster oven!) Inside the phone booth, he begins dialing his commander's number—the boss is going to be so pleased!—but the brake on that cheap imported Soviet pram springs loose, and it goes weaving down the hill into traffic, finally dropping its precious cargo upon a London sidewalk. Alas, there goes the toaster oven.

This exercise in bizarre twists of expectations provides a rare opportunity for the heroes to nick the spy trade's murderous pram-pushers underground network. This is for certain a niche market, and the spies like tattoos and ballroom dancing, so Steed and Emma start there, leading the viewer into yet another delightfully satirical spy spoof.

As the tone of the episode might indicate from its beginning, the story contains a parade of eccentrics, each more charming than the last, presented in a chain that drives the narrative. Buttoned up in a button-down shirt and woolly cardigan and wearing Buddy Holly-style glasses, the tattoo artist is only eccentric due to the fact that you'll not find anyone like him today. He appears obsessed with putting rosebuds somewhere unmentionable on Mrs. Peel—her cheeks perhaps? He spends his spare time practicing tattoos on garlic sausages and manages to scrawl out a message on the delicate skin of one after he's fatally shot.

Captain Noble (played by John Woodnutt) starts out by being strangled by the enemy agent who lost his pram and subsequently spends the remainder of the episode speaking in an incomprehensible laryngitic rasp that only Steed appears to understand. Emma however requires that he whistle his messages in Morse code over the telephone.

The stuffy clerk at Lichen and Company menswear, having been presented with a returned suit riddled with bullet holes, seems unconcerned with the possibility of murder and merely complains about having to mend the suit and claim the deposit. For his diligence and dedication to his job he is rewarded with a fatal knife blow to the gut before he can produce Peever's address for Steed. But the suit produces a shoe repair ticket from Piedi's, and Emma goes shoe-shopping.

Piedi has chosen his profession with great care and precision. The Italian shoemaker, whose name means 'feet,' is nothing less than a card-carrying, certifiable foot-fetishist who proceeds to gasp breathlessly over Mrs. Peel's feet for the better part of five minutes. He's a spoof of a Latin lover, the perfect one for you if your feet happen to need romancing. He's crushed when Emma finally announces she's not there for shoes, and he subsequently loses all interest, though he reveals the purpose for the shoes worn by the dead agent—they're dance shoes for lessons at Terpsichorean Training Techniques. And Emma quickly goes undercover as a dance instructor.

Chester Read is the final eccentric, a bandleader for the dance studio. Perpetually drunk, he 'conducts' a series of photographs of himself playing different instruments with a tape recorder providing the actual music. I have to say I've always wondered the most about old Chester. What is his story? Was he a great bandleader of the 1940s? A master instrumentalist now so tragically washed up that the only job he can get is conducting a tape recorder at a criminal dance studio? No—turns out he's the commander of the operation, the one that the agent was trying to phone when he lost his pram in the beginning; the drunkenness is a ruse. All of these eccentrics are introduced in the first twenty minutes, by the way, as *The Avengers* one-two-cha-cha-cha into the ballroom of spies, whose crooked scheme is to entrap lonely men via their dance school, men who are then eliminated and replaced by enemy agents who assume their identities.

There's so much subtle humor in this episode, like Steed looking for a rose tattoo on Peever's wrist by pretending to check the time, and Mrs. Peel delicately chipping away at the mold upon the face of Mr. Piedi's murdered inbred-looking assistant with disembodied foot casts scattered nearby.

During the ballroom dancing gala at the end, Emma, unable to lead her dance partner, resorts to shoving him into the next room so he can be conveniently knocked out with a sap. Similarly, in the climactic fight scene, Steed gets to 'dance' one of the villains into a wall.

"Quick-Quick Slow Death" is a charming gem of a story that is often ignored by other books on the subject, which is a surprise since it is chock-full of humor and bizarre deaths, the traits that this season is best known for. This is a tremendously fun episode that proceeds with such confidence and fits so well within the program's new template that it could have been molded for it by the master Piedi himself. Make sure it's on your *Avengers* dance card.

CHAMPAGNE, CARS, CLOTHES, AND CANINES

The Prince of Wales blazer with the black waistcoat is back, and sadly for the last time. It's like saying farewell to an old friend, having harkened back to Season One. (Unfortunately, it becomes a bit of a continuity break, as he's wearing the outfit every time he visits Captain Noble but wears different clothes elsewhere.) Well, technically it peeks out from his overcoat in "The Danger Makers" but it's barely visible. Mrs. Peel dons a stunning outfit in black and white (at least that's how it reads on monochrome film): an overcoat with cross-like stripes that intersect at the waistline; underneath is a knee-length dress with the inverse pattern, switching from primarily white with black stripes, to black with white stripes. She pairs the outfit with the 'target' beret, black and white shoes, and white stockings. Steed wears his gray-blue woolen double-breasted overcoat with black buttons and a black collar, topped with a black bowler. He's probably wearing the navy suit underneath. At Piedi's, Mrs. Peel has her feet stroked while wearing a black blouse with white lace collar and a pale knee-length skirt, a little like her outfit in "Dial a Deadly Number," rather Victorian-retro. She later wears a simple black dress with white bands across the top, over which 'Chemin' is added, and slingback dancing shoes. Steed switches to the dark-gray suit, then, the navy suit. Mrs. Peel switches to a loose white cotton dress and then for the dance-off a sleeveless white chiffon thigh-length dress with horizontal bands of metallic fabric along the skirt and along the neckline. Steed dons formal white tie with a black cloak with white lining and a black top hat. He carries a silver-topped cane.

TAG SCENE

Steed and Emma waltz away together on the floor of the criminal's dance studio.

QUOTES

"That was my lunchtime refreshment!"
"The wearer must have worn his medals very clumsily, sir. I mean, these holes, we'll never get these invisibly mended." "The wearer can't exactly be mended either."
"We dress the entire nation, you know. Why, without us, Ascot race week would look like a nudist convention!"
"Piedi never measures, he moulds! Twin treasures, carissima. Signora, I am at your feet!"
"Oh, you poor, poor man. You mean, if you disappeared tomorrow, no one would know or care?"
"You're number nine!" "And you're dancing with garlic sausage."
"Did you know they've arrested a band leader for being drunk in charge of a pram containing a man in full evening dress, with a plaster cast on his head, tattooed on his right wrist, clutching a dance diploma in one hand and a garlic sausage in the other?"

98 (4.20.20) THE DANGER MAKERS

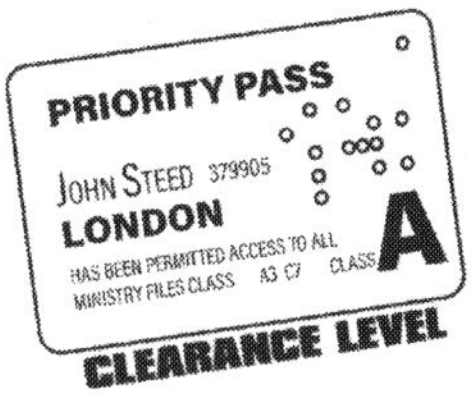

Steed joins a secret society — Emma walks the plank
Written by Roger Marshall
Directed by Charles Crichton

GUEST CAST

Nigel Davenport (Robertson), Douglas Wilmer (Dr. Long), Fabia Drake (Colonel Adams), Moray Watson (Peters), Adrian Ropes (Stanhope), Richard Coleman (R.A.F. Officer), John Gatrell (Lamble)

PRE-TITLE/TEASER

A man riding a motorcycle plays 'chicken' by riding in front of a moving lorry. He narrowly misses. But when he attempts it again with another truck, he is killed. The truck drivers remove his leather jacket to reveal that he is an elderly soldier.

SYNOPSIS

When 60-year old motorcycle enthusiast General Lamble is killed playing chicken with a truck, Steed and Mrs. Peel investigate a secret cabal of thrill seekers addicted to the risk of death. It seems like just mostly an irresponsible addiction to danger until deaths starts to mount up and it is revealed that they plan to launch a suicidal attack on the Tower of London to steal the crown jewels...

REVIEW

An unusual twist, moving from foreign spies to an internal enemy with very different motivations, this is an intriguing episode with a rather new idea, one of the most original for *The Avengers* so far. And, at a time when recent news featured a danger-seeker fatally falling from a high-rise building trying to perform pullups on camera, I'd say it's as relevant as ever. The motivation may be different but the behavior remains the same. This is yet another scintillating and insightful script from Roger Marshall, who can do no wrong in this season.

The pre-title involves an elderly general crashing his motorcycle while trying to outrun a lorry. Investigating the accident, Steed visits a Major Robertson, who tells Steed how much he admires General Lamble while his hands are placed rather conspicuously on a statue of Napoleon. As soon as Steed leaves, the Major's hand begins to shake visibly, and he retreats to his desk where he retrieves a revolver from a drawer. Placing a bullet inside and spinning the chamber, he pulls the trigger. Click. Nothing. He's still alive. He had a five-in-six chance of surviving. He's had his fix of danger for now.

Marshall focuses on the nature of the men's addiction, which is depicted as being like that of recreational drugs. This is something the viewer will almost immediately pick up on as the symptoms of 'danger withdrawal' surface immediately in this scene. Lest the viewer think the men are being depicted as harmless (or at least only self-harming) danger-seekers, eventually it is revealed that no danger is great enough to satisfy their addiction, including murdering a man under the guard of Steed and Mrs. Peel.

Concerned that Lamble will betray them and their plans due to 'turning chicken,' Major Robertson and Peters plan his death. What follows is a remarkable scene made all the more intense by Crichton's superb direction. As if planning the death of one of their own isn't enough, the two men conclude their conversation with an unspoken challenge to see who can hold a live grenade the longest before throwing it away. Other men in this program would toast an agreement like that with a glass of sherry, but these overly testosterone-infused men are likely meant to be larger than life parodic action heroes—a cautionary tale of what goes wrong if one becomes so obsessed with excitement that they can no longer handle the quiet moments of life. They are so extreme that they almost make Steed look dilettante by comparison. Fortunately, he and Mrs. Peel are the rational ones, maintaining a perfect balance between the excitement of their work and the tamer moments in life—after all what's the point of all the danger and excitement if you can't enjoy a nice bottle of champagne afterwards?

After killing Lamble, Major Robertson performs a funerary trumpet fanfare in honor of his fallen associate. Steed is hiding in Robertson's office and witnesses the bizarre lonely ritual, starting he and Mrs. Peel off on the right track, delving beneath the surface of the cult. And here it is where Diana Rigg really shines. As Mrs. Peel, she latches on to the psychology of the danger makers immediately, winning Major Robertson over in a great exchange of dialogue and proving herself worthy of their organization. She not only understands why they are malfunctioning psychologically but also knows how to get into their heads and say exactly what they want to hear.

It works, and her initiation ritual is one of the most intense moments in sixties television. Forced to navigate see-saws while holding two rings over electrified rails that zig-zag from one end of the room to the other—each rail is different in orientation, requiring that her arms be held at different angles—this leaves Mrs. Peel's life in more immediate danger than perhaps any other time in the show's history, but it is nevertheless the perfect test for her skills. She survives the test and enters the club, for what it's worth. But you might have sweated a few bullets by then. It's an amazing television moment. It has to be said, however, that Steed's gun-grabbing deception might be an even better trick.

That the episode ends with the danger makers' machoistic ideas of glory and honor being smashed by their leader's cowardly defeat is just the kind of appropriate irony that is required. And everything comes to a nice rounded finale with a joyful scene of swordplay that proves that the only type of danger and fighting worth the bother is ***The Avengers*** kind, the kind where the bad guys are defeated and the good guys drink champagne to their own health—or in this case, ride off on go-karts.

One flaw that stands out is the death of Stanhope. He seems to die for no reason. He is killed before he can tell Steed anything—as usual—but the photograph with the evidence that Steed needs is left in his hand as if it doesn't matter. Indeed, how did the Major know that Stanhope was going to betray him anyway? He apparently never saw Stanhope take the photograph. Perhaps we should assume that killing Stanhope was simply a sociopathic thrill that Robertson couldn't resist. The ultimate plan to steal the crown jewels in the Tower of London seems a little less than the great thrill these men might require as well.

In many ways, this episode has a plot that is a throwback to earlier seasons, dealing with mundane issues rather than the fantastic, which is great because this season is the most balanced overall, cycling back and forth between the absurd and the more grounded, giving each equal attention. But in this episode's case the story is given an even more emboldened oomph that strengthens it in a way that a third season episode could never have mustered. Part of the reason for that is the very nature of the production, moving from videotape to film, but the rest of the formula to this season's success is a new and more daring devil-may-care attitude by producers Fennell and Clemens that really gives it its gas. They pushed the envelope hard practically every week so that every concept, whether mundane or not, was amplified by the direction, the humor, the surrealism, the action, or the sheer audacity of its execution. To say this was 'no holds barred' television might seem a little incredible to modern viewers, and admittedly what was daring in 1966 is a long way from what is daring now, but if one is left in any doubt about the show's boldness they only had to wait one more week for the final proof. That two episodes in a row would involve exclusive clubs that go to extremes was likely deliberate, and in the latter case, it would not be the action and violence that was turned up to eleven but something much more salacious.

EPISODE NOTES

In one interesting piece of continuity, Steed goes back to RAF Hamelin—the first time was in "The

Hour That Never Was"—and it's much more active this time as if the decision to close the base has been reversed in the wake of the events of that prior episode, but no one appears to recognize him. We're left to presume that all the traitors have been cleared out and replaced with new staff, none of whom know Steed.

CHAMPAGNE, CARS, CLOTHES, AND CANINES

Mrs. Peel wears a cream blouse and hip-hugger pants with a white jacket with black trim and cuffs. She tops it off with the 'target' beret. Steed wears his brown serge suit; then, a tan overcoat over his check blazer and black waistcoat, with an army helmet (though the blazer is only barely visible as Macnee leans forward). The overcoat is swiftly replaced by the pale blue one with the black collar. Mrs. Peel then debuts one of her most iconic outfits: a crepe catsuit in black and white, a sleeveless top with a plunging V-neck with black trim, and hip-hugging pants in black with white cuffs. It's a pity this is its one and only appearance in the series. It would have played well even on color film. This is quickly followed by the return of the snakeskin jacket from "Two's a Crowd" and the vinyl-fronted jumpsuit from "The Town of No Return," which she wears while completing her testing session. The Edward Rayne boots turn out not to have exactly the best grip!

Steed drives the 1927 Bentley 3 Litre (UW 4887). The motorcycle in the pre-title is a 1960 Triumph Thunderbird (452 YMF).

TAG SCENE

Steed and Emma depart on matching go-karts.

QUOTES

"Whatever you do, don't touch the wrapped ones." "Why not?" "Because I like them."
"Clearer?" "Much. A bunch of schizoid paranoiac psychopaths." "And incidentally dangerous."
"You could call it an addiction to danger. And just as the drug addict needs larger and stronger doses to satisfy his craving..." "...Your men need more and more danger."
"Now, for my little band, the dangers will act as the spur. They will face death. Some of them will certainly die, but that will not matter. It will only make it the sweeter."
"Major, your hand isn't shaking at all. It's as steady as a rock. Where's the danger in this? I'm handcuffed, you've got a gun. There's more danger in... well, in stamp-collecting!"
"How did you get out?" "I knotted some sheets and climbed out of the window." "Oh, that old thing."
"Well, originality didn't seem important at the time."

99 (4.21.21) A TOUCH OF BRIMSTONE

Steed joins the Hellfire Club — Emma becomes Queen of Sin
Written by Brian Clemens
Directed by James Hill

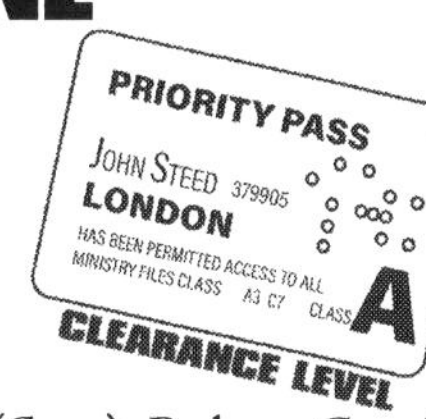

GUEST CAST

Peter Wyngarde (John Cartney), Colin Jeavons (Darcy), Carol Cleveland (Sara), Robert Cawdron (Horace), Michael Latimer (Roger Winthrop), Jeremy Young (Willy Frant), Bill Wallis (Tubby Bunn), Steve Plytas (Kartovski), Art Thomas (Pierre), Alf Joint (Big Man), Bill Reed (Huge Man)

PRE-TITLE/TEASER

An elegantly-dressed man (Cartney) pushes a luxurious armchair into the view of a television set. He watches a political program while eating chocolates. On the program, a foreign diplomat speaks about his desire for better relations between his country and the UK—until he lights up a cigar and it explodes, embarrassingly but harmlessly, in his face. Cartney smiles mischievously in response.

SYNOPSIS

A private club of hedonists, dressed in 18th century clothes and secretly engaging in orgiastic rituals, recreates the historic Hellfire Club. Led by the decadent John Cartney, they plot to sabotage diplomatic affairs with a series of embarrassing pranks. Steed and Mrs. Peel begin an investigation but are too late to prevent the next sabotage from causing a death by electrocution. Now, infiltrating the club directly, they discover the Hellfire Club plan to destroy the government with an underground explosion...

REVIEW

You could scour the history of ***The Avengers*** (and indeed all of sixties British television) and not find an episode more scurrilous, more scandalous, more notorious than "A Touch of Brimstone." The previous episode had shown the viewers that new producers Wintle, Fennell, and Clemens were willing to push the limits of acceptability on television when they depicted a cult of danger-seeking extremists, but this could scarcely have prepared audiences for what came next.

The Avengers had possessed a kinky streak from nearly the beginning, with its earliest origination at least being the black leather suit worn by Honor Blackman in the second season. Aside from this, the mere fact of a woman being the equal of a man in a regular program, fighting alongside him (often fighting better than him), being a widow and yet in a close unmarried relationship with the male lead was already pushing the boundaries for a sixties show. This wasn't helped by the fact that Honor Blackman went on to play a character in the 1964 James Bond film ***Goldfinger*** that was specifically written as a lesbian in the original novel by Ian Fleming. Though her sexual orientation was played down significantly for the film, the character was still highly suggestive, and the way in which Blackman chose to play the part was only superficially dissimilar to her portrayal of Cathy Gale. Though Mrs. Gale was never suggested to be a lesbian—merely an assertive, independent, and strong-willed woman—all of these challenges to gender roles were likely preying on the minds of viewers of the day. Though they no doubt thrilled to all of it, the counter-culture movement and sexual liberation being in full swing by this time, their cups of salaciousness were likely already on the verge of brimming over.

Therefore, that the producers should choose to switch gears to a more libertine direction must have shocked television viewers and challenged the resolve of even the ITV studio executives who were eager for ratings in their never-ending competition with the BBC for television supremacy. Say what you will about how tame this episode might be today; it was kinky beyond words in 1966. The legends were, as many readers will already be aware, that American television executives at ABC refused to air this episode and yet sat around and privately watched it rapt with attention.

Despite this notorious reputation, during the unfolding spectacle of debauchery, there are a few chances to advance the finer points of ***The Avengers*** legacy. The opening pre-title sets the tone as Cartney pushes an overstuffed chair into a shadowy room and indulgently drinks sherry and eats chocolate while watching the results of his latest prank on television—highly suggestive of the dark libertine drama that was to follow. Later on, James Hill's direction takes full advantage of the darkened subterranean sets and the film noir lighting that dominates them. (I'm reminded of the sewers in ***The Third Man***.) Peter Wyngarde, later to be better known for playing Jason King in ***Department S***, plays the role of Cartney as if made for it, his slightly effete aristocratic air being his bread-and-butter.

Though little happens in the way of camaraderie between the two regulars, Emma playfully teases Steed about her newfound romantic possibilities with Cartney (which, in the end, go precisely nowhere), telling him how well they got along with kittenish glee. Steed, for his part, raises an excited eyebrow when first hearing about the Hellfire Club. He also raises the bar of his own daring when he joins the club with panache, proving that if there's anything anyone else can do, Steed and Mrs. Peel can do it better. He's not really a hedonist, a bon vivant maybe, but no hedonist, and yet you can tell he's enjoying the process. And when he's asked if he's ever committed an 'ultimate sin,' his answer is 'no,' but the hint of a smirk about his lips betrays his wider experience, far wider than his interviewers can possibly know.

Mrs. Peel seems less comfortable joining the hedonists. In some ways, Emma seems to be slightly out of her depth for the first time in this season, overwhelmed perhaps by the extremeness of the situation and undermined by so much focus on the dominance of the men. Libertine is definitely not her style, which makes her upcoming outrageous getup all the more stirring. It's an odd twist of expectations to play at this late a stage in the season—a fully liberated woman, more capable than any of the men in the room, forced into the role of a subservient, if elevated, object of desire. Diana Rigg had toned down the severity of Honor Blackman's Cathy Gale in her portrayal of Emma Peel. She was more amiable, more feminine, but still indomitable and at least the equal of any man depicted from week-to-week. The relationship between Emma and Steed had dissolved the prior tension between the regulars and was more easy-going and romantic. Thus, it must have been all the more shocking to see her as she appeared next.

Kittenish Mrs. Peel, already having betrayed wry knowing smiles to the audience for the past twenty weeks, was now a sadomasochistic fetishist's wet dream, with luxurious dark hair piled upon her head, bejeweled eyelids, a tight black corset, knee-high leather boots, elbow-length leather gloves and spiked collar, and a snake wrapped around one wrist. As the camera pans over her body, a roomful of eager men soundlessly ogle her uninterrupted for the better part of thirty seconds. The viewers probably didn't even need Wyngarde's punctuating line of "She's yours, to do with what you will" to shock them at this point, or possibly didn't even notice it due to the resulting shock. While the average viewer in 1960s Britain probably didn't know exactly what the hell was going on or what it signified (S&M-wise), they certainly knew that it was pushing something, and pushing hard.

Adding to all this a slightly effeminate Lord Darcy with a male housekeeper who dotes upon him, a serious session of snogging between Cartney and Sara (Carol Cleveland), interrupted by his need to sadistically push her down with a stamp of his boot, and the drunken revelry at the first meeting of the Hellfire Club, and it's easy to see the approximate point where ABC executives said 'no thanks' to this uninhibited tale of debauchery—with no need to get to the cracks of a whip that punctuated the finale at "The Night of All Sins."

But, you may ask, is the story any good? A just question this is, and I'm sorry to say, not really. As far as the narrative of a typical episode of *The Avengers* goes, this would be distinctly average at best. Stripped of its Bacchanalia and the incumbent salacious overflow, there's just not a lot going on here, with only the boilerplate plot of a secret cabal planning to blow up the government to drive the narrative. While you can certainly say this about many episodes of *The Avengers*—that stripped of its superficial fun the plots are simplistic—the basic problem with "A Touch of Brimstone" is that by putting the emphasis on orgiastic kink it limits its appeal to those audience members who find such things appealing.

I may be underestimating the percentage of viewers who will find sadomasochistic adventures more enjoyable than the usual champagne-infused action hijinks of Steed and Mrs. Peel, but I suspect that most viewers were happier and found the episodes much more satisfying when the program returned to more familiar (and safer) ground. Having said that, "A Touch of Brimstone" is nevertheless historic on multiple levels and legendary in a way that few examples of television manage, so while I'm calling out my safe word for this week, I will admit that this is highly compelling television and thus required viewing.

CHAMPAGNE, CARS, CLOTHES, AND CANINES

The episode begins with Mrs. Peel in 'Flash,' her blue lamé pantsuit (from "Castle De'Ath") and Steed in tuxedo and black tie. Lots of the usual outfits and suits appear here, but the main ones you'll want to hear about are their Regency Lady and Dandy costumes, and, of course, the 'Queen of Sin' fetish outfit that was designed by Diana Rigg herself (described above). It would not have necessarily been unusual to let the star of the show design her outfit under these circumstances. Obviously, the costume was quite racy, especially for the day, and it would have to be something that Rigg would be comfortable wearing. Overall, she was fine with exposing as much as she did; the part that made her most uncomfortable was having a snake on her arm for hours at a time. (I can relate.) Steed's 18th-century dandy outfit includes a chestnut jacket featuring wide lapels and a knee-length skirt, plus a white shirt with blousy sleeves and frilled cuffs. His waistcoat has a fleur-de-lys pattern, and he wears a white cravat and pale trousers. Mrs. Peel also wears a Regency period costume in white, brown, and green with ruched silk trim and a pale silk bow across the breast, and she carries a matching reticule on a long string. Other than this, Mrs. Peel debuts one more outfit: a simple white cotton knee-length dress with elaborate embroidering around the neckline and the sleeves.

TAG SCENE

Steed and Emma depart down a country lane in a carriage drawn by four horses.

QUOTES

"Nowhere seems to be sacrosanct now, not even the House of Lords. A whoopee cushion under the woolsack. Some took it as a vote of sanction."
"I've come here to appeal to you, Mr. Cartney." "You certainly do that."
"I'm afraid he's busy, he won't have time to see you." "He's expecting me." "Mrs. Peel, this is a surprise!" "*Half*-expecting."
"We believe in the power of evil, Mr. Steed. We believe in the...ultimate sins. Have you ever committed an ultimate sin, Mr. Steed?" "No, but I'm always open to suggestions."
"She's yours to do with what you will!"
"The choice of weapons is yours." "Feather dusters at four-hundred yards?"
"Very impressive. Now, what are you like with the big boys?"

100 (4.22.22) WHAT THE BUTLER SAW

Steed becomes a gentleman's gentleman — Emma faces a fate worse than death
Written by Brian Clemens
Directed by Bill Bain

GUEST CAST

Thorley Walters (Hemming), John Le Mesurier (Benson), Denis Quilley (Group Captain Miles), Kynaston Reeves (Major General Goddard), Howard Marion Crawford (Brigadier Goddard), Humphrey Lestocq (Vice Admiral Willows), Ewan Hooper (Sergeant Moran), Leon Sinden (Squadron Leader Hogg), David Swift (Barber), Norman Scace (Reeves), Peter Hughes (Walters)

PRE-TITLE/TEASER

A butler asks his wealthy employer for a pay increase, complaining of the conditions. Instead of agreeing, the man rings a bell to call for the head butler, who brings him a silver tray holding a gun with a silencer. The rich man aims and fires at the first butler, killing him immediately.

SYNOPSIS

Steed and Emma suspect that certain important military figures are leaking information to a foreign power. As a result, Steed goes undercover at a butler training school in order to become the butler for a man of strategic importance. And Emma must deal with the womanizing Group Captain Miles...

REVIEW

After the excesses of the previous two weeks, "What the Butler Saw" is precisely the kind of lighter, fluffier story audiences would have needed to calm down after the buzz subsided. The title is not nearly as suggestive as it sounds, and instead of further peccadilloes of a sexual nature, we're treated to another enjoyable spy spoof. Style-wise, this is much more of a return to the likes of "Two's a Crowd," "The Girl from Auntie," or "Quick-Quick Slow Death," rather than "Dial a Deadly Number," "The Danger Makers," or the lascivious "A Touch of Brimstone." Thus, ***The Avengers*** celebrates its one-hundredth episode with humor and wit in a fun-filled story.

Steed begins by scoping out the army, navy, and air force to find out which branch is the hiding place of the traitor, and he engages in a rarity for him, that of outright disguise. In each case, he pretends to be a stereotypical example of a member of each of the armed services—the neat mustache and stiff upper lip of the army, the bushy beard of the navy, and the wing-like face-smothering handlebar mustache of the RAF, along with incomprehensible banter that would give Biggles and Algy a run for their money.

Ultimately, Steed enrolls at the Butlers & Gentlemen's Gentlemen Association to try and secure an inside view of the treasonous aristocracy, allowing for the show to once again explore the absurdity of turning traditional activities into ritualistic ones, motions that are typically natural becoming mechanistic and stiff. It is after all a Brian Clemens script; his scripts are known for playing up the essential British quirkiness of the show. The rigid and unflappable, formal English butler, usually with a name like Jenkins or James or Alfred, was the ultimate stereotype for a British male in the sixties—in the eyes of Americans, in particular. So, I suppose it was inevitable that it would be covered at some point.

Meanwhile, Mrs. Peel goes into action with her Operation Fascination, an attempt to draw the attention of Group Captain Miles, one of the suspected traitors. It's a charming set piece but the placement of dozens of photographic portraits of herself in his study seems a little lacking in subtlety for her. Regardless, it works, and the Captain is hooked. They engage in an uncomfortably silly romance involving a spoof scene of Casanova romantic tactics, complete with settees whose arms throw the potential conquest into a supine position that is perfect for kissing.

Naturally, Steed graduates early after his forged references make him ideal for the corrupt goals of the villains. And he is instantly made the butler for Group Captain Miles while Miles attempts to seduce Mrs. Peel. This prompts Steed's jealous attempts to short-circuit their romantic interlude with constant interruptions. Turns out, the good Captain's Casanova reputation is a burden that he's eager to shed, and he and Mrs. Peel end up playing a cozy game of Ludo in front of a roaring fireplace.

The potential for butler spies has not been explored anywhere else, before or since, that I'm aware of. It's an area of exploration probably limited to about a generation, and thus, for television, only the sixties, since that was the beginning of the spy show craze and the tail end of the golden era of English butlers. The profession today seldom carries the same cultural symbolism that it once did when it was inextricably bound to the aristocracy and peerage and would seem even more quaint than Steed's bowler hat and umbrella if presented in a similar context today.

Aside from the humorous butler scenes, there are a few other notable moments, such as the two RAF officers who seal themselves together into a gigantic plastic sheet like a condom in order to foil hidden microphones while they have a private conversation, their voices reduced to a comically incomprehensible burbling. They later form a threesome in yet another giant condom.

Not to be outdone in outrageousness, while spying out the laundry room, Steed finds the nice butler Hemmings dead in a man-sized washing machine, his face tumbling wide-eyed and half-comically among the suds. The final fight scene is also gloriously bizarre. Emma and 'the master' of the operation fight on the butler practice set with Mrs. Peel slamming one faux door after another in his face. When a girl says 'no,' it means no!

The problem is that the plot, while an original twist on an unoriginal idea, is circuitous and hard to unravel, finally leading after much meandering to a scheme to install miniature tape recorders inside each military officer's uniform (and a Cockney former military man who wants his revenge). This leaves the story to largely make good with a series of humorous vignettes mixed with outrageous butler-induced deaths, which is not a bad thing but just slightly lightweight after the previous two episodes.

CHAMPAGNE, CARS, CLOTHES, AND CANINES

As far as Steed is concerned, this episode is known for his foray into every branch of the British armed forces, each time as the epitome of a stereotype: first as a bushy-bearded Navy commander; then, as an Army major from a tank regiment, with a neatly trimmed mustache; and, finally, as a Royal Air Force squadron leader with a handlebar mustache practically big enough to drive a motorcycle with. He finally abandons this routine and assumes the role of a butler—which is simultaneously less funny and something of a relief—with a long-sleeved white shirt with wing collar and black tie, black waistcoat and tail coat with black trousers. He also wears his light-gray suit with the pale blue overcoat with black collar. He finishes the tag scene in his chalk-striped navy suit.

Mrs. Peel, on the other hand, dresses in a fascinating array of clothing as part of her Operation Fascination—which works on the viewers as well as her target—including a collarless pale-yellow jacket with diamond-shaped frogs, designed by John Bates and called 'VIP', and a sleeveless pale-green and white dress with a Peter Pan collar worn under her black-and-white coat with cross-like stripes. The dress is chevroned at the waist and laced down the front in a crisscross pattern. Also, in a rare occurrence, perhaps unique, she wears dark shades. She finishes the episode in her black leather jumpsuit with a soft white blouse with a rollneck collar and cloth buttons down the front.

She drives her Lotus Elan S2 convertible (with the top up!) and Steed hitches a lift. The helicopter is a 1963 Brantly B-2A helicopter (G-ASHD)—the first helicopter featured in *The Avengers*.

TAG SCENE

Steed and Emma depart in a helicopter, saying that "in spite of all possible suspects... the butler did it."

QUOTES

"Better, brighter, more beautiful butling!"

"It'll not be easy, you'll find the course an arduous one, but you'll learn many things. You'll start at the bottom, learning how to polish the master's shoes."

"You know, forged references are the best recommendations you could have had. Now, I'm going to give you the chance to earn some real money, Steed."

"Kindly confine your activities to the garden, and don't blow up the roses again!"

"Steed, why don't you say it? Go on, I know you're dying to say it." "Say what?" "That in spite of all possible suspects…" "The butler did it!"

101 (4.23.23) THE HOUSE THAT JACK BUILT

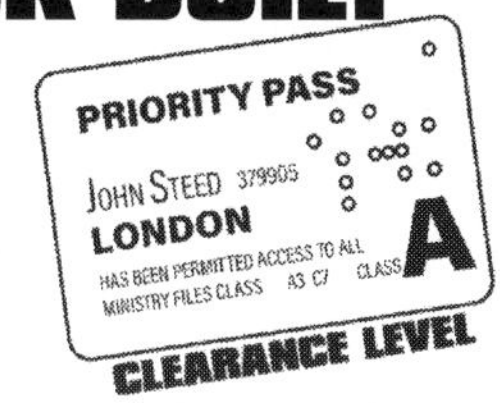

Steed takes a wrong turning — Emma holds the key to all
Written by Brian Clemens
Directed by Don Leaver

GUEST CAST

Michael Goodliffe (Professor Keller), Griffith Davies (Burton), Michael Wynne (Withers), Keith Pyott (Pennington)

PRE-TITLE/TEASER

A convict escapes from prison and flees into a nearby wood while the prison guards pursue him with dogs. Desperate, the convict tackles a guard and takes his shotgun. He then stumbles upon an abandoned manse. He breaks a window and enters. Once inside, he is bewildered by an attacking lion and fires the shotgun at it in terror.

SYNOPSIS

Mrs. Peel receives a letter from her lawyer informing her that she has inherited a house from her uncle Jack. After going to take a look at the property, she enters a maze of rooms and confusing dimensional anomalies designed to drive her mad. Steed becomes suspicious when he discovers that the key to the mysterious house has ruined the holiday snapshots he's developing, but will he arrive in time…?

REVIEW

You're a convict, and you've just escaped from prison. The guards and their dogs are after you, but you manage to evade them, knocking out a guard and stealing his shotgun. Now, you've got to find a place to hide out until things cool off. Thankfully, there's a beautiful country estate just ahead. It looks abandoned. Perfect! Once inside, however, you find the situation getting hotter instead; it's one that requires facing off against film projections of lions that waste your ammo, mysterious laughs that come from nowhere, and rooms that move. Soon, you have become the victim of a trap planned for someone else, but she's due along any minute to rescue you, even though you'll be insane by then.

This seems to be a love or hate it episode with most of the haters finding the tedium of Emma's navigating through the mechanized house the main point of concern. I count myself in the former group and would point out that frustration is the point, and if it didn't transfer to the audience, then they wouldn't find themselves able to identify with the character, audience identification being one of the main foundations of drama.

Diana Rigg, for her part, is doing a great job, running the gamut of the expected emotions in such a situation, going from concerned to frightened, frustrated to angry, and from resolved to despondent, but turning on the intelligence when needed to solve the puzzles. And her look at Steed upon his arrival is a remarkable representation of relief, gratitude, and affection—his simple act of honking her car horn having been the impetus she needed in a brief moment of despair.

For once, we have a red herring of a villain, and it makes sense and works completely. Withers (or Pongo, as Steed knows him) is the only notable eccentric in this episode—a scout master that goes around in knee pants—and he is the chief suspect in the early moments of the story. After Mrs. Peel has expressed mainly annoyance at his presence rather than concern—irritatedly flicking his knife aside in one scene while driving—he is however quickly eliminated from the puzzle. Necessary in the early moments in order to avoid total absence of dialogue for a substantial stretch of time and a total lack of apparent threat, his disappearance briefly transfers suspicions to the other man within the house, the escaped convict Burton from the pre-title, who we know is there but may have forgotten about. Like Withers, Burton (named only in the credits) is also utterly essential to the story, existing to demonstrate Mrs. Peel's superior abilities. When the man has failed and become a blithering idiot within days, Emma comes in and solves the whole conundrum within hours. When he falls to his feet sobbing, her reaction betrays simultaneous sympathy and irritation.

The mechanisms of the house seem at least plausible; given enough time and attention to detail, it seems likely that the engineering could be accomplished, but there are moments when the disorientating dimensional anomalies seem less probable. Even if the rooms are rotating on canisters, it seems unlikely that they could rotate in a 180-degree turn before Emma could open the door to the next section, especially without her noticing the centrifugal force applied in the process.

Despite this, the weird humming props and dazzle camouflage design patterns along the floor and walls have a compelling attraction, one that demands your attention while the mystery is being sorted. Don Leaver accentuated the disorientation by choosing to periodically shoot with Dutch angles, an entirely appropriate directorial move in this situation as it's intended to illustrate a state of uneasiness or vertigo. Adding to this is the discordant organ score. For much of the episode, the soundtrack lacks music, as the weird sound effects and bizarre mechanics whirl and bleep. Then, the crazy organ starts in and shrieks at the viewer in random blasts like screams—a proxy for Mrs. Peel (who surely would never scream). The mysterious growls and distorted laughter coming from the walls are eerie too, and the viewer is likely to be on edge throughout, the tension mitigated only by the knowledge that Steed is on his way.

Don Leaver's direction is as precise as ever, and this episode needed that kind of handling. It is a very structured piece with precise timing needed in order to frustrate the viewer to just the right amount before allowing for release of tension. On the scripting side of things, all of the ideas involving the key activating traps and closing down roads along the way to the house is admirably conceived, demonstrating that writer Brian Clemens had thought of nearly everything, making the whole of the narrative quite the well-constructed puzzle. The first-time viewer is unlikely to be more than a step and a half ahead of Mrs. Peel at any time.

My only significant issue is the relatively weak motivation by Professor Keller, as I find it very hard to believe that a man could be such a sourpuss that he would spend millions of pounds and a year of his life building a mechanical monstrosity to torture someone…all just because he got the sack. I always find it amazing that diabolical masterminds absolutely *never* cool off. You and I both know that if this were one of us ordinary folks, three months into the project we'd be throwing our hands in the air, proclaiming, "I've got less than a year to live. Screw this—I'm going to Disney World!" But diabolical masterminds like Keller are made of sterner stuff, with iron will just like their metal creations. Ultimately, given his limited screen time however, Keller is just a pale one-dimensional shadow of Dr. Armstrong from "The Cybernauts."

Despite this minor drawback, the whole of the production is one that works, works well, and would have worked, with limited tweaking to the script, in any number of programs, from ***The Outer Limits*** to ***Mission: Impossible*** to ***Doctor Who***. I'll go one step further and say that it's a masterpiece of its type of entertainment, and it's difficult to imagine it being done much differently. While it might not be a very good episode to start out with if you're not already a fan, it's required viewing for the initiated.

EPISODE NOTES

Director Don Leaver was possibly chosen for this production due to it largely being set-based, as he was one of the two directors (along with Bill Bain) retained from the videotaped, studio-bound era of Dr. Keel and Cathy Gale. Leaver spoke about this, saying that he and Bain received little respect from Julian Wintle and the film department for their directorial abilities, remarking that they were tolerated rather than welcomed.

The exteriors for the house were shot at Shenley Lodge, Shenley. However, like "The Thirteenth Hole," there are a number of unconvincing rear-screen shots involving Mrs. Peel and Withers at Ivinghoe Beacon.

Some have called the key magical because it interferes with both film and compasses, but if it emits both electromagnetic radiation and particle radiation, then it's entirely possible it could do this. In fact, particle radiation would fog the film in the manner depicted in the episode. However, as someone who has used the odd film changing bag, one thing's for certain, Steed's 'portable darkroom' would have been very leaky, but it possibly wouldn't have mattered much since print film is very slow speed.

CHAMPAGNE, CARS, CLOTHES, AND CANINES

Not much of a fashion episode for either Steed or Mrs. Peel, but she does debut a new outfit that would carry her through the remainder of the season, and it's a pretty iconic one: a cream-colored jacket of cotton twill with matching trousers and a black belt. Double-breasted with large black buttons in two columns, full collar, and flap pocket covers. It is both flared and vented. In this episode, she wears it with a white rollneck jumper. She wears this piece in all of the remaining episodes of the season, regardless of transmission or production order, and in "The Strange Case of the Missing Corpse." Since she remains trapped in Pendlesham for the entire episode, she wears no other outfit, but she does wear her honeycomb print headscarf with it on her trip down in her Lotus Elan and again in the tag scene, though without the jacket.

Steed is not in this one much, but he wears a black jumper in the opening and his navy three-piece suit in the tag scene. He drives the 1927 Bentley 3 Litre down to Pendlesham wearing his tan overcoat, with his brown serge suit and circle-patterned tie underneath.

Sadly, despite photography being developed, there are no cameras to identify, only a very old enlarger. Weirdly, Steed's using a bromide paper (typically a very old black-and-white print film) and a color chemical bleach.

TAG SCENE

Steed and Emma depart on a tandem bicycle.

QUOTES

"You give me the fright of my life and then you have the audacity to ask a favour! Where to?"

"When the experiment is concluded, the machine will continue to function perfectly, but you, Mrs. Peel...you will be quite, quite mad!"

"Suicide box. Once. Inside. Gas. Released. You. Will. Feel. No. Pain. No. Pain."

"You've made a mistake. You've told me what to expect. Now, whatever happens, I'll know it's a trick. I *can* reason it out."

"What happened to the shining armor?" "It's still at the laundry. Never mind, I'll give you a ride home on the old horse."

102 (4.24.24) A SENSE OF HISTORY

Steed dons a gown — Emma becomes a don
Written by Martin Woodhouse
Directed by Peter Graham Scott

GUEST CAST

Nigel Stock (Richard Carlyon), John Barron (Henge), John Glyn-Jones (Grindley), John Ringham (Professor Acheson), Patrick Mower (Duboys), Robin Phillips (John Pettit), Peter Blythe (Millerson), Peter Bourne (Allen), Jacqueline Pearce (Marianne)

PRE-TITLE/TEASER

An elderly man drives his limousine down a country lane. Encountering a fallen man in the middle of the road, he stops the car to investigate. The man turns out to be fine; it's a Rag Week prank. Several other masked men arrive with bows and arrows gesturing for a donation. The old man gives them some money and returns to his car, but is brought down by an arrow in his back before he can close the door.

SYNOPSIS

An archery death puts Steed and Emma into the midst of a group of students at St. Bode's Academy who clash with the economic theories of one of the academy's professors. As Steed and Emma investigate, and more murders occur, the historical issue reaches a surprising crescendo. But which professor is driving the unrest of the students…?

REVIEW

Rag week gone wrong? ***The Avengers*** deal with a group of university upstarts who use rag week as an excuse for a lot more than harmless mayhem. The average American viewer may not get some of the oddities of British university behavior. The larger theme however is a very familiar one—the impetuousness of youth challenging the established knowledge of the older generations. This puts Steed and Mrs. Peel on very unusual ground for the series. Used to being seen as the paragons of cool that they were, they are awkwardly shoehorned into a position much more associated with the older (and squarer) generations of the 1960s. This puts the writing into an awkward position also, forcing Martin Woodhouse to justify the victory of Steed and Mrs. Peel on the basis of sociopathy and self-deception rampant among the university brats. This, in itself, is not necessarily a bad thing, in fact it's the only possible course, and we have a fairly straightforward basis for the narrative, driven by a more sophisticated core conflict between Marxist and Fascist economic theory. There is a suggestion of the Leopold and Loeb murderers about the activities of the students. With their bland assumption of superiority, they have jettisoned the ethics of prior generations and substituted it with Nietzschean philosophy. This pushes Steed into a paternal position in which he becomes slightly sadistic; he threatens to break Duboys' arm.

It's screamingly obvious that someone other than the students has to be behind the villainous scheme. Who could it be? Let's see. You've got students and teachers. It's not the students, so it must be a teacher. And which one do they all admire so much? Professor Acheson. He's the only teacher that appears to use a bow and arrow as well. Well, that was easy to work out! Or not. Thankfully, there *is* a twist of expectations, and the leader is *not* who you might expect. I'm not sure if the twist works that well—given that the mysterious leader has the appearance and charisma of Gargamel, leaving one to question his ability to inspire such insane loyalty—but at least it's a twist. It does seem rather improbable however that the entire basis of the scheme is to alter history by killing a man before he can release his economic theories. Did no one take photocopies back then? Does he not have papers that can be released after his death? Do people really sit around and debate whether or not history can be changed by one man?

In one odd unexplained anomaly, Steed and Carlyon spent their nights camping out together in a gypsy caravan in the middle of a country lane. (Where does Mrs. Peel stay?) Perhaps it's more understandable considering that Carlyon first appears shut inside a car boot under a tarpaulin. *Clearly*, he's eccentric about his vehicles. And it makes even more sense as a visual when the Rag Week Ruffians attack with bows-and-arrows shouting like Indians in an old western. Fortunately, students are no match for Steed. He's not in a charitable mood and sends the young pups scurrying within moments.

There is precious little wit and humor, no surrealism—unless you count incongruent gypsy caravan hideouts and students with fright masks attacking with bows—and no eccentrics, unless you count eccentric economic theories involving Europia. (This theory is perhaps a foreshadowing of the European Union?) This leaves the story to work mainly on good acting and direction. Fortunately, it has both in abundance.

A young Patrick Mower is playing the young rogue character to the hilt, and many of the best parts of the episode feature his capable acting. And the cast, in general, is a very strong one, featuring such luminaries as Nigel Stock, John Barron, and John Ringham. A young Jacqueline Pearce also makes a low-key appearance as one of the students.

All the direction this season is generally superb, although, in this case, director Peter Graham Scott uses the cliché of a thunderstorm as the backdrop for the scene in which Pettit is killed and slightly obvious visuals like panning across a bust of Napoleon onto Duboys while he is giving speech as part of an initiation ritual.

The finale involves a Robin Hood theme (possibly a metaphor for liberal economic theory), and this setting provides a great deal of visual interest—costumes, food, and firelight. And, of course, Emma Peel dresses as the titular hero, a point which apparently gets a lot of people hot and bothered for reasons that are beyond my comprehension. It's the gender-bending aspect, I suppose, though these days it won't ruffle anyone's feathers. In story, the purpose is to put her in direct competition with Duboys, and naturally, the two Hoods fight at the end with the female version winning. And this is about as satisfying as "A Sense of History" gets, for there is no motivation to solve the tedious debate between economic theories. That is of no consequence to the viewer, and the matter is ultimately resolved as it always is—with judo and fisticuffs. This leaves the episode slightly off-kilter and unsatisfying but allows it to survive mainly on good visuals and fine acting.

CHAMPAGNE, CARS, CLOTHES, AND CANINES

Mrs. Peel starts where she left off in the prior episode: wearing the cream jacket and the honeycomb-print headscarf and driving her Lotus Elan, though switching out the trousers for houndstooth woolen hip-hugger pants; later, worn with black academic robes over the top (as a disguise?). Steed debuts what looks like a new overcoat, this time darker (possibly khaki) and in a serge or worsted weave, and a black bowler; possibly the navy chalk-striped suit is underneath because later he wears this suit with the same black academic robes as Mrs. Peel.

But let's cut to the chase— What you're really here to learn about is Mrs. Peel's Robin Hood outfit. It's strikingly skimpy, showing about half of her posterior. It pairs a white shirt in a man's cut with blousy sleeves and tight cuffs with a laced dark-blue tunic with brown scalloped trim. She finishes the ensemble off with black boots and briefs, and a matching cap with quite a feathery plume jutting from the top. She also carries a small blade, possibly a dirk, which she never uses.

Steed wears a Sheriff of Nottingham costume that's equally striking, with its black sword and scabbard, voluminous cloak, and fur hat, not to mention the fake van dyke beard. He drives a Land Rover (VX 897) that would return in the following season.

In the tag scene, Mrs. Peel wears her leather pants with a white rollneck jumper, and Steed wears his dark gray suit. The motorcycle is a 1962 BSA A50 Star Twin (FYK 76C) and sidecar. Don't think I can blame Steed for not wanting to feel the wind in his face. It looked to be quite a misty, rainy day.

TAG SCENE

Steed and Emma ride off on a motorcycle with Steed in the sidecar.

QUOTES

"I think what Pettit was trying to suggest, sir, is that, for the past fifty-three minutes you have assaulted our ears with a load of stupid, pretentious old rubbish!"
"Advanced research into the co-relationship of the lesser-crested newt and Mrs. Sybil Peabody." "Mrs. Sybil Peabody?" "An aunt of mine. Drinks like a fish."
"Well, if Duboys gives you any more trouble, just report him to the proctor." "I'll do better than that. I'll break his arm."
"That the entire future of Europe is in your hands ... beyond that, your lips are sealed. That in due course the full account of your heroism will be revealed to him. And add that if he hasn't heard from you within the week, he must presume that you have died for your country." "I say, that's very good! What!"
"That looks a bit droopy." "Wait till it's challenged!"

103 (4.25.25) HOW TO SUCCEED....AT MURDER

Steed becomes a perfect boss — Emma goes seeking charm
Written by Brian Clemens
Directed by Don Leaver

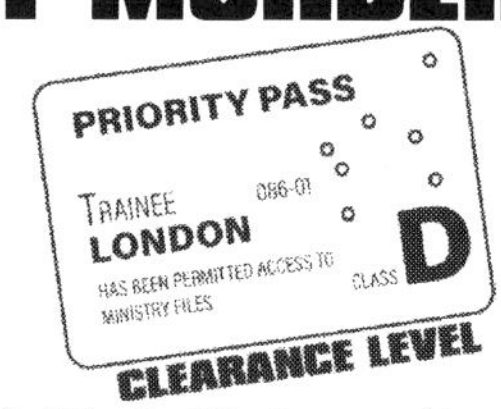

GUEST CAST

Sarah Lawson (Mary), Angela Browne (Sara), Anne Cunningham (Gladys), Zeph Gladstone (Liz), Artro Morris (Henry), Jerome Willis (Joshua Rudge), Christopher Benjamin (Hooter), Kevin Brennan (Sir George Morton), David Garth (Barton), Robert Dean (Finlay), Sidonie Bond (Annie)

PRE-TITLE/TEASER

A businessman complains to his secretary that he cannot understand her filing system and demands that she come in and explain it. Instead, she puts on a hardhat and engages a plunger detonator, blowing up both him and his office. She then carries on with her work as if nothing happened.

SYNOPSIS

Company employers are dropping dead all over town, and their secretaries are taking over. Steed and Emma eventually find a link between the murders at a fitness sorority for young ladies, where all the secretaries just happen to be a member. Mrs. Peel goes undercover as secretary as well and discovers that all the women are taking orders from a ventriloquist's doll named Henrietta, but, unsurprisingly, there's also a man in the room...

REVIEW

The story starts right out with a relatively charming pre-title sequence, one that is very much in the style of this season and the next, and then it quickly goes south from there. Watching the secretary pull out an army helmet and plunger detonator and in cartoonish fashion blow up her obnoxious boss's office, continuing with her typing as if nothing happened, is as absurdly surrealistic as it is amusing.

This is about fourteen years before ***9 to 5***, a seminal women's liberation comedy that starred Lily Tomlin, Dolly Parton, and Jane Fonda as office secretaries trying to get the better of their egotistical and sexist boss. It's difficult to know if the writers behind that film were in any way influenced by "How to Succeed....at Murder," an absurd sixties pastiche of female emancipation, but there are some interesting parallels, such as the idea that the women know more about the business than the men, the patriarchal and sexist attitudes of the bosses, and the employer deaths. Although in ***9 to 5*** no boss actually dies, here the bosses are exploded, strangled with nylon stockings, shot with tiny poison darts from charm bracelets, and suffocated with noxious nose snoods. (That last one is so specialized to this hour of television that I'm in no position to explain it. You'll just have to watch.)

We actually have a potentially good premise for supporting the burgeoning women's liberation movement by presenting a plethora of capable women that are smart, educated, talented, and fully the equal or superior to the men around them. This would have gone a long way to proving that Cathy Gale and Emma Peel were not the female equivalents of a superspade. So, why, oh why, does Clemens then choose to ruin it all by thumbing his nose at equal rights for women?

You could not have possibly made the women look more stupid for taking orders from a ventriloquist's dummy except by making that puppet controlled by a man from within the very room in which they're sitting. *It's a ventriloquist's dummy!* That means there's a ventriloquist *in the room*. It's not controlled by the women taking orders from it, so who could it be...? Possibly the *only* man in the room? The fact that these otherwise intelligent women need Steed to point this out to them makes it even more denigrating. He and Emma instantly see it when they walk into the room. It's astronomically improbable that all these women would never think to ask who is pulling the strings.

Granted, anyone who has no qualms about killing people in order to take over a company is a sociopath and thus deserves to be mocked and made to look stupid—perhaps writer Brian Clemens thought this made up for the humiliation of the women—but, by having set up the whole basis of the story around secretaries rising up against their condescending employers in an apparent liberation attempt, it ultimately gives the whole story a sexist air that delegitimizes any positive intention—instead appearing to claim women are not yet worthy of their equal rights.

Rather than giving women's liberation a boost, the story seems to be presenting a parading pastiche of all men's fear about equal rights for women, throwing the story's tone back to the suffragette era. (The women shout "Ruination to all men!" as their motto.) It certainly doesn't help that bad male behaviors and attitudes about women are emphasized as well, and Steed is shown inviting a secretary to sit in his lap and later tickling one to get information out of her. (This isn't 'kinky,' it's just sexist.) Steed would later be shown to be very amenable to giving the occasional pat on the bum to many sexy women, including Tara King. (The first notable subsequent example of such behavior is the promotional film "The Strange Case of the Missing Corpse" in which a scantily-clad Valerie Van Ost is the recipient of this dubious honor.) This is not the way we'd prefer to think of Steed. He's many things, even caddish on occasion, but not sexist. The result is the detriment of the show, Steed's character, and Clemens' writing. Whether Clemens intended the story to come across this way or not is unknown by me. In his defense, I will note that the men in the story are depicted as not much better than the women, and at least Mrs. Peel rises above it all unsullied. Perhaps Clemens merely thought he was being sardonically humorous or satirical. Regardless, the story doesn't quite work on any level, having only a few brief moments of amusement if one aggressively navigates around its many obvious faults.

Henry is a bizarre type of eccentric, a sort of Norman Bates operating by proxy through a puppet. He presents himself as the typical henpecked mild-mannered type and as useless and incompetent, but he is really controlling everything from behind the scenes. He's also completely insane. Thus, the point that Clemens' script apparently makes is that the least competent man is the superior of the most capable woman. But even if the women are so naïve as to think that taking orders from a puppet makes sense, at least they can bedazzle their bosses with an absurdly overcomplicated filing system. This is the only 'superpower' Clemens seemed content granting them—as if making the filing system *incomprehensible* has anything to do with competence or efficiency.

No fourth season episode of *The Avengers* is totally without merit, and I'll admit that there is some (mostly wasted) potential here. The idea of people taking orders from a ventriloquist's dummy is a bizarre idea that fits right in with the show's established template. The most charming and funny set piece however is Mrs. Peel's visit to Perfumier Extraordinary. Christopher Benjamin's J.J. Hooter is such an over-the-top eccentric that…well, how to explain? In a performance like this, one could go with subtlety (which is where *The Avengers* often ends up in this era) and become wryly funny. Or one could go further into the territory of silly and thus become less funny, clownish, childish even. Or one could go even further than that into a performance that is so absurdly caricaturized that the character becomes a send up of itself, a spoof of that very stereotype, and thus gets funny again. The final option is where Benjamin ends up, and it is indeed hilarious. Sadly, this is largely the extent of amusement available in this episode.

We've had a remarkable run up to this point. This season is composed of many great episodes only briefly interrupted by periodic mediocrity, and then you have this episode, and it's like the stereotypical sound of the record needle scratching across in mid-song, right near the end. Still, it's not as bad as some other seasons. Tara King's era would have several skips of the record far worse than this one, some that would leave the record permanently scratched, whereas this episode is a less disturbing break after which the season gets right back in the groove and finishes strong.

CHAMPAGNE, CARS, CLOTHES, AND CANINES

Steed wears his light gray suit and matching bowler hat; later, the tan overcoat on top; and still later, he wears his navy three-piece suit, followed by the brown serge suit. Mrs. Peel debuts a long-sleeved dark dot dress with integrated white facing. On her visit to Mr. Hooter, she wears a cream PVC jacket with the houndstooth hip-hugger pants (same as in "A Sense of History"). Underneath the jacket must be her black sleeveless shirt with a scooped neck, as she's wearing it while painting her abstract painting. Later, she wears a black-checked, knee-length white skirt with a wide white belt and a roll neck jumper. Finally, a variation on the cream jacket with six black buttons arrives, this one with a light checked pattern. She also wears black tights at the exercise studio.

Steed drives his 1927 Bentley 3 Litre.

TAG SCENE

In the back of a camper van, Steed and Emma read books on ventriloquism and then demonstrate their newfound talents to one another. The van drives off suddenly.

QUOTES

"Leap into My Fervid Arms!"
"That is the function of this organization, Mrs. Peel. To take woman out of the secretary's chair and put her behind the executive desk. To bring men to heel and put women to the pinnacle of power."
"20th century Amazons?"
"Ruination to all men!"
"Who's pulling the strings?"
"We do have our uses, madam."

104 (4.26.26) HONEY FOR THE PRINCE

Steed becomes a genie — Emma joins a harem
Written by Brian Clemens
Directed by James Hill

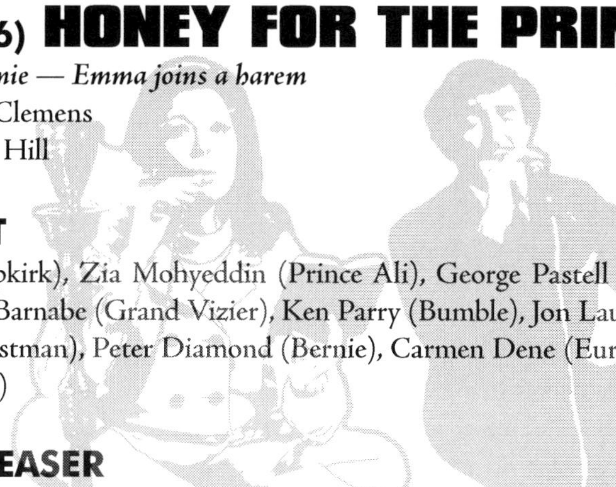

GUEST CAST

Ron Moody (Hopkirk), Zia Mohyeddin (Prince Ali), George Pastell (Arkadi), Roland Curram (Vincent), Bruno Barnabe (Grand Vizier), Ken Parry (Bumble), Jon Laurimore (Ronny Westcott), Reg Pritchard (Postman), Peter Diamond (Bernie), Carmen Dene (Eurasian Girl), Richard Graydon (George Reed)

PRE-TITLE/TEASER

The camera pans over a vast room filled with Middle Eastern artifacts. Two men arrive and begin to search. One of the men finds a genie lamp and rubs it vigorously. A third man with a machine gun suddenly appears in a puff of smoke and guns the other two down.

SYNOPSIS

Investigating the murder of an agent, Steed and Emma trace the death to a honey supplier and an agency called Quite Quite Fantastic Inc that fulfills the fantasies of their clients. Meanwhile, Baravian prince Ali has arrived to finalize a deal that will provide oil concessions to Britain in exchange for their military protection. Unfortunately, the losing competitor for the oil concession deal is now planning to use the QQF for more murderous purposes…

REVIEW

This classic episode starts out in the finest way possible, presenting itself as almost a distillation of all the great established points of the season—bizarre eccentric villains, unique intriguing core concepts, fantasy elements, wit and humor, and the camaraderie between the stars. In the pre-title, the secret agents investigating the QQF find a genie's lamp. Rubbing the lamp produces an assassin wielding a machine gun that immediately and viciously rubs them out.

This is followed by an utterly charming scene in which Steed and Emma stroll through a park in evening wear, possibly after having an enjoyable night out on the town. Steed carries a balloon and Emma a teddy bear. Childlike in tone, never has their relationship appeared so easygoing and intimate. Though they are unstoppable superspies, here they play and laugh with one another, arm in arm. The relationship is plainly that of best friends…for this brief lighthearted moment. When they return to Steed's flat, however, it appears to have been burgled, and their charming respite is terminated by an oncoming spy investigation. Thankfully, for us, the fun is just beginning.

Much like "The Girl from Auntie" or "Quick-Quick Slow Death," the story is another procession of eccentrics, though they each drive the narrative less directly. B. Bumble of B. Bumble and Company is a gentle, harmless eccentric type who is passionate about honeybees. He is rotund and wears a striped jumper, giving him an appearance similar to that of his tiny charges, and his sympathetic talk of having to operate on a sick bee brings a warm smile to Mrs. Peel's face.

Ron Moody is wonderful as Hopkirk, a passionate eccentric working tirelessly to bring fantasies to life for all the Walter Mittys of the world. His operation—the Quite Quite Fantastic Incorporated—is something of a ***Fantasy Island*** for its day and he its Mr. Rourke. Though, I dare say, for the average fan of sixties spy shows, this episode will read as a much better execution of the concept. Hopkirk's death is as delightfully ironic as it is tragic; he encourages his assassin to put more emotion into his murderous intent, using his final moments as an acting coach. It's another example of the show's mixture of humor with violence. Fortunately, before he dies, he has the opportunity to share a hookah with Mrs. Peel in a charming scene.

Arkadi is an intriguing, indulgent, and vain villain that appears to spend more time prepping and primping for his scheme's execution than actually carrying it out, leaving most of the legwork to his assistants while he enjoys steam baths, backrubs, and mink glove massages from a beautiful dark-haired woman who appears to dote lovingly over him. Lord knows why! Money, I suppose. This concept would be repeated with inferior results in "Who Was That Man I Saw You With?" during the Tara King era.

Nothing however could prepare the viewers for Emma's Dance of the Seven Veils and the charming 'retarded' act that follows. Her performance is not so much striking for her terpsichorean talent but the sheer verve of it being presented at all, accentuated by cuts to shots of the reactions of her enraptured audience. Immediately thereafter accepted as Ali's 321st wife and having infiltrated his harem, Emma quickly finds herself on the 'duty roster'—and for more than just spy work. This no doubt forces her to redouble her efforts to find the assassin before she is required to fulfill her new-found wifely (ehem!) obligations. Fortunately, Arkadi's assassin is quickly flushed out, and Mrs. Peel proves herself as a duelist. (Finally, all that fencing practice comes in handy.) Thankfully, this frees her from her bedroom duties, and she and Steed rush to stop the fleeing Arkadi back at the QQF. In the end, it all rounds out nicely with Steed knocking out the fleeing Arkadi with his umbrella after being summoned by Emma with the genie's lamp. Hoist on his own petard! And the heroes naturally depart on a 'magic carpet,' which turns out to be atop an open-bed truck racing down a country lane.

The downside of this otherwise superb hour of television might be the stereotypical way in which Middle Eastern people are presented. This is likely the last decade in which such could be done without comment, after which it soon became unacceptable. To be fair, however, the stereotype was not ridiculously out of date in the sixties, and it is somewhat alleviated by the humorous twist of having the Prince Ali charmingly obsessed with cricket and English traditions. This leaves the Grand Vizier, played by Englishman Bruno Barnabe in brown makeup, to be the primary Arab cliché, and his boundless obsequiousness is played for its full comic potential.

"Honey for the Prince" is a wonderful well-written story, in which all the components dove-tail nicely, and is punctuated throughout with endearing set pieces. It remains a true classic for the series and a strong finale for perhaps the greatest season of the show.

CHAMPAGNE, CARS, CLOTHES, AND CANINES

As referenced above, Steed and Mrs. Peel return from a night on the town, apparently; he's wearing his tuxedo and black tie with a white shirt with thin stripes underneath and his matching black silk overcoat; and she's wearing a white evening gown with matching wrap. Both sleeveless and collarless, the top of the gown is a delicate semi-sheer lace with floral patterns (her white pumps match this pattern) with the simple white fabric underneath, and at the waist there is a large bow in front. Steed's balloon appears to depict a stylized map of the world. At B. Bumble & Co., Mrs. Peel wears a checked cream-colored jacket, a white jumper with rollneck, white hip-hugging pants, a wide black belt, and the Edward Rayne boots. Later, she ditches the jacket. Of course, the show-stopper is Mrs. Peel's harem girl's outfit—six veils covering a bejeweled white bodice with hanging ornaments, blousy sheer harem pants and white briefs, probably made of silk. She performs the dance barefoot.

In the tag scene, Mrs. Peel's plain cream jacket returns with the checked pants and a black roll-neck jumper. Steed returns to a variation of his brown hunting jacket outfit from "A Surfeit of H2O," this time paired with what appears to be the black waistcoat with silver buttons, or possibly a variation thereof. The truck bearing the 'flying carpet' is a 1958 Austin A55 ½-Ton Pickup.

TAG SCENE

Steed and Emma depart on a 'flying carpet,' that is, a carpet on top of a speeding truck.

QUOTES

"Got it! You're a secret agent. Yes, indeed, ideal for you, licensed to kill, pitting your wits against a diabolical mastermind. Make a change from your everyday humdrum existence."
"Uh, what is it to be? The fantasy, what am I to be?" "Chief eunuch in a harem."
"I'm most terribly sorry, Colonel. It's another body entirely."
"Steed, sorry about the body, but it was too big to sweep under the carpet."
"No, thank you. I haven't yet exhausted reality."
"No, no, man, you're not putting enough into it. You won't get any satisfaction out of your fantasy unless you put something into it. Think. Think *murderously*!"
"Tell me, Mrs. Peel, what size do you take in Turkish trousers?"
"What's your party turn, 'Giselle'?"

THE STRANGE CASE OF THE MISSING CORPSE

This brief vignette was shot on color film on the set of "Honey for the Prince." This film was lost for many years, presumably buried in the archives at ABC/Thames Television, but it was found in 1999.

Over the years, many different stories have been told about this footage, and its origins are somewhat obscure. It has been claimed that it was initially filmed as test footage to see how the show would look in color, though this seems unlikely as the sets and clothing are curiously lacking in rich color tones, and it's improbable that such tests would be necessary in any case—everyone at ABC Television was likely already familiar with what color looked like! Color tests in film production are typically limited to specialized situations, seeking out a specific look for a movie or television program, or for testing purposes at film manufacturers. Rarely does anyone test to see how a specific *program* will look in color, they simply design it to look good with the available film stocks.

The most common theory is that it was shot specifically for the American market in order to show that ***The Avengers*** were returning the following year in color. This seems the most plausible theory. This move was extremely important in order to guarantee future sales to America. By 1966, all new programs at the major American networks were in color, and the fourth season of ***The Avengers*** was one of the very last programs offered in monochrome as a series premiere. ABC in America would have insisted that any further product purchased be in color. The fact that the vignette was shot using the set of the final episode for the season suggests financial economy as a motivation, just the kind of thing you'd be thinking of if you were trying to create a promotional film.

Many other sources, including the Dave Rogers books, have reported this film as being originally twenty minutes long and a 'mini-episode.' However, nothing of the available footage, which runs to approximately three minutes, supports this. It is clearly a pastiche of the common themes of the series with precious little plot to accompany it. It's difficult to see how anything here could have originally been expanded out to such a duration. It also seems unlikely that ABC would have run anything that lengthy as a promotional.

The tone of the vignette is silly and fun, and both Macnee and Rigg seem to be having a blast taking the mickey out of the program. Two other facts about this film stand out. First, it features Valerie Van Ost as the 'corpse.' (She would later appear in "Dead Man's Treasure"—very much alive.) Here, she is wearing naught but an overlong sweater and fishnets. And, secondly, it is the only color depiction of Mrs. Peel's season four black leather fighting suit. Later outfits for Mrs. Peel would be designed by Alun Hughes and would be made of softer fabrics with much brighter hues. It's actually easy to see why in this short film, as the black leather looks rather drab in color, whereas it looks inky-black and shiny on black and white film. Perhaps the 'color test' served its purpose after all.

It may turn out that a longer version of this footage exists, but I wouldn't hold my breath if I were you.

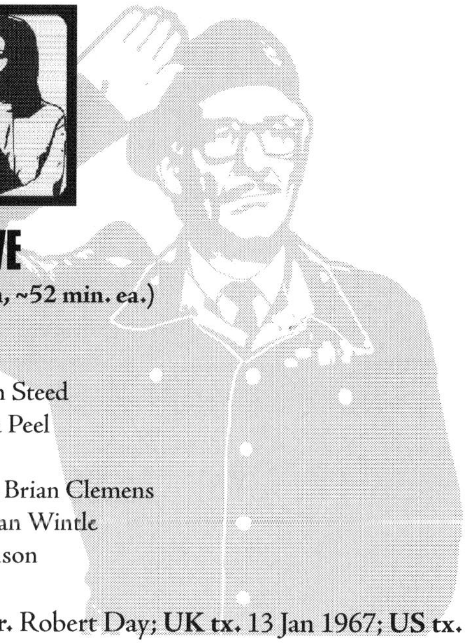

SEASON FIVE

16 episodes (35mm color film, ~52 min. ea.)

Regular Cast
Patrick Macnee—John Steed
Diana Rigg—Emma Peel

Producers: Albert Fennell and Brian Clemens
Executive Producer: Julian Wintle
Music: Laurie Johnson

105. **From Venus With Love—w.** Philip Levene; **dir.** Robert Day; **UK tx.** 13 Jan 1967; **US tx.** 20 Jan 1967; **filmed** Nov 1966
106. **The Fear Merchants—w.** Philip Levene; **dir.** Gordon Flemyng; **UK tx.** 20 Jan 1967; **US tx.** 27 Jan 1967; **filmed** Oct 1966
107. **Escape in Time—w.** Philip Levene; **dir.** John Krish; **UK tx.** 27 Jan 1967; **US tx.** 10 Feb 1967; **filmed** Oct 1966
108. **The See-Through Man—w.** Philip Levene; **dir.** Robert Asher; **UK tx.** 3 Feb 1967; **US tx.** 3 Feb 1967; **filmed** Dec 1966
109. **The Bird Who Knew Too Much—w.** Brian Clemens (s. Alan Patillo); **dir.** Roy Rossotti; **UK tx.** 10 Feb 1967; **US tx.** 10 Mar 1967; **filmed** Nov 1966
110. **The Winged Avenger—w.** Richard Harris; **dir.** Gordon Flemyng and Peter Duffell; **UK tx.** 17 Feb 1967; **US tx.** 17 Feb 1967; **filmed** Dec 1966
111. **The Living Dead—w.** Brian Clemens (s. Anthony Marriott); **dir.** John Krish; **UK tx.** 24 Feb 1967; **US tx.** 3 Mar 1967; **filmed** Dec 1966-Jan 1967
112. **The Hidden Tiger—w.** Philip Levene; **dir.** Sidney Hayers; **UK tx.** 3 Mar 1967; **US tx.** 17 Mar 1967; **filmed** Jan 1967
113. **The Correct Way to Kill—w.** Brian Clemens; **dir.** Charles Crichton; **UK tx.** 10 Mar 1967; **US tx.** 24 Mar 1967; **filmed** Jan 1967
114. **Never, Never Say Die—w.** Philip Levene; **dir.** Robert Day; **UK tx.** 17 Mar 1967; **US tx.** 31 Mar 1967; **filmed** Jan-Feb 1967
115. **Epic—w.** Brian Clemens; **dir.** James Hill; **UK tx.** 31 Mar 1967; **US tx.** 14 Apr 1967; **filmed** Feb 1967
116. **The Superlative Seven—w.** Brian Clemens; **dir.** Sidney Hayers; **UK tx.** 7 Apr 1967; **US tx.** 21 Apr 1967; **filmed** Feb-Mar 1967
117. **A Funny Thing Happened on The Way to The Station—w.** Brian Sheriff (R. Marshall & B. Clemens); **dir.** John Krish; **UK tx.** 14 Apr 1967; **US tx.** 28 Apr 1967; **filmed** Mar 1967
118. **Something Nasty in the Nursery—w.** Philip Levene; **dir.** James Hill; **UK tx.** 21 Apr 1967; **US tx.** 5 May 1967; **filmed** Mar-Apr 1967
119. **The Joker—w.** Brian Clemens; **dir.** Sidney Hayers; **UK tx.** 28 Apr 1967; **US tx.** 12 May 1967; **filmed** Mar-Apr 1967
120. **Who's Who??? —w.** Philip Levene; **dir.** John Moxey; **UK tx.** 5 May 1967; **US tx.** 19 May 1967; **filmed** Apr 1967

SEASON NOTES

Twenty-one black-and-white Diana Rigg episodes (out of the twenty-six produced for British television) were transmitted from 28 March to 1 September 1966 on ABC, as one of the American network's last black-and-white programs. In the wake of this cooperative and financial success, Associated British Corporation had already planned to produce twenty-six episodes, and were apparently hopeful of a full season order of that number from America.

ABC was not interested in that number for the moment, and the reasons for such are related to the vagaries of American television that might have been lost on the program's British producers. ABC had no intention of immediately placing a foreign show on their fall season primetime lineup. *The Avengers* was a weird show by most definitions in the 1960s, weird in a wonderful way, and it was cutting edge. And ABC didn't put 'weird shows' in their fall lineup willy-nilly. What this meant was that if *The Avengers* was going to make it into primetime at all it was going to be a replacement series in a less competitive time slot. This is what had happened with season four, and ABC had only purchased as many episodes as they did for reasons of mere economy—twenty-one episodes is a very long summer replacement series, and during the early weeks of its run, it probably took the place of something canceled from the fall season as well. Either way, this did at least prove that ABC believed in the show.

Unfortunately, the reticence from the American network meant that they instead asked for a mere sixteen episodes to run as a midseason replacement to air in the winter and spring of 1967. This smaller order meant that sixteen episodes were filmed between October 1966 and April 1967 before production was shut down for a six-week break, awaiting further financial instructions from the various ITV stations throughout England and the final ratings from the American network ABC.

For now, however, *The Avengers* got as close as it ever got to being a cohesive set of stories with a singular outlook. Fifteen of the sixteen episodes were written or co-written by Philip Levene or Brian Clemens, and they were certainly among the most solid batches of episodes made for the show. The uniformity comes at the cost of a degree of freshness and multiple points of view from a diverse slate of writers, and this forces the series into something of a surrealistic and humorous bottleneck that would ultimately become difficult to escape. Nevertheless, contemporary fans tend to either judge season four or five the best, and this one certainly has much with which to recommend it, with several episodes as strong contenders for the crème de la crème. Indeed, the program was classier than ever and looked fantastic in color.

Generally, the scripts were even more direct and less complicated than last season. In most cases, they could be reduced down to a single idea-of-the-week. The episodes would variously involve UFOs, phobias, time travel, invisibility, talking birds, comic books, ghosts, killer cats, doppelgänger robots, epic films, trains, nannies, and brain-switching. Even the otherwise more psychological and abstract "The Joker" incorporated a playing card theme into its plotline. It was however not just the concept du jour that heavily characterized this surreal season.

There were many visual changes enacted to take full advantage of this new colorful world for *The Avengers*. The production team made one major change to the look of the show—Diana Rigg's costumes. Out went the uncomfortable black leather fighting gear, and in came colorful Alun Hughes-designed jumpsuits. The other significant changes to Season Five came in flashy new direction, clearly Hitchcockian in inspiration whereas season four had been film noir, new flats for Steed and Emma to occupy, and a noticeable number of established guest stars.

Earlier seasons of *The Avengers* had featured strong actors, but starting with this year, the producers actively used known stars in a bid for ratings—and with the greatly expanded budget built upon American money, they could afford it. Among the already established stars, often from the world of comedy, to appear in either cameos or as villain-of-the-week were Barbara Shelley, Ronnie

Barker, Ron Moody, Roy Kinnear, Jon Pertwee, Warren Mitchell, Patricia Haines, Freddie Jones, Brian Blessed and Christopher Lee. These prominent actors, many of whom were returning from prior seasons, provided a constant stream of identifiably quirky foes: the myopic eye doctor in "From Venus With Love"; the catlike Cheshire in "The Hidden Tiger"; the Ticket Collector in "A Funny Thing Happened on the Way to the Station"; and Christopher Lee's indefatigable man in "Never, Never Say Die."

One stylistic influence came from what might have been an unexpected source at the time but is relatively obvious in retrospect. ***The Avengers*** had discovered the campy but fun comic book series ***Batman*** in the interim between seasons. That iconic comic book-inspired American series—also broadcast on ABC—had been imported by various ITV stations, and its English premiere came in May 1966, shortly before filming began on this season of ***The Avengers***. Although the influence was perhaps not immediately obvious to the casual viewer, it was there and transparently obvious to the more observant fans, and in "The Winged Avenger," the visual style is blatantly comic book-inspired, applying various 'pows,' 'zaps,' 'kabooms' to the spy superheroes' Kung fu-fighting. That episode didn't do anything greatly different from other shows of the period, it just thrust the influence in your face by way of parody whereas the other fifteen episodes merely flirted with its tone. But the end result was a season that was more over-the-top and outrageous than ever with a strong fantasy aspect that will eventually get Fennell and Clemens in trouble.

Transmission of these sixteen episodes came very soon behind each other in the UK and the US with high hopes for high ratings and that elusive fall primetime season order from America. "From Venus With Love" opened the series in the UK on 14 January 1967, and in the US on 20 January. This early premiere in the United States was apparently a late decision. ABC had originally wanted to start the show in March or April, but instead decided to begin broadcast earlier in the winter. This was likely due to another program bombing in the ratings, freeing up an earlier slot. The transmission order was not identical, but schedules in both countries finished with "Who's Who???" in May 1967, which was the closest the series would come to a simultaneous broadcast on both sides of the Atlantic.

These broadcasts were unquestionably the zenith for the series, though no one knew it at the time. The upper echelon at Associated British Corporation and ITV, their eyes still on the prize of a fall premiere on ABC in America, would again be frustrated, for the order was a mere fifteen to be broadcast in the winter of 1968. Associated British Corporation would perhaps be surprised at the obstacles that they would face in the months ahead as they attempted to fulfill that order, but, for the time being, ***The Avengers*** was a cult darling for many and possibly the most exciting and fun program on television.

ICONIC TITLES

This is the title sequence that casual viewers will likely find most familiar, and it is the first one that is entirely live action and in color. Probably inspired by the champagne toast in the American introduction to the previous season, this version begins similarly. It is preceded by a caption card declaring "The Avengers in Color." On an open set with a grey backdrop, John Steed marches out in silhouette holding a champagne bottle, briefly photographed at a distance through champagne glasses upon a table. Mrs. Peel then fires her revolver at the cork of the bottle causing it to explode with a fountain of bubbly. They both walk casually to the table and pour themselves glasses of champagne, toasting as the screen fades to black. The music is a jazzy solo percussive beat.

The screen fades up to reveal the surface of a Chippendale-style desk. Two empty champagne glasses, Steed's hat and umbrella, and Emma's golden revolver lie upon its surface. A wider shot reveals that the feet of the characters casually rest upon the desk as well. They rise, and Steed dons and doffs his bowler and then raises his umbrella in silhouette. Mrs. Peel emerges from behind an overstuffed red chair and aims her revolver after pausing to delicately brush her hair out of her eyes. Steed then uses his sword-stick to toss a red carnation to Emma, who places the flower in the button hole of his lapel. They then practice their fighting moves in series of fast cuts to the music, with Emma appearing in silhouette. During this sequence, only the two leads and the names of the producers—Albert Fennell, Brian Clemens, and Julian Wintle—are seen. The title of the episode is withheld until after the pre-title sequence, and the writer and director are credited during the end titles. The Laurie Johnson music for this sequence is identical to the previous season.

Special taglines were used in this season only, wittily summarizing the activities of the two leads during the events of the episode, e.g. "Steed hunts a big cat — Emma is badly scratched" for "The Hidden Tiger." They are shown immediately following the episode title. According to certain sources, taglines were written for all seasons starting with Season Three, but they were only onscreen for this season. All of these taglines have been included within this volume.

The end titles are mainly composed of Steed and Mrs. Peel again practicing martial arts moves in silhouette against a cobalt blue floor and brownish-grey backdrop. Steed performs unusual strikes with his umbrella while Mrs. Peel practices her judo and kung-fu.

CHAMPAGNE, CARS, CLOTHES, AND CANINES

In this season, both Diana Rigg and Patrick Macnee experience a fashion explosion, now in full color[1], with Rigg's outfits being designed by Alun Hughes, and Macnee's by Pierre Cardin, while still being cut by his usual tailor, Mr. James at Bailey and Weatherill of Regent Street.

For Rigg, Hughes produced a series of colorful, soft-fabric outfits, so many that she could often change several times an episode, perhaps even more than Honor Blackman did during Season Three. This was partially an appeasement to Rigg, who was already expressing dissatisfaction with the shooting schedule. Leather was gone completely and what replaced it were more functional catsuits made of comfortable stretch jersey and cotton, called "Emmapeelers," perfect for throwing villains over your shoulder.

While filming was already in progress, but before the episodes started airing on either side of the Atlantic, Patrick Macnee collaborated in a famous photoshoot with superstar model Twiggy at Teddington Studios on 4 January 1967. This was a wonderful promotional effort, and Twiggy was seen showcasing many of the beautiful and fashionable clothes that Alun Hughes had designed for Diana Rigg's onscreen ensemble, and Macnee, of course, modeled his own clothes as designed by Pierre Cardin, many of which would end up in the series. However, these Cardin-designed clothes, in an attempt to become more modern, would lose their Edwardian touch and inherent Englishness, and in many cases, would come across as rather indulgent. This was accentuated by the loss of a casual clothing line, as Steed would often be seen relaxing in full suits rather than a soft jumper and slacks. Resultingly, there would later be a significant backlash. (See Season Seven.)

Cars would also become an even bigger element of the show, with new cars being introduced for the cast: a green 1930 Bentley Speed Six for Steed and a 1967 Lotus Elan S3 convertible for Mrs. Peel. The Lotus's color is officially "powder blue" but it comes across on film as more of a steely gray-blue color. Just as before, this new car was a promotional gift from Lotus, who rightly saw the TV series as an excellent showcase for their brand. These two cars would become the two main vehicles

---

1 Note that I'm viewing the fashions depicted in the series using the 2015 Canal+ Blu-rays, and thus the colors may vary from what you remember them, given that film colors shift depending on how they are scanned or telecined and then color-graded for DVD/Blu-ray mastering. My background is in graphic design and art, and I'm also an avid film photographer, so I will describe the clothing as best as I can, interpreting the colors with my knowledge of historical film emulsions and how they represent (or skew) color.

they would drive throughout the remainder of the Emma Peel era, and they would appear in almost every episode, though Steed would occasionally bring out another vintage vehicle for some fun.

Steed's flat at 5 Westminster Mews would now feature a large painting over the mantlepiece, which is "The Charge of the Light Brigade in the Battle of Balaclava on 25 October 1854" painted by Robert Alexander Hillingford in 1899. This painting had been previously seen in "The Danger Makers" in the villains' office. (Did Steed loot it?)

Champagne would now be formally a part of the title sequence for the first time—if you discount the American intro from Season Four—though the Avengers would still only drink it in a handful of episodes. No Avengers dogs in sight for a while yet.

Fashion designer for Diana Rigg: Alun Hughes
Fashion designer for Patrick Macnee: Pierre Cardin

Best Dressed: "The Winged Avenger"
Worst Dressed: "Epic" (but only by comparison)

AVENGERS CARS

JOHN STEED

1930 Bentley Speed Six (RX 6180)—racing green—in "From Venus with Love," "Escape in Time," "The See-Through Man," "The Bird Who Knew Too Much," "The Winged Avengers," "The Living Dead," "The Hidden Tiger," "Epic," "Something Nasty in the Nursery," "The Joker," and "Who's Who???"
1925 Bentley 3 Litre Green Label (YK 6781) —racing green—in "The Fear Merchants."
1908 Unic taxi (MD 1480)—red—in "Escape in Time."
1909 Rolls-Royce 40/50 Silver Ghost (R 1909) —pale-yellow—in "The See-Through Man."
Land Rover (OPC 104D) in "The Hidden Tiger."
Land Rover (VX 897) in "Never, Never Say Die."

EMMA PEEL

1967 Lotus Elan S3 Convertible (SJH 499D)—"powder blue" or steely gray—in "From Venus with Love," "The Fear Merchants," "Escape in Time," "The See-Through Man," "The Bird Who Knew Too Much," "The Winged Avengers," "The Living Dead," "The Hidden Tiger," "Never, Never Say Die," "Epic," "Something Nasty in the Nursery," and "The Joker."

THE MOST FANTASTIC EPISODES OF THE SEASON

1. "Something Nasty in the Nursery"
2. "The Hidden Tiger"
3. "A Funny Thing Happened on the Way to the Station"
4. "The Joker"
5. "Who's Who???"

105 (5.4.1) FROM VENUS WITH LOVE

Steed is shot full of holes — Emma sees stars
Written by Philip Levene
Directed by Robert Day

GUEST CAST

Barbara Shelley (Venus), Philip Locke (Primble), Jon Pertwee (Brigadier Whitehead), Derek Newark (Crawford), Jeremy Lloyd (Bertram Smith), Adrian Ropes (Jennings), Arthur Cox (Clarke), Paul Gillard (Cosgrove), Michael Lynch (Hadley), Kenneth Benda (Mansford)

PRE-TITLE/TEASER

An astronomer observes Venus from his home. As he takes photos, the temperature begins to rise, causing him to sweat and his glass of beer to boil. An odd whirring noise grows steadily louder until he is struck by a tremendous blast of light. He falls to the floor, apparently dead, his hair now completely white.

"MRS. PEEL–WE'RE NEEDED"

Emma practices her fencing moves alone in her apartment. Steed enters suddenly and parries her fencing foil with his umbrella. Stuck to the umbrella's ferrule is a notecard reading "Mrs. Peel We're Needed!"

SYNOPSIS

After two astronomers are found dead with bleached white manes of hair, some preliminary investigation puts Steed and Emma in touch with the British Venusian Society. When Emma sees a UFO and strange noises are heard on a recording left by another victim, there is speculation that Venus is invading Earth. However, the trail eventually leads Steed and Emma to optician Dr. Primble, who has a little more than an eye exam planned for Emma...

REVIEW

This episode is an auspicious start to one of the greatest seasons in television history and sets a style and tone that would persist somewhat consistently for the remainder of the series. More observant viewers will notice a shift from the previous season, which had a slightly more grounded tone that was only occasionally broken by fantasy-oriented or comedic episodes like "The Girl from Auntie" or "What the Butler Saw." The tone for this season would adhere much more closely to those two examples and yet eventually amplify everything enormously. Ultimately, this escalation towards fantasy would cause ITV executives to bristle and then fire producers Fennell and Clemens, but this episode is still comparatively sedate. Nevertheless, all of the classic *Avengers* elements are already present: bizarre deaths; eccentric characters; highly specialized clubs and society groups; pseudo-science-fiction; and a growing self-awareness and embracing of the show's more absurd qualities.

The plot is not necessarily the best one in the show's history, and the scope is surprisingly narrow, focusing entirely on astronomers and a tiny group of believers in extraterrestrials who all suffer under the outdated notion that Venus might support extraterrestrial life—an idea that likely strained credibility even in 1967. This amounts to an enormous feint, a misdirection to disguise a plot with equally minor scope. In some ways, it's almost disappointing to have the aliens not pan out. It's also hard to believe that a car with a DeLorean finish, no matter how mirrored, could look like the object (literally, a ball of glowing light) that Emma sees in several of the UFO attacks. It then proceeds to evade Emma in multiple improbable incidences that equally defy believability. After all, if there was a glowing silver car with a laser gun on its hood hiding behind a hay bale in a barn, I think I'd notice. Nevertheless, there is an oddly compelling nature to these scenes as Emma flees a telephone call with Steed to pursue the elusive alien 'spacecraft.' And the featured location footage is a particularly beautiful tour of the English countryside.

The main characters spend most of their time apart, limiting the banter between them, but there is more than enough amusing characterization and witty lines to sustain the dialogue. Emma and Steed are each given their own classic eccentric to investigate. Particularly wonderful performances from the guest cast are those by Jeremy Lloyd and Jon Pertwee, playing two of the best eccentrics to have ever graced the program. Emma meets chimney sweep Bertram Fortescue Winthrop Smythe (Jeremy Lloyd), an eccentric man with a noble heritage who prefers chimneys to lordly manors; he remains undercover as the sooty-faced Bert Smith who waxes lyrical about how a chimney is an ersatz telescope. Meanwhile, Steed investigates Brigadier Whitehead (played by an exuberant Jon Pertwee), a World War II hero who spends all his waking hours recording his memoirs and ultimately exits the story 'white-headed.'

Venus (no relation to a certain blond nightclub singer) is played by Barbara Shelley, who originally appeared in the missing episode "Dragonsfield." Although we cannot view that particular performance in which she played a beautiful scientist gone rogue in a cyber suit that gave her super strength, we can at least appreciate her in full color in this week's episode. As the leader of the British Venusian Society, Venus is a more subtly odd character than the others—presumably because she has to at least appear somewhat normal for her stalwart assistant Crawford (played by Derek Newark with his usual gruffness). Venus not only believes in UFOs, aliens, and golden auras but also wants to start her own space program based on her astronomical society dues, and it's genuinely difficult to decide which of her delusions is the most implausible! (Some fifty years later, I'm inclined to choose the space program. Aliens somehow seem more likely to arrive.) Because her society requires excellent vision for all their members, she also insists on sending Steed to an eye doctor, one that is also a member.

Thus, it is only natural (by *Avengers* logic) that when Steed meets Dr. Primble (Philip Locke), the ophthalmic surgeon is nearly blind, barely capable of seeing with coke bottle glasses. He is truly an eye doctor in need of his own services, and Steed quickly goes to work helping him find his missing contact lens. Having Steed identify hats and bowlers for his eye test was a stroke of genius and part of that cheeky self-awareness that appears so frequently in this season—the bowler hat being emblematic of the show's eccentricity and old-world charm as well as a symbol of the then-fading gentry of 1960s England. When Emma visits Dr. Primble, however, he quickly veers from a harmless myopic eccentric to a sadistic torturer. In horrifically kinky *Avengers* fashion, Emma is harnessed to a chair with leather straps and threatened with a powerful laser, which easily arcs through multiple metal eye charts that offer her fragile protection. The laser effects are particularly good for the era. Inevitably, as is so often the case in this show, there is a hoist-on-his-own-petard moment, and Dr. Primble exits life 'white-headed' just like his victims, but not before Steed's bowler hat receives the same treatment.

This episode is a very solid start to a great season, but there are even better things to come.

EPISODE NOTES

On a musical note, Laurie Johnson seems to be experimenting with some variations on Gustav Holst's "Venus, the Bringer of Peace" from ***The Planets***, which is as obvious as it is inspired. He also adds new cues that sell the mystery of potential space visitors quite well. This is also Cyd Child's debut as Diana Rigg's stunt double, and her first job was to dive through a window with flaming curtains!

CHAMPAGNE, CARS, CLOTHES, AND... CAMERAS!

This episode introduces several of Steed's new suits in turn: a navy wool three-piece single-breasted suit with a very subtle checked pattern (from the title sequence), so dark that in certain lighting conditions, it can appear to be black, much as the prior navy suits did when filmed in monochrome; two new silk tuxedos (one a deep blue and one crimson) with velvet bowties; a gray single-breasted three-piece suit in a gray herringbone pattern with three buttons; a brown-and-green single-breasted tartan blazer worn with checked trousers, a green tie, and a white shirt; and a charcoal chalk-striped three-piece single-breasted wool suit.

Not to be outdone, Mrs. Peel debuts six iconic outfits: her first set of "Emmapeelers," a cobalt blue jersey catsuit, zipped up the front with a large, round zipper ring, with dark gold stripes down each sleeve and the outside of each leg, and matching boots; crimson-red pajamas (or palazzo pants and blouse) in an elaborate Chinese silk; a simple knee-length A-line dress in camel, though not too simple as the vertical seams are designed to give it some structure, paired in one scene with a matching coat fastened with three buttons at the waistline; a wide, A-line coat in navy, which looks a bit like a reimagined peacoat to my eye, fastened at the waistline with three round black buttons (tying it in design-wise with the camel coat), and paired with matching trousers and a vibrant purple rollneck jumper underneath; a tan and white catsuit with a high-neck ring collar and white flashing on the inside of the legs, zippered up the front, and closed at both the collar and the waist with a square ring (this outfit is seen in every episode since it's worn in the title sequence); and a knee-length lavender crepe dress with a straight hem and a matching structured coat with purple trim descending from the shoulders to the closure at the waistline with a single button and a square frog.[2]

If I had to pick a favorite, I'd say the navy coat. It flows very well in the scene when Mrs. Peel is chasing after the "UFO." But these are all stunning new clothes, presented for the first time in vibrant color (though many in the UK didn't see the colour)[3], and it's easy to see how they might be all the fashion rage in 1960s Britain and America.

Both the 1930 Bentley Speed Six and the 1967 Lotus Elan S3 make prominent appearances, making this episode an excellent introduction all around. (Mrs. Peel also uses a radio phone in her car.)

Cosgrove was apparently not very flush with cash; his camera is a cheap Soviet knockoff of a Leica, a 1950s Zorki 1 35mm rangefinder camera, whereas Hadley, being a wealthy business tycoon, not only has a much bigger telescope but the crème de la crème of medium format cameras of the day, a Hasselblad 500C SLR.

TAG SCENE

Steed plays around with Emma's fencing foil in her apartment while Emma gets dressed for dinner. Steed then teases her about having dinner on Venus, despite the fact that his claret "doesn't travel."

QUOTES

"Astronomy's my second love, after chimneys, of course. The two go hand-in-hand, really."

"You are a keen astronomer?" "Dedicated. I cut my baby teeth on a telescope."

"Your occupation?" "Following father's footsteps. He spent his life depositing money, I spend mine withdrawing it."

"I can't manage duty watch tonight—battle of Palermo. Nearly bought it there, had the luck of the devil."

"Well, it's quicker than the peroxide rinse."

---

2 This last one was one of Rigg's favorites and it was sold in her fashion line in sizes 10-16 at the price of £5.

3 Americans saw the color, but Britons didn't see the colour. Sorry, I'll get me coat.

106 (5.1.2) THE FEAR MERCHANTS

Steed puts out a light — Emma takes fright
Written by Philip Levene
Directed by Gordon Flemyng

GUEST CAST

Patrick Cargill (Pemberton), Brian Wilde (Raven), Annette Carell (Dr. Voss), Garfield Morgan (Gilbert), Andrew Keir (Crawley), Jeremy Burnham (Gordon White), Edward Burnham (Meadows), Bernard Horsfall (Fox), Ruth Trouncer (Dr. Hill), Declan Mulholland (Saunders), Philip Ross (Hospital Attendant)

PRE-TITLE/TEASER

A middle-aged man wakes up in the middle of an empty sports stadium wearing only his dressing gown. Terrified, he imagines the roaring of a sports crowd. He collapses in agony apparently suffering a mental breakdown as a mysterious man watches from a distance.

"MRS. PEEL–WE'RE NEEDED"

Mrs. Peel finds a wrapped silver chocolate box in her apartment, but inside there is only a note reading "Mrs. Peel We're Needed!"

SYNOPSIS

One by one, powerful business tycoons are being driven mad in order to try and corner the ceramics market. After tracing the attacks to a Business Efficiency Bureau, Steed may be in store for an unexpected burial, and Emma is forced to face the ultimate fear…

REVIEW

This episode falls short because of the essentially poor quality of its central premise. The idea that these corporate presidents or other stalwart business executives would suffer from phobias so strong as to drive them mad is hard to swallow. The suggestion presented is that we all have these fears and may not know it, but with the right psychological conditions we would be driven 'round the bend in a heartbeat.

How these phobias can be determined through a simple questionnaire is a question that is never answered—probably because it's not possible. After all, if I were to say on a questionnaire that I don't like Brazilian Snapping Dung Beetles, for example, it doesn't mean I'm going to fall into a faint if I see one or certainly not go stark raving mad for that matter. In any case, even if we allow for the unconvincing premise, the episode seems to be largely composed of various otherwise stalwart men being harassed by white mice, bird shadows, and unconvincing plastic spiders, somehow losing their grip on reality in the process. I suppose it could be considered funny, but the direction and Laurie Johnson's piercing fearful music for each 'attack' doesn't really permit it, forcing the viewer to take it seriously.

Andrew Keir, dressed in natty business attire with a neat mustache, is great in the short few minutes he has available; his rich voice is immediately recognizable. Patrick Cargill as Pemberton turns in a solid performance as the efficiency expert, albeit stereotypically cold and dispassionate. In general, the Business Efficiency Bureau are an effete lot, looking a little like Carnaby Street hipsters wearing fashionable colorful shades and Pierre Cardin business suits.

If you're looking for more high points, you can check out the scene where Pemberton's thug attempts to bury Steed in a quarry. It has a feeling of genuine threat. The scene's realism foreshadows similar situations that would be faced by the characters in *The New Avengers* ten years later. There is also a charming scene in which the investigating duo enjoy cups of coffee nicked from Crawley's car. The opening shot of their posteriors, shown in isolation bent over the chassis as they gawk over the power of the engine, is cheeky and sexy at the same time. The eccentric Raven, who is obsessed with ceramic perfection, is also a strong character. Gordon Flemyng's direction is periodically excellent; the fly's eye view during the spider attack on Raven is inspired though appearing for less than a second. It's sad that the spider itself is clearly on a string.

Unfortunately, this is all so much fluff in a story that doesn't really achieve believability. The only moment that really convinces me is when the subject turns to the "universal fear, the ultimate in horror—pain" and it comes down to Emma being threatened with torture. This, I can believe. Men being terrified into insanity by speeding cars, wide-open spaces, and plastic spiders, no. The idea that Pemberton has his own fears is a worthy twist that unfortunately also fails. I mean, if you're afraid of the dark, why would you wear sunglasses? How does Steed guess? Am I missing something, or does this just not make sense?

Like all fifth season episodes, this one has the natural ebullience, charm, and high production values that make it at least palatable, but a thorough re-thinking of the premise might have turned it from merely acceptable to exceptional.

CHAMPAGNE, CARS, CLOTHES, AND CANINES

The episode starts out with Mrs. Peel in her lavender crepe dress and Steed in his gray herringbone suit with pale blue shirt, dark blue silk tie, and black bowler. Steed then switches to a double-breasted suit in navy with a subtle chalk-stripe in dark gray (so subtle it doesn't resolve except in closeups) and six black buttons. He pairs it with a white shirt and a purple tie. Mrs. Peel wears an ivory sundress with a matching khaki coat with white trim. Steed later switches to his charcoal chalk-stripe suit with a white shirt and gray knit tie. Mrs. Peel then debuts her next set of Emmapeelers: a purple (cobalt blue) catsuit, sleeveless with circular cutouts at the hips and a fob watch on a chain between them, and blue-green stripes down the outside of the legs, paired with matching front-zipped jacket with a rollneck collar. Steed debuts three new outfits in rapid succession: a gray three-piece, single-breasted suit with a silk collar and a purple tie, a fawn overcoat and beige bowler, and a navy three-piece, single-breasted with a single button. Mrs. Peel's lavender crepe dress reappears, but not before she debuts another iconic stunner (which, sadly, only appears in this episode): a suede forest-green catsuit with cutouts on either side of the waist and full-length sleeves and matching gloves and boots. Steed finishes off the episode proper in a brown herringbone three-piece, single-breasted suit with a sage felt collar and a matching bowler.

Steed's 1925 Bentley 3 Litre Green Label (YK 6781) appears for the only time in the series, and we get a very good look at the front with its Union Flag waving proudly. Mrs. Peel's Lotus Elan S3 also returns.

Mrs. Peel frightens Steed at the end with her lack of champagne, which turns out to be a ruse as she reveals a bottle. Presumably they drink it, but we don't see this. They do have tea and coffee in the car, however.

TAG SCENE

Steed and Emma arrive at Emma's apartment and he jokingly checks the apartment for every conceivable threat. Emma then finds what appears to be the same box of chocolates from earlier, but this time it really has chocolates inside. She then turns the tables on Steed by bluffing him into thinking they have no more champagne.

QUOTES

"Our territory is the mind. Our merchandise is fear. The inner fabric of us all, Mrs. Peel. The dark balloon we try to hide. Prick it and…well, you'll see."

"You wanted your competitors eliminated. We have carried out your instructions."

"I know. It goes around and around, and it all comes out there."

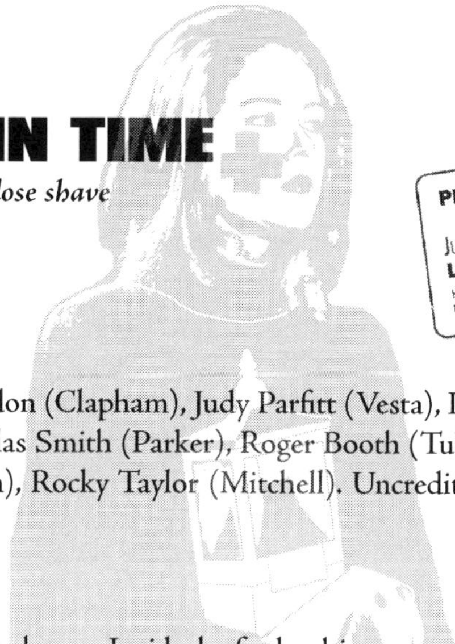

107 (5.2.3) ESCAPE IN TIME

Steed visits the barber — Emma has a close shave

Written by Philip Levene

Directed by John Krish

GUEST CAST

Peter Bowles (Thyssen), Geoffrey Bayldon (Clapham), Judy Parfitt (Vesta), Imogen Hassall (Anjali), Edward Caddick (Sweeney), Nicholas Smith (Parker), Roger Booth (Tubby Vincent), Richard Montez (Josino), Clifford Earl (Paxton), Rocky Taylor (Mitchell). Uncredited: Terence Plummer (Headsman)

PRE-TITLE/TEASER

An agent breaks into a luxurious country house. Inside, he finds a bizarre rotating plinth with busts of men from various historical eras. Entering a strangely painted corridor, he finds himself spinning through time to emerge in a room resembling the 17th century where he is shot dead with a pistol by a man in a historical costume.

"MRS. PEEL–WE'RE NEEDED"

While putting on silver shoes in her apartment, Mrs. Peel receives an invitation to a "Grand Hunt Ball."

SYNOPSIS

Emma and Steed investigate an incident in which one of their agents has been shot by a 16th century bullet. Via a barbershop and by way of an Indian curio shop, they discover that a man called Thyssen is offering escape 'through time' to criminals on the run. The price is half the loot. Unfortunately, as she is exploring the possibilities of the 1790s, Emma is instead sent to the time of Matthew Thyssen, master of torment and the inventor of the rack…

REVIEW

Doctor Who's territory is being invaded in this humorous story of time travel by slot machine, in which pure chance (or perhaps whim) decides which murderous Thyssen will kill you. Generally, we are to be thankful, I believe, that the reality of time travel is not truly explored in this episode. In a season of many over-the-top concepts, I think that that particular fantasy technology would have been too much. It seems that the producers agreed with me and evaded it, eventually steering the series back in the direction of the mundane for Season Six.

Although the concept of time travel turns out to be a deception and a red herring, it gives the series a chance to stretch its legs and do mock period pieces in full color, something that would not have been nearly as effective in the black and white Cathy Gale era. There are many changes of scene before the time travel concept is explored as well. The production takes full advantage, producing some wonderful sets and costumes possibly borrowed from the film studios throughout England at this time. Whatever their source, the quality is very high. Though the "outside" street scenes with the shops are never completely convincing, they are highly detailed and beautifully constructed even when viewed in high-definition.

This episode is largely set-based, but this is counter-balanced with superb location filming, including a particularly prominent scene that is one of the most bizarre moments in the entire series—virtually a Jodorowski-like moment in which Emma, after retrieving a plush crocodile from the road, is chased over the hilly countryside by a man in fox-hunting gear on a motorcycle. There is a terrific stunt where she tumbles down a massive bank and yet maintains her grip on her crocodile. Why the crocodile? The enemy agents are heavily invested in plush toy futures.[4]

There's a wonderful exchange of dialogue when Matthew is preparing to torture Emma with her feet are in the stocks. This scene is very reminiscent of the previous episode's interrogation scene with Emma reacting casually to the thought of torture. There's also a whole array of good fight scenes scattered throughout. Both Peter Bowles and Diana Rigg seem to be having a ball, particularly the former as he goes from one version of Thyssen to another. Peter Bowles does a fine job as both the stuttering Waldo Thyssen and as the sadistic Matthew Thyssen, though I am perplexed as to why the latter steps out of a wooden steambath when he first appears.

"Escape in Time" is an excellent example of an episode not to be taken seriously (nothing in this season really should be), never quite rising to the top with the rest of the cream but managing a wonderful effervescence typical of nearly every episode during this remarkable season.

CHAMPAGNE, CARS, CLOTHES, AND CANINES

Mrs. Peel debuts four completely new outfits. Firstly, hot pink palazzo pants with a silk top in a deep-plum color with a dark cerulean-blue lining. The dress is sleeveless and collarless with a scooped boatneck, and she adds metallic silver pumps. Secondly, she dons a cerulean-blue quilted jacket, with off-center zipper, over black trousers and a black jumper with black gloves. I've heard it called quilted silk, but to me it looks like a faux soft leather. Thirdly, for her travel through time, she dons a dark-rose Georgian silk dress with a large purple bow tied at the breast and elaborate floral brocading, topped with a powdered wig and fake mole, for her trip to 1790, which is, of course, diverted to 1570; thus, the outfit becomes anachronistic. The last outfit is a purple, blue, and white-striped long-sleeved dress that always reminds me of the clothes worn by the residents of the Village in ***The Prisoner***. This dress would show up several more times over this season.

Steed starts out in the gray herringbone three-breasted suit with a white shirt and blue tie, and then, switches to a pale gray suit with a gray-brown felt collar and a buff-colored bowler. There are a lot of gray suits in this season, and it can be hard to distinguish them at times. The navy suit with black bowler also returns. Steed then ends up in a Georgian nobleman's outfit in a desaturated gray-plum color with elaborate light gray frogs and a dark gray collar. Underneath, he wears black tights, a white, laced shirt and a brocaded waistcoat in a cream color, and on his feet are black buckled shoes.

Mrs. Peel, of course, once again drives her Lotus. The motorcycle that chases her is a 1965 Triumph Tiger Cub. Steed's 1930 Bentley Speed Six returns, along with his taupe blazer and green waistcoat from "The Fear Merchants." But the episode ends with the appearance of a red 1908 Unic taxi (MD 1480) which blasts poor Steed's face with soot. Dang fossil fuels!

TAG SCENE

Mrs. Peel finds her silver shoes leading her in a trail to Steed, who then takes her for a ride in an antique car, which needs to be push-started and consequently blows soot in Steed's face.

---

4 For those who are keeping score at home, the chain of plush toys is apparently crocodile to giraffe to kangaroo to pink-spotted white elephant with howdah.

QUOTES

"Remarkable, quite remarkable. That you can sew! Known you all this time, never knew that you could sew." "Well, our relationship hasn't been exactly domestic, has it?"
"I appreciate your appreciation."
"I could think of some names to call you too. Short, up-to-date, highly-descriptive names."
"Oh, I prefer his Samuel. He's a lovable little rogue." "No, no, no, his Matthew's much more in character." "I think I see your point."
"Didn't we get the vote?"

108 (5.5.4) THE SEE-THROUGH MAN

Steed makes a bomb — Emma is put to sleep
Written by Philip Levene
Directed by Robert Asher

GUEST CAST

Moira Lister (Elena), Warren Mitchell (Brodny), Roy Kinnear (Quilby), Jonathan Elsom (Ackroyd), John Nettleton (Sir Andrew Ford), Harvey Hall (Ulric), David Glover (Wilton)

PRE-TITLE/TEASER

A Ministry clerk walks through the halls of the Ministry and appears to be covertly followed by an invisible person. In the file room, he investigates, seeing cabinet drawers open by themselves. He is suddenly struck and knocked out, and the assailant escapes invisibly through the door.

"MRS. PEEL–WE'RE NEEDED"

Emma examines slides through her microscope, and just as Steed arrives, she discovers that one reveals the message "Mrs. Peel – We're Needed."

SYNOPSIS

After a couple of raids are made on ministry files, Steed and Emma discover that the files being explored are those of an eccentric inventor's invisibility formula. When Emma sees a 'headless' man and Steed visits the home of Professor Quilby, it begins to look like the Eastern Drug Company have purchased a copy of the substance for £100,000. However, when dealing with invisibility, what you see is not always what you get…

REVIEW

Take one absurd science-fiction concept, add a couple of eccentrics, a dash of zaniness, a good dose of comedy, throw in a few action scenes, mix thoroughly, and stand well back—the result is "The See-Through Man," a delightfully silly story with an outrageous performance from Warren Mitchell. This episode captures the spirit of the fifth season as well as any episode could.

The invisibility theme is clearly spoofing the classic Universal films, ***The Invisible Man*** and ***The Invisible Man Returns***, both based loosely on the novel by H.G. Wells. And perhaps, more pointedly, they are referencing the ATV serial ***The Invisible Man*** which ran from 1958-59. That series very obviously featured a short man dressed in a stuffed suit about four sizes too large for him in order to make him look like a 'headless' man walking about. Instead, he looks like a short man in a stuffed suit.

The Avengers re-used the idea, and guess what? Vazin really is a short man in a stuffed suit! Since the idea is that the invisibility is faked, I have to believe this stuffed suit business is an intentional reference. It seems unlikely that the dry cleaners merely over-starched his shirts.

My only issue is that I fail to see how the enemy agents could install all the electronics and servos necessary in the top-secret Ministry of Defense file rooms in order to make doors and cabinets appear to open. Even if you let that one by, how do the agents not notice these alterations to their equipment? But "The See-Through Man" is about as close as the series got to a broad comedy, and if we are to enjoy it, we must let such minor trivia slide.

Warren Mitchell was making his fourth and final appearance in the series, the second as Brodny. *The Avengers* never bothered very much with continuity, being the most episodic of episodic television, and their villains tended to die at the end of each episode, leaving few to return. As one of the few 'villains' to return, Mitchell puts even more over-the-top zing into the character, and he becomes more of a buffoonish target for derision than in "Two's a Crowd."

Roy Kinnear plays his character Quilby with considerably more subtlety, which is to say that he's still comically over-the-top. Possibly inspired by his character in the Beatles film *Help!*, he is the stereotypical crackpot scientist that invents one magical formula after another, submitting them annually to the Ministry of Defense. (You know, the kind of scientist that has never actually existed despite being depicted in every comedy film on the subject.) Except that the MOD never quite believe any of these inventions actually work, and Quilby is always rejected. This is understandable due to the number of uncontrolled explosions emerging on a regular basis from his laboratory. Quilby is played with the same humorous alacrity that only Kinnear can manage, and thus, the character works in a way that wouldn't have been possible with an actor of lesser comedic stature. Some of the best lines are his in this comedy pastiche of *The Avengers* at its height.

This is a wonderful episode to enjoy as long as you don't take it very seriously.

EPISODE NOTES

Not counting regulars and what I consider short-lived regulars or semi-regulars—One-Ten, Carol Wilson, Dr. Martin King and Venus Smith— Brodney is one of a mere handful of repeating characters in *The Avengers*. That very short list includes Dr. Richard Tredding (Philip Stone), Spicer (Godfrey Quigley), Detective Superintendent Wilson (Alister Williamson), two of Steed's mysterious overseers, One-Six (Michael Gover) and Charles (Paul Whitsun-Jones), and Dr. Armstrong's assistant Benson (Frederick Jaeger). And the first three characters only returned because "Hot Snow" and "Brought to Book" are effectively a two-parter.

CHAMPAGNE, CARS, CLOTHES, AND CANINES

Mrs. Peel debuts four new outfits: a hot pink sleeveless sundress in a very flattering cut; a structured Dannimac raincoat in a cream pique fabric with large flap pockets at the breast and faux pockets at the hips, worn with navy trousers, jumper, and wool gloves; a yellow, gold, and pink print dress in a modish paisley pattern, long-sleeved with a mini-skirt; and a purple jersey catsuit in separates with cobalt-blue trim at the collar, placket, and sleeve hems, with matching boots. The striped action dress also reappears. Mrs. Peel's Lotus makes another appearance.

Steed wears his brown three-piece, the pale gray double-breasted suit, and the deep-blue tux, and he debuts two more: yet another gray three-piece herringbone and a charcoal overcoat.

TAG SCENE

Steed and Emma return to her apartment, where she discovers that her invisible experiment "really worked." She mimes using her now 'invisible' equipment and places a slide under the microscope. When Steed peers at it, it announces "I'm Hungry." They then take Steed's 1909 Rolls-Royce 40/50

Silver Ghost (R 1909) to lunch. But it needs push-starting, and, unfortunately, once started, it takes off by itself and they are forced to pursue it helplessly into the distance.

QUOTES

"Idiots!—of course, it worked." "You tried it?" "No, it's too risky. Cells might disintegrate."
"It could have been natural causes." "Are they ever?"
"You take a teaspoon full of it at bedtime. When you wake up, all your problems have vanished, and so have you."
"So, this is our invisible formula...electronics."

109 (5.3.5) THE BIRD WHO KNEW TOO MUCH

Steed fancies pigeons *Emma gets the bird*
Written by Brian Clemens (Based upon a story by Alan Pattillo)
Directed by Roy Rossotti

GUEST CAST

Ron Moody (Jordan), Ilona Rodgers (Samantha Slade), Kenneth Cope (Tom Savage), Michael Coles (Verret), John Wood (Twitter), Anthony Valentine (Cunliffe), Clive Colin-Bowler (Robin), John Lee (Mark Pearson)

PRE-TITLE/TEASER

An agent runs in a grassy field pursued by a young man in a buff jumper with a tommy gun. He escapes to a fire lookout tower to make a phone call. However, the young man riddles him with holes, and the dead agent spills seeds from the holes in his clothing.

"MRS. PEEL–WE'RE NEEDED"

Emma opens her curtains to greet a glorious morning. Instead, she is greeted by a message arrow fired by Steed, who then steps inside through the window. The arrow sticks in the wall with a note reading "Mrs. Peel We're Needed!"

SYNOPSIS

Someone is taking aerial pictures of a top-secret military establishment and leaking the information to the other side, but how? After detours to a bird exhibition and a modeling studio, the *Avengers* discover that the real information is known only by Captain Crusoe. The twist is that Captain Crusoe is a parrot…

REVIEW

The title of this episode is a pun on the title of the Alfred Hitchcock movie ***The Man Who Knew Too Much***, filmed twice by Hitchcock, once in 1934 and once in 1956 starring James Stewart and Doris Day. This is not a proper spoof of those films but the overall tone suggests the high style of the 1950s Hitchcock era, spy thrillers full of subtle juxtapositions of surreal violence and humor. The volume of both of these elements has been turned up for this story (and this season), particularly the surrealism. If you throw in eccentrics, you have ***The Avengers*** in a nutshell during this era.

The pre-title starts right out with one of the best examples. A western spy is pursued by a sadistic enemy agent. We know he is sadistic because he is constantly smiling even when firing his machine gun. The spy is finally cornered in a forest fire lookout tower and shot multiple times. As is usual for *The Avengers*, blood is almost never shown, but, in a surreal twist, thousands of seeds pour out of the holes in the dead man's coat—birdseed substituted for blood.

In another example, the next 'counter-counter-counter' espionage agent is pursued by the same sadistic enemy (perpetually dressed in a comfy buff cardigan) over a large arrangement of construction scaffolding, traversing it as if it were a jungle gymnasium. He finally falls into a huge vat of wet cement. Later, Steed must wait until the man is chipped out of a solid block of concrete to identify the body, with the man's feet sticking out the bottom.

Assuming that sadistic smiling enemy agents cannot be considered eccentrics, the lone example would therefore be Ron Moody as Jordan. (He appropriately receives top billing.) Now, Jordan is a type that has to be seen to be believed. He is a bird instructor, teaching parrots and budgerigars to repeat specific phrases upon a signal from a tuned musical triangle. Thus, he wears a mortarboard cap with a stuffed canary on top to signify his station. Why the canary? We are never told.

However, my favorite scene is the one in which Steed does some modeling and has a blast, ending up with a bomb in his umbrella. As a photog myself, I enjoyed seeing the Hasselblad 500c with the 150mm lens. Emma, in search of Captain Crusoe, has a similar session later.

Direction-wise, the camera setups are sterling in quality and go a long way towards selling that auteur Hitchcock style that the production team clearly favored. So many directors were pouring out of the British film industry and into television. The luxury of working on film in British television in the sixties would have been highly attractive to them. Roy Rossotti never directed *The Avengers* again, and it's the show's loss. Along with great direction, there are many well photographed and exciting fight sequences to enjoy throughout this episode. One such sequence takes place between Emma and the comfy cardigan guy on the high diving board of an Olympic-sized swimming pool. Naturally, he ends up taking the dive. The final fight scene has Emma struggling with a bad guy within a stagecoach, like college students crammed within the confines of a Volkswagen bug.

In many ways, this is the prototype episode for this season, and many consider it an excellent introduction to the series. I'm inclined to agree despite some reservations about the plot consistency, which never quite seems to gel beyond a series of enjoyable set pieces.

CHAMPAGNE, CARS, CLOTHES, AND CANINES

Mrs. Peel debuts a purple and navy print dress in an art nouveau pattern over a pair of navy shorts. The bottom of the dress is sheer and flows nicely. The straps match that of her lilac crepe dress, for fashion continuity's sake. (This is the same dress worn by Twiggy in her photoshoot with Patrick Macnee.) She also wears her tan dress and overcoat for the bulk of the episode, but there three more outfits that debut: a Union flag dress, flamboyant hat, and pitchfork for her agricultural modeling session; a very angelic-looking white dress with lacework along the hems, and long-sleeves; and, for the tag scene, a purple garter suit with white trim and white garter boots attached with metal rings. Perhaps Alun Hughes's most avant garde outfit, it's paired with a custom white hood or muffler to protect from the wind while driving (presumably). The lavender crepe dress also reappears worn with a purple, pink, and blue jacket, along with the blue and gold-striped Emmapeeler. Steed rescues her and gives her some champagne.

Steed debuts yet another gray suit with gray bowler and a dark gray double-breasted woolen overcoat. The pale gray double-breasted suit comes back, along with the brown three-piece, and the gray three-piece single-breasted, which was the victim of a continuity error with another gray suit with triangular pockets. Can't say I blame the wardrobe department with all these gray suits going around. It's sort of ironic that upon switching to color film, they kept putting Macnee in gray.

Steed's Bentley Speed Six returns as does Mrs. Peel's Lotus.

TAG SCENE

Emma opens her curtains and is again greeted with a message arrow from Steed, this time inviting her to dinner with a bird he hasn't shot yet. They leave in another of Steed's antique cars—a red 1908 Unic 12/14 hp (MV 9942)—which, humorously, can only drive backwards.

QUOTES

"Do you know they brought the whole Eastern rocket program over in the eye of a needle?"
"New habit—climbing through windows. Lucky for you, I'm a devious fellow."

110 (5.6.6) THE WINGED AVENGER

Steed goes birdwatching — Emma does a comic strip
Written by Richard Harris
Directed by Gordon Flemyng and Peter Duffell

GUEST CAST

Nigel Green (Sir Lexius Cray), Jack MacGowran (Professor Poole), Neil Hallett (Arnie Packer), Colin Jeavons (Stanton), Roy Patrick (Julian), John Garrie (Tay-Ling), Donald Pickering (Peter Roberts), William Fox (Simon Roberts), A.J. Brown (Dawson), Hilary Wontner (Dumayn), John Crocker (Fothers), Ann Sydney (Gerda)

PRE-TITLE/TEASER

A man costumed as a hawk-like comic book character scales the wall of an office building. Inside, business owner, Simon Roberts, is in conference with his son, and they decide to fire an employee. The son performs the firing and his father praises him and sends him along. The hawk-man then climbs through the window and claws the older Roberts to death.

"MRS. PEEL–WE'RE NEEDED"

Emma works on an abstract painting in her apartment which suddenly appears to be already signed with her name, "Mrs. Peel." Steed then appears and completes the message, saying, "We're Needed."

SYNOPSIS

Several business executives have been mysteriously clawed to death in high-rise buildings. Steed and Emma initially suspect a killer bird, but the mystery becomes clearer when the eccentric inventor of a pair of magnetic boots appears and points the finger at a pair of comic book writers…

REVIEW

This episode is a fun but flawed spoof of comic strips and of ***Batman*** (mostly the TV series) in particular. The best aspect of the story is the eccentrics, more than you can shake a talon at. In many ways, this episode almost entirely centers around its eccentrics, much like "Quick-Quick Slow Death."

Professor Poole is an aviphile wacko with an aquiline nose who—in love with the sight of birds flying—constantly endeavors to create wings that will enable human flight. He spends his afternoons flapping about in his front yard wearing Da Vinci-style wings before relaxing at night by hanging from the ceiling like a bat. This character is one of a string of eccentrics in ***The Avengers*** that appear to have limitless financial resources for their eccentric indulgences.

Rock climbing enthusiast Sir Lexius Cray is the next *Avengers* eccentric on that list. He is another of *The Avengers'* growing list of idle rich, a wealthy aristocrat with a lofty bearing that can afford to have a climbing wall in his morning room with simulated ice and snow for his virtual reality conquest of Mt. Everest, maintained by his lugubrious servant. (Something of a throwback to last season's "The Grave-diggers.") Just as suddenly, Cray produces a darker side, regally executed by Nigel Green, as he feigns irritation at Mrs. Peel's delving into his business. He calls for his trained hawk with a murderous glint in his eye. But, wait, he's not the villain either!

This is part of this era's trend of regularly using red herrings to throw off the expectations of the audience. Unfortunately, the red herring of Cray's hawk is ineffective because we know from the beginning that a man in a suit is doing the ripping. Thus, there is no real mystery to this story, just tension. Tension as to whether Steed and Emma will catch up to him or not. As in fan favorite "The Hidden Tiger," it might have been better to hide the identity of the antagonist until the very end, while playing up the possibility of Cray's trained hawk. I also note that if Steed and Emma had been more observant, then they would have noticed the scratched-out names of Simon Roberts and Son outside the building. Hawks don't tend to deface public buildings. Nests in the water tower, yes. Defacing corporate signs, no.

Then, there's the central eccentric, the birdman himself. He and his writing partner are both comic book obsessives, fancying themselves as auteurs rather than writers of derivative schlock—a bit ahead of their time—but Packer has gone completely around the bend, thinking he's "creator and creation fused into one being." Rarely has *The Avengers* dealt with insanity so directly—he is a card-carrying delusional paranoid schizophrenic, having long ago leapt with abandon into the murky ink wells of the comic book fantasy world. Similarly, the episode itself does its own deep dive into the world of comic books. With more than a few dialogue-based jabs at comic book verbosity, Mrs. Peel's comment "Meanwhile, back at the apartment…" could well be an attempt to send-up the comics or *The Avengers* itself, which would explore comic book style humor all season long.

However, the final upside-down battle on the ceiling between Emma and Packer is not nearly as well done as people might have you believe. They gently shove each other as though they're afraid they'll be dislodged, while Emma's one stray buckle neatly hangs as if starched and Packer's cape confusingly hangs around his ankles against gravity. Only when Steed arrives does it really get going and the *Batman* influence hangs on the show's sleeve. Steed wallops the costumed critter using pre-drawn cartoon placards (which he brings with him for mysterious reasons), all with a requisite 'pow!' 'splat!' and a 'bam!' However, it's really short-lived and certainly could have gone on longer with a more elaborate and convincing fight scene. British comic artist master, Frank Bellamy, provided the artwork, and their tie in with the equivalent scenes is a clever touch. But how did Packer know to draw the scenes ahead of time? Now, that's really planning ahead. He storyboards all his attacks for a pre-meditated clawing.

In deference to the comic book theme, the pre-title with Roberts and son seems to spoof a typical *Father Knows Best* or *Leave It to Beaver* scene, channeling the American domestic comedy shows of the 1950s. "You run along, son, and enjoy yourself." It's done completely straight and all the funnier for it.

The tag scene is very cute. Steed 'draws' up a gourmet dinner, complete with a benevolent 'ping!' Watch for the almost-blooper as Diana Rigg is somewhat surprised by the ferocity with which the champagne bottle explodes its cork. This is a very enjoyable episode, but I cannot help but wonder with all the hints at *Batman* throughout the season that the one truly transparent spoof thereof couldn't have been more effective in the end. This is a good one for fans but perhaps not the best one with which to start out if you're new to the series.

CHAMPAGNE, CARS, CLOTHES, AND CANINES

Mrs. Peel debuts another five spectacular outfits this episode: a pale champagne-colored linen suit;

an orange hooded coat, navy jumper and trousers, and brown hiking boots for her visit to Sir Lexius Cray; a maroon and beige Emmapeeler jumpsuit with a heavy-woven fabric, almost quilted; a navy jumper and trousers (they appear navy in some shots and black in others) with a sea foam green suede jacket, matching belt, and thigh-high boots; and finally a cobalt-blue and hot-pink Emmapeeler jumpsuit, very similar to the others, with a zippered front and ring clasp at the waist, this time with a matching hot-pink train engineer's cap. (In the mid-1960s, it was a notable fashion trend to reimagine and repurpose working-class uniform hats as ladies wear.)

No new outfits for Steed, but his brown-and-green tartan blazer, checked trousers, and dark green tie return, along with the charcoal chalk-striped suit, the gray three-piece with triangular pockets, and the first gray herringbone suit.

Both the Bentley Speed Six and the Lotus Elan appear.

TAG SCENE

Steed and Emma return to her apartment, where Emma opens the champagne while Steed works on a charcoal drawing of their next meal. The meal turns out to be real when he wheels a serving trolley into the room, already decked out with real food. "The benevolent Avenger strikes again! Ping!"

QUOTES

"He'd been clawed to death, as though by some bird, some huge obscene bird!"
"Nothing stands in my way. Least of all, you, Mrs. Peel. Least of all, you!"
"Packer's really got his wings clipped."
"EEE-URP!"
"The benevolent Avenger strikes again!" [Ping!]

111 (5.7.7) THE LIVING DEAD

Steed finds a mine of information — Emma goes underground
Written by Brian Clemens, based on a story by Anthony Marriott
Directed by John Krish

GUEST CAST

Julian Glover (Masgard), Pamela Ann Davy (Mandy), Howard Marion Crawford (Geoffrey), Jack Woolgar (Kermit), Jack Watson (Hopper), Edward Underdown (Rupert), John Cater (Olliphant), Vernon Dobtcheff (Spencer), Alister Williamson (Tom)

PRE-TITLE/TEASER

A drunken man leaves a pub in a quaint English village. He stumbles through a graveyard with a bottle of wine, giggling, until he sees a grave open by itself. A gaunt man dressed in white emerges from the grave, walks to the church, and begins ringing the church bell. Terrified, the drunken man returns to the pub screaming hysterically about a ghost, but inside the church, there is nothing and the bell seems to be ringing by itself.

"MRS. PEEL–WE'RE NEEDED"

Emma drives her Lotus down a country lane and comes to a traffic light which turns red. She stops and is surprised to see it light up with the words "Mrs. Peel." Steed then drives up behind her in his

Bentley and the now blue traffic light[5] reads "We're Needed."

SYNOPSIS

Despite the drunken state of the witness, a sighting of a ghost brings not only the *Avengers* to a remote village with a disused mine but also ghost hunting representatives from rival agencies FOG (Friends of Ghosts) and SMOG (Scientific Measurement of Ghosts). When the SMOG agent is killed and Mrs. Peel is kidnapped by a ghost, Steed investigates a mining disaster of five years ago and Mrs. Peel finds herself in a secret city under the village...

REVIEW

Not until the 1977 *Doctor Who* story "Underworld" would two halves of a story again be so disparate in their level of engagement. Although this story isn't quite as bad as that particular segment of *Doctor Who*'s illustrious history, there is nothing to save "The Living Dead" from plunging into a dull underworld of its own, both literally and figuratively.

The first half is a lot of fun with the beginnings of a good old-fashioned ghost story full of outrageous spectral deaths and (ultimately unfulfilled) supernatural promise. You see, these ghosts are killing people, and it's up to the *Avengers* to investigate. But ectoplasmic news spreads quickly, and two ghost-hunting investigators turn up, one a believer, one not. Pamela Ann Davy—one of the more humorous of the *Avengers* eccentrics—gets higher than a kite breathing the spectral essence as FOG member Mandy, alternately using baby-doll eyes to get her way and sighing ecstatically at the perceived ectoplasmic residue in the bell tower in a kind of prequel to *Ghostbusters*.

You have to admire this show for its over-the-top gall. Only in *The Avengers* would you find the corpse of the skeptic from SMOG hanging on a bell pull with a massive Scottish Claymore in his back. (That ghost went medieval on him!) Given the lack of blood, it's so gruesome and unreal that it's comical. That trait would serve the show even further in later episodes.

The whole farce is likely a failed spoof of the Hammer films of the day, particularly one known as *The Plague of the Zombies*, which had just come out the year before. That plot involved an English lord using voodoo to raise the dead for slave labor in his tin mine. I suspect that this film consciously or unconsciously inspired Brian Clemens. All the elements are here—the mine, the 'living dead,' the rich English lord covering it up (albeit unwittingly in this case), and the confused village inhabitants down the pub speculating on whether the dead really do walk.

Had this continued to its logical conclusion, with faux voodoo ceremonies and fake walking corpses covering up a spy game, we might have had a brilliant pastiche of the film. Just imagine the reaction of Steed and Emma to walking corpses or ghosts. Instead, with its rather pedestrian take-over-the-world-with-an-underground-army plot—really, that old trope again!—the end result comes across as two half-baked ideas stitched together worse than Frankenstein's monster. Talk about a wasted opportunity.

Sadly, elements of a mystery at the beginning, like the apparent overuse of sun-tan lotion, also fail to resolve into anything significant, leaving more loose ends dangling than any show really should. It doesn't help that the hysterically goofy Mandy suddenly transforms into a one-dimensional baddie either. The talent of Julian Glover, himself later a Hammer star, is mostly wasted as the sadistic Masgard. He is professional as always but is attempting to deliver dialogue that just doesn't have any life in it. Equally, John Krish makes a valiant effort with the direction in the first half. The lighting in the graveyard and in many other scenes is beautiful, but, in the second half, there's only so much you can do with grey cinderblocks.

The final moments do have their charm—Steed's calm reaction to a firing squad, for example—

---

5 Although I tried to research the reason for the light being blue rather than green, I was, unfortunately, unable to come up with any definitive answer. It's Avengersland. What can we say?

but this script reeks of an idea that simply wasn't thought through. Having said that, the first half is reasonably entertaining and there's enough of the grand *Avengers* style to make it at least palatable.

CHAMPAGNE, CARS, CLOTHES, AND... CAMERAS!

Both Mrs. Peel's Lotus and Steed's Bentley make an appearance right away in the "Mrs. Peel-We're Needed" sequence. Mrs. Peel debuts a white jumper with a soft cerulean blue cardigan while Steed wears his navy chalk-striped single-breasted, three-piece suit with a light blue shirt and a red tie, paired with a dark gray bowler. He switches to the gray herringbone suit with a black bowler for the graveyard scene while Mrs. Peel dons an A-line coat in a sage green with matching trousers and a pale-yellow rollneck jumper. The cut of the coat is very similar to some of the other coats in her collection with three round buttons fastened at the waist. I guess they decided to go home and change first.

Once again in synchronization, Steed changes to the brown tartan blazer, yellow shirt, and green tie, and Mrs. Peel to a heavy woolen coat in an orange, red, and pink check over her hot-pink sundress. Steed's gray three-piece suit returns along with Mrs. Peel's blue and gold-striped Emmapeeler. For the tag scene Steed wears his fawn overcoat and Mrs. Peel wears white mechanic's overalls.

Steed also gets to wear a white lab coat and gas mask over his suit. SMOG member Spencer uses a 4x5 large format folding view camera, probably Graflex, but the label is never clearly visible.

TAG SCENE

Steed paces around his green Bentley Speed Six[6] while Emma prowls underneath pretending to be a Cockney-voiced mechanic and claiming he has "ghosts in his engine." She then emerges with two glasses of champagne and they toast one another.

QUOTES

"Transparent? You could read a newspaper through him!"
"This ghost made more of a 'ding-dong' than a bump. It started swinging on the bell rope, kicked up quite a racket. Loud enough to wake the, uh…well, pretty loud anyway."

112 (5.8.8) THE HIDDEN TIGER

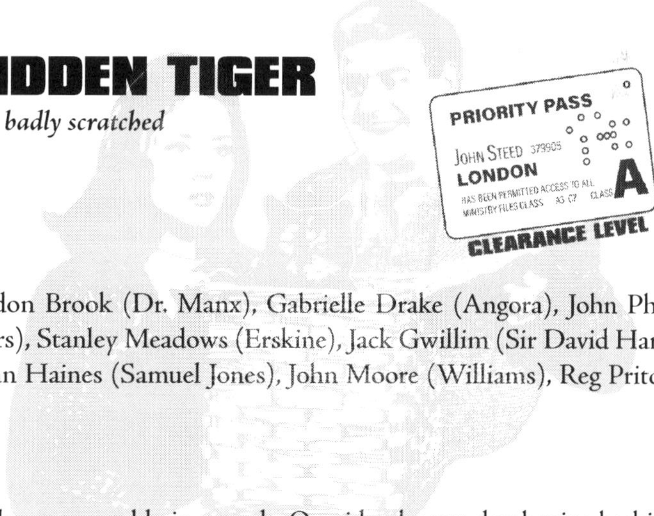

Steed hunts a big cat — Emma is badly scratched
Written by Philip Levene
Directed by Sidney Hayers

GUEST CAST

Ronnie Barker (Cheshire), Lyndon Brook (Dr. Manx), Gabrielle Drake (Angora), John Phillips (Nesbitt), Michael Forrest (Peters), Stanley Meadows (Erskine), Jack Gwillim (Sir David Harper), Frederick Treves (Dawson), Brian Haines (Samuel Jones), John Moore (Williams), Reg Pritchard (Bellamy)

PRE-TITLE/TEASER

In a country mansion, a butler clears up a table in a study. Outside, the pet dog begins barking in alarm, drawing the butler's attention. He goes to the window and closes it but is quickly shocked by the sight of something which then assaults him and claws him to death.

6 I've always thought this scene would make more sense with the Rolls-Royce Silver Ghost.

"MRS. PEEL–WE'RE NEEDED"

As Mrs. Peel remodels her apartment while drinking champagne, she begins by removing the wallpaper, revealing the words "Mrs. Peel" underneath. Steed then appears and tears off more wallpaper revealing the remainder of his message, "– We're Needed."[7]

SYNOPSIS

Something is mauling men to death, and Steed suspects it must be a huge jungle cat. He takes on the services of safari expert Major Nesbit, but Nesbit is the animal's next target. Steed learns all the victims were on the board of directors for PURRR, the Philanthropic Union for the Rescue, Relief, and Recuperation of Cats, and sends Mrs. Peel to investigate. But their leader Cheshire smells a rat and sends a cat to keep Mrs. Peel cozy on those long winter nights...

REVIEW

This is a terrific episode with a double act of piercing music from the esteemed Laurie Johnson and piercing teeth from our feline friends. The pre-title is chilling and well directed, the tiger skin wall rug is a touch of brilliance—although in retrospect I'm reminded of a similar scene in ***Night of the Demon***, which, come to think of it, may have inspired the entire premise. The multiple double-entendres and cat puns—the Identi-Cat system, Psy-Cat therapy, and the fleet of milk floats driving into the PURRR headquarters—are hysterical and among the sauciest and cleverest comedy of the series. Ronnie Barker is sublimely funny in this story, and his bizarre catlike mannerisms are a major selling point as he strokes his hair forward and proclaims the coming day of the cat. His character is very aptly named, but, personally, I'd peg him as a fat grey British shorthair.

The typical *Avengers* wit is on maximum overdrive throughout the entire episode. Diana Rigg and Patrick Macnee are terrific in this story, hamming it up as they search for fictional cats with Cheshire's assistance. (Naturally, Steed's cat is called 'Emma,' and Emma's is named 'Little John.') The direction is particularly beautiful with many great location scenes in the English countryside, and the color film is brightly saturated as befitting the more cartoonish nature of the show during this period.

Unlike "The Winged Avenger," the nature of the attacks is kept a mystery until PURRR arrives on the scene. Aside from the slightly annoying and screechy music for each cat attack, my only other reservation is the generally unrealistic central premise. As in "The Fear Merchants," one negates the other. One could simply accept the cat-attacks as silly and enjoyable nonsense, but the music prevents it. Even if you get past the unrealistic attacks on humans, there's the death of a prize steer to consider. In other words, the idea that an ordinary housecat in *any* state of mind could kill a massive animal like that is just—well, a load of bull. Nevertheless, one man gets caught in a bear trap before enduring a cat scratching fever, and another man dies in a kitty-caused car crash, adding some believability to the feline power to cause chaos. In any case, the threat of death faced by Steed from the claws of a mad glaring in the final moments seems more legit. And by the time we've gotten that far, we have been thrilled with so much wonderful direction, humor and wit, and so many classic eccentrics that we shouldn't care. And this is why this episode works better than similar plotlines like "The Winged Avenger."

The tag scene features Steed playing with green paint rather than helping Emma redecorate her apartment. With childlike glee, he of course paints pussy cats and a heart with an arrow through it (more hints of romance?) before spilling red paint on the floor. Even if you're not a cat lover, "The Hidden Tiger" will no doubt please long-time fans and newbies alike.

---

7 This scene is so inexplicably surreal that it makes me wonder if it inspired the ***Doctor Who*** episode, "Blink," in which something very similar happens to Sally Sparrow.

EPISODE NOTES

The PURRR exteriors were shot on location at North Mymms Park, Welham Green.

CHAMPAGNE, CARS, CLOTHES, AND... CAMERAS!

Mrs. Peel starts out in her blue and hot-pink-striped Emmapeeler and Steed in his midnight-blue single-breasted, three-piece suit with a pale-blue shirt and blue cravat with white spots. Mrs. Peel debuts four new outfits in this episode: a thickly-woven camel coat with a pink rollneck jumper and a knee-length skirt; a tweed hunting blazer over a white rollneck jumper and tan trousers; a bright yellow structured jacket with buttons down the front and another white rollneck; and, of course, a black catsuit with silver zipper placket and trim. All of Steed's outfits are from prior episodes. His Bentley Speed Six returns as does Mrs. Peel's Lotus.

We also see Mrs. Peel's former fur-lined red jacket from Season Four, now in color and worn by Gabrielle Drake.[8] Speaking of Angora, she uses a Leica III 35mm rangefinder in a brown leather case. (I wonder if this is the same one used by Cathy Gale in Season Two.)

Steed enjoys a glass of champagne while speaking to Mrs. Peel over a walkie-talkie. All in all, a pretty good champagne episode when both of them drink it, albeit separately in this case.

TAG SCENE

Steed and Emma continue her remodeling project at her apartment, but Steed cannot help but play—painting cartoonish cats, his name, and a heart pierced by an arrow on the walls. He finally steps right into the paint tray, causing a "cat-tastrophe" by spilling the red paint.

QUOTES

"*Humour In Milk. Milk and Its Derivatives*. Do you mean to say you've waded all the way through these?" "I think the word is 'skimmed.'"

"The name of your beloved pussy?" "Emma."

"A cuddly bronze tabby—what a joy for you it must be when she is curled up in your lap!" "Yeah, well, I never thought of it that way."

"No, Little John's nose is much more aristrocratic."

"Tell me, has your Little John any other peculiarities?" "Well, he's very bad-tempered first thing in the morning...until he's had his first glass of champagne."

"That is our treatment room." "And who is *that* getting the treatment?"

"Shall I put the cat out?" "Do."

"Let's put a pigeon amongst the pussies."

---

8 I guess we can assume Mrs. Peel left it at a charity shop and Angora picked it up for a bargain. I always felt like it makes the line "Don't forget your coat, Mrs. Peel" seem especially catty.

113 (5.9.9) THE CORRECT WAY TO KILL

Steed changes partner — Emma joins the enemy
Written by Brian Clemens
Directed by Charles Chrichton

GUEST CAST

Anna Quayle (Olga), Michael Gough (Nutski), Philip Madoc (Ivan), Terence Alexander (Ponsonby), Peter Barkworth (Percy), Graham Armitage (Algy), Timothy Bateson (Merryweather), Joanna Jones (Hilda), Edwin Apps (Winters), John G. Heller (Groski)

PRE-TITLE/TEASER

A Russian agent awaits a contact in a foggy darkened alley. Finally, his British counterparts arrive; they are very apologetic for being late. But all politeness is dispensed when the Russian attempts to buy information and is unceremoniously shot by the British agents.

"MRS. PEEL–WE'RE NEEDED"

In town, Emma buys a newspaper and is surprised to find that Steed has taken out a full-page ad announcing, "Mrs. Peel–We're Needed!"

SYNOPSIS

Two enemy agents are murdered in London by well-dressed impeccably-mannered killers, and Steed is immediately suspected by his rivals from the other side. An uneasy peace with the forces behind the iron curtain sees Steed and Emma temporarily partnered with enemy agents. The confusing plot twists threaten their uneasy alliance however. Why are crates of umbrellas being shipped to a chiropodist? And what does the aristocratic group SNOB have to do with anything…?

REVIEW

This story is the first of three Emma Peel episodes that were remakes of episodes from the black and white and videotaped Cathy Gale era. (The other two remakes were "The Joker" and "The £50,000 Breakfast." While "The Superlative Seven" is a loose remake of "Dressed to Kill," these three episodes were almost line-for-line the same.) The transition to color was an opportunity to use tested scripts with an updated production standard. This is a tactic that was often used in American television such as ***Bewitched***, a show which seemed to do so for want of fresh ideas rather than updated production standards and justly received criticism for it as a result.

In this case, the original was an excellent episode called "The Charmers." I enjoyed that one immensely and was largely immune to the cramped sets and murky 405-line videotape as I'm well-adjusted to such things, having grown up on it, but modern viewers might find it impenetrable.

Thankfully, "The Correct Way to Kill" is beautifully shot on color film and hasn't lost an ounce of wit in the translation to the Emma Peel era. It's a story that simultaneously spoofs both British and Russian stereotypes brilliantly, doling out some delightful gags in the process. The pre-title starts right out with one of the strongest of the Clemens-style hyperreal presentations of British traditions, two congenial assassins in sharp suits, bowler hats, and umbrellas, one of whom cannot speak until he has been introduced. This becomes the theme of the episode, introducing us to SNOB (Sociability, Nobility, Omnipotence and Breeding Inc.), an organization apparently created to sustain the traditions of the fading English gentry—to which Steed adheres obeisantly himself.

Ostensibly, the students (or perhaps conscripts) are practicing how to hail a cab by raising their umbrellas, but the Nazi connotations of the arm positions are instead transparently obvious to the viewer, especially when the shout of "Hail!" is added to the process. The addition of "Omnipotence" to the company's name wasn't lost on me either. Their motto "Seek, hate, kill!" even sounds remarkably like "Sieg heil!" when shouted, and Nutski is almost a homonym of Nazi. It's perhaps a little obvious. The question is what kind of message was Clemens attempting to send?—a general indictment of snobbery among the upper class, or that of extreme right-wing views and their fascist tendencies? Edward VIII? Ironically, Ponsonby-Frythe is left in admiration of Steed, whose gentility exceeds that of the students by a country mile, and this admiration at times seems to vaguely border on attraction.

My favorite scene is the one in which Mrs. Peel rummages through Nutski's safe for clues. She finds photographs of herself and Steed. The back of Steed's photo says "Dangerous – Handle with Care" but hers reads "Very Dangerous – Do Not Handle at All." (Also, I always wonder if that stuffed crocodile in Nutski's office is the same one that was in "One for the Mortuary.")

The action scenes are excellent, a significant upgrade to the original. There is a vicious slasher of a duel, contrasted with an elegant and perfectly choreographed one. Ray Austin, the stunt arranger at the time—later to become a superb director in his own right—can be justly proud for his work on this particular episode. The casting is also superb, guest-starring the likes of Michael Gough, Peter Barkworth, and Philip Madoc.

In the area of sexual innuendoes, the tag scene is one of the most delightful in the series with Steed and Mrs. Peel hinting that his night with cold-as-Siberia Olga, who is also a first-rate bricklayer, might have required the inclusion of "a certain bourgeois decadent capitalist touch."

CHAMPAGNE, CARS, CLOTHES, AND CANINES

Mrs. Peel starts right out buying her newspaper while wearing the same tweed hunting blazer she wore in "The Hidden Tiger" although this time with a bright yellow cap in the same cut as the hot pink one worn in "The Winged Avenger." She later switches to a navy sports blazer with a V-neck cut with a knee-length orange skirt and a matching orange-and-black scarf. Once again, the navy jacket has two round buttons at the waist like many of her other coats in this collection. Her gloves are a pop-art bicolored beige and white.

Steed debuts yet another three-piece, single-breasted gray suit, one in an already massive collection, this time with darker gray chalk-stripes, a blue cravat and hankie. His bowler matches the stripes in the suit, and his brolly matches the lighter gray. He quickly switches to the navy suit from the title sequence with a purple cravat and white shirt, and this is followed by the charcoal chalk-striped suit, later paired with a lovely grey marle overcoat.

Mrs. Peel then debuts a lavender pantsuit with a plum-purple rollneck jumper and white boots, followed by a new Emmapeeler, a stretch jersey orange catsuit with navy stripes. She then elegantly wears white fencing garb before debuting a red coat with white trim that looks a bit like a reimagined jodhpuri suit with the same round buttons as many of her other outfits. Steed finishes off in his light gray double-breasted suit with a matching Russian-style fur cap.

Neither of their vehicles appears in this episode.

TAG SCENE

Emma arrives at Steed's apartment to find him wearing a Russian fur cap. He then espouses the virtues of his date with Olga but finally admits that it lacked "a certain bourgeois capitalistic decadence."

QUOTES

"You British—you'll be the death of me!"

"Nonsense. Mrs. Peel will vouch for me. I haven't killed anyone all week."

"Very well, the Horse Guards will be infiltrated… perhaps with a horse."
"It will be a pleasure working with you, Mrs. Peel." "It will be a change."
"When I heard of this assignment, my first impulse was to kill you. But the glorious Motherland says I am to work with you." "And Mother's always right."
"They did it to Ivan, they'll do it to Olga." "Do what to Olga?" "Pop her into an umbrella crate." "Furled or unfurled?"

114 (5.10.10) NEVER, NEVER SAY DIE

Steed meets a dead man — Emma fights the corpse
Written by Philip Levene
Directed by Robert Day

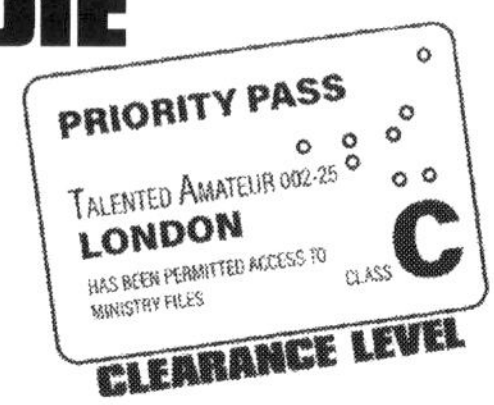

GUEST CAST

Christopher Lee (Professor Stone), Jeremy Young (Dr. Penrose), Patricia English (Dr. James), David Kernan (Eccles), Christopher Benjamin (Whittle), John Junkin (Sergeant), Peter Dennis (Private), Geoffrey Reed (Carter), Alan Chuntz (Selby), Arnold Ridley (Elderly Gent), David Gregory (Young Man), Karen Ford (Nurse)

Note: the three speaking actors who play Eccles' international chess partners are uncredited. The actor playing Twiggy remains unknown.

PRE-TITLE/TEASER

A tall lugubrious man stalks the damp countryside and steps in front of a car on the road. The driver cannot stop in time and strikes and (apparently) kills him. The man is taken to the hospital and pronounced dead. Nevertheless, the nurse and driver are both shocked to see the dead man rise and walk off under his own power.

"MRS. PEEL–WE'RE NEEDED"

Back in her newly remodeled apartment, Emma sits in a comfortable armchair watching a repeat of "The Cybernauts" on her television set. She is surprised to see Steed break in on the broadcast and announce "Mrs. Peel, we're needed."

SYNOPSIS

Steed and Mrs. Peel visit the countryside on the track of an indestructible man who inexplicably wanders about destroying radios and survives both impacts with cars and machine gun fire. Steed witnesses a mob of white-suited men capture the man and follows them to the Neoteric Research Unit, whose director is an exact double of the steely-eyed man…

REVIEW

"Never, Never Say Die" is certainly not one to take too seriously in its first half. The first twenty minutes are particularly humorous with a plethora of witty lines. Dr. Frank N. Stone goes around smashing radios which blare perky BBC lift-music. I certainly can't blame him. Besides that, there's the hysterical joke of a driver hitting and (ostensibly) killing the same victim twice in his car. We, the audience, know that somehow the victim is invulnerable to harm, even if we don't know the means, but the reaction of Christopher Benjamin to having 'killed' a man twice is priceless. I've rarely laughed so hard.

Of course, the whole premise is a thinly veiled reference to Hammer's Frankenstein films, and there are also a few shots that are strikingly similar to ***Dracula*** (aka ***Horror of Dracula***), Hammer's first Dracula film from 1958. Appropriately, Stone's dramatic first appearance in black tie is played with bland aristocratic politeness and stony implacability by renowned Hammer star Christopher Lee, currently on break from the cape.

Some have seen this episode as a Cybernauts story with humanoid robots, and there are connections, as the clip from "The Cybernauts" at the beginning implies. But I think it's much more appropriate that this episode is seen as a spoof of the Hammer Frankenstein or Mummy films, in which Lee also starred. After all, all of this rigmarole is the consequence of an experiment gone wrong. The inspiration is one dimensional however, all of it based in Lee sending himself up. Sadly, that single inspiration fades quickly into witless clichés and substandard dialogue, only sustained by the lone eccentric Eccles and the thrill of watching Steed and Emma at wit's end in a losing fight against unstoppable robot foes. The second half, as a result, is comparatively dull.

EPISODE NOTES

The idea behind realistically human robots holding the consciousness of their creator was already employed in the ***Star Trek*** episode "What Are Little Girls Made Of?" in the previous year, though it's uncertain whether this could have inspired Philip Levene's writing, since ***Star Trek*** did not premiere in the United Kingdom until 1969.

CHAMPAGNE, CARS, CLOTHES, AND CANINES

Mrs. Peel debuts only two new outfits in this episode: a tan suede coat with a high collar paired with an oatmeal heavy-knit rollneck jumper, tan trousers, and white boots; and later another Emmapeeler, cobalt-blue with white trim and zippered white placket. Steed has no new outfits this episode but starts out in his gray herringbone single-breasted, three-piece suit. The brown tartan blazer also features heavily. In the tag scene, his fawn overcoat returns.

For his part, Christopher Lee wears a heavy woolen navy overcoat and crimson rollneck jumper, both of which apparently magically repair bullet holes. Very fashion forward!

Mrs. Peel's Lotus returns in a fair need of a wash—it's a very muddy episode—but Steed's Bentley is still absent.

There is a canine, but she's neither Steed's nor Emma's, but the beloved companion of George Eccles, Twiggy, clearly named after the fashion star, who would also wear Mrs. Peel's tan coat in the famous photo session with Patrick Macnee (the model, not the dog, obviously).

TAG SCENE

Steed and Emma sit in Emma's apartment watching television, constantly changing channels with the remote until Steed rises and complains about the quality of the entertainment. Settling on the Political Party Broadcast, Emma remarks that they've narrowly avoided the disaster of "plastic politicians." Steed responds with "who would know the difference?"

QUOTES

"No body? But there's always a body!"
"It looks as though the dear departed has departed."
"Casualty—found unconscious about a mile from here. He'd been attacked." "By a banana?"

115 (5.11.11) EPIC

Steed catches a falling star — Emma makes a movie
Written by Brian Clemens
Directed by James Hill

GUEST CAST

Peter Wyngarde (Stewart Kirby), Isa Miranda (Damita Syn), Kenneth J. Warren (Z. Z. Von Schnerk), David Lodge (Policeman), Anthony Dawes (Actor)

PRE-TITLE/TEASER

The camera settles upon a golden trophy; it reads: "Given to Z.Z. von SCHNERK for The Best Cinematogaph[9] [sic] Film of 1931." The director Z.Z. von Schnerk then auditions an apparent substitute for Steed as his actors gush their approval. Agreeing to test the potential actor, they then shoot him dead, reminding him that it's "a non-speaking part" as he falls.

"MRS. PEEL–WE'RE NEEDED"[10]

Steed visits Emma at her apartment, but Emma immediately emerges and announces, "Sorry, Steed, I'm needed elsewhere."

SYNOPSIS

A trio of mad film fanatics kidnap Emma Peel and bring her to an exact duplicate of her own apartment at an abandoned film studio. They then proceed to film bizarre and pointless footage of her in a mock film inspired by various epic movies…

REVIEW

There's ample indication that Brian Clemens may have intended "Epic" to be the ultimate fifth season episode, a perfect encapsulation of his vision for *The Avengers*. Indeed, most of the elements are here—an oversimplified plot, eccentrics, humor (or attempts thereof), rampant hyperreality with dashes of surrealism thrown in—but instead of becoming the paragon of *Avengers* episodes, we are instead shown exactly how grotesque the concept is when carried to an illogical extreme. When the next batch of episodes started filming, were ITV executives thinking of "Epic" when they asked Fennell and Clemens to tone it down? Could this be the precise moment that initiated a backlash that led to their firing? Of course, it's difficult to tell, but there are few moments in this series with more potential for irritating established fans of the more centered, realistic version of the series that had dominated for the previous four seasons.

The meager narrative involves an insane director and his cadre of crazed film actors that intend to kill Mrs. Peel and film the process in order to create the greatest epic of all time. But apparently 'greatest epic of all time' is a code word for randomly and incoherently combining every genre known to cinema into a cyclone of film industry clichés. Thus, what Clemens has really written is a pastiched *Avengers* snuff film that dumbs the program down as far as possible. As such, "Epic" has gained tremendous notoriety for being a love-it-or-hate-it affair. Some have proclaimed it 'fun,' others have called it a turgid mess. Certainly, there are some fans of its broad humor, but you will not count me among its adherents. In truth, it does very little right and is only partially saved by some occasionally intriguing direction from James Hill—the wedding and funeral scenes are perhaps in-

---

9 I can't help but think this is an in-joke rather than a typo. Cinemato*gaffe* perhaps?

10 Almost not a "Mrs. Peel–We're Needed" scene since it continues directly into the story proper, such as it is.

spired by Ingmar Bergman and are beautifully shot. We also get to see more of the film backlot than we might otherwise except in an hour-long studio tour. (You even see the brick wall prop used in "The Correct Way to Kill.") Aside from that, there is a smattering of good lines, and that's it; the rest is dreck.

Horrid acting abounds! The guest actors clearly decided to have fun and take the mickey out of the whole thing. In other words, they're enjoying themselves and we're not. Z.Z. Von Schnerk is a transparent spoof of Erich von Stroheim, played with abandon in a pantomime style. He is shaven-headed, mustachioed, and when he's not complaining about 'pink pages,' he raves about the life of the artiste and making the ultimate moving picture. Even worse is the character of Stewart Kirby, a washed-up alcoholic actor type. By Wyngarde's own admission, Kirby is a parody of himself (at the time) and that of many other actors—one that goes straight to the bottle in between takes. (I always imagine Peter O'Toole doing this.) Much is made of Wyngarde playing eleven roles in this episode, but, truthfully, it's only one. He's playing Stewart Kirby playing those eleven caricatures. So, it's not really the same thing. But the whole episode is a procession of clichés that doesn't end until the episode does. If it were done today, "Epic" would have likely added a Bollywood dance sequence with Wyngarde in a cross-dressing version of "Dola Re Dola" from *Devdas*. That's how over-the-top the whole mess is.

Even Patrick Macnee and Diana Rigg seem uninspired and lackluster in their performances, drowned in the excesses of the guest actors. Rigg's one-liners are delivered too lackadaisically to seem like real wit. This is undoubtedly the only time I will criticize Diana Rigg's performance in this series, but here she really seems to be sleepwalking her way through. Oddly enough, the most amusing performance belongs to guest star David Lodge as the eager actor playing a policeman who ably delivers the episode's best line. But even he is a strange anomaly in this episode. This hyperreal era of *The Avengers* didn't tend to include policemen, so we have an actor *playing* a policeman not an actual policeman.

The script piles on highly-derivative jokes about the silent film era, and the narrative meanders along meaninglessly, one film studio gag after another, going from drama to epic to western to war until we are struck with the silliest moment in an already silly episode as Mrs. Peel obligingly growls for her captors in imitation of the MGM lion logo. This manages to be the least funny moment of not only this episode but perhaps of the entire series. It is sophomoric at best, moronic at worst—a degradation of our stylish heroine which seems to leap out of the screen and contaminate the viewer. Meanwhile, Steed dithers dull-witted at home, seemingly paralyzed into inaction. I know the feeling.

At the finale, what could have been a very tense and exciting scene—the buzz saw and pendulum scene—is completely defused by poor direction; the conveyer which threatens to send Mrs. Peel into the buzz saw seems to slow down as it closes in and then retracts between shots. Clever cutting between shots and taut timing in the action could have had the audience biting their nails, but the tension is completely defused instead. I was never convinced her head would reach the saw. Indeed, this is how the episode presents itself, as a hyperreality pastiche that never once convinces us that anything is real at all. While some might argue that this is the point, I say that since there's no threat, there's no tension, just 'fun and games' that aren't fun. Instead of the 'ultimate *Avengers* episode,' we instead have the ultimate anti-*Avengers* episode, one that allows its fantasy elements to overwhelm reality completely and thus suck all the tension and drama right out of it.

As I mentioned, there are plenty of fans who adore this episode, and you might be one of them. You'll just have to watch it and see which side of the controversy you embrace.

EPISODES NOTES

One good excuse for sitting through this is for the commentary by Peter Wyngarde on the Blu-ray. It's much better than his performance in the episode!

CHAMPAGNE, CARS, CLOTHES... AND CAMERAS!

Mrs. Peel wears a lavender skirt and jacket with a white rollneck jumper (it's a very similar outfit to her lavender pantsuit) and Steed wears his fawn overcoat while they're on their way in her Lotus to investigate the mysterious message from Kirby. Later, she switches to a bright-green structured jacket with very large buttons, matching trousers, presumably the same white jumper, and white boots. This becomes the outfit of the episode since she ends up trapped at the nightmarish Z.Z. von Schnerk Studio—at least until the tag scene in which a continuity break occurs.[11]

The car in which she is kidnapped is a 1958 Austin FX3 Taxi (VGF 345). The wedding vehicle is a green Rolls-Royce (EXY 649), much like many of the cars Steed drives, thus highly suggestive of their relationship and her perceptions of him, since this is a very dreamlike sequence. The hearse is a 1951 Rolls-Royce Silver Wraith (MUL 296). The Lotus in which she tries to escape is the same car as usual, though the color looks oddly bluer than normal in the studio lighting

Steed's Bentley Speed Six returns along with his double-breasted gray suit.

Lots of cameras on display, most of them 35mm cinema cameras, though some are not. In the scene in which Mrs. Peel leaves her faux apartment, one of the cameras facing her is a large format view camera, for still photography. The others are cine cameras and they are seen later in the episode. The camera carried by Schnerk is a Mitchell BNC 35mm camera, whereas the giant camera he uses in the final scene looks to be a much older (and larger) Mitchell 35mm camera, perhaps from the 1950s or earlier, but it also looks a bit like a 35mm three-strip Technicolor camera—which might make some sense (even though such cameras were no longer in general use[12]) as Schnerk was clearly intended to be a director who had reached peak popularity in the silent era. Presumably this last camera was an older model no longer in use, perhaps borrowed from somewhere else in the studio.

TAG SCENE

Apparently back in Emma's apartment, Steed and Emma search the newspaper for a decent film. Finally, they give up and decide to spend the evening at home. Emma then kicks over a wall, revealing that they're actually in the duplicate of her apartment at Z. Z. von Schnerk's studio.

QUOTES

"He's very good, I'll give him that. Specializes in corpses, does he?"

"It's time I started planning the climax of this picture, the agonizing climax. The real death of Emma Peel."

"I think I'm in danger of becoming a split personality."

"Gloat all you like, but just remember, *I'm* the star of this picture."

---

11 The tag scene's purple jumper and lavender pants are from the outfit worn in "The Correct Way to Kill" albeit without the jacket. A sign as to how many of these scenes were filmed out of order with separate production units. One unit would be filming the guest stars on one part of the set while the regulars would be filming with the other unit elsewhere. This was a necessary move to keep up with single-camera film production, and sometimes the continuity errors show.

12 Color film had long ago switched to the Eastmancolor process in which all three color dye layers were combined into a single strip during manufacture. By 1967, Technicolor was a proprietary color film printing process—the equivalent of post-production digital color grading today.

116 (5.12.12) THE SUPERLATIVE SEVEN

Steed flies to nowhere — Emma does her party piece
Written by Brian Clemens
Directed by Sidney Hayers

GUEST CAST

Charlotte Rampling (Hana), Brian Blessed (Mark Dayton), James Maxwell (Jason Wade), Hugh Manning (Max Hardy), Leon Greene (Freddy Richards), Gary Hope (Joe Smith), Donald Sutherland (Jessel), John Hollis (Kanwitch), Margaret Heale (Stewardess), Terry Plummer (Toy Sung)

PRE-TITLE/TEASER

In an elaborate red and white dojo, two men test martial arts practitioners against a champion. Both aspirants succeed spectacularly, but their leaders require one more "final test."

"STEED–YOU'RE NEEDED"

Steed goes duck-hunting, but when he shoots his target, what falls out of the sky is a yellow rubber duck with "Steed" printed on it. Emma reveals herself in the bushes nearby and says, "You're needed."[13]

SYNOPSIS

Steed and six other specialized combatants are all invited to a fancy-dress party aboard a plane. After taking to the air and discovering that there is no pilot, the plane operating on remote control, the invitees realize that all their invitations bear a different name for their host. When the plane lands on an uncharted island, they are forced to fight for their lives…

REVIEW

A solid episode that does much to salve the wounds from the previous hour, but still not exactly top notch in my opinion. The idea to bring various combat specialists together to battle a 'superior' warrior seems like an exciting idea, but it doesn't really work perfectly as scripted. After all, if you're banking everything on one guy beating six others, then no matter how good that one guy is, it's still a very chancy thing indeed.

The challengers all seem one-dimensional and, in some cases, silly—Steed has the skills of all of them. How exactly does a bullfighter make for a worthy opponent against a skilled assassin? And the strongman looks more like a 98-pound weakling. As if to emphasize the point, he dresses from the neck down in long johns under his leopard skin, as if he's embarrassed of his physique. It's very unconvincing. Couldn't they have at least gotten Dave Prowse? I think I would have enjoyed that.

Surprisingly, despite the subject being superlative warriors, there's not much action in this one. You see, this killer is a sneaky sort, stabbing people in the back and using subterfuge, which makes sense if you're coming up against a cadre of expert fighters. Nevertheless, there are a couple of neat twists in the plot that really help make things interesting. The killer fakes his own death to throw suspicion onto the others, and when he's really killed, he seemingly comes back to life to fight again. You'll just have to watch to see how he does it.

The main problem however, comes in the heavy use of clichés without any effort to transcend or better them. The *And Then There Were None* plot device had been used countless times in productions far and wide even by the mid-sixties, and some unique twists to shake up this trope might have

13 This is the only time that the "Mrs. Peel–You're Needed" scene was reversed.

gone a long way to brightening the originality of the story. Brian Clemens seems to be lazily satisfied with it remaining a pastiche instead. In any case, it does make a fine vehicle for showcasing Patrick Macnee.

Donald Sutherland does a good job playing a rather bizarre character named Jessel with an unidentifiable accent. He works mainly in isolation with John Hollis, who is making one of several appearances in the series. The episode terminates with Jessel trying to grab weapons from a table as Hana shoots them away, with the end result being Jessel getting knocked out by Steed with a massive candlestick holder. This nearly pointless scene is one of the more bizarre moments in the series.

This is one of those episodes that gives a member of the regular cast a week off. In the heavy schedule of this era, they typically worked eleven- and twelve-hour days, so scheduled breaks like this were necessary for mental and physical health. Thus, there is a reverse of the "Mrs. Peel – We're needed" teaser, and Emma does an impressive duck call in the process. Steed, having been called to duty, goes it alone this time, but Mrs. Peel turns up at the end to help put away the crooks in something of a reversal of "The House That Jack Built" and "The Joker."

CHAMPAGNE, CARS, CLOTHES, AND CANINES

Our story begins with Steed in his taupe blazer and green waistcoat while Mrs. Peel quacks beautifully in her check hunting blazer and white rollneck jumper. She quickly introduces a canary-yellow coat with matching skirt, and this is the only debut outfit of the episode for her, this being an Emma-lite episode. The coat is structured with triangular darts pointing inwards to the waist with two large buttons. But it's Steed who wins the show's fashion award for this week with his wonderful Wellington general costume from Waterloo during the Napoleonic Wars—red coat with navy blue facing, elaborate frogs, and incredible embroidery, gold epaulettes with tassels, white trousers, coat, and gloves, and a black bicorn hat with red and white feathers. It may technically be a costume, but we should all kill to cosplay this well at anything. He looks incredibly dashing, and Macnee's glee at wearing something so magnificent shines through. Towards the end, Mrs. Peel shows up wearing her orange catsuit from "The Correct Way to Kill."

No car for Steed since he spends his time flying, but Mrs. Peel takes him to the airport in her Lotus. He and the others drink lots of champagne at the party during the flight, and both he and Mrs. Peel drink champagne in the tag scene, making this a very champagne-heavy episode indeed.

TAG SCENE

The duck-hunting scene continues, this time with Emma wielding the gun and firing at a duck. Instead of a juicy roaster falling from the sky, a cadre of plush teddy bears plummet. Steed appears and pulls a champagne bottle from one of the teddies and Emma fires again at the sky to produce two champagne glasses.

QUOTES

"That's quite a lot of... That's a very impressive record."

117 (5.13.13) A FUNNY THING HAPPENED ON THE WAY TO THE STATION

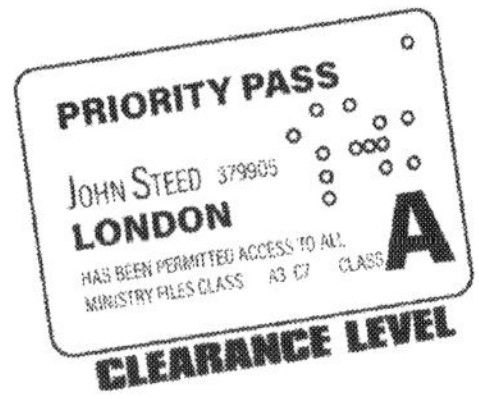

Steed goes off the rails — Emma finds her station in life
Written by Brian Sheriff (Roger Marshall & Brian Clemens)
Directed by John Krish

GUEST CAST

James Hayter (Ticket Collector), John Laurie (Crewe), Drewe Henley (Groom), Isla Blair (Bride), Tim Barrett (Salt), Richard Caldicot (Admiral), Dyson Lovell (Warren), Peter J. Elliott (Attendant), Michael Nightingale (Lucas), Noel Davis (Secretary)

PRE-TITLE/TEASER

At a railway station, a secret agent flees from his pursuers among parked trains. He hides in one of the cars but his dropped hat gives him away. Nevertheless, he slips up on one of his pursuers and strangles him with his necktie before slipping away.

"MRS. PEEL–WE'RE NEEDED"

Emma emerges from her bedroom to find a miniature toy train going round and round on its track. The freight car carries a notecard reading "Mrs. Peel," and then Steed appears, saying, "We're Needed."

SYNOPSIS

After failing to meet fellow agent Lucas at the train station, Steed and Mrs. Peel discover that an organization is using the railway system to pass encoded messages on ticket stubs. As they gradually uncover clues involving derelict train stations and another secret signaling system, they ultimately expose a plot to assassinate the Prime Minister...

REVIEW

What at first seems like a case of pick-a-location-and-write-a-story-around-it, turns into one of the most enjoyable *Avengers* stories ever. The pre-title is wonderfully well shot, completely silent except for the music, cutting expertly between closeups and wide-angle shots of the converging lines of the railroad tracks. Just the kind of directorial flourish that this season is known for. The British film industry was shrinking during this time, and many very talented and experienced directors were pouring into television, John Krish among them. The film industry's loss was television's gain.

The set design is also remarkable in this episode. Admiral Cartney's office is a beautifully crafted set that looks like the stern of a sailing ship. The curved ceiling and sloping panels are exquisitely done. (I could be mistaken, but this looks very much like the same naval set that was used in "What the Butler Saw.") Equally, the British rail cars are perfectly recreated in that classic style of the 1960s that no longer exists.

In an episode that almost loses itself in a self-awareness of its own absurdity (a common enough feature in this season), it is Diana Rigg that seems to be having the most fun not taking anything seriously. The bizarre impulse to close the shades in the rail car as she dispatches the Bride seems almost improvised for comedic effect. In one of the most bizarre fight scenes in the show, she alternately flings villains over her shoulder and crockery across the room. It was a new experience for audiences to see a woman fighting the spies while a helpless man cringes in the corner, and the delightful John Laurie (as Crewe) hams up this opportunity as much as possible as her temporary assistant. You see, he desperately wanted revenge for the destruction of his railroad signal box. He is the 1960s version of the elderly trainspotter type, and he's ill-equipped to pursue revenge, relying upon Mrs. Peel to fulfill that function.

On the down side, this script lacks some of the classic traits of the series, such as a larger-than-life criminal organization and villain, but it survives this oversight on pure charm quite admirably.

EPISODE NOTES

Longtime writer for *The Avengers* Roger Marshall had chafed at the changes to the tone of the series introduced by Albert Fennell and Brian Clemens over the past two years, and he left without completing this script. Brian Clemens finished the story and put it out under the pseudonym Brian Sheriff. Aside from the rewrite of "Death of a Great Dane" into "The £50,000 Breakfast," Marshall never worked on the program again, which is a real shame.

CHAMPAGNE, CARS, CLOTHES, AND CANINES

The first episode with no clothing debuts for Mrs. Peel. It appears she had run the gamut of her wardrobe by the time filming of this episode came around, though there are further new outfits coming up, particularly in the next season, which starts with a slew of them—six of them in "Return of the Cybernauts" alone (further proof of the gap and replanning between Seasons Five and Six). For now, she wears the teal suede jacket from "The Winged Avengers" along with a white jumper and matching train engineer's cap. It's a very charming combination, especially for a train-oriented episode. Her black catsuit with the silver placket and zipper later turns up for the finale.

No fashion debuts for Steed either, but his brown tartan blazer and tan trousers return. He also wears the gray suit with triangular pockets, this time with an olive-green white-spotted tie and matching handkerchief. His black brolly includes a handy audio-recording device underneath the whangee handle (always a whangee, my friends). He chooses to meet the PM wearing his charcoal chalk-striped suit, a light-blue shirt, and a dark-blue tie.

No cars this episode. All their travel is by train.

TAG SCENE

Steed and Emma wait in her apartment for a formal visit by the Prime Minister to thank them for saving his life. They marvel at his surprisingly large (or small) size and ponder their prospects for OBEs and an eventual damehood for Emma (quite prescient!), before admitting that neither of them actually voted for him.[14] They quietly slip out the back door.

QUOTES

"And from all this twiddley-twiddley, you learned that someone important is traveling — the prime minister?"

(Emma nearly tripping over a corpse in Steed's study) "You really must have a word with that cleaning lady of yours." "He tried to kill me." "Antisocial!"

"What are you hanging about for?"

"He doesn't look as small as he does on television." "Really? I think he looks smaller." "I must have a bigger set."

---

14 For viewers who live outside the UK: You don't actually vote for a prime minister in the UK, unless, of course, you live in his or her constituency. When saying this, it generally means voting for the prime minister's party and platform. Though the PM in this episode was entirely fictional, he could have been based on then PM Harold Wilson, which would imply that Steed and Mrs. Peel favored the Conservative party.

118 (5.14.14) SOMETHING NASTY IN THE NURSERY

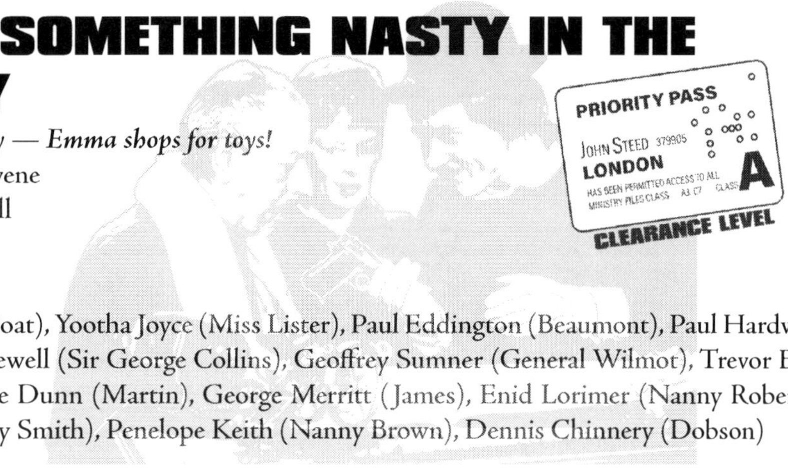

Steed acquires a nanny — Emma shops for toys!
Written by Philip Levene
Directed by James Hill

GUEST CAST

Dudley Foster (Mr. Goat), Yootha Joyce (Miss Lister), Paul Eddington (Beaumont), Paul Hardwick (Webster), Patrick Newell (Sir George Collins), Geoffrey Sumner (General Wilmot), Trevor Bannister (Gordon), Clive Dunn (Martin), George Merritt (James), Enid Lorimer (Nanny Roberts), Louie Ramsay (Nanny Smith), Penelope Keith (Nanny Brown), Dennis Chinnery (Dobson)

PRE-TITLE/TEASER

A man desperately flees from a mysterious wheelchair-riding pursuer. He reaches the house of General Wilmot and finds an open window. Inside, he phones for help but is surprised when a blue-and-yellow ball is thrown through the window. Picking it up, he immediately begins to hallucinate that he is back to childhood. An old woman in an electric wheelchair, apparently his old nanny, arrives and fatally shoots him. He collapses while sucking his thumb.

"MRS. PEEL–WE'RE NEEDED"

Emma finds a toy carousel in her apartment. As it spins around, she finds a notecard attached, reading "Mrs. Peel." Steed pops inside and says, "We're Needed."

SYNOPSIS

A government agent named Dobson is found dead (sucking his thumb) in the home of General Wilmot. This turns out the be the first clue in a plot to capture top secret government information on the location of ballistic missiles. Steed and Emma investigate and find that the victims—high-ranking government officials otherwise beyond reproach—are reduced to a state of mental childhood by a hallucinogenic drug, and the information is coaxed out of them by their former nanny…

REVIEW

One thing *The Avengers* does better than any other series is tread a fine line between comedy and deadly violence. It had always done this, even with the first series, as we are now discovering due to recent recoveries, but, in this season, it is taken to a new level, twisting our expectations completely and playing off the show's own accumulated myths. "Something Nasty in the Nursery" is a perfect example, and this is what makes it so great.

In no scene is this more evident than the scene in which Steed visits Martin's Toy Shop for the second time. The owner Martin has just received a broken jack-in-the-box for repair from a mysterious nanny. Naturally, we know something is amiss because we only see the feet and legs of the nanny as she approaches. She deposits the jack-in-the-box upon the counter and then departs in a Morris Mini van. (Apparently, all nannies use them.) And thus, this scene begins in a state of suspense.

Steed arrives. And when we see only Martin's prone legs visible from behind the counter, our expectations are that he is going to find yet another body of a victim he has not reached in time. The show had become renowned for that particular screenwriting trope by this time. But, in a twist of expectations, Martin sits up. Steed and the viewers are thus relieved of the suspense. The threat appears to have passed for the moment, though this is a mere feint. As Martin struggles to open the jack-in-the-box, the tension rises once more. Just as he is about to reveal a vital clue to Steed, Martin pries loose the lid of the box. A mechanical arm springs up and fires a gun point-blank into Martin's chest. He gasps as he tries to complete his sentence. The director cuts to a shot of Steed looking shocked, and at that moment it hits home. Even as we are surrounded by toys and delightful eccentrics, we realize that this is morbidly serious spy work. This poor man is dying. It's a very real scene set amidst the comedic aspects of the story. Martin was a very nice and funny man, and now he's dead. I cannot emphasize enough the precision with which this scene is executed. The subtle comic gasp from Martin, the faint narrowing of Patrick Macnee's eyes, the precision of the cuts from shot to shot. The combination of humor and violence is decisive and emotionally manipulative. We swing from suspense, to anticipation, to surprise, to humor, to sympathy in a brief few seconds. James Hill is to be commended for this masterly scene alone.

Similarly, in the pre-title, as Dobson escapes an old nanny in an electric wheelchair, we have our paradigm shifted as the director uses childhood imagery in combination with brutal violence. As Dobson is gunned down in a crib, we almost feel as if the nanny is shooting a real child. Obviously, it is insidiously cruel turning someone into a mental child and then executing them, and yet as he falls, he's sucking his thumb, which provokes amusement.

One more example, the concept of the nanny training school Guild of Noble Nannies, evokes humor as nannies march back and forth with prams as if going into battle against bratty babies and diaper rash. What an absurdly organized and militaristic approach to something so innately nurturing!

The concept of reverting government officials to childhood in order to gather top secret information is highly fresh, and all the regulars and guest stars turn in superb performances. The only minor flaw is one scene in which the villains explain their scheme to the viewers by way of each other. But, to be fair, I cannot think of a better way of doing this except by explaining it to the protagonists, as James Bond villains do. Thus, it is to be forgiven. In short, this story is the surreal, kooky version of *The Avengers* at its finest.

CHAMPAGNE, CARS, CLOTHES, AND CANINES

The only fashion debut for Mrs. Peel this episode is a blue catsuit, not an Emmapeeler, at least not nearly in the same style. It has white lacing across a faux placket and also along the sleeves, with a large circular metal buckle at the waist. In my opinion, this isn't one of Alun Hughes's best designs. It only showed up in one more episode, "Mission.... Highly Improbable." In the tag scene, she returns to her striped action dress, which would return only two more times.

No fashion debuts for Steed, though he wears a wide array of outfits from his wardrobe, including the charcoal chalk-striped suit, the brown tartan blazer, and the gray chalk-striped suit (which is growing on me).

Both Steed's Bentley Speed Six and Mrs. Peel's Lotus appear. Nanny Goat's preferred means of transport is a blue-green 1961 Morris Mini Van (994 JOD).

TAG SCENE

When Steed and Emma experiment with a crystal ball, Emma provides Steed with a reading which tracks closely with events similar to their usual adventures, but she refuses to reveal the final outcome, saying "Watch next week." When Steed tries his hand, whatever he sees is so provocative that Emma is forced to cover the crystal ball with a black cloth.

QUOTES

"That smell—it's like lavender." "The General's aftershave?" "Fragrant general."
"You're not my nanny!"
"Someone always gets to them first."

119 (5.15.15) **THE JOKER**

Steed trumps an ace — Emma plays a lone hand
Written by Brian Clemens
Directed by Sidney Hayers

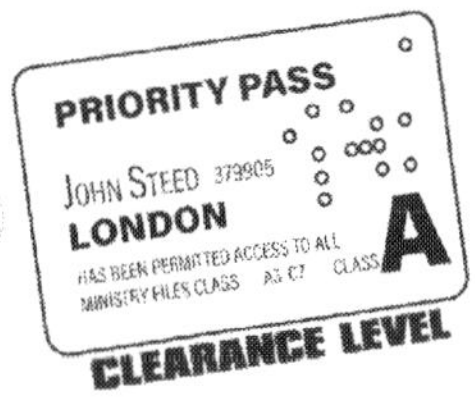

GUEST CAST

Peter Jeffrey (Prendergast), Sally Nesbitt (Ola), Ronald Lacey (Strange young man), John Stone (Major George Fancy)

PRE-TITLE/TEASER

Inside a mysterious old house, the hands of an unseen person with sharp scissors cut a photo of Emma out of an issue of Bridge Players' magazine. As the hands cut, they betray increasing agitation. The photo is finally cut to shreds before the still unseen person stabs the wooden table in fury.

"MRS. PEEL–WE'RE NEEDED"

Emma rings the doorbell of Steed's apartment. Running down the stairs to answer the door, Steed trips and falls, spraining his ankle, and Emma breaks in and rushes to his aid. Naturally, he announces "Mrs. Peel, you're needed."

SYNOPSIS

After receiving an invitation from a fellow bridge enthusiast to spend a weekend at his home, Emma leaves Steed behind nursing a sprained ankle. Soon after arriving and finding the owner not at home, Emma is mildly irritated by the bizarre and unwelcome occupants of the house before discovering that she is being spied upon and tormented by an old enemy...

REVIEW

The pre-title opens with doughy hands fingering a photo of Emma. They grab scissors that caress the photo before they begin to cut furiously. The frenzied psychotic rage that follows concludes with an exasperated stab into the table. Thus, we are given a glimpse into a disturbed mind before the story even begins.

This is an extremely well-directed and eerie episode with Hammer-like flourishes and a strong structural similarity to "The House That Jack Built." As an almost scene-for-scene remake of the Cathy Gale third season episode "Don't Look Behind You," "The Joker" is an engaging psychological thriller, and the clear spiritual ancestor to both of them is the Universal horror film ***The Old Dark House***.

Clemens and Hayers exceed the third season original with a better villain, masterly direction, much higher production values, and some of the oddest eccentrics in the history of the show. Certainly, Sally Nesbitt as Ola—the weirdly immature resident nutcase with a penchant for dentistry, genealogy and the Italian language[15]—is much more than most ordinary people could endure. Indeed, Emma seems more annoyed with the goings-on than frightened, but even her patience is tried when 'strange young man' Ronald Lacey turns up rather ineptly pretending to be a German baron. Lacey takes an exasperatingly grating personality (and a sexual predator-type creepiness) to a new level with Peter Lorre-inspired wheezes and leering. Fortunately, Emma knows just how to handle his lasciviousness.

---

15 In deference to Ola's prior incarnation in "Don't Look Behind You," her Italian phrase of choice is the much more pedestrian "Dove l'ingresso?" which means "Where's the entrance?"

Despite his brief appearance, Prendergast makes a good villain with some interesting ties to Emma's past. Because of the superb direction, I am reminded of *Psycho* as the unseen villain spies on Emma through conveniently-positioned glory holes, not the first or the last time that Hitchcock's directorial style would be referenced in this season or the next two. Indeed, the feel of the narrative is that of a massive peepshow arranged for the benefit of the villain. Just as we do in Hitchcock's *Rear Window*, the viewer will delight nevertheless in the voyeurism, made tamer because we know who is being toyed with and that she is more than capable of defending herself.

Although the entire episode—to drive the admittedly thin narrative—relies upon the quirkiness of its characters and the bizarreness of the situations rather than any of the more overt surrealism so typical of this season, one of the oddest moments of the show comes when Steed dances behind a giant joker card to knock Prendergast out! It is a moment that will have the viewer simultaneously surprised, bewildered, and relieved upon first viewing, and references Steed's late arrival in the aforementioned "The House that Jack Built" at the same time.

My only questions are: How did Prendergast gain access to Sir Rusicana's house? Who are Ola and the 'strange young man'? Is Ola really Sir Rusicana's ward or just some kook that Prendergast picked up?

EPISODE NOTES

The lack of overscan on the Blu-ray release reveals that the hands cutting Emma's photograph in the pre-title are not that of any of the actors, Peter Jeffrey or otherwise. They look to be the hands of a slightly pudgy woman, possibly a production assistant or an extra hired to be a 'hand model.' (The side of her face is caught on a several frames.) On many episodes throughout this era, the lack of overscan also periodically reveals boom mics that otherwise would have remained hidden on 1960s television sets.

CHAMPAGNE, CARS, CLOTHES, AND CANINES

No fashion debuts for Mrs. Peel and only one for Steed, the latter being a brown pin-striped single-breasted suit (yes, pin-striped, not chalk-striped). Mrs. Peel wears her A-line pale-green coat and matching pants with a bright yellow jumper and matching shoes. She also returns to her Chinese silk pajamas with silver slippers for her stay at Sir Cavalier's house. They're so fashionable, they could hardly be considered casual, but they do lend her a slight air of vulnerability which might not be achievable otherwise.

Both Steed's Bentley Speed Six and Mrs. Peel's Lotus appear. She generously loans Ola the Lotus. (Certainly more trusting than I would have been!)

TAG SCENE

Steed plays solitaire and Emma cannot resist offering advice. When he attempts to perform a card trick on her, she turns the tables on him, producing two Jokers to match the vintage year of the champagne bottle he produces.

QUOTES

"This place is the end of the world, isn't it? I'm not surprised you got lost."

"The words are so nice and r-r-r-rolly. Dove l'ingrrresso? You could almost say that around a lollipop, couldn't you?"

"Have I shown you my teeth?" "Frequently."

"Oh, dear!—do you think I frightened him?"

120 (5.16.16) WHO'S WHO???

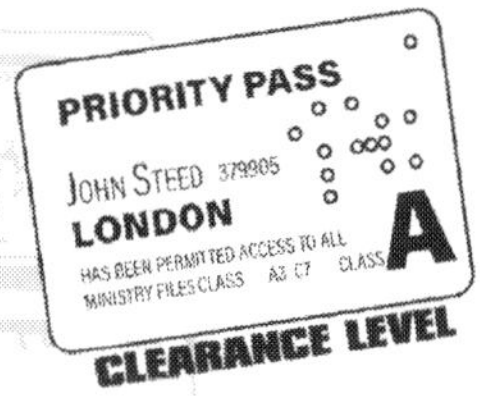

Steed goes out of his mind — Emma is beside herself
Written by Philip Levene
Directed by John Moxey

GUEST CAST

Patricia Haines (Lola), Freddie Jones (Basil), Campbell Singer (Major "B"), Peter Reynolds (Tulip), Arnold Diamond (Krelmar), Philip Levene (Daffodil), Malcolm Taylor (Hooper)

PRE-TITLE/TEASER

A secret agent—codenamed 'Rose'—from the 'floral network' arrives in a warehouse. Apparently called there by a faked note from Steed, he snoops around until he is surprised and fatally shot by two enemy agents—Basil and Lola. They then stage the body in as bizarre a manner as they can imagine in order to attract Steed and Mrs. Peel's attention: the corpse is placed in towering trousers and stilts and regally posed upon a stack of crates which almost reach the ceiling. The final touch is a pistol propped upright with the barrel pointing upwards and a fresh cut rose stuck inside.[16]

"MRS. PEEL–WE'RE NEEDED"

Emma gazes into the mirror in her apartment and Steed appears in the reflection and announces, "Mrs. Peel, we're needed."

SYNOPSIS

Steed and Emma are lured to a warehouse by a bizarre death—the corpse of an agent on gigantic stilts. Clues lead Steed to a faux stilt manufacturer, where he is knocked out and brain-swapped with a foreign agent named Basil. Mrs. Peel is then lured to the same location and swaps bodies with the female agent Lola. Leaving the real Steed and Emma tied up, the enemies use their perfect disguises to devastate the secret agent 'floral network' from the inside…

REVIEW

This over-the-top but fun episode is the latest one to capitalize on its own myths. The two enemy agents, Basil and Lola, in one of the greatest pre-title sequences of the series, prepare the most bizarre death that they can conceive in order to draw Steed and Emma to the scene. The enemies of the *Avengers* know by now that any crime this surreal draws them like sniffing bloodhounds. This self-awareness of the show's own absurdities was a feature of this season but in this case was a bold wink to the fans, who no doubt enjoyed this subtle breaking of the fourth wall. The fourth wall is again broken with the 'important announcements' to the audience. They are deliberately silly and unnecessary, but that is the point. It's another playful wink to the audience.

The brain-switching stuff is completely absurd, and yet typical of this season, so I won't dwell on it. The point is that it's fun. Basil and Lola, having switched bodies with Steed and Emma knock off each agent one by one in order to create a floral bouquet, piling up the bodies in Steed's study. Macnee and Rigg are excellent at playing the 'possessed' bodies of their characters, changing their posture and diction perfectly. Freddie Jones and Patricia Haines are equally superb. I never fail to be amused as Jones (as Steed) expresses ire at his posh apartment being trashed and his cigars smoked.

Absurd though body-swapping is, we get some priceless scenes as a result. Emma chews gum and

16 This is, of course, the same iconic image that is used for the opening "The Avengers in Colour" title cards seen just before the title sequence.

gyrates her hips to go-go music. Likewise, Steed kisses Emma and bites the ends off his cigars. Their bodies behave in remarkably libertine ways for a sixties TV series. It's fun, but it's almost too much. The viewers perhaps never expected this sort of thing to happen but perhaps secretly always wished for it. Now, having received it, we are amused but might find ourselves preferring that the characters return to their demurer, are-they-or-aren't-they status.

"Who's Who???" is possibly the most fantasy-oriented story the series has ever produced. Nevertheless, it is superlative silly fun with superb performances from the regulars and supporting cast. My only question is: When Steed (in Basil's body) gets a migraine, how does he know that a bottle of migraine pills is in his coat pocket?

CHAMPAGNE, CARS, CLOTHES, AND CANINES

Technically, there are no fashion debuts either for Mrs. Peel or for Steed, although, confusingly, Mrs. Peel wears Lola's outfit and Steed Basil's. They are as follows: a blue woolen skirt and fitted jacket with a small silver brooch and five large buttons down the front with faux flap pockets at the waist (it's difficult to tell whether the outfit is composed of separates or functioned as a unified piece, though I assume it's the former, which makes it slightly racy since Lola is apparently wearing nothing under the jacket); and an ill-fitting blue serge suit with a vertical-striped white shirt and crooked blue bowtie, respectively. Steed sort of debuts a charcoal pin-striped, single-breasted, two-piece suit in a modern 1960s cut, with a white shirt, a silver tie, and a black bowler—but this is mostly worn when Basil is occupying his body and only briefly by the real Steed just after they switch back. The modern cut is likely meant to show that Basil has slightly more modern tastes even when imitating Steed; the tie is worn quite loose most of the time.

Both Steed's Bentley Speed Six and Mrs. Peel's Lotus appear again, sometimes driven by the enemy agents, or their bodies—I forget which and when.

Basil and Lola drink plenty of Steed's good champagne, but neither Steed nor Mrs. Peel get any. Well... at least their bodies did, even if they weren't 'there' to taste it.

TAG SCENE

Steed calls at Emma's apartment and finds it full of bouquets of flowers gifted by the surviving members of the Floral Network. Emma then reminds Steed that it's a special occasion, her birthday. Steed at first feigns ignorance but then reveals he's planned a luxurious trip as a gift, and Emma responds by revealing she believed in him all along. Her bags are already packed. They then exchange terms of endearment in imitation of their enemy agent counterparts: "Come along, Basil baby," "Coming, honey child."

QUOTES

"What sort of a fiend are we dealing with. A man that would bite the end off a cigar is capable of anything."

"Steed has poise, a touch of the aristocrat. You slouch like a peasant!"

"One shouldn't take a man for granted but one does. Come along, Basil, baby." "Coming, honey child."

ARE THERE SIX OR SEVEN SEASONS?

This is a fine question, one that addresses an issue first raised by the Cornell, Day, and Topping book, *The Avengers Dossier,* in 1998. That was (and is) an intriguing book that in part prompted my decision to create a website for *The Avengers* shortly thereafter. They raised the issue and argued mightily (and in my opinion, successfully) in favor of seven seasons. Unfortunately, while well-researched and logically organized, the book was beset with typographical and superficial errors within the guest cast lists and in other areas, and I feel this may have undermined their case despite its compelling nature. Nevertheless, I accepted their argument and chose to present the episodes within the seven seasons paradigm when I created my website. I will elucidate in due course as to why, but first, here is a history of the broadcast of *The Avengers* in both the United Kingdom and the United States, which will likely give you some idea of how American money and the number of episodes ordered from America in each batch influenced how the program aired in both countries.

(Note that much of the narrative contained within this article is a repeat of that which is found in the season notes for seasons four through seven. However, this is required for purposes of clarity. Also, for practical reasons, given the ease of confusion between ABC in the UK and ABC in the US, i.e. the ITV production company versus the American network, in this section I'm going to always refer to 'Associated British Corporation' for the UK television production company and to 'ABC' for the American network. It should also be noted that Associated British Corporation merged with Associated-Rediffusion in 1968 and became Thames Television, though no episode of *The Avengers* went out explicitly under the name of that production company despite some episodes being filmed after the transition. Thus, I will not be referencing Thames Television in this section. Nevertheless, the transition from Associated British Corporation to Thames was going on behind the scenes while *The Avengers* was going through its own difficult transition period, and how much this affected the production is hard to assess.)

It is probably difficult for even most Americans to understand where *The Avengers* ranked on American television in the sixties. While there is no question that the show was very popular immediately with American audiences, the program was in fact (only) a 'replacement series' for its first three seasons on ABC. A mid-season replacement series is a program that is aired in place of a failed fall program, usually one canceled by the network due to low ratings around December, and a summer replacement series is one that replaces summer programming when most television is composed of re-runs or syndicated shows. Many popular programs, such as *Northern Exposure,* began life as a summer replacement series. And this is also how *The Avengers* started on American television. These summer replacement series tend to have the quality of cult hits, often quirky or artistic programs that are thought to have limited appeal, the kinds of shows that the network is uncertain about and unwilling to risk exposing to the harsh unforgiving light of a fall premiere.

In a practical sense, what this really meant was that the magic number required from ABC was only about sixteen episodes—either a run from January to April, or one from May to August. The slightly longer first replacement series run in 1966, composed of twenty-one black and white episodes, had largely been a fluke. The Associated British Corporation had simply planned for and filmed a twenty-six-episode series regardless of what ABC had been expected to order, always with the intention of airing everything that they filmed on ITV. They could afford to do that because black and white film was comparatively less expensive than color. ABC had merely taken advantage of what must have seemed like a low-cost, low-risk series to fill a much-needed slot that spring and summer.

As a result, only twenty-one episodes of this black and white Diana Rigg series were aired in the United States. The episodes not aired were "A Surfeit of H_2O," "Silent Dust," "Quick-Quick Slow Death," "A Touch of Brimstone," and "Honey for the Prince." Thus, the seasons on either side of the Atlantic were transmitted as follows, with the American season airing much later than in the UK:

UK FOURTH SEASON	US FIRST SEASON
28 Sep 1965—"The Town of No Return"	28 Mar 1966—"The Cybernauts"
7 Oct 1965—"The Grave-diggers"	4 Apr 1966—"Small Game for Big Hunters"
14 Oct 1965—"The Cybernauts"	11 Apr 1966—"Death at Bargain Prices"
21 Oct 1965—"Death at Bargain Prices"	25 Apr 1966—"The Hour That Never Was"
28 Oct 1965—"Castle De'ath"	2 May 1966—"Castle De'ath"
4 Nov 1965—"The Master Minds"	9 May 1966—"Two's A Crowd"
12 Nov 1965—"The Murder Market"	16 May 1966—"The House That Jack Built"
19 Nov 1965—"A Surfeit of H_2O"	30 May 1966—"The Murder Market"
26 Nov 1965—"The Hour That Never Was"	6 Jun 1966—"The Girl from Auntie"
3 Dec 1965—"Dial a Deadly Number"	13 Jun 1966—"How to Succeed....At Murder"
10 Dec 1965—"Man-Eater of Surrey Green"	20 Jun 1966—"A Sense of History"
17 Dec 1965—"Two's A Crowd"	27 Jun 1966—"Room Without a View"
23 Dec 1965—"Too Many Christmas Trees"	4 Jul 1966—"The Danger Makers"
31 Dec 1965—"Silent Dust"	11 Jul 1966—"The Master Minds"
8 Jan 1966—"Room Without a View"	24 Jul 1966—"Dial a Deadly Number"
15 Jan 1966—"Small Game for Big Hunters"	28 Jul 1966—"What the Butler Saw"
21 Jan 1966—"The Girl from Auntie"	4 Aug 1966—"The Grave-diggers"
28 Jan 1966—"The Thirteenth Hole"	11 Aug 1966—"Too Many Christmas Trees"
4 Feb 1966—"Quick-Quick Slow Death"	18 Aug 1966—"The Thirteenth Hole"
11 Feb 1966—"The Danger Makers"	25 Aug 1966—"Man-Eater of Surrey Green"
18 Feb 1966—"A Touch of Brimstone"	1 Sep 1966—"The Town of No Return"
25 Feb 1966—"What the Butler Saw"	
4 Mar 1966—"The House That Jack Built"	
11 Mar 1966—"A Sense of History"	
18 Mar 1966—"How to Succeed....At Murder"	
25 Mar 1966—"Honey for the Prince"	

This black and white filmed season was a success in both countries, and the American ABC executives were eager for more—but *only* in color. By this time, all three American networks were premiering new seasons and series only in color, and the black and white Diana Rigg episodes were one of the last seasons of anything to premiere on an American network in monochrome. Associated British Corporation happily complied with the request for color filming, and a short promotional trailer called "The Strange Case of the Missing Corpse" was produced to assure American viewers that the show would be returning the following year in color.

Now, however, with the series being shot in color, costs would rise enormously, and Associated British Corporation would increasingly find themselves unable to continue filming without a steady stream of revenue coming from America. Naturally, Associated British Corporation wanted the show to go primetime and become a fall season premiere on ABC. Such a nice fat twenty-six-episode order would have been difficult to resist—the ultimate feather-in-the-cap for the show and for independent television in the UK. However, a certain naïveté veiled their understanding about the strictures of American television and exactly what was required for that full season order, and it was to remain elusive for the next two years.

The truth be told, no one hems-and-haws more about programming than American television executives, and ABC were loath to put an imported show into the regular fall lineup. Thus, they dithered some more and ordered only another sixteen episodes from their British counterparts to be aired in the winter and spring of 1967 as a mid-season replacement. These episodes were filmed from September 1966 to April 1967 and delivered in time for a very successful season in both countries. Shortly after completing these episodes, production in England shut down for a six-week filming break, while the season finished airing, without any knowledge at that time how many ABC would order next or if they would order at all. These first sixteen color episodes would become the closest the show ever came to being simultaneously broadcast in both the United Kingdom and the United States.

UK FIFTH SEASON	US SECOND SEASON
13 Jan 1967—"From Venus With Love"	20 Jan 1967—"From Venus With Love"
20 Jan 1967—"The Fear Merchants"	27 Jan 1967—"The Fear Merchants"
27 Jan 1967—"Escape in Time"	3 Feb 1967—"The See-Through Man"
3 Feb 1967—"The See-Through Man"	10 Feb 1967—"Escape in Time"
10 Feb 1967—"The Bird Who Knew Too Much"	17 Feb 1967—"The Winged Avenger"
17 Feb 1967—"The Winged Avenger"	3 Mar 1967—"The Living Dead"
24 Feb 1967—"The Living Dead"	10 Mar 1967—"The Bird Who Knew Too Much"
3 Mar 1967—"The Hidden Tiger"	17 Mar 1967—"The Hidden Tiger"
10 Mar 1967—"The Correct Way to Kill"	24 Mar 1967—"The Correct Way to Kill"
17 Mar 1967—"Never, Never Say Die"	31 Mar 1967—"Never, Never Say Die"
31 Mar 1967—"Epic"	14 Apr 1967—"Epic"
7 Apr 1967—"The Superlative Seven"	21 Apr 1967—"The Superlative Seven"
14 Apr 1967—"A Funny Thing Happened on..."	28 Apr 1967—"A Funny Thing Happened on..."
21 Apr 1967—"Something Nasty in the Nursery"	5 May 1967—"Something Nasty in the Nursery"
28 Apr 1967—"The Joker"	12 May 1967—"The Joker"
5 May 1967—"Who's Who???"	19 May 1967—"Who's Who???"

When the production returned to filming in June of 1967, both Patrick Macnee and Diana Rigg were contracted for a further ten episodes. A batch of fifteen was the expected number required for another order from America, with the possibility of something longer always conceivable but frustratingly just out of reach. They began filming in earnest, but this was when Diana Rigg dropped her bombshell. She was tired of the long working hours and the short pay. She claimed she was living "the life of a mole" and "paid less than the cameraman" in quotes that received much publicity at the time. Eager to please their star-of-the moment, Associated British Corporation opened their pocketbooks and gave Rigg her raise, but she nevertheless informed them that she would not be signing another contract and would conclude her run with the program at the end of the already contracted ten episodes.

By this time, ITV had already scheduled and promoted a 1967 fall season of *The Avengers*, and when the next order of a further fifteen episodes came through from America, there was a scrambling to make sure that their rapidly approaching deadlines were met.

What transpired next is somewhat enshrouded in mystery, partly due to many of the parties wishing to avoid any libelous talk by revealing details. Suffice to say that sometime in September of 1967—while the production team were likely hard at work on "The Forget-Me-Knot"—Brian Clemens and Albert Fennell were fired from their posts as producers. The executives at ITV and Associated British Corporation had been unhappy with the over-the-top fantasy tone that the program had taken. How much the ownership changes at the company—which was merging with Associated-Rediffusion to become Thames Television—were a part of this is unknown, but it seems likely that such turmoil only added to the confusion and changing tastes in the higher echelons.

Diana Rigg was also dismissed with only eight of her contracted episodes in the can and some work completed on "The Forget-Me-Knot." They subsequently rehired John Bryce, who had previously been the producer for the final stretch of Season Two and all of Season Three, and then set off on a whirlwind effort to find Patrick Macnee's new costar. Dozens of women were auditioned and tested, with Bryce and studio executives finally settling on twenty-year-old Canadian actress Linda Thorson. How much input American executives at ABC had into this decision has been a matter of considerable debate over the past several decades, but it is generally believed that they only had a say in the last four candidates, showing their preference for Linda Thorson.

What is most important for this article however is that the completed batch of eight episodes, comprising "Return of the Cybernauts" through "Mission...Highly Improbable," aired on ITV that fall as the sixth season of *The Avengers*, partially networked. ITV did not even consider rescheduling the season probably because they hoped to load episodes on the back end as they became available. Nevertheless, the scrambling behind the scenes would prove not sufficient to produce further episodes in time to fill out this season, which would end up truncated. However, there was thought to be just enough time to deliver episodes to ABC in America for a winter season of fifteen new adventures.

Filming began anew with Tara King as Steed's new assistant—Thorson choosing her character's name based on her love of the American Civil War film *Gone with the Wind*. Bryce and his crew commenced filming with the story "Invitation to a Killing" in October 1967. This episode was originally intended to be a ninety-minute introduction to Tara King and filming took almost the entire month; next, they moved on to "Invasion of the Earthmen" in November. How much they finally completed is somewhat obscure, but it is thought that three whole episodes—or perhaps just rushes from the third—were completed by December 1967. The ITV studio executives, having seen at least "Invitation to a Killing" and "Invasion of the Earthmen" were apparently not pleased. Whatever it was about the status of these episodes that appalled them is not specifically known, though the usual reason given is a lack of wit and that typical *Avengers* 'spark.' In any case, filming was again halted.

Contrite, with deadlines looming and a heavily-truncated fall season likely leaving a bitter taste in their mouths for its brevity, Associated British Corporation asked Brian Clemens to return and save the show. Clemens agreed upon the condition that Albert Fennell also be asked to resume his post. Reinstated as co-producers, Clemens and Fennell quickly went to work, asking Diana Rigg back for a brief filming and immediately reviving "The Forget-Me-Knot" to give Mrs. Peel a farewell story. After this, they quickly completed another seven episodes by March 1968, salvaging "Invasion of the Earthmen" and "Have Guns – Will Haggle" (using footage from "Invitation to a Killing") along the way. These episodes formed the second half of a third American season along with the final eight color Diana Rigg stories that had aired on ITV in the fall of 1967. They would air in the US from January to May 1968 on ABC, just as the prior American season had done.

These charts illustrate how these episodes aired in the UK and the US.

UK SIXTH SEASON	US THIRD SEASON
28 Sep 1967—"Return of the Cybernauts"	10 Jan 1968—"Mission...Highly Improbable"
5 Oct 1967—"Death's Door"	17 Jan 1968—"The Positive Negative Man"
12 Oct 1967—"The £50,000 Breakfast"	24 Jan 1968—"You Have Just Been Murdered"
19 Oct 1967—"Dead Man's Treasure"	31 Jan 1968—"Death's Door"
26 Oct 1967—"You Have Just Been Murdered"	7 Feb 1968—"Murdersville"
3 Nov 1967—"The Positive Negative Man"	21 Feb 1968—"Return of the Cybernauts"
10 Nov 1967—"Murdersville"	28 Feb 1968—"The £50,000 Breakfast"
17 Nov 1967—"Mission...Highly Improbable"	13 Mar 1968—"Dead Man's Treasure"
	20 Mar 1968—"The Forget-Me-Knot"
	27 Mar 1968—"Invasion of the Earthmen"
	3 Apr 1968—"The Curious Case of the Countless Clues"
	10 Apr 1968—"Split!"
	24 Apr 1968—"Get-A-Way!"
	1 May 1968—"Have Gun - Will Haggle"
	8 May 1968—"Look – (stop me if you've..."

Having saved the day, the reward for Clemens and Fennell was to continue working without break until March 1969 when the final episode of the series, "Bizarre," was completed. This was necessary as the long-desired order from ABC in America had finally come through—a full order of twenty-six episodes to be aired as part of the new fall season in 1968-69.

Americans had already been introduced to Tara King (and Patrick Newell as Mother), but British viewers had not yet had the pleasure. This was to be rectified starting in the fall of 1968 as both ITV in the UK and ABC in the US were once again in relative synchronization. The ABC fall season began with "Game" on 23 Sep 1968, while the ITV season began with "The Forget-Me-Knot" two days later on 25 Sep 1968.

Finally, Britons would say their farewells to Mrs. Peel, a full year after her final episode started filming. After getting short shrift with only eight episodes the prior year, British viewers would now have a glut of thirty-three episodes and the show would air for eight months. Meanwhile, in America, the series went up against number one show ***Rowan & Martin's Laugh-In. Rowan & Martin*** would subsequently proceed to sock-it-to ***The Avengers*** in the ratings, and ITV executives would suddenly have a harsh education on the fragility of their popularity on American television. Fickle American viewers had spoken, and thus Steed and company had finally met a villain they couldn't beat.

While very popular, ***The Avengers*** was still very much a cult on American television, and its newfound primetime prominence would prove to be its undoing as it came up against a much larger cult, one that was more culturally familiar. ABC would later politely inform the television executives in England that they would require no further episodes of ***The Avengers***, and the final episode would flicker across television screens on both sides of the Atlantic—exactly one month apart.

UK SEVENTH SEASON	US FOURTH SEASON
25 Sep 1968—"The Forget-Me-Knot"	23 Sep 1968—"Game"
2 Oct 1968—"Game"	30 Sep 1968—"Super Secret Cypher Snatch"
9 Oct 1968—"Super Secret Cypher Snatch"	7 Oct 1968—"You'll Catch Your Death"
16 Oct 1968—"You'll Catch Your Death"	28 Oct 1968—"Noon Doomsday"
23 Oct 1968—"Split!"	4 Nov 1968—"Legacy of Death"
30 Oct 1968—"Whoever Shot Poor George..."	11 Nov 1968—"They Keep Killing Steed"
6 Nov 1968—"False Witness"	18 Nov 1968—"Wish You Were Here"
13 Nov 1968—"All Done With Mirrors"	25 Nov 1968—"False Witness"
20 Nov 1968—"Legacy of Death"	2 Dec 1968—"All Done With Mirrors"
27 Nov 1968—"Noon Doomsday"	9 Dec 1968—"Whoever Shot Poor George...?"
4 Dec 1968—"Look – (stop me if you've..."	16 Dec 1968—"The Rotters"
11 Dec 1968—"Have Gun - Will Haggle"	30 Dec 1968—"Killer"
18 Dec 1968—"They Keep Killing Steed"	6 Jan 1969—"My Wildest Dream"
1 Jan 1969—"The Interrogators"	20 Jan 1969—"The Interrogators"
8 Jan 1969—"The Rotters"	27 Jan 1969—"The Morning After"[17]
15 Jan 1969—"Invasion of the Earthmen"	3 Feb 1969—"Love All"
22 Jan 1969—"Killer"	10 Feb 1969—"Take Me To Your Leader"
29 Jan 1969—"The Morning After"	17 Feb 1969—"Fog"
5 Feb 1969—"The Curious Case of the Countless..."	24 Feb 1969—"Stay Tuned"
12 Feb 1969—"Wish You Were Here"	3 Mar 1969—"Who Was That Man I Saw You With?"
19 Feb 1969—"Love All"	10 Mar 1969—"Pandora"
26 Feb 1969—"Stay Tuned"	17 Mar 1969—"Homicide and Old Lace"
5 Mar 1969—"Take Me To Your Leader"	24 Mar 1969—"Thingumajig"
12 Mar 1969—"Fog"	31 Mar 1969—"Requiem"
19 Mar 1969—"Who Was That Man I Saw You...?"	14 Apr 1969—"Take-Over"
26 Mar 1969—"Homicide and Old Lace"	21 Apr 1969—"Bizarre"
2 Apr 1969—"Thingumajig"	
7 Apr 1969—"My Wildest Dream"	
16 Apr 1969—"Requiem"	
23 Apr 1969—"Take-Over"	
30 Apr 1969—"Pandora"	
14 May 1969—"Get-A-Way!"	
21 May 1969—"Bizarre"	

17 "The Morning After" was scheduled for this date but may not have been broadcast.

It was over. *The Avengers* was finished. Associated British Corporation/Thames Television could not afford to continue to produce the show—an expensive one, shot in full color on 35mm film—without guaranteed foreign sales. There was also no question of returning the program to videotape and lower production values. In any case, the show was considered tired by many, having reached a crescendo of absurdity and having run the gamut of nearly every conceivable storyline. Undoubtedly, Brian Clemens and Albert Fennell were also tired, having worked continuously for well over a year without break in order to fill orders for a season that had ultimately foundered in the United States. In the end, any ideas about continuing to produce the show were abandoned.

It was the Cornell, Martin, and Day book ***The Avengers Dossier*** that first broke this interpretation of events and proposed the concept of seven seasons for ***The Avengers***. However, their book contained the occasional contradiction. For example, in June of 1967 when their filming break ended, the production team couldn't have planned to send the first sixteen color Rigg episodes to America as part of a twenty-six-episode season if those sixteen had just finished airing on ABC in May of 1967. ***The Avengers Dossier*** mistakenly claims this to be the case, when it's far more likely that Associated British Corporation didn't know how big an order they were going to get. And it ultimately ended up being only fifteen.

Nevertheless, the logic behind the book's assertions is indisputable. When putting together a transmission-order episode guide, here are the facts we can glean from the scenario described above. (And I congratulate you for your wherewithal in staying with me this long.)

- In *both* the UK and the US, the two batches of color Diana Rigg episodes were billed and aired as separate seasons.
- Five months separated broadcast of the two batches of color Diana Rigg episodes in the UK. Even today, when the BBC breaks ***Doctor Who*** seasons in half, a five-month hiatus would likely be considered too long to be part of one season. In fact, ITV specifically billed the second batch of color Diana Rigg episodes as a separate season.
- In British television, the number of episodes frequently has *nothing to do* with what constitutes a season. British viewers (and fans of British television) will no doubt know exactly what I'm talking about. The model at the BBC for many years was to produce six episodes and then hem-and-haw for ages about whether to make any more. For example, all of ***Red Dwarf***'s history is composed of seasons of eight or fewer episodes.
- While combining the color Diana Rigg episodes together into one batch might make sense intuitively, it does not make sense historically. It is not at all a representation of how the episodes were broadcast—in either the UK or the US, or any other country on initial broadcast, for that matter.
- There were stylistic changes in between the batches of color Diana Rigg episodes. The "Mrs. Peel–We're Needed" opening scenes and the tag lines disappear. The episodes are generally toned down and more mundane on the balance with only three episodes having fantasy/science-fiction themes, the remainder being more grounded, much like a third or fourth season episode. Eccentrics became rarer and less absurd. This all points to changes in direction in between seasons, possibly Fennell and Clemens listening to the complaints of their bosses.
- If one is willing to combine two different production blocks—the first sixteen color Rigg episodes and the next eight—into one season despite being separate during production, then why not combine the first seven Tara Kings into that same batch since they were filmed with the last eight color Rigg episodes? The point is that it's logically inconsistent to divide or combine production blocks in order to fit a preconceived notion of how the episodes belong together—even when considering a production-order guide.

- If you create a transmission-order list, then everything can be sorted out based on British transmission dates, which are obtainable by finding the ITV broadcaster that aired the episodes the earliest.

These facts logically defeat the default six-season approach, which I would politely suggest continues purely based upon its simplicity of presentation and a generous portion of cultural inertia. The Dave Rogers books are still very popular and for a long time they were the only resource available to fans, and the decision to organize the episodes that way—in a *transmission-order* episode guide, I hasten to point out—could only have been an arbitrary one by Rogers, one that has since become deeply-seated in the minds of fans. Subsequent books used his material as reference and repeated his arbitrary decision. (I say all this with great respect for Rogers' contribution to research on the series.)

Some have argued that since there was a transmission gap in the first season of the series, then by the logic presented here, a transmission-order guide should have eight seasons—two seasons for Dr. Keel, in other words. Unfortunately, the reasons for that split are completely different from the reason for splitting up the Diana Rigg episodes. The twenty-four color Diana Rigg episodes were the result of two completely separate production blocks, the production having stopped to await a further order from America and instructions from their ITV executives. They didn't even know for certain if they would continue at all—the fact that Macnee and Rigg were only contracted for ten more episodes, not fifteen or sixteen, proves this.

Recording of the Keel season was complete when the Equity strike began in the fall of 1961 and when the decision was taken (under duress) by Associated British Corporation to defer their timeslot to an Associated-Rediffusion show called ***Deadline Midnight***—part of the give-and-take process among the throng of independent ITV broadcasters in the 1960s. When the last four episodes of Season One began airing in December of that year, they had already been in the can for over two months. It is highly unlikely that those episodes were intended to be part of a separate season when recorded, though ITV may have half-heartedly promoted them as 'new episodes' merely to remind viewers that the program was back. Ironically, if ***The Avengers*** had been more popular at the time, it would have never taken a backseat to another show in the first place. Nevertheless, I find the logic arguing for two Keel seasons deeply flawed. I can scarcely believe that anyone working on the show at the time would have thought of it that way.

In any case, there is a difference between intent and *actual outcome*. Some have pointed to paperwork showing that Brian Clemens intended for the color Diana Rigg episodes to be part of one whole season. Well, he might well have intended it that way, but that's not how it turned out, neither in production nor upon transmission. He was probably always planning the show with the hope that ABC in America would order a full season (24-26 episodes) for primetime and a fall premiere, but they kept ordering only 15-16 episodes instead, forcing production to stop at that number until the ratings could once again be assessed and more funds could be obtained.

One of the main points here that readers will need to digest is the fact that the show was largely being driven by demand from ABC in America from season four onwards. Since ABC only needed sixteen (or thereabouts) episodes at a time, this drove production and the way the show was aired on ITV. Despite this, for reasons of hubris or impatience, ITV chose to hurry things along and go against the grain of the production's timeline. In my opinion, they should have never have pressured the production like they did. If they had waited for a winter 1968 season to synchronize with America, just as they had done in the winter of 1967, then I wouldn't need to write this chapter at all. We would instead be talking about seven seasons but split as follows: seasons one through four just as they are; sixteen color Diana Rigg episodes for Season Five; eight color Diana Rigg and seven Linda Thorson episodes for Season Six; and finally, twenty-six color Linda Thorson episodes for Season Seven. And, frankly, it seems to me there would be no argument about it. But the fact that Season

Six was only eight episodes changes nothing because the logic behind the seven-season arrangement is the same in both scenarios.

On the other hand, I understand very well the reasons for the persistence of the six-season episode guide. In its own way, it can also be 'logical.' The points in its favor are:

- It's much easier to re-package the color Diana Rigg episodes as one unit for video releases.
- The number of episodes of the 'fifth season' in this scenario is relatively equal to the other seasons, thus making the number of episodes for syndication comparable.
- Intuitively, it just feels more comfortable. All those color Diana Riggs belong together, right? They're all in color, they're all Diana Rigg. What's the problem?
- There is admittedly some wiggle room when it comes to what we might consider a 'season.'
- If you're doing a production-order episode guide, then this is a logical way to do it—as logical as any other way, that is.

And this is the path that the corporate rights holder has chosen to take for those very reasons. So, where does this leave us?

Let me make a few predictions (and I write this with a wink!):

1. You're going to go right on saying that ***The Avengers*** has six seasons.
2. You're going to go right on combining all the color Diana Rigg episodes into one season called 'the fifth season,' and you're going to go right on saying that the Tara King episodes are 'the sixth season.'
3. The official products related to ***The Avengers***, as owned by Studio Canal, are going to go right on saying that the show has *six* seasons.
4. There are going to be more books published in the future that will insist upon the first three points above.
5. Nevertheless, *you're still going to wonder if I'm right!*

For now, however, I've decided that my book will be the exception to this predicted outcome, and it alone will go against the grain. Seven seasons, it is! Paul Cornell, Martin Day, Keith Topping...I've got your back.

EEE-URP!

SEASON SIX

8 episodes (35mm color film, ~52 min. ea.)

Regular Cast
Patrick Macnee—John Steed
Diana Rigg—Emma Peel

Producers: Albert Fennell and Brian Clemens
Executive Producer: Julian Wintle
Music: Laurie Johnson

121. **Return of the Cybernauts—w.** Philip Levene; **dir.** Robert Day; **UK tx.** 28 Sep 1967; **US tx.** 21 Feb 1968; **filmed** May-Jun 1967
122. **Death's Door—w.** Philip Levene; **dir.** Sidney Hayers; **UK tx.** 5 Oct 1967; **US tx.** 31 Jan 1968; **filmed** May-Jun 1967
123. **The £50,000 Breakfast—w.** Roger Marshall (story by R. Marshall & J. Scott); **dir.** Robert Day; **UK tx.** 12 Oct 1967; **US tx.** 28 Feb 1968; **filmed** Jun-Jul 1967
124. **Dead Man's Treasure—w.** Michael Winder; **dir.** Sidney Hayers; **UK tx.** 19 Oct 1967; **US tx.** 13 Mar 1968; **filmed** Jun-Jul 1967
125. **You Have Just Been Murdered—w.** Philip Levene; **dir.** Robert Asher; **UK tx.** 26 Oct 1967; **US tx.** 24 Jan 1968; **filmed** Jul-Aug 1967
126. **The Positive Negative Man—w.** Tony Williamson; **dir.** Robert Day; **UK tx.** 3 Nov 1967; **US tx.** 17 Jan 1968; **filmed** Jul-Aug 1967
127. **Murdersville—w.** Brian Clemens; **dir.** Robert Asher; **UK tx.** 10 Nov 1967; **US tx.** 7 Feb 1968; **filmed** Aug 1967
128. **Mission...Highly Improbable—w.** Philip Levene; **dir.** Robert Day; **UK tx.** 17 Nov 1967; **US tx.** 10 Jan 1968; **filmed** Aug-Sep 1967

SEASON NOTES

In April 1967, ABC were forced to shut down production due to uncertainty about the next order expected from America. To complicate matters even further, the show's main stars, Patrick Macnee and Diana Rigg, were both contracted to film a further ten episodes, but were left in limbo for several weeks as the Associated British Corporation considered whether to take the actors up on their options.

To contemporary readers, this may seem like fait accompli, a remedial decision, a mere formality. *The Avengers* was a hugely successful show with many fans, so why shouldn't it return? The problem, so common with British dramas in this era, was production cost, and Associated British Corporation was not the most cash-rich television production company in the game. Their bid to produce *The Avengers* at a level of production that would satisfy American broadcasters was an attempt to become more financially successful, something that ITC Entertainment and Lew Grade had already achieved with series like *The Saint, Danger Man,* and Gerry Anderson's various puppet series. This was the new game in independent television in Britain—go mid-Atlantic and conquer markets on both sides of the ocean by dramatically increasing production values. Despite Lew Grade's business having the upper hand over them for the moment, the production values on *The Avengers* were perhaps higher than any other regular show on British television at the time, but this was currently dependent on the money that was flowing in from the States. And they desperately wanted even more to flow in.

The American network ABC had dithered for two years now, constantly dangling the promised full season order like a carrot-on-a-stick, while they hemmed-and-hawed about whether the ratings were sufficient for a prime-time risk. Sadly, this was all too frequent a problem in the era; rare was it that British television was treated with the proper respect by their American counterparts. Thankfully, *The Avengers* had now been an American summer (or winter) replacement series for two seasons and had performed remarkably well. The sixteen color episodes that made up the second American season performed even better in the Nielsens than the monochrome series had despite its dead-time Friday night slot, and American ABC were happy to order another fifteen hours, and therein lay the problem.

Macnee and Rigg were both contracted for ten more episodes, not fifteen, and while Macnee was happy to sign up for more, Diana Rigg was not. She had become fatigued of the eleven- and twelve-hour days required by the role and perhaps felt an artist's calling for higher things, better roles and prestige, before she became typecast. After fighting for a raise, she informed the producers that she would not return for any more than she was contracted.

This was devastating to the production team, who then had to engage in a mad flurry of activity in order to find her replacement in time for the next order. Dozens of women were auditioned for the part, and many of them were screen-tested—notably Lyn Ashley, Diane Clare, Susan Engel, and Jane Murdoch, whose screen tests survive on mute film. We know that these tests were taking place around September 1967, so the process was largely concurrent with (or just after completion of) the filming on the latest batch of episodes. This may explain Patrick Macnee's absence from the screen tests, which took place with American actor James Maxwell as Steed. Regardless, as many have said, the rush to fill the role was detrimental to the success of the show at this critical time.

The producers had taken the layoff between seasons to reevaluate the show in light of increased criticism from the network heads at Associated British Corporation. Firstly, it was decided that the show had become too fantasy-oriented and had lost touch with its spy drama roots, once grounded in more serious and deadly espionage work, though interlaced with wit and characterized by a tongue firmly planted in cheek. In light of the changes that followed, it will be immediately obvious to viewers the difference, both substantive and superficial in this new short season.

To fit with American running times and avoid the threat of the US network making cuts to the episodes—American TV had more minutes of commercials per hour than England—Clemens and Fennell decided to drop the "Mrs. Peel—We're needed" teasers and approximately one minute from each script. Gone also were the cheeky two-liner captions that followed the title. Sadly, they also said farewell to Roger Marshall, who left over disagreements regarding his script "A Funny Thing Happened on the Way to the Station." Marshall was one of the finest screenwriters working on the show and was a major contributor from the second series onwards. His loss was thus keenly felt, especially since the tone was to return to something much more in his idiom.

On that note, despite beginning with the fantasy-oriented "Return of the Cybernauts," which is more akin to "Who's Who???" in tone and its liberal interpretation of science, the stories of Season Six are notably more realist and humorless than their predecessors. And indeed, the three episodes that truly have some fantasy element are nowhere as flamboyant in execution as the fifth season. Make no mistake, they're excellent stories all, just played considerably straighter, in a style more comparative to the third season than the fifth.

Nevertheless, something very surprising happened behind the scenes. It was then in September of 1967—shortly before the heavily promoted return of the series and the season premiere of the sixth season—that production of the ninth episode "The Forget-Me-Knot" was halted. A tenth, probably "Split!," was cancelled. Diana Rigg was dismissed. Since she didn't want to do the show any longer, they deemed that her services were longer needed and they would soon have her replacement. She left having filmed only eight of the ten episodes remaining in her contract, with the ninth only partially complete.

Perhaps even more shockingly, with only eight episodes in the can for the next American order, Albert Fennell and Brian Clemens—whose guiding light had produced the dramatic upswing in the show's production values and popularity during seasons four and five—were moved off the show. This can only be described as a major shakedown, the likes of which are rarely seen in an already successful series. Season Three's John Bryce was installed as producer, and later that October, the press and public were introduced to Rigg's replacement—twenty-year-old Linda Thorson.

And, from here, Bryce, Thorson and the rest of the production team would attempt to complete the next batch of episodes for the required American order. To their great surprise, and that of their bosses, this would prove much more complicated than previously thought. These moves would not be in time in order to fill out an autumn 1967 season on ITV, which ended up truncated at only eight episodes before the show once again went off the air. There was still plenty of time to produce another seven episodes before American television ran out of the eight already produced. Nevertheless, substantial challenges still awaited the show.

ICONIC TITLES

The title sequence for this season is identical to the previous season. However, the taglines were dropped.

CHAMPAGNE, CAR, CLOTHES, AND CANINES

Diana Rigg's clothes change notably in this season. For one thing, all those rollneck jumpers, worn under practically everything, are out, replaced with softer blouses and structured jackets and coats. The hem-lines on her skirt generally go from knee-length to mini, and there are fewer Emmapeelers and catsuits. It seems that Ms. Rigg was settling into what she liked to wear most. Patrick Macnee does not debut very many new outfits, but those he does bring into his wardrobe are more casual-wear and two-piece suits rather than three-piece. Also, there are fewer tiepins and other accessories. The bowlers and brollies, however, remain. In general, they appear to be simplifying his wardrobe. Champagne flows in more of a trickle. And Steed reveals why he no longer has any dogs.

Fashion designer for Diana Rigg: Alun Hughes
Fashion designer for Patrick Macnee: Pierre Cardin

Best Dressed: "Return of the Cybernauts"
Worst Dressed: "Dead Man's Treasure"

AVENGERS CARS

JOHN STEED

1930 Bentley Speed Six (RX 6180) in "Return of the Cybernauts," "Death's Door," "The £50,000 Breakfast," and "You Have Just Been Murdered."
1927 Bentley 3 Litre (YT 3942)—racing green—in "The Positive Negative Man" and "Mission… Highly Improbable."

EMMA PEEL

1967 Lotus Elan S3 Convertible (SJH 499D)—"powder blue" or a steely-gray—in "Return of the Cybernauts," "Death's Door," "You Have Just Been Murdered," "The Positive Negative Man," "Murdersville," and "Mission…Highly Improbable."

THE MOST FANTASTIC EPISODES OF THE SEASON

1. "The Positive Negative Man"
2. "Return of the Cybernauts"
3. "Mission…Highly Improbable"
4. "Dead Man's Treasure"
5. "The £50,000 Breakfast"

121 (6.2.1) RETURN OF THE CYBERNAUTS

Steed pulls some strings — Emma becomes a puppet
Written by Philip Levene
Directed by Robert Day

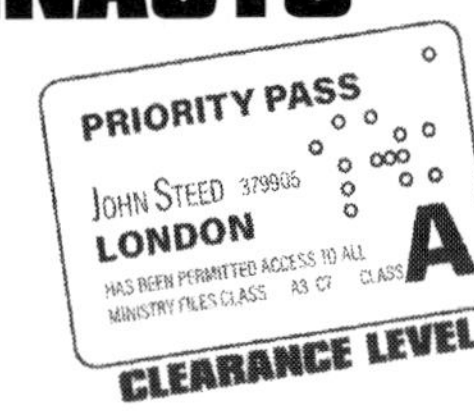

GUEST CAST

Peter Cushing (Paul Beresford), Frederick Jaeger (Benson), Charles Tingwell (Dr. Neville), Fulton Mackay (Professor Chadwick), Roger Hammond (Dr. Russell), Anthony Dutton (Dr. Garnett), Noel Coleman (Conroy), Aimi MacDonald (Rosie), Redmond Philips (Hunt), Terry Richards (Cybernaut)

PRE-TITLE/TEASER

An unseen person shuffles through several electronic identity cards, all of which bear different photos, including photos of Steed and Emma, until finally settling on the card of an imminent scientist. Then, after inserting it into a machine, the machine clicks and whirs, and a Cybernaut crashes into a country mansion and knocks the targeted scientist unconscious in a dramatic kidnapping.

SYNOPSIS

Steed and Mrs. Peel have become friends with wealthy art collector Paul Beresford. Unknown to them, Beresford is the brother of the late Dr. Armstrong, infamous Cybernaut inventor. Beresford is hellbent on vengeance for Steed and Emma. While simultaneously courting their friendship, Beresford continues to wreak havoc with the Cybernauts until he is ready to enact his revenge...

REVIEW

Transparently, "Return of the Cybernauts" is a tip of the fedora to Hammer's gothic horror films, especially the Frankenstein and Mummy movies. The comparisons had been made extensively since the airing of "The Cybernauts" nearly two years earlier. They were emphasized once again in "Never, Never Say Die" with Christopher Lee as a different sort of robot. This time around, as if to even more boldly underscore those connections, the production team secured the services of the highest profile Hammer film star of the day—Peter Cushing.

Though director Robert Day never directed a Hammer film—he was primarily known for directing the sixties cycle of Tarzan films—he was no stranger to horror, having directed a few in the late 1950s including ***Corridors of Blood*** starring Christopher Lee. Despite this, given Hammer films being ubiquitous in England at the time, it is likely that there was at least some influence from their style. Pursuant to this, though the pre-title is likely intended to reference the opening of its predecessor "The Cybernauts," it also happens to be very structurally similar to a scene in ***The Curse of the Mummy's Tomb***, in which the mummy crashes into an office with a comparatively devastating effect. It's a terrible film only noteworthy for this moment direction-wise. I struggle to see why Day would have referenced it, but my mind nevertheless instantly recalls the moment. It may be my fault, not his.

Likewise, seeing Cushing as Beresford struggle against the crushing grip of a Cybernaut in the episode's climax is unavoidably reminiscent of John Banning (also played by Cushing) struggling in the deadly grip of the mummy in Hammer's ***The Mummy*** from 1959. Whether these scenes are referenced intentionally or subconsciously is something we'll probably never know, but they might exemplify the extent to which Hammer studios impacted the collective British psyche in the 1950s and 60s.

What matters is that Cushing is sublime as Beresford, essentially playing the role with the same malignancy of Dr. Frankenstein in *The Curse of Frankenstein*, ignoring morality ruthlessly in pursuit of his goals. Alternately exuding gentrified charm and a scornful disregard for human life, he simultaneously courts the friendship of Steed and romances Emma while plotting to make both of them suffer.

Observing the demonstration of the mind-control device, he is malevolently delighted to control another human being like a puppet. He then callously kills the scientist simply to test the device. Such as the man is, dispensing with the help is a small price to pay for a brief moment of perverse pleasure. As he relishes his victory over Mrs. Peel in the end, he is pure evil, leering at her with a combination of disdain and lasciviousness. It is a chilling performance—the type for which he was well known. Admittedly, he is one-dimensional, being obsessed only with revenge, but what a dimension!

In a turn not too dissimilar from "The Winged Avenger" and a reversal from its Cybernaut predecessor, "Return of the Cybernauts" wastes no time in revealing the robotic monsters and the villain controlling them. This is probably because it was unlikely that viewers familiar with their first appearance wouldn't catch on to the smashed doors and the snapped necks of the victims. Besides, we ought to know that Peter Cushing is up to something anyway. However, the important point is that Steed and Emma don't know, and they being kept in the dark is the source of the tension in this hour of television. The twist here is that they're metaphorically sleeping with the enemy, giving Steed a chance to demonstrate some jealousy over Emma's increasingly cozy relationship with Beresford. In the meantime, we get some of the most enduring images of sixties television as the Cybernauts induce car stoppages more effective than a 21st century London wheel clamp and give you a convertible whether you want it or not!

The lone eccentric is Rosie, who is actually more of a kooky and politically incorrect character than an eccentric. She is hysterical however in a 1960s sort of way that may never exist again. Enjoy her, cherish her. She is a lost breed like the Braque Dupuy, crystalline and frozen in time on celluloid, forever 1967. Feminists, leave her alone. I love you too, but let Rosie live. No one that funny should be put out to pasture just yet.

It's a good thing that we have lots of action and special effects and characters like Rosie because otherwise this is a rather straightforward revenge story, and the science is admittedly pure fantasy. The scientists are magicians not technicians. Like the brain-swapping done with aluminum space helmets descending from the ceiling on stovepipes when the series left off almost five months earlier, there are a lot of questions as to how an ostensibly ordinary wristwatch (with rather unimpressive transistors in it) could possibly control all the complexities of the human body. But let us not contemplate how a simple remote control, that looks like it could barely change the channels on your television set, may be used to control Mrs. Peel as she drives a car. Let's just have fun.

This is an episode which may fall apart if perused too carefully, distracting us from the pure delight of its superficial trappings. Those trappings may be like icing drenched upon a pound cake, but, my God, what sweetness! If I may confess enthusiastically, this is one of my all-time favorites of the series. The Cybernauts were one of the most popular villains of *The Avengers*, and they were one of only two villains to return.

CHAMPAGNE, CARS, CLOTHES, AND CANINES

Steed begins the episode by donning his deep-blue tuxedo and Mrs. Peel showcases a stunning dark-green velvet evening dress with long sleeves and a mini-skirt. There are three bright white buttons on the cuffs. This is one of her more dramatic outfits and it's a bit of a pity that it absorbs so much light and the contrast on the Blu-ray is crushed out quite a bit in the shadows, making it read poorly. Nevertheless, its beauty flashes forward in several shots. In their trip back to Beresford's in the Bentley Speed Six, Steed debuts a new black overcoat, and then later a brown sports coat with beige trousers. The pale gray suit with triangular pockets returns with a gold tie while Mrs. Peel debuts a new camel coat with a wide collar and five buttons down the left breast. As usual, the bottom of the coat is about level with the skirt hem and also A-line giving it some flow when she turns. Later, she debuts another outfit: a dark-wine colored dress with a mini-skirt and a black velvet coat in the same pattern as her previous green dress. She returns to green (and white) to tend to Steed. It's another Emmapeeler catsuit, though with a collar and white trim, piping, false belt, and shoulder panels, and matching white boots. This is followed by a white silk embroidered minidress with a concentric circle pattern, buttoned up over the left breast with round pearl buttons.

This brings us to perhaps Mrs. Peel's most memorable outfit to debut this episode: a hot-pink sleeveless minidress worn with an orange-red woolen coat with a coarse weave and plaid pattern; much like her outfit in "Castle De'Ath" the plaid of the skirt of the coat and the upper portion are in contrasting orientations. The look is finished off with a wide dark-red belt and pink and gold shoes. In the tag scene her striped action dress returns.

Since I adore her kooky character, I'll describe Aimi MacDonald's outfit. It's a tightly-fitted orange-striped white string vest with orange trim paired with an orange mini-skirt, just as sixties as her.

Mrs. Peel's Lotus also makes an appearance as she drives herself to Beresford's under his mental control.

On an art note, Michael Gough was required to return to Elstree on 4 May 1967 to have a mold made of his head for the faux bronze bust of his likeness. The bust was made from plaster-of-Paris and painted to look like bronze.

TAG SCENE

Steed is attempting to fix Emma's toaster. He completes his work, claiming it will "work as it's never done before." However, it instead launches "into orbit" leaving the burned toast behind. Emma quips, "shall I butter them or preserve them for posterity?"

QUOTES

"He's charming, witty and intelligent. There's nothing to dislike about him, is there?" "No, but if I try hard enough, I'm sure I'll find something."
"You are men of ideas. Produce me an idea, a new idea, a rhapsody of suffering."
"...if you think I'm that kind of a girl, well, you're absolutely right. He didn't take me up on it though, kept on asking me for more fruitcake. He's so kinky!"
"I love men with big shoulders. They really...SEND ME!"
"I could tell I'd inflamed him. His eyes were all misty with desire."
"Well, this ice should—" "—should be in a glass with a large whiskey wrapped around it."

122 (6.1.2) DEATH'S DOOR

Steed relives a nightmare — Emma sees daylight
Written by Philip Levene
Directed by Sidney Hayers

GUEST CAST

Clifford Evans (Boyd), William Lucas (Stapley), Allan Cuthbertson (Lord Melford), Marne Maitland (Becker), Paul Dawkins (Dr. Evans), Michel Faure (Pavret), Peter Thomas (Saunders), William Lyon Brown (Dalby), Terry Yorke (Haynes), Terry Maidment (Jepson)

PRE-TITLE/TEASER

A flock of British civil servants arrive for an auspicious meeting surrounded by a flurry of photojournalists and the glare of their flashbulbs. However, the political star of the moment balks as he approaches the conference room. He turns in fear and hurriedly strides out of the room.

SYNOPSIS

There is a European Union conference about to start, but someone is invading the dreams of the British delegates in order to undermine their self-esteem. When two delegates attempt to enter but break down and run, Steed and Emma must find the culprits and put an end to their scheme before all the attendees take flight from the conference…

REVIEW

There's something good in almost every episode of *The Avengers*. As I've pointed out before, this is because (particularly in this era) there is a natural high-style and flourish to the stories, an auteur sophistication that makes the mundane more exciting. Nevertheless, in keeping with the more low-key approach in this new season, this particular installment is more akin to the fourth season or perhaps even the third in tone and pace. Normally, this would be fine by me as I adore those seasons, but the new and casual viewer might find this episode lacking in eccentrics, action and witticisms. This is likely something of a death knell for any episode of *The Avengers*. In short, "Death's Door" falls backwards in style too much, and resultingly moves as slowly as the slowest videotaped episodes from seasons one through three. Not to mention the fact that Steed and Emma are performing a bizarrely out-of-character bureaucratic function in this narrative—managing a conference for a series of delegates who also happen to be having prophetic dreams.

Fortunately, the basic concept behind the story is an intriguing and thoughtful one, and this does help to sustain the hour. The dreams of the delegates are being manipulated—or perhaps 'manufactured' is a better word—so as to appear to predict future events which are then contrived by enemy agents. Since the dreams are always terminated by a fatal accident, the delegates are sent fleeing from the conference in terror lest such accidents actually occur. The dream sequences are superbly executed, a clear example of the program choosing to underscore traits for which it is well known. Much is made of *Avengers* surrealism, and this episode takes its cue from the master himself, Salvador Dali.

Despite this, I find myself with little else to say about "Death's Door." It is essentially all-style-no-substance in the most literal fashion, having only the surrealistic dream sequences as a major point of interest, and, alas, the delegates cannot dream continuously. The generic villains are also armed with nearly fatal blandness. There is however one particularly exciting scene on a shooting range with Steed becoming Becker's new target.

The episode has its good points, but if it had been part of the third season it might have stood out a little more. Here, it is sustained mostly by its superior production standards. Oddly, it possesses a prophetic quality of its own, a harbinger of things to come, as it possesses a tone that seems to belong more to the seventh season of the series despite the presence of Diana Rigg to contradict this.

EPISODE NOTES

Peter Thomas (from "Small Game for Big Hunters") returns in another silent role, that of a chauffeur. He does get more screentime though.

CHAMPAGNE, CARS, CLOTHES, AND… CAMERAS!

This episode starts out with one of the less impressive Mrs. Peel debuts: a fawn-colored long-sleeved minidress with cream shoulder panels, fastened at the collar with one button, and a cream belt. It comes across as quite bland, and it's not a personal favorite. Fortunately, the next outfit is a substantial step up—a soft orange structured jacket with a collar and diagonal ribs leading to a single button at mid-chest. She pairs it with a matching skirt and appears to be wearing a soft orange blouse or shirt underneath.

Steed's Bentley features more prominently than usual and is almost the subject of an accident along a country road when its brakes fail. Steed also rides in a 1964 Daimler 4.5 Litre Limousine (AUV 719B).

Mrs. Peels debuts another outfit, a cream-colored high-collar, sleeveless blouse with light-green plaid, paired with a cerulean-blue skirt. Later, over the blouse and skirt, she wears a matching cerulean coat with two plaid cream belts and plaid shoulder panels under the wide collar. Not one of the most successful outfits, in my opinion, but the coat improves it. (It also appears green during the limousine ride and gets a dose of muddy water from a speeding car.) Steed retreats to relative safety by returning to his pinstriped charcoal suit with a muted gray-blue tie and handkerchief and later his brown tartan blazer with a dark-red cravat and gold stickpin. This last one is probably his most elegant iteration of the outfit yet, and it's easy to see why it was a Macnee favorite. He wore it in some form or other in twelve episodes.

Mrs. Peel debuts another catsuit in a soft jersey fabric with white lacings up the front and along the sleeves. This is very similar to a blue and white catsuit she wore in "Something Nasty in the Nursery." After dispatching the criminals in the finale, she relaxes in the tag scene wearing a blue, green, dark-red, and purple long-sleeved silk blouse and palazzo pants in a very hip 1960s stained glass pattern. Her Lotus Elan also appears briefly.

With the press' flash bulbs popping everywhere, this is easily the most camera-heavy episode yet, and there are way too many cameras to identify properly, but there are multiple press cameras scattered throughout several scenes: a Graflex Speed Graphic 4x5, a couple of MPP Micropress cameras (a British company making cameras from Graflex parts), a Rolleiflex 3.5 twin lens reflex (featuring very prominently in one shot), a MamiyaFlex TLR, a Mamiya C22 TLR, and a Yashica 635 TLR (which was capable of shooting both 120 and 35mm film). Later, there are a Bolex H16 16mm cine camera and a couple of unidentified 35mm SLR stills cameras.

TAG SCENE

Steed lies asleep in his study as Emma tries to awake him. When he wakes up, he recounts his dream of being in a harem. But when Emma reveals that her dream is for Steed to take her to the theatre, it turns out he's already bought the tickets.

QUOTES

"There was that horoscope of mine. Told me I'd collide with a tall dark stranger." "And?" "I ran into the back of your car, remember?"

"I wonder, Mr. Steed, would you oblige me and set up a new target?"

"Your nightmare was a reality, but they made you believe it was a dream. Then, it was easy enough to make the dream come true."

"I'm afraid that broke his dream."

123 (6.4.3) THE £50,000 BREAKFAST

Steed dabbles in Tycoonery — Emma in Chicanery
Written by Roger Marshall
(based on a story by Roger Marshall and Jeremy Scott)
Directed by Robert Day

GUEST CAST

Cecil Parker (Glover), Yolande Turner (Miss Pegram), David Langton (Sir James Arnall), Pauline Delany (Mrs. Rhodes), Anneke Wills (Judy), Cardew Robinson (Minister), Eric Woofe (1st Assistant), Philippe Monnet (2nd Assistant), Richard Curnock (Rhodes), Jon Laurimore (Security Man), Richard Owens (Mechanic), Michael Rothwell (Kennel Man), Yole Marinelli (Jerezina), Christopher Greatorex (1st Doctor), Nigel Lambert (2nd Doctor)

PRE-TITLE/TEASER

A man drives a 1961 Austin A55 Cambridge 'Countryman' Mark II (257 BLM) along a country road while talking to an unseen person in the passenger seat named Charlie. When a farm vehicle causes the driver to crash into a hay bale, the passenger is revealed to be a ventriloquist's dummy, and when the still unconscious driver is examined at the hospital, he is found to have many diamonds in his stomach.

SYNOPSIS

After a man named Rhodes is taken to a hospital for injuries suffered in a car crash and £50,000 in diamonds is found in his stomach, Steed and Mrs. Peel investigate Rhodes' ventriloquist shop and then the Litoff organization. However, a Miss Pegram is ostensibly running the show, and Mr. Litoff is only heard over an intercom. After Mrs. Rhodes attempts to blackmail Miss Pegram and is killed, the body of Mr. Litoff is found in the grave of his own dog Bellhound. It then becomes clear that a lot more than £50,000 is at stake...

REVIEW

This is the third and final remake of a Cathy Gale era episode (not counting the quasi-remake of "Dressed to Kill"). All three of these stories were superb and well worth re-exploring given the immensely improved production standards afforded them. Although "The Correct Way to Kill" and "The Joker" were both enhanced enormously by the high-quality production alone, the writing was not changed or improved significantly. On the other hand, "The £50,000 Breakfast" experiences some notable script restructuring, possibly designed in part to take advantage of the increased amount of location filming and certainly to introduce more of swinging sixties London to the bigger picture. Filmed during the summer of 1967, which undoubtedly allowed the film crew to get out more often in the fine weather, I will note that the location filming is of especially high-quality. In general, during this season, location filming becomes stronger and more realist (you wouldn't have likely seen a junkyard and its mechanic in greasy overalls during the fifth season), and it depicts a London that is less abandoned, more populated, busier. Although the excellent pre-title shows us a minor car accident on a country road, the rest of the story is considerably more urban...and indeed urbane. The theme is more James Bond in tone.

Having said this, the reality is that all of this extra reality is something of a come-down from the extravagance of the prior season. True, the third season's stories were considerably less surreal and more grounded in mundane spy work than was Season Five, and that was indeed an excellent season, but I can't help but think that the producers were overdoing it a bit with the sixth. Viewers would likely have noticed the shift in tone right away and perhaps missed the over-the-top ***Batman*** references of the prior season.

Coming full circle, I'm quite in awe of the writing in the Cathy Gale era. The third season was in fact the one that crystallized the hip new style, one that depicted a liberated female martial arts expert fighting diabolical masterminds with her acidic Chelsea wit while drenched in the jazz chops of Johnny Dankworth. This story maintains that structure for the most part though it is a little light on wit and eccentrics, and this is largely true of this entire season. Fortunately, there is more extravagance to come.

Some changes from the original story are Frederick Jaeger's Getz being replaced by Miss Pegram, played by Yolande Turner as a liberated female running the show at a major investments firm. Rhodes (the lone eccentric that carries on conversations with his ventriloquist dummy) now has a shop full of them (the dummies, that is), and the beginning of the narrative is pushed back to before his auto accident, as opposed to "Death of a Great Dane" which begins with the character already in hospital. There's a very nicely directed scene in the ventriloquist shop with the camera slowly panning over numerous dummies before settling on the faces of the masked killers.

CHAMPAGNE, CARS, CLOTHES, AND CANINES

Steed drives his green Bentley Speed Six carrying Mrs. Peel directly into view, and she's wearing a matching green outfit. It's a heavy-woven woolen coat in an oversized herringbone pattern over a dark-green sundress in the same cut as the pink one in "Return of the Cybernauts." The outfit is completed with pale-yellow stockings and yellow and green shoes. Steed's navy three-piece suit returns for the first time since "The Fear Merchants." This would be its last appearance. The only new outfit Steed debuts is a very casual one: black trousers and a dark-green polo shirt.

Mrs. Peel, on the other hand, debuts four more outfits in this episode. Starting with a sleeveless white dress in a plaid pattern and a belt. Again, like other outfits in this collection, the plaid patterns are oriented in contrasting patterns between the dress and the belt, and it is later worn with a tan coat in much the same cut as the fawn and tan outfit worn in "Death's Door." This is followed by a pink woolen coat fastened with two large buttons at the breast with a wide dark-red belt (probably worn with a matching blouse or jumper and a skirt, though the outfit is never seen at full length except at a distance); a gray jacket and tweed flat cap with a white blouse, tan jodhpurs, and black riding boots; and, finally, a very simple and casual orange long-sleeved dress. Her black catsuit with silver trim appears again as does Steed's deep-blue tuxedo.

Dogs have a significant role in this episode, but just like "Death of a Great Dane," they are not Steed's, and unlike "Death of a Great Dane," they are not Great Danes, but Borzois—a Russian wolfhound breed. The surviving dogs have black and white coats, but one has a smidge of reddish-brown about the face whereas the other does not. Steed refers to having a similar dog once, but remarks that they need "an awful lot of exercise." He later comments that he'd prefer to not have dogs "either in my domain or upon my neckties," thus explaining why he no longer keeps one as a pet. Perhaps spy work made it too demanding to keep up with a dog; after all, he was always trying to get Dr. Keel to take care of Puppy.

Lots of smoking, drinking, and drug use in one scene—the smoke is literally hanging in the air—but no champagne. Mrs. Peel's Lotus does not appear.

TAG SCENE

Emma reveals that she has rescued the villains' dogs and then negotiates with Steed to keep them by offering him a gift—a necktie adorned with a drawing of a dog. Steed responds that because he's an Englishman, he's a dog lover, but he prefers "not to have dogs either in my domain or upon my necktie." (Now, we finally know why he got rid of his prior dogs.)

QUOTES

"Oh well, shall we rewind it, or go on to Popeye?"
"He obviously inherited the talent, or..." "Or what?" "He likes rich food."
"It's the power that excites me. I want to be ill-mannered, and rude and uncouth, and order people about, especially women. I look forward to being excessively rude to a considerable number of handsome women!"

124 (6.3.4) DEAD MAN'S TREASURE

Steed rallies around — Emma drives for her life
Written by Michael Winder
Directed by Sidney Hayers

GUEST CAST

Norman Bowler (Mike), Valerie Van Ost (Penny), Edwin Richfield (Alex), Neil McCarthy (Carl), Arthur Lowe (Benstead), Ivor Dean (Bates), Rio Fanning (Danvers), Penny Bird (Miss Peabody), Gerry Crampton (1st Guest), Peter J. Elliott (2nd Guest)

PRE-TITLE/TEASER

A car chase is in progress along a country road. The first driver escapes his pursuers and makes his way to a country estate. Wounded and bleeding, he breaks in to an office and fills out an invitation to John Steed, leaving it stained with his bloody fingerprints. He then returns to his car and rejoins the chase, with his pursuers unaware of what he's done.

SYNOPSIS

A dying agent hides secret documents in a treasure chest containing the bounty for a road race and treasure hunt. After the sponsor of the race is killed by enemy agents for not revealing the location of the treasure, Steed and Emma must complete the course and find the secret papers before the enemy does...

REVIEW

"Dead Man's Treasure" is a delightful episode in all regards. After establishing that top secret spy information is stored in a box intended as the prize for a rally, the race through the English countryside becomes a loose structure for this episode. Though it has barely an ounce of plot, this is more than made up for by the fun of the rally as the two sets of opposing agents search for clues to the box's location and subvert their opponents' progress with all kinds of dirty tricks. This gives the production ample opportunities for location filming, all of which is beautiful, let down slightly by rear-screen projection that at times is rather obvious.

The motivation of three villains is never fully explained. I'm assuming it's not the thousand guineas they're after, thus they must want the spy information that Danvers put in the box, just like Steed and Emma, but we are never privy to the specifics or what the information entails, and this leaves the motivation as lightweight as possible. Thus, the whole of the narrative is driven by the McGuffin of the mysterious red box.

Typically, the wit suffers when Steed and Emma are kept apart, but their pairing with prominent co-stars makes up for it. Valerie Van Ost is great and fortuitously useful as Steed's companion for the day, Black Fiancée Penny. All of her fiancés (too many to count) have died in a bizarre series of fatal accidents. Despite these apparent tragedies, she inexplicably manages to remain a bubblehead-ed sixties blond and as innocent and carefree as ever. This prompts many witty lines as she gives the rundown on each of her deceased lovers. (Shades of Maggie O'Connell in ***Northern Exposure***.) Emma's partner Mike engages less well on the humor side but still manages to distinguish himself as a mischievously ruthless driver. And the twist of his being a villain distinguishes him even more.

Racing eccentric Benstead's racing simulator is a worthy idea for the era that would largely precede video games and other commercial simulators. The twist of delivering an electric shock to the participant would later be used in the James Bond film, ***Never Say Never Again***. Nevertheless, I am mildly bothered by the fact that there would even be a fatal voltage available. I mean, if you were building such a machine, why would you even allow for the possibility? When Emma gets to the final clue first, we are led to a shocking climax as she is forced to play the simulator game with the voltage at full power. She doesn't even shed a single bead of sweat. That's our girl! It's an intense moment as the race for her life is intercut with Penny haplessly futzing up the controls and forcing Emma to drive in reverse. Thus, create tension, increase it, increase it some more, add a complication and increase it until the audience can barely stand it, and then finally relieve it. Steed gives her a warm kiss on the cheek when it's over. We all should.

This episode also contains the first conspicuous example of blood being used in the series, appearing in copious amounts on both an invitation and the wall of Steed's apartment—another sign of the pivot towards more realism in the series. The tag scene is likely the silliest in the series' history. Then again, it's not the first time Emma has worn a mustache in the program.

CHAMPAGNE, CARS, CLOTHES, AND CANINES

The episode proper begins right away with champagne, as Mrs. Peel brings over a bottle for Steed. There are no fashion debuts for Mrs. Peel in this episode, and Steed premieres only one outfit: a deep-purple silk dressing gown with dark-purple spots. Mrs. Peel's white silk embroidered mini-dress (from "Return of the Cybernauts") appears again, but the main outfit she wears throughout the car chase is her tan coat, tan trousers, and green-and-blue scarf from "Return of the Cybernauts." She also wears an intriguing watch with an octagonal dial. Steed's primary outfit is the charcoal three-piece chalk-striped suit with a white shirt and silvery-gray knit tie, naturally with his gray bowler. But he seldom wears the latter—naturally because of wind risk.

Given that it's a chase, this episode is all about cars, not fashion. Steed naturally drives a vintage car, but it's not the Bentley Speed Six that he's been driving all season, instead it's the 1927 Bentley 3 Litre which hasn't been seen since "How to Succeed.... At Murder" (turns out it's green also). Sadly, the windscreen gets smashed. Mrs. Peel runs the race with her partner, Major Mike Colbourne, in a burgundy 1966 Mercedes-Benz 250 SE Cabriolet (LUC 507D). The villains, played by Edwin Richfield and Neil McCarthy, pursue their quarry in a 1961 Jaguar E-Type Open Two-Seater (648 CYV).

The racing car simulator is a Lotus Formula Junior Racing Simulator, naturally on loan from Lotus for promotional purposes, though I doubt that the very clunky controls used by the cast on set have anything to do with the functioning of it.[1]

Coming full circle, the episode ends with a "consolation prize" in the form of another bottle of champagne, thus repaying Mrs. Peel for her earlier gift.

---

1 The idea of the car simulator producing electric shocks when the driver makes a mistake would later be copied in the James Bond film *Never Say Never Again*, in which "Domination," a nuclear war videogame designed by Largo, produces electric shocks whenever the player receives a significant loss to their territory.

TAG SCENE

Emma visits Steed at his flat where he demonstrates his new and exceptionally powerful (and exceptionally loud) electric shaver. Intrigued by the fact that the shaver has a 'reverse' setting, Emma tries it out and accidentally gives herself a handlebar mustache.

QUOTES

"Perhaps I'm intruding?" *(hands Steed a bottle of champagne)* "You're not intruding."
"Rattle of ambassadorial decoration, the drone of speeches—" "—all proceeding at the pace of an infirm, gravely debilitated, very old snail."
"What a beauty!" "Oh, I do agree." "Marvelous chassis." "Well, I wouldn't be quite so bold as to say that, but..." "Her suspension is pretty complex too." "Eh?"
"You're right. Let's just stay good friends."
"Five thousand shaves to the gallon. One million whisker service only once a year. Fast down the straights, nippy 'round the curves. Four forward speeds and reverse."

125 (6.5.5) YOU HAVE JUST BEEN MURDERED

Steed chases a million — Emma walks off with it
Written by Philip Levene
Directed by Robert Asher

GUEST CAST

Barrie Ingham (Unwin), Robert Flemyng (Lord Maxted), George Murcell (Needle), Leslie French (Rathbone), Geoffrey Chater (Jarvis), Simon Oates (Skelton), Clifford Cox (Chalmers), John Baker (Hallam), Les Crawford (Morgan), Frank Maher (Nicholls), Peter J. Elliott (Williams)

PRE-TITLE/TEASER

A middle-aged man enters an office at night. A tall, blond invader strides into the room, threatening him with a gun. The first man bargains for his life offering money and possessions. Silently, the blond man pulls the trigger anyway, but the gun doesn't fire. It's empty. The intruder exits, but not before leaving a card that reads: "You have just been murdered"

SYNOPSIS

Millionaires are enduring staged 'murders' as a means of blackmail by a criminal organization. They are only threatened with actual death, but the would-be deceased are coerced into giving up a million pounds each to avoid the next murder attempt becoming real. Steed attempts to help, but the men are too frightened to talk. Eventually, Emma tracks the crooks down by following the final case of money as it is delivered. Unfortunately, Steed doesn't know that finding these villains is like looking for a needle in a haystack, and Emma is actually carrying a bomb...

REVIEW

Although the central plot premise has been tried in a number of sixties and seventies TV series, it has a typical original *Avengers* style twist to it that makes the somewhat tired blackmail plot sing in a way that it couldn't elsewhere. "You Have Just Been Murdered" is a bit repetitive in some regards—the narrative being composed of various faux murders relentlessly interspersed with actual ones—but the murders at least incorporate a variety of styles, sustaining the viewers' interest.

The villains have a sense of humor—whereas they usually just have an eccentric nature—and it's quite refreshing. George Murcell as Needle is a slimy sort, a type that manages to be greasy, sleazy and slick all at the same time. He cracks jokes and continuously smokes an odious cigar. A throwback to Mr. Teddy Bear from Season Two, he is hardly the usual eccentric or sophisticated megalomaniacal mastermind of prior filmed seasons. But then this is Mafia-style blackmail. Needle exhibits dry wit with his joke about being both literally and figuratively "a needle in a haystack." While something of a sophomoric joke, hearing Emma finish his line while actually in a giant 'haystack' is still amusing. It's just the kind of humor that *The Avengers* manages to get away with on a fairly regular basis, its classiness counter-balancing the occasional cartoonish joke. For his part, Simon Oates is stalwart and steely-eyed as the silent Skelton, arrogantly flicking a card in the direction of his would-be victim when his task is completed.

This episode has some of the very best fight scenes in the series. Emma is attacked with a scythe by Nicholls in an action scene that alternates between silly and deadly serious. In the end, Mrs. Peel reaps the harvest rather than Nicholls, who instead dies with the scythe in his back. She later subdues another man in scuba gear as he attempts to recover the blackmail money in a river.

Essentially, this is a strong script in the style of the Cathy Gale era, excellently written while more serious and mundane, but the direction is also slightly pedestrian and straightforward as Robert Asher seems merely focused on getting the job done without much flourish. The episode's greatest weakness, however, might be that Steed and Emma could have been almost any two generic secret agents investigating, what with the surrealism, witticisms and eccentrics toned down or nearly eliminated. On this basis, it becomes hard to understand why Fennell and Clemens were fired and replaced with John Bryce (the month before this episode debuted to British audiences), considering that they had already moved in the direction desired by the ITV executives. This dispute regarding artistic vision was quickly remedied by the successive season, but by then the dynamic tried-and-true partnership of Steed and Emma was no more, forcing everyone to start over just when the show was required to be at the top of its game.

I'm particularly enamored of the tag scene in this episode. Steed counts up 999,999 half-pennies but needs one half-penny from Emma to become a "half-penny millionaire." According to my knowledge of pre-decimalization British money, that would be about £2,083 and some change. Well, it's enough for a few more bottles of champagne anyway.

EPISODE NOTES

There is visible blood on the scythe. The cash amount is represented as £1000,000, which I assume means one million albeit with a missing comma.

CHAMPAGNE, CARS, CLOTHES, AND CANINES

Mrs. Peel debuts a very elegant white A-line minidress with a matching white coat in crepe and lined with white feathers about the shoulders and a faux belt with a silver buckle. The outfit is completed with silver shoes. When the minidress underneath the coat is revealed at the cocktail party (plenty of champagne and very old sherry here), it is a dramatic crocheted weave in a chevron pattern. One of Ms. Rigg's most stunning outfits, and yet seldom commented on. The direction of her fashions seems to be increasingly more conservative and sophisticated rather than pop art and hipster, but there are still elements of simplicity in many of her garments and there is always a lack of pretention.

She would debut three more outfits this episode: a lemon-yellow high-collared minidress with a faux belt (quite the theme this season) and shoulder panels in a desaturated tone (the color of the dress is fine but the cut isn't particularly flattering); she goes into action in a black soft-leather catsuit (the first time we've seen her in leather for a while) with silver trim, belt, and boots, and two biker chains dangling across the breast and the abdomen (perhaps her most 'metal' outfit so far); and (another less successful piece) a striped sky-blue long-sleeved blouse with a cream-colored structured low-cut vest, which is buttoned at the waist with three buttons, and a matching skirt (probably a mini). The purple and hot pink Emmapeeler also returns, but it gets wet in the river.

Steed sticks to his regular outfits, favoring the brown checked tartan blazer with houndstooth trousers and a pinstriped shirt, the gray three-piece single-breasted suit, and the gray chalk-striped suit.

The Lotus and the Bentley both return. Steed uses a radio phone in his car.

The only dogs that appear chase poor Emma up a tree! (They appear to be Belgian Malinois.)

TAG SCENE

Steed shows Emma the vast fortune he has saved: box after box containing 10,000 half-pennies each, making him a half-penny millionaire.

QUOTES

"I wonder how he'll arrive—in a hearse?"
"Are we viewing comfortably? Good. Then, I'll begin."
"In the last twenty-four hours, you've been murdered four times. Now, on any one of those occasions it could have actually happened."
"Dying is a very serious business. It's so permanent."
"Who ever heard of nine-hundred-ninety-nine thousand nine-hundred and ninety-nine-a-naire?"

126 (6.7.6) THE POSITIVE NEGATIVE MAN

Steed makes the sparks fly — Emma gets switched on

Written by Tony Williamson

Directed by Robert Day

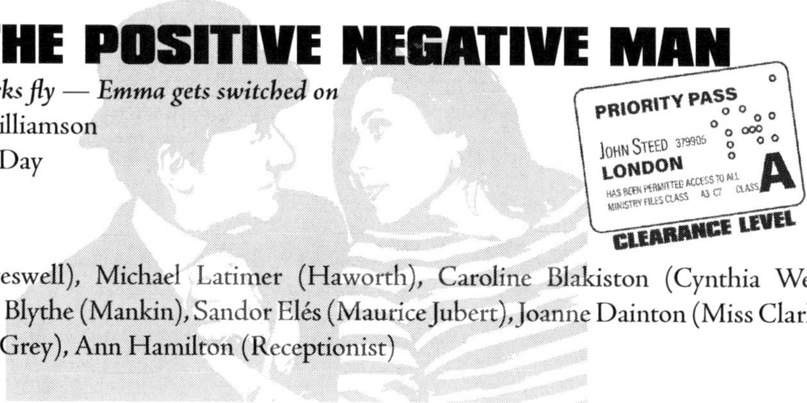

GUEST CAST

Ray McAnally (Creswell), Michael Latimer (Haworth), Caroline Blakiston (Cynthia Wentworth-Howe), Peter Blythe (Mankin), Sandor Elés (Maurice Jubert), Joanne Dainton (Miss Clarke), Bill Wallis (Charles Grey), Ann Hamilton (Receptionist)

PRE-TITLE/TEASER

A man sits at a drafting table on hot evening. He takes a break from his drawing, lights a pipe, before being startled by a peculiar sound. A strange man with pale blue skin slowly and silently enters the room. He touches the draughtsman in the chest and blasts him into the nearby wall.

SYNOPSIS

When a series of scientists that were once part of a broadcast power research team are found dead, Steed and Emma investigate activities at the Risely Dale research center. After both Steed and Emma have had shocking experiences involving a man in blue-grey makeup, the sole remaining member of the team, Dr. Creswell, is revealed to be the man behind the plot. When Creswell sends his electrifying companion to capture Mrs. Peel, she ends up becoming deadly bait charged with 25,000 volts, and surely, Steed will come and rescue her...

REVIEW

I'll state from the outset that this is one of my very favorite episodes. In fact, I'm highly tempted to nominate "The Positive Negative Man" for the Best of Show award. In any case, this is an excellent episode to start out with as it has all the typical traits associated with the show and is viscerally exciting. Chock-full of wit, perhaps more than may be found in this entire season, it is in many ways the quintessential *Avengers* episode. The balance between fantasy and spy adventure is nearly perfect. Though the plot is straight-forward enough, it has its roots in real science. Broadcast power is a genuine possibility and is still theoretically possible, and we are given an original twist on it here.

The 'monster' of this episode is Haworth, who creeps about in cyan-colored makeup with a crackling thimble on his fingertip. This thimble produces a surprising amount of anxiety to the viewer as it homes in on its hapless targets. We're aware that it's more than capable of throwing a man across the room and stopping his heart. I still get chills when viewing the pre-title. As the camera zooms in on the first victim, Laurie Johnson's music hits a deliberately discordant note that always sets my hair on end. In these many electrifying attacks, Robert Day does a marvelous job with the direction. There's not much artistic flourish, but this is more than made up for by the sustained tension and suspense. There is a particularly exciting sequence as Dr. Mankin is chased along disused railroad tracks, finally meeting a grisly end on a barbed wire fence. Michael Latimer is perfectly cast as Haworth because he lacks any degree of gravitas when out of his makeup. Resultingly, it's easy to see his attraction to the power and perceived respect he receives when he becomes the 'superman' he claims to be.

After Mrs. Peel finally meets a man she can't defeat, she ends up wrapped in silver Bacofoil with hysterically unnecessary eyeholes. This allows for more of the storied combination of humor and violence so well known in the series. Looking like some bizarre crested silver chicken, ready to be popped into the fryer, it provides Steed with a chance to playfully tease her before setting her free. The final fight scene that follows is one of the most well-choreographed in the series. Steed exchanges some brutal blows in a particularly nasty brawl that ends with Creswell being knocked through a window. In contrast, Mrs. Peel and Haworth engage in a balletic balancing act as Mrs. Peel desperately tries to avoid her only unprotected foot being forced onto the floor.

The lone eccentric is Cynthia Wentworth-Howe as the Ministry's 'top-hush secretary,' whose ultimate ambition is to become as bureaucratic as humanly possible as a 'button lip.' Cynthia isn't the most flamboyant of *Avengers* eccentrics, but odd she is. She doesn't approve of levity by her own admission, and yet by being so serious she manages to be funny. In a touch of kinkiness, she stores her keys to top secret facilities in a garter belt.

By this time in the show, Diana Rigg and Patrick Macnee have their banter down perfectly, and given the superb dialogue and witticisms provided by Tony Williamson, they seem to be gelling on every level possible and working together perfectly as a team. Speaking of banter, the closing tag scene is likely the finest of the entire series. Steed is magnetically stuck to his car, giving Mrs. Peel a chance to return his earlier teasing. I cannot help but giggle helplessly at this dialogue every time. Asking whether someone is "AC or DC" is a question that was about as kinky as you could get in 1967. Though David Bowie wasn't yet a bisexual sensation as Ziggy Stardust, the implication is more than obvious to modern viewers, especially when Steed responds with "I've never had occasion to find out!" Oh my—do you think they knew what they were saying! The intensity of their collective magnetism seems to be off the scale in this moment. And just when you think it can't get any better, Patrick Macnee appears to sum up this era of the series with one pithy line—"Don't fight it, Mrs. Peel, we're inseparable!" If only it were true.

CHAMPAGNE, CARS, CLOTHES, AND CANINES

Mrs. Peel straight away debuts a new outfit, and I wish I could say it's a stunner, but it's not. It's a straight-cut long-sleeved minidress in a sort of mustard-yellow with greenish-yellow trim and collar. The collar also has way too much of a sailor collar cut to it. Next is a very simple and yet stylish number: a bright-red coat with an A-line flare at the bottom and a matching skirt underneath. She pairs it with a white jumper. The coat is a very similar cut to several others she wears this season and the color—which is a strong "fire engine" red—makes it a standout. It also has a beautiful matching red silk lining. This is followed by another beautiful and elegant outfit, a floral minidress in purples, reds, and pinks. Like many of Mrs. Peel's dresses, it's long-sleeved. It has silver buttons and she wears it with lavender shoes. The orange and blue-striped Emmapeeler shows up for the final action sequence, and she finishes off the episode in her iconic striped action dress.

Steed debuts only one new outfit this episode and it's a navy-blue, two-piece, single-breasted suit. He wears it with a white shirt and a muted gray-blue tie. In order to protect himself from electricity, he finishes the outfit off with black rubber galoshes, "the English gentleman's best friend, guaranteed to protect you against the vagaries of our delightful climate and also 25,000 volts." For the tag scene, he returns to the brown tartan blazer

The Lotus Elan features prominently in this episode, and the Bentley 3 Litre also makes a welcome return and is seen extensively throughout. And it's the latter that both Steed and Emma become electromagnetically stuck to.

The little blue Morris van is also rather iconic in its own right, projecting a surprising amount of menace for something that looks like it was designed for a cartoon—it's actually a 1963 Morris 6CWT O-Type Van (CMF 263A).[2]

TAG SCENE

Outside Risely Dale, Steed finds that the electricity from the Positive-Negative Man has inexplicably caused him to become magnetically stuck to his own car. When Emma offers him a hand she becomes stuck too, and Steed declares, "Don't fight it, Mrs. Peel. We're inseparable." (Possibly the greatest of all tag scenes!)

QUOTES

"Well, Grey wasn't killed for the plans of a fiendishly new electric fan."

"You seem to have pyromaniac mice!"

"You don't happen to be carrying around a large brandy, do you?" "No, I'm traveling light. What happened?"

"Mrs. Peel, do you know anyone who wants to buy a vintage Bentley in the new two-toned shade of green and slightly-singed?"

"I have just survived an electrifying experience, and I'll swap you the details for—" "—a large brandy?"

"I knew you had sterling qualities but bright silver! Where are you hallmarked?"

"You ruined his make-up!"

2 Many might refer to it as a "Morris Minor," and it is indeed very similar, as the basic design and chassis are based on the Morris Minor, though it's still a different model.

127 (6.6.7) MURDERSVILLE

Emma marries Steed — Steed becomes a father
Written by Brian Clemens
Directed by Robert Asher

GUEST CAST

Colin Blakely (Mickle), John Ronane (Hubert), Ronald Hines (Dr. Haymes), John Sharp (Prewitt), Sheila Fearn (Jenny), Eric Flynn (Croft), Norman Chappell (Forbes), Robert Cawdron (Banks), Marika Mann (Miss Avril), Irene Bradshaw (Maggie), Joseph Greig (Higgins), Geoffrey Colville (Jeremy Purser), Langton Jones (Chapman), Tony Caunter (Miller), John Chandos (Morgan), Andrew Laurence (Williams)

PRE-TITLE/TEASER

In the improbably named town Little Storping in-the-Swuff, two men drink their pints of beer and play dominoes outside the pub while having an innocuous conversation. Suddenly, a third man is thrown violently through the door of the pub and is shot and killed by an assassin wearing a business suit.

SYNOPSIS

Mrs. Peel's childhood friend Major Croft is retiring to the isolated community of Little Storping in-the-Swuff, where his valet Forbes has vanished. While looking for him, Croft himself then disappears, and Mrs. Peel finds Forbes' body. The fact that the town inhabitants are particularly unwelcoming makes Mrs. Peel's visit less than pleasant, and she quickly finds herself eager to escape their questionable hospitality...

REVIEW

This story begins with a perplexing pre-title that underwhelms and intrigues at the same time. Their having failed to react emotionally to a violent murder, the congenial veneer of the locals is already disingenuous from the outset. That veneer is finally smashed altogether when they later turn into sociopathic man-apes, destroying the property of new resident Major Croft, who happens to be Emma's friend. The two villagers (played throughout with considerable odiousness by John Ronane and Colin Blakely) have accents that are West Country in origin, and I assume that this is the intended location of Little Storping in-the-Swuff despite the episode having been filmed on-location in Aldbury, northwest of London.

Emma is working solo for the majority of this episode, visiting Little Storping on her own—Patrick Macnee's apparent vacation being responsible for Steed's absence (and indeed a serious plot flaw). Once it becomes obvious that there is a conspiracy very much in the style of many *Avengers* episodes, it seems very odd that Emma would call the police instead of Steed. The latter option certainly would have saved her a lot of trouble. Sadly, this action by Mrs. Peel is so painfully out of character that it sticks out like a sore thumb—the script is clearly being adjusted to fit Macnee's availability. This is not without merit, however, as the fight scenes between Emma and the villagers are exciting even if the end result is one of futility.

The futility of escape experienced by Emma and the suspicious conspiratorial behavior of the locals are both highly reminiscent of *The Prisoner*, which was to premiere some weeks after this episode was filmed. This seeming connection—however coincidental—is amplified by the fact that the pub owner in this episode (John Sharp) and the shop keeper in *The Prisoner* (Denis Shaw) are played by actors who are very similar in appearance and demeanor.

While the concept of "Murdersville" in general is a promising one, the narrative manages to please only on a superficial level, rarely rising to the level of vitality and political intrigue that its spiritual sibling managed consistently in its seventeen-episode run. I suspect that the lack of Steed throughout most of the story and the consequent lack of wit derived from their usual banter is responsible. Indeed, he is missing for the first two thirds, and it is only when they are once again together that the pace picks up. Until then, we're just marking time while Emma experiences a frustration that transfers all too well to the viewer. There is no forward momentum for quite a long while.

Fortunately, that apparent 'marking time' involves a stunning helicopter chase that surely must have cost the production a large amount of money. Likewise, the scenes in the makeshift dungeon (composed of artifacts from the local museum) are bizarre and subtly humorous. Emma is fastened to the wall with a chastity belt, and all the other abstaining villagers (pardon the double entendre) are shackled with a variety of medieval devices. Once Steed finally arrives, their final struggle against the villains turns into a bit of a slapstick pie fight, relieving the palpable tedium of the prior forty-eight minutes.

The tag scene however is possibly the best moment in the episode, as Mrs. Peel struggles to remove a knight's helm that she extemporaneously donned during the fight, spurred by an impulse that she cannot entirely explain. (This writer presumes that she has an innate and irrepressible sense of humor that surfaces in moments of extreme danger—laughing at the jaws of death, as it were. God love her.) Naturally, she sips champagne through a straw while Steed attempts to remove the stubborn head gear. It's an adorable moment. The distressing thing about this episode is the amount of time it took to get to anything that fun.

CHAMPAGNE, CARS, CLOTHES, AND CANINES

Steed only debuts one outfit this episode, and it's a dark-gray single-breasted, two-piece suit. He wears it with a cerulean-blue tie, a white shirt, a gray bowler and brolly, and black Chelsea boots. Mrs. Peel has no new outfits this episode, but her purple and blue-striped Emmapeeler returns and becomes the outfit of the episode for her.

To greet Mrs. Peel's childhood friend, Major Paul Croft, in the first scene proper, they drink a 1927 champagne (and Steed complains about it not being the 1926 that he asked for); looking carefully, the "Meudon & Heim" label is barely visible, which is a faux brand with a fake label often seen in the series. Usually, it was Moët & Chandon with the fake label stuck over the bottle or the box as needed.

Mrs. Peel drives Paul down to Little Storping in her Lotus, but the rear-screen projection may play tricks on your eyes, because her outfit appears to morph into the orange and navy-striped Emmapeeler until she gets out of the car and the colors have been magically restored. Her car also skews towards green in these shots. Later, this color-change trick reoccurs in other car scenes. Of course, by the end, she pairs this outfit with a knight's helm, and, tragically, it simply doesn't work as an ensemble; even swapping it out for her white patterned dress doesn't fix the problem, but undoubtedly sipping champagne through a straw makes up for it.

On a different vehicle note, the helicopter used in this episode is an Aérospatiale SE-3130 Alouette II (G-AVEE) manufactured by SUD Aviation. It had been previously used in ***The Prisoner*** (under a different registration), and it's distinctive whir will be familiar to viewers of that program, particularly in that show's first episode. It was also used in several more ITV shows, including ***The Baron, Man in a Suitcase, Department S,*** and ***The Champions.***

TAG SCENE

Having donned a knight's helm in the final battle, Emma has become stuck and now sips champagne with a straw through the grate of the helm while Steed tries to figure out how to free her. He does so, but in his eagerness to demonstrate the helm's ease of use, he becomes stuck himself.

QUOTES

"It may surprise you too know that I've had very little experience with this type of garment."
"Not only are we going to be late for this party, but the ambassador is going to take it as a personal affront. We all know his reputation as a womanizer, but to turn up in armor. It really is very inconvenient."

128 (6.8.8) MISSION...HIGHLY IMPROBABLE

Steed falls into enemy hands — Emma is cut down to size
Written by Philip Levene
Directed by Robert Day

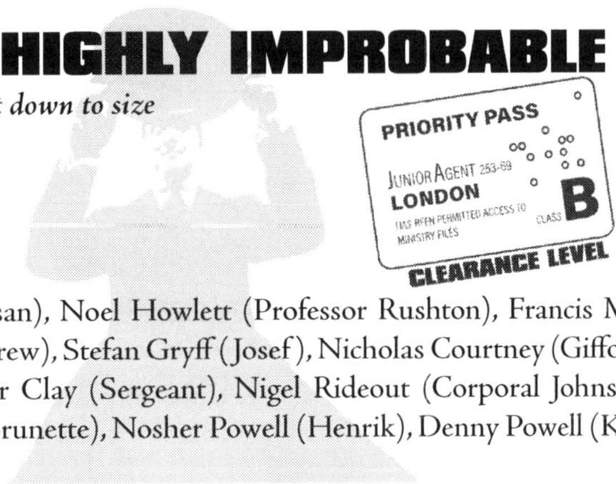

GUEST CAST

Ronald Radd (Shaffer), Jane Merrow (Susan), Noel Howlett (Professor Rushton), Francis Matthews (Chivers), Richard Leech (Colonel Drew), Stefan Gryff (Josef), Nicholas Courtney (Gifford), Kevin Stoney (Sir Gerald Bancroft), Peter Clay (Sergeant), Nigel Rideout (Corporal Johnson), Cynthia Bizeray (Blonde), Nicole Shelby (Brunette), Nosher Powell (Henrik), Denny Powell (Karl)

PRE-TITLE/TEASER

A military troop on motorcycles is escorting an important politician to a nearby demonstration, but the politician's Rolls-Royce suddenly and inexplicably disappears in the middle of the road.

SYNOPSIS

Professor Rushton has developed a shrinking ray, and his assistant Chivers is determined to use it for personal gain. Having already shrunk Sir Gerald Bancroft, he proceeds to shrink army security man Gifford and flush him down a garage drain. However, the more sinister part of the plan is to steal a brand new British Army tank by reducing it enormously in size...

REVIEW

This episode features a return to the high-fantasy elements of the prior season, proving that Fennell and Clemens still weren't completely keen on the more mundane spy stories that their bosses were. On the other hand, it could have been the result of a backlog of scripts that were written before that particular mandate. In any case, I sincerely hope it wasn't what got them fired because this is a delightful story. Ultimately, despite the tiff between Fennell-Clemens and their bosses, this season was to serve as a proforma for the following one—a mixture of the more fantastic with the more mundane with the fantasy being more blunted than it had been in the recent past.

The plot is not exactly brilliant; it is straightforward and linear, made rudimentary by the simplicity of the technology used by the criminals to carry out their goals. It moves at an even and moderate pace with little action. Apparently, the primary goal was to show off the special effects and make sure that both Steed and Emma shrink at least once. However, as usual, the point of this era is pure escapist fun and the enjoyment of seeing Steed and Mrs. Peel working together and engaging in witty banter. There is plenty of that here...for the more patient of the viewers.

Speaking of which, this episode shows Steed and Mrs. Peel working together well despite one or the other being vertically challenged at various points in the narrative. It's obvious that at this point Macnee and Rigg had tremendous chemistry, which, in this outing, resulted in some wonderful dialogue and teamwork...eventually. I say 'eventually' because it takes so long before they are together after the initial setup—a full thirty-seven minutes into the program, by which time Steed has been shrunk and needs Mrs. Peel's help.

This initiates a particularly lovely sequence in which "a tiny dream" of Steed frees Emma using a letter opener and helps her fight off crooks by stabbing them with the nib of a fountain pen. And this is where the story's real charm begins. Likely, British viewers would have been reminded of the 1958 George Pal film ***Tom Thumb*** (a largely British production). The special effects in this episode are as enchanting as that of the film, a testament to the production quality of the series in this remarkable era.

The direction from Robert Day is again ordinary, probably due to focusing on the special effects, but there is one particular shot that stands out—an upward view of Steed framed against a bright cloudy blue sky in extreme wide-angle as he places his bowler over the miniscule bodies of the enemy agents. I can imagine the film crew spending an hour or more just setting up that shot, changing lenses and whatnot. I'm glad they took the time. These little things matter.

Francis Matthews as Chivers and Ronald Radd as Shaffer are an engaging double act of sociopathy (Radd making a welcome return to the series). Nicholas Courtney, less than six months away from a role that would prove iconic for him (that of Brigadier Lethbridge-Stewart in ***Doctor Who***), has a brief and fatal role as Captain Gifford. Though there is little time to distinguish himself before he is washed down the drain, he manages to make an impression very similar to what was to come—a hard-nosed, no-nonsense military man, albeit without a mustache this time.

Chances are... highly probable that you will enjoy this episode as much as I have.

CHAMPAGNE, CARS, CLOTHES, AND CANINES

Steed brings out the brown tartan blazer again and the grey suit from "Murdersville" but he would also debut two more: another single-breasted, two-piece navy suit, worn with a pale-blue shirt and a bright-red spotted tie; and yet another gray single-breasted suit with a gray shirt and a blue tie.

Mrs. Peel would finish the season off with four more new outfits: a pale-green sleeveless sundress with a white trim in a crisscross pattern across the shoulders and chest (the length is uncertain); a mint-green blouse with a subtle stripe pattern, tan trousers, black belt, and white shoes; a spring-green coat, buttoned at the collar with a single button and at the waist with a faux belt, and a matching A-line skirt, slightly above knee-length (since we never see the outfit without the coat, it's also possible that it's a matching minidress); and, finally, a lovely and elegant yellow sleeveless minidress with ribbing down the front in a sort of faux placket and another faux belt integrated into the dress. There is also a possible continuity error in which a pale-pink blouse shows up, but it's only barely visible in a few shots during her phone call with tiny Steed. The Emmapeeler/catsuit of the episode is the cerulean blue one with white lacing and trim.

Steed's Bentley 3 Litre returns again, and Mrs. Peel's Lotus also appears. The light armored army vehicle, that is shrunk while Steed is inside, is a 1952 Alvis FV 603 Saracen Series II personnel carrier. While shrunken, Steed takes a ride in a 1966 Mercedes-Benz 230 SL convertible (LGK 75D). Gifford (Nicholas Courtney) drives a 1961 Triumph Thunderbird motorcycle.

Steed's mantelpiece painting is replaced by a landscape that looks like it could be by a Dutch Golden Age artist like Meindert Hobbema or Jacob van Ruisdael, but a painting by John Constable would be more appropriately British.

TAG SCENE

Back in Emma's apartment, Steed is helping her rearrange her furniture while they have a conversation about the potential benefits of shrink ray technology. When it starts to rain, Steed offers Emma his brolly, which turns out to be as small as a cocktail umbrella—a possible side effect from his having been shrunk recently.

QUOTES

"It's a dream, a dream. A tiny dream."

"Well, I must say, Mrs. Peel, the pen is mightier than the sword." "Well, between us, we've written them off."

"I can tell you one thing, Doctor. We are going to be big men!"

"Have you got them, Steed?" "Yes, Mrs. Peel. I think we've cut them down to size."

"A MAN'S HEARTBEAT. AS DISTINCTIVE AS HIS FINGERPRINT."

SEASON SEVEN

33 episodes (35mm color film, ~52 min. ea.)

Regular Cast
Patrick Macnee—John Steed
Linda Thorson—Tara King
Diana Rigg—Emma Peel (episode 129)
Patrick Newell—Mother (episodes 129, 131, 132, 135, 136, 138, 141-143, 145, 148–154, 157, 159, 161)
Rhonda Parker—Rhonda (uncredited, episodes 135, 136, 138, 143, 149, 152, 154, 157)

Producers: Albert Fennell and Brian Clemens
Producer (uncredited): John Bryce (episodes 140, 144, and 154)
Executive in charge of production: Gordon L.T. Scott
Consultant to the series: Julian Wintle (episodes 129, 132–134, 139, 140, 144, 147, 156, 160)
Story Consultant: Philip Levene (episodes 129–134, 136, 139, 140, 144, 147, 156, 160)
Script Editor: Terry Nation (episodes 135, 137, 138, 141–143, 145, 146, 148–155, 157–159, 161)
Music: Laurie Johnson (episodes 129, 133–135, 137, 139–141, 143–150, 152, 154–161)
Music Supervisor: Laurie Johnson (episodes 130, 131, 136, 138, 142, 151, 153)
Score: Howard Blake (episodes 130, 131, 136, 138, 142, 151, 153)
Additional Music: Howard Blake (episodes 148, 156)

129. **The Forget-Me-Knot—w.** Brian Clemens; **dir.** James Hill; **UK tx.** 25 Sep 1968; **US tx.** 20 Mar 1968; **filmed** Sep 1967 & Dec 1967-Jan 1968
130. **Game—w.** Richard Harris; **dir.** Robert Fuest; **UK tx.** 2 Oct 1968; **US tx.** 23 Sep 1968; **filmed** May-Jul 1968
131. **Super Secret Cypher Snatch—w.** Tony Williamson; **dir.** John Hough; **UK tx.** 9 Oct 1968; **US tx.** 30 Sep 1968; **filmed** May-Jul 1968
132. **You'll Catch Your Death—w.** Jeremy Burnham; **dir.** Paul Dickson; **UK tx.** 16 Oct 1968; **US tx.** 7 Oct 1968; **filmed** Apr-Jun 1968
133. **Split! —w.** Brian Clemens (& Dennis Spooner); **dir.** Roy Baker; **UK tx.** 23 Oct 1968; **US tx.** 10 Apr 1968; **filmed** Jan-Feb 1968
134. **Whoever Shot Poor George Oblique Stroke XR40? —w.** Tony Williamson; **dir.** Cyril Frankel; **UK tx.** 30 Oct 1968; **US tx.** 9 Dec 1968; **filmed** Mar-May 1968
135. **False Witness—w.** Jeremy Burnham; **dir.** Charles Crichton; **UK tx.** 6 Nov 1968; **US tx.** 25 Nov 1968; **filmed** Jun-Jul 1968
136. **All Done with Mirrors—w.** Leigh Vance; **dir.** Ray Austin; **UK tx.** 13 Nov 1968; **US tx.** 2 Dec 1968; **filmed** Apr-Jun 1968
137. **Legacy of Death—w.** Terry Nation; **dir.** Don Chaffey; **UK tx.** 20 Nov 1968; **US tx.** 4 Nov 1968; **filmed** Jul-Aug 1968
138. **Noon Doomsday—w.** Terry Nation; **dir.** Peter Sykes; **UK tx.** 27 Nov 1968; **US tx.** 28 Oct 1968; **filmed** Jul 1968
139. **Look – (stop me if you've heard this one) But There Were These Two Fellers... —w.** Dennis Spooner; **dir.** James Hill; **UK tx.** 4 Dec 1968; **US tx.** 8 May 1968; **filmed** Feb-Mar 1968

140. **Have Guns – Will Haggle—w.** Donald James; **dir.** Ray Austin; **UK tx.** 11 Dec 1968; **US tx.** 1 May 1968; **filmed** Oct-Nov 1967 & Sep 1968
141. **They Keep Killing Steed—w.** Brian Clemens; **dir.** Robert Fuest; **UK tx.** 18 Dec 1968; **US tx.** 11 Nov 1968; **filmed** Jul-Sep 1968
142. **The Interrogators—w.** Richard Harris & Brian Clemens; **dir.** Charles Crichton; **UK tx.** 1 Jan 1969; **US tx.** 20 Jan 1969; **filmed** Sep-Oct 1968
143. **The Rotters—w.** Dave Freeman; **dir.** Robert Fuest; **UK tx.** 8 Jan 1969; **US tx.** 16 Dec 1968; **filmed** Sep-Oct 1968
144. **Invasion of the Earthmen—w.** Terry Nation; **dir.** Don Sharp; **UK tx.** 15 Jan 1969; **US tx.** 27 Mar 1968; **filmed** Nov 1967-Jan 1968
145. **Killer—w.** Tony Williamson; **dir.** Cliff Owen; **UK tx.** 22 Jan 1969; **US tx.** 30 Dec 1968; **filmed** Aug-Oct 1968
146. **The Morning After—w.** Brian Clemens; **dir.** John Hough; **UK tx.** 29 Jan 1969; **US tx.** (27 Jan 1969)*; **filmed** Oct-Nov 1968
147. **The Curious Case of the Countless Clues—w.** Philip Levene; **dir.** Don Sharp; **UK tx.** 5 Feb 1969; **US tx.** 3 Apr 1968; **filmed** Dec 1967-Jan 1968
148. **Wish You Were Here—w.** Tony Williamson; **dir.** Don Chaffey; **UK tx.** 12 Feb 1969; **US tx.** 18 Nov 1968; **filmed** Aug-Sep 1968
149. **Love All—w.** Jeremy Burnham; **dir.** Peter Sykes; **UK tx.** 19 Feb 1969; **US tx.** 3 Feb 1969; **filmed** Oct-Nov 1968
150. **Stay Tuned—w.** Tony Williamson; **dir.** Don Chaffey; **UK tx.** 26 Feb 1969; **US tx.** 24 Feb 1969; **filmed** Nov-Dec 1968
151. **Take Me to Your Leader—w.** Terry Nation; **dir.** Robert Fuest; **UK tx.** 5 Mar 1969; **US tx.** 10 Feb 1969; **filmed** Nov 1968
152. **Fog—w.** Jeremy Burnham; **dir.** John Hough; **UK tx.** 12 Mar 1969; **US tx.** 17 Feb 1969; **filmed** Nov 1968-Jan 1969
153. **Who Was That Man I Saw You With?** —w. Jeremy Burnham; dir. Don Chaffey; **UK tx.** 19 Mar 1969; **US tx.** 3 Mar 1969; **filmed** Dec 1968-Jan 1969
154. **Homicide and Old Lace—w.** Malcolm Hulke & Terrance Dicks; **dir.** John Hough; **UK tx.** 26 Mar 1969; **US tx.** 17 Mar 1969; **filmed** Nov-Dec 1967 & Jan 1969
155. **Thingumajig—w.** Terry Nation; **dir.** Leslie Norman; **UK tx.** 2 Apr 1969; **US tx.** 24 Mar 1969; **filmed** Jan-Feb 1969
156. **My Wildest Dream—w.** Philip Levene; **dir.** Robert Fuest; **UK tx.** 7 Apr 1969; **US tx.** 6 Jan 1969; **filmed** Mar-Apr 1968
157. **Requiem—w.** Brian Clemens; **dir.** Don Chaffey; **UK tx.** 16 Apr 1969; **US tx.** 31 Mar 1969; **filmed** Jan-Feb 1969
158. **Take-Over—w.** Terry Nation; **dir.** Robert Fuest; **UK tx.** 23 Apr 1969; **US tx.** 14 Apr 1969; **filmed** Jan-Feb 1969
159. **Pandora—w.** Brian Clemens; **dir.** Robert Fuest; **UK tx.** 30 Apr 1969; **US tx.** 10 Mar 1969; **filmed** Jan 1969
160. **Get-A-Way!** **—w.** Philip Levene; **dir.** Don Sharp; **UK tx.** 14 May 1969; **US tx.** 24 Apr 1968; **filmed** Jan-Feb 1968
161. **Bizarre—w.** Brian Clemens; **dir.** Leslie Norman; **UK tx.** 21 May 1969; **US tx.** 21 Apr 1969; **filmed** Feb-Mar 1969

* "The Morning After" was scheduled for this date but may not have been actually broadcast.

SEASON NOTES

Starting out with Linda Thorson as Tara King and John Bryce as producer, filming began in October 1967, by all measures too late to contribute to the ongoing season on ITV but with plenty of time to make the American order for the winter of 1968. Producer John Bryce was concerned about Linda Thorson being dark-haired and thus too similar to Diana Rigg, and he required that she bleach her hair blond. The decision turned catastrophic as poor Ms. Thorson's hair reacted badly to the bleaching process and began to break and fall out, forcing her to wear a wig. It didn't help that the British press were also very negative in their response to her casting.

The production unit working on *The Avengers* during this period was reportedly very unhappy, and few had agreed with the decision to remove Brian Clemens and Albert Fennell. Regarding this, stunt double Cyd Child remarked that "it felt totally wrong. You felt you were working on something that wasn't going to work. And that wasn't the way that it had been with *The Avengers*." She further commented that she too had to bleach her hair so she could double for Thorson and experienced the same hair loss.

By December of 1967, Bryce would only have two episodes completed and one more filmed with the rushes awaiting editing. These episodes were "Invitation to a Killing," "Invasion of the Earthmen," and "The Great Great Britain Crime." His bosses took a look at these episodes and decided they didn't like what they saw. The modern viewer will have approximately half of this material to second guess. The entirety of "Invasion of the Earthmen" still exists, and the bulk of "Invitation to a Killing" survives as "Have Guns – Will Haggle," while fragments of "The Great Great Britain Crime" are viewable in between Mother's story time driveling in "Homicide and Old Lace." Viewing the material as it survives, it appears that no second-guessing is required. The material is mostly subpar, and two-thirds of these episodes form the bottom tier of this season, with the balance being merely on the upper side of mediocre.

No doubt they also were worried about the time remaining. Bryce still had four episodes to complete, and at a rate of one per month, it didn't look likely he would meet their goals. A certain degree of handwringing higher up in management swiftly resulted in the reversal of their prior decision. John Bryce was dismissed and Brian Clemens was asked back from his work on the ITC show *The Champions* with Dennis Spooner. He agreed on the contingent that Albert Fennell also be asked to return.

Reinstated, and also vindicated, Clemens and Fennell quickly went to work. By this time, it was early December 1967, and new episodes were required by at least March, and the final episodes would need to be delivered to ABC by May. Summoning Diana Rigg back, they resumed production on "The Forget-Me-Knot," filming a special 'hand-off' scene so that Mrs. Peel could remind Ms. King to stir Steed's tea anti-clockwise. They returned Linda Thorson to her natural hair color, but she was still required to wear brown wigs for the first production block until her hair's length had been restored.

Moving on, they quickly realized that they couldn't possibly finish in time without using some of the material already filmed by John Bryce. (And indeed, they likely could have ill-afforded the loss of funds used in the filming of that material.) They viewed "Invasion of the Earthmen" and found that episode to be mostly acceptable, and with minor edits, new music, and new scenes to explain Linda Thorson's changing hair, the episode was approved for broadcast. Aggressive edits were made to "Invitation to a Killing," and additional material was shot, ultimately cutting it down from the intended ninety minutes to fifty-two in order for it to fit into an hour-long timeslot.

From here, they completed four more full episodes by March of 1968—"The Curious Case of the Countless Clues," "Split!," "Get-A-Way!," and "Look – (stop me if you've heard this one) But There Were These Two Fellers…" These episodes were variable in quality, and some of them show signs of the rush behind their development, but, by all accounts, Brian Clemens and Albert Fennell had pulled off something of a miracle. Combined with the final eight Diana Rigg episodes that were broadcast on ITV the prior autumn, these seven new episodes were enough to satisfy ABC's order. The third season of ***The Avengers*** in America was saved, and the ratings were better than ever.

The result of this mad rush and confusion was that the long-pursued twenty-six-episode order from ABC in America finally came through. ABC wanted a full season to premiere in the autumn of 1968. Thus, for their having saved the prior season, the reward for Clemens and Fennell was to work without break for the next year while preparing this new batch of episodes. As they say, be careful what you wish for...

Because ABC had previously only ordered another fifteen episodes, Linda Thorson was hired for an initial seven episodes, and Macnee's contract was extended by only five (from his original ten). Everyone, it seems, was on trial, kept on pins-and-needles by the suspense based on the Nielsen's and American funding. This was all relieved as the larger order came through. Thorson's and Macnee's contracts were appropriately extended to accommodate this new season and filming continued unabated. At this point, confidence seemed to have been restored to the previously troubled production, and it shows in the episodes produced. Indeed, many of the episodes in the second production block are among the finest in the season with "All Done with Mirrors," "Super Secret Cypher Snatch," "Game," "False Witness," "Noon Doomsday," "They Keep Killing Steed," and "Killer" all being solid examples of the series.

During this period, Linda Thorson would finally find her footing after being tossed back and forth between various versions of Tara King's persona over many weeks. This Tara-of-the-week personality could only be blamed on the producers and writers, who apparently didn't know what they wanted. Many examples of this inconsistency can be noted. At one point, Tara was more sedentary, answering Steed's phone for the most part, and then, in a complete reversal of apparent competency, she was laid up with a twisted ankle and yet still managed to stop several would-be assassins with devastating martial arts skills. Later, she was easily captured and then rescued, and then, in another complete turnabout, she was required to handle the entirety of her adventure without assistance—which nevertheless required Steed to be *very* worried. And then there was the infamous brick-in-the-handbag 'feminine' mode of fighting. So, which was it to be? Was she a competent fighter out in the field? Or was she mostly a bookish type that assisted behind the scenes? As for their relationship...Was she a companion for Steed? A romantic partner? A secretary? Could she be the witty foil that her predecessors had been?

Early on, the romantic relationship between her and Steed blew hot and cold from episode to episode before finally settling on a surprisingly familiar mode of expression—the old standby of are-they-or-aren't-they? Though from Tara's side the romantic uncertainty did seem to veer more towards hot in its expression—Thorson clearly played Tara as if she was in love with Steed—there are episodes in which they seemed to barely look at one another.

Finally, this sturm und drang about how Tara compared to Emma Peel and Cathy Gale seemed to clear, and they realized that there was nothing wrong with Tara simply being like her predecessors—a tough, skilled agent who could get along in the field as well as any of them. Nevertheless, many of the more eclectic personality traits survived in the final mix, and we're left to conclude that Tara is simply kookier than her predecessors with tastes and tactics that are more unconventional. It's difficult to understand why it took them so long to make these decisions about her character, and the indecision certainly cost Tara some initial popularity.

The scripts would blow equally hot and cold. Though Brian Clemens frequently went on record as saying that the writing was at its best during this season, this is a statement which frankly doesn't hold up under analysis. If anything, the writing was at its most inconsistent. Some are among the best the show has to offer, others are rotten beyond description. "Fog" is a lamentable mess of a script, "Pandora" is an exercise in tedium, and "Whoever Shot Poor George Oblique Stroke XR40?" is a failed science-fiction comedy. Finally, the less said about the ham-fisted hatchet job that is "Homicide and Old Lace" the better. On the other hand, the scripts for "The Interrogators" and "Super Secret

Cypher Snatch" would hold up against any era of the program. The show frequently seemed to lose its direction under script editor Terry Nation's guiding pen, whose ideas, though well-intentioned, seemed ill-suited to the program's nature. Wit and humor seemed to be hit or miss, surrealism came and went in spurts, and some episodes seemed more suited to ***Doctor Who*** than to ***The Avengers***.

One aspect of the program that was not ambivalent is the skillful and artistic direction and cinematography on display. Suddenly, more than ever, ***The Avengers*** was cinematic eye candy. Though television viewers in the 1960s were unlikely able to see the subtlety involved, it is more noticeable than ever on today's high-definition television sets. Directors like Peter Sykes, John Hough, Charles Crichton, Robert Fuest, and Ray Austin were pulling out the stops to make ***The Avengers*** as visually engaging as possible.

The third production block would not fare as well however. Despite some classics like "Love All" and "The Interrogators," most of the remainder of the season would suffer from considerable mediocrity, as if the program were running out of steam. Blights like "Homicide and Old Lace" and "Fog" were no help, and, whether you go by production or transmission order, the series would end on "Bizarre," which can only be described as a failed pastiche of ***The Avengers*** in its heyday. Even its name seems half-baked, as if no one could think of anything better with which to sum it up. Possibly intended to be a grand finale, rarely has a series ender fallen so flat, and, in a tag scene better suited for ***Sid and Marty Krofft***, Steed and Tara are blasted off into space in a rocket that Steed built in his backyard.

When the final series debuted in the fall of 1968 on both ITV and ABC, American viewers had already been introduced to Tara King and Mother (via those final seven episodes broadcast in the winter of 1968). However, in the United Kingdom, all of Tara King's episodes (totaling thirty-three) had been held back. British viewers would finally say goodbye to Emma Peel, one full year after her farewell episode had started filming, and they would view the earliest Tara King episodes some six months after they finished airing in America. These new episodes were not at all well-received by British critics, who generally disliked Linda Thorson's portrayal and were not kind to the production in general. Despite this, ratings in the UK were solid; viewers were tuning in, and all of the UK would be treated to a glut of the show which would air continuously for eight months.

All of it was a moot point however, as the series tanked in the ratings in America, and it should have been a no-brainer as to why. ***Rowan & Martin's Laugh In***, which ran opposite on NBC, was the number one show on American television that season, and ***Gunsmoke***, a well-established show with fans that simply didn't budge for anything, managed to be number six. Together, they pulled in an 80 share, meaning that 80% of all viewers tuned in were watching one of those two shows. It should not be a surprise therefore that against such overbearing competition ***The Avengers*** only managed a 14 share—with the balance being UHF channels like PBS. While today a 14 share is pretty good given that we have dozens of channels and streaming services at our disposal, in the late sixties it was truly awful. As Brian Clemens put it, "it was an accolade that they thought we could do something against them, but, at the same time, it was our death knell."

Rather ironically, under ordinary circumstances a show performing that badly in the ratings would have been pulled from the lineup mid-season and replaced with something else. ***The Avengers*** had received its first shot based on the failure of another program, so the tables were now turned, and the reason for its final season playing out in full was probably a rather ignoble one—whatever ABC put there was going to be killed off, and it was better to sacrifice a foreign show on which comparatively little money had been spent than a more expensive homegrown program. Thus, ***The Avengers*** on American television had come full circle, and it would go from a replacement to the replaced. Executives at ABC would call their British counterparts and politely inform them that they would require no further episodes of ***The Avengers***.

While many would subsequently blame Linda Thorson, or Patrick Newell, Clemens or Fennell, or even Patrick Macnee, it is doubtful that any of them had anything to do with the season's failure.

The reasons for the show choking at the big game were likely no one's fault in particular. Despite some minor hiccups during the early episodes of the season, the quality of the production had remained stronger than ever.

The demand for twenty-six scripts over a very short period—just as practically every storyline had already been explored—was possibly a significant factor. This was compounded by shifts in tone due to the selection of Terry Nation as script editor, a writer who seldom seemed to completely understand what the show was about. Though, to their credit, the screenwriters did their best and frequently pulled out some great ideas.

More importantly, the show had been under tremendous pressure for at least two years, and unfortunate events, such as Diana Rigg's departure, had unfolded at just the right time to disrupt the production precisely when they needed to be at the top of their game. If anyone should be blamed, it was Associated British Corporation executives, who insisted on the show being in primetime in America in the first place. Their odd decision to change horses in the middle of battle was also a critical one that had set the stage for failure. The best men for the job were clearly Clemens and Fennell, and their turning the show about face instantly when rehired was likely the only reason that it made it to ABC's fall lineup at all.

In the end, the best answer is probably that *The Avengers* was a cult show, and cult shows are fragile. The worst thing that could have happened to *The Avengers* was to go mainstream, and this is what it did. If it had remained a replacement series on ABC, the pressure for high ratings against stiff competition would have been eased, and we might have had several more seasons. Or if more reasonable competition for the show had been selected by ABC, we might be talking about ten or eleven seasons instead of debating about only six or seven.

Nevertheless, it is the cult nature of *The Avengers* that has in the end preserved it. It is the reason we still talk about it instead of *Laugh In*. While *Laugh In* is still a fondly remembered show, a quick Google search will reveal no websites and no luscious coffee table books dedicated to it. Perhaps, some fifty years later, *The Avengers* finally socked it to them.

INTRODUCING TARA KING

Tara was John Steed's final regular partner during *The Avengers*. And, for the first time in the series, she was a full professional agent working within the Ministry alongside Steed, and perhaps appropriately, she was just as eclectic a persona as Steed.

Though she was a professional secret agent like Steed, she was a distinctly junior one, having just completed her training as 'Agent 69' in "The Forget-Me-Knot." Although immediately assigned to Steed by episode's end, she also came with a new boss in the form of Mother. Though the reasons for this are unknown, it is possible that Tara's early activities within the Ministry were perceived to require more of a guiding hand.

Tara was dark-haired and pretty with blue eyes. Though she appeared to be of average build, she was incredibly athletic, capable of many judo throws, somersaults, front rolls, and other martial arts forms. Like Steed, she fought with an improvisational style, often utilizing surrounding props and improvised weapons, including the oft referenced 'brick in the handbag.' She once shorted out a deadly electronic device by showering it with champagne. She was also a trained pilot and highly skilled with a variety of firearms.

Style-wise, her clothes and home décor were equally eclectic. Her wardrobe was a collision of fashion ideas but was mostly composed of pop-art inspired garments with vibrant colors. Many of her outfits were more akin to costumes, and in one episode, she spent the first third dressed in a bizarre superhero outfit. Nevertheless, she was also capable of a more glamorous appearance when called for. She occasionally wore a blond wig (for a 'disguise').

Her flat at 9 Primrose Crescent was similarly diverse, and its décor encompassed a vast array of curios, including many items of Victoriana—examples include a wooden spinning wheel, a variety of old shop signs, African paintings, a penny farthing bicycle, and several mounted stag heads. The apartment was accessed from the street but apparently had an upper floor with a separate exit at a higher level, though this scarcely correlated with the footage of the exterior, which was consistent with an ordinary terraced house.

Tara possessed many professional spy skills aside from martial arts. She was an excellent safe cracker and lock picker. She was also good at interrogating as well as at resisting interrogation. Despite her relative inexperience, she also had access to 'red card' clearance just like Steed, something that had been established to be exceptionally rare. She appeared to have no special ability at linguistics however.

Tara was depicted as being enamored of Steed, and her responses to him were often that of a young schoolgirl in love, and though it is uncertain whether Steed felt as intensely about her, he clearly demonstrated affection and concern about her wellbeing on many occasions. Tara was last seen blasting off into orbit with Steed in a rocket of Steed's own making.

MOTHER

Mother was the supervisor for John Steed and Tara King during the Tara King era of the original *Avengers* series. Seemingly a paraplegic, he was required to use a wheelchair for mobility and seldom left his makeshift headquarters, which were usually a station set up for him in a variety of incongruous locations, from a swimming pool to a double decker London bus to a field of flowers.

He was dark-haired, short, and immensely overweight, possibly owing to his physical incapacitation as well as a tendency to be a bit of a gourmand and bon vivant. His personality was frequently and intensely curmudgeonly, and many a subordinate was subjected to a dressing down at his privilege. He seemed to respect John Steed and Tara however, and this may explain why he so frequently worked with them. Clearly, nepotism was not a concern for Mother, as he also had a nephew named Watney who was employed by the Ministry.

Mother was assisted by Rhonda, a tall, perpetually silent blonde woman, who was required to obeisantly abide his condescension and primarily acted as a lackey. It was suggested that she was also highly skilled at martial arts however, and thus she could function as a bodyguard. Though she never spoke in the entirety of her onscreen appearances, it was implied that Rhonda could speak and simply preferred not to do so.

'Mother' was a codename, and his real name was never revealed, much like that of One-Ten and the rest of the 'One' series in the early seasons of the program. Another Ministry official, code-named 'Father,' appeared in the episode "Stay Tuned" as a replacement for Mother. She was a blind woman whose sense of hearing was especially acute.

ICONIC TITLES

For this season, two entirely new title sequences were created. The first one was originally used for the Tara King episodes in the American market's third season—composed of "Invasion of the Earthmen" through "Look – (stop me if you've heard this one) But There Were These Two Fellers..." It is uncertain exactly how many episodes went out with these titles, but we know that the second version of titles was shot in July 1968, well in advance of the British airings of Tara King, and this second version was used for all broadcasts in the UK. Nevertheless, some prints of the first six episodes still have the first sequence in place, and this version of the titles dominated syndication in America prior to the release of the series on DVD in the early 2000s. Most of the title sequences for these episodes have now been replaced with the newer version. However, the episode "Split!" includes the earlier version on the official StudioCanal DVDs. Even in the UK, prints of "The Forget-Me-Knot" used the end titles of the first sequence, possibly to emphasize that it was a transition between the two eras of the series, beginning with Emma Peel's title sequence and ending with Tara's. It must have been very confusing to UK viewers when the opening sequence never appeared on *any* broadcast and indeed the end sequence was never seen again!

The first version of the titles was shot in studio in January 1968 at Elstree and was directed by Harry Booth. It starts with the "The Avengers in Color" placard appearing over a painter's palette with a pearl necklace, a silver revolver, and a carnation on top. In animation, a row of black figures looking like target practice sheets flows from right to left in a countdown. A gun sight chases across the figures in the opposite direction before settling on a figure with a heart at its center. The program title appears in white against a red background. (This is preceded by a subliminal shot of two red hearts against a white background that only appears for a few frames.) The same gun sight then tracks across red figures with black bowler hats atop them. When the target again settles on a figure with a heart, the film cuts to a closeup shot of Patrick Macnee from behind. He turns to the camera and removes his bowler. The gun sight then tracks curvier figures in red until it settles once more upon a heart, and the film cuts to another subliminal shot of red pop-art lips, and then to a closeup of Linda Thorson wearing a dark orange mini dress and coat with a white turtleneck underneath. The animated gun sight chases them around briefly before Steed uses his bowler as a distraction, resulting in a bullet hole in the hat's crown. One version of this sequence has gunshot sound effects, the other just music. The entire sequence was shot upon an empty soundstage with a pale orange backdrop. The end titles continue this sequence with Tara handing Steed his ruined hat, which he places on his head after a long pause of consternation. They then appear to casually dodge more gunfire in a coordinated routine around the soundstage before settling close together as Tara romantically strokes Steed's lapel. The Laurie Johnson theme song is very similar to the prior three seasons but is even more upbeat with a glassier sound and a fast trumpet solo.

The second title sequence used during the Tara King era was primarily shot on a bright sunny day in Aldenham Park on 3 July 1968 and was directed by Robert Fuest. It begins with "The Avengers in Color" placard over a shot of a grassy field with a halberd stuck in the ground by its spiked tip. A broadsword is propped against the halberd, and both are draped in colorful ribbons and a pearl necklace with Steed's bowler hat lying nearby. The film then depicts rows of knight's armor with colorful plumes emerging from their helms. More halberds are stuck in the ground next to the suits of armor. John Steed crouches upon the grass and then raises a shield (decorated with a rampant golden lion) against a sword attack. The sword scrapes a carnation from the shield's surface, and the program title appears superimposed atop it in a freeze frame. Steed then points the sword at a suit of armor, which falls over revealing that the helm is full of red carnations. He then smiles towards Tara King, who rises from the grassy field in a black low-cut evening dress and a pearl necklace. She runs through a door frame, closing the door behind her, and catches the bouquet of carnations tossed to her by Steed. Suddenly dressed in casual clothes, Tara then runs across a bridge and through a row of knight's armor to greet Steed with the carnations in her hands. The Laurie Johnson theme song is the same as in the first version of the titles. Inexplicably, the end titles are composed of hands performing various card shuffling tricks against a black velvet backdrop. What this has to do with the opening sequence is anyone's guess.

Both of the opening title sequences have the names of the lead actors and producers only, each time freezing the action for the superimposed caption.

CHAMPAGNE, CARS, CLOTHES, AND CANINES

At first glance, it might not look like much changed for this season regarding fashion. However, behind the scenes, there was in fact a seismic shift occurring, and it centered as much around Patrick Macnee as his new co-star, Linda Thorson. As bizarre as it might seem today, questions about Steed's apparent masculinity had been raised from almost the very beginning of the series and great pains had often been taken to decrease any possibility of perceived foppishness or gender transgression.[1] Howard Thomas, the ABC chief executive, once again raised the point prior to production of this season, and great pains were taken to consciously elevate Steed's manliness.

The association of the series with Pierre Cardin had not helped. As I noted in my fashion commentary for Season Five, Cardin's distinctly French take on the character meant that his clothes had lost their essential Edwardian Englishness and had simultaneously become more effete. The loss of a casual clothes line had not helped either, resulting in Steed lounging around in purple silk tuxedos instead of a black cardigan and slacks. (It's hard to imagine anything more effete than lounging around in a purple silk tuxedo!) With the apparent blessing of the ABC executives, by the end of the first production block, Macnee had dispensed with Cardin's services and was designing his own wardrobe and receiving credit for it in the end credits. Casual clothes would return, although they would never be the same again. The wacky late-1960s had to inflict its style upon these decisions as well, and it has to be said that Macnee's choices were not always the best, sometimes resulting in outrageous patterns and garish colors.

This new outlook affected Thorson as well, forcing her character of Tara King to go in an even more feminine direction than had Diana Rigg, and she resultingly became the young ingenue to a much older man (Macnee was in his mid-forties at the time), immediately playing on Steed's greatest weakness, that of women—which we were apparently hearing about for the first time—and wearing more colorful and free-flowing clothes with floral patterns. And pink, lots of pink.

Both Macnee and Thorson were given amphetamines to help them lose weight, and reportedly Macnee lost nearly thirty pounds and needed to have all his suits taken in. And the newest version of the title sequence emphasized all these collected changes. Macnee is slimmer, wearing a gray suit with very little color, and playing around with medieval knight iconography as Thorson chases across the landscape either wearing a floral blouse with balloon sleeves or a long slinky black evening dress with string pearls, her arms clutching a bouquet of red flowers. If anything, this season is almost heavy-handed with its reinforcement of traditional gender roles.

As for cars, they are more prominent than ever. Each of the regulars have three to play with, including Mother. Champagne flows like never before—literally in a champagne fountain—and Steed acquires a new pet dog, albeit only briefly.

Fashion designer for Linda Thorson: Alun Hughes
Fashion designer for Patrick Macnee: Pierre Cardin and Himself

Best Dressed: "Love All"
Worst Dressed: (tie) "Invasion of the Earthmen," "Legacy of Death"

AVENGERS CARS

JOHN STEED

1927 Bentley 3 Litre (YT 3942)—racing green with red seats—in "The Forget-Me-Knot," "Split!," "Have Guns–Will Haggle," and "The Curious Case of the Countless Clues."
1923 Rolls-Royce Silver Ghost 40/50 (KK 4976)—pale yellow with black seats—in "Game,"

---

1 The tag scene joke at the end of "The Positive Negative Man" about "AC or DC" was one that the production team themselves often bantered about. The fact that it actually made it into the show was evidence of how frequently it was raised.

"Super Secret Cypher Snatch," "You'll Catch Your Death," "Whoever Shot Poor George Oblique Stroke XR40," "False Witness," "All Done With Mirrors," "Legacy of Death," "Look – (Stop Me If You've Heard This One) But There Were These Two Fellers…," "The Interrogators," "The Rotters," "Wish You Were Here," "Love All," "Stay Tuned," "Take Me To Your Leader," "Fog," "My Wildest Dream," "Get-A-Way!," and "Bizarre."
1929 Rolls-Royce New Phantom Mark I (UU 3864) in "Who Was That Man I Saw You With?," "Homicide and Old Lace," "Thingumajig," "Requiem," and "Take-Over."

TARA KING

Lotus Elan +2 (NPW 999F)—orange-red—in "Have Guns–Will Haggle" and "Homicide and Old Lace" ("The Great Great Britain Crime")
AC 428 convertible (LPH 800D)—dark maroon with black top—in "The Forget-Me-Knot," "Super Secret Cypher Snatch," "You'll Catch Your Death," "Split!," "Whoever Shot Poor George Oblique Stroke XR40," "Look – (Stop Me If You've Heard This One) But There Were These Two Fellers…," "Invasion of the Earthmen" (driven by Steed), "My Wildest Dream," and "Get-A-Way!".
Lotus Europa (PPW 999F)—orange-red—in "False Witness," "Legacy of Death," "The Rotters," "Wish You Were Here," "Love All," "Stay Tuned," "Who Was That Man I Saw You With?," "Thingumajig," "Requiem," and "Pandora."

MOTHER

Bentley Continental (3 HKM) in "Super Secret Cypher Snatch."
1954 Leyland Titan PD2 double-decker bus (OLD 666) in "False Witness."
BMC Mini Moke (THX 77F) in "Fog."

LADY DIANA

1968 MG C Roadster[2] (BWM 300G)—pale green ("Snowberry White")—in "Killer."

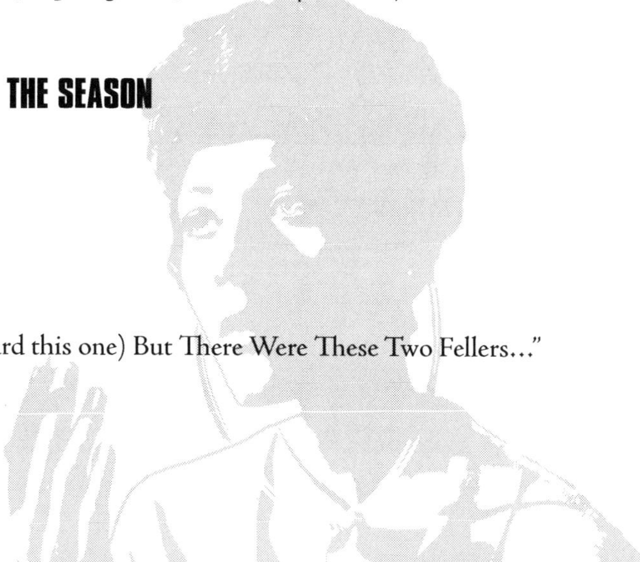

THE MOST FANTASTIC EPISODES OF THE SEASON

1. "Super Secret Cypher Snatch"
2. "Love All"
3. "Game"
4. "The Interrogators"
5. "Killer"
6. "They Keep Killing Steed"
7. "Look – (stop me if you've heard this one) But There Were These Two Fellers…"
8. "False Witness"
9. "Noon Doomsday"
10. "My Wildest Dream"

---

2 This is often referred to as an MGC 'convertible,' but further research reveals it to be an open-top car, not a convertible. This particular MG model was called the MG C Roadster and it was distinguished from the MG B by the oval bulge in the bonnet with an accentuating chrome strip. The bulge was a design change necessary to accommodate the 6-cylinder inline engine. The regular MG C was a coupe. Although the paint color is called "white" in other books, the official MG car color is "Snowberry White" which is actually a very pale green.

129 (7.1.1) THE FORGET-ME-KNOT

Written by Brian Clemens
Directed by James Hill

GUEST CAST

Patrick Kavanagh (Sean), Patrick Newell (Mother), Jeremy Burnham (Simon Filson), Jeremy Young (George Burton), Alan Lake (Karl), Douglas Sheldon (Brad), John Lee (Dr. Soames), Beth Owen (Sally), Leon Lissek (Taxi Driver), Tony Thawnton (Jenkins), Edward Higgins (The Gardener)

PRE-TITLE/TEASER

In a darkened wine cellar, two men engage in a violent fistfight. When the fight comes to a draw, one man pulls a high-tech gun from his coat and shoots the other. Despite being shot, the second man flees the basement and hails a taxi, but he quickly finds that he has total amnesia.

SYNOPSIS

Steed and Emma find fellow agent Sean Mortimer wandering in the street with a serious case of amnesia, claiming that there's a traitor in the organization. Steed goes to tell Mother, but while he's gone the enemy strikes again, taking Mortimer and wiping out Emma's memory too. When he returns to his apartment to help Emma, Steed is ambushed and his memory is wiped also. Emma is taken and Steed is left behind. Slowly regaining his memory, he finds his way to see the new trainee Tara. With her help, Steed discovers that there's a traitor in the Ministry, and he's very close to Mother…

REVIEW

First things first. As you're probably already aware, this is the episode in which Diana Rigg departs the series performing her memorable hand-off to Linda Thorson, who would star as Tara King over the next thirty-two episodes. Rigg's performance in Emma's departing scene is very touching, sweet, and especially sensitive, and she dutifully reminds Tara to stir Steed's tea anti-clockwise perhaps as one last effort to make sure he is taken care of. She appears to be so verklempt at leaving Steed that she can only speak in a whisper, her eyes watery upon turning to leave. This is also the one and only time in the series that Steed calls her Emma instead of "Mrs. Peel." Linda Thorson suggested in interviews that Diana Rigg's emotional response was not acting, she really was saddened for leaving the show. Having Mrs. Peel's husband revealed as a Steed-lookalike is also a charming touch, and this suggests the source for her attraction to Steed.

We'll never forget Mrs. Peel, but we'll also never forget that she was essentially (re)married off, ostensibly re-conscripted to domestic housekeeping and cookie-baking just because her husband suddenly reappeared. What?—she can't be a secret agent anymore because she's married? There was apparently a limit to how liberated women could be in the 1960s after all. And so, this scene perfectly expresses the ennui we feel for the lurking changes, juxtaposed as it is with appreciation for the episode's one charming trait. Yes, I said 'one charming trait' because there really isn't much else to recommend.

Linda Thorson is actually pretty darn good in this story, but there is still a fundamental difference in persona and a lack of the cool detached Chelsea wit for which her predecessors were well-known, and fundamentally the nature of Steed's assistant is dramatically altered. It had been established from the very beginning that Dr. Keel, Cathy Gale, and Emma Peel were all "talented amateurs," experts in their fields without any special spy training. All of them were recruited by Steed himself without apparent Ministry approval. They were best friends, not co-workers. They worked together because they liked being together, not because they were ordered to do so. Now, this had all changed. Not only was Tara a full agent, just like Steed, but she was seen completing her training in some kind of ***Get Smart*** training camp with instructors disguised as trees right out of the ***Wizard of Oz***.

Underscoring this was the presence of Mother played by Patrick Newell. Patrick Newell does a fine job but the character himself was to be mostly a pompous windbag that would only occasionally demonstrate charisma throughout the remainder of the series. As the future would show for the most part, the direction his new role indicated would fail; there was no need to turn backwards in the direction of his predecessors One-Ten (Douglas Muir) and Charles (Paul Whitsun-Jones). This was supposedly encouraged by American executives at ABC who liked Mother. Bluntly, the show didn't need it.

With regard to the more aesthetic qualities of the episodes, although there is some dramatic lighting and fine direction in the opening scene, director James Hill appears to leave his creativity at home, the remainder of the story being rather pedestrian in appearance. To be fair, this might have been due to the break in production that left this episode unfinished for several months.

Narrative-wise, another problem is that the identity of the traitor is painfully obvious from the beginning. Burton clearly doesn't like Steed very much, and we know that Steed is great. Thus, by his casting aspersions on the lead character, the viewers already know Burton's on shaky ground. The script's not particularly clever either, sporting a dreadful amount of padding in only fifty-two minutes. It's pretty hard to move a plot when no one can remember anything. Everyone largely sits around trying to remember who they are and what they were doing just now, and then later trying to remember what they were just trying to remember.

It's also very surprising how inconsistently the forgetfulness drug works. Some people forget everything, others just some things, others just things that are convenient to the plot. For example, Mrs. Peel and Mortimer seem to forget their entire life stories. They spend all their time locked up, trying to remember their names. Tara, on the other hand, forgets just the conversation she had with Steed twenty minutes earlier. And Steed recovers amazingly quickly despite getting several full-strength shots of the drug. Just one or two lines dropped in might have been all that was necessary in order to explain why it works differently on different people. (Try DNA, that's always a good one.) And what is the point of all this memory loss? The traitors don't seem to have a real plan; they just go around shooting everyone with dementia darts.

In the end, this episode—aside from Mrs. Peel's exit—is appropriately forgettable. But, worse still, is the sinking feeling that the program itself is now turning anti-clockwise.

CHAMPAGNE, CARS, CLOTHES, AND CANINES

Mrs. Peel wears her scarlet-red coat again but this time with matching pants and a tan jumper, so it makes it almost an entirely different outfit. Tara King arrives for her first scene wearing a khaki corduroy jacket and trousers with a black jumper and black beret. Her face is smeared with face paint as she undergoes training. It's definitely a look we never got with her predecessors, and there's something to say for that. Nevertheless, it foreshadowed the fact that Ms. King's wardrobe would be more youthful and hip. Her color of the episode is a bright-green; first, a green jacket with matching trousers and a black jumper; and, then, a blouse and miniskirt in the exact same color, sometimes paired with a camel-colored overcoat and a blue-and-green print scarf, and sometimes worn with beige shoes and sometimes with black boots. She also wears a midnight-blue dressing gown with her hair wrapped up in a pale-blue towel, and in the final moments, a pale-tan sleeveless V-neck (very short) pantsuit with thigh-high black boots and long gloves. She wears a cheetah print fur coat over it. For the title sequence, which is generally only seen for the closing credits in this episode (depending on where and when it was syndicated), she wears a muted-orange jacket and miniskirt over a cream-colored rollneck jumper with orange heels. I've never been wild about the color of this last outfit, as I always felt it blended in too much with the dark-orange color of the cyclorama backdrop.

Steed debuts one outfit in the end titles: a grey three-piece suit fastened with a single jacket button, but otherwise he wears mainly his pale-gray two-piece suit with a pale-blue shirt, a blue spotted tie, a pale-gray bowler and matching umbrella. We get a good look at his Chelsea boots when he puts Tara's card in one. They're sort of a pale greenish-gray.

The villains have quite the look themselves with tweed jackets, rollneck jumpers, houndstooth driving caps, black boots and leather motorcycle gauntlets, and goggles with deep-red lenses. They drive a BSA A10 (431 BY) with sidecar and a Triumph T100 (NKM 741).

The 1927 Bentley 3 Litre makes a welcome return, and it looks like it has received a new paint job—the green appears brighter and shinier. Steed briefly drives a 1966 Rover 2000 Mark I. And Tara's maroon AC 428 convertible makes its debut appearance. It was a promotional gift from AC Cars, who were eager to get in on some of Lotus's action. Mrs. Peel's husband Peter drives a champagne-colored 1967 Rolls-Royce Silver Shadow Drophead Coupé Mulliner Park Ward convertible (YMB 20F). He wears a navy-blue double-breasted overcoat with matching trousers, bowler hat, and umbrella. His shirt is white and his tie red.

TAG SCENE

Steed makes the arrangements for Emma's departure from Ministry service and her replacement. Her husband, Peter Peel, has been found alive in the Amazonian jungle. Emma is planning to meet him at Steed's apartment, and they bid each other farewell. As Emma leaves, she tells Tara that Steed likes his tea stirred anti-clockwise, and when she meets her husband, he looks and dresses exactly like Steed.

QUOTES

"Even the biggest idols can have feet of clay."
"I'd rather she didn't have any happy memories."
"Peter Peel Alive: Air ace found in Amazonian jungle. Wife Emma waits."
"Always keep your bowler on in times of stress and watch out for diabolical masterminds."

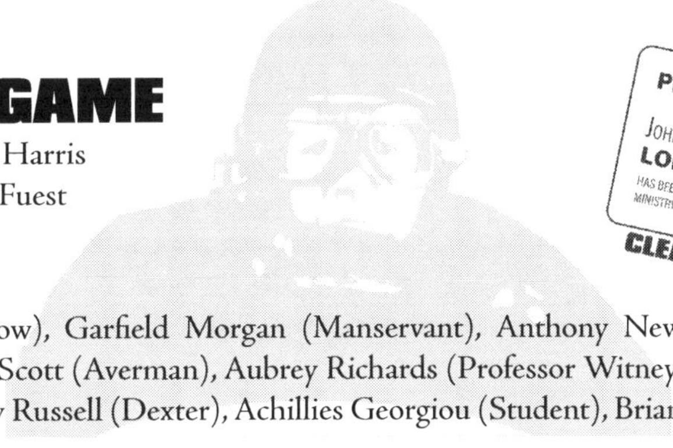

130 (7.13.2) GAME

Written by Richard Harris
Directed by Robert Fuest

GUEST CAST

Peter Jeffrey (Bristow), Garfield Morgan (Manservant), Anthony Newlands (Brigadier Wishforth-Brown), Alex Scott (Averman), Aubrey Richards (Professor Witney), Desmond Walter-Ellis (Manager), Geoffrey Russell (Dexter), Achillies Georgiou (Student), Brian Badcoe (Cooty Gibson)

PRE-TITLE/TEASER

A race car driver drives an apparent racing simulator, having been given only one minute to complete his race by an unseen man. After driving several laps around the track, illustrated by a model, he loses control and crashes. When he falls out of the car, he is suddenly in a completely different location with jigsaw puzzle pieces filling the lenses of his goggles.

SYNOPSIS

Steed and Tara are surprised by the deaths of several former officers Steed served alongside in the military. They are being killed by a villain who is forcing them to play life-scaled games tailored to their profession, in this case with death as their ultimate reward. Unable to save his colleagues,

Steed is forced to play the final game of "Super Secret Agent" in order to rescue Tara from a giant hourglass...

REVIEW

This is the first episode of the fourth (and final) season to be broadcast in the United States, and it followed "The Forget-Me-Knot" in the United Kingdom's final season as well. It's easy to see why. By the time of this episode's filming, the issues that had arisen in the first filming block—script issues, production chaos, Tara's ill-defined character, her confusing relationship with Steed, and Linda Thorson's tortured hair which forced her to wear wigs—were resolved, and there were several good (possibly great) stories in the can, mostly filmed in the second production block. "Game" is one of them.

As they say, all you need is an original idea, not necessarily your own. As such, this episode is a masterpiece of artistic and entertaining gloss. Richard Harris had previously written the over-the-top comic book spoof "The Winged Avenger," a story that involves one death by comic book character after another, a comic book villain who is only defeated once someone beats him at his own game. Here, he produces a superficially similar story involving the repetitive deaths of unwilling participants whose high-risk games fail to pay off. Steed and Tara finally beat the mastermind behind it all by taking his challenge and winning. The villains in both stories are eccentric oddballs who are obsessed with childlike subjects, comic books and board games respectively.

Robert Fuest hides this simplistic approach behind a façade of high directorial style. Like all of Fuest's episodes in this season, "Game" is beautifully and creatively shot, lending this mostly superficial revenge story credibility. Although betraying its lack of budget by depicting a race car driver by way of a toy car on a tabletop track, intercut with a real man in a life-size race car simulator, the pre-title sequence makes up for this with flair as the driver is thrown to the ground, revealing puzzle pieces inside his goggles.

Steed and Tara's relationship seems to crystallize at this point in the season, becoming a matter of Steed rescuing his assistant far more often than he did in the past. The relationship is definitely that of a junior agent to a senior one, but Steed does slap Tara's bottom in this episode, which is too much. I imagine either Cathy Gale or Emma Peel would have sent him flying if they had been on the receiving end of such rudeness.

The Super Secret Agent Game in particular is a triumph, giving Steed a chance to show off by running rings around all of Bristow's traps. The final fight scene again embraces the ***Batman*** style of Harris' previous script, as Steed and Tara stand back-to-back punching foes. All of it is immensely entertaining. It's not flawless and it's not high art, but it is a jolly good time, just the way you would want to start out a new season. It's unfortunate that this high quality couldn't be maintained throughout.

CHAMPAGNE, CARS, CLOTHES, AND CANINES

Tara immediately introduces a new outfit: a canary-yellow jacket with a sloping V-neck and no lapels, navy trim, and two silver buttons. She wears it with a matching (very short) miniskirt and a collarless blue polo shirt with white trim. Later, the outfit is seen without the jacket. Steed wears a brand-new light-gray three-piece single-breasted suit with a white shirt, a silver-blue silk tie, and a matching gray bowler. This was also the suit worn in the updated title sequence, albeit with a pale-blue shirt, pink paisley tie, and, of course, a bright-red carnation. The suit would be worn in nine more episodes throughout the season. Tara changes to a barely-there sweater minidress in a robin's egg blue and a long, beaded necklace, and then, in fairly rapid succession: a hot pink long-sleeved blouse and black trousers and vest; a lime-green jacket and miniskirt; a hot-pink minidress with long-sleeves and a V-neck; and then a black vest with black culottes, a lavender blouse, a purple scarf, and black knee-high boots.

Meanwhile, Steed also debuts a brown three-piece suit (sort of a chocolatey color) a white shirt and brown tie with dark brown spots (which would return in a further twelve episodes); a dark-blue three-piece suit with pale-blue shirt and crimson tie; and a taupe three-piece suit with a dark-brown felt collar, cream-yellow shirt, and brown paisley tie, plus matching taupe bowler. This last one comes across as much classier on film than it might seem in the description. And that is quite a number of debut outfits for one episode! Then it all goes bad in the tag scene, in which Steed wears a garish gray-blue and brown print shirt in a vine pattern and Tara wears a canary-yellow long-sleeved, button-down blouse and a green miniskirt.

The 1923 Rolls-Royce Silver Ghost makes for a welcome return.

TAG SCENE

Steed and Tara relax at his flat playing a board game, but Tara finds the rules incomprehensible as they are always in Steed's favor. When she demands an explanation, he reveals that the game is called Steed-opoly.

QUOTES

"Tell me, what do you do on long winter nights?" "I ride a bicycle."
"Excellent. Excellent! He's really entering into the spirit of the thing!"
"You cheated! You cheated! Cheat! Cheat! Cheat!"

131 (7.12.3) SUPER SECRET CYPHER SNATCH

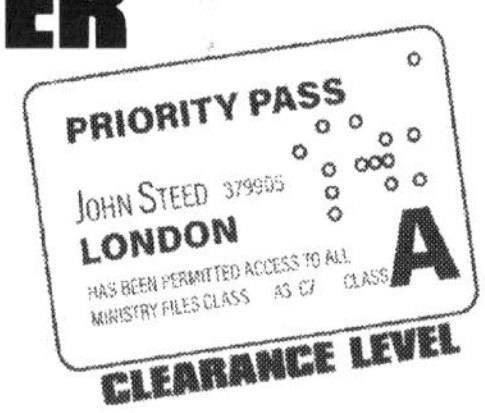

Written by Tony Williamson
Directed by John Hough

GUEST CAST

Allan Cuthbertson (Webster), Ivor Dean (Ferret), Angela Scoular (Myla), Simon Oates (Maskin), Donald Gee (Vickers), John Carlisle (Peters), Nicholas Smith (Lather), Alec Ross (1st Guard), Lionel Wheeler (2nd Guard), Anne Rutter (Betty), Clifford Earl (Jarret), Anthony Blackshaw (Davis), David Quilter (Wilson)

PRE-TITLE/TEASER

An old woman rides a bicycle past a Ministry agent on a country lane. When the agent receives a radio call from headquarters he is admonished for letting the old woman pass. He chases the cyclist down on his motorcycle, and, of course, it's an enemy agent bearing stolen secrets awaiting an escape by helicopter. The two agents engage in an epic fight with the helicopter flying overhead before they both draw their handguns. The enemy agent misses, but the Ministry agent fires back, killing him, and then forces the helicopter to leave by firing numerous shots.

SYNOPSIS

The leaking of top-secret cyphers from the Ministry of Defense has prompted an internal investigation, but agents seem to vanish before beginning their assignments. Photographic evidence proves they had been there, but the entire staff of Cypher HQ insist they have never seen the missing agents...

REVIEW

This is one of the few seventh season episodes that features all the classic attributes of *The Avengers* at its peak—fun, suspense, eccentrics, surrealism, excellent direction and scripting, wit, and good action scenes. The core idea is slightly strained. I don't find the idea of paralysis gas all that believable, but thankfully the other aspects of the story more than make up for any defects in the spy idea-of-the-week.

John Hough's direction is particularly good, some of it as good as any high-budget James Bond film. The dramatic pre-title sequence is of remarkably high cinematic quality. A motorcyclist (played by a young David Quilter) wearing a red helmet with eyes painted on the back—Get it? He has eyes in the back of his head—lets a man in drag riding a bicycle escape their spy dragnet. He catches up with the 'old woman' and they engage in an epic fight with an enemy helicopter hovering overhead. I find myself in cheerful admiration of the fact that Hough chose to—in the middle of this epic fight—have the cross-dressing man slap the motorcyclist with his egg basket. This is ***The Avengers,*** folks! It is full of humor mixed with violence. It turns out that the old pepperpot was peddling more than bicycles. The motorcyclist, having defeated the cross-dressing agent and driven the helicopter off, finds that the basket is full of photographed secret cipher information.

Equally good direction is in evidence when Classy Glass is setting up for its raid upon the Cypher Headquarters. The array of shots, alternating between wide angle and extreme closeups, really sells the images on an artistic level. There is one subtly odd scene, the significance of which modern viewers might miss, as we find out why Mother is always surrounded by telephones. Mother and Rhonda sit in a car in the middle of a field of flowers (possibly the same as the one in the title sequence and at the end of "All Done with Mirrors") and in a reality-defying moment receive a phone call from Steed, which Steed rings on a 1920s candlestick phone in his own car many miles away.

Eccentrics-wise, it is during Steed's trip to Classy Glass Cleaners Ltd that he meets one of the best *Avengers* eccentrics, the duplicitous Lather, played by Nicholas Smith who later became famous for playing Mr. Rumbold in ***Are You Being Served?*** Quite naturally he refuses to serve Steed's fictional estate. Allegedly, all the windows save one are boarded up and such a sight would surely cause all of his employees to fall into a nervous faint with the resulting shock. Lather is, of course, the actual villain and dispatches his foes with fatal applications of window-cleaning supplies—a camel skin towel and cream rinse suffocation hit job… with a hot air finish. Steed also endures an attack by homicidal window cleaners, and a ladder passes straight through his windscreen, taking his bowler hat off as it does so. This ironically ruins his beautiful window but doesn't prevent him from picking up Tara after work.

Peters, the flamboyant photographer, who really missed his calling in fashion, might even be *The Avengers'* first (or second) gay character. Unfortunately, he dies a rather ignoble death by window-cleaner. Naturally, he had to go as he was the only character that would be able to spot the anomalies in the photographic evidence. It's a delightful idea; the characters are completely still in the photographs. No, they're not made still by the photography, but frozen still *before* being photographed. So, how would one be able to tell? It's a gimmick that is slightly goofy but manages to work anyway.

A fun and delightful romp, "Super Secret Cypher Snatch" is a triumph for the Tara King era, proof that they could come up with the goods when they really tried.

CHAMPAGNE, CARS, CLOTHES, AND… CAMERAS!

Steed's gray suit from the first version of the title sequences returns, albeit with a pale-lavender shirt and a pink tie. Tara wears a sky-blue long-sleeved minidress with pink shoes and a blue and pink scarf. Then, a white long-sleeved blouse, with black slacks, boots, blue-and-white cravat, yellow-brown snakeskin belt, and a black vest (fastened with a chain); and a navy shirt with the rest of the outfit the same. Steed trades his suit out for another ugly brown-and-black striped cardigan with a black placket and tan trousers. And Tara then adds a deep-green fitted jacket with triangular pockets to the prior outfit before changing for her new job to a pink minidress with orange trim and placket and a long orange-and-pink scarf in diagonal stripes. Steed adds another brown serge three-piece suit (with a confusing weave that suggests stripes or bands and even looks like herringbone in some shots) with a brownish-green suede collar, a white shirt, and a brown paisley tie (another winner that would come back seven times). For her next day at the office, Tara wears a long-sleeved lime-green minidress with yellow collar, placket, and cuffs, and matching knee-high boots. While investigating the photos, Steed wears a brown long-sleeved shirt, striped brown trousers, and a brown scarf; and, while undercover, he wears white overalls. For the tag scene, Tara wears a low-cut ankle-length black evening dress with a green feather boa, while Steed returns to his blue three-piece suit from "Game."

This episode contains the (semi-)famous meeting in the field of flowers, in which all of the regulars' cars are parked facing one another. Mother sits in his Bentley Continental, though it's unclear if he ever actually drives it (or rides in it), Tara sits atop the hood of her AC 428 convertible, and Steed stands in front of the 1923 Rolls-Royce Silver Ghost.

The motorcycle the agent rides in the pre-title is a blue 1967 BSA B25 Starfire (MOJ 771F) with a bright red-and-silver BSA star logo. The same model bike returns in "Take Me To Your Leader" though with a different registration. The helicopter is a Hughes 269B helicopter (G-AVZC), and this is one of several appearances in this season.

The cameras carried by Peters were only glimpsed for the most part, with a Mamiya Press camera being visible, and only the barest few frames of some kind of TLR can be spied, probably a Rolleiflex. The 35mm SLR camera he uses remains unidentified. One thing's for certain, he's merely playing at an actor's idea of a photographer. When he takes a photo of Tara, it's so close, the best he could possibly have managed to get is a blurry photo of her nose.

TAG SCENE

At Steed's flat, Tara is dismayed at her inability to master hypnosis. Steed insists it's simple and demonstrates his technique by attempting to hypnotize Tara with a swinging pocket watch. However, he instead accidentally hypnotizes himself and then obeys all Tara's commands. But when she orders him to take her to dinner, his hypnosis act is revealed to be a ruse, and he only agrees when Tara says she'll pay.

QUOTES

"We only use the finest camel skins, you know." "Camel skins?" "Hold twice as much water."
"There are no shortcuts to the top of our ladder."
"The sight of all those boarded windows...men have cracked under less!"
"Air conditioning, at last!" "Compliments of Classy Glass, the people who really care about windows."
"It is a perfectly ordinary, perfectly boring day."
"Never leave your ladder unattended."

132 (7.10.4) YOU'LL CATCH YOUR DEATH

Written by Jeremy Burnham
Directed by Paul Dickson

GUEST CAST

Roland Culver (Colonel Timothy), Valentine Dyall (Butler), Fulton Mackay (Glover), Sylvia Kay (Matron), Patrick Newell (Mother), Dudley Sutton (Dexter), Peter Bourne (Preece), Charles Lloyd Pack (Dr. Fawcett), Henry McGee (Maidwell), Hamilton Dyce (Camrose), Bruno Barnabe (Farrar), Fiona Hartford (Janice), Geoffrey Chater (Seaton), Jennifer Clulow (Georgina), Emma Cochrane (Melanie), Willoughby Gray (Padley), Andrew Laurence (Herrick), Douglas Blackwell (Postman)

PRE-TITLE/TEASER

A man is receiving a medical checkup from his doctor as a courier arrives with a letter. After the courier drops the letter through the letterbox, the nurse delivers it to the doctor, and once he opens it, he begins to sneeze violently, finally collapsing and dying.

SYNOPSIS

Ear, nose and throat specialists are sneezing themselves to death and all because of mysteriously 'empty' white envelopes. After Tara gets captured by the enemy, Steed traces the envelopes to a nursing school and discovers that they aren't quite empty after all—they contain a concentrated viral strain that kills nearly instantly. He soon finds the perpetrators, but can he stop them before Tara catches cold…?

REVIEW

Frankly, this is an unimaginatively-scripted episode, largely a predictable run-around that offers little more than one uninteresting death scene after another by obviously overdubbed scream-sneezes. You can see how tired the script-writing was getting by this stage as every cliché in the book is being used without all the usual classic *Avengers* elements that enlivened the best stories.

Speaking of wheezing sneeze-fits, I have serious questions about the method of assassination. As is often the case during this era, the methods used by the villains work only as well as allowed by plot convenience. It just doesn't seem likely that a simple envelope could contain a germ, and even if it could, surely anyone who handled the envelope would catch the virus, not just the first person to open it. Very few viruses can survive long outside a host anyway. And even if you let that one by, Steed opens an envelope himself and doesn't get affected, apparently because he 'dumps' the contents onto someone else. It's sad when the success of our heroes is only accomplished by the contrivances of the writing.

On the upshot, Linda Thorson again impresses me in this episode. This is the first episode in the second production block of the season, and she does indeed seem to have settled down into a consistent character. I'm still frustrated however by the need to put her in costumes rather than the stylish outfits of her predecessors. It seems that designer Alun Hughes (and/or the producers) suddenly decided that the *Avengers* girl needed to be kooky and comedic in the way that she dressed rather than stylishly practical. This could have worked fine, but I personally find that it seldom does.

I am however amused by the generally good pop-art design, such as a giant sculpted nose on the wall in the ear, nose, and throat office, out of which Tara later sneezes herself, and one of the more bizarre examples of Mother's roaming headquarters with multiple brightly-colored stepladders scattered around.[3] It's a typical bit of over-the-top whimsy for the series, which is now all-too often in short supply. Sadly, it's not quite enough to enliven this story overmuch. I suppose it's pretty hard to make a story about germ warfare fun; and ultimately, it all takes a turn for the deadly serious at the end.

This episode certainly isn't the worst of the series, just slightly languid, suffering under a mild brain-haze not unlike the kind delivered by multiple dollops of cough syrup when under the weather.

CHAMPAGNE, CARS, CLOTHES, AND CANINES

Not a stellar episode as far as fashion goes. They put Tara in a cranberry-colored pantsuit, with a matching fitted jacket with five round, black snaps and triangular snap pockets, a white blouse, and a wide polka-dotted clown tie (somewhat like a collision between Diane Keaton in ***Annie Hall*** and Colin Baker's Doctor in ***Doctor Who***) with a short crop of dark hair setting the whole ensemble off. This is the first time we've seen her real hair this season due to the bleaching crisis (mentioned in the season notes), going by production order, so this explains the short hair, fair enough, but the suit is a much less understandable decision. Not to be outdone, Steed wears another cardigan exactly like the one in "Super Secret Cypher Snatch" except in blue tones instead of brown. It's only slightly more palatable in this color. No better in the tag scene is his dark-green rollneck jumper and matching cardigan, with (speaking of clown clothes) brown vertically-striped trousers, nor is Tara's brown dress with white trim and white fur coat that looks like it was made out of a freshly sheared sheep.

Virtually none of the new fashions in this episode work for the characters in my opinion; the suits almost never seem to suit Thorson's figure, and putting Macnee in outrageous 1960s designs and garish colors undercuts his gravitas and style. Unfortunately, there is more of this to come. On the other hand, Steed does debut a new charcoal single-breasted, three-piece suit, which is just fine, and Tara brings back the yellow jacket with navy blouse and hat (from "Game"), although the colors of these disappear during car rides, making the outfit look black and white.

Both the AC 428 and the Rolls-Royce Silver Ghost reappear, and there is a fairly extended chase sequence in which Tara pursues one of the letter-bearing assassins. The villains, for their part, like to be chauffeured around in a luxurious 1965 Rolls-Royce Silver Cloud III Sports Saloon (CDK 978C), albeit while dressed as chauffeurs.

TAG SCENE

At Steed's flat, Tara has a bad cold and rests her feet in a bowl of hot water. Steed nurses her back to health with his Auntie Ermintrude's patent cold cure remedy, a nasty looking green liquid poured into a tumbler. Tara remarks that the drink tastes rather good but refuses it after Steed admits that his auntie died of a cold. He then begins to sneeze himself and joins Tara by placing his own feet in a hot water bowl.

QUOTES

"It seems there's nothing deadlier than the mail."
"If you want to play games, lady, we must get you a copy of the rules."
"The oldest motive, the oldest cliché, they knew too much."
"Always keep a hold on nurse for fear of catching something worse!"
"By the way, you forgot your mail!"

---

3 This scene took place in a one of Elstree's concrete water tanks, which had been drained for the filming. Many years later, this site would be re-developed and end up as the location for the ***Big Brother*** television series.

133 (7.4.5) **SPLIT!**

Written by Brian Clemens
Directed by Roy Baker

GUEST CAST

Nigel Davenport (Lord Barnes), Julian Glover (Peter Rooke), Bernard Archard (Dr. Constantine), John G. Heller (Hinnel), Jayne Sofiano (Petra), Steven Scott (Kartovski), Maurice Good (Harry Mercer), Iain Anders (Frank Compton), Christopher Benjamin (Swindin), John Kidd (The Butler)

PRE-TITLE/TEASER

At the top secret and very high security Ministry of T.S.I., Harry writes at a desk in the Executive Rest Room. He has a brief conversation with Frank, and then after receiving a mysterious phone call, he suffers a psychotic episode that causes his writing to become an incomprehensible scrawl on his papers. When Frank returns, Harry shoots him. However, moments later, he doesn't even remember having committed the murder.

SYNOPSIS

Someone is transferring the personality of a Soviet agent into the minds of loyal Ministry agents and then using those involuntary traitors to commit murders from the inside. As the number of traitors and murders rack up, Steed and Tara discover that the Soviet agent is Boris Kartovski, a man whom Steed near-fatally wounded in Berlin in 1963. After dealing with the perpetrators, they now must stop Rooke who is also about to go over the edge...

REVIEW

It has to be said from the outset that the agent with an induced schizoid personality is somewhat of a novel twist on the double agent theme. Granted, I'm aware of the comparisons to ***The Manchurian Candidate***, but this isn't merely pre-programmed instructions but a wholesale change of personality. Okay, based on the pre-title and premise, I'd say I'm interested. Sadly, as intriguing as this schizoid idea is, it's hardly enough to sustain an hour of television on its own.

The problem with the stories during this troubled era in the program's history is that they all too often tend to have nothing other than the big-idea-of-the-week to sustain them. So much of this season seems to be using "You Have Just Been Murdered" as the template—alas, without Mrs. Peel. That was a reasonably good story, supported by a good guest cast, some fine humor and witticisms, several mildly eccentric villains, and a few fun action scenes. Not a masterpiece but a stalwart example of ***The Avengers*** at its peak. Why does the seventh season struggle to maintain such a simple format?

But, even if you're a fan of this one and you're shouting at the book, "No, no, no, you're wrong! It's much better than that!"—well, just hear me out. Let me put it to you this way. You give me a good premise, written by Brian Clemens, directed by Roy Baker, and guest starring Bernard Archard, Christopher Benjamin, *and* Julian Glover, and frankly, I expect *acres* better than this. Such an episode should be knocking my socks off! Something happened. The celebrated wit is turned off—completely. The tone is grim. All the characters, whether schizoid or not, are languid and dull. The guest stars are among the crème de la crème of what was available at the time, and yet they struggle to bring their characters to life. Even Christopher Benjamin's handwriting analyst seems weighted down by the banality of it all. And why are characters like that limited to such brief scenes in this season? Can you imagine Benjamin's scene being that short in the fourth season? The one exception to my guest star criticism is likely Glover, who manages to pour his all into his final scene, but it's striking that it requires that much effort to cut through the morass of doldrum.

This is a bit of a Tara-light story—or perhaps I should say a Tara-as-light-secretary story. Thus, she spends an awful lot of time hanging around Steed's apartment with little involvement, shuffling files and making his phone calls. The only time she ventures out, she ends up getting captured. Next week, she'll be making tea, toasting scones and giving Steed backrubs when he gets home from work! Portentously, we are seeing what I call the Tara-of-the-week, in which her personality and role in the series shift from episode-to-episode as they were figuring her out. What they wanted her to do, and what they wanted her personality to be, shifted depending on the writer. To be fair, however, this is still very early in the production order, and indeed the production was very chaotic during this time. Linda Thorson was frequently brilliant when given something good to work with, but so much time is wasted before we get there.

Lastly, the usually reliable Laurie Johnson produces some annoyingly repetitive music which beats out a piercing refrain every time a schizoid agent's clawing hand is shown. Basically, it's all about marking time for the big action-scene climax, which at this point seems obligatory. Thankfully, it's a good one, but, having wasted the first forty-seven minutes, "Split!" is such a snoozer of a plot that it's no wonder that the real villain is nearly in a coma when Steed and Tara discover him. And a bit of action isn't enough to wake him or us up.

CHAMPAGNE, CARS, CLOTHES, AND CANINES

Tara gets a new double-breasted, knee-length bright-red coat with two columns of brass buttons down the front. She pairs it with brown gloves and boots and a patterned cream scarf. Steed debuts a new pale-gray three-piece suit with pale yellow shirt and a copper-colored silk tie. Nice cufflinks too. Tara strikes back with a brown sleeveless minidress. The cut is perfect for her figure, even if the color is a bit drab. Her next move is a woolen miniskirt in a deep maroon color with a matching single-breasted jacket with bright buttons—she pairs it with a cream handbag and gloves. Steed blocks her with a new gray three-piece suit with a white shirt and a metallic-blue tie—still great cufflinks—and a really nice chalk-striped charcoal overcoat. But Tara returns fire with a gold miniskirt, white blouse, and gold fitted jacket and orange creamsicle scarf. Unfortunately, Steed responds with an olive-green patterned shirt and a brown blazer and checked trousers, and he's all out of ammo. Tara wins the day (by a hair) with her pink evening gown, headscarf, diamante shoes, and white handbag and gloves, which lend her an elegance that was sometimes difficult for her to maintain. At least they get to have champagne at the end.

The 1927 Bentley 3 Litre returns for the second time this season (and Steed again uses his car phone), as does the AC 428 convertible, which Tara again uses to chase after the criminals (only to get herself chloroformed).

TAG SCENE

Tara visits Steed at his flat, and he asks her what she'd like to drink, remarking that he has "everything." After Tara concocts an absurdly unrealistic recipe for a drink—"a tall crystal glass of crushed ice, permeated with grenadine, laced with a mixture of Cantonese sake and crème de violette, topped with a measure of calvados, a tablespoon of Devonshire cream, and a fresh, unripe strawberry"—Steed admits he doesn't have any of that, only chilled champagne in a desk drawer full of ice.

QUOTES

"I can't promise you'll play the violin again..."
"Clearly the handwriting of a strong, weak, happy, sad, anxious, carefree man."

134 (7.9.6) WHOEVER SHOT POOR GEORGE OBLIQUE STROKE XR40?

Written by Tony Williamson
Directed by Cyril Frankel

GUEST CAST

Dennis Price (Jason), Clifford Evans (Pelley), Judy Parfitt (Loris), Anthony Nicholls (Ardmore), Frank Windsor (Tobin), Adrian Ropes (Baines), Arthur Cox (Anaesthetist), Tony Wright (Keller), John Porter-Davison (Jacobs), Jacky Allouis (Jill), Valerie Leon (Betty)

PRE-TITLE/TEASER

At the Ministry of Technology Administration—Cybernetic & Computor [sic] Division, a most desperate call is made with the technician declaring that George "must be throwing some sort of fit." As the technicians try to respond to the situation, an intruder leaps into the computer room and blasts George with a shotgun. George, who is actually a computer/robot, prints a ticker tape-style readout, which declares, "Attention!—I have a message of the most vital importance. Help—"

SYNOPSIS

A supercomputer called George Oblique Stroke XR40 is shot while solving a complex equation, and as it dies it names Pelley, one of its creators, as a traitor. As scientists operate and Steed investigates, more attempts are made on George's life and Tara goes undercover to get to the bottom of things...

REVIEW

This episode falls into the lower third of this season and the series, easily one of the worst, failing in almost every department. The script is a dull plodding run-around with a pathetic series of remarkably unfunny computer gags involving George's (the computer's) surgical operations. It's perplexing to contemplate exactly what they were going for when they created this episode—a comedic farce? In of itself, a full-on comedy is not necessarily a bad thing—it was done with reasonable success in "Look – (stop me if you've heard this one)...," but the steady stream of one-liners and would-be witticisms fall as consistently flat as the pulse on a heartbeat monitor, the patient dying on the script-writer's table before anyone actually turned on a camera.

On the other hand, what is perhaps most surprising about this episode is Linda Thorson. Despite spending the first ten minutes in a down-market Eartha Kitt-era Catwoman suit that looks like it was culled from the kid's section at K-mart, she is brilliant throughout and particularly good as Prunella. It seems that Thorson is finally hitting her stride. It's too bad that such a gem of a performance is wasted in such a poor episode. Macnee is also his usual reliable self, putting in a performance that is at turns jovial and vicious (threatening to set a man on fire in one scene). Another slight positive aspect is the direction, which is fairly good; Cyril Frankel manages a few artistic angles that soften the blows of tedium. Sadly, neither Thorson nor Macnee nor Frankel can pull this hour back from the brink of death.

It's the story that is the problem; the usually reliable Tony Williamson should have performed a little more surgery on the plot before submitting it, and frankly, Fennell or Clemens should have caught the problems before the script proceeded so far in the schedule. Ultimately, the tiresome comedic attempts to resuscitate George, relentlessly hammering upon our heads with pseudo-scientific computer jokes for three-quarters of an hour, could be considered an allegory on the failure of the episode in general. Instead, each time, both George and the episode just come back more stupid than ever. "Whoever Shot Poor George Oblique Stroke XR40?" is an episode that should have been put out of our misery.

CHAMPAGNE, CARS, CLOTHES, AND CANINES

We start with our heroes wearing not exactly their best yet again. Steed brings out the chocolate-colored two-piece suit with a matching paisley tie, and Tara wears the aforementioned fancy-dress party outfit. The latter lacks any sparkle at all: a simple full body stocking (catsuit?) in a black jersey with a green feather boa and 'tail' with black boots and a steel-gray and black feather mask.[4] She subsequently wears a nurse's surgical gown and mask, then a hot-pink minidress with a wrap top gathered at the waist under a faux belt with a white string of pearls. This is followed by: a maroon suit, soft-rose scarf with a black pattern, knee-length black boots, and her black fedora; a salmon-orange collarless t-shirt with white trim, black pants, and a yellow jacket; and a black knee-length evening dress with a plunging V-neckline and hoop earrings made from white pearls. Somewhere in here, Steed wears a black golf shirt and trousers with a tan cardigan. He also wears his blue three-piece suit with a pale-blue shirt and black paisley tie. They finish off the episode with Steed's experimental explosion and a bottle of Meudon & Heim champagne (again, a prop label, probably actually filled with Moët & Chandon).

The Rolls-Royce Silver Ghost appears and is admired by one of the villains outside Sir Wilfred's house. Tara briefly drives the AC 428.

TAG SCENE

At Steed's flat, he reveals to Tara that George Oblique Stroke XR40 gave him the recipe for the most "deliciously potent cocktail in the world." When he completes this experimental libation, however, it explodes violently, forcing them to break out a bottle of Meudon & Heim champagne instead.

QUOTES

"It's George—I think he's throwing some sort of fit!"
"I shall need two technical nurses, a stand-by programmer, and an electrical anesthetist."
"What on Earth did you hit him with?" "With a great deal of venom."
"Hands behind your back. Chin out."

135 (7.14.7) FALSE WITNESS

Written by Jeremy Burnham
Directed by Charles Crichton

GUEST CAST

John Bennett (Sykes), Barry Warren (Melville), Tony Steedman (Sir Joseph), Patrick Newell (Mother), William Job (Lord Edgefield), Dan Meaden (Sloman), Michael Lees (Plummer), Simon Lack (Nesbitt), Arthur Pentelow (Dr. Grant), Peter Jesson (Penman), Rio Fanning (Lane), John Atkinson (Brayshaw), Larry Burns (Gould), Jimmy Gardner (Little Man), Terry Eliot (Amanda)

---

4 The mask was apparently to make it easier to hide Cyd Child's face when she performed the two magnificent stairwell tumbles. The tumble was due to Tara getting whacked in the head. Realism wasn't the show's usual bag, but at least it was depicting what getting hit in the head actually looks and feels like.

PRE-TITLE/TEASER

Penman, a spy, creeps into a London parking garage on a mission to search an enemy spy's car. His lookout, Melville, stands by the phone booth ready to warn him if anyone should enter the garage. However, when Melville sees a chauffeur approaching and calls, he lies and tells Penman that "no one is coming." Penman leaves the car, thinking he's safe, but the chauffeur spots him and immediately shoots him. Penman struggles to escape, finally collapsing next to the phone booth, dying and wondering why Melville didn't warn him.

SYNOPSIS

The Ministry's case against Lord Edgefield, a peer accused of blackmail, hits a snag when witnesses go back on their own testimony and one of Steed's fellow agents Melville begins lying about the department's own covert investigation. Tara follows a link to DreemyKreem Dairies, where Edgefield has contracted a milk delivery for all the men who could destroy him...

REVIEW

Milk baths for Tara? Or is it the butter machine for our heroine? This is a fairly average entry in the seventh season but one that has several positives going for it—among them, some superb direction from Charles Crichton, good acting from Linda Thorson, and a chance to show the serious side of spy work in Steed's powerful punch to Melville. Despite this, "False Witness" never really boils over into an example of true greatness, instead just simmering beneath the surface with mundanity, albeit superbly executed mundanity.

The main problem is curiously hard to identify, but I tend to blame the seventh season's all-too frequent lack of eccentrics, wit and surrealism. There is no surrealism, unless you count Mother's office being on a double-decker bus, constantly on the move throughout London's streets—which is really just hyperreal. This allows for Crichton to shoot frequently on location around London, which is admittedly a special treat. However, most of the humor simply falls flat, and the whole affair seems a bit small-scale, just a scheme to keep Lord Edgefield out of jail. In that regard, it's not unlike an episode of the second or third season. That's not necessarily a bad thing, but it has been executed much better elsewhere on many occasions.

The reverse truth serum is an interesting idea and is mostly used to good effect. (Sometimes I think a large percentage of our politicians—and many of their constituents—have drunk about a gallon of this stuff!) However, the milky madness works inconsistently, like most such things in *The Avengers*. And the barrage of lying from Tara gets a bit wearing and silly. Quite unlike Melville, she can behave with integrity but not speak the truth, causing her (and us) great frustration. The final fight scene (with Tara stowed in an automated butter churn) makes up for the story's faults, and Steed finishes off the villains, who have been given a taste of their own medicine.

The story's saving graces are to be found in the acting and the direction. They guarantee that the production as a whole lies somewhere north of mediocre. And, in fact, if you're a fan of many of the other spy series of the 1960s, this might be exactly your cup of Earl Grey. (No milk, please.)

CHAMPAGNE, CARS, CLOTHES, AND CANINES

The episode proper opens with Steed and Tara playing a dice game. She wears a new tan zipper jacket with faux belt, tan boots, and red pants (she doesn't seem to be wearing anything under the jacket), while he wears his blue suit with a sky-blue shirt and a deep-plum tie. The Rolls-Royce Silver Ghost makes a quick appearance taking Steed to his appointment with Mother in his latest mobile headquarters, a red double-decker London bus with the conspicuous registration of OLD 666. Despite the humorously satanic plate number, it seems rather comfortable and well-appointed. (The weather wasn't cooperating though—there's rain all over the windows.) Later, Steed and Melville escape the gun-crazy chauffeur (what is it with chauffeur outfits in this season?) in the Silver Ghost. Steed's chocolate-brown suit reappears with a gold tie. (It's not a favorite for me, the more I look at it.) Ill-advised, Tara responds with a periwinkle-blue vest and culottes over a 'Native American' print blouse. Nope, it's not happening. (So, love all.) Steed eventually debuts a new dark-gray (or charcoal) three-piece suit with a pale-lavender shirt and pink paisley tie—and the brown serge suit with the confusing weave reappears. Finally, for the tag scene, Tara wears purple palazzo pants and a deep-plum blouse with sheer sleeves. Again, nope. Steed wears a crimson silk tuxedo, similar to what he wore in "From Venus With Love," though it's a different outfit, and once again, it's way too Hugh Hefner and not sophisticated enough, in my opinion.

Tara drives her Lotus Europa for the first time this season, and she shadows the DreemyKreem villains as they make their deliveries in their 1963 Austin J2 M16 Milk Float (KWC 739).

There's a dog here, a dirty-looking, cream-colored bichon frise, owned by Plummer and named Suzie. The poor little yapper drinks some of the drugged milk and becomes a liar as well.

The villains toast to their victory with champagne (explaining to each other about their own scheme), and they seem to prefer Meudon & Heim rather than their own milk. It's easy to see why.

TAG SCENE

Tara visits Steed's flat and finds him buttering dozens of slices of bread. When Tara insists that he promised to take her out to dinner, he contradicts everything she says and even says he doesn't like her new outfit. He finally admits he cannot tell a lie and announces that he's already booked a table and that she looks ravishing. The stacks of buttered bread are for "itinerant cats."

QUOTES

"What did you do that for?" "For services not rendered."
"Worried about lack of vitamins?" "Desperately. I'm just wasting away."
"Special delivery, Lane. Sir Joseph Tarleton. Two pints, please."
"It's says, 'Request Stop,' we're refusing your request."

136 (7.11.8) ALL DONE WITH MIRRORS

Written by Leigh Vance
Directed by Ray Austin

GUEST CAST

Dinsdale Landen (Watney), Peter Copley (Sparshott), Edwin Richfield (Barlow), Michael Trubshawe (Col. Withers), Patrick Newell (Mother), Joanna Jones (Pandora), Nora Nicholson (Miss Emily), Tenniel Evans (Carswell), Liane Aukin (Miss Tiddiman), Anthony Dutton (Seligman), Peter Thomas (Kettridge), Graham Ashley (Markin), Michael Nightingale (Real Colonel), Robert Sidaway (Real Barlow), Desmond Jordan (Guthrie), David Grey (Williams), Peter Elliot (Arkin), John Bown (Roger)

PRE-TITLE/TEASER

A Ministry spy named Roger follows an enemy agent named Arkin in his car into a pleasant wooded area. After consulting with Mother by radio, he tracks Arkin on foot, but the enemy agent appears to be having a conversation with an unseen person in the middle of a clearing. Confused, he shoots Arkin, but after briefly examining the body, he is himself shot by an unseen assailant.

SYNOPSIS

Steed's failure to find the source of leaked secrets at a government think tank has led to his being placed under house arrest. Tara and fellow agent Watney are sent to the coastal installation but find that the killers responsible can vanish into thin air...

REVIEW

This is a very stylish episode, one that serves as a vehicle for Tara King to almost go solo. The plot is very linear and just about non-existent, mostly serving as an excuse for Steed (and presumably Patrick Macnee) to have a vacation and simultaneously show unwarranted concern for Tara. Is she a fully autonomous agent or his girlfriend? Make up your mind. Although, while re-watching the episodes in production order, I have praised Linda Thorson in recent episodes for improving enormously, at the time of this episode's filming, I still don't think she quite had the screen presence to fill the gap as yet. Thus, the lack of Steed makes the story sag in its first two-thirds. Pairing Tara with a buffoon was an equally poor idea. Watching Watney interrogate the scientists is like watching a bad Inspector Clouseau impersonation.

The tendency to trick people into falling off cliffs in this episode results in Tara falling to her apparent death, and in an unbelievable twist of unreality, she survives without a scratch. Playing with the laws of physics is no way to pump her up as a character.

What good we do have is some lovely direction and location filming. In a smart move, Ray Austin did a lot of shooting on location in two very picturesque settings. Therefore, we get lovely white cliffs in the south of England and a wonderful lighthouse in Devon twenty-seven miles south of Torquay. (Astonishingly, these two locations are some two-hundred-forty miles apart!) There is a particularly beautiful shot through Guthrie's eyeglasses as he is about to fall off a cliff, highly reminiscent of a classic scene from Hitchcock's ***Strangers on a Train***. Perhaps too referential but it intrigues nevertheless.

Though Thorson's stunt double Cyd Child is a bit too obvious in several shots, there is an incredible action scene on the lawn of a country estate between Tara and a bearded baddie. Worse still, is the obvious stunt rolls as a man falls down the steps inside the lighthouse while deliberately and obviously accelerating his rolls. These minor but noticeable gaffes are especially surprising considering that the director is the show's former stunt arranger.

I can't help but giggle at Tara teasing Steed using the 'retro-meter,' cajoling him into taking her to dinner later. Part B of this conversation takes place in the tag scene, in which they eat filet mignon at a table in the middle of a field of flowers, which may be the same field as used in the opening titles. Interestingly, the core concept of transmitting signals by light waves isn't so far-fetched. Sound can be transmitted via laser, although it cannot be transmitted audibly into thin air as yet.

"All Done with Mirrors" tends to be a popular episode with many fans, but overall I find it to be something of a stylishly-filmed mixed bag.

CHAMPAGNE, CARS, CLOTHES, AND CANINES

Steed debuts a new brown tartan blazer, which replaces the one he'd worn since Season Five, with a matching waistcoat and trousers. It's a beautiful fabric, but it once again makes analysis difficult as there is almost a moiré-like effect depending on how far away the camera is. Tara wears a red tartan skirt with a dark-teal stretch shirt. (She would later pair the skirt with a matching tartan top in "The Rotters," but more on that later.) For her mission, she switches to a muted-green jacket and trousers with a white blouse and matching scarf and beret; the trousers are belted with a gold chain belt with oversized oval links. The jacket is simultaneously casual and hip and yet has detailed stitching, shiny snap buttons, and a great fit. One of her more successful outfits. For the tag scene, she wears a full-length evening gown with diamante embroidery; the sleeves, back, and neckline are sheer showing her skin through the embroidery. She pairs the outfit with black shoes. Steed wears a new midnight-blue tuxedo with a double-cuffed shirt, a silver necklace with a dark-red gemstone (possibly a garnet), and a gigantic black bowtie. And, of course, there's a bottle of champagne standing by.

For this episode, her vehicle of choice is an army-green 1966 Morris Mini Moke Pick-up (LYP 794D) from the Carmadoc Research Establishment. She is knocked off the cliff by a Triumph Tiger Cub 200 motorcycle, but as a consolation she is taken home by Steed in his Rolls-Royce Silver Ghost and cooked a juicy rare filet steak on its engine.

TAG SCENE

Steed and Tara meet for a candlelit dinner in the middle of a bright sunny field full of flowers where Steed reveals that he has cooked their steaks on the engine of his 1923 Rolls-Royce Silver Ghost.

QUOTES

"I'm innocent, entirely innocent!" "Yes, but for how long?"
"I'm awfully flattered, really, you dashing in to the rescue like this."
"Don't worry. I won't haunt you, if you promise to take me out to dinner tonight."

137 (7.16.9) LEGACY OF DEATH

Steed inherits a dagger—Tara undergoes the feather torture
Written by Terry Nation
Directed by Don Chaffey

GUEST CAST

Stratford Johns (Sidney), Ronald Lacey (Humbert), Ferdy Mayne (Baron Von Orlak), Kynaston Reeves (Dickens), Richard Hurndall (Farrer), John Hollis (Zoltan), Leon Thau (Ho Lung), Tutte Lemkov (Gorky), Peter Swanwick (Oppenheimer), Vic Wise (Slattery), Teddy Kiss (Winkler), Michael Bilton (Dr. Winter)

PRE-TITLE/TEASER

In an ornate room full of Oriental treasures, the elderly owner of the house is expecting to be assassinated. Assisted by his butler, he steps into a casket where he pretends to be dead. The would-be assassins—who appear to be caricatures of Kasper Gutman and Joel Cairo—arrive, and finding him dead, retrieve his Last Will and Testament.

SYNOPSIS

Steed inherits an ornate dagger from a recently deceased and anonymous benefactor. Immediately afterwards, Steed is besieged by various baneful visitors, including a wild-eyed Russian named Gorky, who are desperate to take the dagger for themselves. Almost all of them end up dead in Steed's drawing room. Attempting to trace the origin of the objet d'art results in Steed's model plane flying being interrupted by a quasi-Sam Spade cosplay...

REVIEW

This is an obvious parody of *The Maltese Falcon*, full of mildly amusing comedy that is all-too frequently tired and contrived. Now, I'm as big a fan of John Huston's classic as you will find. I watch the film at least biannually. However, I fail to find this crude spoof any better than cartoonish in its execution. At best, it can be considered another of the ongoing failures in Terry Nation's attempts to capture the true *Avengers* spirit. At worst, it's a failed comedy that has nothing to do with it.

The various characters are mostly two-dimensional caricatures, Gorky especially so. He sports an absurd parlor version of a Russian accent, and in stereotypical Russian fashion must throw every glass he drinks from into the fireplace. I fail to understand the humor here, which is built upon embarrassing stereotypes of foreigners. Equally, Ronald Lacey, who practically made a career out of Peter Lorre impersonations, nevertheless seems to be channeling Renfield rather than Joel Cairo. For his part, Stratford Johns fails to capture any of the gravitas, guile and humor of his model, Kasper Gutman (played by Sydney Greenstreet in *The Maltese Falcon*), coming across instead as merely sweaty and crude. In general, the acting is so pantomime-like as to uncomfortably remind one of "Epic" from two seasons ago—never a good comparison!

There were some moments that I found humorous, such as when a would-be assassin leaps from the roof in an attempt to ambush Steed and Tara only to miss and fall flat on his face, knocking himself out. As a result, Steed and Tara get their chances to share witty retorts right out of a James Bond script, but the rest of the story's comedy falls just as flat as the aforementioned villain. And the fatally embarrassing tickle-torture of Sidney is a deal-breaker from my perspective.

The introduction of the Baron von Orlak is one of the more bizarre moments in this season, starting with a Chinese man masked like a Buddhist asura tossing miniature throwing axes to pin Tara's sleeve to a crate. The episode picks up at this point and becomes slightly more engaging, but it is too late to save it.

Anyone familiar with the story's vastly superior point of reference will guess that the prize will not be retrieved at the end[5], leaving the finale to be obvious. This episode has its adherents, and you might be one of them. I wouldn't count on it because I find it to be mostly an hour of distilled tedium.

CHAMPAGNE, CARS, CLOTHES, AND CANINES

Steed debuts a new blue single-breasted three-piece suit, buttoned with a single button, with a pale lilac shirt and a tie the color of port wine—beautiful diamond tiepin too. Tara visits in her Lotus Europa while wearing a Confederate soldier outfit from the American Civil War on her way to a fancy-dress party. She does bring champagne, however. He shares the champagne with Gorky (and loses all his champagne glasses in the process). Tara's next fancy-dress outfit is a cerulean-blue and pink kimono, followed by emerald-green pants and vest with a collared purple blouse with frilled cuffs. The villains escape in a yellow 1958 Land Rover 109" Series II with cherry-picker. For the tag scene, Tara wears a rosy-pink minidress with a fleshy-pink trench coat, and Steed brings out the green-and-brown vine print eyesore again. Neither is a winner.

TAG SCENE

Tara visits Steed at his flat where he is dismayed about having built his model plane improperly. After insisting that he's fixed the problem, a test flight ends with the plane crashing through the window.

QUOTES

"This man has been shot, Mr. Steed...Never mind, we can work wonders today. Soon have him up and about.""This man is dead, doctor."
"But after I've been subtle, then can I kill him?"

---

5 As a side note, wine, if it still is to be drinkable, is not more than 0.1% acetic acid and not sufficiently acidic to dissolve a pearl, at least not nearly as quickly as seen in this episode.

"A very inferior type of assassin…""They just don't make them like they used to…""It's the age of the amateur…""No pride in their craft."

138 (7.15.10) NOON DOOMSDAY

Tara hits the hay—Steed faces a gunfight at high noon…
Written by Terry Nation
Directed by Peter Sykes

GUEST CAST

Ray Brooks (Farrington), T.P. McKenna (Grant), Griffith Jones (Baines), Lyndon Brook (Lyall), Peter Bromilow (Kafka), Patrick Newell (Mother), Peter Halliday (Perrier), Anthony Ainley (Sunley), John Glyn-Jones (Hyde), David Glover (Carson), Lawrence James (Cornwall), Alfred Maron (Taxi Driver)

PRE-TITLE/TEASER

Two horsemen ride through the forested English countryside to an abandoned train station. There, they reveal that they are assassins planning to kill Steed at twelve noon.

SYNOPSIS

After breaking his leg, Steed finds himself inside Department S, a sort of high-security hospital. When Tara comes to visit, things immediately start to go awry. After the facility's guard is killed, they soon realize that an old enemy is planning for his revenge against Steed at noon, and only Tara and Sunley seem to be willing to defend him…

REVIEW

This might be Terry Nation's best effort for ***The Avengers***.[6] It is perhaps the only time he managed to get the feel of the series (mostly) right, and this does much to bring this season out of the doldrums.

If you've ever wondered what happened when a secret agent was laid up with an injured leg, wonder no further. They go to an undisclosed location surrounded by minefields and electrified fences and convalesce with champagne secreted in by their friends. At least in ***The Avengers*** they do. This humorous idea turns out to be less humorous than one might imagine, but it does give the show an opportunity to feature a lot of bizarre agents holed up in the hospital. This is partially wasted, and it's easy to imagine that they'd be orders of magnitude more bizarre in prior seasons. But never mind.

Given the threat to Steed, the only one of them besides Tara that seems to be willing to help is Sunley (played by a very young Anthony Ainley), who is so heavily bandaged that he is practically mummified and therefore useless. Frankly, the situation is not entirely convincing. It's hard to imagine hardened agents unwilling to go to bat for one of their own. That is an example of how Nation just missed getting the feel of ***The Avengers*** right. He comes closest here but strikes just south of the bullseye.

By turning Steed and Tara against each other over the issue of who should be protected, we are also left confused by their apparent irrationality in the face of extreme peril. Steed must lock Tara up to protect her so she can't defend him? Tara must protect Steed by knocking him out so he can't defend himself? What! Did anyone actually think this through? It's hard to imagine secret agents

---

6 While this might indeed be Terry Nation's best script for the show, then again it might be because Brian Clemens rewrote it extensively and apparently gave Nation a bit of a dressing down for forcing him to function as a script editor for the script editor.

thinking with their emotions like this. As Steed is injured (and then knocked out by Tara), the many exciting fight scenes mostly involve her, but Steed appropriately gets to finish off Kafka with a spear gun hidden inside his walker.

The apparent *High Noon* spoof that starts the episode seems to go nowhere. Perhaps convinced that doing any approximation of a western was dubious at best, the parody never quite launches, merely allowed to remain a superficial comparison. I think this is a wise decision. The script focuses instead on the apparent eccentricity of the villains. Thus, after riding in on horses through the hilly English countryside, the villains announce that they will kill Steed at noon and then proceed to spend the bulk of the episode holed up in an abandoned train station, where one practices his shooting and the other contemplates what he will get his niece for her birthday.

The best aspect of this story is a plethora of beautiful and artistic direction that so characterizes this season and the previous two, and Peter Sykes spends a lot of time shooting in a similar style to contemporary auteur directors. Most of the episode is wisely shot on location, and the aforementioned train station and the exteriors for Department S are very picturesque, giving Sykes opportunities to place his camera looking down the converging lines of railroad tracks and through wagon wheels in a barn.

In light of the superior taut and artistic direction and some fine performances by the regular cast, I'm willing to ignore this story's minor flaws. This is a fine addition to *The Avengers* cannon, surviving mainly on style rather than substance, though like so many this season it just misses true greatness.

EPISODE NOTES

Much of this episode was filmed at Brian Clemens' farm in Ampthill in Bedfordshire. The train station was filmed near Leighton Buzzard at the then abandoned Stanbridge Station, which has since been demolished. Reportedly, Linda Thorson didn't like to be stunt-doubled and thus performed one of Tara's leaps herself, a sixteen-footer into some cardboard boxes without an injury. However, she did suffer a severe rope burn to her hands later that forced the filming to stop for the day.

CHAMPAGNE, CARS, CLOTHES, AND CANINES

Tara wears an orange, pink, cobalt-blue, and muted-green blouse in a floral print that makes her look a bit like the Scooby-Doo van. There are also thin white stripes in the green sections of the print. She pairs it with a cranberry-red vest, matching pants, and a thin black belt. The vest is clasped at the abdomen with a thin silver chain. (This is also the final outfit she wears in the second title sequence.) It's pretty typical of Tara's wardrobe and, as usual, lacks all the grace and style of her predecessors. But, to be fair, she was a much younger character, and thus would have been in tune with the hipster fashions of the day. And many viewers today might appreciate the audacity and novelty of such clothes. Steed's white raw silk Nehru jacket and matching trousers come across as slightly better but are still a far cry from his usual sense of style. For the tag scene, Tara wears a sparkly white evening gown with gold over the bust, a plunging neckline, spaghetti straps, and a floral decolletage in front. She looks like Macy's wrapped her as a wedding gift. Steed wears his midnight-blue tuxedo with a ruffed-front white shirt.

No cars in this episode. Steed's laid up for the majority of the narrative and Tara walks or runs about, but the villains ride horses and have a helicopter, a Hughes 269B (G-AVUM). (The Hughes helicopter was rented for the day from Gregory Air Services in Denham.)

There are several bottles of champagne. Tara smuggles one in for Steed who gifts Tara with another bottle at the end. Not to mention the fact that Mother temporarily turned Steed's flat into a display of fine liqueurs and cordials during his occupancy.

TAG SCENE

Tara visits Steed at his flat where he reveals that he has an enormous wrapped gift for her. It turns out to be a bottle of champagne with a large gem attached, a sun hat, cigars, a floral-patterned parasol, and a 'luminous' sundial that chimes the hour.

QUOTES

"We kill John Steed at twelve noon."
"What's more vulnerable than a wounded agent?" "Two wounded agents."
"It's Angela's birthday on Saturday…I wonder if she's too old for a doll's house."
"With a boy, it's easy. Just lay down a hog's head of good claret, and by the time he's old enough to enjoy it, the wine is at its most drinkable. But, a girl…I wonder if she's too old for a teddy bear?"

139 (7.7.11) LOOK – (stop me if you've heard this one) BUT THERE WERE THESE TWO FELLERS…

Written by Dennis Spooner
Directed by James Hill

GUEST CAST

Jimmy Jewel (Maxie Martin), Julian Chagrin (Jennings), Bernard Cribbins (Bradley Marler), John Cleese (Marcus Rugman), William Kendall (Lord Dessington), John Woodvine (Seagrave), Garry Marsh (Brigadier Wiltshire), Gaby Vargas (Miss Charles), Bill Shine (Cleghorn), Richard Young (Sir Jeremy Broadfoot), Robert James (Merlin), Talfryn Thomas (Fiery Frederick), Jay Denyer (Tenor), Johnny Vyvyan (Escapologist), Len Belmont (Ventriloquist)

PRE-TITLE/TEASER

At the Caritol Land and Development Corporation, a secretary sets a table for a board meeting and then asks her boss if she may leave early. Once she has left, the building is invaded by two men who dress as clowns and shoot the executive with a gun that goes 'bang' and then dance away vaudeville style.

SYNOPSIS

Steed and Tara end up tracing a clown murderer, whose face is painted on an egg, that was smashed by a vaudeville quick change artist, that takes his orders from a businessman running a Punch and Judy puppet stand, that is located in a clown rest home, that is inhabited by a group of out-of-work vaudeville acts. Oh, yes, and Tara's going to be burned in half by a stage magician wielding a blowtorch if Steed can't save her…

REVIEW

There are so many bizarre moments in this one. It's as if they saved up all the seventh season's allotment of eccentrics, bizarreness and wit for this one effort. In many ways, I would have preferred that they spread it out. But, judging the episode on its own merit, it descends with abandon into pure comedy, mostly successfully.

Eccentrics abound, mostly composed of former vaudeville stars who are angrily killing the board members of a company who has shut down all their theatres. So, there is a valid reason for their eccentricities… I think. Here, the eccentrics are so bizarre that they make John Cleese at the peak of his comedic powers seem normal by comparison. The clown assassins, Maxie Martin and Jennings, murder each victim with joke guns that really go bang, bombs with the word "Bomb" painted on the side, and by pulling the carpet out from under their victims, tumbling them out the window—exiting vaudeville-style stage-left after each murder.

Bernard Cribbins plays a gag writer with an alacrity that's infectious even if his jokes only bring the faintest of smiles to Steed's face. Talfryn Thomas spreads a sadistic snaggle-toothed grin as he attempts to cut Tara in half with a blowtorch. And if you're already a fan of *The Avengers,* how can you not like the bizarreness of clown henchmen taking orders from a Punch and Judy puppet stand?

This story is, like "Game," the rough equivalent of "The Winged Avenger" from the fifth season, an episode that takes the style of the current season and amplifies it beyond all reason. The style of this season so far has been more similar to the third than anything from the Emma Peel era. If this were a third season episode, the villains would have indeed been vaudeville acts, but they would have committed their murders in plain clothes and denied their criminality when Steed and Mrs. Gale turned up to question them at the theatre. We would have had the obligatory scene where Steed shows up and catches part of their act before ducking backstage. Here, the villains commit their heinous murders in their clown outfits in broad daylight.

The absurdity reaches a peak when John Cleese shows up. He's Marcus Rugman, the manager for the Ministry clown makeup registry office. (Yes, the Ministry has a clown makeup registry office!) Each clown's makeup is registered by being painted upon a single (raw) egg. Each egg is placed in a slot in rows upon rickety wooden shelves with narrow corridors between them—so narrow that one must carefully tread a white line to pass through. You cannot make these things up! Cleese's anxiety over the protection of his precious eggs is palpable, and it's easy to see why given the way the eggs are stored. So quite naturally, it's a guarantee that he'll end up doing a silly walk upon a banana peel and smash them all. The worry could have been eliminated by so many options: stronger, more secure shelves; padded boxes for storage; or even hard-boiling the eggs first. But that is the nature of this story, nothing really makes sense in order to sell the comedy.

Once the veil of fun is parted, problems do abound however. The killers are remarkably conspicuous and using them seems like a great risk. The idea that all clowns look alike doesn't quite fly, since people are likely to start feeling wary of any clowns in general once murders have been associated with them. The vaude-villains aren't very smart either. Do they really think they're going to get their theatres back by killing the people who own them? And they incompetently leave multiple clues that allow Steed and Tara to home in on them. Surely, paid professional assassins would have been a better ploy.

Fantasy increases when Maxie practices his quick-change artist routine on Steed in what is surely one of the most bizarre fight scenes of the series. He changes from clown to charwoman, to ballet dancer, to cowboy, to sea captain, to boxer, to Cyrano de Bergerac, as he and Steed tangle. For once, Steed doesn't seem to know what to make of his opponent except simply punch whatever costumed nut pops in front of him. Finally wrapping things up, Steed and Tara find that the puppet master is the straightest man of all, Seagrave, played by one of the most straight-faced actors in the business, John Woodvine. Steed and Tara then do a little exit stage left of their own. It's fun, certainly, but there's also a veneer of melancholy about it that is hard to explain. Perhaps it's the music.

This is a fine story for a one-off experiment, but to focus purely on the comedy aspects of the series is not something I'd care to witness more than once. It's amazing to me that the show dropped so far off track that this broad comedy would be more appealing than what we were getting. Can we not regain that homeostasis, or is it lost forever?

CHAMPAGNE, CARS, CLOTHES, AND CANINES

Steed's brown serge suit returns, and it has quite become my favorite of the season. Meanwhile, Tara debuts a robin's egg blue overcoat with matching miniskirt and a dark-chocolate rollneck jumper and matching leather gloves. Later, she switches this out for a beige rollneck with sky-blue culottes with a matching jacket (and a pink clown nose). Steed debuts a new single-breasted three-piece suit in a very dark charcoal (reads as almost black on film) with a double-breasted waistcoat, a white shirt, and a charcoal-colored tie. One of his more stylish offerings this season, though a tad funerary. Tara then wears a dark-teal jacket and matching culottes with a black crewneck shirt, black boots, and a wide black belt with a round, gold buckle. Steed rescues Tara as "Gentleman Jack" in a new dark-navy double-breasted three-piece suit, white shirt, metallic blue tie with gold and ruby stickpin (the same one as in the second title sequence), and black bowler and umbrella. In the tag scene, she wears a white satin minidress, very short skirt, enormous flared sleeve cuffs with white lacing, a low neckline, and a black choker. She carries a gold handbag.

The AC 428 returns with the top up and Steed accidentally gives it "extra air-conditioning" by poking the cloth roof with a sword. The Rolls-Royce Silver Ghost also makes an appearance when Steed races to Tara's rescue.

TAG SCENE

Steed relaxes in his flat reading ***Le Lotus Bleu,*** a Tintin adventure. When Tara arrives dressed elegantly for the opera, she is dismayed that Steed is still dressed in his casual clothes, but he performs several quick changes of costume, briefly dressing in a traditional Chinese hanfu and Tartar hat, then as a 19th-century British naval admiral, then an indigenous American with a full headdress. He finally settles on what appears to be the proper couture, a tuxedo, but when they turn to leave, he reveals that the back of the jacket has a lighted "Eat at Joe's" sign attached.

QUOTES

"You like that one!" "It has a certain humorous shape."
"Vauda Villa—A Resting Place for Artistes Whose Services Are Not In Immediate Demand."
"They're all eccentrics, all of them...except for me, of course."

140 (7.6.12) HAVE GUNS–WILL HAGGLE

Written by Donald James
Directed by Ray Austin

GUEST CAST

Johnny Sekka (Colonel Nsonga), Nicola Pagett (Adriana), Jonathan Burn (Conrad), Timothy Bateson (Spencer), Michael Turner (Crayford), Robert Gillespie (Lift Attendant), Roy Stewart (Giles), Peter J. Elliott (Brad)

PRE-TITLE/TEASER

At the high security State Ordinance Depot, a cadre of men wearing blue jumpers and clown masks use a trampoline to jump over the security fence. Once inside, they break into a warehouse, overwhelming the guard and knocking him unconscious, and begin to steal a collection of high-powered firearms. But the guard wakes up and demands that one of the intruders hit him repeatedly.

SYNOPSIS

A dramatic theft of three-thousand highly secret new rifles brings Steed and Tara on the scene. The guns have many potential buyers on the black market, including Colonel Nsonga and Steed. After arranging to represent Colonel Nsonga's own president at the same auction the Colonel is attending, Steed must rescue Tara from a hut that's about to send her and the guns sky high...

REVIEW

"Have Guns–Will Haggle" is a surprisingly good effort, especially considering its troubled past. It was one of the episodes filmed when John Bryce was producer and was originally entitled "Invitation to a Killing," scheduled as the first episode of the seventh season. While it fairs much better than the forgettable "Invasion of the Earthmen," there is still a lot lost in the translation to the new era. Because of the production chaos involved behind the scenes, it's inevitable that the story would show evidence of cutting and pasting, and here again we have Tara in a blond wig and salmon-colored padded jacket—not very flattering. On the other hand, the plot, which is not exactly awe inspiring in its complexity, hangs together fairly well.

With the pre-title, we have hipster criminals wearing clown fright masks, turtleneck jumpers and navy-blue high-top trainers trampolining their way into a high-security weapons storage facility, having presumably put their gymnast training time in prior (given the outrageous flips that they engage in). Their leaders are Colonel Nsonga and Lady Adriana Beardsley. Johnny Sekka as Nsonga is the first person of color with lines since Paul Danquah in the fourth season's "Small Game for Big Hunters." Unknown to many at the time, there was a guideline among *The Avengers* production team that called for no black people. While the reasons for this were likely more to do with maintaining a very traditional (and fantastic) vision of England rather than outright racism, it was a sad artistic decision to make, and I'm glad that it at least ended in this particular season. In the end, Nsonga and Lady Beardsley are decent villains, but neither is anywhere near the level of the diabolical masterminds from the past, nor even the caliber of early seventies Bond villains. (That includes you, Dr. Kananga.)

In production order, this is the first episode of *The Avengers* that was directed by Ray Austin. Austin had worked on the series for several years as the stunt arranger but had been progressing steadily towards directing. Ultimately, he would go on to direct some of the most vivid and engaging episodes of television on both sides of the Atlantic. Here, he seems to be holding back slightly, possibly still somewhat in the learning phase of his career, but later on, he would become one of the most artistic and capable television directors around. Aside from the obvious athletic stunts being featured (trampolining in high-top trainers), the episode does have its additional artistic elements. For example, I found myself wanting Tara to stop jumping so that I could observe the beautiful light behind her that threatened to peak through dark moody clouds. The actions sequences and car chases are particularly good as well.

Ultimately, this is a reasonably good episode of the series, but at the risk of sounding like a broken record (indeed, you'll hear me say this many times during this season), "Have Guns–Will Haggle" is merely one of the best examples of the mundanity of the seventh season. It features the usual toning down of the fantasy elements and the celebrated wit, while beefing up the typical spy themes. It's a malaise that was acquired when Bryce started filming this episode, so it's no wonder that it couldn't be fully reversed merely with editing. The surprising thing is that it persisted for so long even after Clemens and Fennell took over.

CHAMPAGNE, CARS, CLOTHES, AND CANINES

Tara starts out in a black leotard and rollneck jumper with a tam o'shanter hat in a red plaid (and clown mask). Steed wears a new pinstriped charcoal overcoat over his light-gray suit from "Split!"

There are a lot of overcoats because apparently it was pretty cold that autumn in 1967. Tara wears a heavy overcoat herself—a tan number with a black jumper, boots, and gloves. Steed switches to a different dark gray overcoat over the same suit as before. Later, without the overcoat, you can see that Tara wears a tan miniskirt underneath with her wide black belt with ring buckle (as in "Look – (stop me if you've heard this one) But There Were These Two Fellers..."). Then, a salmon-pink overcoat with miniskirt underneath (with the blond wig) and pink pumps. Pink seems to be the color of the episode, because she quickly swaps this out for an even warmer plush pink faux fur overcoat with metallic silver bands and a high upturned collar. Underneath, she wears pink tights and matching boots (and the blond wig). We never see what top she wears with it because she switches into her red tartan skirt and frill-fronted white shirt from "All Done with Mirrors" (though to be fair, this is its first appearance in production order). Steed introduces a new dark-navy single-breasted three-piece suit with a white shirt and a dark-blue cravat with white spots with a pearl tiepin (this outfit's only appearance in the series). In the tag scene, Tara dons mustard-yellow culottes with a purple blouse while Steed brings out the eye-blight that is the dark-green-and-brown vine pattern shirt. I can't understand why they couldn't nail the more casual clothes in this season.

This is the only appearance by the orange-red Lotus Elan +2 in the series, and it is involved in quite an exciting chase scene with several dangerous stunts, one of which involves Tara's assailant being thrown from the Lotus to the asphalt, and the stuntman has to quickly get out of the way so she can roar off, immediately after which he jumps into his own car and chases after her. The pursuing vehicle is a 1965 Jaguar Mark 2 (BNF 642C). The 1927 Bentley 3 Litre makes its third of four appearances in this season.

TAG SCENE

Tara visits Steed at his flat to find that he is expecting a gift from the reigning monarch, something "from our country and of our country." They speculate wildly about fancy clocks and uncut diamonds, but when Steed opens the door to receive their prize, he is greeted by a terrifying roar.

QUOTES

"You had to endure fifty-two approved tests?"
"Say, I thought we were chasing an FF70 oblique stroke 9074 XXV Mark Ten."
"What about me? You've got to make it look good like last time. A violent attack."

141 (7.17.13) THEY KEEP KILLING STEED

Written by Brian Clemens
Directed by Robert Fuest

GUEST CAST

Ian Ogilvy (Baron Von Curt), Ray McAnally (Arcos), Norman Jones (Zerson), Bernard Horsfall (Captain Smythe), Patrick Newell (Mother), with William Ellis, Hal Galili, Nicole Shelby, Rosemary Donnelly, Gloria Connell, Michael Corcoran, Ross Hutchinson, Reg Whitehead, Anthony Sheppard, Angharad Rees, George Ghent

PRE-TITLE/TEASER

An enemy agent waits in an abandoned quarry surrounded by junk and debris. Another man emerges from an old car and calls him inside. Within the car is a hidden entrance to am underground laboratory where they have attempted to alter a man's face to look like John Steed. Unfortunately, they consider their results flawed and shoot the test subject dead. They can't work from photos; they need the real Steed.

SYNOPSIS

An enemy scientist named Arcos kidnaps Steed in order to perfect his quick-molding face change technique, which requires the original in order to produce accurate doppelgangers. Arcos wants these doubles so that he may infiltrate a peace conference. Steed manages to switch both the molds and documentation so that five men are assigned to become Steed, and four of them infiltrate the conference simultaneously. But it is when the real Steed breaks out that the confusion really begins...

REVIEW

From the opening pre-title, in which the face of Steed is pried from a giant ping-pong ball space helmet (that looks suspiciously like the one worn by Klaatu in ***The Day the Earth Stood Still***), it is clear that we're in for a special treat. We are quickly told by Ray McAnally (with a suspect German accent) that this apparent duplicate is inaccurate, and then the man with his imperfect Steed face, whoever he might be, is quickly dispensed with by pistol fire. You see, they realized that they cannot create a proper mold for Steed's face from photographs. While any artist worth his salt knows that working in three dimensions from photographs is a bad idea, these baddies needed to experiment and then kill someone to find that out. It turns out that four years of atelier instruction would have served them better than all that science. Thus, the real Steed is captured in order to make a proper maquette, and our story is launched.

The premise is just intriguing enough to sell to the viewer, a good example of toning down the science-fiction ideas from the fifth season yet keeping them slightly outlandish. Thus, while largely mundane, the usual *Avengers* strangeness crops up regularly in this episode. Mother's office is at the bottom of a lake. (Turn left at the salmon nets.) The villains are hanging out in an underground bunker in a quarry. (The entrance is through the door of an abandoned car.)

The script is an especially fine one from Brian Clemens. It is cleverly devised to show the simultaneous execution and unraveling of the villains' plot, yet without spoiling it completely. The monkey wrench is thrown into the works before the machine starts running, but the outcome is still not certain. Thus, we are left with tension and relief at once, relief that the good guys have a small advantage from the outset.

The direction from Robert Fuest, one of the standout directors in this season, is especially good also. Despite his tendency to go for needlessly artistic shots and maybe a few too many Dutch angles, he manages a taut narrative with an economy of shots that put the viewer in the middle of the action. It is a cinematic style of direction, the kind that elevates ***The Avengers*** into territory that was not only superior to most television in Britain at the time (including series that were shot on film) but also to most television in general. Even the American television of the day—American drama inevitably being shot on 35mm film—seldom had such an artistic eye. It's hard to emphasize enough how ahead of its time was ***The Avengers*** in this regard.

Linda Thorson is exceptional in this episode. There is a lovely scene when an apparent Steed shows up and Tara is uncertain whether he is real or not. For perhaps the first time, I'm finally convinced in this scene that these two have had a long-term and close partnership. Likewise, this is one of few episodes from this season that has almost the same feel as the Emma Peel era. One of the strongest episodes from this season, "They Keep Killing Steed" comes just short of true greatness.

Ian Ogilvy—about nine years away from playing Simon Templar in ***Return of the Saint***—makes a guest appearance as a smooth-talking German baron and playboy who has his sights on Tara. He is quickly roped into spy work instead as an ersatz partner for Tara.

CHAMPAGNE, CARS, CLOTHES, AND CANINES

The failed Steed doppelganger in the pre-title wears a pale-yellow suit shirt, olive tie, and pale gray trousers. He is disheveled with the tie loosened and the top button of his shirt unbuttoned—a great way to know it's not really Steed. He also looks a bit sweaty and puffy. Tara opens with a hot-pink miniskirt and a matching long sleeveless cardigan, that is cut more like a vest, with a dark purple-blue blouse. Steed (the real one) brings out his taupe double-breasted suit with a pale-gold shirt and brown paisley tie. For her pairing with the Baron, Tara wears matching cerulean-blue trousers and a vest with a gold frog at the waist and a bright-red blouse underneath. As usual, her sleeve cuffs are rather loose and blousy. The Baron wears a cobalt-blue double-breasted jacket with bright round buttons, gray slacks, and a sky-blue rollneck jumper. Tara's next outfit is a dark-tan distressed cropped leather jacket with studs, a pale-cream blouse, and black stretch pants.

Here's where things get really confusing—Steed's doppelgangers and what they wear! One double, of course, dies immediately. Another wears a taupe suit that matches Steed's. One of his rivals wears a pale-gray two-piece suit with a white shirt and a deep-crimson tie, and the taupe doppelganger quickly dispatches him. The second rival wears a blue two-piece suit with a pale-blue shirt and a red tie, a black bowler and umbrella. The taupe doppelganger wins out again. Quite right, he has the best suit! Once the real Steed escapes, this leaves us with no way to tell the remaining two Steeds apart except for the subtle acting cues by Macnee. If we've followed events this far, we should have covered all the Steeds, but then, "the woods are full of them!" One taupe doppelganger dies and it turns out there's another one, and then another one, which, of course, turns out to be Arcos. Where did they get all those taupe suits and can I have one?

In the tag scene, Steed (the real one) wears another outrageously ugly 1960s flower-power casual shirt (far out, man!) with cream trousers, socks, and slip-on loafers, while Tara wears a sheer black bathing costume and mauve-tinted shades.

Technically, there are no Avengers cars in this episode, but the Baron drives a black 1936 Mercedes-Benz 540 K Roadster (NTR 164) with red seats. (I'll consider him an honorary Avenger as his fencing skills are top notch.) Steed is kidnapped in a pale-blue 1964 Morris Oxford Series VI taxi (GMX 575B). The secret entrance to the villains' lair is a dilapidated black 1948 Austin FX3 taxi.

TAG SCENE

Steed and Tara relax on a sunny beach under giant parasols. Lamenting how little time they normally have for relaxation, Tara thinks it was mean of Mother to make them come back so soon from their assignment. Suddenly, thunder crashes to signal an oncoming thunderstorm, and it is revealed that they actually are in Tara's apartment on an elaborate set designed to mimic the beach.

QUOTES

"These holiday romances, they never last."

"Straight downstream, turn left at the salmon nets."

"Remember that time in Tibet, we rescued that little llama, remember, friend of the Dalai's?...Oh my goodness, it wasn't you at all!"

142 (7.21.14) THE INTERROGATORS

Written by Richard Harris & Brian Clemens
Directed by Charles Crichton

GUEST CAST

Christopher Lee (Colonel Mannering), David Sumner (Minnow), Philip Bond (Caspar), Patrick Newell (Mother), Glynn Edwards (Blackie), Neil McCarthy (Rasker), Neil Stacey (Mullard), Neil Wilson (Norton), Cardew Robinson (Mr. Puffin), Cecil Cheng (Captain Soo), Mark Elwes (Naval Officer), David Richards (R.A.F. Officer)

PRE-TITLE/TEASER

Two men, one in a military uniform, sit casually reading their newspapers at a bar, while screams of agony spill from a door behind them. The apparent torture victim comes out holding his mouth in pain, and the army officer is asked inside next. Sitting in an apparent dentist chair with an apparent dentist, after giving his name, rank, and serial number, the officer refuses to answer any further questions and the scene quickly turns into an interrogation session with two communist Chinese soldiers in attendance. Finally, a rather severe English army officer intervenes, but he only repeats the threats made by his subordinates.

SYNOPSIS

Military intelligence officers have gone missing from active service, and their contacts are being steadily killed off. It turns out they're under house interrogation by officers under the command of Colonel Mannering. However, Steed and Tara find themselves asking why the men under torture are happy to take tea breaks with the Colonel…

REVIEW

The strength of this episode is its plot. The core premise is original and engaging, and for once, we can actually believe that it could occur with agents in the real world. This seriousness is underscored by Steed's anger as he pins Minnow to the wall and threatens to choke him unless he explains his betrayal. The scene that sells the concept the best is when Colonel Mannering confronts Tara and we see the full scheme played out. His confidence man bluffs and misdirection are in full evidence, suckering her in immediately despite her skepticism, making her play the game without realizing it. It's actually sickeningly real. When the villains' secret department is invaded by Mother's agents, including Steed, the evil genius takes a sharper, more brilliant turn, bluffing the unwilling agents into fighting for him under the ruse of it being yet another training exercise. Christopher Lee is of course beyond reproach, relying mostly on his natural gravitas, but it is in this moment that he becomes satanic in his malignant deception, much like many of the roles that he was known for at the time.

The interrogations themselves are hyperreal, mixing casual banter between the men with punishing blows and torture that the men accept as all part of the process. They're still mostly tame, perhaps too tame to be plausible. However, even this can be explained by the fact that they don't confess during torture but afterwards. All in all, this is a brilliant scheme from the minds of Harris and Clemens.

Aside from the ingenious story, the best parts of this episode are the scenes involving its eccentric agents, all of whom are to be betrayed by the confessions of the men being interrogated. Each are shot and killed as they are engaged in their own (often bizarre) pastimes. Izzy Pound and His Incredible Marching Sound has to be one of the most eccentric of eccentrics. He is the most conspicuous secret agent of all time.[7] Steed first finds him marching back and forth in a quarry wearing harlequin trousers, a trilby with a Union Jack tied on, and simultaneously playing an accordion and a trumpet horrendously off-key. His blaring of the patriotic song "Rule, Britannia!" is so loud that he cannot hear Steed shouting as he approaches. We're almost relieved when he's shot and the racket ceases, and the cacophony he unleashes as he rolls down the hill dead is both sickening and silly. Naturally, Steed and Tara get there too late almost every time, Tara finally catching up with balloon seller P. Puffin, whose teeth stick out so far that he'd be well-advised not to get too close to his own wares. The battle among the balloons with the approaching enemy agent that follows is brief but exemplified by notable camera artistry.

By this time, the show had regained its homeostasis, a different balance from what we had before, but a stability nevertheless. This is a good example of the seventh season at its peak. It's a story that works consistently despite not being too strong on the typical elements that have been toned down during this late *Avengers* era.

EPISODE NOTES

In the scene in which Izzy Pound's corpse is revealed to Caspar, a boom mic is very visibly in shot for several frames, corresponding with Mother's line, "Feel his pulse." Presumably, this was the sound man moving the mic closer to Mother when he says his lines, since Patrick Newell was sitting down and Philip Bond was standing.

CHAMPAGNE, CARS, CLOTHES, AND CANINES

The Rolls-Royce Silver Ghost makes a very early appearance in this episode and we get to see the interior in closeup. (Later, Steed uses it to follow Caspar.) Steed is wearing his gray suit and Tara pops out of the secret phone booth entrance in a chocolate-brown minidress with white trim and a matching scarf with diagonal chocolate-and-white stripes and brown pumps. Mediocre. This is followed by a bizarre plaid tweed jacket in pale-green, blue, and white that makes her look like she sacrificed her couch for a new outfit. (I swear we had a couch in that exact fabric in the 1970s!) It's worn with a white jumper and navy pants. Going from ostentatious to bland, this is soon substituted for a black jumper and trousers that is eventually greatly improved by her beautiful green fitted jacket (from "Super Secret Cypher Snatch"). Likewise, Steed wears his blue three-piece suit from that same episode with a black paisley tie. For the tag scene, Tara dons a black evening gown with sequins and sheer sleeves.

The helicopter used to follow the pigeon is a Brantly B2B (G-AVCA), hired from British Executive Air Services.[8] The "closed van" in which Tara was kidnapped is a 1968 BMC EA 350.[9]

Drinks in the bar, but no champagne.

TAG SCENE

At Tara's apartment, Steed is interrogating her over the secret recipe in her soup. It turns out to be merely a dollop of yoghurt.

---

7 One has to wonder how these agents are at all functional given that they're a bizarre instrumentalist, a football player, and a balloon vender. And why do they spent all their time practicing their craft in open fields?

8 Due to inclement weather and other scheduling issues, the filming of the helicopter was delayed several times, ultimately resulting in director Charles Crichton scrapping six scenes.

9 The Royal Mail once owned scads of these, and they were a common sight throughout Britain for most of the '70s and '80s.

QUOTES

"I think you'd better watch your step. Any man who smokes such a revolting mixture must be evil incarnate!"
"She's a woman." "She's also brighter, sharper and more intelligent."
"Follow that pigeon!"

143 (7.20.15) THE ROTTERS

Written by Dave Freeman
Directed by Robert Fuest

GUEST CAST

Gerald Sim (Kenneth), Jerome Willis (George), Eric Barker (Reggie Pym), John Nettleton (Palmer), Patrick Newell (Mother), Frank Middlemass (Mervyn Sawbow), and Dervis Ward, Harold Innocent (Wainwright), Tony Gilpin, Amy Dalby, John Stone, Charles Morgan, Harry Hutchinson, Noel Davis, John Scott

PRE-TITLE/TEASER

An elderly man flees an unseen threat in the countryside, making his way to the Department of Forestry Research. He locks himself inside the building and then his office, but the door instantly disintegrates revealing two men wearing tweed jackets and flat caps. They shoot him and smile smarmily as he collapses and dies.

SYNOPSIS

Two upper-class villains from the firm of Wormdoom Ltd. are murdering former colleagues of the Institute of Timber Technology with the assistance of a spray gun that instantly rots wood. Now, someone has stumbled upon their find, or possibly one of them is betraying the others...

REVIEW

Any episode with an eccentric agency named Wormdoom Ltd can't be all bad. Its upper-class-twit-of-the-year owners are caddish, smarmy and condescending, truly capturing the qualities of the slang term "rotters," which is used as a double meaning in this episode. With their matching brown tweed jackets and driving caps, they kill their prey with a sociopathic charm that is simultaneously sleazy and scornful. Yes, the rot is on the inside as well as the out.

Their top-secret technology rots wood instantly. Is this too fantastic an idea? Well, considering we had brain-swapping and shrink rays in the previous two seasons, I don't think so, but it is a little more over-the-top than usual for this season. The speed with which the wood is destroyed is probably what makes it seem like too much. I think I would have preferred it if the wood corrupted quickly, weakening enough that one could easily crash through. A prop made of balsa wood could easily have been used. It's also hard to comprehend how selective this insta-rot fungus is. Why wouldn't it just keep going once released?

While this is admittedly a superficial complaint, the use of an instant rot-inducer produces many contrived scenarios in which a character attempts to hide within a wooden structure only to have it instantaneously destroyed around them. In other words, the technology is not nearly as useful as the writer makes it out to be. The villains real plan, once revealed, is equally contrived. They plan to replace all the post office boxes with dry rot fungus sprayers that will instantly rot away the entire country. Sounds more like a *Doctor Who* plot.

Given the woody theme for this episode, with whom should Tara fight? Why a lumberjack, of course! Strangely, she defeats him, and he does an aboutface and steals her car instead, passing through a gate which is instantly destroyed by dry rot. He also abandons his own truck in the process. There's never an explanation for this bizarre behavior by a stalwart timber industry worker, and this sort of scripting failure is no substitute for eccentric behavior.

The plot is a typical one for *The Avengers*—too typical—a narrative in which villains are attempting to wipe out members of an elite group that all have a particular association. Steed and Tara do not connect all the dots in time to stop most of the murders, only catching up with the antagonists at the end. This plot was used far more successfully in episodes like "The Positive Negative Man," which is almost identical in its narrative structure. (Perhaps this is why they chose to extensively re-use the music from that particular episode.) That one was helped along by its tidal wave of high-quality witticisms and the spectacular chemistry between the leads. Here, the same plot is not afforded these luxuries, having lost them somewhere along the way, exterminated by John Bryce and not yet completely resurrected by Fennell and Clemens.

Robert Fuest is his usual artistic self for this episode, but he really doesn't have much to work with. There is a fantastic church bell tower with lovely texture. In the first scene with Mother, he has the entire set wrapped in plastic, creating a mod glow amid glittering light. And then there are some lovely shots inside a forest. However, that's all I have to recommend as eye candy.

Ultimately, this story never really gelled for me. This is Dave Freeman's only screenplay for *The Avengers*, and it's a worthy idea, but plot difficulties bring it too far down for direction and acting to prop it back up again.

CHAMPAGNE, CARS, CLOTHES, AND CANINES

Steed's chocolate-brown suit reappears. Despite all the fungus in this episode, it's still not growing on me. Tara debuts a purple overcoat over a lavender blouse and red trousers. This is followed by a new green minidress with white collar and shoulder patches (later worn with a black macintosh). Steed's gray suit from the title sequence returns, and I'm beginning to appreciate its merits, but it can't beat the taupe suit, which appears next. Still my favorite. This is followed by the blue three-piece suit. In the tag scene, Steed relaxes in a dark-orange jumper, tan trousers, and a bright-green scarf. Tara wears another chocolate-brown dress with the 'Native American' geometric print blouse (last seen in "False Witness"). (The 'casual' clothes simply don't improve.)

Tara drives the Lotus Europa to meet Professor Palmer and it is later stolen by the axe-swinging looney, and Steed drives Tara to save Mr. Pym in his Rolls-Royce Silver Ghost.

TAG SCENE

At Steed's flat, Tara is in the kitchen reading out a recipe as Steed relaxes on the couch reading a book. Having verified that the recipe for "Steed's crusted omelet of the mushroom" is correct, Tara retrieves a giant mushroom the height of a bar stool from the den and returns to the kitchen.

QUOTES

"We don't deal in secrets in this department. We plant trees. When they grow up, we cut them down." "What a full rich life you must lead."

"I detest imitations...I loathe anything inferior."

"You weren't thinking of trying to clobber me with that bottle, were you?" "Well, it had crossed my mind. I get so few pleasures down here."

"I say, have you seen what they did to my mother's piano?" "Seen what they did! I was under it!"

144 (7.2.16) INVASION OF THE EARTHMEN

Written by Terry Nation
Directed by Don Sharp

GUEST CAST

William Lucas (Brett), Christian Roberts (Huxton), Lucy Fleming (Emily), Christopher Chittell (Bassin), Warren Clarke (Trump), Wendy Allnut (Sarah), George Roubicek (Grant)

PRE-TITLE/TEASER

A spy breaks through a fence with wire cutters. Creeping into the lush landscape, he briefly spies on a group of young people wearing orange jumpers before he's caught in a bear trap and pursued by a massive boa constrictor. The young people do nothing to help him and only smile in amusement.

SYNOPSIS

Steed and Tara investigate the death of a fellow agent, which reveals a plot by the Alpha Academy to use the youth of England to conquer space. As a result, both Steed and Tara end up in a tunnel that will produce their secret fears while the academy members hunt them down...

REVIEW

This episode starts out right away with a pre-title carrying all the detrimental characteristics of this much-maligned story in microcosm. The on-screen title has very little to do with what we're seeing, as a man cuts through a fence only to get caught in a bear trap and threatened by a massive python while a cadre of blonde Hitler youths grin sadistically at his despair. It's impenetrable, murky and unintelligible, and yet not particularly engaging either, much like the story in general. In fact, the event is nearly irrelevant to the plot, to the contrary of almost every other pre-title in this program's history, all of which served to establish the premise of the story in one brief scene.

This episode exists in a bizarre twilight zone—somewhere between the third and fourth seasons in style and timbre—and stands as the most complete example as to why John Bryce was replaced once again by Fennell and Clemens after a chaotic start to the Tara King era. The script is uneven, the pace languid, and the premise uninspired. Even the production quality seems to have taken a step backward, often looking more like the *early* sixties than the late sixties. The direction, lighting, sets, and characters are all dull, flat and lifeless.

The departure of Roger Marshall had left a gap in *The Avengers*' slate of screenwriters, and, as a result, there was a culling from the best British television writers of the day, which the show could easily command with its international success. If one were to put together such a list, Terry Nation would easily rise to the top as one of the most prominent. He was unquestionably a very fine writer, responsible for many of the great episodes of this golden age of television. Nevertheless, I would say without reservation that he never got the hang of writing for *The Avengers*, and it's easy to see why here.

The Avengers does not lend itself well to Nation's well-trod tropes. He trots out Nazi-lookalikes and fascist villains—something that he is well-known for in his work for *Doctor Who* and *Blake's 7*. And the idea of a tunnel which produces your ultimate fears (and deadly mutations), through which the cast must travel, is also distilled Nation hokum, reminiscent of his first Daleks serial for *Doctor Who*. Unfortunately, both concepts are much less well realized here. The fascist antagonists are ineffectual and dull-witted, relying purely on sadism to distinguish themselves. In the aforementioned tunnel of doom, Steed and Tara encounter only a pool of acid and some fake-looking bugs. Maybe they're averse to bad special effects and poor-quality props. I can certainly relate. On a positive note, however, some of the location shooting is pretty nice though.[10]

The 'humpty-dumpty' astronaut is the episode's only surrealistic element, being completely out of place in every scene in which he appears. Personally, I have an odd and perhaps misplaced affection for this rotund space dweller, who magically appears behind blackboards in schoolrooms. He is the one anarchic element residing in an hour of doldrums. The early fifties appearance of his space suit with his smiling emoji face is a bit of schlocky charm amidst a story that is as dull and stiff as a 1950s London stockbroker. And, endearingly, we never receive any explanation for his appearances.

The main problem of this episode stems from the production chaos that plagued the story. Because this was a Clemens and Fennell re-working of an episode originally planned and partially completed by John Bryce's production team, the editing is rather poor and suggests a cut-and-paste job. Such is the reason for Tara's "disguise," which consists merely of a blonde wig and a frumpy padded coat. She later switches out her costume for something seemingly more appropriate for Robin Hood. There is none of the classic *Avengers* banter as Steed and Tara have yet to work out any organic chemistry. The situation will improve notably as this season progresses, but for now we're stuck with a dull mess that never rises above mere competence.

CHAMPAGNE, CARS, CLOTHES, AND CANINES

Tara starts out in a brown halter neck minidress which is later paired with a checked brown-and-yellow double-breasted coat and the notorious blond wig. Though the cut of the coat is pretty good, this is a serious contender for worst outfit of the season (just like the episode). Again, the fabric looks like it was stolen from the living room sofa. It's pretty sad when Tara's best outfit of the episode is a forest-green terrycloth bathrobe and a white towel headwrap. She later wears a white blouse with a soft kid leather waistcoat with brass buttons, matching trousers and boots, and a chain link belt (and the blond wig), and then, in the tag scene, a bright blue monk's robe lined with blue sequins. Steed makes up for Tara's shortcomings a bit with his lovely brown tartan blazer. Sadly, the hideous olive-green patterned shirt rears its ugly head on Steed for the second time, contaminating the tartan blazer and making this possibly the worst fashion episode overall. The astronaut, for his part, dresses in early Cyberman by Mondas Design Group with a proto-Cyberleader helmet, and it might be the best outfit of the episode.

Steed drives Tara's maroon AC 428[11] with her in the passenger seat. The Hitler Youth villains drive a dark-blue Land Rover (695 EAC).

No champagne, which is a great pity because by now I could use some.

TAG SCENE

Steed attempts to teach some martial arts moves to Tara at his flat. After using her feminine wiles to distract him, Tara quickly masters the lesson.

QUOTES

"...I really saw an inflated astronaut that looked like humpty-dumpty."
"The quarry is our survival area. There, it's kill or be killed."
"Today's youngsters are tomorrow's people." *(You mean they're not people yet?!)*

---

10 The location for the Alpha Academy is Knebworth House near Stevenage.

11 This is because John Bryce had originally decided to dispense with the vintage vehicles and have Steed drive a sports car instead. This decision was reversed when Clemens and Fennell returned to the production, and the car instead became Tara's, essentially replacing the Lotus Elan +2, which, consequently, only shows up in two episodes.

145 (7.19.17) KILLER

Written by Tony Williamson
Directed by Cliff Owen

GUEST CAST

Jennifer Croxton (Lady Diana Forbes-Blakeney), Grant Taylor (Merridon), William Franklyn (Brinstead), Richard Wattis (Clarke), Patrick Newell (Mother), Harry Towb (Paxton), Anthony Valentine (Calvin) with John Bailey, Michael Ward, James Bree, Michael McStay, Charles Houston, Jonathan Elsom, Clive Graham, Oliver MacGreevy

PRE-TITLE/TEASER

A scientist explains to Mr. Merridon that his design is perfect and that the new invention is the center of a complex with air-conditioning, heating, and fail-safe circuits. Satisfied that everything is working properly with Remak, Mr. Merridon sends the scientist inside, and Remak is revealed to be a room filled with glowing light where the scientist is killed.

SYNOPSIS

Investigating the death of an agent found packaged in plastic wrap and pink ribbons in a graveyard, Steed and Lady Diana Forbes-Blakeney are unable to stop their own agents encountering a deadly enemy called Remak. Each one ends up being killed in outrageous ways. Armed with the clues of those that came before him, Steed is forced to confront Remak himself and finds something he didn't expect...

REVIEW

The idea of a computer that's programmed to kill, process and package agents is delightfully absurd and so very sixties. This story is the inverse of "Whoever Shot Poor George Oblique Stroke XR40?" Instead of a tiresome failed comedy about a sick computer, this computer is genuinely frightening, dispensing death rather than being on the edge of it. The pre-title is appropriately chilling, as a nebbish computer designer is thrown to the mercy of his own creation and fatally irradiated by a purple light, leaving us uncertain as to what is going on but in no doubt as to its deadliness.

Tara goes on holiday with a "pink and purple" pass in the first few moments[12], and Steed gets a replacement partner. Jennifer Croxton does a wonderful job as Lady Diana Forbes-Blakeney. She is assertive and dynamic in a way that Tara is not. I don't mean to be negative about Linda Thorson, who improved massively over the course of this season, particularly once the second filming block began, but she didn't have the nuances down and never quite mastered them during her run as an *Avengers* girl. To be even more fair, I don't think Croxton quite achieves the high-water mark either—Diana Rigg was still more subtle and charismatic—but Croxton's Lady Diana comes much closer than Thorson, and I cannot help but think the name is a reference to Thorson's predecessor.

What is slightly problematic is that it's hard to imagine all these otherwise intelligent but overly eager agents rushing with abandon to try and destroy Remak. "Killer" has a huge guest cast, and they are needed with all the agents getting processed by Remak. Does Britain have any agents left? Steed's final confrontation with Remak is satisfying however, as he uses his usual guile to outwit the computer, dumping one prop after another in succession—bowler hat, umbrella, overcoat, suit coat, etc—stripping himself of every tool he has to win the day. Thankfully, like all good 1960s computers,

---

12 Linda Thorson's absence was due to an illness that affected filming on this and "The Morning After."

Remak has a self-destruct mechanism, which Steed operates to produce a much-needed 'blue screen of death.'

Apart from one terribly overexposed shot about twenty-seven minutes in, "Killer" is stylishly directed throughout, including a dizzying rappel down the side of a building in one scene and the terrific final confrontation with Steed amid mod sets and mood lighting. This is one of a small crop of episodes that rises above the rest—one of the seventh season's triumphs.

CHAMPAGNE, CARS, CLOTHES, AND CANINES

Tara begins the episode in her sky-blue knit minidress from "Game" (also with matching cardigan) and she ends it in a pink blouse and deep-red high-waisted trousers. The rest is about Lady Diana Forbes-Blakeney, and I wish I could say it's a huge improvement on the designs this season, but I cannot. Nevertheless, it is palatable. Her first outfit is a purple blouse and magenta skirt with a sky-blue neckscarf and matching calf-high boots and a magenta belt with a large brass buckle. (Again, Velma from Scooby-Doo vibes.) She follows this up with a bright-yellow long-sleeved blouse, gray pants, and a navy-blue cravat with white spots. (Reportedly, Croxton did not like this outfit.) Next is a brown and red herringbone overcoat with bright-red buttons, belt buckle, and boots, followed by a dark-red coat with an A-line skirt, and a black jumper, matching black fedora, hot-pink trousers and matching boots. The coat has stitching that sculpts it along the bust and three large round buttons. This is probably Lady Diana's most distinctive look. Unfortunately, the fedora gets bullet holes in it along with Steed's bowler. She drives a pea-green MG C Roadster and is pretty good with a samurai sword.

Steed wears his chocolate-brown suit, then the blue three-piece with pale-blue patterned shirt and sky-blue paisley tie, and then the pale-gray suit. He later wears a bulky gray overcoat over the charcoal suit with matching bowler hat, and it is this suit that is slowly sacrificed to Remak. He ends the episode in his brown serge suit. He also drives the Rolls-Royce Silver Ghost.

The Hughes 269B helicopter (G-AVZC) from "Super Secret Cypher Snatch" and "Split!" returns. The villains drive a beige Commer HX441 coach (616 BYP).

Steed and Tara share a glass of champagne before she goes away on vacation in the opening scene.

TAG SCENE

Steed arrives at his flat to find dozens of postcards from Tara... and Tara herself. He welcomes her back from her holiday and she gives him a present, which turns out to be a tiny box containing an inflatable dinghy that immediately inflates and fills the entire room.

QUOTES

"In alphabetical order, he was clubbed, poisoned, shot, spiked, stabbed, strangled, and suffocated... and his eardrums are damaged." "His neck's broken as well."

"Perhaps he was killed by a consortium of crazed creditors."

"Why didn't he wait?" "Why can't any of them wait?"

"Lovely cleaning job." "And the bullet holes have been invisibly mended."

146 (7.22.18) THE MORNING AFTER

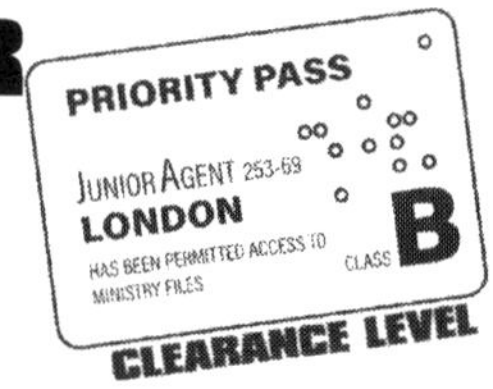

Written by Brian Clemens
Directed by John Hough

GUEST CAST

Peter Barkworth (Merlin), Penelope Horner (Jenny), Joss Ackland (Brigadier Hansing), Brian Blessed (Sergeant Hearn), Donald Douglas (Major Parsons), Philip Dunbar (Yates), Jonathan Scott (Cartney)

PRE-TITLE/TEASER

At the high security establishment, the Ministry of T.S.I.[13], a guard is distracted by a party favor bleating around a corner. When he investigates, he is knocked out by a man wearing a clown mask. When a fellow guard investigates, he is given a hotseat by the clown and knocked out as well. When two more guards investigate, they grab him only to find that he has been replaced by a dummy and stuffed suit. Elsewhere Steed and Tara await Merlin, the apparent double agent who has stolen a newly developed sleep gas, and when he arrives, they quickly disarm him. But he knocks both of them out with the sleep gas before becoming trapped and succumbing to the gas himself.

SYNOPSIS

During an attempt to apprehend an enemy agent called Merlin, Steed and Tara are knocked out by the villain's stolen sleep gas. Merlin also falls prey to the gas, and the trio sleep for 24 hours. When they awake, they find the entire town evacuated and under martial law. It turns out that the entire city is threatened by an atom bomb. Or is it…?

REVIEW

This is an inventive and engaging story that a vacationing Linda Thorson unfortunately misses. Therefore, in an odd turn, Tara spends the entire episode sleeping on a couch, waking only to save Steed from a villain before falling right back to sleep.

Merlin, played by the wonderful Peter Barkworth, is a charismatic and duplicitous character and greatly enlivens his scenes as he banters and negotiates with Steed for his release, alternately helping and then hindering him while they are handcuffed together. There is little explanation for his eccentric modus operandi however, which, as revealed in the pre-title, consists of wearing a clown mask and giving army guards hotseats. Given the usual point of the pre-title scene to establish a basis for the story, it seems oddly separated from the rest of the narrative.

This is one of those episodes during this era that capitalizes on the show's own mythical status, this time showing a major English city normally as busy as an anthill—and possibly serving as an ersatz London (though it was filmed in St. Albans and Watford)—in a state of abandon, and the mystery of why is a significant part of the plot.

In any case, the state of desertion allows for some great direction from John Hough, who alternately depicts the streets by sending the camera creeping along to capture the shifting perspectives of the buildings and with closeups of the cast in shallow depth of field. However, in order to keep the emptiness intact, no major or recognizable landmarks are shown (possibly the result of filming in St. Albans and Watford). The emptiness cannot last, however, as the military eventually have to show up. The city isn't entirely abandoned after all. Thunderous as usual, a slimmer beardless Brian Bless-

---

13 The T.S.I. from "Split!" returns (or at least the signs), and the location for the filming is right behind the film cutting rooms at Elstree.

ed shows up with them. He is his usual loud-mouthed brilliant self, presumably chosen to break the frequent disquiet of the more forlorn scenes.

It has to be said that this plot hasn't a shred of originality. It had been done before and would be done many times after in various other productions. A variation would even be done again in *The New Avengers*. That episode is called "Sleeper" and is delightful. "The Morning After" is good too, but I'll leave you to decide which you prefer.

EPISODE NOTES

It is during this season that *The Avengers* was going up against the American comedy-variety show *Rowan & Martin's Laugh-In* on NBC, and Patrick Macnee's wry comment of "sock it to me" was a direct reference to the competition. Sadly, for *The Avengers, Laugh-In* did indeed sock it to them, and ABC cancelled *The Avengers* months later due to disappointing ratings.

CHAMPAGNE, CARS, CLOTHES, AND CANINES

Steed begins the episode in his chocolate-brown suit (his brown Chelsea boots are clasped with copper-colored cord or chains) and Tara debuts a new scarlet-red jacket with high-waisted trousers and a white blouse with a bow. The jacket is stitched in white to form trim and piping. She wears the outfit with tan boots. Since they spend most of the episode in an abandoned London, with Tara sleeping, the only other outfits are in the tag scene, in which Steed wears his midnight-blue tuxedo with the necklace from "All Done With Mirrors" and Tara debuts a metallic green-and-blue peacock print dress with a halter-neck. A bit garish.

Steed's Rolls-Royce Silver Ghost returns but has to be abandoned when the street is blocked. The van with the radar dish on top is a 1964 Volkswagen Delivery Van T1.

No champagne but some Craig's Scotch Whisky, as drunk by Brian Blessed (while on duty).

TAG SCENE

Steed is relaxing at home in front of the television, remarking "sock it to me" as he turns it off. Tara arrives bearing a gift from Merlin, the box of which appears to be empty. Steed then receives a phone call alerting him that Merlin has stolen a box of luminous dust from a top-secret establishment, and they immediately suspect their gift contains some of the stuff.

QUOTES

"Your friend wasn't very brave." "He's a big disappointment to me."
"Sock it to me."

147 (7.3.19) THE CURIOUS CASE OF THE COUNTLESS CLUES

Written by Philip Levene
Directed by Don Sharp

GUEST CAST

Anthony Bate (Earle), Kenneth Cope (Gardiner), Tony Selby (Stanley), Peter Jones (Doyle), Tracy Reed (Janice), Edward De Souza (Flanders), George A. Cooper (Burgess), Reginald Jessup (Dawson)

PRE-TITLE/TEASER

Police inspectors investigate a murder in the victim's flat. After one inspector analyzes every clue to the praise of his colleague, the owner of the flat comes in and is quickly shot by the inspectors, who have apparently planned out every aspect of the murder they'd intended to commit. The victim's body falls neatly within the chalk outline already on the floor.

SYNOPSIS

A series of rich men are all being blackmailed. The blackmailers commit murders and then plant evidence that incriminates the men at the crime scene. After Steed gets too close to the truth, they attempt to blackmail him as well, with Tara as the intended murder victim...

REVIEW

After an intriguing pre-title, this episode quickly becomes mired in a tiresome blackmail trope that languidly creeps along in the early seventh season style with nary a plot twist in sight. This story's one saving grace would normally be the attempt to create a classic ***Avengers*** eccentric. However, in this case, the eccentric has deluded himself into thinking he's Sherlock Holmes, an investigator that the Ministry periodically uses, and alas his Holmesian kitsch falls flat throughout.

The relationship between Steed and Tara feels remarkably nascent in this episode, veering between overly casual and too formal. Never once do their interactions recall any of the spirited wit and banter of prior assistants. This is not helped by the fact that Linda Thorson plays Tara variably from practically scene to scene.

The best twist to this otherwise flaccid episode is when Steed is to be blackmailed with the death of Tara King. It's a worthy effort that we really should have seen coming all along, and when it arrives, it is executed with a decent amount of tension and grit. Transparently, Tara's leg is injured to facilitate the story's climax, but she has a great fight scene at the end, utilizing all kinds of props; it almost works at selling the character, but they seem to be trying too hard. The story picks up at this point, but it is too little, too late.

"The Curious Case of the Countless Clues" is not offensively bad, just dull, failing to rise above mediocrity. Tara's action scene vehicle at the finale notwithstanding, it lacks almost every one of the key elements that made ***The Avengers*** unique and could therefore have been shoe-horned into just about any standard sixties spy show without too much rejigging.

CHAMPAGNE, CARS, CLOTHES, AND CANINES

Tara opens the episode in a beige rollneck jumper and a tan suede miniskirt. It's very bland. Steed wears his chalk-striped charcoal suit with a light gray bowler, a white shirt, and a blue tie. He drives the 1927 Bentley 3 Litre for the final time in the series (in transmission order). He then switches to a dark-gray two-piece suit. Tara's next outfit is a collarless sleeveless minidress made out of pale-gray raw silk, which frankly reads like coarse muslin onscreen. It's very bland. Steed brings out the brown tartan blazer and olive tie again; he wears them with tan trousers and a pale-green shirt. Tara's third ensemble is a pale-orange romper, zipped up the back, with a massive butterfly collar and a built-in faux belt. (Since the zipper reaches down past the beltline, I don't think the outfit is composed of separates.) Despite the collar and puffed sleeves, it's very bland. Steed wears a dark-gray two-piece suit again but with a pale-gold shirt and a copper-colored tie. Nice gold cufflinks. He later adds a heavy fawn overcoat and matching bowler. Sadly, the episode once again ends with that green-and-brown vine print shirt, not hidden well enough under the tartan blazer. Tara wears deep-green slacks and a dark-teal jersey t-shirt. It's very bland.

This is a car-heavy episode, with many older models to spot. The villains drive a black 1964 Citroën DS 19 Safari (AYR 141B), a red 1955 Land Rover Series I 107" (641 CVX), and a 1955

Bentley S1 Saloon. The latter becomes part of the plot by switching out its registration plate (285 FLA) before committing a murder. Tara is laid up for the entire episode so she doesn't get to drive anywhere. Speaking of driving, when Steed's Bentley breaks down, there is some very convincing day-for-night shooting. I genuinely thought it was a night shoot at first.

TAG SCENE

Tara performs a successful 'operation' on Steed's bowler in her apartment and then proves to Steed that her ankle is mended by cartwheeling across the room.

QUOTES

"No, Sir Arthur, he's a sort of…he's kind of… I really must ask him!"
"I see you've changed your secretary. The last one was brunette."
"Who knows why Steed killed you? The fact remains that he did."

148 (7.18.20) WISH YOU WERE HERE

Written by Tony Williamson
Directed by Don Chaffey

GUEST CAST

Liam Redmond (Charles Merrydale), Robert Urquhart (Maxwell), Brook Williams (Basil), Dudley Foster (Parker), Patrick Newell (Mother), Gary Watson (Kendrick), Richard Caldicot (Mellor), Derek Newark (Vickers), David Garth (Brevitt), Louise Pajo (Miss Craven), John Cazabon (Mr. Maple), Sandra Fehr (Attractive Girl)

PRE-TITLE/TEASER

Two middle-aged men, Brevitt and Charles, argue about how they're going to escape. Both of them want to leave, but Charles thinks the risk is too great and they'd never make it. Finally, Brevitt makes a break for it, and they're revealed to be in a luxurious hotel. When Brevitt demands that he be allowed to leave, to his surprise, the concierge graciously agrees. However, as soon as he walks out the front door, he takes a terrible tumble and injures his leg. An apparent accident, for which the concierge apologizes as Brevitt is carried back to his room.

SYNOPSIS

After Tara learns her uncle has been on holiday for a month and is no longer traceable, she travels to a resort to investigate. Finding that her uncle is being held prisoner, they attempt to escape only to have numerous strange accidents prevent them from doing so. They finally decide to take over the hotel kitchen in an attempt to undermine the hotel operations, but there is a double agent in their midst…

REVIEW

This appears to be a seriocomic spoof of fellow sixties spy show ***The Prisoner***. It is full of slapstick attempts to escape, extremely obvious undercover villains, and Mother's bungling nephew, and ultimately is incredibly unlike ***The Avengers***. ***The Prisoner*** was deadly serious—albeit with dry wit peppered throughout—and the counter-measures to stop escapes were direct, frequently violent, and indeed dreamlike. However, in this take-off version the escapes are stopped entirely by apparent accidents. This has notable potential which the story strangely never fulfills. It's hard to understand how the various contrived obstacles could be imagined and executed so quickly, always the correct one to prevent departure at any given moment. It doesn't help that most of the episode is composed of new visitors arriving, all in fresh need of being convinced by the others that escape is impossible, locking us into a cycle of tedium.

I appreciate the use of comedy in the series, and usually it works as a mélange with all the other typical *Avengers* elements, but this time it might have worked far better if they had simply dropped the comedic aspects and made a tour de force that captured the spirit of its model. That being said, the idea of taking over the kitchen is the episode's one moment of true inspiration and greatly enlivens the final moments of the story. The attack of the kitchen implements that follows is genuinely funny. The frying pan on top of the head routine never fails to amuse. It's too bad it took so long to reach that point.

CHAMPAGNE, CARS, CLOTHES, AND CANINES

Tara starts out wearing her green-and-yellow minidress (from "Super Secret Cypher Snatch") and Steed wears his chocolate-brown three-piece suit. For her trip to the Prisoner Hotel, Tara changes into a green rollneck jumper, matching pants, and a green-and-white striped cardigan, and after she gets doused by the 'careless' window cleaner, she wears a cerulean-blue bathrobe with an eye-like print. Steed switches to his pale-gray three-piece suit with a white shirt and pink tie. Tara steals an outfit from a closet, and it's a black-and-white maid's uniform with vertical stripes and high-waisted slacks. She then wears a white chef's tunic with full-size toque. Steed declines to join her, having already dressed as a chef in Season Three's "Death à la Carte." For the tag scene, Tara wears a white blouse and navy slacks with a navy-blue cravat with white spots.

Steed drives his Rolls-Royce, and Tara's Lotus Europa reappears as well.

TAG SCENE

At Steed's flat, he nervously contemplates opening an interior door when he is interrupted by his doorbell and Tara's arrival. He tells her that he's being kept prisoner in his own home. When Tara says she's willing to take his place, Steed happily pops off to the pub, leaving Tara with the occupant of the room beyond the door: the neighbor's baby, who immediately begins crying.

QUOTES

"What on Earth are you doing in this part of the world! And what stupid and idiotic impulse brought you here?"
"I'm not your uncle! I'm your Mother!"
"Active girl—no wonder she's gone to bed!"

149 (7.23.21) LOVE ALL

Written by Jeremy Burnham
Directed by Peter Sykes

GUEST CAST

Veronica Strong (Martha), Terence Alexander (Bromfield), Robert Harris (Sir Rodney), Patrick Newell (Mother), Patsy Rowlands (Thelma), with Brian Oulton, Frank Gatliff, Ann Rye, Zulema Dene, Peter Stephens, Norman Pitt, John Cobner, Robin Tolhurst, Larry Taylor, David Baron

PRE-TITLE/TEASER

A top civil servant holds a meeting in a government building, admonishing all of the attendees against revealing any of the secrets discussed. The meeting breaks up and the civil servant returns to his office. The char woman comes in straight after and they greet each other as lovers, and, sitting in his lap, she immediately wants to know everything about the meeting and all his secrets.

SYNOPSIS

Security lapses are occurring amongst top civil servants. It turns out that the men are telling their secrets to the same char woman that they've all fallen in love with. The question is why are these middle-aged men falling for this rather homely and ordinary woman, and can Steed stop the villains before Tara commits a love-sick suicide over her own new lover…?

REVIEW

From the opening pre-title, as an executive civil servant falls into the arms of a Pythonesque char woman with a partially-burned cigarette constantly hanging off her lip, you know this one is going to be different and special. The skillful direction and the moody cimbalom music together provide significant atmosphere that captures the pathos and plight of the men involved, their unrequited love being taken advantage by a vicious snake of a woman and her fellow agents. It's quite sad seeing the poor Sir Rodney driving along lonely streets obsessively looking for his love's residence, even as her sociopathic manipulation is well in evidence to the viewer. This is an unusual departure from the typical approach of ***The Avengers***, and, unlike several departures in this season, it comes across as exceedingly fresh. Veronica Strong's transformation from one version of her character to another is exceptionally well realized—accomplished only with makeup, clothing changes, and acting.

The core concept is highly original—making civil servants reveal secrets through love-sick persuasion. At the same time, the absurdity of it all is played up. The male civil servants are all confirmed 'woman haters'—a Victorian concept that was often a code word for homosexual—and yet they are falling deeply in love with a woman who deliberately dresses as blandly as possible, making herself appear lowly and plain. One could easily ask why she does this. The answer, of course, is to sustain typical *Avengers* eccentricity. Let it slide, dear reader, let it slide! Enjoy the nonsense with the same abandon as the poor tortured love-sick souls of the beleaguered men under the influence of her love charm.

The eccentrics continue in force within Casanova Ink, a romance novel company where the stories are all composed by a computer.[14] The computer—named Rosemary Z. Glade—has all known romantic narratives programmed into its database. Rosemary is merely a piano prop with narrative tropes printed on its keys; it is operated by pressing the keys in various musical sequences. Steed humorously flirts with its operator, Thelma, who provides him with a copy of the computer's latest 'masterpiece,' ***Love on the Moon***. The company's owner and schemer-of-the-week is Mr. Bromfield, and all his employees are deeply and unrequitedly in love with him—such is the man's vanity that he uses his weapon on everyone in his service.

In the usual *Avengers* high fashion, the humor and violence entwine with a remarkably tense moment. Tara sits on a window ledge threatening suicide, also now in love with Bromfield. A great fight scene ensues, and Steed emerges with enough love charms to make everyone fall in love with him, including Bromfield himself. Hoisted with his own petard, he follows Steed out like a lovesick

---

14 I needn't tell you that current technology has caught up with this episode's concept. AI writing programs are already being used by the authorially-challenged to publish books of questionable quality. These writing robots even have names, but so far none of them are called Rosemary Z. Glade that I'm aware of.

puppy. This is a wonderful story that is marred only by one of those contrived scenes when the villains explain their scheme to the audience by way of one another. "Love All" reaches the zenith of the season and remains in my personal top five for this season.

CHAMPAGNE, CARS, CLOTHES, AND CANINES

Tara opens the episode wearing an oatmeal rollneck jumper and a pale-orange miniskirt. This is followed by one of her top outfits: a bright-red blouse with a navy cardigan and matching pants with a black belt and black boots. The cardigan has red piping and trim along the cuffs that match the blouse. Later, she wears another winner, a tan-and-gold A-line overcoat with a lime-green blouse, yellow trousers, and a brown belt, which gets broken in Steed's efforts to save her from jumping out the window. (The coat is very like something Emma Peel would have worn; the rest of the outfit isn't.) She again drives the Lotus Europa, and the exterior of her flat is shown. Steed doesn't debut any new outfits this episode, but he does wear the lovely taupe three-piece suit with a pale-gold pinstriped shirt and a dark-olive tie. For the tag scene, in which Steed 'enjoys' his Beatlemania-like fame, he wears the brown serge suit and Tara wears a black evening gown with a string of pearls.

TAG SCENE

Still wearing the love 'charms' on his waistcoat, Steed arrives at his flat, chased Beatles-style by hundreds of screaming fans who pound at the door. But when he reveals the charms to Tara, she immediately becomes infatuated with him and he has to fend her off as well.

QUOTES

"Hmm, three shots. Very civil, you even shoot people in triplicate."
"Poor Sir Rodney. This is one murder he won't be able to accept responsibility for."
"You see, I've got no personality." "What? None at all?" "Not an iota. My brother says that as a salesman I'm a total disaster. When he's here, he usually shuts me up in the back of the shop."
"They were anathema to him—sheer anathema! Mention women's suffrage and he'd go purple in the face!"
"Just my luck. My first case, a simple parking offence, and I end up chained to a chronic Cassanova."
"Something went wrong that day. Couldn't get the end of the story to work. Instead of boy-gets-girl, it kept coming out girl-gets-gorilla."
"Go on, admit it. I'm irresistible." *(Yes, you are, Steed.)*

150 (7.25.22) STAY TUNED

Written by Tony Williamson
Directed by Don Chaffey

GUEST CAST

Gary Bond (Proctor), Kate O'Mara (Lisa), Patrick Newell (Mother), Iris Russell (Father), Duncan Lamont (Wilks), Howard Marion-Crawford (Collins), Denise Buckley (Sally), Roger Delgado (Kreer), Harold Kasket (Dr. Meitner), Ewan Roberts (Travers), Patrick Westwood (Taxi Driver)

PRE-TITLE/TEASER

At his flat, Steed checks to make sure he has everything for his three-week holiday, suitcases, sporting equipment, tickets, etc. As he opens his door to leave, however, he is greeted by a knockout punch to the face.

SYNOPSIS

Tara knocks on Steed's door as he is leaving for his three-week vacation and informs him that he's already had it. Steed is removed from active duty by Father, and he begins an investigation into what happened during the missing three weeks. Is his amnesia benign or has something more sinister happened to him...?

REVIEW

This one begins with Steed's amnesia and the old trope of the psychiatrist's couch, as the doctor (beset with a German accent) spouts clichés about psychiatry. It's not nearly as terrible as it sounds because Don Chaffey presents this scene with moody lighting in a minimalist set and shoots the psychiatrist in isolation and in extreme close-up. I am again reminded of *The Prisoner*, a program which is something of a spiritual sibling to *The Avengers*, being about an agent on the inside rather than agents on the outside. Surrealism abounds in both shows, but one is deathly serious and the other frequently humorous. Chaffey frequently directed episodes of *The Prisoner*, so the connection is more than superficial. With this in mind, I find the direction in this episode to approach a new high-water mark for the series, and Steed's nighttime wandering in the first third of the story has a remarkable cinematic appeal.

Throughout the first third of the hour, the story has an ingenious plot that manages to beguile us through sleight-of-hand into thinking it hasn't been done before, when in fact we've already seen it more than twice in variations, notably in "My Wildest Dream," which was filmed before this one but broadcast in the UK afterwards. The entire narrative has plot elements lifted wholesale from *The Manchurian Candidate*, especially the finale in which Steed manages to see through the conditioning just enough to evade carrying out the programmed instructions to the letter. And several episodes of *The Prisoner* had played with such themes only the previous year, most notably "A. B. and C." Yet, the immersive quality of the story through excellent direction and mood manages to initially convince us that we're seeing something new. If it could have been sustained, we might have had a remarkable episode. Unfortunately, once the plot of the villains is revealed about halfway through, the illusion is dispelled and the episode descends into a dreariness that Chaffey's artistic direction cannot save.

The major downside of this episode's unusual approach is that it never quite feels like *The Avengers*—a common problem in this season. We're just not used to seeing John Steed so disabled and confused. We're used to a character that is always in charge. Instead, he is wandering the streets like a deer in the headlights and seeking out psychotherapists who recommend tranquilizers. I don't mind this in general terms. Anything can be done if it works. But I'm sorry to say that it never quite does.

"Stay Tuned" isn't bad, just too derivative to be truly effective despite a valiant effort from all involved. Enjoy the night scenes and guest stars and leave your thinking cap off.

EPISODE NOTES

This episode might be notable in particular to *Doctor Who* fans for an unusual convergence of two prominent stars from that series—Roger Delgado (known for his role as The Master) and Kate O'Mara (known for playing another Time Lord called The Rani). Even though their characters appear to live in the same house, they fail to appear in the same scene together—except once Delgado is a corpse. Nevertheless, their presence is something to remark upon for the seeming televisual historical relevance. Roger Delgado, who was a mere two years away from his iconic role as the Doctor's arch nemesis, looks exactly as he did in the series. His role here is criminally small, but he greatly enlivens the scenes in which he appears, engaging in a vicious sword fight with Tara. Not to be outdone, O'Mara has a similarly violent catfight.

CHAMPAGNE, CARS, CLOTHES, AND CANINES

Steed gets his lights punched out in his pale-gray three-piece suit with matching bowler, a white shirt, and a pink tie, and he stays in this outfit for the bulk of the episode, maintaining an unprecedented level of continuity in such a dreamlike story. Tara wears a black rollneck jumper and slacks with an oatmeal jerkin with a chain-link belt made of circular rings. Both Steed and Tara later wear white overalls and face masks (shades of COVID-19). Underneath Tara's overalls are her lime-green jacket and miniskirt (from "Game") with an olive-green scarf. This is later replaced by a bright-green rollneck jumper, matching trousers, and a pale-yellow fitted and belted jacket.

As for the guest stars, Kate O'Mara wears a tiger-print fur coat with a cerulean-blue knee-length dress underneath; the integrated belt is a bright pink. And Roger Delgado wears a dark-green velvet smoking jacket, matching trousers, a white shirt and black bowtie. He also wears a ring pendant dangling from a long chain.

Tara drives her Lotus Europa again (which takes over as her main vehicle in the later episodes), and Steed nearly drives it off the road. Steed rides in a 1965 Austin FX4 taxi, and the Rolls-Royce also makes an appearance.

TAG SCENE

At her home, Tara checks to make sure she has everything for her holiday, and Steed arrives, briefly trying to convince her to go on another mission. However, when this fails, he reveals that the assignment is a trip to Bermuda and she quickly changes her mind and races after him.

QUOTES

"Isn't there some way of making this conflagration spark up a bit quicker?"
"Gosh—then honesty *is* the best policy!"
"You shouldn't touch me. You never know where I might have been."

151 (7.24.23) TAKE ME TO YOUR LEADER

Written by Terry Nation
Directed by Robert Fuest

GUEST CAST

Patrick Barr (Stonehouse), Patrick Newell (Mother), John Ronane (Captain Tim), Michael Robbins (Cavell), Henry Stamper (Major Glasgow) with Penelope Keith, Hugh Cross, Elisabeth Robillard, Michael Hawkins, Sheila Hammond, Bryan Kendrick, Raymond Adamson, Matthew Long, Cliff Diggins, Wilfred Boyle

PRE-TITLE/TEASER

A man stealthily sneaks into a home seeking a red briefcase. He almost takes it but when touched the briefcase cries "Stop, thief!" repeatedly, drawing the attention of the owner, who fatally stabs the intruder with a hidden blade inside a clarinet. He then resets the anti-theft device in the case.

SYNOPSIS

Steed and Tara pursue a talking attaché case across London. The case passes taped instructions to a series of double agents who are acting as couriers in order to throw off pursuit...

REVIEW

This is something of a sustained *Mission Impossible* quasi-parody, the regular cast taking instructions from a computerized attaché case that spouts instructions at regular intervals. The 'sustained' part of that sentence is the most relevant. The sustain is too long, too vacuously scripted. The reality is that the various diversions and plot 'twists' are really just so much marking time before something actually happens, a series of unrelated set pieces that act in a chain leading to some sort of elusive payoff. We know our heroes won't perish in a burst of poison gas, so what is the point of this exercise, you may ask? Not much, just a lot of runaround.

In the midst of this runaround however, we have one of my favorite scenes, occupied front and center by a precocious little girl named Sally, who greatly enlivens her scene with every word of dialogue that she utters. However, this scene simultaneously underscores the previous point. The temporary diversion only briefly delays the chain of events perpetuated by the case's relentless yammering; our brief distraction facilitated by a little girl's budding capitalistic instincts. And every other point of contact is just like that, a brief pause in the chain, easily handled by our heroes, albeit without the witty dialogue.

There are some good points to this episode however. The quirkiness and hyperreality return to some degree. There is a deadly clarinet in one fight scene, and, in another, Tara humorously beans a contact with a giant wrench. The aforementioned kid being used as a contact is a nice touch. And there are some bizarre outfits for undercover agents, including one with "love" studded onto the back of his leather jacket (a nod to the counter-culture movement of the time). Steed and Tara work better together than ever before, like when they instinctually split up without a word after a second case appears. Tara's ingenuity in using the decoy case to escape from the crypt and her deception of a contact to discover the next location are nice touches.

These minor strong points are mitigated by music that is terribly dated (oddly even more so than *The New Avengers*—if that's conceivable), a very ineffective poison gas, and Tara's naiveté in interrogating the enemy. Frankly, Tara's fight with the karate expert is about as obvious as is possible, and the tag scene is just plain stupid. When was the last time we saw Steed with a dog? ("Concerto.")

While no episode directed by Robert Fuest can be a total failure, a story needs something more in the way of a plot to really deeply engage. "Take Me to Your Leader" is a mixed bag that requires viewers to switch their brains off—completely. Nevertheless, I suppose it might promise a superficially fun time for some that do.

CHAMPAGNE, CARS, CLOTHES, AND CANINES

Only one new outfit is debuted in this episode and it's Tara's: a sleeveless chocolate-brown roll neck jumper with matching slacks and cardigan with pale-beige trim. She accessorizes the ensemble with a string of beads. Steed wears his taupe three-piece suit throughout the episode.

The Rolls-Royce Silver Ghost appears again, this time with the black top up. The motorcycle 'Love' villain rides a deep-blue 1967 BSA B25 Starfire (MOJ 767F). There is also a little orange-red 1963 Trojan 200 Type 603.

Perhaps impressed by Fang's spying performance throughout the episode, it appears that Steed has once again taken up the role of caregiver for a dog, and yet, he is back to asking other people to help him care for the poor pup. "You'll find he'll curl up anywhere. Just toss an old mink jacket into a corner and he'll be happy." A feisty German Shepherd, this is Fang's first and only appearance, and apparently he was retained to the end only to provide a joke in the tag scene.

Champagne? Yes! Hidden in one of the cases along with poison gas. Tara saves one—again Meudon & Heim—and gives it to the local vicar.

TAG SCENE

Two red briefcases resembling the locus of the episode play recorded messages from Steed and Tara, one from Steed asking Tara to take care of his dog Fang and one from Tara refusing and saying she's visiting her aunt. Their two messages appear to have anticipated one another, and Steed adds at the end that Fang will insist on inviting all his friends 'round for a visit, as the sound of barking dogs outside grows louder.

QUOTES

"Aaaarrrrgh!! Had to get that out of my system. If I didn't do that at least once every day, I'd massacre them. Oh, you haven't got a little monster...? I mean, a dear sweet child you wish to enroll?"
"Good, then let's talk money and not lollipops." "Ten shillings?" "Twenty-five pounds."
"Don't waste time on little-girl talk. I should think she's one of the Gnomes of Zurich."
"Oh, Mr. Steed, don't shatter a little girl's illusions."
(villain produces a clarinet) "This is no time for a clarinet solo." (clarinet extends a sharpened blade) "'A' sharp, I imagine."

152 (7.26.24) FOG

Written by Jeremy Burnham
Directed by John Hough

GUEST CAST

Nigel Green (The President), Guy Rolfe (Travers), Patrick Newell (Mother), Terence Brady (Carstairs), Paul Whitsun-Jones (Sanders), David Lodge (Maskell), Norman Chappell (Fowler), David Bird, Patsy Smart, John Garrie, Frederick Peisley, Arnold Diamond, John Barrard, Frank Sieman, Virginia Clay, Bernard Severn, Stan Jay, William Lyon Brown

PRE-TITLE/TEASER

On the foggy streets of London, everything seems quite retro, all the way back to Victorian times in fact, and a man with his face hidden takes a finely polished sword from a vendor in the street. He places the sword in a black case, and, as he leaves, a Victorian-era wanted poster tumbles into view warning of the "Gaslight Ghoul."

SYNOPSIS

On the hunt for a mysterious man who is imitating a Victorian murderer called the Gaslight Ghoul, Steed and Tara often get lost in the fog. Eventually, they discover that the man is killing his victims because they are part of a disarmament committee and he's against anti-gun laws...

REVIEW

This "Fog" is impenetrable. While not quite as bad as I remembered it from about two decades ago, this episode still suffers from poor execution and a half-baked plot. Hansom cabs? Murky London fog? Victoriana gone wild? While I do admire the gall for doing this sort of story at all, if it were *Star Trek: The Next Generation*, it would take place on the holodeck—such is the diversion from the usual look and theme of *The Avengers*.

I don't understand what Jeremy Burnham wanted with this script. Was he going for a Jack the Ripper spoof or a serious story with the qualities of a Victorian murder mystery? Or is it just a quirky *Avengers* story about an eccentric that thinks he's a Victorian murderer? Unfortunately, the indecision costs the episode dearly as boredom descends, and we are sorely disappointed when the villain's motivations are revealed, our illusions of anything sophisticated shattered. For the record, he's extreme right-wing and hates gun laws. (Which is maybe not so extreme these days!) Ultimately, it can at best be considered a failed experiment that suffers from the halfhearted attempt to do some vague approximation of a Jack the Ripper story, violently shoehorned into *The Avengers* context.

Originally, many years ago, I wrote that the direction was poor. My exact comment was "because of the cramped 'Victorian' streets and the impenetrable fog, the episode is so claustrophobically-lensed that it looks like it was shot on Ultra-Panavision and then very badly pan-and-scanned." While director John Hough does seem to stick to the longer lenses for this one, I am now shocked by that comment because I find the cinematography to be the episode's one minor saving grace. I can only assume that the vastly improved Blu-rays with their freshly scanned and restored negatives (which I cannot praise enough) are responsible for this stunning about-face. It's amazing that a fresh presentation can so change one's view. Aesthetically, the pale blue light is beautiful, shimmering through a veil of fog, casting a pleasing glow upon everyone. My excuse is that these are nuances that wouldn't have been picked up by earlier telecine equipment. I think that the original comment was largely intended to convey a sense of disorientation conveyed by the fog, which remains well in evidence, likely originally worsened by a zoomed-in, clapped-out film print presented on the original A&E DVDs released in the late 1990s. And it is indeed fair to ask how 1960s UK audiences would have interpreted this on their comparatively tiny screens and flickering black and white sets. Such is the downside of shooting cinematically for television.

The Gaslight Ghoul Club are a very eccentric lot. In this case, they truly have a fog machine, which they overuse just like the production itself. They all sweep about through the fog, darting in and out of Hansom cabs, dressed in late Victorian garb replete with top hats, magician's capes and full beards that look like they've been dyed with black shoe polish. (Are they Victorians or Abe Lincoln impersonators?) It doesn't help that they all look exactly alike. Perhaps this makes the mystery of the murderer more difficult to solve, but it also means that the audience is confused by the revelation at the climax in which the killer almost appears to be the same man that died in the previous scene.

Steed and Tara just seem to amble about, disappearing in and out of fog in a series of almost unrelated set pieces without coherence. They are truly lost in the fog of the plot—as is the viewer. I'm rarely this confused by a story of any television series, but this episode threw me in every way possible. I had to watch it twice and it still didn't make much sense. Frankly, forcing me to delve through this pea souper twice is torture. Speaking of which, the finale takes place in what looks like a down-market sadomasochistic dungeon with printed cardboard walls, and it's seriously hard to know whether this was intentional or not.

Tara also delivers one of the worst puns ever to blight the show, right at the end, a sort of parting shot to all those who have suffered along this far. And the tag scene is simply perplexing. Why would Tara have her air-conditioning on when it's a cold foggy night outside? I'm sorry to say that this episode, while not exactly a disgrace, is a far cry from anything worthy of the great *Avengers* legacy.

EPISODE NOTES

Steed's linguistic skills are seriously called into question when he spouts this gobbledygook: "Venito scuava due... Venito Steedski" ("Came scavenged two... Came Steedski.") What?! He does know that Italian is a different language from Russian, right? He does know his Italian sucks, right?

CHAMPAGNE, CARS, CLOTHES, AND CANINES

The new clothing debuts are crashing to a halt in this production block, but Steed wears his pin-striped charcoal suit with a gray-purple cravat and diamond tiepin, and Tara wears a new black rollneck jumper with black culottes and a black belt. She wears her bright-red coat with black fur trim over this ensemble when going out in the fog. One thing's for sure, Steed's never worn a Gaslight Ghoul outfit until now: Victorian black top hat with a black cape and false beard. It looks like Steed's chocolate-brown suit in the tag scene, but it's hard to tell for certain. They don't drink champagne, but they share snifters of brandy in the fog.

The Rolls-Royce Silver Ghost appears, top up and lights on, and Mother arrives in a BMC Mini Moke, but mostly, it's about hansom cabs for transport.

TAG SCENE

At Tara's home, she and Steed sit enshrouded in a dense fog and struggle to find the glasses for their drinks (and each other). The apparent culprit is Tara's air-conditioning system, which is drawing in the fog (and traffic) from outside.

QUOTES

"Is there a steam pipe broken or something?" "Eh? Oh, that's fog, that's fog, Mr. Haller. We still lead the world in that department."

"...and the fever called living is conquered."

"This could go on forever."

"We haven't much time. I must get you a doctor." "I am a doctor, old boy, but you can send me an undertaker."

"I just can't bear traps." (urgh!)

153 (7.27.25) WHO WAS THAT MAN I SAW YOU WITH?

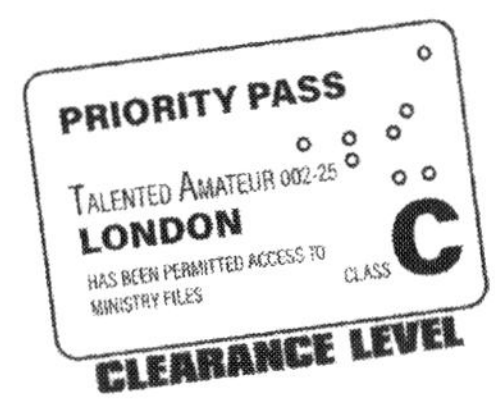

Tara meets a Field Marshall — Steed puts on boxing gloves

Written by Jeremy Burnham

Directed by Don Chaffey

GUEST CAST

William Marlowe (Fairfax), Ralph Michael (General Hesketh), Alan Browning (Zaroff), Alan MacNaughtan (Gilpin), Patrick Newell (Mother), Alan Wheatley (Dangerfield), and Bryan Marshall, Aimee Delamain, Richard Owens, Nita Lorraine, Ralph Ball, Ken Haward, Neville Marten

PRE-TITLE/TEASER

Two Ministry agents investigate a spy named Zarov on a darkened street. After pretending to be dead, Zarov takes one of the agents by surprise and shoots him and then escapes back to his leader. The boss then reveals that the next victim is Tara King and laughs maniacally.

SYNOPSIS

Tara has been assigned to break the security of the top-secret missile defense system called Field Marshall. Unfortunately, a villain called Zaroff has assigned himself to frame Tara as a traitor and then steal the information she has gathered...

REVIEW

This is a mediocre second-tier episode, settling somewhere in the lower middle of the seventh season standard. Though centering a story around Tara was always a risk due to Linda Thorson's relative inexperience, in this case, it shows Thorson at her very best as she tries to prove her innocence. Sadly, this is about the extent of the episode's good points.

Unfortunately, the central premise is unoriginal and fairly obvious. The idea that mere coincidences and circumstantial evidence can add up to something significant enough to raise suspicion is an interesting one, but the problem is that writer Jeremy Burnham chose entirely the wrong direction with which to pursue this narrative. The path chosen relies almost entirely on contrivances and cuts to the film in order to keep the audience in suspense as to whether Tara is truly guilty. When the story requires that shots be cut in order for the premise to work, the writing is weak. For example, when Zaroff calls Tara, prompting her to go to the Maple garage, Tara's part of the conversation is deliberately cut out, her reaction appearing damningly subservient as if she's passively accepting his instructions. The viewer is only left in a fragile state of mystery about her potential guilt because the film is cut this way. Clever writing could eliminate the need for such contrivances.

Furthermore, Tara's immediate need to escape when under house arrest, presumably in order to find evidence for her defense, seems to cement her guilt in the viewer's mind—for all of about two minutes. The reason that this is a problem is because it's *obviously* a red herring. We know they're not going to do this to one of their main characters. It doesn't help that all pretense of her being guilty is given up almost immediately thereafter. And thus, the mystery unravels rather than deepening even as the plot against her unfolds. Burnham is trying to create mystery about something that is inherently lacking in mystery, and then he gives up on it very suddenly as if he realized that he had painted himself into a corner.

A far better solution would have been to make the audience entirely privy to everything from Tara's perspective—put us in her shoes, in other words. Thus, creating suspense and tension instead of mystery. We know she's innocent, there is no pretense about it, but will she be able to prove it? Will all her friends turn away from her? Will she be able to convince Steed at least? They should have forced the audience to identify with Tara and then isolated her (and us) from everyone else.[15] There's so much potential there that could have made this a spectacular story instead of a mediocre one. A fragment of this alternative interpretation finally manifests about forty-one minutes in, by which time, Tara is already in the hands of Zaroff, with Steed knocked out just as he decides he believes her. By then, however, it's too late to build the tension, which ultimately never manifests. Some of this is also Don Chaffey's responsibility of course, and the plot problems could have been mitigated by the way the story was shot. Nevertheless, the foundation of good drama begins with the script.

Other aspects of the story seem equally perplexing. Gilpin's vanity is off the charts, primping and preening for forty-five minutes in a boxing ring. It's still hard to determine what the implied meaning of this might be. Preparing for a fight? Indeed, a fight does take place here later, but it's hard to know why the villains would conduct their business entirely within this squared circle in anticipation of their enemies showing up for a duel. I guess it's no weirder than Mother's headquarters being a haunted house set.

"Who Was That Man I Saw You With?" is a fairly typical seventh season episode that falls far short of its full potential due to problems with its narrative foundation that really started before anyone ever set hands on a camera.

---

15 This is the classic Hitchcock theme explored in so many films, most notably ***North by Northwest***. Or think of ***Rosemary's Baby***, where everyone, including her husband, was involved in a conspiracy against her.

CHAMPAGNE, CARS, CLOTHES, AND CANINES

Tara starts out the episode charmingly dressed in a camouflage jacket, black rollneck jumper, olive-green trousers, and black face paint. She wears a utility belt and holster with a pistol and two grenades. As hard as this is to improve upon, she largely ups it with a purple dressing gown with string feather cuffs, a black rollneck jumper, and a thin blue headband with bow. Once she's finally into real clothes, we find her wearing a lovely teal-green minidress (cut like a long jacket) with scalloped button holes and black buttons, a black rollneck jumper again (probably the same one), and black stockings. Next, she wears a gold blouse with plum-colored floral print, with a navy cardigan, matching flared pants, and brown boots. Then, she wears Kate's blue-and-gold Chinese jacket with dragon print and black buttoned placket, with black flared pants and a wide black belt. In the tag scene, her final outfit is a sheer silver, gold, and black cardigan over a black dress. Steed mostly wears the chocolate-brown suit again, but later switches to the blue one, and finally the midnight-blue tux in the tag scene.

The Lotus Europa reappears, and in its first scene, it's parked outside Tara's apartment again, making me wonder where she parks the AC 428. Steed also drives the Rolls-Royce Silver Ghost.

Loads of cases of Meudon & Heim champagne are delivered to Steed's apartment, and he forms a champagne fountain in the tag scene.

TAG SCENE

In Steed's flat, he carefully stacks glasses to make a champagne fountain, and Tara is very impressed by the result, but "the best is yet to come" as they now get to drink the champagne.

QUOTES

"Let us consider the alternatives. On the basis of your evidence, Tara is either a traitor, or alternately and judging only by the facts...she *is* a traitor."

"I was making life and death decisions when the only choice in life you had to make was whether to eat your baby cereal or spit it out!"

"You know, most people's feet are so ugly. Mine...are so elegant."

"To Tara King, of whom I never suspected funny business for one moment." "Never?" "Well, almost never."

154 (7.30.26) HOMICIDE AND OLD LACE

Written by Malcoln Hulke and Terrance Dicks (uncredited: Brian Clemens)
Directed by John Hough (uncredited: Vernon Sewell)

GUEST CAST

Patrick Newell (Mother), Joyce Carey (Harriet), Mary Merrall (Georgina), Gerald Harper (Colonel Corf), Keith Baxter (Dunbar), Edward Brayshaw (Fuller), and Donald Pickering, Mark London, Kristopher Kum, Bari Jonson, Stephen Hubay, Bryan Mosley, Gertan Klauber, Kevork Malikyan, John Rapley, Anne Rutter

PRE-TITLE/TEASER

Two elderly women, Harriet and Georgina, await a visitor, one whom they have gone through great lengths to bring, but when he finally arrives, they greet him with antique pistols.

SYNOPSIS

On his birthday, Mother meets his aunts Georgina and Harriet and proceeds to tell a story involving Steed and Tara infiltrating the international criminal organization Intercrime…

REVIEW

The Avengers does a clips episode. It's hard to imagine the conversation that must have occurred when Fennell and Clemens sat down to figure out how they were going to make use of the footage from "The Great Great Britain Crime" and complete a much-needed twenty-sixth episode for the final season of the series. There is no doubt that they would have felt rushed to decide something. Cannibalizing the failures of John Bryce's previously filmed material had been accomplished twice already with mixed results—the most successful of which was "Have Guns–Will Haggle," which made use of footage filmed for a planned ninety-minute episode called "Invitation to a Killing."

Despite these cost-cutting efforts, they were still coming up short on episodes, time, and money. They had received an order for twenty-six episodes from ABC in America, and sending only twenty-five episodes was never an option. The season had gotten off to a rough start due to Clemens and Fennell's firing and re-hiring and the lost time incurred; and money and time had already been spent on "The Great Great Britain Crime" during Bryce's brief tenure. Thus, writing and filming an entirely new episode was not an option either. Somehow, they had to make use of the footage that had already been shot. Therefore, any feelings of pressure would have been understandable.

On the other hand, that they decided that Mother should tell the whole story to his aunts on his birthday over "five fingers of Old Red Eye" is truly shocking and not at all understandable, and one is left to imagine that this decision must have been taken over the consumption of large portions of alcoholic beverages and many funny-looking cigarettes. Regardless of the conditions defining their decision, this was in fact the decision that was made, however inconceivable it might be.

While the pre-title is actually quite good in the *Avengers* style, it's dumbfounding how quickly the episode sinks into total oblivion from there. The narrative—or what stands in for one—could at best be considered a loose re-working of the source material, re-interpreted into a broad comedy for which the material was clearly not well-suited. Sadly, the original story—which might well have been superb for all we know—is completely incoherent, and the whole mess is encapsulated within Mother's continually intrusive and remarkably unfunny narration.

Patrick Newell is forced to narrate the story in character, so we are subjected to his usual Mother-as-condescending-blowhard routine, which, as always, utterly fails to allow anything other than puerile humor to surface. John Hough starts far too many shots in an extreme closeup of Newell's rotund jowls, which flap as he spouts Clemens' worst dialogue of the series.

Ironically, the two aunts sum it up best when one asks "What is an impasse?" The other answers that it's "when they run out of plot." And that is exactly what happened here. There is barely a whisper of a plot, and what exists is nonsensical. The story is painful to sit through, and the viewer is subjected to a denigration of *The Avengers* as it is lowered to the level of children's story time with hackneyed acting set to a honky-tonk piano score. The tag scene in particular is egregiously infantile. If you're going to waste your time with something this dull-witted and juvenile, the only reason to watch is to see the surviving footage from "The Great Great Britain Crime," the remainder of which no longer exists as far as anyone knows.

The sad fact is that Intercrime is the second villain to return other than the Cybernauts, having first appeared in the second season Cathy Gale episode "Intercrime." That was a fine episode, one of the best of that era. Sadly, this production is a disgrace and nowhere near a worthy sequel.[16]

---

16 Hi, 2024 Michael here, and my opinion hasn't changed. This one just gets worse every time I see it.

EPISODE NOTES

Only Malcolm Hulke and Terrance Dicks are credited on screen as writers whereas Brian Clemens receives no credit for his Mother-related linking material, which can only be considered a wise decision on his part. Conversely, the linking segments were directed by John Hough, who receives the on-screen credit, with the original "The Great Great Britain Crime" being directed by Vernon Sewell who remained uncredited (to his probable relief). The surviving "Great Great Britain Crime" footage is interspersed with clips from "The Bird Who Knew Too Much," "Murdersville" and "Never Never Say Die," whose actors, directors, and writers are not credited.

CHAMPAGNE, CARS, CLOTHES, AND CANINES

Since the only scenes with Tara in this episode are from the first production block under John Bryce, we're back to the dull browns, beiges, and tans of Tara's wardrobe from this period (all with the blond hair or wig). First, she wears a pale-orange (the color of a cantaloupe) romper paired with thigh-high black PVC boots. The next ensemble is a cream plaid miniskirt, a camel long-sleeved jumper, black belt, white leggings and boots. Third is a bright-orange jumper with a wide black belt. Another pale-orange jumper paired with a leopard-print coat is next and the same PVC boots, and she also briefly wears a double-breasted cream overcoat and then a white lab coat over it, both with the boots. Finally, a pale-gray sleeveless romper, once again with a black belt, the PVC boots, and matching gloves. Steed primarily wears a variety of simple two-piece suits, mostly gray, apparently part of the effort to streamline and modernize his look, which was thankfully reversed when Clemens and Fennell took over again.

TAG SCENE

Steed plays cards with Mother as Rhonda paints an enormous oil painting in the background. Steed admits that he is bothered by the fact that Rhonda has never spoken, and Mother volunteers to have her speak so as to ease Steed's mind. At first her voice sounds very strange, but Mother admits that he was only practicing his ventriloquism.

QUOTES

"Now, look here, aunts. This is *my* story, and if I wish to make Tara King sky-blue pink, I will!"
"What's an impasse?" "It's when they run out of plot."
"They were worse than Philistines. They were villainstines!"

155 (7.29.27) THINGUMAJIG

Written by Terry Nation
Directed by Leslie Norman

GUEST CAST

Dora Reisser (Inge), Jeremy Lloyd (Teddy), Iain Cuthbertson (Kruger), Willoughby Goddard (Truman), Hugh Manning (Major Star), John Horsley (Dr. Grant), Edward Burham (Brett), Vernon Dobtcheff (Stenson), Russell Waters (Pike), Michael McKevitt (Phillips), Neville Hughes (Williams), John Moore (Greer), Harry Shacklock (Bill)

PRE-TITLE/TEASER

In a secret passage behind the old walls of a country church, a woman retrieves a skull from an archaeology site. Immediately, the lights dim and the organ begins to play itself. She screams in terror, but her colleague in the tunnels doesn't hear her. Quickly, he is killed by a flash of light from an unseen force that leaves odd patterns on the dirt floor.

SYNOPSIS

Archaeologists are being killed off under mysterious circumstances as they dig under a 12th century church. Since the vicar is an old friend, he asks Steed to come and investigate the happenings, though he believes that the events are supernatural in nature and Steed does not. The deaths turn out to be caused by a foreign power that has created box-like machines with the power to kill electrically...

REVIEW

This is a truly bizarre episode, another artifact of Terry Nation's attempts to figure out how to write for *The Avengers*. He had script-edited almost the entire season, and some of his odd ideas about what worked were well in evidence before this episode appeared and turned the whole basis of the series on its head for one hour. Now, I should emphasize that this is not necessarily a bad thing. I spend a lot of time talking about how this season kept jumping-the-shark, and it did, but sometimes I admit my complaints could be due to resisting a paradigm shift. Nevertheless, even if we are to allow for a substantive change in the direction of the series, it has to work on some level. In this case, I worry that it doesn't. I confess I still don't fully know the answer to that question.

Having said that, the first thirty minutes are actually really good... for a *Doctor Who* episode. They are remarkably *Doctor Who*-like. A couple of archaeologists get killed mysteriously before Steed arrives on the scene, and when he does, he investigates, setting off on some dialogue that could have easily been written for The Doctor. There is some irony here, because if Mrs. Peel had uttered these same lines it might have worked, but Patrick Macnee seems more than slightly off kilter. Steed is vague about his intentions, keeping the guest cast and the viewers in a state of mystery; he appears overly confident about the situation, and he shrugs off the vicar's supernatural theories as nonsense and proceeds with scientific experiments without explaining anything to his confused companions. As far as the guest cast is concerned, greed drives the archaeologists, who proceed despite the danger, and then there's that quintessential trope in which a victim of the mysterious threat is implored for information he cannot provide, having been driven insensible due to the terror that he has witnessed. Considering Terry Nation wrote the script, none of this is surprising.

It's all notably atmospheric until about halfway, then we see what is causing all this havoc—a little black box. I suppose it could have been intended as a parodic reference to something—Daleks perhaps? How exactly do these odd little boxes drag themselves around? Why not just give them wheels? Could they travel up a flight of stairs? All questions one could ask of the Daleks. Later, a very odd scene ensues, in which Tara is besieged by one of the thingumajigs in her apartment while taking instruction from the allergy-afflicted scientist Truman over the phone. The box dithers around, blasting pre-determined objects in the apartment with electricity as Tara throws power cords from various household appliances at it in order to drain its power, prompting a reverse-the-film effect to make the cords jump into place. A rain of champagne from Tara's well-stocked apartment finally finishes off the metallic beastie, and Tara takes a gulp in celebration. This scene seems to pull humor from the situation like pulling teeth, but it gets the job done somehow.

Kruger is finally hoisted with his own petard after raving like Davros about how his boxes will rule the world, and Steed destroys the thingumajig with a laser gun whilst wearing space goggles. Seriously, where is the TARDIS? But let's jump passed all that for the moment and ask the important question—does it work? Well, I suppose it works about as well as the fifth season's "The Living Dead," which also mostly failed due to a sharp shift in tone in the middle of its narrative. However, I find this one slightly more interesting because the basis is science-fiction (rather than a ghost-story that doesn't pan out). I'll say this for "Thingumajig," it's intriguingly different, even if not entirely successful as an episode of *The Avengers*. And it's always possible that you'll enjoy it even more than me.

CHAMPAGNE, CARS, CLOTHES, AND CANINES

This one starts out with Tara debuting a green rollneck jumper and a black tunic with black buttons, while Steed wears his blue three-piece suit with a crimson tie. Tara follows up with a fawn-colored zippered minidress with intricate embroidery in metallic gold thread (and possibly pearls) along the placket and the lower sleeves; the fabric is somewhat shiny suggesting an artificial fabric like rayon. Just in time for the Thingumajig attack, she changes into a purple blouse under a black vest with plum-colored slacks. In the tag scene, Steed switches into a lovely and comfortable-looking brown suede jacket with soft round buttons. Underneath is an oatmeal rollneck jumper with orange and brown stripes around the collar and gray checked trousers. Tara hangs upside down in a white blouse with a reddish-brown vest (looks like one that possibly shows up later).

Steed briefly drives a 1958 Land Rover 88" Series II ¼-ton 4x4 (HMH 659B); later, his Rolls-Royce returns, as does Tara's Lotus Europa (which is becoming her car of the moment in the later episodes in this season). Lots of champagne, in fact a virtual shower of it is wasted by Tara on the Thingumajig. She does get a swig though.

TAG SCENE

At Steed's flat, he fusses about the reception on his television set as Tara, out the window, tries to adjust the aerial according to his instructions. "Yes, a woman. Long flowing hair… Oh, it's not a woman at all. It's a dog. Looks like an Afghan hound. Only saw her from behind." Unfortunately, the final, perfect position results in Tara hanging precariously in front of the window and Steed has to help her back inside.

QUOTES

"Fetch the doctor. I'll see what happened." (The Doctor?)
"Say nothing, professor. That's the way the cookie crumbles."
"You baptize and bury them, and I'll try and see that the interval between the two is as long as possible."
"A mechanical animal, living on electricity, able to seek it out and devour it!"
"Oh yes, I've given it the power of the movement, and most of all, the will to kill!"

156 (7.8.28) MY WILDEST DREAM

Written by Philip Levene
Directed by Robert Fuest

GUEST CAST

Peter Vaughan (Jaeger), Derek Godfrey (Tobias), Edward Cox (Chilcott), Susan Travers (Nurse Owen), Philip Madoc (Slater), Michael David (Reece), Murray Hayne (Gibbons), Tom Kempinski (Dyson), John Savident (Winthrop), Hugh Moxey (Peregrine)

PRE-TITLE/TEASER

One man stalks another in an elegant apartment. When the stalker reaches the flat's owner, he pulls a knife and stabs violently, but in a quick cut it is revealed that this is merely a hallucinatory exercise and the would-be assassin is in fact stabbing a cloth dummy. When he leaves from having been programmed, still somewhat in a daze, he enters a chauffeured car and finds himself sitting next to the very man he's supposed to kill.

SYNOPSIS

Murders are occurring, and the murderers are claiming it was all a dream. It turns out that someone is manipulating them with aggresso-psycho-therapy to commit the murders for their own gain. Is it the eccentric Jaeger? And is Steed scheduled to be the next victim…?

REVIEW

In production order, this is the first of only two Philip Levene stories this season. Momentarily, the old style is back—at least partially. As such, "My Wildest Dream" is one of the best seventh season stories. Though not entirely original for *The Avengers*, having been explored in Season One's "Tunnel of Fear," murder by hypnosis using aggresso-psycho-therapy gets the usual seventh season approach, which is to tone down everything and subsist off the big-idea-of-the-week. The idea is just strong enough for that, and frankly it comes across as more convincing this time than in the Season One effort. Unfortunately, you can also see most of the plot developments coming from a mile off, and the story lacks the surrealism that the subject matter naturally suggests. Ultimately, this leaves it up to the characters and Robert Fuest to carry it to the next level. Fortunately, they succeed for the most part.

Fuest is his usual brilliant self throughout. The artistic shots and moody lighting, alternating wide angle shots and closeups really sell this adventure. One intriguing and mildly offbeat fight scene is shot in a modish and moodily-lit room with multi-colored glass panels mounted on tables that seem to serve no purpose other than to get smashed. However, the best set is the observation room, which has the word "observation" in very large red and white letters across the back wall. The action scenes are great, and the various stabbings seem quite brutal, which is unusually dark for *The Avengers*.

The twist of expectations that Levene and Fuest give us is the seemingly unavoidable arrive-just-a-second-too-late-to-stop-a-murder scene, which they then reveal to be part of a dream sequence. Winthrop later dies anyway, but the novel innovation is much appreciated. It's also novel to see the suspected villain Jaeger seemingly admit his terrible actions; Steed at first seems very shocked. Jaeger turns out to be innocent, but again, the original twist is nice. Levene is trying to throw us off the scent, which can never hurt.

On the downside, Tara gets an unwanted boyfriend in this one, a tedious whiner of a man named Teddy Chilcott who invades every scene in which he appears. Naturally, he's jealous of Steed, which makes it painfully obvious that he will be used in an assassination attempt. Thankfully, the plan is thwarted by Tara's ingenuity with her footwear and the old carpet trick, all of which manages to be terribly funny. Thus, we are guaranteed that Teddy will not return, an infinitely wise decision. This is easily the last really good one before oblivion calls, but I'm bothered by the fact that additional wit and bizarreness, and maybe sharper pacing, could have elevated it to the level of a masterpiece.

CHAMPAGNE, CARS, CLOTHES, AND CANINES

Tara wears her sheer black, gold, and white cardigan (last seen in "Who Was That Man I Saw You With?" in transmission order, though this would be its first appearance in production order). This time, it's worn buttoned up with only a black brassiere underneath, a matching black skirt, and long dangling diamond earrings. Steed wears his pale-gray three-piece suit with a striped white shirt and dark-crimson tie. At Tara's apartment, she wears a purple satin dressing gown with pale-blue string feather cuffs, and Steed wears his brown serge suit with a pale-gold shirt and copper-brown tie. Tara changes to her brown studded leather jacket (from "They Keep Killing Steed") with brown shorts, a black rollneck jumper, and black boots. Meanwhile, Steed changes to his navy suit with pale-blue shirt and black bowler. This is followed by the blue-and-pink kimono for Tara and the chocolate-brown suit for Steed. Tara's last debut of the episode is a pinstriped white blouse with a sky-blue vest and matching culottes. She pairs this ensemble with a tan belt and shoes. Overall, a good episode, fashion-wise; unfortunately, Steed's striped brown-and-black trousers show up at the end to blight the tag scene.

They do enjoy more Meudon & Heim champagne, however.

The Rolls-Royce returns and Tara gets to drive it while chasing after Dyson. She also gets to drive her own vehicle—the AC 428. Nurse Owen, perhaps appropriately, drives a 1964 Volvo 122 S B18 'Amazon' (BLE 392B).

TAG SCENE

In Steed's flat, Steed tells Tara his darkest secret. When Tara suggests that this may explain his abiding interest in champagne, he denies this overbaked analysis, remarking that "I happen to like it."

QUOTES

"Steed—am I glad to see you!" "Is that a question or a statement?"
"So, you think you're a horse, eh?" "Oh, not often, but 'round about Derby Day I do get a slight twinge in my fetlocks."

157 (7.31.29) REQUIEM

Written by Brian Clemens
Directed by Don Chaffey

GUEST CAST

Angela Douglas (Miranda), John Cairney (Firth), John Paul (Wells), Patrick Newell (Mother), Denis Shaw (Murray), Terence Sewards (Rista), Mike Lewin (Barrett), Kathja Wyeth (Jill), Harvey Ashby (Bobby), John Baker (Vicar)

PRE-TITLE/TEASER

In a London parking garage, two assassins await the arrival of Miss Miranda Loxton, whom they plan to kill. A car matching the description does indeed arrive and the assassins shoot Miss Loxton's bodyguard, but the target herself escapes.

SYNOPSIS

Star witness Miranda Luxton has several hitmen looking for her, and Steed has been assigned for her protection. He takes Miranda to a safe place that only he knows, but Tara is kidnapped and may be tricked into revealing Steed and Miss Luxton's location...

REVIEW

While hardly original or particularly clever, "Requiem" makes for surprisingly entertaining television. Tara's drug-induced dreams are a bit obvious however, and the viewer is never under any illusions that her unfortunate experiences are real. Nevertheless, it's a good episode for Linda Thorson in particular, who has an opportunity to act out a more engaging version of the scenario that framed the much less interesting episode "Pandora." I find it rather unconvincing however that Mother and his crew could set up a decoy house before the villains could drive over.

Don Chaffey's direction is solid, and the production crew does a nice job of apparently destroying Steed's apartment in a surprise explosion, which naturally turns out to be part of Tara's drug-induced delusion. The most charming parts of this episode however involve Steed and his newfound kindred spirit Miranda playing toy soldiers and recreating major battles to pass the time in their self-induced exile. It's a good opportunity to see the kid in Steed. It's a side that wouldn't show again until *The New Avengers* episode "Dirtier by the Dozen."

This is a suitably entertaining hour of television as long as you don't expect too many surprises or much ingenuity.

CHAMPAGNE, CARS, CLOTHES, AND CANINES

Tara begins with a fabulous new debut, a glorious cerulean-blue overcoat in an elegant cut with an A-line skirt, a high collar, and a black integrated belt. It's worn over a flame-red silk long-sleeved blouse with black slacks and boots. The fact that her clothes never change and she doesn't even get any pajamas is a pretty good clue that her situation is a drug-induced illusion. No debuts for Steed but it's always a good day when he wears his taupe suit, which is pretty much the suit he's stuck in for his extended hideaway, with the pale-gold shirt, and the black-and-olive paisley tie. They both finally get a clothing change in the tag scene: Tara in a red double-breasted tunic dress with gold chains over a red-and-white pinstriped blouse with a red butterfly collar and black stockings; and Steed is back in his brown suede jacket, gray trousers, and a cream rollneck jumper.

Steed drives a gray-blue 1966 Austin A60 Cambridge (LGF 942D) and a red 1965 Triumph 2000 Automatic Mark 1 (MBH 545C) (both with red interiors) when escorting Miranda to her secured location. The villains drive a black 1965 Morris LD-M30 1½-Ton Van and a black 1968 Mercedes-Benz 220 (TMP 884F). Tara again drives the Rolls-Royce Silver Ghost, this time under gunpoint by Murray. She also rides to Steed's faux funeral and back in a black 1964 Vanden Plas Princess 4-Litre hearse (BLE 697B). Fortunately, she finally gets back to reality and behind the wheel of her own car, the Lotus Europa, by episode's end.

The champagne is well-stocked for Miranda's hideaway.

TAG SCENE

Tara arrives at Steed's flat to find him tracing his ancestry, including Sir Steedalot, who accidentally created the Round Table. Then, by the most absurdly complicated lineage, he confirms that he has royal blood.

QUOTES

"In loving memory of our dear Mother....The Finest Chap We Ever Knew. Died Suddenly. Explosively. R.I.P."
"Steed had no one and nothing to fear, nothing except my stupidity."

158 (7.32.30) TAKE-OVER

Written by Terry Nation
Directed by Robert Fuest

GUEST CAST

Tom Adams (Grenville), Elizabeth Sellars (Laura), Michael Gwynn (Bill), Hilary Pritchard (Circe), Garfield Morgan (Sexton), Keith Buckley (Lomax), John Comer (Groom), Anthony Sagar (Clifford)

PRE-TITLE/TEASER

Two criminals with a hostage in handcuffs drive down a country road until their car breaks down. While the criminals attempt to repair their car, the hostage escapes and makes for a nearby house across a field. But he doesn't make it very far. One of the villains activates a device hidden in a cigarette lighter which causes the escapee to instantly fall down and die.

SYNOPSIS

A group of criminals invade the home of Bill and Laura Bassett and hold them hostage with microbombs implanted in their necks. Fortunately for the victims, Steed is arriving for a late Christmas celebration…

REVIEW

This is another script from Terry Nation, who has not had a very good track record with writing for *The Avengers*. Thankfully, this episode is directed beautifully by Robert Fuest, which goes a long way towards giving it points of interest. I suspect that they gave Fuest the difficult episodes to shoot precisely because he could make a dull script into something interesting. Watching people trapped in a house by criminals with micro-bombs in their necks is a scenario that provokes continuous tension, and not necessarily in a good way. It could produce an hour of tedium rather than tension in lesser hands. Fortunately, the careful handling of Fuest keeps the story on an even keel. And there are a few interesting characters like the superbly villainous Grenville and the sexy but mad Circe.

The narrative reaches a peak with an especially well-shot and tense sequence involving a hunting expedition that goes wrong—Steed becoming the prey, having unexpectedly dropped in upon his friends who are Grenville's intended victims from the outset. Having said that, it certainly is a strange coincidence that the crooks pick the very day that Steed just happens to be dropping. It's almost as if Terry Nation wrote the story in isolation and then realized that he somehow had to involve Steed.

Although the idea of micro-explosives implanted in a vital organ or blood vessel is an intriguing one, as I've said many times before, Nation never got the feel of the series quite right, and this episode is the final proof of that. It never feels quite like an episode of *The Avengers*, though it comes close to the feel of *The New Avengers*, and thus, is something of a harbinger of things to come and a reasonably entertaining hour of television at the same time.

CHAMPAGNE, CARS, CLOTHES, AND CANINES

As we near the end of the season, there are very few new outfit debuts in this episode, the most interesting of which is Steed's—a hunter-green waterproof jacket, matching canvas trousers, the beige rollneck jumper (from "Thingumajig"), a zippered olive-green suede jacket, with a reddish-brown leather messenger bag, black wellingtons, white leather gloves with brown palms, and a dark-green trilby. He starts out, however, in his chocolate-brown suit with a pale-gold striped shirt and a brown paisley tie. Tara debuts a very wet, bright-yellow plastic mac over a black rollneck jumper, stockings, and boots. Steed later wears his midnight-blue tuxedo at dinner. When Tara arrives at the house later, she wears a soft brown leather tunic with a brass chain at the abdomen, a black rollneck jumper, and matching trousers. In the tag scene, Steed wears the same suede jacket as in the tag scene for "Thingumajig," albeit with a different (unstriped) oatmeal rollneck jumper.

Steed drives his Rolls-Royce Silver Ghost down to the house, but it's not the only vintage car on view; the car in the foyer is a green-and-black 1907 Riley 9hp Vee-Twin (YU 4031). When hunting, the villains drive an army-green 1958 Land Rover 109" Series II pickup (UFK 523).

Champagne at dinner, and lots more drinking too.

TAG SCENE

Steed plays "invisible golf" in Tara's apartment, claiming that it requires far greater concentration than regular golf. When Tara joins the game, she accidentally sends the invisible golf ball through her living room window, and Steed quips that she should have used the number two iron.

QUOTES

"You see, Bill and I were taken prisoner in Nanking. There was no window in the cell. We lost all track of time—""—So, we made our own calendar. Eventually we found that we'd celebrated Christmas in February."

"I spend all my money on new noses.""Well, everyone should have a hobby."

"When I was little, I used to get the most awful pains in my head. I used to think how nice it would be if I could cut a little hole in the temple and take the hurting part out."

"But I'm a generous man, sentimental even. You can go on living."

"It's nice to be nearly a genius when you're as pretty as I am."

159 (7.28.31) PANDORA

Written by Brian Clemens
Directed by Robert Fuest

GUEST CAST

Julian Glover (Rupert), James Cossins (Henry), Kathleen Byron (Miss Faversham), Patrick Newell (Mother), John Laurie (Juniper), Anthony Roye (Pettigrew), Geoffrey Whitehead (Carter), Peter Madden (Lasindall), Reginald Barratt (Xavier Smith), Raymond Burke (Young Gregory)

PRE-TITLE/TEASER

In a stately Edwardian house, two brothers argue about the merits of jazz music. According to the newspapers, the Great War is just about to break out and Rupert reassures his fiancée, Pandora, that the war will not disturb their wedding day. But Pandora is revealed to be just a dressing dummy.

SYNOPSIS

Apparently, Rupert's dotty old uncle has hidden a large fortune as a dowry for Pandora, his wife-to-be. Problem: no Pandora. Thus, Tara—a dead ringer for the bride—is kidnapped by Rupert as part of a plot to have her impersonate his uncle's long-lost love and find the fortune…

REVIEW

This is an ambitiously directed but dreary episode; it is long on atmosphere but tragically short on thrills. Tara spends the entire episode heavily drugged, and Steed spends the same amount of time experiencing contrived concern for Tara's wellbeing, relentlessly reminding us how close they're supposed to be. It's surprising how frequently Tara is chloroformed considering she's so skilled in martial arts. It's too bad those skills were not in evidence in this story as they could have saved us from an hour of tedium.

I imagine the idea was that this story would serve as a significant vehicle for Linda Thorson to almost play a different character. Thorson has repeatedly said that this is her favorite episode, and this is understandable since she does theoretically get the chance to stretch her acting legs so to speak. However, it's unfortunate that the story, and for that matter the entirety of what the series is about, needed to be sacrificed in order to provide the actor with a script that would please her. I mean, couldn't she have gotten a role in ***A Room with a View*** if she really wanted to do an Edwardian period piece? In any case, she spends almost the entire time drugged and disoriented or sleeping, so where is the performance? Just as she wanders into a forbidden room and finds something of mild interest to the audience—if you can consider dry-as-a-bone bleached-white skeletons to be of even mild interest—she is chloroformed yet again and the cycle starts over. I'm getting a bad Hammer film vibe here.

The best thing about this story is the directorial styling of Robert Fuest; he puts the viewer right in the drama with extreme close-ups on the guest stars in the cramped Edwardian quarters and practices his amusing tactic of putting the camera into unusual places. In other good news, Julian Glover is a significant bonus as always. He doesn't exactly have a good story to star in but makes the most of his character. I also enjoyed seeing John Laurie return to the series.

Unfortunately, the finale reminds me just a little too much of a 1951 Donald Duck cartoon called ***Lucky Number***, in which his nephews win a car for him only to have him vindictively destroy it before he realizes its potential. What a bizarre connection to make! To be fair, it's no one's fault but mine that those particular brain cells fire in response to this episode, but it does reveal the frustration felt by the viewer that is prompted by the final moments, our illusions of anything fulfilling or intellectually satisfying ripped to shreds along with a priceless Rembrandt.

Robert Fuest's style goes a long way in lending this lackluster script some artistry, but in the end, it still feels as dull as Tara must have felt when doped up on all that chloroform.

CHAMPAGNE, CARS, CLOTHES, AND CANINES

The color of the day for Tara is purple, but the fashion of the day for 'Pandora' is Edwardian, so we get two purple outfits and four Edwardian ones. When she's chloroformed and kidnapped, she wears a purple zippered top with a hoodie and an integrated belt, and pale-orange trim around the collar, cuffs, and hemline, with canary-yellow slacks and pale-brown leather boots. Her Edwardian outfits are: a high-waisted royal-blue skirt and sky-blue blouse with a long royal-blue necktie; a frill-fronted ankle-length white nightgown worn with a royal-blue-and-green housecoat; a high-waisted royal-blue skirt with a pale-blue long-sleeved blouse with black ankle boots and stockings; and a pink-and-white bridal gown with matching wide-brimmed hat, long white gloves, and pink shawl. The gown is layered with two types of fabric and the white part is sheer and laced, whereas the pink part is opaque. She finishes off the episode in the tag scene with a purple rollneck jumper, fuchsia trousers, and a pink hair bow.

Steed wears his chocolate-brown suit with the pale-gold pinstriped shirt and copper-brown tie. This is followed by the brown serge suit with a white shirt and a brown-and-blue paisley tie, then, the gray three-piece, and then the taupe suit with the pale-gold pinstriped shirt and a black-and-gray floral tie, and finally, the pale-gray suit with a pale-pink shirt and a blue-and-crimson satin tie. So, in an episode which is ostensibly all about Tara's experience, we get a full review of all Steed's greatest hits. He finishes off the tag scene in a fluffy cream cardigan, black trousers, and a multi-colored cravat.

Perhaps despite all expectations—this being an episode with Tara 'trapped' in Edwardian times—her Lotus Europa makes an appearance with a mocked-up skeleton wearing her first outfit from the episode. The villains set it alight with gasoline. We never see it actually burn up, so whether this is its last appearance due to the fire or simply because it's nearly the end of the season cannot be definitively answered.

Tara gets to drink champagne under the worst of all circumstances, while she's imprisoned and drugged—and, again, it's Meudon & Heim, which you'd think would be a dead giveaway that the times aren't what she thinks. I guess we'll assume that it's a very old winery in Avengersland and dates back to well before Edwardian times.

TAG SCENE

At his flat, Steed has a terrible migraine, and when Tara arrives, he asks her to take back her gift—a beautiful mantel clock with chimes as loud as Big Ben! The chimes shatter several champagne glasses next to a bottle of Meudon & Heim.

QUOTES

"Let's be civilized about this. Oh, do get up. Lying there, you look so…so down."
"The fortune, the vast fortune that you've hidden away, set aside against this day. You've tormented Henry and me with it ever since we were children!"

160 (7.5.32) GET-A-WAY!

Written by Philip Levene
Directed by Don Sharp

GUEST CAST

Andrew Keir (Colonel James), Peter Bowles (Ezdorf), Peter Bayliss (Dodge), Neil Hallett (Paul Ryder), Terence Longdon (George Neville), William Wilde (Baxter), Michael Culver (Price), Michael Elwyn (Lt. Edwards), John Hussey (Peters), Barry Linehan (Magnus), Robert Russell (Lubin), Vincent Harding (Rostov), James Belchamber (Bryant)

PRE-TITLE/TEASER

At an ancient monastery, the monks check on their prisoners, and one of them, viewing the interior of a cell on a monitor, finds to his dismay that a prisoner is not inside. When he investigates, the prisoner appears out of nowhere, KO's the monk and escapes. When the monks pursue the escapee to a dead-end at the end of a corridor, he has disappeared into thin air.

SYNOPSIS

One by one, a trio of enemy agents attempt to escape from a maximum-security prison. After two have mysteriously vanished while escaping and later kill their assigned targets, Steed interrogates the last of the spy triumvirate to find the secret of their elusiveness, and the answer is mysteriously difficult to see…

REVIEW

This is the first episode (production-wise) involving a format that would be repeated all too often during *The New Avengers*. Steed meets some old close friends who are then killed as part of a plot by the main antagonists of the story. As always, we've never seen them before (the friends, that is), and thus, the object is to convince us of the pathos of their deaths in a mere few moments. This seldom worked perfectly despite being done many times. Coupled with the seventh season's all too common lack of eccentrics, surrealism and wit otherwise so associated with the series, we're almost dooming the story from the outset.

Having said this, the core idea-of-the-week is at least an intriguing one. The escapist abilities of the criminals are a genuine mystery for the first two-thirds of the story, though the reveal of how it's done is not as satisfying as it could have been—the special effects are not that special. They work far better when it is accomplished with editing and cuts. Speaking of which, the corridor that leads to nowhere in the monastery seems to only exist to give the escapees somewhere to run and perform their disappearing act. I'm also perplexed as to why the escapees don't treat their entire bodies instead of just their backs. Nevertheless, the gimmick does work well enough to set the narrative in motion and sustain suspense.

Another complaint about the situation is that Ezdorf doesn't seem to have a plan for actually killing Steed, just escaping from prison. If he respects Steed so much, then surely, he didn't think he could merely show up at Steed's apartment and kill him with a gun. If it were that simple, he could have strangled him while they were talking in the cell. We're left to assume that he considers his camouflage to be such an advantage that it will insure victory. Fortunately, Steed masters the same technique as Ezdorf. This has the effect of ensuring his survival so that he can try again next week to recover the burnished perfection of the prior era of the show, a constant struggle in this problematic season.

The guest cast this week is high quality indeed, and they breathe needed life into a story that could have been especially dull without careful handling. Andrew Keir and Peter Bowles both make welcome returns to the show and make the most of their roles. One highlight of this episode is the verbal sparring between Steed and Ezdorf.

"Get-a-way!" is a solid enough hour of television, existing in the twilight between two eras, with all the inherent flaws and uncertainties therein, but it's also lamentably straightforward and unexceptional.

CHAMPAGNE, CARS, CLOTHES, AND CANINES

Although this was an early episode production-wise, it still show signs of the move away from some of the early fashion decisions made under John Bryce. Tara debuts five different outfits, most of which have considerably more color and class than her ensembles in other episodes in this recording block. First, she wears a cream silk blouse under a white knee-length knit coat dress with a cowl, paired with white stockings and cream boots; next, a cobalt-blue minidress with hot-pink trim, a red-and-pink scarf, and knee-high black boots; then, a white pinstriped blouse, fawn vest and culottes, with a wide black belt with circular buckle and brown boots; next, a black rollneck jumper, fawn culottes, a black-and-orange print scarf, and a very similar belt; and, finally, a rose-red minidress with orange-red trim and a stripe across the waist.

Steed's brown tartan blazer returns with a pale-green shirt and a forest-green tie; it's been a while. He also wears his fawn overcoat over the pale-gray three-piece suit with a white pinstriped shirt and a copper-colored tie. Unfortunately, the olive-green patterned shirt blights the episode as well.

No champagne, instead they drink more of Craig's Old Scotch in Ezdorf's cell. And, of course, there's plenty of Lizard vodka.

Tara's AC 428 returns for the first time in a while. Perhaps she'd lost her Lotus Europa in the previous episode (in terms of transmission order continuity). Steed's Rolls-Royce returns as well.

TAG SCENE

Tara visits Steed at his flat with her arms loaded with colorful packages. Steed appears to be invisible at first and Tara searches the flat looking for him among ordinary objects. When Tara threatens to not give him his present if he doesn't come out, Steed pops up from behind the settee, remarking that he has a leak in his tuba (which he uses for potted flowers).

QUOTES

"You're getting close, Steed. Very close. But you'll never be close enough."
"It's like a riddle. I was trained never to turn my back on an enemy, because to turn my back put me at my most vulnerable. But, if I turn my back now, I'm at my most invulnerable."

161 (7.33.33) BIZARRE

Written by Brian Clemens
Directed by Leslie Norman

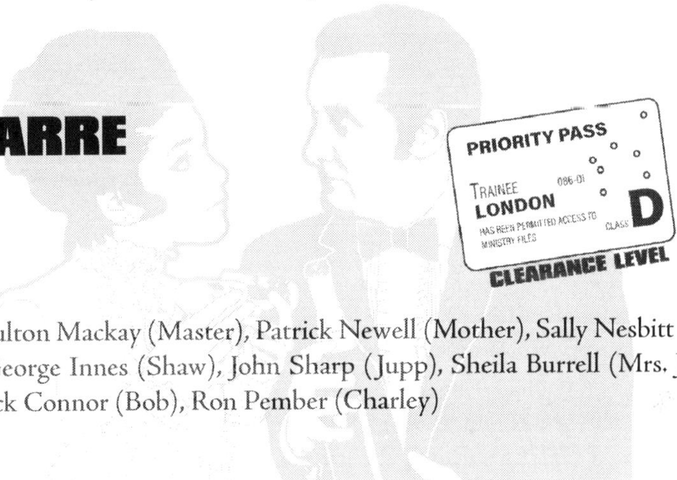

GUEST CAST

Roy Kinnear (Happychap), Fulton Mackay (Master), Patrick Newell (Mother), Sally Nesbitt (Helen), James Kerry (Cordell), George Innes (Shaw), John Sharp (Jupp), Sheila Burrell (Mrs. Jupp), Michael Balfour (Tom), Patrick Connor (Bob), Ron Pember (Charley)

PRE-TITLE/TEASER

A waifish blond woman wearing only a white nightgown wanders in a daze in a snowy field. Barefoot and exhausted, she finally collapses and stares blankly with tears in her eyes.

SYNOPSIS

A woman found unconscious in a field wearing her bedclothes is babbling about dead men who won't stay dead. Captain Carson assists Steed and Tara as they investigate, and they learn the woman was thrown from a train by a man who emerged from a coffin that was bound for Happy Meadows. This graveyard is run by Bagpipes Happychap, who likes to make death 'fun.' Happychap isn't a very good caretaker though, as his "Paradise Plot" is filled with empty coffins. Will Steed have to 'die' in order to solve the mystery of the empty graves…?

REVIEW

As with many episodes from this season, the direction is excellent, but the story is at best lacking. The episode opens with a beautifully-shot and vaguely Bergman-like sequence. Sally Nesbit wanders wearily through a snowy landscape under a bright blue sky. She stumbles directly towards the camera until her face fills the frame. Then, she collapses and awakens in a hospital, screaming hysterically about a "dead man that isn't dead." This leads us on a staccato jumble of set pieces over the next hour, all of which have little relevance to one another and terminate with a rocket journey into space, which remains for what this episode is likely best known—along with its being the last episode of *The Avengers*.

Superficially, the story is actually a fair throwback to the earlier tropes of previous seasons, which makes it perhaps somewhat ironic that it is such a poor episode—not that it doesn't eventually earn it. The first twenty minutes aren't nearly as bad as its reputation, which generally remains that of one of the worst four or five hours of this season, but there is no question that Fennell and Clemens were running out of gas—and ideas—for the season.

Steed spends most of his time confounding Happychap at Paradise Plot, as the latter continually expresses his dismay about the empty graves that are dug up one by one. Meanwhile, Tara stays with Helen, consoling her while she tries to remember anything that might actually advance the plot, of which there is precious little. Mother makes a few tiresome appearances, his grumpy patriarchal shtick now exhausted.

The excellent guest cast, which includes Roy Kinnear and Fulton Mackay (embarrassingly slathered in brown makeup), is wasted on eccentrics that aren't truly eccentric and surrealistic scenarios that aren't truly surreal. It's more like half-baked hyperreality. It's as if *The Avengers* is worn out and merely going through the motions of imitating its former self. It's as if Fennell and Clemens forgot how they did it.

The core concept—that of arranging fake deaths for criminals on the run—is actually frighteningly unoriginal, without even a notable twist. And it's hard to imagine anyone as stupid as Happychap running anything successfully, even a cemetery plot. He, having been exposed by Steed to the ploy behind the empty graves relentlessly for half-an-hour, tells Tara that Steed is dead and in Paradise Plot (and he apparently believes it). We can only assume that this is intended to make *us* believe it's true, only for it to be dispelled thirty seconds later by Steed's reemergence in a down-market version of heterosexual male heaven—an underground cavern lounge, decked out with velvet curtains, and rocking with beat music and swinging sixties girls that don't mind an occasional pat on the bum. How very Austin Powers!

The whole effort terminates with a whimper of defeat as the line of criminals are marched out, shackled in handcuffs. Steed and Tara then unceremoniously blast themselves off into space in a tag scene that really is more appropriate for *The Far Out Space Nuts*. Mother promises us that they'll be back, while the circumstances of their departure assures us the least amount of likelihood that they will be, which is about the most honest part of this episode.

CHAMPAGNE, CARS, CLOTHES, AND... CAMERAS!

White seems to be the theme of this episode. Tara debuts only two new outfits: a white double-breasted overcoat with black buttons (very nice) and a navy scarf with white spots, black trousers, and boots; and, for the tag scene, a white chiffon dress with intricate lacing and pearls over the bust and the collar, and a diamond tiara. The sleeves are sheer with the barest hint of skin underneath. She also spends some time wrapped up in a woolly brown-and-gray plaid blanket while sipping tea.

Steed wears his pale-gray three-piece suit with the pale-pink shirt, pink-and-blue satin tie, and matching gray bowler for his trips to Paradise Plot, but switches to the blue suit with pale-blue shirt and purple tie for his final visit to the afterlife. I guess I can think of worse suits to spend eternity in. He later breaks out his Hugh Hefner imitation once more with the crimson tuxedo and matching bowtie.

The Rolls-Royce Silver Ghost returns. Steed also pilots an Atlas SLV-3 rocket with a brand-new 1969 Sid and Marty Krofft Mark I interior. Jim Cordell drives the same 1958 Land Rover 88" Series II as in "Thingumajig" but with the same registration plate as the Mini Moke in "All Done with Mirrors." He wears a very nice heavy leather overcoat with fur trim.

For all the debauchery in Steed's arranged afterlife, you'd think there'd be more champagne, but no. Maybe that's why he's eager to drink some in celebration with Tara in his homemade rocket.

Mother's camera is probably a Rolleiflex 3.5 twin lens reflex but the label plate is covered over with masking tape. Nevertheless, the rivets on either side of the plate give it away. However, I cannot explain the square metal plate on top of the viewfinder lid with an 'M' logo. Either this was a further modification to hide the fact that it's a Rollei camera, or it could be a copy of a Rollei, or, just maybe, the 'M' stands for Mother. You decide.

TAG SCENE

Steed reveals to Tara that he has built his own rocket ship in his backyard. Mother arrives and compliments Steed on his accomplishment, and then goes outside to take a photo. Tara hits the launch button and the rocket streaks into space, leaving Steed and Tara to toast champagne together. On the ground, Mother breaks the fourth wall and assures the audience that "they'll be back. You can depend on it" before exclaiming, "they're unchaperoned up there!"

QUOTES

"I wonder if it's too late to hand this case over to another department...?"
"Very well. I will arrange for you to leave this life. Dispense with it. Shuffle off this mortal coil."
"...I offer special after-death benefits. Death is only the beginning, Mr. Steed."
"The mind boggles. What would it be like, I wonder, if I'd lived a completely blameless life?"
"Steed is alive and well, but... but he's staying on in paradise."

"THEY'LL BE BACK. YOU CAN DEPEND ON IT."

THE AVENGERS REINCARNATED

Until the 1998 film *The Avengers, The New Avengers* was something of a pariah in *The Avengers* legacy. Generally, it was agreed that the show was inferior to the original. Even Patrick Macnee was said to have ultimately disliked the program, disagreeing sharply with the decisions of the Canadian and French backers on the style of the show, particularly in the faltering second series.

But this was likely no real excuse for the near total disregard shown by fandom for many years. Truthfully, *The New Avengers* did often fall prey to the influences of the day, which, frankly, disallowed any hope of capturing the original style and ambience of the 1960s version. As an example, Steed was a character that was based on the old-world English gentry, a centuries old perception of the ideal British man that had crystallized in the age of the British empire. If this was considered somewhat amusingly quaint and old-fashioned in the late sixties, it was bizarre by the late seventies.

By the time *The New Avengers* was going before the cameras, the world had changed in other ways as well. The counterculture revolution had come and gone and then returned in a brand-new form—it was the second wave of Baby Boomers. Not only was stylish, upper class, aristocratic behavior considered out of vogue, it was thought of as nearly vulgar by the post-sixties hipsters and yuppies-in-training. This left only one option—to convert the characters into hard-nosed, liberated professional spies with kitsch flats in wall-to-wall sea foam green and bead curtains, and to fill the stories with car chases, gun fights, and heavy use of judo moves and karate kicks.

The trappings of the seventies were everywhere in *The New Avengers*. Even the title sequence apparently required that the obligatory crate of fruit fall on top of a racing sports car, intercut between shots of the stars performing their action moves on the dastardly villains and then removing their helmets to shake out their coiffures to a pounding disco bassline. It was so *Charlie's Angels*, so *Starsky and Hutch*, so seventies, so damn American! To some fans of the original series, it might have been seen as remarkably counterfeit.

To compound the problems of a shifting savoir-faire, Steed was moved to the role of a wise patriarch that guided the talents of his younger cohorts. Now, he's an equestrian, lives in a country estate instead of the Mews, and drives Jaguars and Land Rovers instead of a Bentley. From a producer's viewpoint, this was very likely an intelligent move, considering that Patrick Macnee was in his mid-fifties at that time, his role as an active TV secret agent seemingly a bit too far-fetched. The result however, was a far cry from the peak of the original series, in which the theme had been a close-knit pair of unstoppable superspies that were engaged in a gentle and adorable are-they-or-aren't-they relationship. Such a situation with Macnee in the lead was near impossible under the new format, so this ambiguous relationship was transferred to the younger characters, who now commanded most of the action, both the physical and the elusively romantic.

While this may seem to restore the central character motif, in the context of the seventies, an enigmatic relationship takes on a distinctly sexual tone rather than one of innocent flirtatiousness. Mrs. Peel was married, her husband was gone but likely to walk in at any moment. She could have had a light in the window that forced her to hold back, but what was stopping Purdey and Gambit? In any case, this sadly had the unfortunate effect of marginalizing John Steed, who now all too frequently stayed at home answering telephones, brushing down horses with his girlfriend-of-the-week, and receiving old friends that died on his doorstep.

The show managed notable merits however, despite these disappointing changes. In spite of morphing into something closer to *The Professionals* or *The Sweeney* than its predecessor series, the show was not without considerable wit, great writing, and some especially fine direction. It also possessed the notable talents of the superb Joanna Lumley, who proved herself to be exquisitely equal to Diana Rigg and Honor Blackman. Many of the heavily bantered scenes between Purdey and Gambit are amongst the best in any era of the series, new or old. If Diana Rigg was the sixties queen of diamonds—a youthful sophisticated polished aristocrat with simultaneous warmth, charm and approachability—Purdey was the seventies queen of hearts, fun-loving, in touch with her sexuality and with every man at her beck and call.

In the 21st century, if the criticism of *The New Avengers* is to take any positive form, it would be to recognize it as really no different than its predecessor in its origins. Both were distinctly a product of their era. The only meaningful difference in style is that *The New Avengers* suffers from the association, while *The Avengers* benefits. In the past four decades, the sixties have gained a mystique for their diversity, their revolutions, and their mawkish charm—a mixture of quixotic innocence, desperate struggles, and much needed social change. The seventies are more noted for their superficiality and the now maligned "me generation"—not to mention the tacky interior decorating and heavily-coiffed puffy hairdos. The decade of the sixties is looked upon as noble and naïve, the seventies as narcissistic and shallow.

Having recognized this, it should be obvious that one is to dispense with the cosmetic criticisms, and judge the show for its writing, humor, acting, and often superb direction, all characteristics that are far more deserving of the viewer's attention than the peripheral aspects of a bygone generation.

SEASON ONE

13 episodes (35mm color film, ~52 min. ea.)

Regular Cast
Patrick Macnee—John Steed
Gareth Hunt—Mike Gambit
Joanna Lumley—Purdey

Producers: Albert Fennell and Brian Clemens
Music: Laurie Johnson

1. **The Eagle's Nest—w.** Brian Clemens; **dir.** Desmond Davis; **UK tx.** 19 Oct 1976; **US tx.** 5 Sep 1978; **Filmed:** Apr 1976
2. **House of Cards—w.** Brian Clemens; **dir.** Ray Austin; **UK tx.** 26 Oct 1976; **US tx.** 20 Oct 1978; **Filmed:** May 1976
3. **The Last of the Cybernauts...?? —w.** Brian Clemens; **dir.** Sidney Hayers; **UK tx.** 2 Nov 1976; **US tx.** 9 Mar 1979; **Filmed:** May 1976
4. **The Midas Touch—w.** Brian Clemens; **dir.** Robert Fuest; **UK tx.** 9 Nov 1976; **US tx.** 1 Dec 1978; **Filmed:** Apr 1976
5. **Cat Amongst the Pigeons—w.** Dennis Spooner; **dir.** John Hough; **UK tx.** 16 Nov 1976; **US tx.** 17 Nov 1978; **Filmed:** Jun 1976
6. **Target! —w.** Dennis Spooner; **dir.** Ray Austin; **UK tx.** 23 Nov 1976; **US tx.** 12 Sep 1978; **Filmed:** Jul 1976; **Filmed:** Jul 1976
7. **To Catch a Rat—w.** Terence Feeley; **dir.** James Hill; **UK tx.** 30 Nov 1976; **US tx.** 16 Feb 1979; **Filmed:** Jun 1976
8. **The Tale of the Big Why—w.** Brian Clemens; **dir.** Robert Fuest; **UK tx.** 7 Dec 1976; **US tx.** 2 Feb 1979; **Filmed:** Aug 1976
9. **Faces—w.** Brian Clemens & Dennis Spooner; **dir.** James Hill; **UK tx.** 14 Dec 1976; **US tx.** 13 Oct 1978; **Filmed:** Jul 1976
10. **Gnaws—w.** Dennis Spooner; **dir.** Ray Austin; **UK tx.** 21 Dec 1976; **US tx.** 29 Dec 1978; **Filmed:** Oct 1976
11. **Dirtier by the Dozen—w.** Brian Clemens; **dir.** Sidney Hayers; **UK tx.** 5 Jan 1976; **US tx.** 22 Dec 1978; **Filmed:** Oct 1976
12. **Sleeper—w.** Brian Clemens; **dir.** Graeme Clifford; **UK tx.** 12 Jan 1977; **US tx.** 6 Oct 1978; **Filmed:** Sep 1976
13. **Three Handed Game—w.** Dennis Spooner & Brian Clemens; **dir.** Ray Austin; **UK tx.** 19 Jan 1977; **US tx.** 12 Jan 1979; **Filmed:** Aug 1976

SEASON NOTES

Truth be told, it all starts out rather well, picking up more-or-less where *The Avengers* left off, mostly back to a more grounded spy series with hints of the bizarre. Eccentrics weren't often to be found however; they'd departed for greener pastures, as the seventies were about grittiness and hardboiled reality not humorous fishes-out-of-water. But the wit and banter were there in spades, mostly exchanged between Gambit and Purdey. The music was still composed by the esteemed Laurie Johnson, who had been composing the music since the fourth season of *The Avengers*, but the classy jazz themes of the past were gone, replaced by questionable (and sometimes appalling) disco-funk.

In this fresh new season, the lion's share of episodes was written by Brian Clemens and Dennis Spooner, with the spare picked up by Terence Feeley, all of whom had now written for the show since its first year. Directors Ray Austin and Robert Fuest would return, along with John Hough, James Hill, and Sidney Hayers, who would be joined by first time *Avengers* directors Graeme Clifford and Desmond Davis. The result is a season of remarkable uniformity in tone, with ideas that are diverse and engaging. Classics include "House of Cards," "The Midas Touch," "The Tale of the Big Why," and "Sleeper." Ian Hendry would return, albeit in a completely different role with a depressingly fatalistic end—as if to carelessly smash the hopes and dreams for a return of Dr. Keel, the 'forgotten Avenger.' And other guest stars would return: Peter Cushing, Peter Jeffrey, Ronald Lacey, Kevin Stoney, Frederick Jaeger, and Ronald Leigh-Hunt. Though, like Ian Hendry's appearance, this would seldom create any sense of continuity. (For example, Frederick Jaeger is *not* in "The Last of the Cybernauts…?")

Often this new incarnation would feel quite like the original series, and just as often it would not, but this should not trouble the viewer because this first season of *The New Avengers* is highly enjoyable whether its feet are firmly placed in the past or the present.

INTRODUCING MIKE GAMBIT

Gambit was something of a mystery throughout his adventures with John Steed and Purdey. Although he was officially part of the Ministry and a full agent like Steed—albeit a more junior one—his past was never explored in any substantive depth. Nevertheless, various hints are thrown out during the twenty-six onscreen episodes. Before becoming a spy, he had been a Major in the British Army's Parachute Regiment. He was apparently a race car driver for a time, claiming that he crashed at all the big Formula One races. He was an expert at lock-picking and housebreaking and could fly a helicopter. He was also clearly something of a cinema buff. He appeared to have had a largely working-class background and education but was otherwise very knowledgeable.

Mainly, Gambit appeared to fulfill the same function that John Steed had (to a more limited extent) during his time in the original series. Gambit was very fit and had thick, dark wavy hair. He was suave, masculine, handsome and devastatingly capable in martial arts. His role largely seemed to be fighting the strongest men, charming female witnesses and providing protection to his friends. He and Purdey even managed to dispatch a Cybernaut together.

He was clearly romantically (or at least sexually) interested in Purdey for a time, though it remained to be seen how strongly he felt about this because he largely played the role of the stereotypical womanizer, clearly playing the field with any woman that was interested. It is possible that he and

Purdey could have never formalized a relationship due to their professional cooperation, and thus their involvement never went beyond flirting.

In the second season, Gambit often appeared to take even more of a lone wolf role, periodically separating from Steed and Purdey to go it alone, particularly in "Complex" and "The Gladiators." His interactions with Purdey also became less flirtatious, possibly an indication that he was beginning to respect her more as a professional and a capable spy rather than merely a potential pickup. He was last seen still trying to escape Canada in 1977.

INTRODUCING PURDEY

Purdey was a spy and a martial arts expert assigned to work with John Steed and Mike Gambit. Her official capacity within the Ministry was never fully explained but she appeared to not be within the mold of the 'talented amateur' as Cathy Gale and Emma Peel had been. Likely, she was a junior agent much like Tara King. She was tall, leggy, and blonde with a high intellect, an insouciant wit, and a playful side. She enjoyed motorbiking and redecorating her stylish seventies apartment after it had been smashed by Cybernauts and other villains.

She fought with the French kickboxing style of Savate (sometimes referred to as 'Panache' or 'La Panache'), a style which appeared to combine elements picked up from her time with the Royal Ballet. (She had been kicked out for being too tall.) She spoke fluent French when visiting France in several episodes and went convincingly undercover within a criminal organization in "Faces," adopting a credible accent and demonstrating convincing acting skills, though she seldom otherwise exhibited traditional spy skills at subterfuge and espionage. She also had the ability to read in Russian and Arabic.

She appeared to be a fully liberated woman of the seventies with the intelligence and wit to easily banter with her male colleagues. Occasionally, she seemed to find Mike Gambit attractive but showed no special interest in starting a romance with him, and their relationship remained primarily professional; aside from their regular work, it was based on a series of witty teasing exchanges. She was also never seen to have a current romantic involvement with any other man, though flashbacks in "Obsession" revealed a former relationship that caused her intense emotional pain.

Purdey only went by the one name, and it was generally presumed that this was her surname.

ICONIC TITLES

There are two title sequences used in the first season of *The New Avengers*. The first version begins with a circular aperture in which the three lead actors briefly pose in costume. This is followed by a shot of John Steed tipping his bowler hat to the audience. The remainder of the title sequence is composed of a series of clips from the first few episodes, most of them from "The Midas Touch." This sequence was used for "The Eagle's Nest," "House of Cards," "The Last of the Cybernauts...?," "The Midas Touch," "Cat Amongst the Pigeons," "Target!," and "To Catch a Rat." The theme song by Laurie Johnson starts with a brief fanfare that recalls his theme for seasons four through seven of *The Avengers* and then departs into a much more funk and disco-oriented sound with a marching drumbeat.

The second version of the title sequence is partially animated and partially live action. It begins with a brand-new and stylized logo based on a lion rampant in the red, blue, and white colors of the Union Flag. The lion morphs into the shape of John Steed silhouetted in red and then back into the shape of the lion, and a brief live-action clip of Patrick Macnee in action is shown through the 'window' of the lion using optical printing. Macnee's credit is superimposed over the top. This process is repeated for Gareth Hunt and Joanna Lumley individually with Hunt's figure being blue and Lumley's white. At the end of the sequence, the three iconic figures merge back into the red, blue, and white lion logo over the credit for producers Albert Fennell and Brian Clemens. This version of the title sequence was used for the remainder of the series. The music is the same as the first version.

CHAMPAGNE, CARS, CLOTHES, AND CANINES

Joanna Lumley's fashions were initially designed by Catherine Buckley, though these designs were soon found to be rather impractical for an action series. Buckley, a real artisan, made elaborate clothes sometimes using vintage material. Such materials had little endurance and Buckley often advised against washing or dry cleaning. This makes it hard to imagine how such clothing could be worn anywhere, whether in real life or on a television series.

Meanwhile, Gareth Hunt initial desire to wear plain clothes such as jeans and bomber jackets was rejected and he was dressed much like Steed in three-piece suits with high-end shirts and ties, although the jeans and bomber jacket did show up a few times. At Macnee's insistence, Steed remained his stylish self, of course, though Macnee's clothes were now provided by Saville Row clothiers Gieves and Hawkes. Steed and Gambit's outfits would tend to be consistent and operate mostly on a rotation, whereas Purdey would typically debut several outfits in a single episode, much as had been the case in the original series with Mrs. Gale, Mrs. Peel, and Tara King.

Steed's cars would change completely, however. With one exception, the vintage cars were gone, and he was now driving modern Jaguars, Range Rovers, and the very modern but rather inauspicious-looking bright-yellow Rover 3500 (also known as an SD1, manufactured from 1976 to 1981). Nevertheless, this car had more power underneath the hood than one might expect, as it had a V8 engine with 155 hp and a top speed of 123 mph.

There are no Avengers dogs this season, and the champagne budget was down due to inflation, but a few cameras might show up.

Best Dressed: "House of Cards"
Worst Dressed: "Sleeper"

AVENGERS CARS

JOHN STEED

Rover 3500 aka SD1 (MOC 229P)—yellow—in "The Eagle's Nest" and "The Midas Touch."
Jaguar XJ12C (NWK 60P)—racing green[1]—in "House of Cards," "The Last of the Cybernauts…??," "To Catch a Rat," "Sleeper," and "Three Handed Game."
Range Rover (TXC 922J)—dark-green—in "Cat Amongst the Pigeons," "Target!," and "The Tale of the Big Why."

PURDEY

MGB (MOC 232P)—pale yellow-brown—in "House of Cards," "The Last of the Cybernauts …??,"

---

1 Honestly, the color seems to change from episode to episode, sometimes appearing dark-green, sometimes gray-green, sometimes racing green. The colors on the DVDs are very inconsistent. Unfortunately, given that the only sources for these episodes are DVDs which are sourced from 1990s-era telecines, the colors are frequently skewed badly in one direction or the other depending on which DVD set you own, either too warm or too cool, or just plain wrong. Thus, it is often very difficult to determine the colors of individual clothing pieces or cars.

"The Midas Touch," "Target!," "Faces," "Dirtier by the Dozen," "Sleeper," and "Three Handed Game."
Yamaha DT250 enduro motorcycle (LLC 950P)—yellow—in "Cat Amongst the Pigeons."
Honda 125 motorcycle (OLR 471P)—dark-red and black—in "The Tale of the Big Why."

MIKE GAMBIT

Jaguar XJS (NRW 875P)—orange-red—in "The Eagle's Nest," "The Midas Touch," "The Last of the Cybernauts…??," "Cat Amongst the Pigeons," "Target!", and "Three Handed Game."
Range Rover (LOK 537P)—white—in "Cat Amongst the Pigeons," "To Catch a Rat," and "The Tale of the Big Why."

THE MOST FANTASTIC EPISODES OF THE SEASON

1. "The Tale of the Big Why"
2. "Sleeper"
3. "House of Cards"
4. "The Midas Touch"
5. "Target!"

1 (1.1.1) THE EAGLE'S NEST

Written by Brian Clemens
Directed by Desmond Davis

GUEST CAST

Peter Cushing (Von Claus), Derek Farr (Father Trasker), Frank Gatliff (Karl), Sydney Bromley (Hara), Trevor Baxter (Brown-Fitcth), Joyce Carey (Lady with Dog), Neil Phillips (Main), Brian Anthony (Stannard), Ronald Forfar (Jud), Jerold Wells (Barker), Trudi Van Doorne (Gerda), Peter Porteous (Nazi Corporal), Charles Bolton (Ralph)

PRE-TITLE

Agent George Stannard flees across a high coastal cliff pursued by two men who cast fishing lures at him shredding his jacket. Nevertheless, he manages to reach a nearby castle monastery, interrupting the monks during their service and asking for sanctuary. The monks do nothing to help and allow his pursuers to capture and imprison him in one of the castle's cells. There, he is interrogated by a man dressed in a white monk's cowl. However, in the midst of this interview, he manages to escape and flees once again to the cliff where, faced again with his captors, he takes a daring leap from the edge.

SYNOPSIS

Investigating the death of fellow agent Stannard and the kidnapping of the world's foremost authority on suspended animation, Steed, Gambit, and Purdey travel to the small island of St. Dorca where they find the remnants of the Third Reich ready to rise again...

REVIEW

This episode sets the tone for the series. Gambit and Purdey begin their witty by-play, and Steed establishes himself as the brains of the operation with the younger agents doing most of the legwork. On the whole, it works well, even if the overall style isn't very reminiscent of the original series. While Mike Gambit sticks to the tried-and-true judo, more tone-setting is done by introducing Purdey's kick-style of martial arts, which she implies is adapted from her time with the Royal Ballet, though it's actually the French martial art form of Savate.

The story is fairly generic, playing off an old conspiracy trope that Adolf Hitler survived World War II and was living somewhere in the world waiting for his followers to resurrect him.[2] Just one day before this episode aired, the novel for ***The Boys from Brazil*** came out, which presents a variation on this trope. The theme mirrors an earlier (and missing) ***Avengers*** episode called "Dead of Winter," which featured neo-Nazis freezing their own men as part of a plot to take over the world. So, it's fascinating to think that ***The Avengers*** was doing this type of storyline ahead of everyone else.

Peter Cushing is his usual superb self, and for a twist, they make him the honest and ethical doctor instead of the villain. Brian Clemens makes a nice stab at the almost obligatory ***Avengers*** eccentric in the form of Hara, who has the shortest short-term memory in the world and looks like ***Monty Python***'s "It's" man. However, the use of fishing poles by the villains is *perhaps* a miscalculated attempt at the surrealism of the original series.[3] I can never quite decide if I like it or not. It's definitely original.

---

2 Savvy viewers will receive a hint about the goings-on at the monastery in the opening pre-title, the "holiest day" in their calendar—April 20, the birthday of Adolph Hitler.

3 There is a plausible explanation, however: the island has been isolated for so long that ammo is very low.

Perhaps the most notable change in *The New Avengers* is that it really dates itself in a way that the original series never did. I think the reason for this is that *The Avengers* was so ahead of its time in production quality. Few shows looked as professional and expensive as it did in its hey-day, whether a British show or an American one. The concept was fresh too. On the other hand, *The New Avengers* looks exactly like a mid-seventies television show, on either side of the Atlantic—very generic in that sense. The production's only other disturbing flaw is the horrendously dated music, a sign of things to come. Sleazy saxophones, pounding bass, a funky guitar, some of this works well enough, but the theme introducing Steed at the beginning is the worst of all, sounding like 1970s shopping music.

Nevertheless, a very solid and enjoyable introduction to the show and the characters.

CHAMPAGNE, CARS, CLOTHES, AND CANINES

Steed begins the episode wearing a navy-blue single-breasted three-piece woolen suit with a matching bowler and brolly. The shirt is sky-blue and the tie is a metallic copper color. (This suit would become a major outfit, appearing in eleven episodes.) Gambit is first seen wearing a pale-gold shirt with French cuffs, worn with a dark-brown waistcoat and a brown tie with a gold concentric circle pattern; when he throws Purdey out of bed, he has added the jacket for this outfit, also dark-brown; his boots are black. Purdey is first seen wearing white satin sheets with a blue floral pattern. When she gets dressed, she is wearing a raw silk double-breasted embroidered jacket and matching trousers (designed by Catherine Buckley). This is a strong start. It remains to be seen how well this ensemble will hold up under action hijinks. She later adds a luxurious white fur coat while Steed dons a fawn-colored overcoat with an orange-brown collar. When playing the violin, Steed wears a pale-gray single-breasted three-piece suit with a white shirt and a brass-colored tie. (This too would be a major outfit, appearing in twelve episodes.)

Purdey is next seen wearing a black-and-blue wetsuit over her next outfit: a metallic-green silk blouse and matching floral skirt over a green body stocking with a plunging neckline, a matching silk neckscarf, and red high-heeled boots. The ensemble was again designed by Catherine Buckley, and it's easy to see the impracticality of it, given that there was no way it was fitting under that wetsuit. While very beautiful, the blouse is a loose, flowing thing with multi-colored threads, and it's easy to imagine it getting caught on anything and everything and torn to pieces. Fortunately, she dispenses with the blouse, opting for just the tights when engaging in melee. Later, she wears a German Army gray, red, and black greatcoat over the tights. Steed gets a third suit: a gray checked woolen single-breasted three-piece with a cream shirt and red-and-blue paisley tie. (The checks are a sort of micro-houndstooth pattern.) His matching bowler has a radio in it. Gambit also gets a change, a checked pale-brown single-breasted three-piece suit with a pale-brown shirt with French cuffs and a muted-brown tie. This would be his action suit, and the trousers are flared, the back of the waistcoat is gold, and the jacket has a ticket pocket. He also wears a black wetsuit over a cream rollneck jumper. Steed ends up in a brown monk's habit, but doesn't know to wear a Nazi uniform underneath it instead of his gray checked suit. And that's quite enough fashion debuts for one episode.

Right away, Steed drives his newest vehicle, a yellow 1976 Rover 3500/SD1. It's hard to imagine picking a car that is less suited to his established character. He's also bad at parking—his left rear tire is parked on the curb. Gambit drives his orange-red Jaguar XJS, but as it's blocked in, he also briefly steals and drives a white 1971 Citroën DS 21 in pursuit of Von Claus, which he subsequently crashes.

At least the series starts out with one canine, though it's not Steed's, but "Posey-poof," a dark-gray poodle owned by George Stannard's elderly neighbor. Steed stumbles right into the poor dog, perhaps having flashbacks to his bygone days of dog ownership in the process.

QUOTES

"It's called 'Sins of Youth.'" "That's not a color, that's an accusation."
"You are to be executed immediately." "Well, thank goodness, you broke it to me gently."
"I abhor violence, and loud gunshots make me blink."
"Where'd you learn that, the Royal Marines?" "The Royal Ballet. They threw me out."
"I want Purdey." "Who doesn't?"

2 (1.3.2) HOUSE OF CARDS

Written by Brian Clemens
Directed by Desmond Davis

GUEST CAST

Peter Jeffrey (Perov), Frank Thornton (Roland), Lyndon Brook (Cartney), Derek Francis (The Bishop), Mark Burns (Spence), Geraldine Moffatt (Jo), Annette André (Suzy), Ina Skriver (Olga), Murray Brown (David), Gordon Sterne (Vasil), Dan Meaden (Boris), Jeremy Wilkin (Tulliver), Anthony Bailey (Frederick)

PRE-TITLE

Steed and Purdey greet an apparent rock star at the airport, and their contingent includes buxom, young ladies dressed in sky-blue shorts and white t-shirts with 'Mike' printed on them. The young ladies swarm the young star, who is actually Mike Gambit in disguise, of course, and chase him all over the concourse, but this is all a distraction to facilitate the defection of a scientist from behind the iron curtain.

SYNOPSIS

Professor Vasil is defecting, and Steed, Purdey, and Gambit are charged with protecting him. After rescuing Vasil from a forced repatriation by Soviet agents, they come across a vast network of spies and pre-programmed assassins—"Sleepers"—triggered by hypnotic suggestion through ordinary playing cards. This 'House of Cards' network is run by Ivan Perov, who at first appears to commit suicide from the shame of his failure in the Vasil affair. However, this turns out to be a ruse in order to continue his operations in secret…

REVIEW

This episode starts out with a spectacular opening sequence—the kind that likely would never have been possible in the original series—and proceeds as a relatively straightforward spy story. In order to add a twist, the script folds in some elements of ***The Manchurian Candidate***, a film that would not have been commercially available at the time, which likely means that the screenwriters were working off their memories or from the original novel. The difference is that only the top half of the cards—with the name of the target written on the back—are distributed in order to activate their assassins.

One of the best scenes is a humorous vignette in which Steed describes his prior horses to Joanna, who mistakenly believes he is talking about the photos of his previous partners-in-action—Cathy Gale, Emma Peel, and Tara King. It's a cute scene, and a welcome nod to the past, with the lines perfectly tailored to add to the confusion. However, one scene that seems difficult to swallow is Steed's confrontation with Joanna as her plot to assassinate him is revealed by Purdey. Even considering his romantic interest in Jo, he hesitates a little too much to be believable for such an experienced agent. Does he really think Purdey would come in with a gun if she wasn't sure of her facts?

The final twist to the story is clever and provides ample opportunities for more excellent Purdey-Gambit banter. This is one of the better stories in the series.

CHAMPAGNE, CARS, CLOTHES, AND CANINES

The episode opens with Steed again wearing his navy suit, with a pale-blue shirt and a navy tie with white spots (again the poor quality of the early standard-definition telecines of these episodes makes color identification difficult, and the suit often reads as black or possibly slate, but since Macnee tends to wear blue suits with blue shirts and ties, navy-blue is what I'm going with. This is consistent with prior outfits in the original series.) Purdey opens in the same outfit as the other young women, except for her the colors are reversed—her shirt is sky-blue and her shorts are white. She also wears white boots. Gambit's outfit is a pale-gold pirate shirt, pale-blue jeans with a variety of patches all over them, and a leather belt cinched around the waist above the shirt, and makeup. Steed gets to debut a new suit: a tweed checked yellow-brown jacket with a forest-green waistcoat, cream trousers, a cerulean-blue shirt, and a nut-brown tie. (A real winner, in my opinion.)

Meanwhile, Purdey debuts a gold lamé karate gi with mauve trim in her sparring session, and Gambit wears a new navy-blue chalked-striped single-breasted three-piece suit with a pale-blue shirt and a navy tie with white dots, a sort of reflection of many of Steed's earlier outfits. Purdey's next outfit is quite the stunner—a white laced long-sleeved blouse with a patchwork split midi skirt in red, blue, pink, green, and purple patches, with a matching long neckscarf. This was the Catherine Buckley outfit that was infamously labeled with an advisement that it couldn't be washed or dry-cleaned in any way because it was made from vintage early 20th-century jacquard materials. It's quite a beautiful piece but again it's easy to see the impracticality for an action character, and it does give her a granola-ish, Stevie Nicks vibe that again didn't really match the persona of a superspy.

Not to be outdone, Steed debuts another outfit, a nut-brown single-breasted, two-piece suit with cream trousers, a blue shirt, and a brown tie with white spots; and then, a deep-green velvet tuxedo with a white shirt and an enormous velvet bowtie. Meanwhile, Purdey wears a lovely white, silver, and lilac Edwardian-style dress with sheer blousy sleeves and multiple skirt layers each cut to a different angle. The lilac is printed on the torso and the collar is high. It is paired with white boots. (This is another Catherine Buckley creation.) In rapid succession, Purdey debuts blue-and-white lingerie with a champagne-colored silk dressing gown; a royal-blue jumpsuit with a green print; and a gold satin dress with a floral print and spaghetti straps paired with cream high heels. Steed debuts a taupe riding jacket paired with a muted-gold waistcoat with brass buttons, beige twill trousers, a white shirt with French cuffs and silver cufflinks, and a navy-blue tie with white spots. And, finally, Gambit debuts a black tuxedo with silk collar, white frill-front shirt, black silk cummerbund, and a black bow tie. And that is a lot of debuts for one episode.

Purdey's pale-yellow MGB debuts as does Steed's dark-green Jaguar XJ12C. Lots of champagne at the casino. The helicopter that Perov uses is a Bell 47G-5A. Eagle-eyed viewers will also see a Piper PA-23-250 Aztec plane.

Poor Steed hopes to get champagne while having a quiet evening with Joanna but it turns out to be drugged (or does it?) and he misses out.

QUOTES

"Oh, very spirited, very special, fantastic creature!—had to take the whip to her though sometimes."
"Excellent, great action! But liked her oats too much. I sold her to an Arab prince. I think he had to eventually shoot her."
"I never did tell you about my marriage, my one and only marriage. I married a job. I married a profession. I've been very faithful."

3 (1.4.3) THE LAST OF THE CYBERNAUTS...??

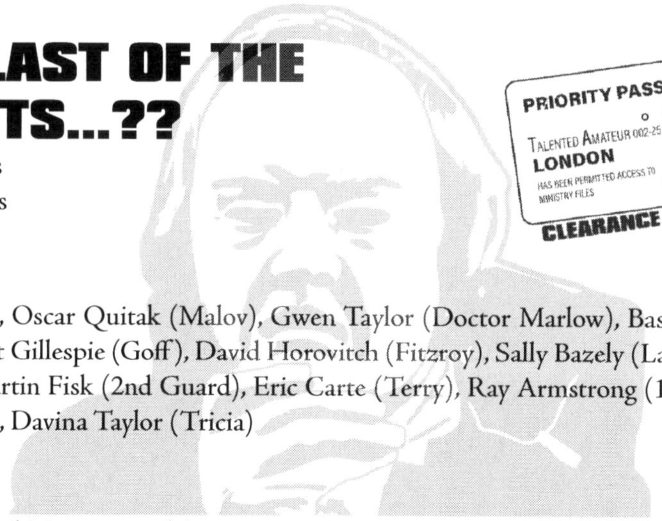

Written by Brian Clemens
Directed by Sidney Hayers

GUEST CAST

Robert Lang (Felix Kane), Oscar Quitak (Malov), Gwen Taylor (Doctor Marlow), Basil Hoskins (Professor Mason), Robert Gillespie (Goff), David Horovitch (Fitzroy), Sally Bazely (Laura), Pearl Hackney (Mrs. Weir), Martin Fisk (2nd Guard), Eric Carte (Terry), Ray Armstrong (1st Guard), Rocky Taylor (Cybernaut), Davina Taylor (Tricia)

PRE-TITLE

Steed, Gambit, Purdey, and Tricia are celebrating Steed's birthday at his home when a mortally wounded agent, Channing, limps inside and announces that he's found the double-agent, Felix Kane, and warns that Kane is meeting a contact in a carpark the next day. The following day, Steed, Gambit, and Purdey all wait in the carpark—Steed in his Jaguar and Gambit and Purdey in Gambit's Range Rover. When the contact is made, Steed and friends attempt to block the escape of both Kane and his contact, and a car chase ensues which causes Kane to crash his car into a petrol truck.

SYNOPSIS

During a car chase involving the *Avengers* and a double agent named Felix Kane, Kane's car slides out of control and into a gasoline tanker. In the resulting collision, Kane is disabled and horribly disfigured. When a former assistant of the infamous Cybernaut engineer and questionable genius Dr. Armstrong is released from prison, he is employed by Kane to revive the Cybernauts and take his revenge on the *Avengers*...

REVIEW

This one begins with the inevitable seventies car chase in the pre-title, which, frankly, manifests as an incomprehensible morass of squealing tires and zoomed in camera shots that leave the viewer with little conception as to how the all-important accident actually happens. The result, nevertheless, is the disfigurement of the antagonist of the story and the return of *The Avengers*' most iconic villain, which is incomprehensibly revealed nearly instantly by the on-screen title. Thus, this story does not bother much with subtlety, becoming merely an obvious revenge story, much like both of its predecessors.

Having said that, superficially-speaking, "The Last of the Cybernauts...?" is a weakly-satisfying creation. The latest evolution of Cybernaut technology is something that even the casual viewer could easily guess. It is, in fact, a well-known trope in modern science-fiction that someone eventually gets turned into a cybernetic being. However, this episode deserves some credit for having done it before *Doctor Who*'s Cyberman concept. Incidentally, the Cybernauts from *The Avengers* predate the first appearance of the Cybermen in *Doctor Who* as well.

The problem isn't in the concept's originality however, it's a matter of a plot that insists on the same silly revenge narrative as the two previous stories, coming across as linear, crude, and as direct as a Cybernaut on a mission. (Isn't it funny how TV villains absolutely never cool off, no matter how much time passes?) Frankly, the prior two stories were excellent superficial entertainment that managed all the same Cybernaut tropes as this one, albeit with a great deal more panache. Ultimately, it all ends when Robert Lang—in a tin-man suit and wearing an auburn fright wig, sunglasses and a boiler suit—is defeated with spray cans of "plastic skin." There is never any explanation given as to why this works, possibly because of the somewhat annoying tendency for *The New Avengers* to have absolutely no sort of epilogue at all.

On the other hand, all of the Cybernaut attacks are exciting and nostalgic (the one on the stairs possibly exceeds anything in the original series), as are the fan-pleasing references to Mrs. Peel and her prior adventures with Steed, but the best part is some highly entertaining Gambit and Purdey banter, lacing the entire episode with layers of wit.

I have a confession to make. If you're already a fan, you'll probably like this episode more than me, even though I'm quite the fan of the first two Cybernaut stories.

CHAMPAGNE, CARS, CLOTHES, AND CANINES

There are many, many clothing changes in this episode, including returns of outfits that already appeared in the prior two episodes (including prominently the pre-title in which they all first appear in the same outfits from the casino scene in "House of Cards"), so I'll confine my comments to the debuts by the regulars. Purdey wears a hot-pink shirt or blouse in the carpark; at the second birthday party a year later, she wears a pink-and-white laced bodysuit with a halter top, matching cravat, and flared pants legs; then, a chocolate-brown jacket with cream stitched trim, flared lapels, matching pants, and a white blouse with a butterfly collar so wide she could take off; then, a halter neck blouse in gold-and-brown metallic fabric with chocolate-brown culottes and calf-high boots; then, a pale-gold plastic cape and midi skirt with rose-colored patterns, a mauve long-sleeved blouse, and black boots; then, a brown rollneck jumper with a white patterned skirt, a wide black belt, and a copper necklace; then, a pink, purple, and white patterned sundress; then, a lavender leotard with a purple knit jumper; and, finally, a blue-and-green leotard with a sheer flowing skirt and matching cape tied at the neck. Phew, that girl has one hell of a wardrobe!

Steed debuts a new navy-blue (again, reads as black or gray onscreen) single-breasted, three-piece suit with a pale-blue shirt, and first with a red tie, then a navy tie with white spots. Next, he debuts a dark-gray single-breasted, three-piece suit with a pale-blue shirt and a metallic gold tie. Both suits are paired with a black bowler and brolly. Gambit debuts one outfit, a single-breasted, three-piece light-brown suit; it has a single vent, a slit breast pocket, flap pockets at the waist, and an extra ticket pocket. It's worn with a pale-brown shirt and olive-brown tie.

At one point, Steed plays with a Stylophone toy synthesizer, and one wonders if it was even Macnee's hands playing the thing given his almost notorious lack of musical ability.

In one of the few champagne moments this season, they drink the sparkly beverage at both of Steed's birthday parties. No word on the vintage or marque.

QUOTES

"Steed never worries." "It's a feature of the man." "He never, ever worries. Not unless he's worried." "Which means it's serious." "Very, very serious."

"I am wearing my face of pleasure, please, do not force me to assume this mask."

"What happened?" "I'm very disappointed. 'What happened?' That's a terribly corny thing to say, Steed."

"You must stop being so gallant, Steed. We're liberated now."

"You dented it, Mike. You actually dented it! Poor clever little fist."

"I'm not lurking." "Well, not now, but you were. Your whole attitude is one of pure and positive *lurk*!"

4 (1.2.4) THE MIDAS TOUCH

Written by Brian Clemens
Directed by Robert Fuest

GUEST CAST

John Carson (Freddy), Ed Devereaux (Vann), Ronald Lacey (Hong Kong Harry), David Swift (Turner), Jeremy Child (Lieutenant), Robert Mill (Curator), Ray Edwards (Garvin), Gilles Millinaire (Midas), Pik-Sen Lim (Sing), Chris Tranchell (Doctor), Lionel Guyett (Tayman), Geoffrey Bateman (Simpson), Tim Condren (Boz), Peter Winter (Morgan), Bruce Bould (Froggart), Bruno Elrington (Choy)

PRE-TITLE

In an arctic location, a man signals to base on a telegraph in Morse code. Another man slips inside and smashes the telegraph before the message can be completed. Elsewhere, in England at night, Steed returns from a dinner at The Cock Pit restaurant with a classy female companion and runs into his friend and former agent, Freddy, who is clearly down on his luck since leaving the Ministry. They have an awkward exchange in which Steed offers him money but is turned down. The next morning, Freddy awakens in an abandoned industrial complex and witnesses an invasion of military vehicles. Led by an elegantly-dressed man, they charge into the complex and smash through a door as Freddy watches in fear.

SYNOPSIS

A former agent who resigned in disgrace clues Steed into a project called Midas that is bringing foreign arms dealers into England. The gold-obsessed Professor Turner has infected a man code-named Midas with dozens of deadly diseases, while preserving his immunity, in order to use him as a kind of guided missile of pestilence. After test-running Midas at a party, he is sent to assassinate a foreign monarch by merely kissing her hand…

REVIEW

This episode starts with something we never saw before in the original series, a disgraced agent, who, looking quite a bit like a hobo, turns up to 'embarrass' Steed on a date, simply by showing his face. Steed is much more gracious than a stereotypical member of the aristocracy might have been. No kicking to the curb, so to speak, for which I'm extremely grateful. Before this, we are shown an arctic base, a radio smashed by a rifle butt, and afterwards, we see the villain ordering a door to be kicked in for the purpose of re-capturing a massive white rat. And thus, the pre-title concludes, an odd mélange that exposes the basis of the story without us truly realizing it at the time.

On first examination, "The Midas Touch" might not seem like a very original story. Some forty-one years after its airing, we have seen an extraordinary number of television episodes and films that depict the use of weaponized bacteria or viruses, often in a post-apocalyptic setting. Already, there had been ***Survivors***, and since this episode aired, there have been ***The Stand***, ***28 Days Later*** and ***Twelve Monkeys***, among many others. Despite this, "Midas" stands out as unique in its method of using plague as a weapon. In every other example I can think of, the plague is simply unleashed, and in an uncontrolled manner results in that post-apocalyptic world. Here, the villains are much cleverer, creating a weaponized plague that is contained within a single individual, a human guided missile to be launched at a given target. Thus, this story has more to do with "Return of the Cybernauts" or "The Positive Negative Man" than it does any other futurist plague film.

Aside from a fairly original take on biological warfare, this episode is known for its striking and strange images, an unusual take on the cliched car chase scene, and Joanna Lumley's intriguing wardrobe malfunction (and a striking reveal of underwear). Few scenes in either *The Avengers* or *The New Avengers* have the visual punch of Midas spiking the punch bowl at a raucous hedonistic costume party, one that takes place under psychedelic red and blue lighting with music that sounds suspiciously like instrumental Atomic Rooster. This moment is the episode's directorial tour de force.[4]

The car chase includes all the 1970s clichés—squealing tires, swerving unnecessarily amidst bridge support columns, cutting corners when turning, driving on the sidewalks and in back alleys, and the obligatory box of fruit being dropped on the hood by an irritated fruit seller who shakes his fist in the air at the fleeing vehicles—but they are all intercut with Gambit and Purdey having a casual debate about who directed *The Treasure of the Sierra Madre*. This scene concludes with another obligatory seventies action show cliché—the foot chase through an abandoned industrial complex, with the actors running side-by-side full-speed towards the camera. Thankfully, this scene morphs into a tense and atmospheric sniper shoot-out with our heroes in serious danger. It ends with Purdey all-too effectively finishing off the sniper.

The plot however is almost as disjointed as the pre-title scene, seemingly juxtaposing diverse elements that really didn't require this much work to fuse together. The story's visual strength, bizarrely incongruent elements, and humor—deftly directed with flourish by Robert Fuest as usual—make up for this however, giving the episode's seventies action show clichés enough twists to become exceptional rather than ordinary.

My only minor complaint is perhaps Ronald Lacey's return as yet another Peter Lorre take-off, this time poorly made-up as an Asian character called Hong Kong Harry. His breathless wheezes are unwelcomed in every scene. By the way, beriberi is not an infectious disease.

CHAMPAGNE, CARS, CLOTHES, AND CANINES

Purdey debuts a cream patterned blouse and matching mini-shorts (or hot pants) with a sheer, laced split dress. When running, the dress flows to her sides and exposes the shorts.[5] This is followed by a pale-yellow crocheted jumper with a mid-length split skirt and a white-and-yellow crocheted coat and matching boots and hat. The crocheting is very fuzzy, almost like she's a soft, lumpy cactus. Last is a reimagined designer army jacket in a camouflage pattern with matching trousers, an army-green t-shirt, and black boots. Steed wears his dark-green velvet jacket in the pre-title, his navy-blue suit (from "The Last of the Cybernauts…??") with a blue floral tie, and his gray checked suit (from "The Eagle's Nest"). Gambit wears his chalk-striped navy-blue suit (from "House of Cards") and his brown suit from ("The Eagle's Nest"). Purdey also wears her high-collared dress (from "House of Cards") with silver-and-blue heels.

Steed's Rover, Gambit's Jaguar, and Purdey's MGB all appear.

QUOTES

"Difficult decision—him or you."

"He sort of fell for me—""—In the worst possible way."

"Steed, you're becoming a roué."

"Our tests are only preliminary, you understand, but so far, it appears these people died of typhus, typhoid, malaria, pneumonia, smallpox, black water fever, and beriberi. Yes, Mr. Gambit, they died of everything."

"You should take up motor racing.""I did—Le Mans, Spa, Monza, Daytona—I crashed at them all."

---

4 I'm pleasantly reminded of the Andy Warhol-style party scene with the sibling artists Hansel and Gretel in *Midnight Cowboy*, in which Elephant's Memory music forms the soundtrack.

5 It's a very iconic outfit for Purdey as it appears in many clips of her climbing over a fence (including the title sequence and in other places) and providing a generous view of (shall we say?) her undercarriage—though I hasten to add that this is PG-rated.

5 (1.6.5) CAT AMONGST THE PIGEONS

Written by Dennis Spooner
Directed by John Hough

GUEST CAST

Vladek Sheybal (Zarcardi), Matthew Long (Turner), Basil Dignam (Rydercroft), Peter Copley (Waterlow), Hugh Walters (Lewington), Gordon Rollings (Bridlington), Joe Black (Hudson), Patrick Connor (Foster), Kevin Stoney (Tomkins), Andrew Bradford (Merton), Brian Jackson (Controller)

PRE-TITLE

In a suburban home, a man is the caretaker for thousands of caged birds. Leaving briefly to empty waste, he hears an eerie whistling and when he returns all the birds have vanished from their cages. Steed's fellow agent, Merton, is parked along a country road and hears the same eerie whistling. He contacts Steed via radio phone and tells him that Rydercroft is going to be killed at twelve-noon, but before he can elaborate he is attacked by something that drives him off the edge of a cliff.

SYNOPSIS

Ecologists, ornithologists and other experts are dropping dead with mysterious scratches upon their bodies. After one such man is killed in a plane crash with no explanation, Steed, Purdey, and Gambit discover that there is a strange noise associated with these attacks—an eerie flute-like sound—and, after several links, they trace the sound to Zarcardi, an expert trainer of birds, who may have developed a new way of controlling them...

REVIEW

This episode seems suspiciously familiar—perhaps because we've seen it before, with cats instead of birds in "The Hidden Tiger." One could argue that it has all the required elements: a bizarre central premise, several eccentrics, atmosphere, wit and humor and an odd former stage performer as the villain. Frankly, it instead manages considerably more creeps and thrills than did "The Hidden Tiger," perhaps by relying rather obviously on its similarity to Hitchcock's classic horror film *The Birds*. Indeed, on that latter comparison, Laurie Johnson chose to include minimalistic music, quite likely in order to allow the natural eerie silence and whistling flute from Zarcardi to dominate the soundtrack, just as Hitchcock did in his version. Despite the eeriness, the humor is still there but is blunted by comparison to the classic series.

This itself is not a problem. In fact, it creates a unique blend of characteristics that makes the episode more appealing than it might have been otherwise. Unfortunately, while the episode enjoys all the benefits of its Hitchcock model, the creeps and thrills, it suffers all the disadvantages of its *Avengers* predecessor, lack of believability in an even more serious context. While "The Hidden Tiger" benefitted from that season's sense of unreality and fantasy, "Cat Amongst the Pigeons" seems more divided, as if the half-believable premise is at odds with its atmosphere and seriousness. It's hard to understand how birds can be controlled with a flute, regardless of training, let alone able to cause hawks to steal paperwork from an administrative inbox (one that is cheekily decked out with a Union Flag). It's even more difficult to understand why ornithologists would be so terrified of birds that an attack causes them to die of shock. Equally confusing is Zarcardi's death, which is presented with absolutely no epilogue or explanation. Thus, his psychotic behavior and motive are never fully explored.

That said, this is a superficially enjoyable story. The guest cast is relatively impressive credentials-wise (although Kevin Stoney has only a tiny role), and the direction is good as well. Purdey, who spends the episode whizzing around on a dirt bike with her name on her helmet, has some nice dialogue with the eccentric and acrophobic Lewington. My main issue is that the finale is rather abrupt, a strange trait of *The New Avengers*, especially considering that *The Avengers* was so well known for its tag scenes.

CHAMPAGNE, CARS, CLOTHES, AND CANINES

The fashion debuts slow down as the season progresses, but, in his first scene, Gambit debuts a very nice light-brown double-breasted suit with very wide lapels, a white shirt, and dark-brown tie. At the same time, Purdey debuts a sleeveless, knee-length black-and-white dress with a V-neck and a matching faux neckscarf that forms out of the placket with matching white trim; followed later by a pale-pink T-shirt with jeans, eventually paired with a white motorcycle helmet bearing her name on the front; and, finally, an off-the-shoulder, backless, green, black, and white floral print dress in satin by designer Lee Bender. Steed wears his first navy-blue suit, his pale-gray suit, and his brown riding jacket, while Gambit also wears the checked brown suit.

Steed's racing green Range Rover makes its debut in this episode, where he is unfortunately attacked by a bird of prey while driving. Gambit's Jaguar returns. And Purdey's motorcycle is a yellow Yamaha DT250 enduro, which makes its first and last appearance in the series. She even rides it in her green floral dress! Rydercroft's plane is a Piper PA-28-140 Cherokee (G-ATUC). The crash site is very well-staged and they remembered to get the registration right.

No dogs, just lots of birds, and later, a sizeable glaring of cats. And the chief predator bird used by Zacardi appears to be a Eurasian Sparrowhawk.

QUOTES

"Purdey, hold the fort, man the battlements, lower the drawbridge." "And feed the dogs."
"Are you seeking sanctuary?"
"Pussies?" "Galore!"

6 (1.7.6) TARGET!

Written by Brian Clemens
Directed by Robert Fuest

GUEST CAST

Keith Barron (Draker), Robert Beatty (Ilenko), Roy Boyd (Bradshaw), Frederick Jaeger (Jones), Malcolm Stoddard (Myers), Deep Roy (Klokoe), John Paul (Kendrick), Bruce Purchase (Lopez), Dennis Blanch (Talmadge), Robert Tayman (Palmer)

PRE-TITLE

On a spy test range, one agent takes the course and quickly gets 'shot' (with a red paint spot), thus failing the test. After being checked by the doctor, he begins to leave but becomes dizzy and passes out. Another agent experiences the same thing, followed by a third, whom the doctor has just declared "will live to be ninety."

SYNOPSIS

Agents are dropping like flies as soon as they go on leave, apparently of natural causes. Steed and company find that all of the dead agents went through the same training course and medical examination, just prior to leaving. Following a lead on a deadly fast-acting poison that leaves no trace, Steed realizes that the test range is hitting them with the poison via paintball dye. And Purdey is set to complete the course next...

REVIEW

This is a reasonably satisfying but predictable hour of television. The test range village is a nice spy idea that's used to good effect throughout the episode, although it does limit the scope—so many scenes take place there. Some of it is a bit silly and cheeky—the target range is full of fake graffiti with phrases like "Kilroy was here—and got wasted." It's also terribly predictable that both Purdey and Gambit end up taking the course.

The most baffling part for me, however, is the fact that no one makes the connection between the course and all the deaths. Seriously, every single man that dies went through the course mere hours earlier, and nobody sees it. Gambit has every single piece of the puzzle laid out before him—he even accidentally kills Bradshaw in a 'joke' on the test range—and he still doesn't get it.[6] I guess he really is the brawn not the brains of this operation! Brian Clemens also made the doctor (played by John Paul) small in the hat size. He's so incompetent that he actually believes that all these relatively young, fit men are dying one after the other because they've all been working too hard. Such is the contrivance necessary to keep a secret from the cast that is easily seen by the audience.

Fortunately, there's still a tense moment when Gambit has to make it through successfully in order to save both Purdey and Steed. This scene is so good as to make the rest of the episode seem like a mere warmup. Robert Fuest directs this story with flourish, which he mostly reserves for the test range scenes, in which he has the gall to blow up a police box with a bomb in a baby pram. Clearly, not a *Doctor Who* fan![7] There's nothing really wrong with "Target!" that couldn't have been overcome with a little more intelligence delivered to its protagonists—or perhaps the script. It's brainless fun that could have been a little smarter but still manages to be effective.

CHAMPAGNE, CARS, CLOTHES, AND CANINES

Purdey's first debut ensemble of the episode is a multi-colored horizontally-striped rollneck jumper with a crimson cardigan with matching trim, worn with blue jeans and brown boots. Next, she wears a bright-green dress with white shoulder trim and cuffs, matching green pumps, and a white tasseled scarf. This is followed by a pink buttoned blouse with short sleeves and the word "SPORT" printed across the back in white, with a multi-colored pleated skirt and a wide white belt with a multi-colored tassel hanging from it and flowing with the skirt. After being drugged from running the testing course, she falls asleep in her flat wearing a white silk camisole with sheer white stockings (and it is this outfit she has to wear in her car ride to the testing range for the antidote). Gambit wears his chocolate-brown suit (from "House of Cards") with a white shirt and brown tie with cream diamond pattern, followed by his brown suit (from "The Last of the Cybernauts...??") with a green cravat. Steed wears several outfits over the course of the episode, including his pale-gray suit (his mannequin also wears a duplicate)[8] with a white shirt and a gold metallic tie, his checked gray suit, his navy-blue suit, and his tweed jacket.

---

6 I'm perplexed as to why Bradshaw's terrified reaction to the thought of the testing course being turned on him doesn't immediately trigger any suspicion from Gambit. After all, why should Bradshaw be afraid of paintball guns?

7 If you look very closely, you can see the St. John Ambulance badge on the police box, just as it's seen in the William Hartnell, Matt Smith, and Peter Capaldi eras of the show.

8 I cannot find a reference to it anywhere, but I could swear that the mannequin version of Steed in the final act (the one holding the bowler hat with the antidote) is the real Patrick Macnee made up to look like a mannequin. In one brief shot, he looks like he's moving slightly.

Steed's Range Rover appears along with Purdey's MGB and Gambit's Jaguar—the latter only very briefly at the test range as Purdey is leaving.

QUOTES

"I got ninety-nine percent." "Yes, but it's the one percent that kills you."
"Some party!" "Yes, lucky for you, we brought a bottle."

7 (1.5.7) TO CATCH A RAT

Written by Terence Feely
Directed by James Hill

GUEST CAST

Ian Hendry (Gunner), Edward Judd (Cromwell), Robert Flemyng (Quaintance), Barry Jackson (Cledge), Anthony Sharp (Grant), Jeremy Hawk (Finder), Bernice Stegers (Operator), Jo Kendall (Nurse), Dallas Cavell (Farmer), Sally-Jane Spencer (Mother)

PRE-TITLE

Early in the morning, a man drives a Volkswagen Beetle through a forest listening to the American Forces Network on the radio, which proclaims the date as July 19th 1960. He passes through a border checkpoint into East Germany, parks the car, and enters an abandoned building with his face still hidden in shadows. There, another man hidden inside reveals himself, holding a gun on the first man and calling him a "white rat" and a traitor. After threatening to take him back to London, they exchange gunfire, and the first man is shot but manages to escape in his car. Elsewhere, at Der Leipziger Zirkus, trapeze artists practice their act and ask about "white rat," but when they begin their trapeze act they miss connecting with one another, and one falls to the floor without a net.

SYNOPSIS

After being betrayed fifteen years ago, agent Gunner lost his memory, living out a quiet life in the intervening years as an eccentric amnesiac. Now, he's starting to remember and still thinks he's on the mission he started in 1960, but the same double-agent that betrayed him is also active and is eager to shut Gunner down before he remembers too much. And does the Ministry have yet another traitor in its midst…?

REVIEW

This episode will probably always be remembered as the one when Ian Hendry (the first *Avenger*) returned to the show, but there's actually not much more to recommend here than that. This is actually a rather smart spy story, straight-forward and well-executed, albeit without much in the way of wit (despite some decent Gambit and Purdey banter in a church). The problem is that it oddly seems to run out of steam about two-thirds of the way in and falls into a trap of cliched spy drama tropes. The real traitor is *way* too obvious, and Purdey is way too naïve about this to be believed. Every frame of the finale is also extraordinarily predictable.

On the other hand, Ian Hendry is excellent in this story, playing a much more emotionally complex character than in his original role as Dr. Keel, a tortured type who struggles against his memory loss and dysfunction constantly as he single-mindedly strives to complete his mission. Despite this, he is playing a character whose destiny is screamingly obvious to the viewer from the outset. The fact that he is doomed to die is one cliché that I wish writer Terence Feely had bent over backwards to avoid.

This is not a terrible episode but one that appears to fritter away so much potential derived from a return of *The Avengers'* first star. One has to ask why it couldn't have simply been a story about Dr. David Keel actually coming back to work with Steed again. That might also seem obvious and a bit fanfic, but in retrospect it seems like a good way to juice up a story that has little flair otherwise.

CHAMPAGNE, CARS, CLOTHES, AND CANINES

Gambit debuts a very nice suede long coat with brown buttons; he wears a white rollneck jumper and brown trousers underneath. He also wears his chocolate-brown suit with a pinstriped white shirt and brown tie with cream diamond pattern, and later, his checked brown suit. Purdey debuts a black bomber jacket with a white fleece lining, plus jeans, a pale-blue rollneck jumper, black boots, and a blue-and-white striped scarf; then, an orange, red, green, and black wrap dress with a Japanese-style print evocative of gingko leaves and bearing white cherry blossoms (another Catherine Buckley original, and one of her classiest); unfortunately, this is followed by a fashion misstep—a purple velvet smoking jacket and trousers with a white shirt with wide lavender stripes and a wide white tie. The suit also has pinstriping that may be areas where the fabric pile is shortened to form ridges (it's hard to tell with a standard definition image). It's too much, and it doesn't help that everything is a bit oversized and ill-fitted; the tie and the collar are way too big. Then again, it was the 1970s. She also wears her striped jumper and crimson cardigan from "Target!" Steed wears his dark-navy suit with a white shirt and navy tie with white spots; then, the pale-gray suit with a pale-blue shirt and a metallic-green tie (though the tie does seem to switch a couple of times), and he also debuts a dark-green waistcoat over a light-blue shirt and tan riding trousers, as he gives a fine filly a brushing down… with Helga who doesn't speak a word of English.

Gambit's Ranger Rover and Steed's Jaguar both return. Cromwell apparently drives a red 1975 Triumph Stag Mark 2.

QUOTES

"Take your hands off me, you brute! You can't make me do it! I'll never marry you, never! I hate you!"
"Quick thinking, eh? I got us out of a tricky situation without any embarrassment."
"Rats can hide, but not from me. We both know that, don't we? I've put my mark on you. I'm going to cut off your tail, destroy you."
"I know it's seventeen years late, but welcome back."
"You're dying to know, aren't you? How I knew about the scar on Cromwell's leg? You're just bursting with curiosity, aren't you?"

8 (1.9.8) THE TALE OF THE BIG WHY

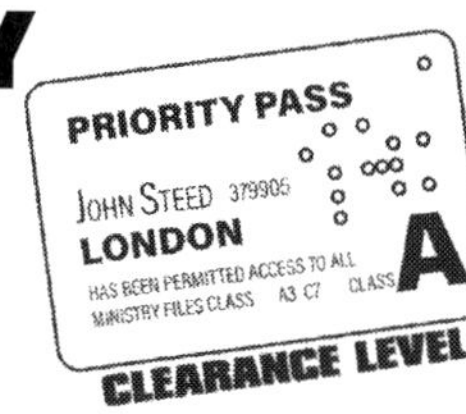

Written by Brian Clemens
Directed by Robert Fuest

GUEST CAST

Derek Waring (Harmer), Jenny Runacre (Irene), George Cooper (Brandon), Roy Marsden (Turner), Gary Waldhorn (Roach), Rowland Davis (Poole), Geoffrey Toone (Minister), Maeve Alexander (Mrs. Turner)

PRE-TITLE

Two men, Poole and Roach, argue in an abandoned building. Roach begins threatening Poole with a knife until he finally agrees to work with Roach again. They're going to kidnap Bert Brandon when he's released from prison. Elsewhere, Bert Brandon is in his prison cell with Mike Gambit (apparently in disguise as a fellow prisoner). Back at the Ministry, Steed and another Ministry official discuss what to do, anticipating Bert's departure from prison. Meanwhile, Purdey waits outside the prison on her motorcycle and surveils the scene. Poole and Roach wait until they see Brandon, who leaves in his car. Poole and Roach attempt to follow in their car, but a blue prison van deliberately blocks them from exiting. Revving her motorcycle, Purdey zips straight towards the van, seemingly intending to crash into it.

SYNOPSIS

The Avengers race against two murderous criminals named Roach and Poole to uncover hidden evidence buried somewhere in the country by a man imprisoned for espionage. A clue emerges in the form of western novel *Tale of the Big Y* as to the evidence's whereabouts, but there are no clues as to what the evidence will prove, or what government is involved…

REVIEW

This is one of the best episodes of the season, and the program appears to be hitting its stride. Purdey spends much of the early parts of the episode on her dirt bike, which in the 1970s was almost as hip as a dune buggy. In a minor breaking-the-fourth-wall moment, she wears *The New Avengers* lion logo (from the new title sequence) along with her name on the back of her leather jacket. Later, she is seen gluing her stairway banister back together, in a moment that prompts thoughts about how secret agents manage to repeatedly repair all the damage incurred in their apartments from episode to episode. She must have required a complete remodeling job after the Kane/Cybernaut attack. I wonder if they get a regular redecorating stipend from the Ministry?

The plot is an excellent mystery story with good plot twists. We have no idea what Gambit, Purdey and Steed and their rivals are searching for until the very end (which culminates with a surprising traitor). Steed seems more comfortable than ever in his elder agent role (a role he seemed shoehorned into earlier in the series), and there's a very tangible chemistry between the regulars. This action-oriented episode has lovely direction by Robert Fuest—particularly intriguing are shots through a beer glass at a pub that mark the time between separate shots. There is a very realistic car crash, followed by a ransacking of the Brandon's person and vehicle. The animalistic way in which they rip off his clothes, even tearing with their teeth, is quite disturbing! His car is then disassembled in the middle of a wheat field in a remarkably well-directed sequence. And few action sequences could be more seventies than the surreal Purdey hostage situation with a novelty laughing bag.

This is one of those few episodes where *The New Avengers* rises above merely a good seventies television show into an exceptional one, just as its predecessor frequently did in its era. It is frequently entertaining merely for its surface details—direction, humor and wit, and action—but also manages to impress for an intelligent script. Not to mention the fact that though there isn't a proper epilogue to the story per se, for once, the narrative structure, with its falling action in the final act, makes it seem as though one isn't necessary. The final wrap-up with Harmer feels like a denouement.

CHAMPAGNE, CARS, CLOTHES, AND CANINES

Only a few fashion debuts this episode. Gambit gets to trade in his three-piece suits for a prison uniform in dark-gray (which might have actually pleased Gareth Hunt); it is worn with a pale-gray shirt. He also wears his chalk-striped navy suit, followed later by his brown suede coat with brown trousers, a pale-yellow shirt with white collar, and a lime-green tie.

Purdey gets to wear one of her coolest ensembles, a set of black overalls with red-and-white trim at the cuffs and a patch at the left pocket. The top is short-sleeved and is worn over a white long-sleeved rollneck jumper, and it has the red, white, and blue 'New Avengers' lion logo on the back with her name in large white letters. She also wears a white motorcycle helmet, black leather gauntlets, and black riding boots. She, of course, wears this while riding her Honda 125 motorcycle. (This is its first and last appearance in the series, possibly because it's damaged in her encounter with Poole and Roach.) Next, she wears a bright-red structured woolen coat with long cloth belt tied around the waist. It's worn over a black skirt or dress (it's impossible to tell for certain what kind of outfit is underneath) with matching red pumps. Finally, she wears a pink, green, and white floral sleeveless dress tied at the shoulders; it is knee-length and has a V-neck. Steed wears several outfits throughout, including his tweed checked jacket and cream trousers, the pale-gray suit, and the dark-navy suit.

Steed and Gambit drive their respective Range Rovers. The airplanes seen in the episode are two de Havilland DH82A Tiger Moth biplanes, a red-and-white one (G-ANOH) and a yellow one (G-AOMX). Poole and Roach drive a white 1972 Citroën DS 20 Safari.

Steed gets to enjoy champagne at the end, and Gambit and Purdy attempt to drink some but miss out when they're ordered to pick up Turner. Steed and Harmer drink their glasses while they're gone.

QUOTES

"That's not corny. That's downright dangerous."

"Think of your soul, Gambit, think of your soul." (Gambit looks at sole of his shoe)

"I'm not a frog!"

"Gambit, you're the nearest. Disarm him, will you?"

"What, I asked myself, is a Ministry undersecretary doing with a loaded gun? He might hurt himself, I thought."

9 (1.8.9) FACES

Written by Brian Clemens & Dennis Spooner
Directed by James Hill

GUEST CAST

David De Keyser (Prator), Edward Petherbridge (Mullins), Richard Leech (Craig), Neil Hallett (Clifford), Annabel Leventon (Wendy), David Webb (Bilston), Donald Hewlett (Torrance), J.G. Devlin (Tramp), Jill Melford (Sheila), Michael Sheard (Peters), Robert Putt (Attendant)

PRE-TITLE

Two scruffy derelict men sit around a campfire in the forest discussing their association over a freshly killed rabbit that one of them has just shot with his bow-and-arrow. Hearing a car horn, they approach the nearby road and observe a man in a chauffeured car who looks very like one of the tramps. Elsewhere, the same man from the car prepares to dive from the diving board at his backyard swimming pool. Just as he launches from the springboard, one of the derelicts, Mullins, shoots him with his bow.

SYNOPSIS

A long-running scheme of finding vagrants who resemble top officials and replacing the originals is underway, using a shady plastic surgeon to assure the results. When Steed uncovers the plan, and realizes the sensitive nature of the case, he leaves Purdey out of the assignment and sends Gambit to pose as a drunk who could be recruited to replace himself. To help Gambit, Purdey goes undercover herself as a woman that requires a new identity. Meanwhile, a real vagrant has already been found to replace Steed...

REVIEW

There are likely many fans of *The New Avengers* that regard this episode highly. Unfortunately, despite multiple viewings, I cannot count myself among their number. At the most superficial level, it is entertaining, but I find the plot to be of the most contrived nature possible and not at all convincing. Frankly, the idea of having a plastic surgeon alter people's faces in order to replace highly skilled agents is more than a little far-fetched. After all, Steed, Gambit, and Purdey, amongst the many others, are all talented agents, whose skills would take years not weeks to cultivate, especially if lowly drunken bums are the ones receiving the training. The bulk of the training would consist of knowledge and skills not superficial physical traits. Once these doppelgängers are in place, they actually have to perform the jobs of the people they replace, competently at the very least.

There is one glaring plot hole also. When the doppelgänger for Steed's friend is altered after his death to make it look as though he'd had his appendix out, it should be pointed out that *corpses don't heal*, so it would be impossible for the appendix to be cut out and the wound then heal into a scar! Furthermore, there was hardly likely to have been an investigation if the crooks had simply left well enough alone. Instead, the whole case starts because they broke into the morgue and tampered with the body, leaving a very obvious clue for Steed to find.

In many ways, the story stinks of a typical French farce, in which all the main characters end up thinking one another is up to something that they're not. Left out of Steed's plot, Purdey infiltrates the villains' establishment on her own, posing as a cockney whore who wants a face change to escape her 'boyfriend,' while Gambit does the same as an Irish vagrant under Steed's instructions. Neither knows what the other is up to. Nevertheless, I find it nigh on impossible to believe that Gambit and Purdey, once in training for weeks on end to replace themselves, would not recognize each other at some point during this lengthy process. Neither character is likely to be that good an actor (or that imperceptive).

Purdey, driven by 'womanly emotions' and her suppressed feelings for Gambit, and thinking that Steed is also dead and replaced by a double, then blows her cover by confessing to the very first doppelgänger within the Ministry. Then, she finds out (as we already knew half an hour earlier) that she was wrong about both Steed and Gambit's doppelgängers as well. Gambit fooled her by impersonating his own doppelgänger, just as she did, and lucky Steed dodged a bullet and is still alive. So, Steed and Gambit are both undercover, and Purdey is just wrong, wrong, wrong! After all, she had to be, otherwise we wouldn't have had a plot. This all appears to be for the purpose of pumping up Steed as a character. We mustn't allow the little children to seem smarter than the great Steed, mustn't we? But this comes at the expense of Purdey.

One could easily imagine a narrative in which Gambit and Purdey recognize each other during their respective training sessions and then secretly unravel the villains' organization from the inside. This would have been far more believable to me and much more respectful of Purdey's character, who is instead denigrated by being portrayed as gullible, lacking in perception, and unable to make sound decisions due to being incapable of controlling her emotions. This is in addition to the fact that she is left out of the plan by the rather sexist decision of Steed, who apparently thinks the mission is too dangerous for a woman. Perhaps it was her punishment for devising the worst secret agent disguise ever—her absurd 'Mother Hubbard' outfit, a coarse decision that seems to be aiming for *Avengers* eccentricity but misses wholesale. The whole episode is just like that, aiming for something that it misses by a country mile.

CHAMPAGNE, CARS, CLOTHES, AND CANINES

Okay, here's where it gets really crazy with lots of outfits and costumes to go over. As usual, it's Purdey in the lead. First, she debuts a short-sleeved gray knit sun dress with an abstract green, white, and red 'Aztec' pattern along the trim and a thin cord belt. Then, it's a luxurious pink dress with white trim and a knit cardigan worn over a white blouse and accessorized with a deep-red coral bracelet and a white pearl necklace. Followed by a black leotard with a beige jumper and a thin pink belt. Then, a red, green, and white knee-length floral print dress with long, wide sleeves.

Then, the costumes begin. Gambit wears a filthy gray shirt, green jacket and trousers with a pale-brown scarf, while Steed dresses in a navy suit that is almost as dirty and disheveled with a pale-blue shirt, red suspenders, round spectacles, and a battered black fedora hat. Later, Purdey wears a lavender-and-blue diaphanous dress, gathered over the bust almost like a halter neck but with a sheer cape over the shoulders. She wears it with silver heels. This is both one of her regular outfits and a disguise that she wears when she's posing as her double of herself with a rather tragic blond wig. This is followed by a rather quaint 'Salvation Army' ensemble that makes her look like an early 20th-century school matron, a severe black garment with a matching black bonnet with red ribbon and rectangular eyeglasses. (Underneath, she wears her white silk camisole from "Target!") Finally, she dresses as a street hooker with a hot-pink sleeveless dress made of a ribbed stretch fabric, a dull blond wig, a brown-and-gray fur coat, a gold belt, and many long dangling gold necklaces.

Steed wears his tweed jacket and cream trousers and later his navy suit with a white shirt and a purple tie. Gambit wears his navy chalk-striped suit and later, while shooting with Steed, his brown checked suit without the jacket but with his pale-yellow shirt with white collar and white French cuffs and a wide olive tie.

As far as cars go, only Purdey's MGB shows up.

QUOTES

"I'm not annoyed with you, Gambit. You can't help your background."

"I'll bet he's halfway through my 61' claret."

10 (1.12.10) GNAWS

Written by Dennis Spooner
Directed by Ray Austin

GUEST CAST

Julian Holloway (Thornton), Peter Cellier (Carter), Jeremy Young (Chislenko), Patrick Malahide (George), Keith Marsh (Tramp Joe), Ken Wynne (Tramp Arthur), Morgan Shepherd (Walters), John Watts (Harlow), Keith Alexander (Malloy), Ronnie Laughlin (Motor Mechanic)
Uncredited: Anulka Dubinska (Pretty Girl)

PRE-TITLE

A well-dressed man, Thornton, enters a laboratory, puts on his glasses, and begins reading some documents. He is surprised by Harlow, an agent from the Ministry hiding in the darkened room, who has been following him. Apparently, the documents were taken without authorization, and Harlow is there to arrest him. However, Thornton takes Harlow by surprise, delivering a fatal blow to the back of the head. Gambit and Purdey soon find Harlow's body in a nearby wood. Elsewhere, Thornton and Carter argue about stealing top secret papers. Thornton wants Carter to perform the dirty deed, and he ultimately does so under Thorton's precise instructions, but a security guard interrupts the crime in progress and Carter is forced to knock him out.

SYNOPSIS

An accident in a lab results in a radioactive growth concentrate being washed down the sink. Days later, seismic readings show something large in the sewers and most of the local vermin population has vanished. *The Avengers* work with a foreign embassy and the two unscrupulous scientists responsible for the accident to destroy whatever threat lurks in London's sewers...

REVIEW

When the classic *Doctor Who* series did the giant rat thing in 1977's "The Talons of Weng-Chiang," it had its mawkish charm, with a giant brown plush rat toy with bucked-teeth sewn out of white cloth chewing fruitlessly away at Louise Jameson, who screamed completely out of character. (Honestly, you half expect to see the operator's arms sticking into view!) Here, it is unforgiveable in a program that was supposed to have risen far above such budget limitations. It's even worse that a writer the caliber of Dennis Spooner penned it, that a director as talented as Ray Austin was saddled with it.

Austin was at least wise enough to know that an early appearance of a giant rat would dispel all suspense and credibility (with the obviously fake animal in full view). Sadly, waiting until the end to show the beastly special effects abomination[9] turned out to be just as bad an idea, because after so much buildup (some of it reasonably good) we are left disappointed and laughing by the time the finale eventually arrives. This climactic sewer rat battle was accomplished by the only means available to television in the 1970s, a normal-sized rat shot in extreme closeup on a model set intercut with closeups of parts of a rat prop in isolation.

In the interim, about the best we have in this story are a few chilling attacks on random individuals, where the beast attacking them remains off camera. Given that we're to briefly believe that the creature is a giant shark, these scenes work on some fundamental level where the audience is afraid of being eaten by a giant shark in a sewer. (Show me a man who is not afraid of being eaten by a giant shark in a sewer, and I'll show you a fool.) Otherwise, we're just marking time for the big climax, as one man after another gets dragged away screaming into the murky water. Since the finale is terrible, we're left with nothing but work in getting there and no payoff.

But this is hardly the biggest sin of "Gnaws." And, no, it's not the name either, though the jokey reference to the prior year's hit film from Steven Spielberg is pretty terrible too. (The connection is ineptly sold by a brief diversion from a vagrant who proclaims the creature a 'giant shark.') Its biggest downside is that it manages to be quite dull almost all the way through.

What conclusions we are left with in this rather torrid episode is perhaps the notion that the whole idea should never have been attempted in the first place. The problem with this production isn't the actors, the director, or the props designers. It isn't the dialogue, humor, or wit, or lack thereof. It's the fact that the script got off the planning table at all without someone realizing that it couldn't be executed effectively. That, in 1976, you could come to Fennell and Clemens and say you wanted to "see Joanna Lumley in an a-line skirt fighting a giant rat in the sewers" is truly remarkable. Can you imagine anyone suggesting that Diana Rigg do this?

Ray Austin strains mightily, the cast gives it a real go, but you cannot make this story fly. It is hopelessly bogged down. That the aforementioned "The Talons of Weng-Chiang" managed to be a superior example of the same subject—albeit only as a minimal part of its narrative—is a testament to the fact that budget is no substitute for a good script (or a good script idea).

---

9 The general murkiness of the sewer is part of the problem here, and a new scan from the original negatives could help out enormously. It wouldn't make the 'giant' rat any more convincing, but it could help us see the other more important characters more clearly as well as the sets.

CHAMPAGNE, CARS, CLOTHES, AND CANINES

There are seven fashion debuts in this episode, and one is for Gambit, and as for the others, I'll give you three guesses as to who. In the scene in which they discover Harlow's body, Gambit debuts a casual brown corduroy jacket worn with wide epaulettes, worn with a pinstriped white shirt and a dark-brown tie. In the same scene, Purdey debuts a brown rollneck jumper with a matching cardigan and a long black pleated skirt. Soon, she wears a Burberry's trench-style overcoat in beige with a Burberry's brown-and-beige plaid scarf, matching umbrella, and brown leather ankle boots. In the same scene, Gambit wears his chalk-striped navy-blue suit without the waistcoat; later, he wears his pale-gray suit with the ticket pocket, and then, he's back to the corduroy jacket with matching trousers and a cream rollneck jumper. Purdey wears a black very short-sleeved dress with a hot-pink collar and sleeve trim. (I cannot rule out the possibility that this is the same dress worn under the Burberry's overcoat with the pink trim hidden by the scarf.) It is accessorized with a multi-colored headband.

For her first trip into the sewers, she chooses to wear pale blue jeans, a long-sleeved blue-and-white striped rugby shirt, and bright-yellow belt and boots. Once cleaned up from her fight in the sewer with Chislenko, she goes to bed in a cream-colored and very frilly ruched nightie. (So, agents actually get to sleep occasionally. That's healthy.) She also re-wears the Buckley patchwork split midi skirt and scarf (from "House of Cards") with a long-sleeved lavender shirt. Remarkably, this is the outfit she ends up wearing for her second foray in to the sewer. (Poor Ms. Buckley must have been horrified. I mean, you couldn't even dry clean that outfit!) And her shoes are fancy red pumps to boot. Probably having had to discard that outfit, for the brief tag scene at dinner, she switches to a cream-colored blouse and matching cravat with a gold-and-peach multi-layered skirt.

None of the *Avengers* cars appear in this episode. After all, there's no driving in the sewers. I mean, where would they put the traffic signals?

QUOTES

"He died with his boots off?"

"Well, well, what is steel-hearted Purdey doing here?" "I'm a woman, and women are allowed their idiosyncrasies."

"Assume the position. I assume you know how to assume?"

"I saw it! I saw its jaws, its teeth like razors!"

11 (1.13.11) DIRTIER BY THE DOZEN

Written by Brian Clemens
Directed by Sidney Hayers

GUEST CAST

John Castle (Colonel Miller), Shaun Curry (Sergeant Bowdon), Stephen Moore (Major Prentice), Alun Armstrong (Harris), Ballard Berkeley (Colonel Foster), Michael Barrington (Colonel Stevens), Michael Howarth (Tony Noble), John Forbes-Robertson (Doctor), Brian Croucher (Terry), John Labanowski (Keller), David Purcell (Orderly), Francis Mughan (Freddy)

PRE-TITLE

Deep in the jungles of Heatherden Hall in London, a one-eyed psychopath in army fatigues, Colonel 'Mad Jack' Miller, with his fellow soldiers fires his machine gun at similarly dressed men, including a photographer, Travis, who is attempting to film them. The photographer manages to escape, however. Elsewhere, a general and his captain, Tony Noble, arrive at Miller's army base with the general declaring that he will "have Colonel Miller's head on a plate," but finding the base deserted, they search until they are confronted by a soldier with a machine gun who immediately shoots Noble.

SYNOPSIS

Recovering some filmed footage from a dead agent, Gambit discovers that the films are all of a certain British Army regiment fighting all over the world. Steed, Gambit and Purdey soon learn that the regiment, led by Colonel "Mad Jack" Miller, is working secretly as a group of mercenaries...

REVIEW

Frankly, this is mostly a dull episode that lacks every single classic *Avengers* element. Among the attributes that save it from its military-oriented morass of gunfire and explosions are Purdey's eccentric uncle, Steed's toy soldiers, and Purdey using her quick wit to have a whole pub full of soldiers eating out of her hand. The latter scene is easily the best moment in the entire episode.

However, as always, there is some strong Gambit and Purdey witty banter, and Sidney Hayers' direction is interesting in a few instances, including one scene in which he cleverly films Gambit's assailants, revealing one at a time, even though they were standing next to each other the whole time. Immediately thereafter, a rather good action scene follows, and Gambit and Purdey unwillingly play war games in a cross-country chase involving jeeps and mortars. I find it impossible to believe, however, that Purdey cannot comprehend Gambit's warnings to stay out of a minefield.

The core idea isn't so bad, but the villainous Colonel Miller is distilled tedium. Mind-numbingly wearisome, he stomps around, alternately grinning and swaggering. He may be mad, but he also completely lacks gravitas, coming across as a stereotypical military heavyweight who never quite intimidates in the way that he intends. Definitely not one of John Castle's finest hours. The final frames are remarkably cheesy, in a horrid seventies way that fails completely to capture the essence of the original series. Somehow this scene—consisting of Joanna Lumley riding a rope ladder hanging from a helicopter while drinking champagne—comes across as more *Absolutely Fabulous* than *The Avengers*.

CHAMPAGNE, CARS, CLOTHES, AND... CAMERAS!

Gambit starts out immediately in his brown corduroy jacket with matching trousers (from "Gnaws") and a cream rollneck jumper. In the scene in which Gambit and Purdey review Travis's films, she debuts a new beige Safari suit with a beige blouse, muted orange trousers, and matching knee-high boots; later, she pairs it with a brown wide-brimmed hat with an enormous leopard-print band. He wears his gray checked suit. Later, Gambit gets to play the full soldier routine and wears two different uniforms: first, he dresses as a Scottish regiment of the British Army with khaki jacket, tartan (or diced) regimental cap, and black trousers; and then, he wears British army camo fatigues with a black beret, and later the standard-issue army-green woolen jumper with padded shoulders. Purdey's final outfit debut of the episode is a bright-red ankle-length dress with a cowl collar and a pleated split skirt. It's paired with matching red boots. Steed wears mainly his navy-blue suit with a white shirt and a navy tie with white spots and later his tweed jacket and cream trousers.

Yes, there's champagne in the cheesiest possible way, drunk by Purdey while dangling from a rope ladder attached to a helicopter. I do admire her dexterity, however. It's pretty hard to do anything while dangling from a rope ladder attached to a helicopter. It's also the closest we get to an epilogue.

By the way, the helicopter is a Bell 206B JetRanger II (G-BBEU). Out of the cars, only Purdey's MGB appears in this episode, this time with the top up as it appears to have been a rather rainy autumn day. Colonel Miller rides in a 1962 Land-Rover 88" Series IIa (45 BE 72).

The camera used by Travis is a Bolex H16 cine camera.

QUOTES

"What I need is a woman's eye." "That's not what I've heard."
"I'll buy you a dog." "Two heads are better than one." "I'm definitely not buying you another head!"
"Esprit de corps with a vengeance!"
"Exactly. You are a general, and I have been looking for a general. I'm an ambitious man, and you are the key to my ambition."
"Now, what should we do? Start building a nest?"
"Pretend it's a chastity belt." "I'll get the key. Don't go away."

12 (1.11.12) SLEEPER

Written by Brian Clemens
Directed by Graeme Clifford

GUEST CAST

Keith Buckley (Brady), Arthur Dignam (Dr. Graham), Mark Jones (Chuck), Prentis Hancock (Bart), Sara Kestelman (Tina), Gavin Campbell (Fred), David Schofield (Ben), George Sweeney (Phil), Peter Godfrey (Pilot), Leo Dolan (Bill), Jason White (Policeman), Tony McHale (Policeman)

PRE-TITLE

Professor Merker lands at Westland Heliport and is greeted rather rudely by another gentleman who immediately attacks him and knocks him out, taking his clothes and case. Nearby, as they prepare to test a new sleeping gas, Purdey, Gambit, and Steed get their inoculations in order to make them immune. The test is successful and the test subjects pass out while those who received the inoculation are unaffected. However, the man who knocked out Professor Merker is there, observing.

SYNOPSIS

After a secret chemical that can put a mass number of people to sleep is stolen, Steed, Gambit, and Purdey, inoculated against the chemical as part of the demonstration, are the only people in the city that can stop the crooks from stealing all of London blind…

REVIEW

"Sleeper" would hardly have been an unoriginal idea in 1977, having already been done with "The Morning After" in the original series. And 1970s audiences would have been well familiar with post-apocalyptic films and television shows that depicted London or some other city in a similar state of abandonment. Nevertheless, originality is hardly a required quality, and this is a stylishly-directed and charming episode, one of the most enjoyable in the season.

The villains would have likely reminded audiences of the day of the Black September Organization from the Munich Olympics. Indeed, they are crude and unimaginative, choosing to use their newfound weapon merely to rob banks. I'm also surprised that the man who stole the sleeper dust doesn't realize that there could be other people awake; he did after all directly witness people being inoculated in the demonstration he attended. Despite this, and the fact that it lacks all the classic traits of the original series, the story more than makes up for it with wit and gags.

My favorite scene is Purdey impersonating a mannequin with slippery silk pajama bottoms. It is one of the funniest scenes in an *Avengers* episode. Purdey then has the opportunity to kick Prentis Hancock across the street, and after knocking him out, she steals his belt to keep her pajama bottoms anchored in place. It's funny and sexy at the same time. Thus, it is the little touches that make this episode so entertaining. Gambit, in almost unexpected gentlemanly manner, arranges a sleeping woman's skirt to preserve her modesty. In another scene, Steed and Gambit drink stolen beers straight from the bottle, and then, the two agents disguised as sleepers outwit the dull-witted thugs at a bus stop. Also memorable is Purdey hailing a cop car only to have the policeman fall asleep in their approach, nearly running her down and crashing. The final convergence of the heroes might seem a little contrived, but it's the perfect ending for an episode that thrives on its humor.

One of the most enjoyable aspects of this story is the fact that there is so much of London on display—skillfully directed by Graeme Clifford. This was a real rarity for the original series in particular, mitigated somewhat by increased on-location shooting in the final season. However, the locations included here are limited to back alleys and industrial parks. Stylish sixties London was gone, and in its place, was a gritty, slightly rundown city in the midst of economic stagnation. (We do however see Steed and Gambit visit the BT Tower restaurant.) If not for this and Gambit's garish sea-green apartment, the emptiness could almost make you forget it was the 1970s, but failing to do so would be forgivable in this otherwise highly enjoyable hour of television.

CHAMPAGNE, CARS, CLOTHES, AND... CAMERAS!

Early in the episode, Steed wears his navy-blue suit with a white shirt and a navy-tie with white spots, Gambit wears his brown double-breasted suit (from "Cat Amongst the Pigeons"), and Purdey wears her floral dress (from "Faces"). Steed's outfit doesn't change until the end, but Gambit changes his suit for the brown suede coat and trousers. But since Purdey slept in her pajamas, she ends up trapped in them throughout the vast majority of the episode—they're cerulean-blue silk pajamas with white abstract patterns (maybe clouds?) on the back and wrapping over to the right side. Both the short sleeves and the trousers are flared. Steed and Gambit wear army camo jackets and army-green balaclavas to disguise themselves as bank robbers, while Purdey wears a gray jacket, a white jumper with an enormous rollneck, a black balaclava, and a steel-gray helmet to disguise herself as the helicopter pilot.

This is quite the car-spotting episode since it takes place in a sleeping London. Steed's Jaguar appears, and they all ride home in it from dinner, and he and Gambit drive around London in it extensively after the sleep gas is used. Purdey's MGB also returns, albeit only briefly as she's left her keys inside her flat and cannot unlock the door, forcing her to 'borrow' a red 1966 Morris Mini Minor Mk1 (FHO 650D), which is still occupied by a sleeping gentleman. The bank robbers chase her in a 1973 Volvo 144 GL (WJH 291M). The helicopter used by the villains (and stolen by the Avengers) is a yellow-and-white Bell 206B JetRanger II.

No champagne, but Steed and Gambit do grab some emergency beer from a nearby pub. And I spied cameras on Frank Hardy's desk! One of them is a Soviet-made Zorki rangefinder. Sadly, the others are too blurry to identify with any certainty.

QUOTES

"It's suddenly gone all quiet."
"Shall we use the siren?" "If it's good enough for Kojak, it's good enough for us."
"Well, after all, Sunday is the day of rest."

13 (1.10.13) THREE HANDED GAME

Written by Dennis Spooner & Brian Clemens
Directed by Ray Austin

GUEST CAST

David Wood (Ranson), Michael Petrovich (Larry), Stephen Greif (Juventor), Tony Vogel (Ivan), Gary Raymond (Masgard), Terry Wood (Meroff), Annie Lambert (Helen), Ronald Leigh-Hunt (General), John Paul (Doctor), Hugh Morton (Professor), Noel Trevarthen (Tony Fields), Bill Bailey (Cary)

PRE-TITLE

Deep in the Atlantic ocean, a submarine cruises along. Inside, instructions are given to an agent with an eidetic memory. The process continues with two more agents, a woman and a man, in New York City and Washington DC respectively. Back at the Ministry in London, their memorized words are edited together by Steed to complete the message. The general asks if their eidetic resources can be used again, but Steed replies that they agreed to use them only once and then disband them. Elsewhere, an eccentric professor explains to two enemy agents, Juventor and Ivan, how he discovered the idea of storing information in the human brain and then demonstrates the process by transferring information to Juventor. Having acquired the necessary information, Juventor immediately shoots him. This is followed by a tap dancer, Ranson, returning to his dressing room after a performance to be punched and knocked out by Ivan.

SYNOPSIS

The 'Three Handed Game' is a trio of agents with eidetic memories. Each has memorized every third word in a secret American defense document. As a result, each is being targeted by the mercenary arms dealer Juventor and his mind-stealing machine...

REVIEW

For one week, ***The New Avengers*** takes a turn of several degrees towards its predecessor, in a story that lifts minor elements of "Who's Who???" and "Look – (stop me if you've heard this one) But There Were These Two Fellers..." and combines them with seventies televisual blandness. That clowns and tap-dancing should show up in ***The New Avengers*** at all might seem enough of a surrealistic turn to re-capture some of the show's historical surfeit of such, but that Steed would chase down a Formula 1 drag racer in his Jag in one scene seems more like an advert for the auto manufacturer than a genuine stab at the show's prior style.

And, thus, ***The New Avengers*** strangely gets it both right and wrong simultaneously—as is frequently the case. This season had begun largely in its own sphere, somewhere between the final season of ***The Avengers*** and 1976, formerly classy spy shtick lightly dipped in late seventies schmaltz, a crackly shell of the 'Me Generation' enwrapping luscious sixties spy hijinks. ***The New Avengers*** was no doubt more hard-boiled than its predecessor, even considering the jackknifing turn towards periodic realism in the Tara King era, but it now sharply tacked back in the direction of the original series as if Fennell and Clemens were suddenly struck with a fit of nostalgia—*amnesiac* nostalgia. That this episode falls just short of re-capturing that spirit could be seen as either forgetfulness for the producers on how it was done or ill-considered second-guessing of the decision partway through the process. Thus, the brain drain of ***The Avengers*** legacy continues.

Frankly, I'm surprised that this episode was directed by Ray Austin; its humdrum shooting style and dreary sets betray a much more pedestrian director. Are we seeing the budget fall apart in this story? Or is this the new vogue in direction with urban decay as its theme? Too many scenes take place in drab rooms with a lonely table and chairs—and a radiator to which the villains can chain braindead captured agents.

Nevertheless, there are some moments of humor and wit. Purdey looks far too happy dressed as a clown as she dances across the dressing room floor. The episode terminates with an odd dance-fight on stage, in which she combines her terpsichorean muse with La Panache and ballet, all with great panache, in one of the more bizarre fight scenes of either series, which owes far more to the aforementioned "Look – (stop me..." episode than it does anything from the Mrs. Peel (or Mrs. Gale) era of the original series. And it does deserve a round of applause.

Is this a season finale or a series ender...?

CHAMPAGNE, CARS, CLOTHES, AND CANINES

Nothing much going on here with clothing debuts. It seems that the clothing budget has dried up. In fact, Gambit poses in the nude in one scene and covers up with a red blanket when Purdey arrives. Purdey does, however, debut a new red-orange short-sleeved print dress, with a similar aesthetic to the prior orange and black wrap dress (in "To Catch a Rat"), this one with a V-neck, black trim, and a crisscrossing cummerbund. She wears it with a black choker and knee-high black boots and later with clown makeup and a ginger wig. Steed and Gambit open the episode wearing their deep-green and black tuxedos with frill-fronted white shirts and bowties while Purdey wears her Catherine Buckley Edwardian-inspired high-collared dress. Steed's pale-gray suit returns, and later, his navy suit. Not to be outdone, Gambit's navy chalk-striped suit also returns, and later, his brown suede coat. Purdey's crimson cardigan and multi-color striped skirt also reappear, worn separately.

Both Juventor and Ivan dress well in suits, which gives Tony Vogel, with his unkempt beard and unibrow, the look of a sexy caveman forced to smarten himself up while visiting the far future. This impression is only heightened by his laconic nature and his psychopathic crudeness.

Both Steed and Gambit's Jaguars show up as does Purdey's MGB. Steed's Jag gets a real workout when he chases after Tony Fields on a Formula 2 racetrack. Unfortunately, Gambit's Jaguar has its tires shot out by Ivan. Fellow agent Larry drives a white 1975 Bedford CF panel van with a silver-and-orange 1975 Honda TL 125 motorcycle tucked inside, and, unlike Gambit and Purdey, he is able to chase after the villains on the motorcycle when his van's tires are also shot out. Juventor and Ivan drive a 1975 Daimler Sovereign Series II (XYP 14N). Tony Fields's racecar is an orange-red 1975 March 752.

QUOTES

"And stop staring at me. We're supposed to be watching the embassy."
"You are a very attractive man, Mike." "I never argue with a beautiful woman."
"I could tap before I could walk."

SEASON TWO

13 episodes (35mm color film, ~53 min. ea.)

Regular Cast
Patrick Macnee—John Steed
Gareth Hunt—Mike Gambit
Joanna Lumley—Purdey

Producers: Albert Fennell and Brian Clemens
Music: Laurie Johnson

14. **Dead Men Are Dangerous—w.** Brian Clemens; **dir.** Sidney Hayers; **UK tx.** 8 Sep 1977; **US tx.** 24 Nov 1978; **Filmed:** Mar 1977
15. **Angels of Death—w.** Terence Feeley & Brian Clemens; **dir.** Ernest Day; **UK tx.** 15 Sep 1977; **US tx.** 29 Sep 1978; **Filmed:** Apr 1977
16. **Medium Rare—w.** Dennis Spooner; **dir.** Ray Austin; **UK tx.** 22 Sep 1977; **US tx.** 26 Jan 1979; **Filmed:** Apr 1977
17. **The Lion and the Unicorn—w.** John Goldsmith; **dir.** Ray Austin; **UK tx.** 29 Sep 1978; **US tx.** 15 Dec 1978; **Filmed:** May 1977
18. **Obsession—w.** Brian Clemens; **dir.** Ernest Day; **UK tx.** 6 Oct 1977; **US tx.** 10 Nov 1978; **Filmed:** May 1977
19. **Trap—w.** Brian Clemens; **dir.** Ray Austin; **UK tx.** 13 Oct 1977; **US tx.** 2 Mar 1979; **Filmed:** Mar 1977
20. **Hostage—w.** Brian Clemens; **dir.** Sidney Hayers; **UK tx.** 21 Oct 1977; **US tx.** 8 Dec 1978; **Filmed:** Feb 1977
21. **K is for Kill: Part One – The Tiger Awakes—w.** Brian Clemens; **dir.** Yvon Marie Coulais; **UK tx.** 27 Oct 1977; **US tx.** 23 Mar 1979; **Filmed:** Jun 1977
22. **K is for Kill: Part Two – Tiger by the Tail—w.** Brian Clemens; **dir.** Yvon Marie Coulais; **UK tx.** 3 Nov 1977; **US tx.** 23 Mar 1979; **Filmed:** Jun 1977
23. **Complex—w.** Dennis Spooner; **dir.** Richard Gilbert; **UK tx.** 10 Nov 1977; **US tx.** 5 Jan 1979; **Filmed:** Jul 1977
24. **The Gladiators—w.** Brian Clemens; **dir.** Claude Fournier; **UK tx.** 18 Nov 1977; **US tx.** 19 Jan 1979; **Filmed:** Jul 1977
25. **Forward Base—w.** Dennis Spooner; **dir.** Don Thompson; **UK tx.** 24 Nov 1977; **US tx.** 3 Nov 1978; **Filmed:** Aug 1977
26. **Emily—w.** Dennis Spooner; **dir.** Don Thompson; **UK tx.** 1 Dec 1977; **US tx.** 9 Feb 1979; **Filmed:** Aug 1977

SEASON NOTES

Season One of *The New Avengers* had gone well. It had seemed bright, shiny and new, and the characters had gelled against all expectations. Viewers were likely pleasantly surprised, even if not completely enthralled. The program had not made nearly the splash in the public's imagination as the original series, though it performed well. Steed had maintained a certain genteel gravitas despite slight marginalization and subtle character shifts. Mike Gambit had been established as the new male strongarm of the group with martial arts skills that were nearly unstoppable when they could be brought to bear. Purdey had established herself as the new insouciant female superspy with the skills to match, forever engaged in witty banter and a quasi-romantic tug-of-war with Gambit. The stories were generally strong and well-directed. While attempts to raise the ghosts of the past had usually fallen flat, the program had forged ahead on its own merit, marking new territory in an era of television that was more than slightly hostile to the concept in the first place.

The seventies were grittier than ever by 1978, realism was in like gangbusters, even in sitcoms, and the series had begun to curve back in on itself in an arc towards its roots, one that would eventually have Steed driving a little yellow hatchback instead of a Bentley. This hammering against the late sixties concept of *The Avengers* in its heyday would seemingly pound the show into something more resembling *The Professionals,* and indeed, *The New Avengers* became a clear ancestor to that series, with Brian Clemens and Albert Fennell no doubt keen to abandon the increasingly troubled *Avengers* franchise and commit themselves to their own baby, which was ultimately more suited to this decade of television anyway.

In the meantime, changes were afoot. Realism creeped in in all kinds of ways, like wood rot, eating away at the core ideas of the series. Mike Gambit's much-vaunted fighting skills would suddenly atrophy as if superspies could no longer be super. He would spend his time becoming more of an ersatz rogue and lone wolf, the one to go it alone when the others lacked the initiative, or the stamina. Purdey would slowly attenuate into a more domestic and passive role as well, with less emphasis on fighting skills and more emphasis on taking care of her men, as if female superspies weren't supposed to have such skills anymore, they were supposed to be companions. Was she going to be Steed's lover or Gambit's? The irony was that they spent their time apart more than ever, the one episode with them mostly all together being the one that blunted their spy skills the most—the two-parter, "K is for Kill." Add to this ongoing money troubles, a move to France, and then a move to Canada, and the series was suddenly in deep trouble, a complete loss of identity (and finances) looming on the horizon.

That the season ended in a different country with a tone that would be unrecognizable to any fan of the original series, a fiddle music score in place of the swing jazz chops of Johnny Dankworth or Laurie Johnson, was a virtual disgrace. Not only was the *idealized version* of England and Englishness that made the world swoon in the sixties gone but so was England! They were in Canada and driving on the right-hand side of the road, which was about the only bit of surrealism that had survived the seventies realism overdrive.

The problems driving this unfortunate turn of events were entirely financial and almost pathetic, and it's easy to see why the producers and studio executives behind the production finally said enough is enough and moved on. Fans of *The Avengers* may or may not have cried when "Emily" flickered across television screens in the winter of 1978/79, but, if they did, it was most likely because they saw the show they loved turned into something unrecognizable rather than because it was ending.

On the other hand, there is good news. Season Two of *The New Avengers* is not without redemption. There are good episodes to be seen here, and some capture the spirit of the original show better than did Season One. "Angels of Death" is a remarkably good psychological spy story, which feeds Steed's image of grit and determination better than anything since the early days. Equally, "Hostage" is a striking story with its style rooted in that of the videotaped era, a script that could easily fit in with the first or the third season. And the Canadian experience wasn't all bad. "Forward Base," despite its isolation on Ward's Island along Lake Ontario, manages a light-hearted charm seldom seen since the days of Mrs. Peel. "Complex" rather obviously manages to evoke "The House That Jack Built," seemingly without the shame that comes with knowing fans will recognize the plot structure faster than the computer can spring its next trap, but it works well enough despite this.

On the other hand, the new batch of French and Canadian directors brought in were unexceptional and merely competent. Ray Austin and Sidney Hayers resurfaced for a couple of new episodes each but vanished when the Canadian backers demanded that local talent be used. The wit and banter wilted as if untended. There was no surrealism, just cartoonish French farce-style humor. Season Two is indeed a mixed bag. Fans will no doubt have their favorites and their least favorites, which may or may not correspond to mine. While you may not agree with many of my reviews, you're certain to see the show's inexorable decline, which starts out slowly and then proceeds in fits and starts until the program finally runs out of gas somewhere on a Canadian highway.

CHAMPAGNE, CARS, CLOTHES, AND CANINES

The main difference between this season and the previous one are that Jillie Murphy is now the designer for Joanna Lumley's wardrobe, and Gareth Hunt increasingly wears casual clothes, as had been his wish from the beginning. Patrick Macnee's clothes and all the cast's cars remain largely the same, barring Purdey's new yellow Triumph TR7—and except of course when they move to Canada, in which all their regular cars disappear, replaced by (presumably) rented vehicles. As before, Gambit takes a liking to stealing cars whenever he needs one, which is more often than ever.

Best Dressed: "Complex"
Worst Dressed: "The Gladiators"

AVENGERS CARS

JOHN STEED

Rover 3500 (MOC 229P)—yellow—in "Medium Rare," "The Lion and the Unicorn," and "Hostage."
Jaguar XJ12C (NWK 60P)—racing green—in "Dead Men Are Dangerous," "Angels of Death," and "Trap."
Range Rover (TXC 922J)—dark-green—in "Obsession."
1927 Bentley 3 Litre (YT 3942)—racing green—in "K is for Kill" Part 1.

PURDEY

Honda 125 motorcycle (OLR 471P)—orange and black—in "Obsession."
Triumph TR7 (OGW 562R)—bright-yellow—in "Medium Rare," "Trap," and "Hostage."

MIKE GAMBIT

Jaguar XJS (NRW 875P)—orange-red—in "Medium Rare," "The Lion and the Unicorn," and "Hostage."
Range Rover (LOK 537P)—white—in "Obsession" and "Trap."

THE MOST FANTASTIC EPISODES OF THE SEASON

1. "Hostage"
2. "Dead Men Are Dangerous"
3. "Angels of Death"
4. "Forward Base"
5. "Complex"

14 (2.3.1) DEAD MEN ARE DANGEROUS

Written by Brian Clemens
Directed by Sidney Hayers

GUEST CAST

Clive Revill (Mark), Richard Murdoch (Perry), Gabrielle Drake (Penny), Terry Taplin (Hara), Michael Turner (Dr. Culver), Trevor Adams (Sandy), Roger Avon (Headmaster), Gabor Vernon (Russian Doctor)

PRE-TITLE

Steed drives Mark Crayford across the border and beyond the iron curtain in East Germany. They park and walk into the woods nearby where border guards are patrolling back and forth. It appears at first that Crayford is to undertake a mission on the other side, but Steed soon intuits that he is planning instead to defect. An argument ensues and Crayford draws a gun, becoming increasingly angry. Finally, he fires at Steed, but misses. Steed fires back and hits him in the chest.

SYNOPSIS

After shooting and mortally-wounding an Eastern agent and long-standing rival, Steed faces repeated attempts on his life—not just the threat of death but threats to all his most treasured possessions, including his friends…

REVIEW

The New Avengers re-launches for a new year on a very strong note. This episode features a novel approach to the standard revenge plot so often explored by *The Avengers*. Here, Steed is the specific target, but the enemy takes aim at all the things he loves before he decides to target Steed himself, prompting a series of destructive events as Steed's treasures are taken from him one by one. We are almost in tears as we realize that it was his old Bentley that was blown up in one attack. Thus, the story could be perceived as simultaneously attacking Steed and our pre-conceptions of what the series is about. This in itself is not a bad idea. *The New Avengers* had every right to find its own voice. Indeed, if every episode this season had been up to this standard, we'd have no complaints about this at all. Though this was not to be the case, for now, what we have is a very enjoyable episode that offers deeper insight into Steed's background than any prior story. He clearly cares more about his friends' welfare than any of the art treasures he has gathered since his meager beginnings in *The Avengers*.

All of the regular cast seem to be even more deeply into their roles. Gareth Hunt has clearly been working out more (as one shirtless scene demonstrates), and perhaps oddly, Purdey seems to have developed a mild attraction to Steed, manifesting with some casual flirtation. There is clearly a drive to push Steed and Purdey closer together, indicated by a line of dialogue in which she is declared as something he cares about the most, and the viewer is left with a degree of anxiety about whether this is truly the best direction for the series to pursue. After all, what will happen to the brilliant Gambit and Purdey byplay?

I'm a little skeptical of the creeping bullet that moves steadily towards Mark's heart—over a lengthy period of over ten years!—but a good script, which is what we have here, can gloss over such over-the-top spy nonsense. I'm perhaps even more bothered, however, by the blunted wit, lack of humor, and even more hard-boiled spy drama that indicates the direction of this second season of the program. Nevertheless, the finale is exceptionally tense and well-directed.

CHAMPAGNE, CARS, CLOTHES, AND CANINES

In the pre-title, Steed wears a navy-blue suit, a pale-blue shirt and a brown tie with a beige overcoat and a flat driving cap. In the cricketing scene, he wears cricketing gear and batting pads with a cream woolen cable-stitched jumper. Gambit dresses similarly but with cream trousers and jumper and a flat cap much like Steed's in the pre-title sequence, and Purdey debuts a new dress, a knee-length multi-colored striped short-sleeved dress in much the same style as her similar outfit worn last season in "Target!" and "To Catch a Rat." She wears it with cricketers batting pads. Later, in Steed's Jaguar, he wears a black velvet tuxedo (again, with an enormous velvet bowtie) and she wears a very long cream-white dress with a multi-colored floral print spattered about the chest and shoulders. It's gathered at both the neck and the waist. Later, she dons her gold lamé karate gi over a pink t-shirt while sparring with Gambit, who also wears a karate gi, though a white one. And then still later, she wears a white blouse with a bright-red cardigan (or jumper) tied around her shoulders and a long red multi-layered skirt with a subtle floral print in dark purple with a white hem; the fabric is tightly pleated.

Gambit debuts a new gray two-piece single-breasted suit in a worsted wool, with a blue shirt and a diagonally striped blue-and-gray tie. (The ties are clearly getting wider as the seventies wear on.) Later, he wears a navy-blue buttoned cardigan with a white checked shirt and checked brown trousers. (It seems as though more casual outfits are winning out for Gareth Hunt as he originally wanted, so casual that he's at one point shirtless with blue jeans on his sofa.) Steed wears his pale-gray suit from Season One for the vast majority of the episode, and we see that the waistcoat is backed with silvery-gray silk with a subtle dot pattern.

Steed's racing green Jaguar returns, and he also drives a 1964 Mercedes-Benz 190 (B NP 374) in the pre-title. Unfortunately, this is the episode where the Bentley gets destroyed in an explosion in his garage, and only the radiator grille and hood ornament are seen to survive. Gambit manages to cling to the villains' pale-yellow 1972 Fiat 124 1200 2a for a Herculean amount of time as they attempt to flee, and for this exceptionally long rodeo ride he claims the top prize of one registration plate—HHX 449K.

QUOTES

"You know what I'm going to miss most of all? That old punt up the river and the taste of warm bitter beer." "You shouldn't talk like that—as though you weren't coming back."
"I've stood in your shadow ever since we were kids, Steed."
"Steed, a man who's been awarded the military cross does not say 'What metal?'" "*Which* metal?"
"Your assassin is a very poor shot." "Or the best there is."

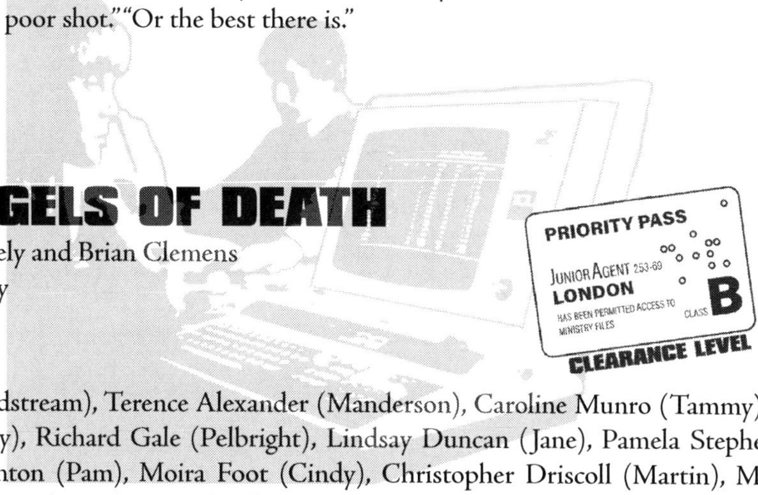

15 (2.5.2) ANGELS OF DEATH

Written by Terence Feely and Brian Clemens
Directed by Ernest Day

GUEST CAST

Dinsdale Landen (Coldstream), Terence Alexander (Manderson), Caroline Munro (Tammy), Michael Latimer (Reresby), Richard Gale (Pelbright), Lindsay Duncan (Jane), Pamela Stephenson (Wendy), Annette Lynton (Pam), Moira Foot (Cindy), Christopher Driscoll (Martin), Melissa Stribling (Sally Manderson), Anthony Bailey (Simon Carter), Hedger Wallace (Colonel Tomson), Jennie Goossens (Mrs. Pelbright)

PRE-TITLE

Purdey tours Paris and having visited the Basilique du Sacré-Cœur de Montmartre, she descends the steps to the Rue du Cardinal Dubois and has her paper cameo cut by a French street artist. However, she is under surveillance by a Soviet agent. Back at their hotel room, she meets with Steed, who reveals the hidden message beneath her cameo and reports the information over the phone with a scrambled line. They then place a mannequin of Steed in the window and leave in disguise as a French priest and nun before discarding their cassock and habit almost immediately. Later, in a German forest, they await an articulated lorry at the East German border, and when it arrives, it heads straight for the gate at full speed.

SYNOPSIS

Senior civil servants are dropping dead suddenly of apparent natural causes, but after one agent speaks of visiting a health farm, Steed decides to take his place, and it becomes clear that someone is torturing and conditioning the men by rather sophisticated means…

REVIEW

This episode seems to be a mashup between "The Wringer" and "Target!" The civil servants within the Ministry are dropping dead of natural causes in prominent numbers. It turns out that all of them visited a certain health farm prior to their demise. Inside the facility, having been injected with mind-numbing drugs and plied with orange juice laced with copious amounts of salt, the residents of the health farm are tormented with bizarre outings on a disco set the size of a closet, draped in sparkling Christmas tinsel, with the party music from "The Midas Touch" on a perpetual loop. It does indeed sound like hell. Having undergone their required torture by disco, the men are triggered into death with a pre-determined pattern after having been conditioned while drugged. Not altogether unlike a weekend at Studio 54!

This is not a bad plot and not without its share of tension. Fortunately, in opposition to the previous week's outing, it is not short on humor and wit, which re-surfaces in abundance. Speaking of which, there is an unusual scene for the series—Gambit and Purdey at computers, punching away at the keys to retrieve information, cross-referencing it to determine the traitor. It's peppered with more wit than you were likely to hear in any seventies computer room. And did they actually do the trash compactor scene from *Star Wars* before *Star Wars* did? (sort of.)

This hour of entertainment produces reasonably enjoyable material, and so far, there are no signs of the show's inevitable decline. We do however have our first mention of being in France.

CHAMPAGNE, CARS, CLOTHES, AND CANINES

Purdey wears a pink-and-white short-sleeved shirt with yellow trim and a pale-yellow split skirt with a pink handkerchief. The skirt is pleated in front and she wears it with a thin tan belt. She and Steed then disguise themselves as a French nun and French priest respectively, he with the wide-brimmed black priest's hat and she with a nun's white cornette. Later, she dons a flowing white dress with a pattern of pink lip kisses. (Underneath the removeable skirt are matching shorts, which we'll see later this season.) She then wears a white dress with a pleated skirt with matching scarf, with an unbuttoned cerulean-blue suit shirt over it. Steed next debuts a brand-new slate-gray three-piece single-breasted suit with a white shirt and a dark-brown tie with white diamond pattern. Gambit's next outfit debut is a rusty brown corduroy jacket (or possibly soft suede. It's hard to tell in standard definition.) with a straight collar over a white checked shirt (probably the same one as "Dead Men Are Dangerous") with brown trousers. At the same time, Purdey debuts a sky-blue ankle-length short-sleeved dress gathered and tied at the waist with a cloth cord. She wears it with a matching tied ribbon choker.

But that's not all, they each have two more new outfits. Gambit debuts a zippered dark-navy velour jacket and matching flared trousers with a blue-and-pink vertically-striped shirt. Purdey wears a black knee-length dress with a hot-pink cardigan, matching scarf, leggings, and red shoes. Steed also wears a khaki-green jacket (it comes across as taupe in natural light) with his yellow waistcoat, a white shirt, cream trousers, and a wide green tie. It's an outfit that could have only worked in the 1970s or 1980s, and it never quite works for me. He does wear it, however, with a black bowler that fortunately saves him from a shotgun blast to the chest. Gambit also wears his gray worsted wool suit with a pinstriped white shirt and a very wide maroon tie and a bright-red handkerchief in the breast pocket. Steed also wears his brown suit with the dark-green waistcoat, a white shirt, and a brown tie. I cannot fathom why they're bringing the worst suits back from Season One. Thankfully, the dark-navy three-piece comes back as well with a pale-blue shirt, a gray-blue tie, and a red carnation.

Steed's Jaguar is again the only Avengers car of the episode, but he is briefly forced to 'drive,' and subsequently crash, a red 1973 Morris 2200 Mk 3 (UPA 214M) when Manderson succumbs to the pattern born by a green 1977 Mini 1000 Mk 4, driven by Caroline Munro (as Tammy). His Range Rover also appears in a brief flashback sequence with clips from "Dirtier by the Dozen" and "Target!" The lorry from the pre-title is a Leyland Marathon.

QUOTES

"Gambit, I didn't know you read mathematics!" "I haven't. I do the football pools."
"I'm Jane." "I've got a terrible feeling I should say 'me Tarzan' but I don't think this is the moment."
"Switch it off! Gambit, switch it off, or I'll be playing for the Harlem Globetrotters!"
"Nicest hallucination I've ever had."

16 (2.4.3) MEDIUM RARE

Written by Dennis Spooner
Directed by Ray Austin

GUEST CAST

Jon Finch (Wallace), Mervyn Johns (Elderly Man), Jeremy Wilkin (Richards), Sue Holderness (Victoria Stanton), Neil Hallett (Roberts), Maurice O'Connell (McBain), Diana Churchill (Dowager Lady), Celia Foxe (Model Girl), Steve Ubels (Young Man At Séance), Allen Weston (Mason)

PRE-TITLE

Steed visits Ministry paymaster Mason and offers him a drink, but Mason turns him down expecting a potential informant. After Steed leaves, the informant arrives, receives his payment and then leaves. Elsewhere, he reveals that he was wearing a disguise by removing a fake beard. The next informant, a woman, comes in and receives an even larger payment; however, Mason, quickly intuits that it's the same man in yet another disguise. He takes a gun and follows him. Confronting the disguised informant on an overpass, they fight and Mason is knocked over the edge to the ground beneath.

SYNOPSIS

The paymaster to Ministry informants is Mason. However, after he is found dead, it is revealed that the informants are in fact all the same man, Wallace, in various disguises. Wallace, his cover blown, then decides that the best way to escape his quandary is to frame Steed, and he manages to run rings around Steed and company, that is, until a woman unexpectedly discovers she has prescient abilities...

REVIEW

This is another Dennis Spooner script, a long-time writer for *The Avengers,* who in this incarnation seems to have decided that the proforma of the show is hard-boiled spy drama mixed with goofiness and situations of high-improbability. This probably shouldn't be a surprise given his single seventh season effort, the ridiculous but outrageously funny "Look – (stop me if you've heard this one) But There Were These Two Fellers..."

The goofiness and high-improbability come in the form of psychic medium Victoria Stanton. It may come as a surprise to more casual viewers of the program that this is actually the fourth time that *The Avengers* had dealt with psychic powers or mind control in some form or other. The first occasion was in the first season episode "Tunnel of Fear," in which a master hypnotist uses his abilities to force innocent men to commit robberies. The second was "Warlock," a second season episode from the Cathy Gale era, in which a sorcerer possesses the power of mind control; the third was the fourth season episode "Too Many Christmas Trees," whose cadre of psychics demonstrated similar abilities. Despite the possibility that many will perceive psychic abilities as being outside the province of a spy show, those were all successful episodes, so it was not necessarily a bad idea to give the subject one more go. In one scene, the villains even reference a print of the same black and white portrait of Patrick Macnee that was used by the psychics in "Too Many Christmas Trees." This sort of for-the-fans nostalgia is no excuse, however, for the terrible pun title.

Worse still, is the egregiously bad explanation for Stanton's clairvoyance—the pipes in her apartment are conducting voices from the villains' office for her to hear. We're expected to believe that she's so stupid that she cannot distinguish between voices in her head and voices in the real world—that she cannot distinguish between a conversation by earthly individuals and that of spiritual informants? Thus, not only is her psychic IQ ridiculously low but her regular IQ is as well. Was the apartment empty before the criminals moved in? Did she never hear voices from above when the prior neighbors were there? Sadly, this sting-in-the-tail to the story's credibility, right at the end, dilutes it by at least fifty percent. As I noted earlier, the show had delved into psychic powers before, so there was no need for a mundane explanation. An otherwise respectable spy story is thus ruined.

Nevertheless, the most confusing part of this episode is the marginalization of Purdey. She now hangs around Steed's house playing his piano and reading Arabic newspapers, or spends her afternoons wallpapering her apartment. Why?

CHAMPAGNE, CARS, CLOTHES, AND CANINES

Purdey debuts a rusty-brown and beige checked minidress with a brown sleeveless cardigan. The dress is tied at the waist with a cloth belt. Then, she wears a complete 'New Wave' outfit in cream, with blouse, sleeveless jacket, pleated trousers, and shoes, with a checked brown-and-cream tie. It's very David Bowie, Thin White Duke era. For her next debut she wears a white collarless shirt with the sleeves rolled up and blue overalls. Then, a multi-layer white dress with cream knee-high boots and a multi-colored purple-and-pink patterned knit cardigan with a heavy white scarf; a high-collared black sleeveless ankle-length dress with a floral brooch in dark bronze or tarnished silver; and, finally, a beige corduroy vest, matching jodhpur riding trousers and an oversized jacket with a long white cravat that spreads out in front of the vest.

Meanwhile, Gambit debuts a new a charcoal-gray double-breasted suit with a pale-blue shirt and a blue-and-grey diagonally-striped tie. This is a solid outfit (Gareth Hunt looks good in double-breasted suits); the gray is so dark it almost appears black in some shots. Unfortunately, this is followed by a tragic number: an ugly white checked shirt with a chunky knitted gray-and-white cardigan, and dark-blue trousers with enormous flares. Very 1970s, dated before it came out. Next, is a structured beige jacket with a collar so big that Dumbo could use it to fly, and epaulettes, with a white pinstriped shirt and khaki-green trousers. This is followed by a zippered jacket in army-green, without epaulettes and a shiny fabric (possibly weather-proofed), a pale-blue shirt, and matching green velour trousers.

There are no clothing debuts for Steed in this episode. He wears his charcoal-gray three-piece suit with a white shirt and a brown tie with diamond pattern; this is followed by the navy-blue three-piece with a pale-blue shirt and a dark-plum tie; and still later, with his cream trousers, white shirt, and the yellow waistcoat while brushing down a horse.

Steed's Rover finally returns, but, fortunately, Steed can't drive it because of a flat tire. Gambit gives him a lift in his Jag. It is, however, stolen by Richards. And Purdey drives a bright-red Triumph TR7.

QUOTES

"I'd be very surprised if he did. Steed doesn't like the ballet." "Only ballerinas."
"As a matter of fact, I abhor guns. I don't even have a gun, except for an old Colt .45, and that's just for sentimental reasons."
"It's Steed." "Doesn't sound like him."

17 (2.7.4) THE LION AND THE UNICORN

Written by John Goldsmith
Directed by Ray Austin

GUEST CAST

Jean Claudio (Unicorn), Maurice Marsac (Leparge), Raymond Bussieres (Henri), Jacques Maury (Ritter), Raoul Delfosse (Marco), Gerald Sim (Minister), Henri Czarniak (Grima), Jean-Pierre Bernard (1st Bodyguard), Ludwig Gaum (2nd Bodyguard)

PRE-TITLE

Steed and Purdey use stethoscopes to listen at various doors in a hotel until Purdey accidentally knocks over an ashcan and they are forced to flee for cover as one hotel resident steps outside. The man follows and reaches them as they drive off in Steed's Rover, firing his pistol. More cars pour out of the garage in pursuit, and men on foot fire at them as well. Steed and Purdey flee along a curving country lane with three cars in pursuit until they reach a muddy quarry. They outmaneuver each of their pursuers one-by-one, one crashing into a small lake and the other running off a cliff.

SYNOPSIS

Steed, Gambit, and Purdey capture French counter-agent the Unicorn in Paris, but when a sniper attack on Steed backfires, killing the Unicorn, a desperate ploy engages to convince the enemy that the Unicorn still lives...

REVIEW

Elderly grizzled street venders? Check. Outdoor cafés with fringed umbrellas and wire back chairs? Check. Buckets of champagne? Check. Shots of the Eiffel Tower framing the characters' faces? Check. Yep, it must be Paris!

What starts out as a solid spy drama morphs into a silly French farce with the music set on Porno Funk Factor 10. The Unicorn lasts about ten minutes. (You know that the Unicorn is a corrupt one—a Frenchman who doesn't drink champagne!) He is quickly killed, leading us on a circuitous plot, which mightn't have been too bad if not for several incidents of farcical slapstick humor that fall flat. There is one ridiculous scene in which Purdey guides Gambit in his pursuit of an enemy agent, and somehow, we're to believe that she can see everything for blocks from the top of a mid-rise building. Gambit driving a trike truck in pursuit?—how very French!

Finally, all credibility built for the last forty-nine minutes is lost when Steed bumps Gambit's arm and sets off an explosion in the enemy agents' escape vehicle—while they're standing ten inches away. Unlike their car, they survive unscathed, their clothes in tatters and their faces cartoonishly covered in soot. They don't make bombs like they used to—nor *The Avengers*.

Purdey's retcon into a housewife role continues; in this episode, she brings home the groceries and cooks for the two men. Bad signs.

CHAMPAGNE, CARS, CLOTHES, AND... CAMERAS!

In the pre-title, Purdey debuts a new sky-blue knee-length dress with a laced bodice. Next, she wears a Kansai Yamamoto tunic in eye-wateringly loud colors of red, green, yellow, and red with the designer's name on the back. The built-in skirt is split on the sides. She wears the tunic with matching red scarf and leggings and yellow platform heels with yellow plastic sunglasses on a chain.[1] She carries a knit fabric handbag in a Southwestern American Native print. Later, she hides her hipster outfit under a cobalt-blue boiler suit.

Gambit debuts another zippered velour jacket very similar to the one he wore in "Angels of Death" except in a forest-green color. He wears it with matching trousers with enormous bell bottoms, a black belt and Cuban-heeled boots, and a pale-gray-and-blue striped shirt. Steed wears his brown suit jacket with cream trousers, a pale-blue shirt and brown tie with cream pattern for the bulk of the run time. Finally, in what could almost be considered a tag scene as they head to the Moulin Rouge, Purdey debuts a pink-and-purple print dress with ribbed shoulders, a matching purse with metallic silver strips, and a gigantic pink floral corsage on the right side of her head. Steed and Gambit wear their respective tuxedos, Gambit with a white bowtie so large that it could again enable Dumbo to fly. It was, after all, Paris, so we're required to have a little 1970s fashion flare, though as far as years go, 1977 was more of a table wine than a fine vintage.

The pre-title has the biggest workout the Rover has received so far (with several aerial shots by helicopter). Visually, it's not a very impressive vehicle, but it apparently handled well for the day. Gambit's Jaguar also returns. Purdey drives a bright-red Austin Mini while in Paris, and Gambit's trike truck is an orange-red Piaggio Ape.

Yes, plenty of champagne in a veritable shower from two bottles held by Steed and Gambit as a means of ambushing the Unicorn... and they actually drink some later.

And, finally, we get cameras galore! (And this is also where I curse the lack of high-definition video.) We have for certain a Yashica-D twin-lens reflex camera and a Hasselblad 500 C/M with probably the 80mm f/2.8 lens (the one that the assassin uses), and what looks like a Pentax 35mm SLR camera. The medium format cameras have flash bulb attachments. The rest gets fuzzy (literally), but they appear to be various 35mm SLR cameras and maybe one rangefinder. The Paris street photographer who is photographing a model during the car chase scene is using a very large format view camera which looks to be an 11x14, though he's shooting the model in landscape orientation, which seems a little off for his composition. He covers the model with his dark cloth when she loses her dress.

---

1 This ensemble presages the Memphis Group/MTV years of design with bold patterns and colors. Like most fashionable things in the mid-to-late 1970s, David Bowie did it before everyone else (as far back as 1971), so Purdey is actually a little late to hipsterville.

QUOTES

"Well, I've been pondering long and hard on the problem of how to swap a dead unicorn with a live and very important hostage."

18 (2.6.5) OBSESSION

Written by Brian Clemens
Directed by Ernest Day

GUEST CAST

Martin Shaw (Larry), Mark Kingston (General Canvey), Terence Longdon (Commander East), Lewis Collins (Kilner), Anthony Heaton (Morgan), Tommy Boyle (Wolach), Roy Purcell (Controller)

PRE-TITLE

In a flashback sequence set in 1970, as Purdey prepares to perform for the Royal Ballet in Swan Lake, she is visited by her lover, Larry Doomer, an Air Force officer. Elsewhere, in the middle east, an older man, Larry's father, drives a station wagon across the desert and towards a group of armed and uniformed men wearing traditional Arab keffiyeh. When his car is attacked, he reverses course and they fire at him, but he gets stuck with one tire off the edge of a short cliff and they push the car over and drag him out, largely unharmed. Cutting back to England, in a large open garden space, Purdey and Larry plan their new house and their future together. But, back in the middle east, his father is killed in a firing squad.

SYNOPSIS

In 1970, Purdey's boyfriend, Larry, attempted to kill a middle-eastern emissary after his own father was assassinated. Purdey stopped him, and their relationship dissolved. Seven years later, Larry is still intent on killing the emissary, while Steed and Purdey are assigned to provide protection for the man…

REVIEW

This is a more personal story, involving a romantic angle for one of the main cast. Not at all something that is like *The Avengers*, but at this point, I'm at least marginally thankful for anything that gives Purdey something to do. And her motorbike is back.

Ultimately, the plot is more hard-boiled spy drama that is again sullied by ill-considered decisions from writer Brian Clemens. Once more, Purdey is compromised by 'womanly emotions' that prevent her from thinking rationally. Regarding this, the dialogue at the end is embarrassing and even the actors seem to be uncomfortable speaking it. This is too bad because Steed's novel solution for dealing with the rocket is otherwise brilliant. Equally, Gambit's 'chicken run' with two of the villains is executed quite well. But these scenes only place more of the emphasis on the men, who must pick up the slack while Purdey is 'incapacitated' by her 'female failings.' She may be a secret agent but she's still limited by being female, so this story says. Yes, in the seventies, sexism was still alive and well and living in England! Why on Earth are they jumping the shark with her character?

At least some of the stock footage of RAF jet fighters in this episode comes from a documentary called "The Engineer in the RAF." I know this because a few frames of the on-screen title survive on one of the clips used. Sloppy. The footage otherwise greatly enhances the look of the episode.

Incidentally, I think I've discovered the most irritating sound in the world—the alert on the metal detector used in this episode! Imagine a blood-curdling scream combined with a spectacularly whiny baby, squalling at an impossible volume. Take this for a metaphorical statement on this episode's quality if you wish.

This hour of television is a mixed bag at best, a failed experiment at worst.

EPISODE NOTES

Martin Shaw and Lewis Collins were both just a short way away from starring in the new Fennell and Clemens ITV series *The Professionals*, and their characters' association here could be seen as something of a trial run. By the time this episode aired, the first few episodes of their first season together were already in the can. From the perspective of Fennell and Clemens (and indeed the observant viewer), *The New Avengers* had long ago morphed in the direction that *The Professionals* would formally take, and they likely wondered why they shouldn't just create a new series that had all the elements they were striving for, without all the baggage and expectations associated with *The Avengers* concept. How much of this played into the death of *The New Avengers* is uncertain, but retrospective viewing of its successor series shows how drab that concept would be when the class and panache were formally abandoned.

CHAMPAGNE, CARS, CLOTHES, AND CANINES

It makes sense that they would save a lot of new outfits for this episode since it's a Purdey-centered one. She debuts seven new ensembles, and they are: (in the flashback to 1970) a white ballerina's tutu and leotard for performing in Swan Lake; a cobalt-blue ankle-length dress which is buttoned up the front, with red boots and a choker necklace; a pale-blue nightdress with white frilled trim (also 1970); a brown rollneck jumper and brown checked overcoat (in a diagonal pattern) with a pale-yellow fur hat; a fuchsia dress with a ribbon-tied high collar and a matching cardigan; a cream-colored suit cinched at the waist with a faux belt in satin finish, with a light-brown-and-cream heavy scarf and matching purse (the strap of which matches the belt); and, a white shirt with lace collar and sheer sleeves, with a black waistcoat, black jodhpur trousers, and white cravat (the latter is the same as at the end of "Medium Rare"). Later on, she adds black leather gloves, black boots, and a jacket with a white motorcycle helmet.

Meanwhile, Gambit debuts a cream shirt with a matching ribbed cardigan, paired with a navy-blue cravat with white pinstripes, and brown trousers so flared he could sweep the floor with them. Steed's gray checked suit reappears, this time with a pale-blue silk shirt, a brown tie, and a black bowler hat and brolly. He also wears his blue-gray three-piece with a white shirt and a blue tie with white spots.

Steed's Range Rover appears again, and in his gray checked suit and black bowler, Steed drives everyone to the air base. Gambit's Range Rover also appears briefly. Purdey rides her Honda 125 motorcycle for the first time since "The Tale of the Big Why," and the color of the gas tank appears to have changed from red to orange. The station wagon that Larry's father drives in the pre-title is a red 1965 SAAB 95 Estate. The dispatcher that Doomer has hijacked rides a BSA B25 Starfire motorcycle (WD 22).

Plenty of champagne at Steed's party; everyone has a glass, including Larry Doomer.

QUOTES

"It was years ago—the first time I went over the wall. I picked up three bullets and a fractured thigh. Traumatic. I felt like jelly. As soon as I could walk, they made me go over it again. The best way to destroy a fear is to face it, you see."

"She's Purdey." "She's a woman." *(urgh!)*

19 (2.2.6) TRAP

Written by Brian Clemens
Directed by Ray Austin

GUEST CAST

Terry Wood (Soo Choy), Ferdy Mayne (Arcarti), Robert Rietty (Dom Carlos), Kristopher Kum (Tansing), Yasuko Nagazumi (Yasko), Stuart Damon (Marty Brine), Barry Lowe (Murford), Annegret Easterman (Miranda), Bruce Boa (Mahon), Larry Lamb (Williams), Maj-Britt (Girlfriend)

PRE-TITLE

Agent Williams drives into East Anglia and parks outside the country estate of Soo Choy. After hiking through a wood to the perimeter of the house, he begins surveilling the house with binoculars and listening to the interior with a shotgun microphone, but he is quickly fired upon and forced to flee. Pursued by armed men into the forest, he is shot while climbing to safety over a barbed-wire fence.

SYNOPSIS

After a failed drug drop with CIA agent Marty Brine, Asian villain Soo Choy tricks Steed, Gambit, and Purdey into attending their own executions at his mansion…

REVIEW

This must be one of the most prominent times that an Asian character in a major film or television production was played so blatantly by someone clearly not Asian. Terry Wood is exceptionally tall, fat and about as Western in appearance as imaginable. Yellowface may have been the only option available in the minds of the producers of the day, but the perception here is that they didn't even try to find someone that could pass, let alone convince. The end effect is so abstract as to seem like ***Our Town*** with its imaginary props and furniture, an acting confidence trick with Wood being totally dependent on emboldened sleight-of-hand to sell the character. This is deeply undercut by his youthful lack of experience and gravitas; he was only twenty-nine. The Miles Davis vocal rasp doesn't help in particular, and he at best produces a down-market James Bond villain. At worst, he has all the authenticity of a Chinese takeaway in a small town.

What is good is a scene involving a plane depressurization and crash; one man gets sucked out the open door—again, very Bond. The reference to Purdey possibly being bionic is amusing. (***The Bionic Woman*** would have been a huge hit in the UK around this time, peaking at No. 1 in the ratings.) The struggles of the main characters outside their would-be captor's estate are engaging enough, with the added impairment of Steed's broken arm. But why waste Ray Austin on this drivel?—whose flattering artistically-backlit shots sell the surrounding forest as much as the photogenic faces of the main cast.

Increasingly, it becomes difficult to find something to say about the plots in this season. They run the gamut of spy drama, veering from international criminal syndicates, to drug dealers, to secret agent rivals, and are generic within the language of the genre. They are not incompetently told, nor poorly produced for the most part, and, strangely, they only seem to suffer when unusual or surreal elements are added, as if the traditional *Avengers* approach had become toxic to the series. The celebrated wit is either on or off for the week, without any chance of predicting when it will reemerge. The music continues to relentlessly throb with something akin to instrumental Funkadelic. This story isn't much different. I'm waiting to be truly impressed again, currently firmly convinced that this season of the series is jumping the shark on multiple levels.

CHAMPAGNE, CARS, CLOTHES, AND CANINES

Purdey wears a long-sleeved blouse in an intense blue with a rolled red scarf and gerbera brooch; then, a brown pleated knee-length skirt, matching boots and handbag, a cerulean-blue scarf, and a woolen checked overcoat in blue-and-white; and a black fitted jacket over a white blouse and black trousers. She and Gambit also wear tennis outfits: she in a long-sleeved white shirt with her name across the front, white shorts, red leggings, and white shoes; he in a white polo shirt, white shorts, and a white zippered warmup jacket with navy-blue collar and cuffs. On the plane, Gambit debuts another casual outfit—a brown leather jacket with an ice-blue shirt and gray patterned tie with tan trousers and a long white scarf (which he sacrifices to open the emergency hatch). Later, he adds a cream mackintosh. He also wears his brown checked suit. Steed gets to wear spring-green army fatigues and aviator sunglasses. He also wears his charcoal-gray three-piece suit with a pale-blue shirt, the navy-blue tie with white spots, and a black bowler and brolly.

Purdey's Triumph TR7 appears again, and she drives Marty Brine in it. Also, Gambit's Range Rover appears. Mostly, they fly... and crash rather unconvincingly. (Uncharred debris is spread around undamaged trees, and their worst injury is Steed's broken arm.) Williams drives a blue 1969 Land Rover 109" Series IIa (APB 286H).

QUOTES

"Do you find me boring?" "Not if I put my mind to it."
"She's not bionic, is she? Purdey—I mean she's just so perfect, I thought maybe someone had made her."
"My arm's broken." "Are you sure?" "It is *my* arm!"
"Wait, no, wait! I think you should know one thing." "What is that?" "I don't believe in capital punishment."

20 (2.1.7) HOSTAGE

Written by Brian Clemens
Directed by Sidney Hayers

GUEST CAST

William Franklyn (McKay), Simon Oates (Spelman), Michael Culver (Walters), Anna Palk (Suzy), Barry Stanton (Packer), Richard Ireson (Vernon), George Lane Cooper (Marvin)

PRE-TITLE

At Steed's house, dressed in white tie (Steed with his Military Cross) Steed and Gambit drink before leaving to visit with the ambassador. Once they leave, however, an intruder reveals himself and takes a gun from Steed's bureau desk. Later, at the Ministry, Gambit says farewell to Purdey who is planning to visit her mother, but when she leaves, she is followed by another car, and once at her flat, men ambush her as soon as she comes in.

SYNOPSIS

Everyone thinks that Purdey is spending the week with her mother. Only Steed knows she has really been kidnapped by ruthless criminals and is held for ransom, but the kidnappers have a bigger goal involving Ministry secrets. How far will Steed go to save Purdey? And who is the real traitor within the Ministry...?

REVIEW

And now we're doing an episode of *The Sweeney*. Is Steed a private investigator or a high-level secret agent with the entire Ministry at his disposal? Surely, he could have had a dozen men working on this case, but he shrugs them all off and goes it alone, driving around, dropping ransom money into rubbish bins in front of dingy row houses. No more Bentley, no more Land Rover, no more Jaguar. He's now lurking about in a little yellow hatchback, an apparent traitor. We have sunk so far on the classiness level!

Purdey is doing a great job of fighting off her kidnappers in her apartment—throwing them into pianos, at ballet balance beams, and through endless cascades of beaded curtains—until some big bald joker comes in out of the blue and casually chloroforms her. Ah—the old Tara King standby! Sometimes I wonder why they try anything else on a female secret agent in this series. And now, of course, she has to be rescued. Why did she bother to learn martial arts?

The plot is a fine one, allowing for the seemingly out-of-character moves for Steed, and it has a kind of gritty panache quite unlike that of *The Avengers,* or at least not seen since the very early days. Steed's apparent betrayal is a strong selling point, that we nevertheless know can't be real. Surely, he has an angle, we say quite rightly. Equally, the confrontation between Steed and Gambit seems inevitable from the moment the latter points out that they've never fought before. Unfortunately, this only makes Gambit's martial arts skills seem to decline even more this series—after being built up as unstoppable in the first season—and he goes down with a single blow to the gut.

Though the specific direction of this episode (and series) is a good ninety degrees off from where *The Avengers* was at its peak, this is, in the end, a rather taut hard-nosed spy thriller—with its car chases and squealing tires through suburban country lanes, its urban dinginess, its subterranean funhouse-based villains. The whole thing is enshrouded in urban concrete, just like the criminals. Just as you couldn't find London in *The Avengers,* being only a kind of empty alternate reality version, you can't escape it in *The New Avengers*. You're drenched in it.

For what it is, it's well-done, sometimes very well-done, but it isn't anything that wasn't being done elsewhere on television. *The Avengers* was always exceptional, standing a head taller than everything else in the sixties. *The New Avengers* at its best is just an average well-made seventies program. At its worst..."Emily"?

CHAMPAGNE, CARS, CLOTHES, AND CANINES

The episode opens with both Steed and Gambit wearing white tie formal attire with black coats and trousers, with white shirts and waistcoats. Steed looks to be wearing a crimson-and-purple sash along with the Military Cross, an award given to military officers (and, since 1993, to any rank in the armed forces) for distinguished acts of heroism, but the medal's ribbon isn't the right color; it's a red rather than the appropriate purple-and-white. Later, Gambit wears a pale-khaki-green shirt with a green tie, brown corduroy trousers, and a brown leather belt with gold rectangular buckle. Purdey wears an outfit resembling the wave-patterned jacket seen in "Medium Rare" but this time it's a complete matching outfit worn sometimes with the jacket and sometimes without. The neckline on the long tunic is plunging.

Steed wears a gray bowler which houses a secret compartment containing a pistol. The bowler is from Herbert Johnson & Sons according to the label. Steed also wears his dark-charcoal three-piece suit with a pale-lilac shirt and a navy tie with white spots, and then, later, the deep-green velvet tux, and then, the gray worsted suit with a black bowler, and, finally, the pale-gray three-piece with the gray bowler. Of course, George Lane Cooper (Marvin) is made up to look like Steed and doesn't even come close to capturing his elegance.

Steed's Rover 3500 and Jag, Purdey's Triumph TR7, and Gambit's Jag all return, the first three all in Steed's garage after Purdey is kidnapped. But it is the Rover's time to shine as it's what Steed drives throughout the bulk of the episode.

QUOTES

"I'm going to hang up." "Eh?" "I'm going to hang up and ring the alarm bells unless you can give me proof that she's alright. I'm going to give you three seconds… 1… 2…"

"Do you know you and I have never faced each other?" "You're too young to die, Gambit. Besides, I never fight fair."

"Then, you have to kill me. Once you start, you have to kill me."

"I did warn you. I never fight fair."

"They're probably already in the building. Their guns are trained on you, Spelman, skilled marksmen."

"Desert a lady in distress? My scoutmaster would turn in his grave!"

21 (2.8.8) K IS FOR KILL – Part One: The Tiger Awakes
22 (2.9.9) K IS FOR KILL – Part Two: Tiger by the Tail

Written by Brian Clemens
Directed by Yvon Marie Coulais

GUEST CAST (Part One)

Pierre Vernier (Colonel Martin), Maurice Marsac (General Gaspard), Charles Millot (Stanislav), Paul Emile Deiber (Toy), Christine Delaroche (Jeanine Leparge), Sacha Pitoeff (Kerov), Eric Desmaretz (Ivan), Sylvain Clement (Vassili), Krishna Clough (Soldier), Kenneth Watson (Salvation Army Major), Tony Then (Monk), Eric Allan (Penrose)
Uncredited: Diana Rigg (Mrs. Peel), Sue Lloyd (Mrs. Peel's voice)

GUEST CAST (Part Two)

Pierre Vernier (Colonel Martin), Maurice Marsac (General Gaspard), Charles Millot (Stanislav), Paul Emile Deiber (Toy), Christine Delaroche (Jeanine Leparge), Maxence Mailfort (Turkov), Alberto Simono (Minister), Jacques Monnet (Waiter), Frank Olivier (Minski), Guy Mairesse (Guard), Cyrille Besnard (Secretary)

PRE-TITLE

(Part 1)[2] At a Tibetan Buddhist temple in 1945, a Soviet lieutenant, Stanislav, interrogates one of the monks, rumored to be one-hundred-years-old. Twenty years later, in England, another Soviet

2 This sequence continues after the title sequence, still in 1965, and Steed races out to a phone box to call Mrs. Peel, confirming that this particular incident took place at the time of their association. This is not the end of Mrs. Peel, however, as he later calls her in the 'present day' to catch up.

soldier tracks across a graveyard to a small village, brandishing his machine gun. He enters the local Salvation Army building where a meeting is taking place and machine guns everyone to death, fleeing afterwards to a wall where he begins to tire and jumps off, expiring as soon as he hits the ground. **(Part 2)** Merely a recap of Part 1, with clips, narrated by Patrick Macnee, then lots of explosions, Gambit firing, and a freeze frame.

SYNOPSIS

With expectations of a new world order, decades in the future, the Soviets created a top-secret plan during the last hours of World War II. Conditions having now been met, the sleeper soldiers of the 'K plan' go to work and begin an assault on previously strategic targets in England and France. And their actions might trigger the next world war…

REVIEW

This is the next episode in a set that was shot in France in order to appease the French backers, part of a contract established in 1975 before production on ***The New Avengers*** began. This is presumably also why a French director was used. (For the record, Coulais appears to have dropped off the face of the planet after this was made. I can find no other entries for any films or programs made by this director.)[3] It subsequently transpired that the French backers were "all crooks and vagabonds" according to Brian Clemens. Not all promised monies were received, and this forced the producers to pick up Canadian money and temporarily move production to Canada. This would produce variable results, but that story is for another time.

I have to say that these two episodes expose a couple of facts about ***The New Avengers***: one, the characters and how they operate aren't exactly conducive to large-scale war activities; and two, the show isn't particularly functional as a two-parter. The main cast spend most of the first part hunkered inside, talking to largely a French guest cast and avoiding machine gun fire that periodically breaks out. Occasionally, they venture outside and have a fight with a strategically-placed, solitary soldier in the forest. This in effect blunts their skills, reducing them mostly to mere dialogue, which, frankly, isn't that interesting.

The second point is perhaps best illustrated by the sudden break in the action that forms part one's 'cliffhanger.' One gets the impression that they ended there for no other reason than it was fifty minutes into the footage. Considering the sparsity of substantive narrative in the first hour, it's surprising that they required two episodes at all. Usually, the show does a good job of setting up an hour's narrative with economy, the extra breathing room going to seeming waste in this example. Thus, the first part is setting up the story with a series of Russian attacks on various French and English landmarks, and it all too frequently merely consists of relentlessly rattling machine gun fire.

Otherwise, what we have is a reasonably good story, directed with reasonable skill by the French director Coulais. The on-location filming takes good advantage of its foreign setting without seeming too obviously a landmark tour of France. This is mitigated, however, by some slightly bizarre scenes, including Gambit running like mad to take out a Russian sniper in the trees. He sprints through the forest, giving the soldier ample opportunities to shoot him, and then at the last moment leaps at the tree, bouncing off it, thus flinging the sniper off his perch and to the ground. As Gambit himself says, it's foolish. More importantly, it's a contrivance designed to give the regular cast something to do other than listening to French generals. See point one above.

The second part returns to more familiar territory, taking place mostly in Paris, instead of a forest, giving Joanna Lumley a chance to demonstrate fluent French and to get caught once again by an enemy agent and become a liability in need of rescuing. Shark-jumping with Purdey continues. Is

---

3 Yvon Marie Coulais was born on 3 February 1932 in Parthenay, Deux-Sèvres, France. He died on 8 May 2024. His only other credit was as a producer on Les conquistadores in 1976.

she an agent or a proxy wife for Steed and Gambit? The latter, I suppose. After all, who else do they have to cry over Steed's fake-out death (stopped once again by an object he happened to be carrying in his pocket) with slightly cheesy overly sentimental dialogue? (see below)

Quite often, much is made of the fact that Emma Peel returns to the series in part one. However, her appearance is merely by way of clips from Diana Rigg's time on the sixties show, spiffed up with new dialogue overdubbed by actress (and Rigg soundalike) Sue Lloyd. The appearances are thus necessarily brief, and in the few seconds in which audio is heard while Rigg is on screen, the words clearly don't match her lips. Fennell and Clemens were very keen on persuading Rigg to return to the series but were sadly unsuccessful. Watching it, I find myself only thinking about what might have been, so if you're watching this episode to see Emma Peel, you might be mildly disappointed.

As for humor, there's not a lot. The elderly soldier trumpeter getting bumped off in mid-fanfare? (Miles Davis, he ain't. You'll thank the enemy agent, believe me.) Gambit's injured hands preventing a congratulatory handshake from a general, one that is replaced by French double-cheek air-kisses? The jokey champagne toast post-medal ceremony? Meh.

Ultimately, not bad, but in the end, just a slightly bland, slightly sad imitator of *The Avengers* as it was once known—not much to do with it really.

CHAMPAGNE, CARS, CLOTHES, AND CANINES

Purdey wears a very similar dress to the blue laced-up version last seen in "The Lion and the Unicorn" except in a bright-red. Continuing his trend towards more casual clothes, Gambit dons a beige waterproof jacket with an elastic waist and epaulettes on the shoulders. He wears it with a white checked shirt and brown trousers. Purdey changes to a brown corduroy vest and matching trousers. It's worn with a brown-and-white plaid shirt with a Peter Pan collar, similar to her plaid overcoat in "Trap." (Again, it was the 1970s and everyone wore fabrics that blended in with their couch. Great for camouflage when you've passed out after an all-night cocaine bender. No one will disturb you, because no one will see you.)

Gambit's next outfit has him drenched in grays and whites—a gray shirt and matching trousers with a white jacket, and black belt and boots, while Purdey switches to her white dress with red lips pattern. Later, at the nightclub, she wears a cool-blue bodysuit with a matching jacket and chunky necklace. This is followed by a long-sleeved white blouse, red shorts, and a long red scarf. Meanwhile, Gambit returns to more formalwear with a well-cut brown suit with a white shirt and an ice-blue tie, and Steed, presumably to give his broken arm a break (pardon the pun), ditches the three-piece suits temporarily and wears a charcoal blazer with a cream shirt, gold-and-navy patterned tie and beige trousers. Purdey goes back to her blue laced-up dress. And they all receive Soviet medals and champagne for their service. Otherwise, lots of drinking throughout.

As they're far from home for almost the entirety of the episode, only Steed's 1927 Bentley 3 Litre returns in this episode, but it's only in the 1965 sequence. Is it just me, or are there a lot of jeeps in general in 1970s television?

No dogs, but rabbits and guinea pigs in Tibet.

QUOTES

"I found the way to a man's stomach. It's not through his heart."

"Where were you—on the Somme? I asked the English battalion to cover my left flank. They never turned up." "Perhaps they got lost. Have you looked since?"

"Gambit, we wanted him alive." "Conflict of interest. I wanted *you* alive."

"He was good and honest and true…and he's still alive!"

"I'm a girl, and I will not let that fact go unnoticed."

23 (2.10.10) COMPLEX

Written by Dennis Spooner
Directed by Richard Gilbert

GUEST CAST

Cec Linder (Baker), Harvey Atkin (Talbot), Vlasta Vrana (Karavitch), Rudy Lipp (Koschev), Jan Rubes (Patlenko), Michael Ball (Cope), David Nichols (Greenwood), Suzette Couture (Miss Cummings), Gerald Crack (Berisford Holt)

PRE-TITLE

At the CN Tower in Toronto, agent Keith Greenwood, using telescopic camera equipment mounted on a rifle stock, takes a Polaroid photograph of what he believes is spy X41. At the airport, he observes with binoculars as his briefcase containing the photo is sent through the X-ray machine and heads out on a flight to the UK. Elsewhere, Soviet agents toast to their greatest agent, X41, remarking that he is due to receive a medal. They then receive a message from X41 that an intercept is required in England. In Kent, "the garden of England," Steed, Gambit, and Purdey await the arrival of the critical spy information by paratrooper, but as soon as the paratrooper lands, he is gunned down by a machine gun from the nearby woods and Purdey is grazed by a bullet.

SYNOPSIS

The Soviet Union's most talented spy, X41, is on the loose, according to a photograph acquired by the *Avengers*. This means a trip to Canada (that lasts four episodes) and a confrontation with a killer computer with a fresh appetite for agents...

REVIEW

The New Avengers relaunches with...a guy atop the CN Tower in Toronto with a Polaroid camera-gun. He takes a black and white Polaroid of enemy agent X41. Okay.

So, for the next four episodes, we're in Canada...as the opening placard boldly declares. The show had been on a hard pivot from its roots for this entire season, and, you could argue, from the final year of the original series. *The Avengers* at its peak was a stylized vision of spy work in England that didn't actually exist. Pulling back from that was probably a good idea—the series had peaked at a frenzied fantasy high and had actually been more grounded in seasons prior—but now we are so far away from what made the series wildly popular in the late 1960s that it's scarcely recognizable. We're not even in England anymore. I say this despite a conspicuous sign behind our main characters that announces "Welcome to Kent—the garden of England." Should we believe this? Nothing doing.

As an American, I can tell you that this is a strange experience, and it almost seems as though the *Avengers* have temporarily regained their surrealism merely by way of moving Steed to North America. Seeing him walking about in much more familiar terrain, in clothing that was already dated for the United Kingdom, let alone across the Atlantic, is quite the jolt. I'm half-expecting him to pop into a 7-Eleven for a slush puppie and a lottery scratcher!

Gambit is arrested twice and placed in Canadian jails, trying to convince the policemen that he's a secret agent. There's something not quite congruent here (secret agents don't tend to announce themselves), but it does give the goofy Talbot an opportunity to produce some of the episode's most humorous dialogue, and Gambit the chance to demonstrate some ill-mannered impatience.

The design work for the computer is quite good. The multiple screens in the wall panel must have been expensive and potentially difficult to accomplish for the time, but I struggle to find much else to work with other than this is a fairly run-of-the-mill story, so forgive me if I send it up a bit.

As a megalomaniacal computer (what other kind is there?) enjoys eliminating agents (shades of "The House That Jack Built" and "Killer"), the music temporarily shifts from porno funk to Howard Shore-style musique concrète (Cronenberg era), for which I'm profoundly grateful, as it greatly enhances these scenes with real tension and suspense. One has to wonder though why the Canadian secret service would set up a computer with control of endless traps within their own office building—including elevator cars that have trap doors inside. And I could have done without the air-conditioning vent sucking Purdey's skirt off. It's a hilariously unnecessary Marilyn Monroe-in-reverse moment, one that manages to be neither sexy nor kinky. In revenge for her torn skirt, Purdey sets off the sprinkler system, drenching the computer which then declares, "AM UNDER ATTACK!"

It all ends with a crass impersonation of *The Avengers* high-style amid rain showers and showering sparks inside the building as the computer explodes, screaming "HELP!" on its printout screen. One shot is effectively cinematic as Purdey rapturously enjoys the drenching 'rain' in her sopping wet Jillie Murphy ensemble, framed by bursts of light from the computer's wall of monitors—something of a cross between *The Avengers*, MTV music videos, and an Irish Spring commercial.

EPISODE NOTES

In retrospect, having recently revisited the entirety of ***The Six Million Dollar Man*** and ***The Bionic Woman*** on Blu-ray, this episode has numerous points of reference with ***The Bionic Woman*** episode, "Doomsday is Tomorrow" Part 2, about a computer-controlled complex that Jaime Sommers must infiltrate in order to stop a doomsday clock from going off. In that episode—a real thrill ride with as much action as emotional tension—the computer is also destroyed by activating the sprinkler system. It aired on 26 January 1977, about six months before "Complex" was filmed, so I think it's fair to say that very likely a little bit of copying was going on.[4] Then again, to be even more fair, "Complex" borrows just as much from "The House That Jack Built" and "Killer" as from "Doomsday is Tomorrow." Nevertheless, that doesn't change the fact that the latter is one of the best ***Bionic Woman*** stories ever, and it's superior to this ***New Avengers*** quasi-copy.

CHAMPAGNE, CARS, CLOTHES, AND... CAMERAS!

Purdey debuts a new yellow crocheted minidress worn over a white blouse, with a red-and-white cloth belt and yellow purse. Next, she wears a hot-pink-and-white striped drawstring jacket, with matching jeans and black high heels, and initially with a giant white handbag and then a matching pink purse hung from her neck. Lastly, she debuts a red satin sleeveless dress with a ruched neckline and a scarf-like halter-top tied around her neck. But the real scene stealer is again the Jillie Murphy lips print dress, in which she loses the skirt during her ordeal with X41. Gambit debuts a new blue three-piece single-breasted suit, and then a blue blazer with a pale-blue shirt and a purply-gray tie, and finally, a completely new casual outfit—a brown velour zippered jacket with matching trousers and a pale-brown shirt. This last outfit is a culmination of several prior outfits in various colors, velour jacket, then velour trousers, now both apparently. Steed mostly wears his brown two-piece suit with a white shirt and a very wide brown tie, and his blue three-piece with a pale-blue shirt, navy-blue tie with white spots, and the black bowler and brolly.

The camera used on the CN Tower is apparently a Polaroid Pronto Instant Land Camera with the button on the left face and the "Pronto!" logo blacked out, and a specially modified telescopic lens setup. There were no such lenses made for Polaroid Land Cameras, so no word on precisely what this lens is, but my suspicion is that it was a non-working prop. The telescopic POV shots were, of course, accomplished with a mask over the filmed image.

---

4 After all, ***The Bionic Woman*** was one of the most popular shows on TV that year on both sides of the Atlantic.

For the remainder of the season, no regular Avengers cars appear in the series due to the Canadian filming locations. However, Gambit steals a gray 1977 Chevrolet Impala four-door sedan (MAK 344) to chase down the enemy agents in a blue 1974 Dodge Kary van from The Toronto Star. He crashes into the van in order to stop it. Throughout the bulk of the remainder of the episode, he drives a red 1976 Triumph TR7 'Victory Edition' (MHF 292) with white racing stripes. Apparently, when traveling abroad he has sophisticated tastes. Naturally, it's left-hand drive though. Steed drives a yellow Jaguar XJS (MHF 291), maybe because it reminds him of both his own Jag and his Rover 3500.

Steed and Purdey drink champagne in the computer office building.

QUOTES

"You didn't even have a steel cord in your watch!" "No, I wasn't very helpful. I do apologize." "I accept."
"You know, with that crazy hat and the flashy umbrella, what else could he be but an agent? You should all be like that. Makes my job easier."
"No wonder Talbot's our senior. It's marvelous how he recognizes these British agents. They all look alike to me."

24 (2.11.11) THE GLADIATORS

Written by Brian Clemens
Directed by Claude Fournier

GUEST CAST

Louis Zorich (Karl), Neil Vipond (Chuck Peters), Bill Starr (O'Hara), Peter Boretski (Tarnokoff), Yanci Bukovec (Barnoff), Jan Muzynski (Cresta), Michael Donaghue (Hartley), George Chuvalo (Huge Man), Dwayne McLean (Rogers), Patrick Sinclair (Ivan), Doug Lennox (Nada)

PRE-TITLE

In a pre-title very reminiscent of "The Superlative Seven," trainer and superspy, Karl Sminsky, reviews the fitness levels of his four new supermen, forcing them to duel one another to choose the best fighters for the mission—a fight to the death with only two of them surviving.

SYNOPSIS

Soviet trainer and master spy Karl has an army of gladiators at his disposal, gladiators who have physics-defying skills. They've been unleashed in Canada where the *Avengers* are currently enjoying a soon-to-be interrupted holiday...

REVIEW

Again, we're "Somewhere in Canada," where the *Avengers* are resisting mightily their return flight to the United Kingdom and are now officially on holiday. This episode is an odd variation on "The Superlative Seven"—without any of the fun. It doesn't help that these warriors have physics-defying superpowers, including the ability to deflect bullets (from an automatic rifle!)[5] and slash people with their bare hands. Heck, even the *Six Million Dollar Man* couldn't do that.

Come to think of it, this Canadian segment of the season has a surprisingly similar feel to those bionic shows, and perhaps to Kenneth Johnson-Harve Bennett productions in general. There's that

5 It's a famous stage trick to catch a bullet in your teeth, but this is taking it too far.

barely-on-the-lower-edge-of-professional television quality so apparent in such programs, further cementing the notion that *The New Avengers* had fallen from a very exceptionally high production quality (during *The Avengers* peak) to *here*—hovering somewhere just at or below average despite being touted as the most expensive program on television anywhere.

The acting isn't much better—a virtual parade of ugly men pretending to be the peak of physical perfection, despite being merely at the upper end of fit (sometimes). Even their victims voluntarily leap backwards when struck. The added Cybernaut 'swish' sound doesn't help either, merely seeming to contaminate those superior episodes.

In one distinctly American scene, Gambit steals a police car and chases after one of the super-warriors who has just killed a cop. In this series of Canadian episodes, he continues to play the roguish go-it-alone type, which is not necessarily a bad idea for the character. Another flash-forward to *The Professionals?*

A core problem with this story is that they've created such unstoppable (and physically impossible) enemies that it's hard to imagine how any of the *Avengers* team could come up against them and live, let alone defeat them. Nevertheless, when a confrontation does occur with some of the students, they easily prevail. Thankfully, our heroes are more challenged by the experts in the finale but not so much as you would expect for opponents that can punch through metal doors and deflect bullets. Their final defeat of the master is pathetically silly. Just give him two projectiles to deflect—one of them Steed's hat—and then KO him with a karate chop. Simple. And dull.

There's no wit, and the porno funk music comes back in spurts. "The Gladiators" is not exactly wretched, but it does restart the downward spiral the show was on before the previous two stories. The most important factor however is that the series once again isn't even a vague facsimile of *The Avengers*—Cybernauts chop sound notwithstanding.

CHAMPAGNE, CARS, CLOTHES, AND CANINES

Purdey debuts a frost-green dress with cream-colored, high-heeled sandals and a green choker necklace; then, she wears a red dress with paler red dots with a round ruched collar; and, finally, a symphony in cream—cream high-waisted trousers, cream blouse with Peter Pan collar, a long baggy cream sleeveless knit cardigan, and cream boots, with a cream-and-red plaid tie. With that much cream, you could drink coffee for a month! Meanwhile, Gambit debuts a beige checked two-piece suit with a cream shirt and beige tie; then, he wears the brown leather jacket (from "Trap") with a pale-brown checked shirt with brown corduroy trousers and brown boots. Steed wears his dark-blue blazer with cream trousers, a pale-blue shirt and a wide purple tie; then, his brown suit without the waistcoat. Sminsky wears suits too; otherwise, fashion wise, there's only a lot of tank tops and shirtless men. (There's always an upside.)

Gambit's (presumably rented) red Triumph TR7 returns and is used by him extensively as he continues to largely go it alone as the man in the field. He also steals police car #6418, a 1976 Plymouth Gran Fury (MKJ 634), briefly driving on the wrong side of the road by "force of habit." Steed drives the yellow Jag again.

QUOTES

"A skill that is the amalgam of everything that is best in karate, sumo, jujitsu, the very essence of the mystique of the martial arts of the East. But, nevertheless, a skill, not magic."

"The man perhaps—he looks as though he might be a worthy opponent for our students. But, not the girl, so slim, one blow might demolish her."

"What does Purdey do when Purdey gets annoyed?"

"How would it work with two projectiles? No, it doesn't work with two, does it!" "Oh well, back to the old drawing board."

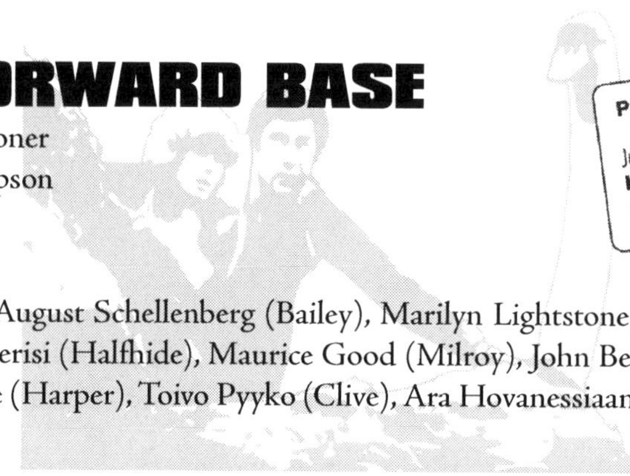

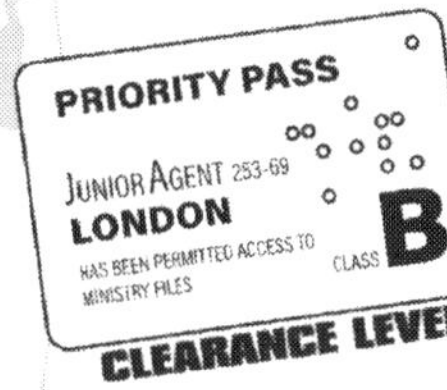

25 (2.12.12) FORWARD BASE

Written by Dennis Spooner
Directed by Don Thompson

GUEST CAST

Jack Creley (Hosking), August Schellenberg (Bailey), Marilyn Lightstone (Ranoff), Nick Nichols (Malachev), David Calderisi (Halfhide), Maurice Good (Milroy), John Bethune (Doctor), Antony Parr (Glover), Les Rubie (Harper), Toivo Pyyko (Clive), Ara Hovanessiaan (Czibor), Richard Moffat (Radio Operator)

PRE-TITLE

In a flashback sequence to Vladivostock, U.S.S.R., on 15 April 1969, the Forward Base commander, Malachev, is awakened by his assistant, Ranov, and informed that five ships have been sunk by a typhoon, the breakwater has been completely destroyed, emergency conditions are into effect up to twelve miles inland, and the army is on standby. Elsewhere, on Lake Ontario, Hosking, a fisherman, is caught up in an unexplained blast of wind and finds his fishing boat suddenly back on shore. Flash forward to Toronto in 1977, and Steed meets with fellow agent Bailey in an apparent shopping mall. Later, Steed, Gambit, and Purdey await the arrival of a plane on Lake Ontario, with Bailey hidden in the nearby brush. Another agent, Czibor, leaves the plane and walks into the woods where he is confronted by Bailey.

SYNOPSIS

Working with Canadian agent Bailey, the *Avengers* intercept a missile guidance system in Lake Ontario. While this provides them with the evidence needed that the Soviets have established a missile base somewhere in North America, finding the precise location proves more difficult…

REVIEW

In general, things are looking up with this episode, which recovers its humor in minor touches, the swan boat chase being one of them. Gambit and Purdey onboard, these swans putter along down the river with a curious poop-pop-pop-poop sound that cannot help but provoke grins. Not to be outdone, Steed goes 'fishing' with a children's magnetic fishing kit, and Purdey breaks the surface of Lake Ontario to visit an underwater base after donning her personalized wetsuit with *The New Avengers* lion logo and her name imprinted thereon.

The avoidance of obvious Canadian landmarks throughout this episode effectively displaces the story to potentially just about anywhere in the Northern hemisphere or other temperate zone.[6] This can only be considered a wise decision given the incongruous nature of seeing the *Avengers* on the streets of Toronto.

The downside is a certain empty rural feel that makes it seem as though the events take place in the middle of nowhere, with the Canadian admiral appearing only on radio to save the day at the end. The Forward Base itself appears to be a single spartan room, in which a Russian agent lazily sits

---

6 In actuality, this episode was mainly filmed on heavily wooded Ward's Island among the Toronto islands along the coast of Lake Ontario. The semi-famous swan-boat scene was filmed on and around the bridge between Ward's Island and Snake Island. Steed was certainly ahead of his time—magnet fishing is a very popular pastime these days, some even have YouTube channels devoted to treasure-hunting using this method, often bringing up safes full of fun things like jewelry and old watches.

listening to classical music while berating his assistant for interrupting him. Thankfully, they have a monitor upon which to project stock underwater film footage. Otherwise we wouldn't be convinced they were under a lake!

This episode manages to hammer together some rough approximation of *The Avengers* as we remember it, reflected through the inexact simulation presented in the first season of this show, filtered through a rather hodgepodge Canadian production team that was doing the filming this time around. Despite being a copy of a copy of a copy, the end result comes agonizingly close to being great—sold short by a clearly declining budget and the exile across the Atlantic.

CHAMPAGNE, CARS, CLOTHES, AND CANINES

Purdey debuts a multicolored Mondrian tracksuit similar in style to the Yamamoto ensemble from "The Lion and the Unicorn" with Memphis Group overtones—it's a mostly white jacket with red sleeves, blue collar and buttons, with matching hem and cuffs, and a green back, worn with red trousers and blue-and-white running shoes. Tragically hipster even in the 1970s, and yet passable for a breakdancer in the 1980s. Next, she tones it down a smidge with a cobalt-blue wetsuit with her name emblazoned across the back; underneath, she wears a navy-blue t-shirt with the "New Avengers" lion logo. With the zippered sleeves and the slim, tight fit, it harkens back to Mrs. Peel's Emmapeelers. Meanwhile, Gambit debuts another lumpy knit cardigan (similar to "Medium Rare") in gray-and-cream with a white shirt with pale-blue checks, and black trousers and black shoes. Steed mostly wears his dark-navy three-piece suit with a pale-blue shirt and navy-blue tie with white spots.

Steed drives a green-and-white Toyota Land Cruiser 4x4 (MMZ 300), while Purdey drives a yellow Toyota Corolla hatchback (LRM 022). There certainly are a lot of yellow hatchbacks in *The New Avengers*. Oh, and everyone gets to drive a swan!

QUOTES

"Fish? Fish are nesting in the trees?" "Of course!"
"Will you drive, or shall I?" "Well, it is a left-handed swan."
"Well, if a job like this can't be fun..."

26 (2.13.13) EMILY

Written by Dennis Spooner
Directed by Don Thompson

GUEST CAST

Jane Mallett (Miss Daly), Les Carlson (Douglas Collings), Richard Davidson (Phillips), Brian Petchey (Reddington), Peter Aykroyd (Mirschtia), Peter Torokvei (Kalenkov), Jack Duffy (Radio Operator), Ed McNamara (Chicken Farmer), Don LeGros (Mechanic), Sandy Crawley (1st Policeman), John Kerr (2nd Policeman), Pat Patterson (3rd Policeman), Bill Ballentine (4th Policeman)

PRE-TITLE

Opening once again in Toronto, Purdey breaks through a door at Puck's Circus, pursued by two men wearing suits. Fleeing through many of the rides at the inactive park, she climbs onto a nearby roof and escapes into the city proper, running through the streets with the men close behind. Finally, she escapes into the front yard of a house, locking the gate to the tall iron fence behind her and pounding on the front door. But the men catch up to her, and locked out, they pull out their pistols, threatening to fire through the fence.

SYNOPSIS

Steed, Gambit, and Purdey chase an agent known as 'The Fox,' and lose him, but not before he leaves a palm print on the roof of a car known as 'Emily.' This prompts a cross-country car chase to fiddle music...

REVIEW

The New Avengers remains in left-hand drive mode, and they get stuck in the mud, not being used to driving in the rugged Canadian landscape. This will make perfect sense to the viewer but clearly had no impact on the producers who instead decided to send the team on a cross-country car chase with little more plot than *Smokey and the Bandit*, accompanied by cornpone music and sawing fiddle. There is no explanation as to why they can't dust the handprint before leaving, necessitating that Steed's bowler hat be placed over it. It's as if by placing his hat in constant view, we'll be reassured that it's still *The Avengers*. Personally, I'm not buying it.

The show is *extremely* uncomfortable in this setting, and this discomfort is underscored by multiple out-of-character gags that leave the viewer just as uncomfortable. The car wash scene is one of the most predictable and least funny jokes in the series. (Purdey leaps on top of a car in order to protect a handprint on its hood and emerges on the other side completely washed and dried.) Gambit and Purdey drinking moonshine with the insane hillbilly and the fight that follows is even more embarrassing. The rest of the gags are similarly puerile.

Excepting Jane Mallett the guest cast is absolutely atrocious. I think most of them must have been pulled off the streets of Toronto. Never in my life have I heard so much wooden acting in a flat Canadian accent. The only thing keeping this episode from sinking into total oblivion is the main cast. Professional as always, they hang on desperately and manage to project a small measure of dignity into an otherwise absurd mess, despite the hard work by the rest of the production to sink the episode further into the mud.

This is likely how the show would have been under continued Canadian funding, and thus, far from feelings of regret at the show's end, I'm left with a deep relief that it ran out of gas. This episode is *The New Avengers* equivalent of "Homicide and Old Lace"—a sad pastiche stuck in a paradigm that operates at right angles to what the series was long about.

CHAMPAGNE, CARS, CLOTHES, AND CANINES

Purdey debuts a new Laura Ashley-style dress (albeit designed by Jillie Murphy) in blue, cyan, and rose; a flowing glamorous frock, gathered at the waist, with slight pleating in the skirt and a ruched neckline, it's worn with grey boots and a big red ribbon tied around her neck like she's someone's present. Later, she wears a disguise as a hotel housekeeper with a red maid's uniform with a white apron and floral headscarf; underneath is a brown plaid ankle-length skirt with a slightly baggy cream sweater and olive-brown scarf. The cheap gag of course being that later the skirt shrinks to mini length and the sweater becomes tight-fitting after she rides through the car wash. (I'm beginning to understand why Joanna Lumley became frustrated during filming of this episode and nearly left the production.) Steed wears his dark-blue blazer with beige trousers, a pale-blue shirt, and wide purple tie (as in "The Gladiators"), and later, he wears his charcoal three-piece with a pale-blue shirt and a navy-blue tie with white spots.

Prior to the arrival of Emily, Purdey's yellow Corolla hatchback and Steed's yellow Jag reappear for a drive through the streets of Toronto while communicating on their car phones. They chase one of the villains, who drives a dark-green 1977 Datson B210 (LYX 913), and Steed's Jag gets stuck.

Emily herself is a brown 1941 Plymouth Deluxe. All the Avengers ride in it throughout the final half of the episode (but it feels like at least the final two-thirds). Despite its many, many faults, this is an excellent car-spotting episode if you're into American models.

QUOTES

"You said 'Emily.'" "The name of the car is Emily, the lady who owns it is Miss Daly."
"Emily will be at her shining best." "Where is she now?" "In the car wash."
"The wax polishing is extra, Purdey, but, in appreciation, I'll do it for nothing."
"I like you so much, I'm going to fight you."

A BRIEF FASHION GUIDE

In this section, I'll give you the rundown on some of Patrick Macnee and Honor Blackman's most famous outfits. Unfortunately, this section would be ponderously lengthy if I tried to index every outfit worn by the main cast, especially since Diana Rigg, Linda Thorson, and Joanna Lumley changed outfits so often. However, Macnee and Blackman at least had some iconic outfits that they wore very regularly, which I will cover below. Details on other clothes worn by the main cast can be found in the respective *Champagne, Cars, Clothes, and Canines* sections.

JOHN STEED'S ICONIC SUIT INDEX

Take a tour inside Patrick Macnee's Regent Street tailors, Bailey and Weatherill, to see a few of his most iconic John Steed suits and ensembles and where they appear in ***The Avengers*** and ***The New Avengers***. Patrick Macnee wore so many great and iconic outfits as John Steed that it's impossible to list them all here, but, hopefully, this section will provide you with a satisfying number of samples.

DARK-GRAY THREE-PIECE SINGLE-BREASTED SUIT WITH LAPELED WAISTCOAT AND CLOTH-COVERED BUTTONS

One of Steed's most iconic suits, and it (or a similar suit) is worn throughout the entirety of ***The Avengers***. The original was worn throughout Seasons One through Three and it had a ticket pocket. Starting with Season Four, a new incarnation arrived with all the same features except for the ticket pocket, and from then on, a version of this suit was in every season, making it the all-time winner.
Featured in— (original suit with ticket pocket) "Toy Trap," "Kill the King," "Dead of Winter," "Mr. Teddy Bear," "Propellant 23," "Bullseye," "Death of a Great Dane," "The Sell-Out," "Death on the Rocks," "Immortal Clay," "School for Traitors," "The White Dwarf," "Man in the Mirror," "Conspiracy of Silence," "Six Hands Across a Table," "Killer Whale," "The Undertakers," "Man with Two Shadows," "The Nutshell," "Death of a Batman," "November 5," "The Gilded Cage," "The Grandeur That Was Rome," "The Golden Fleece," "The White Elephant," "The Little Wonders," "The Wringer," "Mandrake," "The Charmers," and "Lobster Quadrille."
(Without ticket pocket) "The Cybernauts," "Death at Bargain Prices," "Castle De'Ath," "The Murder Market," "Dial a Deadly Number," "Two's a Crowd," "Silent Dust," "The Danger Makers," "A Sense of History," "How to Succeed.... at Murder," "The Fear Merchants," "Escape in Time," "The Bird Who Knew Too Much," "The Living Dead," "Never, Never Say Die," "Something Nasty in the Nursery," the first title sequence for Season Seven, "Super Secret Cypher Snatch," "You'll Catch Your Death," "Look- (stop me if you've heard this one) But There Were These Two Fellers...," "The Interrogators," "Fog," "My Wildest Dream," "and "Pandora."

There was also a charcoal-colored version that appeared in "False Witness," "Killer," and "Wish You Were Here."

PRINCE OF WALES BLAZER WITH BLACK WAISTCOAT WITH SILVER BUTTONS

After the three-piece single-breasted gray suit with the lapeled waistcoat, this beautiful gray Prince of Wales blazer with its striking black waistcoat with bright silver buttons is the second most worn outfit throughout the black-and-white era of the show. An ensemble outfit, it could be mixed and matched, but it was usually worn with cream-colored tweed trousers, a white shirt, and a wide variety of ties. Like the gray suit, we don't know exactly when this outfit first appeared, but the earliest known sighting was in "The Springers."
Featured in— "The Springers," "Toy Trap," "Dead of Winter," "A Change of Bait," "Dragonsfield,"

"Mr. Teddy Bear," "The Decapod," "Bullseye," "The Mauritius Penny," "Death on the Rocks," "The Big Thinker," "Dead on Course," "Immortal Clay," "Warlock," "The Golden Eggs," "Six Hands Across a Table," "Killer Whale," "Brief for Murder," "The Undertakers," "The Nutshell," "Death of a Batman," "The Gilded Cage," "The Medicine Men," "The Golden Fleece," "Don't Look Behind You," "The White Elephant," "Mandrake," "Build a Better Mousetrap," "Esprit de Corps," "The Town of No Return," "The Master Minds," "The Murder Market," "A Surfeit of H2O," "Dial a Deadly Number," "Man-Eater of Surrey Green," "Too Many Christmas Trees," and "Quick-Quick Slow Death."

NAVY-BLUE (OR CHARCOAL) THREE-PIECE SINGLE-BREASTED SUIT WITH DOUBLE-BREASTED WAISTCOAT

Double-breasted waistcoats were a rare offering from John Steed. However, this suit is a standout that goes all the way back to Season One. Because the bulk of its appearances are only during the monochrome era, it's very difficult to determine the color of the suit, though it appears quite dark, so either navy-blue or a dark charcoal are both possibilities. It had a notch collar and four buttons on the waistcoat

Featured in— "One for the Mortuary," "Kill the King," "The Deadly Air," "Dragonsfield," "The Decapod," "Box of Tricks," "Warlock," "Man in the Mirror," "Conspiracy of Silence," "Six Hands Across a Table," and (a very dark charcoal version) in "Look – (Stop Me If You've Heard This One) But There Were These Two Fellers..."

NAVY-BLUE CHALK-STRIPED THREE-PIECE SINGLE-BREASTED SUIT

As iconic as this one is, it only lasted a relatively short time, starting with Season Three and not making the cut into the color era. Nevertheless, it was the standout piece from Seasons Three and Four. Often referred to as a "pin-striped" suit, it's actually chalk-striped, which is a wider, softer line as the name implies.

Featured in— "Brief for Murder," "The Undertakers," "Man with Two Shadows," "Death of a Batman," "November Five," "The Medicine Men," "The Grandeur That Was Rome," "The Golden Fleece," "The Wringer," "The Secrets Broker," "The Outside-In Man," "The Charmers," "Concerto," "Esprit De Corps," "Lobster Quadrille," "The Cybernauts," "Death at Bargain Prices," "The Murder Market," "Dial a Deadly Number," "Two's a Crowd," "Room Without a View," "Small Game for Big Hunters," "What the Butler Saw," and "A Sense of History."

BLACK JACKET WITH SILVER BUTTONS

One of the classiest clothing pieces from Macnee's casual collection. It went with practically everything casual and looked great in black-and-white.

Featured in— "School for Traitors," "The White Dwarf," "A Chorus of Frogs," "Death Of A Batman," "Second Sight," "The Grandeur That Was Rome," "Dressed To Kill," "The White Elephant," "The Outside-In Man," and "The Charmers."

BLACK THREE-PIECE SINGLE-BREASTED SUIT

Another Season Three suit, this one was almost as iconic as the navy-blue chalk-stripe.

Featured in— "November Five," "Second Sight," "The Medicine Men," "The Little Wonders," "The Wringer," "The Secrets Broker," "The Outside-In Man," "The Charmers," and "Lobster Quadrille."

BROWN SERGE THREE-PIECE SINGLE-BREASTED SUIT

Serge is a particularly interesting fabric weave that creates a beautiful pattern on black-and-white film. It's no wonder that they chose it for a major outfit during Season Four. Another version of this suit would appear in Season Seven.

Featured in— "The Gravediggers," "The Cybernauts," "The Master Minds," "A Surfeit of H2O," "Dial

a Deadly Number," "Maneater of Surrey Green," "Room Without a View," "The Girl from Auntie," "The Danger Makers," "The House That Jack Built," "How to Succeed .... at Murder," and " Honey for the Prince."
(Updated version) "Super Secret Cypher Snatch," "False Witness," "Look – (Stop Me If You've Heard This One) But There Were These Two Fell¬ers…," "Killer," "Love All," "My Wildest Dream," and "Pandora."

NAVY-BLUE THREE-PIECE SINGLE-BREASTED WOOL SUIT WITH A SUBTLE CHECK PATTERN

Although Patrick Macnee wore a navy-blue suit in almost every season, this suit, worn only in Seasons Five and Six, had a subtle check pattern that made it stand out. Its primary distinction comes from having been worn in the Seasons Five and Six title sequence and thus it appears in every color Diana Rigg episode.
Featured in— the Season Five title sequence, "Escape in Time," "The Correct Way to Kill," "Who's Who??? ," the Season Six title sequence, "Return of the Cybernauts," and "Death's Door."

BROWN-AND-GREEN TARTAN BLAZER

Another one of Macnee's favorite, worn extensively during Season Five. It's a single-breasted sports blazer with a brown-and-green tartan pattern and three bone buttons. The waistcoat is straight cut and has six buttons. Usually, the ensemble is worn with gray trousers.
Featured in— "From Venus with Love," "The Winged Avenger," "The Living Dead," "The Hidden Tiger," "Never, Never Say Die," "A Funny Thing Happened on the Way to the Station," "Something Nasty in the Nursery," "Death's Door," "The £50,000 Breakfast," "You Have Just Been Murdered," and "The Positive Negative Man."

TAUPE BLAZER AND GREEN WAISTCOAT

Another Season Five favorite and always classy, this blazer echoes the brown-and-green checked blazer, except the colors are separated into two pieces. The blazer is a taupe that can appear brown under certain lighting and the waistcoat is a deep forest-green with brass buttons. This ensemble is usually worn with beige or gray trousers.
Featured in— "The Fear Merchants," "Escape in Time," "The Hidden Tiger," "The Correct Way to Kill," "Never, Never Say Die," "Epic," and "The Superlative Seven."

LIGHT-GRAY THREE-PIECE SINGLE-BREASTED SUIT

A simple suit with no breast pocket but no less iconic due to its appearance in the title sequence to Season Seven.
Featured in— the Season Seven title sequence, "Game," "Super Secret Cypher Snatch," "The Rotters," "Killer," "Wish You Were Here," "Stay Tuned," "Homicide and Old Lace," "Pandora," "Who Was That Man I Saw You With?," and "Bizarre."

TAUPE THREE-PIECE SINGLE-BREASTED SUIT

Despite being worn only in a few episodes of Season Seven, this is one of my personal favorites. The suit fabric has some color while not being too bright or overpowering, and it had a dark felt collar.
Featured in— "Game," "They Keep Killing Steed," "The Rotters," "Love All," "Take Me to Your Leader," and "Requiem."

CATHY GALE'S LEATHER FIGHTING-SUIT EMPORIUM

Everyone knows that Cathy Gale's favorite clothing fabric was leather, and she wore a stunning and intimidating array of all-leather fighting suits, as well as coats, jackets, skirts, and trousers. Here are a few of the most iconic.

V-NECKED TUNIC WITH MATCHING TROUSERS AND KNEE-HIGH BOOTS

This suit was usually paired with a black rollneck jumper. The tunic is long-sleeved and zipped up the back. Debuting in "The Golden Eggs" this was Cathy's first leather fighting suit. It was designed by Audrey Liddle, the head of ABC's wardrobe department. It was actually a dark, muted green rather than black.

Featured in— "The Golden Eggs," "Conspiracy of Silence," "Six Hands Across a Table," "Killer Whale," "The Undertakers," "The Nutshell," "The Golden Fleece," and "Don't Look Behind You."

BOATNECK TUNIC DRESS WITH MATCHING SHORTS AND BOOTS

Designed by Frederick Starke, this dress echoed the earlier V-necked tunic but was cut like a tabard that ran down to the knees and was worn with matching shorts and calf boots. It was zipped up the back and usually worn with a rollneck jumper underneath.

Featured in— "November Five," "The Gilded Cage," "The Medicine Men," "The Secrets Broker," "Trojan Horse," and "The Charmers."

DOUBLE-FRONTED JACKET WITH STUD BUTTONS AND MATCHING TROUSERS

This suit was designed to cross over in the front and fasten with large leather-covered stud buttons on the right-hand side. It is somewhat reminiscent of a bellhop's uniform.

Featured in— "November Five," "Second Sight," "The Gilded Cage," "The Medicine Men," "The White Elephant," "Mandrake," "The Secrets Broker," "Trojan Horse," "The Outside-In Man," and "Esprit De Corps."

EDWARDIAN CHAUFFEUR-INSPIRED JACKET WITH MATCHING TROUSERS

Distinguished by its two columns of stud buttons on either side of the jacket, this fighting suit is again worn with knee-high leather boots and usually a black rollneck jumper. A favorite for Honor Blackman during Season Three.

Featured in— "The Medicine Men," "The Little Wonders," "Mandrake," "The Secrets Broker," and "The Outside-In Man."

BLACK LEATHER VEST WITH SILVER BUTTONS

Evoking the classic look of World War I pilot's uniforms, this iconic vest had eight large silver buttons, a chevroned waist, and a high collar. It could be paired with almost anything, from the roughest jumper to the frilliest blouse, and with tough trousers and knee-high leather boots.

Featured in— "The Undertakers," "Man with Two Shadows," "Death Of A Batman," "The Grandeur That Was Rome," "The Golden Fleece," and "Build a Better Mousetrap."

LEATHER KNEE-LENGTH OVERCOAT WITH BLACK-AND-WHITE FUR TRIM

This magnificent knee-length overcoat had black fur lining with white flecks and wide lapels. It looked amazingly warm and comfortable.

Featured in— "November Five," "Second Sight," "The Secrets Broker," and "The Outside-In Man."

APPENDICES

MAIN CAST BIOGRAPHIES

Ian Hendry, b. 13 January 1931 in Ipswich, Suffolk, England, UK, **d.** 24 December 1984 in London, England, UK

Hendry is probably best known today for films such as ***The Hill, Repulsion,*** and ***Get Carter,*** as well as the television series ***The Lotus Eaters.*** However, his career had started out in a very different way—in estate management for Bidwells. By 1953, he had changed his mind however and decided to attend the Central School of Speech and Drama–London, where he was a fellow student with future ***Lotus Eaters*** costar Wanda Ventham. By the second half of the decade, Hendry was steadily gaining work, with small roles in films like ***Up in the World, The Secret Place,*** and ***Room at the Top.*** He began the 1960s with the historical war film ***Sink the Bismarck!*** Though his part in that film was still not a sizable one, he soon after managed to secure the starring role of Dr. Geoffrey Brent in the Associated British Corporation series ***Police Surgeon.*** Though ultimately unsuccessful, this indirectly led to ***The Avengers*** co-lead role as Dr. David Keel the following year. Though his time in ***The Avengers*** was not as memorable for him as for his successors (as well as Patrick Macnee), it was the cusp of a career apex that would last throughout the 1960s. He immediately went on to several television productions—***Armchair Theatre***: "Afternoon of a Nymph," ***The Ginger Man,*** and ***A Suitable Case for Treatment***—followed by a string of relatively successful films: ***Live Now–Pay Later, Girl in the Headlines, Children of the Damned,*** and ***This Is My Street.*** From there, he would have a significant role in the MGM/Seven-Arts film ***The Hill*** with Sean Connery (on a break from playing James Bond), and it was this tough army prison drama that launched him into international fame. After the critical and commercial success of Roman Polanski's ***Repulsion,*** he would round out the 1960s with the Gerry Anderson film ***Doppelgänger*** (aka ***Journey to the Far Side of the Sun***) in 1969. This was followed by another internationally successful film in 1971—***Get Carter*** with Michael Caine—which would be his most prominent role in any film thus far. (He had been considered for the lead role of Carter but landed with the number two spot.) After ***Get Carter,*** he would start out 1972 with a regular part in ***The Lotus Eaters,*** a television series about expat Britons living on the island of Crete. This was another lead role that would supply significant visibility for the series' short run. Sadly, Hendry's fame would be dampened during the late 1960s and early 1970s by an alcohol addiction and a troubled domestic situation, punctuated by the death of his wife in 1972 at only the age of 38—a tragedy from which he was said to have never fully recovered. Nevertheless, in the mid-1970s, his career seemed to be still on track, though with somewhat less success than in the prior decade. Though films came less frequently, he would star in ***Captain Kronos: Vampire Hunt***er in 1974, and in the Michelangelo Antonioni film ***The Passenger*** with Jack Nicholson in 1975. During this time, he was also a guest star in many British television shows, including ***The Persuaders!, Dial M For Murder, Churchill's People, Thriller, Van Der Valk, Supernatural, The Sweeney, Crown Court, The Enigma Files, Bergerac, The Return of the Saint,*** and ***The Chinese Detective.*** In 1976, he would return to the ***Avengers*** franchise in ***The New Avengers*** episode "To Catch a Rat"—though ***not*** as Dr. Keel. The decade would end on a bittersweet note. He received a regular part in the ATV series ***For Maddie with Love*** in 1980. This show proved to be a substantial challenge for Hendry, and he found himself frequently at odds with the producers and struggling for stamina with the long hours. He returned to drinking and eventually passively quit the show by not showing up after being denied a two-week break. Work became more difficult to find after that, and his last three credits were ***Jemima Short Investigates*** in 1983, ***Brookside*** in 1984, and appropriately enough, an appearance on the

Patrick Macnee episode of *This Is Your Life* on 24 October 1984. He would pass away exactly two months later from a stomach hemorrhage at the age of 53.

Patrick Macnee, b. 6 February 1922 in Paddington, London, England, UK, **d.** 25 June 2015 in Rancho Mirage, California, USA
Starring in 185 episodes of the series, Macnee has remained indelibly associated with ***The Avengers*** for over fifty years, but he nevertheless managed an incredibly diverse career over that time with many other iconic roles to his credit. Born into a wealthy and eccentric family, Macnee studied at the prestigious Eton College. Shortly after graduating, he made his film debut as an extra in ***Pygmalion*** in 1938. He briefly studied at the Webber Douglas School of Singing and Dramatic Art in London on a scholarship before leaving to join a repertory theatre in Hertfordshire. This led to another repertory in Bradford, and then finally, to London's West End. However, just ahead of his West End stage debut, his budding career was interrupted by his service in the Royal Navy during World War II. He started as an ordinary seaman but quickly became a navigator on a motor torpedo boat in the Eighth Gunboat Flotilla, which patrolled the British Channel. Just before D-Day, in a bizarre stroke of luck, he was sidelined in hospital with bronchitis. While he recuperated, his boat and almost the entire crew were lost in action. He left the Navy in 1946 as a full lieutenant. After his naval service, Macnee resumed his acting career, performing in films like ***Scrooge*** (aka ***A Christmas Carol***) in 1951, in which he played the young Ebenezer. Macnee credits his time in Canada for his evolution as an actor and his subsequent success, claiming that "before then, I was a very bad, strictly upper-class English actor." Indeed, when Macnee arrived back in Britain in 1960 following a run of success in Canada, Sydney Newman remembered him from their mutual CBC days, and both Newman and producer Leonard White were keen to cast him in ***The Avengers***. Eight years later and Macnee was a household name and known internationally. It was perhaps only natural therefore that he ended up in America right after the series wrapped its final episode. Settling in California, Macnee acted in plays in Cyprus, Australia, and New Zealand, and appeared in one episode of ***The Virginian*** and the film ***Incense for the Damned*** with Peter Cushing in 1970. He then did ***Sleuth*** on Broadway in 1972, which enjoyed a sixteen-month run and was made into a feature film starring Laurence Olivier and Michael Caine. Afterwards, he moved back into television, primarily in America, building a steady career. During the 1970s, he starred in programs such as ***Night Gallery, Diana*** (where he was reunited with his ***Avengers*** costar Diana Rigg), ***Dial M for Murder, Columbo*** and the 1976 television film ***Sherlock Holmes in New York***, in which he played Dr. Watson. Next, it was two seasons of ***The New Avengers***, the Imperious Leader (and later Count Iblis) in the 1978 ***Battlestar Galactica*** film and subsequent television series, and then ***King Solomon's Treasures*** with David McCallum in 1979. The start of the 1980s brought two especially prominent roles: ***The Sea Wolves*** with Gregory Peck, Roger Moore, and David Niven, and then, ***The Howling*** in 1981, a film in which he received second billing. He then acted in London Weekend Television's mini-series ***Dick Turpin*** in 1981, ***Gavilan*** with Robert Urich in 1982-83, the TV film ***The Return of the Man from U.N.C.L.E.: The Fifteen Years Later Affair, Empire***, the cult film ***This is Spinal Tap*** (as Sir Eton-Hogg), ***Magnum P.I., Hart to Hart, The Love Boat***, and then finally Roger Moore's James Bond swansong ***A View to a Kill*** in 1985, in which he returned to a role involving espionage. The remainder of the decade was extraordinarily busy for Macnee and brought roles in ***Hotel, Lime Street, Alfred Hitchcock Presents, Murphy's Law, War of the Worlds*** (in 1989), ***Around the World in 80 Days*** with Pierce Brosnan, and ***Masque of the Red Death***. The 1990s were only slightly less busy and continued to produce a steady stream of roles on television, including ***The Ray Bradbury Theatre, The Gambler Returns: The Luck of the Draw, Sherlock Holmes and the Leading Lady*** (in which he returned to the role of Dr. Watson), ***P.S.I. Luv U, Sherlock Holmes: Incident at Victoria Falls, Super Force, Murder She Wrote, Coach, Thunder in Paradise, Kung Fu: The Legend Continues, Spy Game, NightMan***, and ***Nancherrow*** (where he was reunited with Joanna Lumley). He also lent his voice to the ill-received

The Avengers Warner Brothers film in 1998 with Ralph Fiennes as John Steed. He had only three credits in the early 2000s: ***Family Law***, an episode of ***Frasier***, and his final film role as Dr. Ballard in ***The Low Budget Time Machine***, after which he effectively retired, occasionally appearing as himself in interviews and retrospectives on his work, including ***The Avengers***.

Ingrid Hafner, b. 13 November 1936 in London, England, UK, **d.** 20 May 1994 in Berkshire, England, UK
Hafner was the only other cast member besides Ian Hendry to move from ***Police Surgeon*** to ***The Avengers***, playing his nurse once again. This time her character was named Carol Wilson, whereas previously she had played Amanda Gibbs. At the time of her casting in the show, she was fresh off a role in the film ***Bluebeard's Ten Honeymoons*** with George Sanders. She would go on to star in ***The Corridor People***, with another former ***Avengers*** actress, Elizabeth Shepherd. And, in the early 1970s, she would be reunited with Hendry in ***The Lotus Eaters***. In the 1980s, she would play Mary in the HTV West series ***Robin of Sherwood***.

Honor Blackman, b. 22 August 1925 in Plaistow, Essex, England, UK, **d.** 5 April 2020 at Lewes, Sussex, England, UK
While Blackman is clearly best known today for two roles, Cathy Gale in ***The Avengers*** and Pussy Galore in the 1964 James Bond film ***Goldfinger***, she has had a long and prestigious career spanning over seven decades. In cinema, her first role was a small uncredited part in ***Fame Is the Spur*** in 1947, but she quickly gained steam, and by 1950 had a much more substantial role in the classic British mystery film ***So Long at the Fair*** with Dirk Bogarde, Jean Simmons and André Morell. In 1958, she appeared in the Roy Baker-directed Titanic film, ***A Night to Remember***, and starred in the comedy ***The Square Peg*** a year later. While she was in ***The Avengers***, in 1964, she squeezed in another role as the goddess Hera in ***Jason and the Argonauts***, which is now considered the best in the cycle of Ray Harryhausen special effects films. After the success of ***The Avengers*** and ***Goldfinger***, she appeared in ***Life at the Top*** with Laurence Harvey, and soon after, she found another iconic role as Lady Julia Daggett in the 1968 western ***Shalako***, which reunited her with Bond star Sean Connery. The end of the decade brought ***The Virgin and the Gypsy***, and later the Dean Martin western-comedy ***Something Big*** in 1971. From here the film roles seemed to decline with movies like Hammer's ***To the Devil a Daughter*** and ***The Cat and the Canary***, but she maintained a strong presence on television from the 1960s to the 2000s, occasionally in America, with credits that include ***The Four Just Men, Danger Man, The Pursuers, The Saint, Ghost Squad, ITV Play of the Week, ABC Stage 67, Armchair Theatre, ITV Playhouse, ITV Sunday Night Theatre, Boney, Columbo, The Lives of Benjamin Franklin, Never the Twain, Lace, The First Olympics: Athens 1896, Minder, Doctor Who, The Upper Hand, Jack and the Beanstalk: The Real Story, Bridget Jones's Diary, Dr. Terrible's House of Horrible, The Royal, Coronation Street***, and ***Casualty***. Her latest credit is the 2015 comedy series ***You, Me & Them***. Honor has always embraced ***The Avengers*** fandom and, well into her nineties, regularly provided interviews in which she freely speaks about her time as both Mrs. Gale and Ms. Galore. She has a website that offers autographed portraits. Alas, Honor passed away in 2020.

Julie Stevens, b. 20 December 1936 in Prestwich, Lancashire, England, UK
Stevens is primarily known for her work in children's television, having appeared in ***Play School*** in 1965 and in ***Play Away*** with Brian Cant and other presenters. She provided the voice for the BBC primary school educational series ***Look and Read***. Her other television credits include ***Our House*** in 1962, ***Z Cars*** in 1963, ***Girls About Town*** in 1970-71, and ***Cabbages and Kings*** from 1972-74. She also starred in the 1964 film ***Carry on Cleo***.
Starred in 6 episodes: "The Decapod," "The Removal Men," "Box of Tricks," "School for Traitors," "Man in the Mirror," "A Chorus of Frogs"

Jon Rollason, b. Jon Roger Rollinson, 9 April 1931, in Birmingham, England, UK, **d.** 20 February 2016 in Llandudno, Wales, UK

Though a regular role continued to evade him, Rollason went on to a moderately successful career in television as a jobbing actor. After ***The Avengers***, he had guest roles in ***No Hiding Place, Swizzlewick, Danger Man, The Baron*** and ***Mogul***. He played a variety of characters in ***Z Cars***, and then returned for both sequel series ***Softy, Softly*** and ***Softly, Softly: Taskforce***. He had a recurring guest role in ***Coronation Street*** from 1963-1971. He also had roles in ***Barlow, Crossroads***, and ***Robin's Nest***. His most memorable guest role—other than ***The Avengers***—is that of the cowardly and obnoxious Harold Chorley in the recently recovered 1968 ***Doctor Who*** serial "The Web of Fear."

Starred in 3 episodes: "Mission to Montreal," "The Sell-Out," "Dead on Course"

Elizabeth Shepherd, b. 12 August 1936 in London, England, UK

Shepherd was originally hired to play Emma Peel in season four but was replaced by Diana Rigg after working on two episodes. Though Shepherd's work on ***The Avengers*** is not possible to view, she played a similar spy role in Granada Television's ***The Corridor People***. Her film credits include ***Blind Corner, The Tomb of Ligeia***, and ***Damien: Omen II***. In more recent years, she has worked mainly out of New York and taught for a time at the Stella Adler Studio of Acting. During the last thirty years, she has also starred in many Canadian-American films such as ***Amelia***.

Starred in 2 episodes: "The Town of No Return," "The Murder Market" (Shepherd's versions of these episodes are no longer extant)

Diana Rigg, b. 20 July 1938 in Doncaster, West Riding of Yorkshire, England, UK, **d.** 10 September 2020 in London, England, UK.

Diana Rigg had been a member of the Royal Shakespeare Company prior to becoming a television actress, making her professional debut with RADA in ***The Caucasian Chalk Circle*** in 1957. She also appeared in an episode of ***Armchair Theatre*** and the play ***King Lear***, both in 1964. She was only twenty-six when she joined the cast of ***The Avengers*** that same year but immediately made a splash with her nuanced portrayal of Mrs. Emma Peel. Since then, Rigg has accrued many noteworthy acting credits in an oeuvre spanning the past five decades and is easily one of the most notable and accomplished actors associated with ***The Avengers***. In the years immediately following the program, she starred in such films as ***A Midsummer Night's Dream, The Assassination Bureau***, and ***On Her Majesty's Secret Service*** (playing the only woman to marry James Bond). Though her film career never really took off, she has continued to entrance audiences on the stage for decades, performing in works as varied as ***Colette, Pygmalion, Night and Day, Macbeth, Who's Afraid of Virginia Woolf, Phaedra***, and ***My Fair Lady***, but it was her performance in an early 1990s revival of the ancient Greek play *Medea* by Euripides that enraptured audiences the most and won her considerable fanfare and a Tony award in 1994. That she was also made Dame in 1994's New Year's Honours, just after several runs of *Medea*, is likely no accident. Amidst her stellar stage career, she has remained no stranger to television, starring in such diverse television mini-series and films as ***Oresteia, Hedda Gabler, King Lear, Bleak House, The Worst Witch, Mrs. 'Arris Goes to Paris, The Fortunes and Misfortunes of Moll Flanders, Rebecca***, and ***Victoria and Albert***. She even tried her own hand in a self-titled American situation comedy, ***Diana***, in 1973-74, which guest-starred Patrick Macnee in one episode. Her latest television role is in *Victoria*, with Jenna Coleman as the titular queen. In the intervening years, she has seldom spoken of *The Avengers*, seemingly eschewing any involvement with its fandom. However, in 2015, in an interview at the British Film Institute, she finally spoke at length about her time as Emma Peel. Also, in recent years, she has joined the casts of other cult programs, such as *Game of Thrones*, and even had a fun villainous turn in *Doctor Who*'s "The Crimson Horror" with Matt Smith and her daughter Rachael Stirling (who has also become an actor of considerable merit). Sadly, Diana died from cancer in 2020.

Linda Thorson, b. Linda Robinson, 18 June 1947 in Toronto, Ontario, Canada
Thorson moved to England in 1965 and studied dance and voice. She was an apprentice at London's Royal Academy of Dramatic Arts when she accepted the role of Tara King in ***The Avengers,*** thus securing her first professional role. Though her stint in the series was short-lived, Thorson stayed in the UK and went on to star in several other British television series throughout the 1970s—***Thriller*** (which reunited her with Brian Clemens), ***BBC Play of the Month, The Howerd Confessions, Return of the Saint,*** and ***Oresteia,*** which reunited her with Diana Rigg. By the 1980s, she was guest-starring in a variety of American television programs, including ***The Two of Us, St. Elsewhere, Spenser: For Hire, Moonlighting, Marblehead Manor,*** and ***Dynasty.*** From 1989 to 1992, she had a regular role in the American soap opera ***One Life to Live.*** Shortly afterwards, she had a guest role as a Cardassian in ***Star Trek: The Next Generation.*** She continued to travel back and forth between her native Canada and the United States, building a television career in both countries throughout the 1990s, appearing in ***Street Legal, E.N.G., Kung Fu: The Legend Continues*** and ***F/X: The Series.*** In 1998, she took a regular role in the CBC series ***Emily of the New Moon*** and a main role in the American basketball series ***The Hoop Life.*** Films throughout the 1970s and 80s included ***Valentino, The Greek Tycoon, Curtains,*** the Tim Matheson film ***Blind Justice,*** and ***Sweet Liberty*** with Alan Alda in 1986. More recently, she starred in the Steven Seagal vehicle ***Half Past Dead,*** the martial arts film ***Max Havoc: Ring of Fire*** and the war movie ***Straight into Darkness.*** It was then that she returned to the United Kingdom and once again began appearing in British television series; she had a regular role in ***Emmerdale*** and a guest part in ***Doctors.*** Then, it was back to Canada where she appeared the following television series: ***Flashpoint; The Listener; Saving Hope; Rookie Blue;*** and ***Transporter: The Series.*** Her most recent work is in the 2016 British romance film, ***The Second Time Around.***

Patrick Newell, b. 27 March 1932 in Hadleigh, Suffolk, England, UK, **d.** 22 July 1988 in Essex, England, UK
Newell usually played overweight pompous types. He once described himself as "an actor with a weight problem—the more he diets, the less work he seems to get." He had minor film roles throughout the late 1950s and 60s, including ***Father Came Too!,*** and ***A Study in Terror.*** In the 1970s, he starred in ***The Magnificent Seven Deadly Sins, The Canterbury Tales,*** and ***Vampira.*** On television, he was in ***The Persuaders!, Danger Man,*** and ***Doctor Who***'s "The Android Invasion," playing the replacement for Brigadier Lethbridge-Stewart.

Gareth Hunt, b. Alan Leonard Hunt, 7 February 1943 in Battersea, London, England, UK, **d.** 14 March 2007 in Redhill, Surrey, England, UK
Aside from his role as Mike Gambit in ***The New Avengers,*** Hunt is likely best known for playing the footman Frederick Norton in ***Upstairs, Downstairs,*** and according to Clemens and Fennell, it was that series about the separation of the classes in Edwardian England that inspired them to hire Hunt in the first place. But, long before both series, he had been building a solid career in television. He appeared as Arak in ***Doctor Who***'s "Planet of the Spiders" (Jon Pertwee's swansong) in 1974 and in the television mini-series ***The Hanged Man.*** He also had guest parts in two other popular series, ***Softly, Softly: Taskforce*** and ***Space: 1999.*** And it was shortly afterwards that the ***Upstairs, Downstairs*** and ***New Avengers*** gigs appeared. He continued to work regularly thereafter in television, appearing in the comedy series ***That Beryl Marston...!, Sunday Night Thriller, Minder,*** and ***Hammer House of Mystery and Suspense.*** Other credits include ***Emu's Wide World, The Castle of Adventure, The New Adventures of Robin Hood, Animal Ark, Eastenders, Night & Day,*** and ***Doctors.*** Throughout the 1980s, he was a familiar face in television advertisements for Nescafé coffee. Though film roles were few, he appeared in the low budget Jack Palance film ***The Incredible Adventures of Marco Polo on His***

Journeys to the Ends of the Earth in 1998. Hunt died in 2007 from pancreatic cancer after a period of declining health and heart problems.

Joanna Lumley, OBE, FRGS, **b.** 1 May 1946 in Srinagar, Jammu and Kashmir, British India
Today, the charming Joanna Lumley is almost certainly best known for her role as Patsy Stone in the hit comedy series ***Absolutely Fabulous***; written by comedy legend Jennifer Saunders, the program ran sporadically throughout the 1990s and the early 2000s with five seasons and eight specials. Lumley won two BAFTA TV awards for her role in the program. To fans of British telefantasy, she is also known for her starring role in ***Sapphire and Steel***, a surrealistic fantasy about interdimensional agents who regulate the flow of time itself; the series ran on ITV in four short seasons from 1979-1982. Other television roles include a regular role in the short-lived (and now mostly missing) series ***It's Awfully Bad for Your Eyes, Darling***, and guest parts in ***Steptoe and Son***, ***Coronation Street***, ***Are You Being Served?***, ***The Cuckoo Waltz***, ***Mistral's Daughter***, ***Oxford Blues***, ***The Two Ronnies***, London Weekend Television's World War II mini-series ***A Perfect Hero***, and ***Lovejoy***. Until the 2017 casting of Jodie Whitaker as the 13th Doctor in ***Doctor Who***, Lumley was the only woman to have ever played the part, albeit in the non-canon charity comedy special ***The Curse of the Fatal Death*** in 1999. In 2000, she was in the pilot of the new Jennifer Saunders series ***Mirrorball***, which ended up not going forward because Saunders decided to revive ***Absolutely Fabulous*** instead. More recently, Lumley also starred in the acclaimed comedy-drama ***The Sensitive Skin*** from 2005-2007 and then in seasons one and two of another Jennifer Saunders comedy series ***Jam & Jerusalem*** in 2006-2007. She is also well-known for her series of travel documentaries, such as ***Joanna Lumley in the Land of the Northern Lights***, ***Joanna Lumley's Greek Odyssey***, ***Joanna Lumley's Trans-Siberian Adventure***, and ***Joanna Lumley's India***, work which has subsequently earned her a fellowship with the Royal Geographical Society. In cinema, Lumley has had several notable roles, including a brief appearance in the 1969 James Bond film ***On Her Majesty's Secret Service***, which also featured Diana Rigg, a small role in Amicus' 1971 film ***The House That Dripped Blood*** with fellow ***Avengers*** alumni Christopher Lee, Peter Cushing, Nyree Dawn Porter and Jon Pertwee, and much more sizable roles in Michael Pertwee's ***Don't Just Lie There, Say Something!*** and as Peter Cushing's granddaughter in Hammer's ***The Satanic Rites of Dracula***, both in 1973. Later, in the early 1980s, she participated in the ill-received post-Sellers ***Pink Panther*** follow-ups, ***Trail of the Pink Panther*** and ***Curse of the Pink Panther***. Notable film roles in the 1990s were ***Cold Comfort Farm*** and ***James and the Giant Peach***. In the 2000s, she appeared in the period drama ***The Cat's Meow*** and the fantasy film ***Ella Enchanted***, and she provided voice work for the Mike Johnson-Tim Burton animated film ***Corpse Bride***. Lumley's most recent films include the failed Terry Jones-penned ***Monty Python*** reunion ***Absolutely Anything***, the ***Absolutely Fabulous*** cinematic release ***Absolutely Fabulous: The Movie***, the romance film ***Me Before You***, and ***Paddington 2***. In 2018, she was the presenter for the BAFTAs, having received a BAFTA fellowship the prior year. Over forty years have passed since her time as one of the ***New Avengers***, and Joanna Lumley remains one of Britain's most recognizable and beloved stars.

THE MASTER MINDS

Sydney Newman, **b.** Sydney Cecil Nudelman 1 April 1917 in Toronto, Ontario, Canada, **d.** 30 October 1997 in Toronto, Ontario, Canada
Starting out as a commercial artist and cartoonist with the ambition of working for Disney, Newman took extensive testing for the Disney corporation and was approved for employment, but, sadly, couldn't obtain the work permit for entry into the United States. He subsequently became an apprentice filmmaker for the Canadian National Film Board. Eventually graduating to become a director, he was sent to New York to work on the staff of NBC, where he fell in love with television,

ultimately working in the News Department, the Drama Department, and the Light Entertainment Department, as well as on classic shows like the ***Milton Berle Show, Philco Playhouse,*** and for Sid Caesar. After working there for thirteen months, he returned to Canada and the National Film Board to find that they weren't interested in television at all. He then went to work for the CBC, where he was eventually promoted to Head of Drama. After the success of a drama called ***Flight into Danger,*** which was shown in the UK, the BBC bought 26 of his serials, and by 1957, he became well known enough in the UK to be hired by ABC Television to work on ***Armchair Theatre*** and later its spinoff, ***Armchair Mystery Theatre,*** an anthology mystery show.

This eventually led to the creation of ***Police Surgeon*** with Julian Bond, but this series quickly failed and was replaced by ***The Avengers,*** which Newman himself devised as Head of Drama. Though subsequently he would have little influence over the show once Leonard White took over as producer, Newman's fame steadily grew until he received a call from Kenneth Adams at BBC Television and was offered a new job as (again) Head of Drama, and though he still had eighteen months left on his contract with ABC, the BBC waited for him! Starting work at the BBC in December of 1962, one of the first shows he devised was ***Doctor Who.*** Later, he was given oversight for the establishment of BBC 2, and he brought his entire ***Armchair Theatre*** staff from ABC to work with him. Ultimately, he was responsible for over 700 shows per year at the BBC, including serials, one-off plays, and television series. He was then offered a job as Chief Producer at Elstree Studios, a decision he later regretted. He later returned to Canada and worked for the Canadian Radio and Television Commission. In 1977, he moved back to Toronto and took a part-time job as the Chief Creative Consultant for the Canadian Film Development Corporation (now called Telefilm Canada) before retiring permanently. He loved painting, sculpting, and driving cars in his spare time.

Leonard White, b. 5 November 1916 in Newhaven, UK, **d.** 2 January 2016 in Seaford, UK
White is primarily known for his work on ***Armchair Theatre,*** for which he produced many episodes during its run, and for his work as co-creator and producer of ***The Avengers,*** but he started out as a stage actor, later working in Signals for the British Army during World War II. After the war, he finished out his Army service by acting in the Army Bureau of Current Affairs. Afterwards, he became a full-time actor, appearing in Christopher Fry's ***A Sleep of Prisoners.*** In 1960, Sydney Newman invited him to join ABC Television as an associate producer, where he also worked on ***Police Surgeon,*** as well as many episodes of the anthology series ***Out of This World*** and ***ITV Playhouse.***

CO-CONSPIRATORS

The purpose for this section is multifold. Firstly, it is primarily intended to provide a reverse-lookup for the talent that worked on the program—writers, directors and actors. ***The Avengers*** was (and is) well-known for capturing some of the finest talent working in the United Kingdom at the time. Looking back, the breadth of talent on display is truly remarkable. Secondly, it is to show the extraordinary number of connections between ***The Avengers*** and countless other television programs and films throughout the British entertainment industry. You will indeed see many of the same television shows come up over and over again; sometimes, it seems as though the entirety of British cinema and television was one great repertory. I simply cannot tell you how many wonderful discoveries I have made by looking at the credits for an actor that I saw on ***The Avengers.*** And thirdly, it is to show how much these talented actors, writers and directors achieved before and after the show—including Academy awards!

The purpose, however, is not to provide a comprehensive biography for each of these talented professionals—one can easily find all that they need to know by scouring IMDB.com or Wikipedia. Thus, I will limit each mini-bio to just a few lines for the vast majority of cases.

THE GUEST ACTORS

Terence Alexander, b. 11 March 1923 in Islington, London, England, UK, **d.** 28 May 2009 in London, England, UK
Alexander starred in the early 1960s adventure series ***Garry Halliday***, but many years after ***The Avengers*** he was probably best known as Charlie Hungerford in the long-running detective series ***Bergerac***. He also had a major role in ***The Forsyte Saga*** and guest roles in ***The Champions*** and ***Doctor Who***.
Guest-starred in (4): "The Town of No Return," "The Correct Way to Kill," "Love All," "Angels of Death"

Patrick Allen, b. John Keith Patrick Allen in 17 March 1927 in Malawi (formerly Nyasaland), **d.** 28 July 2006 in London, England, UK
Born in Nyasaland (now Malawi), Allen featured in many ITV shows during the sixties, including ***The Baron, The Champions, Gideon's Way, The Saint,*** and ***UFO***. His later career was dominated by extensive voice work, and he frequently redubbed numerous actors, most of the time uncredited, including Leon Greene in ***The Devil Rides Out***. He also served as the narrator for ***Force 10 from Navarone***.
Guest-starred in (2): "Kill the King," "The Thirteenth Hole"

Ronald Allen, b. 16 December 1930 in Reading, Berkshire, England, UK, **d.** 18 June 1991 in London, England, UK
Prominent soap star, Ronald Allen starred for two decades as David Hunter in the soap ***Crossroads***. He also starred in ***Compact*** and ***United!*** but is known in America for his recurring part as the evil Uncle Quentin in ***The Comic Strip***'s various "Famous Five" parodies. He guest starred in other television series such as ***The Adventures of Robin Hood, Danger Man,*** and ***Bergerac***.
Guest-starred in (1): "The Secrets Broker"

Bernard Archard, b. 20 August 1916 in Fulham, London, England, UK, **d.** 1 May 2008 in Witham Friary, Somerset, England, UK
Archard's first major role on television was in ***Spycatcher***, which ran from 1959-1961. He was a frequent guest star in British television, including such series as ***Rumpole of the Bailey, Upstairs, Downstairs, Danger Man, Z Cars, Paul Temple, Dixon of Dock Green, The Professionals,*** and ***Emmerdale***. His sepulchral appearance was also put to good use in ***Doctor Who***'s "Pyramids of Mars." He starred in dozens of films, including ***Village of the Damned, The Horror of Frankenstein,*** Roman Polanski's ***Macbeth, Dad's Army, The Sea Wolves, Krull,*** and ***King Solomon's Mines***.
Guest-starred in (2): "The Master Minds," "Split!"

Graham Armitage, b. 24 April 1936 in Manchester, England, UK, **d.** 6 March 1999 in Johannesburg, South Africa
Armitage worked in small parts in B-movies as varied as ***Games Lovers Play*** and ***Kickboxer 5***. He also had small uncredited roles in ***The Spy Who Came in from the Cold, Battle of Britain, Scrooge,*** and ***The Gods Must Be Crazy***. On television, he appeared in ***The Naked Civil Servant*** with John Hurt in 1975.
Guest-starred in (2): "Quick-Quick Slow Death," "The Correct Way to Kill"

Peter Arne, b. 29 September 1918 in Kuala Lumpur, British Malaya, **d.** 1 August 1983 in Knightsbridge, London, England, UK
Arne played many small roles in several great films of the 1970s, including ***Khartoum***, ***Agatha***, and ***The Straw Dogs***. His last role was in ***The Far Pavilions***, which was transmitted after his death in 1983. Arne was murdered by an Italian immigrant and vagrant shortly before he was to begin filming the ***Doctor Who*** serial "Frontios."
Guest-starred in (4): "Death on the Slipway," "Warlock," "The Golden Eggs," "Room Without a View"

John Bailey, b. 26 June 1912 in New Cross, London, England UK, **d.** 18 February 1989 in London, England, UK
Bailey appeared in multiple episodes of ***Doctor Who***—playing the Commander in "The Sensorites," then Edward Waterfield, the father of future companion Victoria Waterfield, in "The Evil of the Daleks," and Sezom in "The Horns of Nimon." As for films, he played the lead in the 'second feature' film, ***The Night Won't Talk***, in 1952, and was the royal physician in Hammer's ***Rasputin the Mad Monk*** with Christopher Lee.
Guest-starred in (4): "A Change of Bait," "Killer Whale," "Dial a Deadly Number," "Killer"

Ronnie Barker, OBE, **b.** 25 September 1929 in Bedford, Bedfordshire, England, UK, **d.** 3 October 2005 in Adderbury, Oxfordshire, England, UK
Barker was clearly best known for ***The Two Ronnies*** with his namesake Ronnie Corbett, which ran on the BBC for twelve series over sixteen years, as well as ***Porridge*** and ***Open All Hours***. At the time of his sole appearance in ***The Avengers***, he would have frequently been seen playing a variety of characters on ***The Frost Report***. He won a BAFTA for best light entertainment performance four times.
Guest-starred in (1): "The Hidden Tiger"

Peter Barkworth, b. 14 January 1929 in Margate, Kent, England, UK, **d.** 21 October 2006 in Hampstead, London, England, UK
Barkworth would later star in the 1970 London Weekend Television war drama ***Manhunt*** and 1979's ***Telford's Change***. He would win two BAFTAs for Best Actor, one in 1975 for ***Crown Matrimonial*** and one in 1978 for his roles in ***Professional Foul*** and ***The Country Party***. He starred in such films as ***Where Eagles Dare***, ***Patton***, ***International Velvet***, and ***Champions***. On television, he is known to ***Doctor Who*** fans as Leader Clent in "The Ice Warriors," a serial that remains partly missing, as well as the fellow Associated British Corporation TV series, ***Public Eye***, and he appeared in the episode "Silver Blaze" as part of Granada Television's ***Sherlock Holmes*** mysteries.
Guest-starred in (4): "Kill the King," "The Medicine Men," "The Correct Way to Kill," "The Morning After"

Anthony Bate, b. 31 August 1927 in Stourbridge, Worcestershire, England, UK, **d.** 19 June 2012 in Newport, Isle of Wight, England, UK
Bate would later become famous for playing Oliver Lacon in the BBC's miniseries adaptations of the John le Carré novels ***Tinker, Tailor, Soldier, Spy***, and ***Smiley's People*** with Sir Alec Guinness. At the time of his first appearance in ***The Avengers***, he would have just completed his tiny roles in two Bob Monkhouse comedy films, ***Dentist in the Chair*** and ***Dentist on the Job***, the former of which was directed by future ***Avengers*** alumnus Don Chaffey. Much later, in 1984, he would appear in the Paul McCartney film ***Give My Regards to Broad Street***.
Guest-starred in (2): "Tunnel of Fear," "The Curious Case of the Countless Clues"

Geoffrey Bayldon, b. 7 January 1924 in Leeds, West Riding of Yorkshire, England, **d.** 10 May 2017 in Leeds, West Yorkshire, England, UK

Despite having had considerable stage experience working for the Royal Shakespeare Company, Bayldon is probably best known for three roles: the Crowman in ***Worzel Gummidge***, Magic Granddad in ***Watch***, and the beloved titular wizard in ***Catweazle***. He also appeared in many notable film roles, including ***King Rat***, ***To Sir, with Love***, the 1967 version of ***Casino Royale*** (as Q), ***The Pink Panther Strikes Again***, both ***Steptoe and Son*** movies, the Hammer films ***Dracula*** and ***Frankenstein Must Be Destroyed***, and the Amicus films ***The House That Dripped Blood***, ***Asylum***, and ***Tales from the Crypt***. His guest roles in television are simply too numerous to list, but he had a memorable turn in the ***Doctor Who*** story "The Creature from the Pit." He remains one of Britain's most loved and well-remembered stars.

Guest-starred in (2): "The Deadly Air," "Escape in Time"

Christopher Benjamin, b. 27 December 1934 in Trowbridge, Wiltshire, England, UK

Benjamin was a regular in ***Dick Turpin*** but was also a very familiar face on British television for decades in a variety of guest roles. He had three memorable turns in ***Doctor Who***: Sir Keith Gold in "Inferno" in 1970; Henry Gordon Jago in "The Talons of Weng-Chiang" in 1977; and Colonel Hugh in "The Unicorn and the Wasp" in 2008. He is also notable for playing a character named Potter in both ***Danger Man*** and ***The Prisoner***, though the latter was a mere fantasy told to school children by No. 6, and thus does not necessarily describe a connection between the two series. On film, he appeared in the 1974 remake of David Lean's ***Brief Encounter*** and the cult film ***Hawk the Slayer*** in 1980.

Guest-starred in (3): "How to Succeed....At Murder," "Never, Never Say Die," "Split!"

John Bennett, b. 8 May 1928 in Beckenham, Kent, England, UK, **d.** 11 April 2005 in London, England, UK

Bennett guest-starred in many dramas of the 1960s and 1970s: ***Danger Man***; ***Doctor Who*** "The Talons of Weng-Chiang"; ***Blake's 7***; and ***Survivors***. He also had a small regular part in ***The Forsyte Saga***, was the Stranger in both series of ***Mulberry***, and was one of the stars of Jimmy McGovern's controversial ***Priest***, but he will always be remembered by many as the voice of Holly in the animation classic, ***Watership Down***.

Guest-starred in (2): "Mission to Montreal," "False Witness"

Caroline Blakiston, b. 13 February 1933 in Chelsea, London, England, UK

Blakiston had many guest roles on television before starring as Sylvia in ***The Racing Game***. In 1983, she played Mon Mothma in ***Star Wars: Return of the Jedi***. She is also well-known for her role in ***Brass*** and her character of Marjorie Ferrar in ***The Forsyte Saga***.

Guest-starred in (3): "Dance with Death," "The Grave-Diggers," "The Positive Negative Man"

Joby Blanshard, b. 17 November 1919 in Beverley, East Riding of Yorkshire, England, UK, **d.** 26 November 1992 in Rotherfield, East Sussex, England, UK

Blanshard starred in thirty-two episodes of ***Doomwatch***.

Guest-starred in (1): "Man-Eater of Surrey Green"

Brian Blessed, OBE, **b.** 9 October 1936 in Mexborough, Yorkshire, England, UK

The booming voice of English actor Brian Blessed is well-known throughout the world probably because of his role as Prince Vultan in the camp classic science-fiction film ***Flash Gordon***; thus, he is fondly remembered for such lines as "Gordon's Alive?!" Nevertheless, Blessed is an actor, writer and presenter with a long list of credits in stage, television and film spanning decades, having paid his

dues mostly on stage and in television throughout the 1960s and 70s. His guest roles in television are extensive and include ***Z Cars, Till Death Us Do Part, Cold Comfort Farm, Randall and Hopkirk (Deceased), Jackanory, Space: 1999, The Sweeney, Blake's 7, Minder,*** and ***I, Claudius***. He also cites his role as Richard IV in ***Blackadder*** as one of his personal favorites. Aside from ***Flash Gordon***, in film, he is known for ***Henry V, Robin Hood: Prince of Thieves***, and ***Hamlet*** and ***King Lear*** (both in 1996). He also provided the voice for Boss Nass in ***Star Wars: The Phantom Menace***. In the field of voice work, Blessed is also known for lending his voice to a considerable number of video games. His stage work includes Baron Bomburst in the 2002 stage version of ***Chitty Chitty Bang Bang***. Aside from acting, he is an avid sportsman, having attempted to climb Mt. Everest without supplemental oxygen on three separate occasions. He is also a third Dan in Judo.
Guest-starred in (2): "The Superlative Seven," "The Morning After"

Bruce Boa, b. 10 July 1930 in Calgary, Alberta, Canada, **d.** 17 April 2004 in Surrey, England, UK
Boa's most recognizable roles can likely be reduced to three: General Rieekan in ***Star Wars: The Empire Strikes Back***; the Marine colonel in ***Full Metal Jacket***; and his obnoxious American tourist in the ***Fawlty Towers*** episode "Waldorf Salad." Nevertheless, he also appeared in many television series, in both the United Kingdom and the United States—***Out of the Unknown, The Champions, The Troubleshooters, The Saint, Ace of Wands, Special Branch, The Onedin Line, Z Cars, The Professionals, The Omega Factor, Remington Steele***, and ***Warship***—usually when a character with an American accent was required.
Guest-starred in (2): "Dead on Course," "Trap"

Philip Bond, b. 1 November 1934 in Burton-on-Trent, Staffordshire, England, UK, **d.** 17 January 2017 in Madeira
Bond was best known for his character of Albert Frazer in ***The Onedin Line***, but early in his career, he played one of the first Thals in the ***Doctor Who*** serial "The Daleks" in 1964. He is the father of actress Samantha Bond, who was Miss Moneypenny in the Pierce Brosnan James Bond films.
Guest-starred in (1): "The Interrogators"

Peter Bowles, b. 16 October 1936 in London, England, UK, **d.** 17 March 2022
Bowles has been a near constant presence on British television in a wide variety of guest roles, in such programs as ***Danger Man, The Saint, The Persuaders!***, and ***The Prisoner*** in the 1960s, usually in rather villainous roles. In the 1970s, he turned his hand to comedy and featured in a variety of comedy series well into the 1980s: ***Rising Damp; Only When I Laugh; The Bounder; Executive Stress***, and ***To the Manor Born***. For this writer, his most powerful role was as a psychopathic immortal being in the ***Space: 1999*** episode "End of Eternity."
Guest-starred in (4): "Second Sight," "Dial a Deadly Number," "Escape in Time," "Get-A-Way!"

Keith Buckley, b. 7 April 1941 in Huddersfield, West Riding of Yorkshire, England, UK, **d.** 1 December 2020
Buckley played small roles in several British films such as ***The Eagle Has Landed, The Spy Who Loved Me, Excalibur***, and Roman Polanski's ***Tess***.
Guest-starred in (2): "Take-Over," "Sleeper"

Alfred Burke, b. 28 February 1918 in Peckham, London, England, UK, **d.** 16 February 2011 in Barnes, London, England, UK
Though Burke was mainly a film actor during the 1950s, 60s, and 70s, he was best known for his role in the drama television series ***Public Eye***. His film credits include ***The Angry Silence, Touch and Go, Interpol, Yangtse Incident, Buccaneers, Children of the Damned***, and the Hammer film ***The Nanny***.

His last film role was Professor Armando Dippet in ***Harry Potter and the Chamber of Secrets***. He was also seen on television in ***Armchair Theatre, The Saint, Randall and Hopkirk (Deceased)***, and ***Minder***.
Guest-starred in (3): "Dragonsfield," "The Mauritius Penny," "The Girl from Auntie"

Patrick Cargill, b. 3 June 1918 in Bexhill-on-Sea, Sussex, England, UK, **d.** 23 May 1996 in Richmond, London, England, UK
Cargill was the star of London Weekend Television's sitcom ***Father, Dear Father***. He was also memorable as the No. 2 that No. 6 made cry in the "Hammer into Anvil" episode of ***The Prisoner***.
Guest-starred in (2): "The Murder Market," "The Fear Merchants"

John Carson, b. 28 February 1927 in Colombo, Ceylon (now Sri Lanka), **d.** 5 November 2016 in Cape Town, South Africa
Carson was a star of many British films during the sixties and seventies, including several Hammer films. Some of his film credits include ***The Night Caller, The Plague of the Zombies, The Man Who Haunted Himself, Taste the Blood of Dracula***, and ***Captain Kronos—Vampire Hunter***. His television credits were extensive and varied—***The Adventures of Robin Hood, The Saint, Adam Adamant Lives!, The Baron, Man in a Suitcase, The Champions, Department S, Emergency–Ward 10, Ivanhoe, William Tell, Armchair Theatre, Maigret, Out of the Unknown, Emma, Dixon of Dock Green, Crown Court, Telford's Change, Secret Army, The Professionals, Tales of the Unexpected, Hammer House of Horror, Doctor Who, Shaka Zulu***, and ***Poirot***. He was known in particular for his rich voice, which had an astonishing similarity to James Mason.
Guest-starred in (4): "A Chorus of Frogs," "Second Sight," "Dial a Deadly Number," "The Midas Touch"

Robert Cawdron, b. December 29, 1921 in Garches, Hauts-de-Seine, France, **d.** September 1997 in Somerset, England, UK
Cawdron's many television credits include ***No Hiding Place, Danger Man, 199 Park Lane, Dixon of Dock Green, The Newcomers, The Saint, Z Cars, Doctor Who, Triton, Department S, Doomwatch, From a Bird's Eye View, The Persuaders!***, and ***The Dick Emery Show***. He also appeared in a few very small film roles in the 1960s, including ***The Blood Beast Terror***.
Guest-starred in (2): "A Touch of Brimstone," "Murdersville"

Cyd Child, b. 24 December 1944 in Chiltern, Buckinghamshire, England, UK
Child went on to perform stunts (many uncredited) in television series and films such as ***Captain Nemo and the Underwater City, No Blade of Grass, The Return of the Pink Panther, Space: 1999, Blake's 7, Superman, Superman II***, and ***For Your Eyes Only***.
Stunt doubled: for Diana Rigg and Linda Thorson, 1967-1969

Carol Cleveland, b. 13 January 1942 in London, England, UK
Cleveland was born in the UK but was raised from a young age in the United States, living in Philadelphia PA, Lubbock TX, and Pasadena CA. She is known mainly for her long association with ***Monty Python***. She was a semi-regular in the famous BBC TV series and also had roles in their films (***Monty Python and the Holy Grail, Monty Python's Life of Brian***, and ***Monty Python's The Meaning of Life***) and various stage revivals, including some of the ***Secret Policeman*** charity concerts and 2014's ***Monty Python Live (Mostly)*** at the O^2 in London. She did have several small film roles prior to ***Monty Python***, including ***Strictly for the Birds, The Pleasure Girls, A Countess from Hong Kong, Mister Ten Per Cent, The Bliss of Mrs. Blossom, The Adding Machine, Moon Zero Two***, and she also starred in ***Vampira*** and ***Brute***.

Guest-starred in (1): "A Touch of Brimstone"

Lewis Collins, b. 27 May 1946 in Bidston, Birkenhead, Cheshire, England, UK, **d.** 27 November 2013 in Los Angeles, California, USA

Collins was easily best known for his starring role in another Clemens-Fennell series, ***The Professionals***, a role which was prefaced by his appearance in ***The New Avengers*** as a guest star playing a similar character with future ***Professionals*** costar Martin Shaw. In the final years of his life, he abandoned acting and moved to Los Angeles to sell computer equipment—not the usual reason an actor moves to Los Angeles!

Guest-starred in (1): "Obsession"

Nicholas Courtney, b. 16 December 1929 in Cairo, Egypt, **d.** 22 February 2011 in London, England, UK

Courtney starred in many television series from the 1960s until his death, including ***The Champions, Randall and Hopkirk (Deceased), Riviera Police, All Creatures Great and Small, Only Fools and Horses, Yes, Prime Minister,*** the 1984 television movie ***To Catch a King,*** and ***The Two Ronnies.*** However, Courtney's most memorable role was certainly Colonel/Brigadier Lethbridge-Stewart in ***Doctor Who.*** His first episode was "The Web of Fear" Episode 3, which is sadly still missing from the BBC archives (having disappeared from an African television archive just after being spotted by missing episodes hunter Philip Morris). Beloved by ***Doctor Who*** fandom, he embraced the fans in return, returning to the show several times throughout the 1980s and 1990s ("Mawdryn Undead," "The Five Doctors," "Battlefield," and the non-canon charity special "Dimensions in Time"), and later starred in several Big Finish ***Doctor Who*** audio productions as well as ***The Sarah Jane Adventures*** with Elisabeth Sladen and David Tennant.

Guest-starred in (2): "Propellant 23," "Mission…Highly Improbable"

Howard Marion Crawford, b. 17 January 1914 in London, England, UK, **d.** 24 November 1969 in Chelsea, London, England, UK

Crawford, best known for playing 'blusterers' and curmudgeonly old man types, played many minor roles over his career, including Dr. Watson in Sheldon Reynold's quaint but enjoyable productions of ***Sherlock Holmes.*** He was also a star in such classics as ***Lawrence of Arabia,*** and had several notable television roles in ***Danger Man.***

Guest-starred in (2): "What the Butler Saw," "The Living Dead"

Jack Creley, b. March 6, 1926 in Chicago, Illinois, USA, **d.** March 10, 2004 in Toronto, Ontario, Canada

Creley had many small film parts, most notably Kubrick's ***Dr. Strangelove (or How I Learned to Stop Worrying and Love the Bomb)*** and ***Videodrome.*** Despite these relatively high-profile films, he's probably best known for a recurring role in the ***Police Academy*** films.

Guest-starred in (1): "Forward Base"

Bernard Cribbins, OBE, **b.** 29 December 1928 in Derker, Oldham, Lancashire, England, UK, **d.** 27 July 2022 in Weybridge, England, UK.

At the time of his appearances in ***The Avengers,*** Cribbins would have been primarily known for his film work, including two ***Carry On*** films, the second ***Doctor Who*** film with Peter Cushing, and the Hammer film ***She.*** Notable subsequent television work would include ***Fawlty Towers, Space: 1999*** (voicing "Brian the Brain"), ***Worzel Gummidge*** (playing Jolly Jack in the final season), ***Last of the Summer Wine,*** and ***Coronation Street.*** In the 2000s, he would return to ***Doctor Who,*** this time playing Wilfrid Mott, the grandfather of companion Donna Noble.

Guest-starred in (2): "The Girl from Auntie," "Look – (stop me if you've heard this one) But There Were These Two Fellers..."
Jennifer Croxton, b. 1944 in Cambridge, Cambridgeshire, England, UK
Croxton starred with future *Avengers* girl Joanna Lumley in the 1971 comedy series ***It's Awfully Bad for Your Eyes, Darling,*** and later in ***I, Claudius.*** She also appeared in the 1968 anthology of plays, ***The Jazz Age.***
Guest-starred in (2): "Killer," "Invitation to a Killing"

Peter Cushing, OBE, **b.** 26 May 1913 in Kenley, Surrey, England, UK, **d.** 11 August 1994 in Canterbury, Kent, England, UK
Cushing should require no introduction to fans of British television and film. He established significant visibility on television in the ***BBC Sunday-Night Theatre*** series of plays from 1951-57, in which he played a wide variety of roles, including his most memorable, the 1954 adaptation of George Orwell's ***1984,*** in which he played Winston Smith. It was shortly after this run on television that he was cast as Baron Frankenstein in Hammer Film Productions' lurid remake of the Frankenstein story, ***The Curse of Frankenstein.*** The film was a huge hit, and Cushing became a major film star. Along with Christopher Lee, he was a marquee actor for Hammer, starring in further such horror classics as ***Dracula, The Hound of the Baskervilles,*** and ***The Mummy.*** In 1968, he would return to the role of Sherlock Holmes for a series of sixteen episodes on the BBC. He is also famous for the title role in the 1960s ***Doctor Who*** films and is fondly remembered by a whole generation of science-fiction fans for his role as Grand Moff Tarkin in ***Star Wars: A New Hope.*** Recently, he proved himself inimitable when his likeness was unconvincingly re-created with CGI and motion capture for ***Rogue One: A Star Wars Story.***
Guest-starred in (1): "Return of the Cybernauts," "The Eagle's Nest"

Allan Cuthbertson, b. 7 April 1920 in Perth, Western Australia, Australia, **d.** 8 February 1988 in London, England, UK
A World War II veteran with the RAAF, Cuthbertson starred in several war movies of the late 1950s, including ***The Guns of Navarone*** and ***Carrington V.C.,*** but he is best known for spoofing his usual military-type characters in the ***Fawlty Towers*** episode "Gourmet Night."
Guest-starred in (4): "The Deadly Air," "Death at Bargain Prices," "Death's Door," "The Super Secret Cypher Snatch"

Iain Cuthbertson, b. 4 January 1930 in Glasgow, Lanarkshire, Scotland, UK, **d.** 4 September 2009 in Glasgow, Scotland, UK
Gravelly-voiced Scottish character actor Cuthbertson appeared in many small roles in television throughout his career, including ***Inspector Morse, Bulman, Ripping Yarns, The Duchess of Duke Street, Adam Adamant Lives!,*** and the ***Doctor Who*** story "The Ribos Operation." He also had more significant roles in ***The Stone Tape, Children of the Stones,*** and ***Danger UXB.***
Guest-starred in (1): "Thingumajig"

Paul Danquah, b. 25 May 1925 in London, England, UK, **d.** 13 August 2015 in Tangier, Morocco
Danquah is one of the few actors to break the (highly questionable and politically incorrect) 'No Coloreds' rule of the Fennell-Clemens era of ***The Avengers.*** He was the son of a Ghanaian politician; his mother was English. Aside from being the first black presenter of a children's program in the UK (***Play School***), he was known for his role in the film version of ***A Taste of Honey*** in 1961. He was the lifelong companion of Peter Pollock and eventually abandoned acting to assume a legal career.
Guest-starred in (1): "Small Game for Big Hunters"

Nigel Davenport, b. 23 May 1928 in Great Shelford, Cambridgeshire, England, UK, **d.** 25 October 2013 in Gloucester, Gloucestershire, England, UK
Davenport started his career in small parts in classic British films like ***Look Back in Anger*** and the Michael Powell film ***Peeping Tom***. He later starred in ***South Riding, Oil Strike North***, and in ***Chariots of Fire*** as Lord Birkenhead. He also appeared on stage with Angela Lansbury in the 1960 Broadway version of ***A Taste of Honey***. One little known fact is that he read the lines for HAL 9000 off-camera during filming of ***2001: A Space Odyssey***. The final voice was supplied by Canadian actor Douglas Rain.
Guest-starred in (2): "The Danger Makers," "Split!"

Ivor Dean, b. 21 December 1917 in London, England, UK, **d.** 10 August 1974 in Truro, Cornwall, UK
Dean was probably best remembered for playing the recurring character of Inspector Teal in ***The Saint***. He provided a very similar performance in ***Randall and Hopkirk (Deceased)*** as Inspector Large.
Guest-starred in (3): "The Removal Men," "Dead Man's Treasure," "Super Secret Cypher Snatch"

Roger Delgado, b. 1 March 1918 in Whitechapel, London, England, UK, **d.** 18 June 1973 in Nevsehir, Turkey
Though Delgado was easily best known for his portrayal of The Master in the long-running science-fiction series ***Doctor Who*** (playing the role throughout the bulk of the Jon Pertwee era in the early 1970s), by that time, he had already established himself with a large number of credits in both television and film, though mostly in small parts and guest roles. He first came to prominence in the early 1960s with his portrayal of a Spanish envoy named Mendoza in the ITC Entertainment television series ***Sir Francis Drake***. From there, he received many small television roles throughout the remainder of the decade, including ***Z Cars, Danger Man, The Saint, The Champions***, and ***Randall and Hopkirk (Deceased)***. Though he greatly enjoyed his role in ***Doctor Who***, Delgado did express lament that so few other parts came his way thereafter, as his appearances in the show were so frequent that many thought he was a regular. He did however receive a part in ***The Persuaders!*** in 1973. His film credits include several Hammer films, such as ***The Terror of the Tongs*** and ***The Mummy's Shroud***, as well as other British films like ***The Road to Hong Kong*** and a small part in ***Antony and Cleopatra*** (1972), which was directed by Charlton Heston. In 1973, he was on location in Turkey filming a Franco-German TV series called ***la Cloche Tibétaine*** when he was killed in a car crash along with two film technicians.
Guest-starred in (2): "Crescent Moon," "Stay Tuned"

Basil Dignam, b. 24 October 1905 in Sheffield, West Riding of Yorkshire, England, UK, **d.** 31 January 1979 in Westminster, London, England, UK
In 1959, English character actor Dignam appeared as the Minister of Labour in ***I'm All Right Jack***. He also had a small uncredited role in ***Lawrence of Arabia***.
Guest-starred in (2): "Trojan Horse," "Cat Amongst the Pigeons"

Fabia Drake, OBE, **b.** 20 January 1904 in Herne Bay, Kent, England, UK, **d.** 28 February 1990 in London, England, UK
Drake had a long career spanning over seven decades. She played Mabel in ***The Jewel in the Crown*** and was a lifelong friend of Sir Lawrence Olivier.
Guest-starred in (1): "The Danger Makers"

Patricia English, b. October 1931 in Detroit, Michigan, USA, **d.** 13 August 2016 in Cornwall, UK
English, with a rather ironic name as it turns out, was born in the United States but immigrated to the United Kingdom after building acting credits in radio and television since the age of five. Aside from ***The Avengers***, she had many roles on television during the 1960s, including ***Mogul, Department S, The Champions,*** and ***The Rat Catchers.***
Guest-starred in (3): "Mission to Montreal," "The Secrets Broker," "Never, Never Say Die"

Clifford Evans, b. 17 February 1912 in Senghenydd, Glamorgan, Wales, **d.** 9 June 1985 in Aberaeron, Cardiganshire, Wales
Welsh actor Evans starred in ***The Power Game*** during the 1960s and in the BBC thriller ***Codename*** in 1970 but is best known for starring in dozens of British films from the 1930s into the late 50s.
Guest-starred in (3): "Dial a Deadly Number," "Death's Door," "Whoever Shot Poor George Oblique Stroke XR40?"

Derek Farr, b. 7 February 1912 in Brentford, Middlesex, England, UK, **d.** 22 March 1986 in Hillingdon, Middlesex, England, UK
Farr is likely best remembered as Group Captain John Whitworth in ***The Dam Busters.***
Guest-starred in (2): "Man-Eater of Surrey Green," "The Eagle's Nest"

Robert Flemyng, OBE, MC, **b.** 3 January 1912 in Liverpool, Lancashire, England, UK, **d.** 22 May 1995 in London, England, UK
Flemyng reached the rank of Colonel in the Royal Army Medical Corps by the age of 33. He was also honored with the Military Cross. As an actor, he appeared in a variety of television and film roles, such as ***Golden Rendezvous, Shadowlands,*** and ***Kafka,*** as well as his final role in the BBC miniseries adaptation of ***The Choir,*** which finished transmission only weeks before he died.
Guest-starred in (2): "You Have Just Been Murdered," "To Catch a Rat"

William Franklyn, b. 22 September 1925 in Kensington, London, England, UK, **d.** 31 October 2006 in London, England, UK
Franklyn was probably best known for voicing the adverts for Schweppes from 1965 to 1973.
Guest-starred in (3): "Silent Dust," "Killer," "Hostage"

Eunice Gayson, b. 17 March 1931 in Croydon, Surrey, England, UK, **d.** 8 June 2018 in London, England, UK.
Gayson played the role of James Bond's girlfriend Sylvia Trench in ***Dr. No*** and ***From Russia With Love.***
Guest-starred in (1): "Quick-Quick Slow Death"

Julian Glover, OBE, **b.** 27 March 1935 in Hampstead, London, England, UK
Glover is best known for his many guest star parts on series such as ***The Champions, Bergerac, Callan, Doctor Who, Space: 1999, By the Sword Divided*** and ***Q.E.D.*** In the US, he starred in television series such as ***Magnum P.I.*** and ***Remington Steele.*** His films include Hammer's 1967 adaptation of ***Quatermass and the Pit, Star Wars: The Empire Strikes Back, For Your Eyes Only,*** and ***Indiana Jones and the Last Crusade.*** More recently, he voiced the giant spider Aragog in ***Harry Potter and the Chamber of Secrets.***
Guest-starred in (4): "Two's a Crowd," "The Living Dead," "Split!," "Pandora"

Maurice Good, b. 8 June 1932 in Dublin, Ireland, UK, **d.** 10 May 2013 in Corner Brook, New-

foundland, Canada
Irish actor Good guest-starred in many television series during the 1960s: ***Z Cars, No Hiding Place, Doctor Who, Emergency–Ward 10, Dixon of Dock Green, Man in a Suitcase,*** and ***The Saint.*** Noteworthy film roles include ***Quatermass and the Pit, The Skull,*** and more dubiously, the 1970 Joan Crawford career finale ***Trog.***
Guest-starred in (3): "Hunt the Man Down," "Don't Look Behind You," "Split!," "Forward Base"

Michael Gough, b. 23 November 1916 in Kuala Lumpur, Federated Malay States, **d.** 17 March 2011 in Wiltshire, England, UK
Though Gough has become a familiar face the world over thanks to his role as Alfred the butler in the ***Batman*** films, long before then he had established himself as a premier character actor of British film and television, usually playing characters of an especially sour demeaner. He had many guest star parts in television and won critical acclaim in the celebrated 1979 BBC TV movie ***Suez 1956.*** He is known to ***Doctor Who*** fans for two noteworthy appearances in that series in 1966 and 1983—"The Celestial Toymaker" and "Arc of Infinity." He also starred in Hammer's 1958 ***Dracula,*** the 1984 miniseries ***Mistral's Daughter,*** and the prehistoric spelunking film, ***Trog,*** in 1970. In the decade prior to his death, he was well-regarded by Hollywood director Tim Burton, who often employed him when he could be persuaded out of retirement.
Guest-starred in (2): "The Cybernauts," "The Correct Way to Kill"

Stephen Greif, b. 26 August 1944 in Sawbridgeworth, Hertfordshire, England, UK, **d.** 23 December 2022
Though his acting credits are actually rather extensive, Greif is probably remembered most for playing the first incarnation of Travis in the cult BBC science-fiction series, ***Blake's 7.*** One notable film role is a small part in ***Nicholas and Alexandra.***
Guest-starred in (1): "Three Handed Game"

Patricia Haines, b. 3 February 1932 in Sheffield, West Riding of Yorkshire, England, UK, **d.** 25 February 1977 in Northampton, Northamptonshire, England, UK
Despite dying from lung cancer at the tragically young age of 45, during her short career Haines accumulated an impressive number of acting credits, mainly in television, including ***Dixon of Dock Green, Steptoe and Son, Danger Man, Public Eye, The Baron, Softly, Softly, Adam Adamant Lives!, The Champions, The Saint, Department S, Randall and Hopkirk (Deceased), Up Pompeii!*** (as Pussius Galoria!), ***Emmerdale Farm, Special Branch, The Protectors,*** and ***Within These Walls.*** Though film roles were not as frequent, she appeared in ***The Night Caller*** in 1965 and ***The Virgin Witch*** in 1971 (directed by fellow ***Avengers*** alumnus, Ray Austin). She was married to actor Bernard Kay.
Guest-starred in (4): "Girl on the Trapeze," "The Nutshell," "The Master Minds," "Who's Who???"

Gerald Harper, b. 15 February 1929 in London, England, UK
Harper, mainly known for television work, is likely best remembered for his starring roles in ***Adam Adamant Lives!*** and ***Hadleigh,*** two nearly consecutive parts that occupied the bulk of his work in the late 1960s and early 70s. Film roles include ***The Admirable Crichton, A Night to Remember, The League of Gentlemen, Tunes of Glory, The Punch and Judy Man, The Shoes of the Fisherman,*** and ***The Lady Vanishes.*** He also had a small uncredited part in ***The Dam Busters.*** Later, in the 1990s, he turned to radio, becoming a regular presenter on BBC 2, offering his "Saturday selection" and giving away champagne and chocolates.
Guest-starred in (3): "Death Dispatch," "The Hour That Never Was," "Homicide and Old Lace," ("The Great Great Britain Crime")

John G. Heller, b. 19 April 1928 in Teplitz-Schönau, Czechoslovakia, **d.** 19 November 1989 in London, England, UK
Heller starred in many British television series over his career, including ***The Onedin Line, Dick Barton: Special Agent, The Sweeney, The Lotus Eaters, Danger Man,*** and ***Emergency–Ward 10.*** He also appeared in the film ***Kelly's Heroes*** and had a small uncredited role in ***The Dirty Dozen.***
Guest-starred in (3): "Man-Eater of Surrey Green," "The Correct Way to Kill," "Split!"

John Hollis, b. 12 November 1927 in Fulham, London, England, UK, **d.** 18 October 2005 in London, England, UK
Hollis played Kaufman in the BBC's two ***Andromeda*** serials, and he was a frequent guest star on many British television programs: ***The Saint; Doctor Who; Blake's 7;*** and ***The Tomorrow People.*** In film, he's perhaps best known for playing Lobot in ***Star Wars: The Empire Strikes Back*** but also had cameos in a variety of films, including ***Captain Kronos: Vampire Hunter,*** and ***Flash Gordon.*** He was one of the Kryptonian elders in the first two Christopher Reeve ***Superman*** films and was dropped by James Bond into an industrial exhaust chimney at the beginning of ***For Your Eyes Only.***
Guest-starred in (4): "Warlock," "The Cybernauts," "The Superlative Seven," "Legacy of Death"

Bernard Horsfall, b. 20 November 1930 in Bishop's Stortford, Hertfordshire, England, UK, **d.** 28 January 2013 in Isle of Skye, Scotland, UK
Horsfall had four particularly noteworthy appearances in ***Doctor Who***: a real-life version of Gulliver from ***Gulliver's Travels*** in "The Mind Robber"; one of the first Time Lords in "The War Games"; a Thal named Taron in "Planet of the Daleks"; and Chancellor Goth in "The Deadly Assassin." His most conspicuous film roles were in ***On Her Majesty's Secret Service, Gandhi,*** and ***Braveheart.*** He returned to the ***Doctor Who*** franchise in the Big Finish audio production called ***Davros*** in 2003.
Guest-starred in (3): "The Cybernauts," "The Fear Merchants," "They Keep Killing Steed"

Prentis Hancock, b. 14 May 1942 in Glasgow, Scotland, UK
Hancock appeared in four ***Doctor Who*** serials during the classic run of the series—"Spearhead from Space," "Planet of the Daleks," "Planet of Evil," and "The Ribos Operation." He is better known however for being a member of the regular cast in season one of ***Space: 1999.***
Guest-starred in (1): "Sleeper"

Barrie Ingham, b. 10 February 1932 in Halifax, West Riding of Yorkshire, England, UK, **d.** 23 January 2015 in Palm Beach Gardens, Florida, USA
Ingham appeared in the 1965 ***Doctor Who and the Daleks*** film and ***The Day of the Jackal,*** and had guest roles in contemporary television—***Randall and Hopkirk (Deceased)*** and ***The Sweeney***—before moving to America for more television work—***George Washington, Remington Steele, The A-Team,*** and ***Days of Our Lives***—as well as providing voiceover for the animated film ***The Great Mouse Detective.***
Guest-starred in (1): "You Have Just Been Murdered"

Gordon Jackson, OBE, **b.** 19 December 1923 in Glasgow, Lanarkshire, Scotland, UK, **d.** 15 January 1990 in London, England, UK
Jackson is best known for being the boss, George Cowley, in the 'CI5' drama ***The Professionals.*** He also had a regular role in ***Upstairs, Downstairs*** as Hudson. Film roles include ***Mutiny on the Bounty, The Great Escape, The Ipcress File, Those Magnificent Men in their Flying Machines, The Prime of Miss Jean Brodie,*** and ***Scrooge.***
Guest-starred in (1): "Castle De'ath"

Frederick Jaeger, b. 29 May 1928 in Berlin, Germany, **d.** 18 June 2004 in Majorca
German-born Jaeger's distinctive voice set him apart from other actors of his era, and like several actors on this list, Jaeger is well-known to ***Doctor Who*** fans for three memorable roles—he was Jano in "The Savages" in 1966, Professor Sorenson in "Planet of Evil" in 1975, and Professor Marius, the man who created K-9, in "The Invisible Enemy" in 1977. Other television appearances include ***Callan, Department S, Special Branch, Dixon of Dock Green, Jason King, The Persuaders!, Pretenders, Doomwatch, Fall of Eagles, The Sweeney, The Return of the Saint, The Professionals,*** and ***The Onedin Line.*** He also had a tiny role in ***Indiana Jones and the Last Crusade*** in 1989.
Guest-starred in (4): "Death of a Great Dane," "The Cybernauts," "Return of the Cybernauts," "Target!"

Colin Jeavons, b. 20 October 1929 in Newport, Monmouthshire, Wales, UK
Jeavons played Lestrade throughout Granada's ***Sherlock Holmes*** productions and was Stamper in the ***House of Cards*** serials. He has two notable ***Doctor Who*** credits, "The Underwater Menace" in 1966, and ***K-9 and Company,*** the much-maligned short-lived spin-off with Elisabeth Sladen as Sarah Jane Smith fighting a witch's coven with assistance from her own robot dog.
Guest-starred in (2): "A Touch of Brimstone," "The Winged Avenger"

Peter Jeffrey, b. 18 April 1929 in Bristol, Gloucestershire, England, UK, **d.** 25 December 1999 in Stratford-upon-Avon, Warwickshire, England, UK
Jeffrey was mainly known for many small film roles in the 1960s and 70s. Notable films include: ***The Abominable Dr. Phibes, The Odessa File, The Return of the Pink Panther, Midnight Express,*** and ***The Adventures of Baron Munchausen.*** On television, he starred as Philip II of Spain in ***Elizabeth R*** and as Oliver Cromwell in ***By the Sword Divided.*** He guest-starred twice in ***Doctor Who,*** in "The Macra Terror" and "The Androids of Tara." In 1985, he appeared in the American miniseries ***Lace II.*** The following decade, he appeared in two celebrated miniseries, ***Middlemarch*** and Dennis Potter's ***Lipstick on Your Collar*** as well as the critical smash ***Our Friends in the North.*** Sadly, Jeffrey passed away from prostate cancer on Christmas Day 1999.
Guest-starred in (4): "Room Without a View," "The Joker," "Game," "House of Cards"

John Junkin, b. 29 January 1930 in Ealing, Middlesex, England, UK, **d.** Florence Nightingale House, Aylesbury, Buckinghamshire, England, UK
Junkin was a comedian and comedy writer who appeared in ***Marty*** and co-wrote ***The World of Beachcomber.*** However, his being taller than Norman Rossington in the Beatles classic film ***A Hard Day's Night*** will always be his most memorable role.
Guest-starred in (2): "Dressed to Kill," "Never, Never Say Die"

Maurice Kaufmann, b. 29 June 1927 in Gorleston, Norfolk, England, UK, **d.** 21 September 1997 in London, England, UK
Kaufmann played one of the leads, Edward Champion, in ***Avengers*** writer Peter Ling's ***Champion House.*** Aside from his one appearance in the show, his other claim to ***Avengers*** fame is being married to Honor Blackman from 1961 to 1975.
Guest-starred in (1): "Quick-Quick Slow Death"

Bernard Kay, b. 23 February 1928 in Bolton, Lancashire, England, UK, **d.** 25 December 2014 in North London, England, UK
Kay was a well-known actor in the UK for the better part of four decades, appearing in multiple guest television roles, mainly in the 1960s and 70s. His credits are too many to list but include ***Emmerdale***

Farm, The Champions, The Cellar and the Almond Tree, Clayhanger, A Very British Coup, Casualty, Casualty 1909, Doctor Who, The Sweeney, Space: 1999, Doctors, Z Cars, Coronation Street, Foyle's War, Dick Barton: Special Agent, and the television mini-series *South Riding*. Notable films include *Doctor Zhivago, Witchfinder General, Sinbad and the Eye of the Tiger*, and the 1977 film *Sweeney!*, which was based on the television series. Like several other fine British actors of the day, he appeared in the furry-flick that punctuated Joan Crawford's career, *Trog*. He was married to Patricia Haines.
Guest-starred in (1): "Bullseye"

Andrew Keir, b. 3 April 1926 in Shotts, Lanarkshire, Scotland, UK, **d.** 5 October 1997 in London, England, UK
Keir is mainly known for his film work, including the titular role in Hammer's 1967 adaptation of *Quatermass and the Pit* and his appearance as the eccentric Father Sandor in *Dracula–Prince of Darkness*. He also appeared in the Roy Baker-directed version of the Titanic story, *A Night to Remember*, and the second 1960s *Doctor Who* film *Daleks–Invasion Earth: 2150 A.D.* For his final role he returned to the role of Professor Quatermass for the 1996 BBC radio serial *The Quatermass Memoirs*.
Guest-starred in (2): "The Fear Merchants," "Get-A-Way!"

David Kernan, b. 23 June 1938 in London, England, UK, **d.** 26 December 2023
Kernan was one of the featured players in *That Was the Week that Was*. He played Private Hitch in *Zulu*. As a singer, he was known for being an interpreter of the songs of Stephen Sondheim.
Guest-starred in (2): "Quick-Quick Slow Death," "Never, Never Say Die"

Roy Kinnear, b. 8 January 1934 in Wigan, Lancashire, England, UK, **d.** 20 September 1988 in Madrid, Spain
Though his television and film credits are quite extensive, Kinnear will likely always be remembered with great fondness for playing the long-suffering father of Veruca Salt in the 1971 children's classic *Willy Wonka & the Chocolate Factory*. He first came into the public eye in Britain with *That Was the Week that Was* in 1962. Subsequently, he never seemed to suffer for work in either television or film, becoming a comedy regular in such shows as *Doctor at Large, Man About the House, George and Mildred*, and *The Dick Emery Show*. He was a long-time collaborator with director Richard Lester, working with him on seven films—*Help!, A Funny Thing Happened On the Way to the Forum, How I Won the War, The Bed Sitting Room, The Three Musketeers, The Four Musketeers*, and *The Return of the Musketeers*. Given that Kinnear was such a delightfully funny actor, it is especially sad that his death was so early and tragic. After falling from a horse during the making of *The Return of the Musketeers* in 1988, he suffered a heart attack and died the next day. Lester, who was a close friend of Kinnear's, is said to have been so upset by his death that he left the film business altogether.
Guest-starred in (4): "Esprit de Corps," "The Hour That Never Was," "The See-Through Man," "Bizarre"

Burt Kwouk, b. 18 July 1930 in Warrington, Cheshire, England, UK, **d.** 24 May 2016 in Hampstead, London, England, UK
Easily best known for playing Cato in the *Pink Panther* films, Kwouk was born in England but raised in Shanghai, China; thus, he acquired his characteristic accent that allowed him to be the go-to actor for any interesting Asian roles in British film and television for decades. This oeuvre included three James Bond films—*Goldfinger, Casino Royale* (1967), and *You Only Live Twice*. In the 1980s, he was known for playing Imperial Japanese Army Major Yamauchi in *Tenko*.
Guest-starred in (3): "Kill the King," "Lobster Quadrille," "The Cybernauts"

Ronald Lacey, b. 28 September 1935 in Harrow, Middlesex, England, UK, **d.** 15 May 1991 in London, England, UK

Lacey strung together a long career based mostly on small roles in both film and television, everything from ***Zulu Dawn*** to ***Firefox*** to ***The Sweeney*** to ***Last of the Summer Wine,*** but he stood out mainly in three different roles: the recurring character Harris in ***Porridge,*** the Bishop of Bath and Wells in ***Blackadder II,*** and Arnold Ernst Toht in ***Raiders of the Lost Ark.*** This last role is no doubt indelible on the memories of at least two generations of movie-goers for the famous (or infamous) "face-melting" scene. Oddly enough, most people don't know that he appeared in the sequel, ***Indiana Jones and the Last Crusade*** (1989), as Heinrich Himmler. In real life, unlike many of his characters, Lacey was far from sinister; he was jovial and very friendly to fans. Sadly, he died of liver cancer in 1991.

Guest-starred in (3): "The Joker," "Legacy of Death," "The Midas Touch"

Avice Landone, b. 1 September 1910 in Quetta, British India, **d.** 12 June 1976 in Richmond upon Thames, Surrey, England, UK

Occasionally credited with the surname 'Landon,' Avice Landone later starred as Mrs. Haddock in the legal comedy ***Misleading Cases.*** One notable film was ***Blood on Satan's Claw*** in 1971.

Guest-starred in (1): "The Secrets Broker"

Philip Latham, b. 17 January 1929 in Essex, United Kingdom, UK, **d.** 20 June 2020 in England, UK

Latham appeared as Count Dracula's manservant Klove in ***Dracula: Prince of Darkness*** with Christopher Lee in 1966. One other notable film role was in ***Force 10 From Navarone.*** His television credits include ***Danger Man, Jesus of Nazareth, Paul of Tarsus, The Treasure Seekers, The Cedar Tree, UFO, The Saint, Maigret, Sergeant Cork, Justice, Love Story, Killers, Hammer House of Horror, No. 10, Nanny,*** and ***The Professionals.***

Guest-starred in (2): "The White Dwarf," "Room Without a View"

John Laurie, b. 25 March 1897 in Dumfries, Scotland, UK, **d.** 23 June 1980 in Chalfont St Peter, Buckinghamshire, England, UK

A wonderful comic actor, Laurie was likely best known for being Private Frazer in the sitcom ***Dad's Army.*** However, he made his acting breakthrough with surprisingly prestigious film company, Alfred Hitchcock, starring in two of Hitchcock's British films, ***Juno and the Paycock*** and ***The 39 Steps.*** In the 1930s and 40s, he worked several times with directors Michael Powell and Emeric Pressburger, appearing in their films ***The Edge of the World, The Life and Death of Colonel Blimp,*** and ***I Know Where I'm Going!.*** During that same decade, he also featured in ***The Way Ahead*** and ***Medal for the General.*** In the 1960s, he was in the Hammer film, ***The Reptile,*** and he starred in the Robert Fuest-directed film ***The Abominable Dr. Phibes*** in 1971.

Guest-starred in (4): "Death of a Great Dane," "Brief for Murder," "A Funny Thing Happened on the Way to the Station," "Pandora"

Christopher Lee, CBE, **b.** 27 May 1922 in Belgravia, London, England, UK, **d.** 7 June 2015 in Chelsea, London, England, UK

Lee needs little introduction. With credits in over two-hundred movies, he first made his mark on horror playing the triumvirate of Hammer monsters—Dracula, Frankenstein's creature, and the Mummy—in many Hammer films from 1957 to 1976. However, perhaps his most praise-worthy Hammer role is his remarkable turn as Duc de Richleau in the 1968 cult-classic, ***The Devil Rides Out.*** In the 1970s, at the tail end of his Hammer career, memorable roles include Lord Summerisle

in *The Wicker Man* and a scientist in ***Return from Witch Mountain***, where he worked alongside Bette Davis, and several television miniseries, including ***Goliath Awaits, The Far Pavilions, Around the World in 80 Days***, and ***Shaka Zulu***. Surviving a dry spell during the 1980s, he remained active through the 1990s, with guest roles in everything from ***Young Indiana Jones*** to Nickelodeon's updated ***Tomorrow People*** and had a recurring character on TNT's 1996-97 ***Robin Hood***. He also starred in two major TV mini-series, ***Ivanhoe*** and ***The Odyssey***, both in 1997. He rounded off the decade with roles in the Hammer-inspired ***Talos the Mummy*** and in Tim Burton's ***Sleepy Hollow***. He then rose to even greater notoriety in the early 2000s for his turn as Count Dooku in the ***Star Wars*** prequels and as Saruman in the classic Oscar-winning ***Lord of the Rings*** films. He later returned to the latter role in the long-winded ***The Hobbit*** series. Aside from ***Sleepy Hollow***, he was a frequent Tim Burton collaborator, starring in six Burton films including ***Charlie and the Chocolate Factory, Alice in Wonderland***, and ***Dark Shadows***. Always a rich bass singer, he branched out into heavy metal music in his late eighties, recording two symphonic metal albums, ***Charlemagne: By the Sword and the Cross*** and ***Charlemagne: The Omens of Death***. He was knighted in 2009. Lee was a noted polyglot, speaking English, Italian, French, Spanish, and German fluently, and having some facility in Swedish, Russian, and Greek. He was sometimes asked to dub roles in other languages during voice-over work. His screen credits are sometimes hard to count, numbering near three-hundred. Although he slowed down significantly in the 2010s, he continued to make cameo appearances and perform voice work until his death in 2015.
Guest starred in (2): "Never, Never Say Die," "The Interrogators"

John Lee, b. 31 March 1928 in Launceston, Tasmania, Australia, **d.** 21 December 2000 in Melbourne, Victoria, Australia
Lee starred in the classic drama ***Warship***.
Guest-starred in (2): "The Bird Who Knew Too Much," "The Forget-Me-Knot"

Ronald Leigh-Hunt, b. 5 October 1920 in London, England, UK, **d.** 12 September 2005 in Isleworth, Middlesex, England, UK
Known for his resonant voice, Leigh-Hunt was typically cast as authority figures. He had numerous television credits including two memorable roles in ***Doctor Who***—"The Seeds of Death" and "Revenge of the Cybermen." Notable film roles include the Steve McQueen vehicle ***Le Mans*** in 1971 and ***The Omen*** in 1976.
Guest-starred in (3): "Dragonsfield," "The Cybernauts," "Three Handed Game"

John Le Mesurier, b. 5 April 1912 in Bedford, Bedfordshire, England, UK, **d.** 15 November 1983 in Ramsgate, Kent, England, UK
Le Mesurier was a familiar face with dozens of credits in film and television over the decades, with nine seasons in ***Dad's Army***. Too many to list here, his film credits include ***I'm All Right Jack, The Punch and Judy Man, Carlton-Browne of the F.O., The Pink Panther, Those Magnificent Men in their Flying Machines***, and ***The Italian Job***.
Guest-starred in (2): "Mandrake," "What the Butler Saw"

Barry Letts, b. 26 March 1925 in Leicester, Leicestershire, England, UK, **d.** 9 October 2009 in England, UK
Letts later left acting permanently to become a BBC staff director and producer. He was the producer, occasional director and writer for the entirety of the Jon Pertwee years of ***Doctor Who***. He was also responsible for the casting of perennial fan-favorite Tom Baker as the fourth Doctor, and he returned to the show to work briefly as executive producer during John Nathan-Turner's first year in the producer's seat. Although ***Doctor Who*** is primarily what he is known for today, he was

also responsible for popular television adaptations of many classic novels in the 1980s—***Great Expectations, The Hound of the Baskervilles, Beau Geste, Jane Eyre, The Invisible Man, The Prisoner of Zenda,*** and ***The Pickwick Papers.***
Guest-starred in (1): "The Wringer"

Marilyn Lightstone, b. 28 June 1940 in Montreal, Quebec, Canada
Lightstone starred as Miss Stacy in the various ***Anne of Green Gables*** productions and provided voices for cartoons such as ***GoBots, Dennis the Menace,*** and ***Heathcliff.***
Guest-starred in (1): "Forward Base"

Jeremy Lloyd, OBE, **b.** 22 July 1930 in Danbury, Essex, England, UK, **d.** 23 December 2014 in London, England, UK
Lloyd is better known for his comedy writing. With David Croft, he created ***Are You Being Served?*** and ***'Allo, 'Allo.*** Film roles include ***The Wrong Box, The Magic Christian,*** and ***Murder on the Orient Express.***
Guest-starred in (2): "From Venus with Love," "Thingumajig"

Sue Lloyd, b. 7 August 1939 in Aldeburgh, Suffolk, England, UK, **d.** 20 October 2011 in London, England, UK
Lloyd's most well-known role was her character Barbara Hunter in the ITV soap opera ***Crossroads.*** Her most prominent film role was likely Jean Courtney in ***The Ipcress File*** (1965), in which she starred with Michael Caine. She was also known for playing Cordelia Winfield in ***The Baron,*** and she had many other guest appearances on television, including ***The Saint, Department S, The Sweeney, The Two Ronnies,*** and ***Bergerac.***
Guest-starred in (2): "A Surfeit of H_2O," "K is for Kill—Part 1: The Tiger" (voice of Mrs. Peel)

Charles Lloyd-Pack, b. 10 October 1902 in East London, England, UK, **d.** 22 December 1983 in London, England, UK
Lloyd-Pack appeared in several notable Hammer films in the 1950s and 60s, including ***Quatermass 2, Dracula, The Revenge of Frankenstein, The Terror of the Tongs,*** and ***The Reptile.*** He also appeared in the Robert Day-directed 1958 film ***Corridors of Blood.*** His son was actor Roger Lloyd-Pack.
Guest-starred in (2): "Silent Dust," "You'll Catch Your Death"

Philip Locke, b. 29 March 1928 in Marylebone, London, England, UK, **d.** 19 April 2004 in Dedham, Essex, England, UK
Locke appeared in many guest roles on television—***The Saint, The Baron, The Champions, Department S, Z Cars, Pennies from Heaven, The Omega Factor, Codename Icarus, The Box of Delights, Bergerac, Inspector Morse, Jeeves and Wooster, Minder, Antony and Cleopatra, Oliver Twist, Ivanhoe,*** and ***Jekyll & Hyde***—and guest-starred in the ***Doctor Who*** serial "Four to Doomsday" in 1982.
Guest-starred in (2): "The Frighteners," "From Venus with Love"

Aimi MacDonald, b. 27 February 1942 in Glasgow, Lanarkshire, Scotland, UK
MacDonald is best known for ***At Last the 1948 Show,*** which she hosted with a very similar personality to her single appearance in ***The Avengers,*** a kooky, liberated 1960s girl with a squeaky voice. Though she is primarily remembered for her bubbly persona to this day, she was also a regular guest star on many 1960s television shows as well as a few notable musicals and cabarets, including ***The Boys from Syracuse*** with Bob Monkhouse and Ronnie Corbett in 1963. Film-wise, she appeared in the horror spoof ***Vampira*** with David Niven, the film version of ***Man About the House,*** and the sex comedy ***Keep It Up Downstairs.***

Guest-starred in (1): "Return of the Cybernauts"

Fulton Mackay, OBE, **b.** 12 August 1922 in Paisley, Renfrewshire, Scotland, UK, **d.** 6 June 1987 in London, England, UK
Scottish actor Mackay was later to become well-known for his role as Mr. Mackay, the prison warden in the classic comedy series ***Porridge*** with Ronnie Barker, which ran from 1973 to 1977. He also briefly reprised this role in the sequel series ***Going Straight*** in 1978. Other television roles include: ***Some Mothers Do 'Ave 'Em***; the Scottish historical drama, ***The Master of Ballantrae; Fraggle Rock;*** and ***Lovejoy.*** He also played Dr. Quinn in the ***Doctor Who*** serial "Doctor Who and the Silurians," and Barry Letts considered him for the lead role when casting the fourth Doctor in 1974. Mackay's film work included ***Gumshoe, Britannia Hospital, Local Hero,*** and ***Defence of the Realm.*** He also wrote plays for the BBC under the pseudonym Aeneas MacBride.
Guest-starred in (3): "Return of the Cybernauts," "You'll Catch Your Death," "Bizarre"

Philip Madoc, b. 5 July 1934 in Twyn-yr-Odyn, Glamorgan, Wales, UK **d.** 5 March 2012 in Northwood, London, England, UK
Madoc starred in the 1970 London Weekend Television war drama ***Manhunt*** and the drama ***Ennal's Point*** in 1982. His credits in ***Doctor Who*** were almost as many as in ***The Avengers,*** appearing in several iconic roles for the series—Eelek in "The Krotons," the War Lord in "The War Games," Doctor Solon in "The Brain of Morbius," and Fenner in "The Power of Kroll." He also had a small part in the Peter Cushing ***Doctor Who*** film ***Daleks–Invasion Earth: 2150 A.D.*** Other film roles include ***Doppelgänger*** with Ian Hendry, ***Hell Boats,*** the Hammer film ***Dr. Jekyll and Sister Hyde, Soft Beds, Hard Battles,*** and ***Operation Daybreak.***
Guest-starred in (5): "The Decapod," "Six Hands Across a Table," "Death of a Batman," "The Correct Way to Kill," "My Wildest Dream"

Patrick Magee, b. 31 March 1922 in Armagh, County Armagh, Northern Ireland, UK, **d.** 14 August 1982 in Fulham, London, England, UK
Northern Irish actor Magee, whose name is frequently confused with the main star of ***The Avengers,*** was better known for roles in two films for Stanley Kubrick, ***A Clockwork Orange*** and ***Barry Lyndon.*** He was also known for genre films such as ***The Masque of Red Death, The Skull,*** and ***Demons of the Mind.*** Later in his career, he appeared in the cult film ***Hawk the Slayer*** and the Oscar-winning ***Chariots of Fire.***
Guest-starred in (2): "Killer Whale," "The Gilded Cage"

Hugh Manning, b. 19 August 1920 in Birmingham, England, UK, **d.** 18 August 2004 in London, England, UK
Manning's most visible role was as the Reverend Donald Hinton in ***Emmerdale Farm,*** which he played from 1977-1989. Some of his film roles were ***The Dam Busters, The House That Dripped Blood, The Mackintosh Man,*** and ***The Elephant Man.***
Guest-starred in (3): "The Thirteenth Hole," "The Superlative Seven," "Thingumajig"

Francis Matthews, b. 2 September 1927 in York, England, UK, **d.** 14 June 2014 in England, UK
Matthews is familiar for several Hammer film roles, including ***The Revenge of Frankenstein, Dracula–Prince of Darkness,*** and ***Rasputin the Mad Monk.*** He also voiced the titular character in Gerry Anderson's puppet series ***Captain Scarlet and the Mysterons.***
Guest-starred in (2): "The Thirteenth Hole," "Mission...Highly Improbable"

Jack May, b. 23 April 1922 in Henley-on-Thames, Oxfordshire, England, UK, **d.** 19 September

1997 in Hove, Sussex, England, UK
May played the valet Simms in ***Adam Adamant Lives!***. On film, he appeared in ***A Funny Thing Happened on the Way to the Forum, How I Won the War, Trog,*** and ***The Seven-Per-Cent Solution.***
Guest-starred in (1): "The Secrets Broker"
Ray McAnally, b. 30 March 1926 in Buncrana, County Donegal, Ireland, **d.** 15 June 1989 in County Wicklow, Ireland
McAnally won a posthumous Best Supporting Actor BAFTA for his role in ***My Left Foot*** in 1990.
Guest-starred in (2): "The Positive Negative Man," "They Keep Killing Steed"

Neil McCarthy, b. 26 July 1932 in Spalding, Lincolnshire, England, UK, **d.** 13 August 1985 in Winchester, Hampshire, England, UK
McCarthy was a very familiar face in television dramas of the era. Though he suffered from acromegaly, which gave his face a very distinctive craggy and lugubrious look, this only made his appearance more memorable, and he never suffered for lack of acting roles, appearing in ***Man of the World, Danger Man, The Saint, Z Cars, Dixon of Dock Green, Randall and Hopkirk (Deceased), Catweazle, My Wife Next Door (A Sense of Movement), Softly, Softly: Taskforce, Department S, Who Pays the Ferryman?, Return of the Saint, Enemy at the Door, The Professionals, Some Mothers Do 'Ave 'Em, Only When I Laugh, The Gentle Touch, Emmerdale Farm,*** the television adaptation of the Lord Peter Wimsey novel, ***The Nine Tailors,*** two ***Doctor Who*** serials, the television miniseries ***Shōgun,*** and ***Daniel Pike.*** He was no stranger to cinema either, appearing in ***Zulu, Where Eagles Dare, Steptoe and Son Ride Again, Clash of the Titans,*** as the villain Calibos, and ***Time Bandits.*** His stern, saturnine countenance belied his gentle demeaner and academic talents. He spoke several languages, including French, Greek, and Latin, and he was a gifted pianist. Sadly, he died quite young at the age of 53 from motor neuron disease.
Guest-starred in (3): "Brought to Book," "Dead Man's Treasure," "The Interrogators"

T. P. McKenna, b. 7 September 1929 in Mullagh, County Cavan, Ireland, **d.** 13 February 2011 in Hampstead, London, England, UK
Irish actor McKenna began his career primarily with stage work, eventually graduating to directing such works as John Millington Synge's ***The Playboy of the Western World*** and Thomas Kilroy's ***The Death and Resurrection of Mr. Roche.*** In 1973, he once more worked with Linda Thorson in Brian Clemens' anthology series ***Thriller*** in the episode "Lady Killer." On film, he appeared in ***Ulysses*** in 1967 and ***A Portrait of the Artist as a Young Man*** in 1977, both based on James Joyce novels. In 1988, he appeared in the ***Doctor Who*** story, "The Greatest Show in the Galaxy."
Guest-starred in (3): "Trojan Horse," "Death at Bargain Prices," "Noon Doomsday"

Warren Mitchell, b. Warren Misell, 14 January 1926 in Stoke Newington, London, England, UK, **d.** 14 November 2015 in Highgate, London, England, UK
Mitchell was easily best known as cockney bigot Alf Garnett in ***Till Death Us Do Part.*** He also appeared in such films as the Hammer film ***The Curse of the Werewolf,*** the Richard Burton spy drama ***The Spy Who Came in from the Cold,*** the Beatles film ***Help!,*** and ***The Assassination Bureau.***
Guest-starred in (4): "The Golden Fleece," "The Charmers," "Two's a Crowd," "The See-Through Man"

Ron Moody, b. 8 January 1924 in Tottenham, Middlesex, England, UK, **d.** 11 June 2015 in London, England, UK
Moody, recognizable for his rich voice, his comic talent, and a devilish twinkle in his eye, was easily best known for his portrayal of Fagin in both the Oscar-winning 1968 film ***Oliver!,*** directed by the great Carol Reed, and the 1983 stage revival. He was however a popular film and television actor

in Britain throughout the 1960s, and his subsequent international fame launched him into American television as well during the 1970s, 80s and 90s. As such, he would star in a diverse array of television programs, including ***Comedy Playhouse, Armchair Theatre, Starsky and Hutch, Tales of the Unexpected, Into the Labyrinth, Nobody's Perfect, Hart to Hart, Highway to Heaven, Last of the Summer Wine, Eastenders, The Bill,*** and ***Casualty.*** Aside from ***Oliver!,*** his many film roles include ***The Twelve Chairs, Flight of the Doves, Legend of the Werewolf, Unidentified Flying Oddball, Wrong Is Right, Where Is Parsifal?, Emily's Ghost, A Kid in King Arthur's Court, The 3 Kings, Revelation, Paradise Grove,*** and ***Lost Dogs.*** He is the most famous actor to turn down the lead role in ***Doctor Who*** (in 1969), something that is noteworthy for the fact that according to friends he regretted this decision for many years thereafter. He called it "the worst decision he ever made." Despite this regret, Moody had a long and storied career and passed away in 2015 at the age of 91.
Guest-starred in (2): "Honey for the Prince," "The Bird Who Knew Too Much"

André Morell, b. 20 August 1909 in London, England, UK, **d.** 28 November 1978 in London, England, UK
Morell is famous for his numerous Hammer film appearances, including ***The Hound of the Baskervilles*** (as Dr. Watson), ***She, Plague of the Zombies,*** and ***The Mummy's Shroud.*** Outside of Hammer, his film career was just as notable, appearing in such films as ***So Long at the Fair, The Bridge on the River Kwai, Ben-Hur, Interpol, The Wrong Box,*** and ***Barry Lyndon.*** He also voiced the character of Elrond in the Ralph Bakshi animated version of ***The Lord of the Rings*** in 1978. On the BBC, he starred in the popular serial ***Quatermass and the Pit*** as Professor Quatermass and in ***1984*** as O'Brien. He became the president of Equity, the actors trade union, in 1973.
Guest-starred in (2): "Death of a Batman," "Death at Bargain Prices"

Garfield Morgan, b. 19 April 1931 in Birmingham, Warwickshire, England, UK, **d.** 5 December 2009 in London, England, UK
Morgan starred as Lewis in the long-running crime drama ***Softly, Softly.*** He also had a role in ***The Odessa File.***
Guest-starred in (3): "The Fear Merchants," "Game," "Take-Over"

Aubrey Morris, b. 1 June 1926 in Portsmouth, Hampshire, England, UK, **d.** 15 July 2015 in Los Angeles, California, USA
Morris, the younger brother of actor Wolfe Morris, was probably best known for his equally eccentric roles in ***A Clockwork Orange*** and ***The Wicker Man,*** two films that have considerable cult followings. However, he had several other interesting credits to his name, including the rather intriguing little-known sci-fi thriller ***The Night Caller*** (directed by Hammer films director John Gilling) and the bizarre Ken Russell film ***Lisztomania,*** which also starred Ringo Starr as the Pope and Roger Daltrey as Franz Liszt! The later years of his life were spent in Los Angeles where he starred in a handful of US productions, including a ***Colombo*** television film and the Dennis Miller film ***Bordello of Blood.***
Guest-starred in (1): "Silent Dust"

Wolfe Morris, b. 5 January 1925 in Portsmouth, Hampshire, England, UK, **d.** 21 July 1996 in Camden, London, England, UK
Making his film debut in ***Ill Met by Moonlight,*** Morris also starred in several other interesting cinema titles—***The Abominable Snowman, The Camp on Blood Island, I Only Arsked!, Nine Hours to Rama, The Best House in London, The Mackintosh Man,*** and ***The Adventure of Sherlock Holmes' Smarter Brother.***
Guest-starred in (3): "The Yellow Needle," "The Decapod," "Two's a Crowd"

Patrick Mower, b. 12 September 1938 in Oxford, Oxfordshire, England, UK
Mower was a regular star in ***Callan*** with Edward Woodward and is also known for his role in Hammer's ***The Devil Rides Out*** in 1968. More recently, he has starred in ***Emmerdale*** since 2000 as Rodney Blackstock.
Guest-starred in (1): "A Sense of History"

George Murcell, b. 30 October 1925 in Naples, Campania, Italy, **d.** 3 December 1998 in Isleworth, Middlesex, England, UK
Murcell usually played sneering villains or murderous rogues throughout his career, and he featured in many television programs of the era, including ***Danger Man, The Baron, The Saint, The Champions, Randall and Hopkirk (Deceased), The Persuaders!,*** and ***Jason King.*** His film roles include ***Hell Drivers, The Battle of the River Plate,*** and ***The Fall of the Roman Empire.*** He later appeared in the ABC television film ***Inside the Third Reich*** as Herman Göring.
Guest-starred in (2): "Square Root of Evil," "You Have Just Been Murdered"

Valentino Musetti, b. 7 January 1943 in Pontremoli, Tuscany, Italy
Musetti is an Italian-born stuntman and racecar driver that appeared in many British television programs throughout the 1960s and 70s. Aside from ***The Avengers,*** he also starred in ***Doctor Who, Space: 1999, Callan, The Professionals, Minder, The New Avengers, Dempsey and Makepeace,*** and ***Midsomer Murders.*** He later appeared in films such as ***Superman II, An American Werewolf in London, Robin Hood: Prince of Thieves,*** and ***Alien 3.*** His name was variously misspelled in the credits for the series as 'Valentine Musetti' or 'Valentino Mussetti.'
Guest-starred in (5): "The Decapod," "Death à la Carte," "The Secrets Broker," "The Outside-In Man," "Lobster Quadrille"

Derek Newark, b. 8 June 1933 in Great Yarmouth, Norfolk, England, UK, **d.** 11 August 1998 in London, England, UK
Newark played heavies in guest star parts in many series of the time and partially spoofed that image as the hard man Spooner in LWT's ***Rising Damp.*** He also has the distinction of being one of the very first guest stars in ***Doctor Who,*** having appeared in the debut serial "An Unearthly Child." He returned to the series for another memorable role as Greg Sutton in 1970's "Inferno."
Guest-starred in (3): "Trojan Horse," "From Venus with Love," "Wish You Were Here"

Anthony Nicholls, b. 16 October 1902 in Windsor, Berkshire, England, UK, **d.** 22 February 1977 in London, England, UK
Nicholls played W. L. Tremayne in ***The Champions.*** He also had guest roles in ***The Saint, Man in a Suitcase, Department S,*** and ***Space: 1999.*** Film roles included the Lawrence Olivier version of ***Othello*** in 1965, ***Battle of Britain*** and ***The Omen.***
Guest-starred in (2): "School for Traitors," "Whoever Shot Poor George Oblique Stroke XR40?"

Simon Oates, b. Arthur Charles Oates, 6 January 1932, London, England, UK, **d.** 20 May 2009 in Eastbourne, East Sussex, England, UK
Simon Oates has perhaps the most unique qualification of any ***Avengers*** guest star—he actually played John Steed in the 1971 stage production of the series with Sue Lloyd and Kate O'Mara. Though he is likely best known for his regular role as Dr. John Ridge in ***Doomwatch,*** he also guest-starred in ***Man in a Suitcase, Department S, Jason King, The Professionals,*** and ***Bergerac.*** He had few film roles, with the dubious pleasure of starring in the 1968 Amicus film, ***The Terrornauts,*** which was described as one of the two worst films the studio ever made. He also reprised his role as Dr.

Ridge for the film version of ***Doomwatch*** in 1972.
Guest-starred in (3): "You Have Just Been Murdered," "Super Secret Cypher Snatch," "Hostage"

Kate O'Mara, b. Frances Meredith Carroll, 10 August 1939 in Leicester, Leicestershire, England, UK, **d.** 30 March 2014 in Sussex, England, UK
Other than the one guest star role in ***The Avengers,*** O'Mara also appeared as the villainess Madame Gerda in the 1971 stage play version with Simon Oates and Sue Lloyd. O'Mara had a diverse career that included many television roles: ***No Hiding Place; Danger Man; Adam Adamant Lives!; The Saint; Z Cars;*** and ***Jason King.*** She had a semi-recurring role as The Rani in ***Doctor Who,*** appearing in "The Mark of the Rani," "Time and the Rani," and the non-canonical charity special "Dimensions in Time." She briefly had a regular role on the American primetime soap ***Dynasty*** as Caress Morell and appeared as Patsy Stone's sister Jackie in ***Absolutely Fabulous.*** She also wrote two novels and two autobiographical books. She was also at one time married to ***Avengers*** guest star Jeremy Lloyd.
Guest-starred in (1): "Stay Tuned"

Geoffrey Palmer, OBE, **b.** 4 June 1927 in London, England, UK, **d.** 5 November 2020 in Lee Common, Buckinghamshire, England, UK
Palmer became a major star in sitcoms—***Butterflies, The Fall and Rise of Reginald Perrin, As Time Goes By*** (9 seasons, with Dame Judi Dench)—and feature films—***A Fish Called Wanda, Mrs. Brown, The Madness of King George,*** and ***Tomorrow Never Dies.*** He remains one of Britain's most distinguished actors.
Guest-starred in (4): "Dance with Death," "Propellant 23," "Man with Two Shadows," "A Surfeit of H_2O"

Judy Parfitt, b. 7 November 1935 in Sheffield, England, UK
After ***The Avengers,*** Parfitt later starred in ***Malice Aforethought*** and ***The Jewel in the Crown*** as well as American films such as ***Dolores Claiborne*** and the Drew Barrymore Cinderella film ***Ever After.***
Guest-starred in (4): "Bullseye," "The White Elephant," "Escape in Time," "Whoever Shot Poor George Oblique Stroke XR40?"

George Pastell, b. 13 December 1923 in Nicosia, Cyprus, **d.** 4 April 1976 in Dade County, Florida, USA
Due to his Mediterranean looks, Pastell was a character actor that was often chosen for Middle Eastern roles. He is well-known for several Hammer film appearances, such as ***The Mummy, The Stranglers of Bombay,*** and ***The Curse of the Mummy's Tomb.*** On television, he made the usual rounds during the 1960s, appearing in ***Danger Man, The Champions, The Saint,*** and ***Department S.*** He also appeared as the villain in ***Doctor Who***'s "The Tomb of the Cybermen."
Guest-starred in (1): "Honey for the Prince"

John Paul, b. 20 April 1921 in Hertfordshire, England, UK, **d.** 23 February 1995 in Buckinghamshire, England, UK
Paul was Dr. Spencer Quist in ***Doomwatch.***
Guest-starred in (3): "Requiem," "Target!," "Three Handed Game"

Jacqueline Pearce, b. 20 December 1943 in Woking, Surrey, England, UK, **d.** 3 September 2018 in Lancashire, England, UK
When she starred in ***The Avengers,*** Pearce was fresh from what was probably her first big career break, starring in two high quality Hammer films, ***The Plague of the Zombies*** and ***The Reptile.*** In the latter film, she played the title character. She would later become famous for her role as Servalan in

Terry Nation's *Blake's 7*.
Guest-starred in (1): "A Sense of History"

Jon Pertwee, b. 7 July 1919 in Chelsea, London, England, UK, **d.** 20 May 1996 in Sherman, Connecticut, USA
At the time of his appearance in ***The Avengers***, Pertwee was best known for his many roles in radio comedies, such as his long-running ***The Navy Lark***, and his comedy films, including three of the ***Carry On*** productions from 1965-66. He would later find even greater success as the third ***Doctor Who*** from 1970-74 and as ***Worzel Gummidge*** in two series produced and screened the late 1970s and the late 1980s respectively.
Guest-starred in (1): "From Venus with Love"

George Pravda, b. 19 June 1916 in Prague, Austria-Hungary, **d.** 1 May 1985 in London, England, UK
Pravda was born in 1916 in Prague, now part of the Czech Republic but once Austria-Hungary. His distinctive voice and accent served him well, no doubt making his casting in ***The Avengers*** as an Eastern European an obvious decision. He appeared in numerous television shows over the 1960s and 70s, such as ***No Hiding Place, The Saint, The Baron, The Prisoner, Special Branch, Department S, Callan, Softly, Softly, Doomwatch, Codename, Public Eye, Spy Trap, Moonbase*** 3, and ***Colditz***. He had three particularly noteworthy appearances in ***Doctor Who***—Denes in the recently recovered "The Enemy of the World," the scientist Jaeger in "The Mutants," and a Time Lord ally of The Doctor, Castellan Spandrell in "The Deadly Assassin." On film, he appeared in the 1965 James Bond film ***Thunderball***, the 1969 Hammer film ***Frankenstein Must Be Destroyed***, the 1973 television version of ***Dracula*** starring Jack Palance, and the 1982 Clint Eastwood Cold War film ***Firefox***.
Guest-starred in (1): "The Radioactive Man"

Dennis Price, b. 23 June 1915 in Twyford, Berkshire, England, UK, **d.** 6 October 1973 in Guernsey, Channel Islands
Price played the suffering boss of ***Jason King*** in that spy-adventure series starring Peter Wyngarde. On film, he played the forgetful would-be aristocrat Louis Mazzini in the Ealing Studios classic ***Kind Hearts and Coronets*** in 1949, a performance that will be perpetually overshadowed by Sir Alec Guinness having played nine characters.
Guest-starred in (1): "Whoever Shot Poor George Oblique Stroke XR40?"

Anna Quayle, b. 6 October 1932 in Birmingham, England, UK, **d.** 16 August 2019 in UK
Quayle starred in the 1976 serial ***The Georgian House*** and later appeared in ***Grange Hill***.
Guest-starred in (1): "The Correct Way to Kill"

Godfrey Quigley, b. 4 May 1923 in Jerusalem, Mandatory Palestine, **d.** 7 September 1994 in Dublin, Ireland
Irish actor Quigley has the honor of being the first actor to be seen in ***The Avengers***, in the episode "Hot Snow," as he walks up Upper Cheyne Row in Chelsea. He would star in several popular films over the coming decades in a variety of small roles, including ***Daleks – Invasion Earth: 2150 A.D., Get Carter, A Clockwork Orange, Barry Lyndon, The Man in the Iron Mask***, and ***Educating Rita***.
Guest-starred in (3): "Hot Snow," "Brought to Book," "The White Elephant"

Ronald Radd, b. 22 January 1929 in Ryhope, Sunderland, County Durham, England, UK, **d.** 23 April 1976 in Toronto, Ontario, Canada
Radd began as a stage actor but tired of theatre by the late 1950s and decided to break into tele-

vision. He appeared in dozens of programs throughout the 1960s and 70s, including ***The Saint, Armchair Theatre, Softly, Softly: Task Force, The Champions, Callan,*** and ***Jason King***. On film, he starred in ***The Camp on Blood Island*** in 1958, with André Morell as a costar and Val Guest directing.
Guest-starred in (3): "Bullseye," "The Outside-In Man," "Mission…Highly Improbable"

Moira Redmond, b. 14 July 1928 in Bognor Regis, Sussex, England, UK, **d.** 16 March 2006 in London, England, UK
Redmond's stage debut was in Peter Brook's revival of ***Titus Andronicus*** with Laurence Olivier. She was also a founding member of the Actors' Company with Ian McKellen. On television, she appeared in ***The Baron, Dixon of Dock Green, I, Claudius,*** and ***The Sweeney***. One film of interest is ***A Shot in the Dark*** in 1964, the second of the 1960s ***Pink Panther*** films with Peter Sellers. Late in her career, she appeared in ***The Alleyn Mysteries*** in 1994.
Guest-starred in (2): "Hot Snow," "Kill the King"

Arnold Ridley, OBE, **b.** 7 January 1896 in Walcot, Bath, Somerset, England, UK, **d.** 12 March 1984 in Hillingdon, London, England, UK
Ridley was Private Godfrey in ***Dad's Army***. He also wrote the play ***Ghost Train***. His grandniece is Daisy Ridley of ***Star Wars*** fame.
Guest-starred in (1): "Never, Never Say Die"

Edwin Richfield, b. 11 September 1921 in London, England, UK, **d.** 2 August 1990 in Shrewsbury, Shropshire, England, UK
Richfield was a well-known actor to viewers of British film and television. He holds the record for the most guest appearances in ***The Avengers*** but is tied with Gerald Sim if ***The New Avengers*** is also included. His extensive television work includes ***R3, 199 Park Lane, Gideon's Way, Danger Man, Dixon of Dock Green, Z Cars, Adam Adamant Lives!, The Baron, Champion House, Out of the Unknown, The Owl Service, UFO, Bergerac, Crossroads, Doctor Who*** ("The Sea Devils" and "The Twin Dilemma"), and ***All Creatures Great and Small***. He was also known for being the titular character in ***The Odd Man***. His film work includes such films as ***X the Unknown, The Secret of Blood Island, The Face of Fu Manchu,*** and ***Quatermass and the Pit***. He had a small, uncredited role in ***Ben-Hur***. He died all too early in 1990 at the age of 68.
Guest-starred in (6): "Girl on the Trapeze," "The Removal Men," "The White Elephant," "Too Many Christmas Trees," "Dead Man's Treasure," "All Done with Mirrors"

George Roubicek, b. 25 May 1935 in Vienna, Austria
Roubicek appeared as a bizarre approximation of an American pilot in the classic ***Doctor Who*** episode "The Tomb of the Cybermen" in 1967.
Guest-starred in (2): "The White Dwarf," "Invasion of the Earthmen"

Peter Sallis, OBE, **b.** 1 February 1921 in Twickenham, Middlesex, England, UK, **d.** 2 June 2017 in Northwood, London, England, UK
Sallis starred in all 31 seasons of the BBC's ***Last of the Summer Wine***—the only actor to appear in all 295 episodes! Other TV roles include ***Danger Man, Catweazle, The Persuaders!,*** and ***The Pallisers***. He also guest-starred in ***Doctor Who***'s "The Ice Warriors." Notable film roles are ***The Curse of the Werewolf, Scream and Scream Again, Taste the Blood of Dracula,*** and ***Wuthering Heights***. In his later years however, he turned more frequently to voice-acting and found international fame as the voice of Wallace in four Nick Park ***Wallace & Gromit*** shorts and one feature film, ***Wallace and Gromit: The Curse of the Were-Rabbit***.
Guest-starred in (1): "The Wringer"

August Schellenberg, b. July 25, 1936 in Montreal, Quebec, Canada, **d.** August 15, 2013 in Dallas, Texas, USA
Schellenberg found mainstream success playing Randolph in all three ***Free Willy*** movies but is best known for being a guest star in three separate roles over five episodes of ***The Littlest Hobo.***
Guest-starred in (1): "Forward Base"

Alex Scott, b. 18 September 1929 in Australia, **d.** 30 June 2015 in Australia
Scott's film roles included notables such as ***Darling, Fahrenheit 451, The Blue Max, The Abominable Dr. Phibes, Twins of Evil,*** and ***The Asphyx.*** He also starred in a 1958 BBC film called ***Yesterday's Enemy*** that Hammer remade without him in 1959.
Guest-starred in (3): "Square Root of Evil," "Too Many Christmas Trees," "Game"

Athene Seyler, CBE, **b.** 31 May 1889 in Hackney, London, England, UK, **d.** 12 September 1990 in Hammersmith, London, England, UK
Seyler starred in many roles on stage and in cinema and television. Her film career was extensive, beginning in the silent era and spanning well into the 1960s. Notable examples include ***The Citadel, The Pickwick Papers, Night of the Demon,*** and ***A Tale of Two Cities.*** Her stage appearances include ***The Rivals, Romeo and Juliet, Harvey,*** and ***Arsenic and Old Lace.*** She was made Commander of the British Empire (CBE) in 1959. By the early 1960s, however, she had switched to a career mostly in television, primarily playing dotty elderly women, just as in ***The Avengers.*** She retired by 1970 and passed away in 1990 at the age of 101.
Guest-starred in (2): "Build a Better Mousetrap," "Man-Eater of Surrey Green"

John Sharp, b. 5 August 1920 in Bradford, West Riding of Yorkshire, England, UK, **d.** 26 November 1992 in London, England, UK
Sharp had quite a film career, with a variety of character roles in ***Mrs. Brown, You've Got a Lovely Daughter, The Wicker Man, Barry Lyndon, Jabberwocky*** and ***Top Secret!*** His television credits were extensive and include ***The Prisoner, Not On Your Nellie, Z Cars, The Sweeney,*** and the 1984 version of ***A Christmas Carol*** with George C. Scott.
Guest-starred in (3): "Traitor in Zebra," "Murdersville," "Bizarre"

Denis Shaw, b. 7 April 1921 in Dulwich, London, England, UK, **d.** 28 February 1971 in London, England, UK
Shaw was a semi-regular on ***The Prisoner*** as the Shopkeeper.
Guest-starred in (1): "Requiem"

Martin Shaw, b. 21 January 1945 in Birmingham, Warwickshire, England, UK
Obviously best known as Doyle in ***The Professionals,*** Shaw is also known for hosting ***Martin Shaw: Aviators,*** a six-part series on the history of aviation, in which Shaw's own plane crash and the subsequent re-build of his plane are covered.
Guest-starred in (1): "Obsession"

Douglas Sheldon, b. 1936 in London, England, UK
Sheldon started out as a pop singer with moderate success and later starred opposite Kate O'Mara in the 1980s BBC soap ***Triangle.***
Guest-starred in (1): "The Forget-Me-Knot"

Barbara Shelley, b. 13 February 1932 in Marylebone, London, England, UK, **d.** 3 January 2021 in

London, England, UK
As Hammer's Number 1 female star, Shelley is a notable film actor. Her Hammer horror films include ***The Gorgon, Dracula–Prince of Darkness, Rasputin - The Mad Monk,*** and ***Quatermass and the Pit.*** Other films outside of Hammer are ***Village of the Damned, The Secret of Blood Island,*** and ***Ghost Story.*** In 1988, she starred as the White Witch in the BBC's ***Chronicles of Narnia*** adaptations.
Guest-starred in (2): "Dragonsfield," "From Venus with Love"

Gerald Sim, b. 4 June 1925 in Liverpool, Lancashire, England, UK, **d.** 11 December 2014 in Northwood, Hillingdon, London, England, UK
Sim starred in ***To the Manor Born,*** and late in his career, he worked with Sir Richard Attenborough in small roles in such films as ***Chaplin*** and ***Shadowlands.*** Shortly thereafter, he retired but returned for the special 25th anniversary episode of ***To the Manor Born*** in 2007.
Guest-starred in (6): "The Radioactive Man," "Mission to Montreal," "The Wringer," "Dial a Deadly Number," "The Rotters," "The Lion and the Unicorn"

Nicholas Smith, b. 5 March 1934 in Banstead, Surrey, England, UK, **d.** 6 December 2015 in Sutton, London, England, UK
Smith was easily best known for playing Mr. Rumbold in the BBC sitcom ***Are You Being Served?.***
Guest-starred in (2): "Escape in Time," "Super Secret Cypher Snatch"

Tony Steedman, b. 21 August 1927 in Warwickshire, England, UK, **d.** 4 February 2001 in Haywards Heath, West Sussex, England, UK
Steedman would later appear in the controversial 1969 series ***Big Breadwinner Hogg*** and two seasons of ***Citizen Smith.*** Steedman immigrated to America and has appeared in series as disparate as ***The A-Team*** and ***Babylon 5.*** On film, he starred as Socrates in ***Bill & Ted's Excellent Adventure.***
Guest-starred in (2): "The Little Wonders," "False Witness"

John Stone, b. May 26, 1924 in Cardiff, Wales, UK, **d.** 2007
Stone played Captain Dillon in 1955's ***Quatermass II*** and was the submarine captain in ***You Only Live Twice.*** His television credits include ***Softly, Softly, The Champions, Doomwatch, Dixon of Dock Green,*** and ***Z Cars.***
Guest-starred in (3): "The Secrets Broker," "The Joker," "The Rotters"

Kevin Stoney, b. 22 January 1921 in Nowgong, Assam, India, **d.** 22 January 2008 in Chiswick, London, England, UK
Stoney was a regular guest actor in a wide variety of 1960s and 1970s British television programs, including ***Doctor Who*** and ***The Prisoner.*** His role in ***Doctor Who***'s "The Daleks' Masterplan" was so memorable and iconic for that show that it persists in memory despite the bulk of the serial being missing. His role in 1968's "The Invasion" was equally indelible. His many other television credits include ***The Adventures of Robin Hood, The Saint, Danger Man, Dr. Finlay's Casebook, Softly, Softly, Man in a Suitcase, The Troubleshooters, Doomwatch, Freewheelers, Z Cars, The Tomorrow People, Ace of Wands, Special Branch, The Onedin Line, Fall of Eagles, Space: 1999, Quatermass, Hammer House of Horror, Bergerac, All Creatures Great and Small, The Bill,*** and ***Inspector Morse.***
Guest-starred in (2): "Mission...Highly Improbable," "Cat Amongst the Pigeons"

Veronica Strong, b. 1938 in Eastry, Kent, England, UK
During the time she appeared in ***The Avengers,*** Strong was mainly a television actor performing in television series such as ***No Hiding Place, The Baron, Doomwatch, Armchair Theatre, Adam Adamant Lives!,*** and ***Dixon of Dock Green.*** She married ***Avengers*** actor and writer Jeremy Burnham in

1966.
Guest-starred in (1): "Love All"

Donald Sutherland, b. 17 July 1935 in Saint John, New Brunswick, Canada, **d.** 20 June 2024 in Miami, Florida, USA
Sutherland was little known at the time he starred in ***The Avengers,*** though he was right on the cusp of a long and stellar film career. A Canadian, he initially built his career upon television in the UK, guest-starring in many shows: ***The Odd Man; The Saint; Man in a Suitcase; Studio 625;*** and ***The Champions.*** For the remainder of the sixties, prominent film roles were relatively few, only ***The Dirty Dozen*** was a highwater mark. His breakthrough in the 1970 film ***M*A*S*H*** changed all that. From there, he went on to star in ***Klute*** with Jane Fonda, then Nicholas Roeg's superb 1973 thriller ***Don't Look Now*** and many other popular films throughout the seventies such as ***The Eagle Has Landed,*** and, as a result, quickly became entrenched as a film icon, a status that continues to this day.
Guest-starred in (1): "The Superlative Seven"

Peter Thomas, b. 23 January 1936 in England, UK, **d.** 5 January 2017 in England, UK
Thomas starred in ***Dixon of Dock Green, Department S, No Hiding Place,*** and "The Savages" during the Hartnell era of ***Doctor Who.*** He was forced to retire from acting in the mid-1970s in order to nurse his severely ill wife.
Guest-starred in (3): "Small Game for Big Hunters," "Death's Door," "All Done with Mirrors"

Talfryn Thomas, b. 31 October 1922 in Swansea, Wales, UK, **d.** 4 November 1982 in Cardiff, Wales, UK
Snaggle-toothed Welsh actor Thomas was primarily known for a variety of supporting roles on television over the 1960s and 70s, mainly those that might take advantage of his Welsh heritage and eccentric appearance. Two regular television roles stand out however, that of Private Cheeseman in ***Dad's Army*** and Tom Price on ***Survivors.*** Aside from his two memorable ***Avengers*** appearances, he also had two similarly notable guest roles in ***Doctor Who,*** a nosy hospital cleaner in "Spearhead from Space" in 1970 and a Welsh miner down the ol' mine in 1973's "The Green Death."
Guest-starred in (2): "A Surfeit of H_2O," "Look – (stop me if you've heard this one) But There Were These Two Fellers..."

Michael Trubshawe, b. 7 December 1905 in Chichester, Sussex, England, UK, **d.** 21 March 1985 in Sussex, England, UK
Trubshawe first served as an officer in the Highland Light Infantry Regiment of the British Army, and it is this special qualification that tended to determine what sort of roles he would play throughout his career in television and film, that of blustery authority figures and retired military men. At the time of his appearances in ***The Avengers,*** he would have been primarily known as a film actor, having appeared in ***The Lavender Hill Mob, The Pink Panther, A Hard Day's Night, Those Magnificent Men in their Flying Machines,*** and ***Bedazzled.*** He was a close personal friend of fellow British actor and former army man David Niven.
Guest-starred in (2): "Dial a Deadly Number," "All Done with Mirrors"

Wanda Ventham, b. 5 August 1935 in Brighton, Sussex, England, UK
Ventham was long a glamorous face in British television, and sometimes it seems as though she was in virtually everything. Her credits are extensive, having appeared in a wide variety of programs, including ***Danger Man, The Saint, The Likely Lads, The Troubleshooters, Department S, Z Cars, The Lotus Eaters, Emmerdale Farm, The Sweeney, Minder,*** and ***Only Fools and Horses,*** but she was perhaps best known for her regular role as Colonel Virginia Lake in the Gerry Anderson live-action

series *UFO* in 1969. Much more recently, she has played the mother of Sherlock Holmes in ***Sherlock***, which stars her own real-life son, Benedict Cumberbatch, as the titular detective.
Guest-starred in (1): "The Grave-diggers"

Bill Wallis, b. 20 November 1936 in Guildford, Surrey, England, UK, **d.** 6 September 2013 in Bath, Somerset, England, UK
Wallis was a guest star in many series in the 1970s and 80s, most notably three parts in ***Blackadder***. He took small roles in Ben Elton's BBC drama ***Stark*** and the hit ***Dangerfield***. He later had a blink-and-you-miss-it part in Terry Gilliam's ***Brazil*** in 1985.
Guest-starred in (2): "A Touch of Brimstone," "The Positive Negative Man"

Barry Warren, b. 12 July 1933 in London, England, UK, **d.** 22 February 1994 in Chichester, Sussex, England, UK
Warren is mainly known for his Hammer film appearances, including ***The Kiss of the Vampire***, ***The Devil-Ship Pirates***, and ***Frankenstein Created Woman***. But he also appeared in many television plays, most notably ***The Wednesday Play***: "For the West," ***ITV Play of the Week***: "Their Obedient Servants," ***BBC Play of the Month***: "Gordon of Khartoum" and ***Armchair Theatre***: "Unscheduled Stop." In film, he played an amusing uncredited set of minor roles in ***Lawrence of Arabia***, stating that he "...played three roles—a British officer with a moustache, a British officer without a moustache, and an Arab Sheik!"
Guest-starred in (2): "Too Many Christmas Trees," "False Witness"

Kenneth J. Warren, b. 25 September 1929, Parramatta, New South Wales, Australia, **d.** 27 August 1973, Effingham, Surrey, England, UK
Warren starred in the film version of ***The Navy Lark***, and in ***Demons of the Mind*** and ***The Creeping Flesh***. His final film role was ***S*P*Y*S*** with Donald Sutherland. He played a suspected brother of Harold in ***Steptoe and Son*** in 1970.
Guest-starred in (4): "Girl on the Trapeze," "Intercrime," "The Little Wonders," "Epic"

Jack Watson, b. 14 May 1915 in Thorney, Cambridgeshire, England, UK, **d.** 4 July 1999 in Bath, Somerset, England, UK
Watson was a ubiquitous presence in British cinema and television for decades, appearing in over 70 films including ***Peeping Tom***, ***This Sporting Life***, ***The Gorgon***, ***The Hill***, ***Grand Prix***, ***Tobruk***, ***The McKenzie Break***, ***Tower of Evil***, ***The Devil's Brigade***, ***The Wild Geese***, and ***The Sea Wolves***. On television, he had a wide variety of guest roles and one recurring role on ***Coronation Street***.
Guest-starred in (2): "Silent Dust," "The Living Dead"

Moray Watson, b. 25 June 1928 in Sunningdale, Berkshire, England, UK, **d.** 2 May 2017 in Hillingdon, Greater London, England, UK
Watson appeared as a regular in ***Catweazle***, ***Quiller***, and ***Rumpole of the Bailey***. On film, he appeared in the 1960 Cary Grant film ***The Grass Is Greener*** and ***The Sea Wolves*** with Gregory Peck, Roger Moore and David Niven.
Guest-starred in (1): "The Danger Makers"

Gordon Whiting, b. 9 May 1918 in London, England, UK, **d.** February 2002 in Surrey, England, UK
Whiting had two roles in the BBC television series ***The Adventures of Robin Hood*** from 1957-1959. He also appeared in ***No Hiding Place***, ***Dixon of Dock Green***, and ***Danger Man***.
Guest-starred in (2): "The Golden Eggs," "The Cybernauts"

Paul Whitsun-Jones, b. 25 April 1923 in Newport, Monmouthshire, Wales, UK, **d.** 14 January 1974 in London, England, UK
Whitsun-Jones played the role of Mr. Bumble in the original 1960 West End production of the musical ***Oliver!***. However, this writer will always remember him as the rotund and maniacal Mussolini-clone, the Marshall, in the ***Doctor Who*** serial "The Mutants" in 1972.
Guest-starred in (4): "Man with Two Shadows," "The Wringer," "Room Without a View," "Fog"

Brian Wilde, b. 13 June 1927 in Ashton-under-Lyne, Lancashire, England, UK, **d.** 20 March 2008 in Ware, Hertfordshire, England, UK
Wilde is best known for starring as "Foggy" Dewhurst for almost all of ***Last of the Summer Wine,*** starting with the 1976 season, a role that he maintained for almost as long as Peter Sallis.'
Guest-starred in (1): "The Fear Merchants"

Anneke Wills, b. Anna Katarina Willys, 20 October 1941 in Fulmer Chase, Buckinghamshire, England, UK
Despite having worked extensively in television from her early teens to her late twenties, Wills is easily best known for her role as Polly Wright in ***Doctor Who*** during the William Hartnell and Patrick Troughton eras. She was married to fellow ***Avengers*** and ***Doctor Who*** guest star Michael Gough from 1962 to 1979, and she retired from acting in 1970 to concentrate on raising a family. By 1980, she left the UK and lived in several countries, including the United States, Canada, and India, where she spent some time in an ashram. She returned to the UK in 1996 and has written two autobiographies since then. She is also a popular convention guest at many ***Doctor Who*** conventions in both the UK and the US and has returned to the show for Big Finish audio productions. Her extensive television credits include ***The Blakes, The Railway Children, Don't Tell Father, Emergency–Ward 10, Gamble for a Throne, No Hiding Place, The Likely Lads, ITV Play of the Week,*** and ***The Saint.*** Her last acting credit before retiring was ***Strange Report*** in 1969-70. Early in her career, she went by Annika Wills or Anneke Willys.
Guest-starred in (2): "Dressed to Kill," "The £50,000 Breakfast"

Douglas Wilmer, b. 8 January 1920 in Brentford, Middlesex, England, UK, **d.** 31 March 2016 in Ipswich, Suffolk, England, UK
Aside from playing ***Sherlock Holmes*** in the 1965 BBC television series, Wilmer is best known for his film work, including ***A Shot in the Dark, Patton, The Vampire Lovers,*** and ***The Golden Voyage of Sinbad.***
Guest-starred in (1): "The Danger Makers"

Frank Windsor, b. 12 July 1927 in Walsall, Staffordshire, England, UK, **d.** 30 September 2020 in London, England, UK
Windsor played the classic television cop Inspector Watt through three series—***Z Cars, Softly, Softly,*** and ***Softly, Softly: Taskforce.***
Guest-starred in (1): "Whoever Shot Poor George Oblique Stroke XR40?"

John Woodnutt, b. 3 March 1924 in London, England, UK, **d.** 2 January 2006 in Denville Hall, Northwood, England, UK
Woodnutt appeared in several BBC classic adaptations of Shakespeare and Antigone, and from 1990-93 played Sir Watkyn in selected episodes of Granada's ***Jeeves & Wooster.*** He had four notable roles in ***Doctor Who***—in "Spearhead from Space" as Hibbert, in "Frontier in Space" as the Draconian Emperor, in "Terror of the Zygons" as Broton and the Duke of Forgill, and in "The Keeper of

Traken" as Seron.
Guest-starred in (1): "Quick-Quick Slow Death"

Catherine Woodville, aka Katherine Woodville, Kate Woodville, **b.** Rosemary Henn Woodville Mason on 12 March 1938 in Ewell, Surrey, England, **d.** 5 June 2013 in Portland, Oregon, USA
Woodville was married to Patrick Macnee from 1965 to 1969. She starred in ***Z Cars*** and ***Danger Man*** in the UK before permanently relocating to the United States in 1967 and subsequently starring in ***Mission: Impossible, It Takes a Thief, Mannix, The Rockford Files, Days of Our Lives,*** and ***Eight Is Enough.*** She is also well-known to ***Star Trek*** fans for her portrayal of Natira in "For the World Is Hollow and I Have Touched the Sky."
Guest-starred in (2): "Hot Snow," "Propellant 23"

John Woodvine, b. 21 July 1929 in Tyne Dock, South Shields, County Durham, England, UK
Woodvine has been a very visible British actor for decades on both sides of the Atlantic. His numerous appearances for television series and TV mini-series have kept him very much in demand. His first major role was as Detective Inspector Alan Witty in ***Z Cars*** from 1968 to 1969. Over the years since, he has been seen in the following mini-series: ***Elizabeth R, Edge of Darkness, The Modern World: Ten Great Writers, Tell Tale Hearts, Oliver's Travels,*** and ***Verdict.*** His latest work is the mini-series, ***Hornblower: The Duchess and the Devil.*** He's also made guest appearances in ***Doctor Who, The Champions, Danger Man, The New Statesman,*** and ***Chelmsford 123.*** One of his most significant movie roles was as Dr. Hirsch in John Landis' ***An American Werewolf in London.***
Guest-starred in (4): "Square Root of Evil," "Dead of Winter," "The Murder Market," "Look – (stop me if you've heard this one) But There Were These Two Fellers..."

Peter Wyngarde, b. 1928 in Marseille, Bouches-du-Rhône, France, d. 15 January 2018 in Chelsea, London, England, UK
Wyngarde was the early 1970s television icon Jason King in ***Department S*** and follow-up series ***Jason King.*** Prior roles had included guest-starring as the No. 2 of the week on ***The Prisoner*** and guest roles on ***The Baron*** and ***The Saint.*** Fined for cottaging in September 1975 and drowning in alcoholism, he was semi-retired for years, working only sporadically, before he returned as the masked Klytus in the camp classic ***Flash Gordon.*** Though this did not quite qualify as a comeback, he worked somewhat more regularly, including stints on ***Doctor Who*** ("Planet of Fire"), ***The Two Ronnies, The Comic Strip Presents...,*** and ***The Lenny Henry Show,*** in performances that generally milked his reputation as a suave decadent type. He managed to live to the ripe age of 90 and acquired a reputation for expertise on many subjects.
Guest-starred in (2): "A Touch of Brimstone," "Epic"

Jeremy Young, b. 1934 in Liverpool, Merseyside, England, UK, **d.** 9 April 2022 in Chelsea, London, UK
Young was one of the stars of the 1960-61 ATV newspaper drama ***Deadline Midnight,*** which briefly displaced ***The Avengers*** in the ITV schedules during October and November of 1961. He would later star in several episodes of the BBC's 1984 adaptation of ***The Tripods*** and a miniseries adaptation of ***Brat Farrar.***
Guest-starred in (4): "A Touch of Brimstone," "Never, Never Say Die," "The Forget-Me-Knot," "Gnaws"

THE SCREENWRITERS

Jeremy Burnham, b. 28 May 1931 in Wharfedale, Yorkshire, England, UK, **d.** 31 December 2020 in UK

Burnham originally started in the business as an actor, performing in many 1950s and 60s television programs from ***Armchair Theatre, Emergency–Ward 10,*** the 1964 version of ***Martin Chuzzlewit, No Hiding Place, United!, The Saint*** and ***The Baron.*** By the late sixties, he turned his hand to screenwriting, and aside from writing for ***The Avengers,*** he penned scripts for ***Paul Temple, Emmerdale, Children of the Stones, Hammer House of Horror,*** and ***Minder.*** He also wrote the screenplay for the Hammer film, ***The Horror of Frankenstein.*** His latest television contribution is ***CI5: The New Professionals.***

Guest-starred in (3): "The Town of No Return," "The Fear Merchants," "The Forget-Me-Knot"

Screenplays (5): "You'll Catch Your Death," "False Witness," "Love All," "Fog," "Who Was That Man I Saw You With?"

Brian Clemens, OBE, **b.** 30 July 1931 in Croydon, Surrey, England, UK, **d.** 10 January 2015 in Bedfordshire, England, UK

Obviously, Clemens was the king of ***Avengers*** writers for having written the largest share of ***Avengers*** episodes; and he was along with Albert Fennell the guiding light for ***The Avengers*** (and ***The New Avengers***) from the fourth season onwards. He was also instrumental in helping to establish the early tone of the series in seasons one and three. However, his writing credits extend far beyond that, having started writing for television in the late 1950s. He wrote nine episodes for ***The Man from Interpol*** in 1960 and then nine episodes for ***Danger Man*** in 1961-62. Other programs include ***Sir Francis Drake, The Baron, The Cheaters, Adam Adamant Lives!, The Champions, The Persuaders!, The Protectors, Bergerac,*** and ***Remington Steele.*** After working on ***The Avengers,*** he created ***Thriller, The Professionals,*** and ***CI5: The New Professionals,*** contributing scripts for those series as well. In cinema, he wrote the script for ***Captain Kronos: Vampire Hunter,*** producing it with Albert Fennell, and also co-wrote ***The Watcher in the Woods.*** He wrote the screenplay for and produced the Hammer film ***Dr. Jekyll & Sister Hyde,*** again with Fennell.

Screenplays (46): "Brought to Book," "One for the Mortuary," "Brief for Murder," "Don't Look Behind You," "Dressed to Kill," "Build a Better Mousetrap," "The Charmers," "The Town of No Return," "Death at Bargain Prices," "A Touch of Brimstone," "What the Butler Saw," "The House That Jack Built," "How to Succeed....at Murder," "Honey for the Prince," "The Bird Who Knew Too Much," "The Living Dead," "The Correct Way to Kill," "Epic," "The Superlative Seven," "The Joker," "Murdersville," "The Forget-Me-Knot," "Split!," "They Keep Killing Steed," "The Interrogators" (with Richard Harris), "The Morning After," "Requiem," "Pandora," "Bizarre," "The Eagle's Nest," "House of Cards," "The Last of the Cybernauts...??," "The Midas Touch," "The Tale of the Big Why," "Faces" (with Dennis Spooner), "Dirtier by the Dozen," "Sleeper," "Three Handed Game" (with Dennis Spooner), "Dead Men Are Dangerous," "Angels of Death" (with Terence Feeley), "Obsession," "Trap," "Hostage," "K is for Kill" (Parts One and Two), "The Gladiators"

Associate Producer: "The Town of No Return" through "Honey for the Prince"

Producer: "From Venus with Love" through "Emily"

Terrance Dicks, b. 10 May 1935 in East Ham, London, England, UK, **d.** 29 August 2019, Hampstead, London, England, UK

Dicks is one of several ***Avengers*** writers that is far better known for ***Doctor Who*** than ***The Avengers,*** having written eight serials for that series as well as serving as script editor for the entirety of the Jon Pertwee era, working closely with producer Barry Letts during that time. He maintained a close association with Letts thereafter, and they would work together frequently. He was script editor for

Moonbase 3 (again produced by Barry Letts), writing one episode for the show. Later, Dicks and Letts would work together on Letts' adaptations of classic novels for the BBC in the early 1980s. Dicks worked as script editor on ***Great Expectations, The Hound of the Baskervilles, Jane Eyre, The Invisible Man, Goodbye Mr. Chips,*** and ***The Pickwick Papers.*** He was also well-known in the 1980s as being the king of the ***Doctor Who*** Target novelisations, writing over sixty titles for the series.
Screenplays (4): "The Mauritius Penny" (with Malcolm Hulke), "Intercrime" (with Malcolm Hulke), "Concerto" (with Malcolm Hulke), "Homicide and Old Lace" ("The Great Great Britain Crime") (with Malcolm Hulke)

Malcolm Hulke, b. 21 November 1924 in Hampstead, London, England, UK, **d.** 6 July 1979 in Cambridgeshire, England, UK
Hulke started his career in television co-writing the successful ***Target Luna, Pathfinders in Space, Pathfinders to Mars*** and ***Pathfinders to Venus*** serials with Eric Paice. These programs were produced by Sydney Newman and were highly successful, establishing Hulke primarily as a science-fiction and fantasy genre writer. He would go on to write for ***Danger Man, No Hiding Place, United!,*** and ***Crossroads.*** But, like many of the writers in this list, it would be ***Doctor Who*** for which he would become best known, co-writing "The Faceless Ones" with David Ellis, and contributing seven more serials during the Patrick Troughton and Jon Pertwee eras—"The War Games" (with Terrance Dicks), "Doctor Who and the Silurians," "The Ambassadors of Death" (uncredited rewrite), "Colony in Space," "The Sea Devils," "Frontier in Space," and "Invasion of the Dinosaurs." He was famous for creating the Silurians, a race of 'aliens' that had been on Earth since the age of the dinosaurs, and their popularity was sufficient for their return in the post-2005 version of the series. He also novelized all his scripts for the Target series of ***Doctor Who*** novels. In the 1970s, he wrote the industry 'Bible' for television writing, ***Writing for Television.*** Sadly, Hulke was not long-lived, passing away in 1979 from lung cancer. He was a close friend of Terrance Dicks, despite their diametrically opposed political views.
Screenplays (9): "The Mauritius Penny" (with Terrance Dicks), "Intercrime (with Terrance Dicks), "The White Dwarf," "The Undertakers," "The Medicine Men," "Trojan Horse," "Concerto" (with Terrance Dicks), "The Grave-Diggers," "Homicide and Old Lace" ("The Great Great Britain Crime") (with Terrance Dicks)

Philip Levene, b. 9 June 1926 in London, England, UK, **d.** 25 March 1973 in London, England, UK
If Brian Clemens is the king of ***Avengers*** writers, then Levene is clearly the crown prince. Levene started out in the industry as an actor in 1955, appearing in small roles on British television and on film, two notable credits being a tiny role in the BBC's ***Quatermass II*** serial in 1955 and an uncredited part in the Hammer film ***X the Unknown*** in 1956. Soon after, he turned to writing with his first professional job being a 1957 episode for ***Hour of Mystery*** called "Sound Alibi." Thereafter, he would work on other series such as ***The Flying Doctor, The Invisible Man, Armchair Theatre, Armchair Mystery Theatre, The Pursuers,*** and ***Ghost Squad.*** Additionally, the German television film ***Ein Augenzeuge*** was based on a translation of his novel. He was one of the most prolific writers for ***The Avengers,*** contributing some of the most memorable scripts and creating perhaps the most iconic foe that the ***Avengers*** ever faced—the Cybernauts. Sadly, Levene died very young, not quite reaching his fifth decade.
Screenplays (19): "The Cybernauts," "Man-Eater of Surrey Green," "Two's a Crowd," "Small Game for Big Hunters," "From Venus with Love," "The Fear Merchants," "Escape in Time," "The See-Through Man," "The Hidden Tiger," "Never, Never Say Die," "Something Nasty in the Nursery," "Who's Who???," "Return of the Cybernauts," "Death's Door," "You Have Just Been Murdered," "Mission...Highly Improbable," "The Curious Case of the Countless Clues," "My Wildest Dream," "Get-A-Way!"

Guest-starred in (1): "Who's Who???"

Peter Ling, b. 27 May 1926 in Thornton Heath, Croydon, London, England, UK, **d.** 14 September 2006 in Hastings, East Sussex, England, UK
Ling is easily best known for having created two popular soap operas, ***Crossroads*** and ***Compact,*** with his writing partner Hazel Adair. He wrote episodes for ***Dixon of Dock Green, Sexton Blake,*** and ***No Hiding Place*** and also penned the perennial fan favorite ***Doctor Who*** serial "The Mind Robber" in 1968. His scripts for ***The Avengers*** tended to have a subtle comedic quality which went a long way towards establishing the series as one that intertwined violence and humor.
Screenplays (3): "Ashes of Roses," "Dance with Death," "Box of Tricks"

John Lucarotti, b. 20 May 1926 in Aldershot, Hampshire, England, UK, **d.** 20 November 1994 in Paris, France
Lucarotti wrote scripts for many television series over the 1960s and 70s, including ***The Protectors, Dr. Finlay's Casebook, United!, Joe 90, Operation Patch, Star Maidens, Treasure Island,*** and ***The Onedin Line.*** Despite all this, he seems to be most remembered for his contributions to ***Doctor Who,*** having written three early historical serials for the program, "Marco Polo," "The Aztecs," and "The Massacre of St. Bartholomew's Eve," which helped to establish that particular subgenre for the series. Another script of his formed the basis for "The Ark in Space," which was rewritten by Robert Holmes.
Screenplays (6): "Double Danger" (adapted from a script by Gerald Verner), "The Far Distant Dead," "Killer Whale," "Death á la Carte," "The White Elephant," "Castle De'ath"

Roger Marshall, b. March, 1934 in Leicester, Leicestershire, England, UK, **d.** 1 April 2020
Marshall went on to create several series—***Zodiac, Public Eye, Kids,*** and ***Mitch***—over the coming decades. He wrote for many other television series as well—***The Sweeney, The Gentle Touch, The Professionals, Travelling Man, Lovejoy, Floodtide, Missing from Home,*** and ***London's Burning.*** His scripts for ***The Avengers*** are easily among the very best with "Dial a Deadly Number" qualifying for a possible Best of Show award.
Screenplays (15): "The Removal Men" (with Jeremy Scott), "Death of a Great Dane" (with Jeremy Scott), "Conspiracy of Silence," "Death of a Batman," "The Gilded Cage," "The Golden Fleece," "Mandrake," "The Hour That Never Was," "Dial a Deadly Number," "Silent Dust," "Room Without a View," "The Girl from Auntie," "The Danger Makers," "A Funny Thing Happened on the Way to the Station" (rewritten by Brian Clemens under the pseudonym Brian Sheriff), "The £50,000 Breakfast" (with Jeremy Scott)

Terry Nation, b. 8 August 1930 in Cardiff, Wales, UK, **d.** 9 March 1997 in Los Angeles, California, USA
Welsh writer Nation is known the world over for having been the creator of the Daleks in ***Doctor Who,*** writing numerous serials for the original run of the show from 1963-1989, including the first Dalek story "The Daleks" in 1964. He also created two well-regarded science-fiction series—***Survivors*** and ***Blake's 7***—and wrote numerous other episodes for television throughout his career, far too many to list here.
Screenplays (6): "Legacy of Death," "Noon Doomsday," "Invasion of the Earthmen," "Take Me to Your Leader," "Thingumajig," "Take-Over"

Eric Paice, b. 13 November 1926 in Pevensey, East Sussex, England, UK, **d.** 6 July 1989 in Cambridge, Cambridgeshire, England, UK
Paice first came to prominence co-writing the successful ***Target Luna, Pathfinders in Space, Pathfind-***

ers to Mars, and *Pathfinders to Venus* serials with Malcolm Hulke. Sydney Newman also produced those serials. Paice also co-created ***Star Maidens*** and ***Buccaneer.*** He later wrote a book called ***The Way to Write for Television.***
Screenplays (8): "Dead of Winter," "The Decapod," "Bullseye," "Death on the Rocks," "Dead on Course," "November Five," "The Little Wonders," "Esprit de Corps"

Dennis Spooner, b. 1 December 1932 in Tottenham, London, England, UK, **d.** 20 September 1986 in Hertfordshire, England, UK
Spooner is somewhat unusual within ***The Avengers*** legend; he is a writer who had almost no professional experience when he began to work on the series. In 1961, he submitted a story outline to the show's producers, they liked it and engaged him to write the full script; and just like that Spooner was a professional screenwriter. Clearly, the production team at Associated British Corporation were excellent talent scouts because Spooner went on to a long career writing for television, becoming a frequent collaborator with Brian Clemens and writing thirteen scripts for both ***The Avengers*** and ***The New Avengers.*** Aside from his association with the two programs, he also penned many scripts for series such as ***No Hiding Place, Fireball XL5, Stingray, Thunderbirds, The Baron, Man in a Suitcase, The Champions, Department S, UFO, Paul Temple, Doomwatch, Jason King, The Professionals, Bergerac,*** and ***Remington Steele.*** He also made highly notable contributions to ***Doctor Who,*** writing several important serials for that series—"The Reign of Terror," "The Romans," "The Time Meddler," and "The Daleks' Master Plan" (with Terry Nation). He also worked on rewrites for "The Power of the Daleks," which was the first serial to feature Patrick Troughton as the lead.
Screenplays (13): "Girl on the Trapeze," "Please Don't Feed the Animals," "Split!" (with Brian Clemens), "Look – (stop me if you've heard this one) But There Were These Two Fellers…," "Cat Amongst the Pigeons," "Target!," "Faces" (with Brian Clemens), "Gnaws," "Three Handed Game" (with Brian Clemens), "Medium Rare," "Complex," "Forward Base," "Emily"

Tony Williamson, b. 18 December 1932 in Manchester, Lancashire, England, UK, **d.** 19 June 1991
Williamson got his start in television writing with ***Shoestring Theatre,*** contributing four scripts to that series from 1961-63. Soon after, he was writing for many other series, including ***Coronation Street, Compact, Armchair Mystery Theatre, The Mask of Janus, The Spies, Danger Man, Adam Adamant Lives!, Dr. Finlay's Casebook, Z Cars, The Champions, Counterstrike, Department S, The Persuaders!,*** and ***Jason King,*** having naturally been asked back repeatedly to write for all the spy and fantasy series on the slate in the United Kingdom in the 1960s and 70s. During the 1970s, he wrote a series of thriller books under the pseudonym Steven Cade and a screenplay for the 1973 film ***Night Watch*** with Elizabeth Taylor and Laurence Harvey. Later, in the early 1980s, he wrote for two Swedish thriller series, ***Fem dagar i december*** and ***Rød snø.*** His final television writing credits were ***Worlds Beyond*** and ***Fire, Ice & Dynamite.***
Screenplays (9): "The Murder Market," "Too Many Christmas Trees," "The Thirteenth Hole," "The Positive Negative Man," "Super Secret Cypher Snatch," "Whoever Shot Poor George Oblique Stroke XR40?," "Killer," "Wish You Were Here," "Stay Tuned"

Martin Woodhouse, b. 29 August 1932 in Romsford, Essex, England, UK, **d.** 15 May 2011 in England, UK
Woodhouse originally trained as a medical doctor, and was also a pilot, an engineer, and a computer designer. He wrote eleven novels. Five of these were techno-thrillers about a man of science hero named Giles Yeoman, three were crime-based, and three were historical fiction novels about Leonardo da Vinci, written with Robert Ross. His stories for ***The Avengers*** frequently explored science or medical subjects. Aside from ***The Avengers,*** he is likely best known for his work on Gerry Anderson's ***Supercar*** with his brother Hugh, and he is credited as a co-creator for the series and as a writer on

twenty-three episodes.
Screenplays (7): "A Chorus of Frogs," "Mr. Teddy Bear," "The Golden Eggs," "The Big Thinker," "Second Sight," "The Wringer," "A Sense of History"

THE DIRECTORS

Jonathan Alwyn, b. 10 October 1930 in London, England, UK, **d.** 29 August 2020
Alwyn directed many television episodes before and since ***The Avengers***, including ***No Hiding Place, Armchair Theatre, Out of This World, Doomwatch, Callan, The Onedin Line***, and ***Juliet Bravo***
Directed (7): "Propellant 23," "Death on the Rocks," "Death Dispatch," "Intercrime," "School for Traitors," "The Secrets Broker," "The Outside-In Man"

Robert Asher, b. 1915 in London, England, UK, **d.** 1979.
Aside from ***The Avengers***, Asher also directed episodes of ***The Baron, The Prisoner, The Saint, The Champions***, and ***The Pathfinders***. He obviously was the go-to director for programs starting with 'The.'
Directed (3): "The See-Through Man," "You Have Just Been Murdered," "Murdersville"

Ray Austin, b. 5 December 1932 in Merton, London, England, UK, **d.** 17 May 2023 in Virginia, USA
Austin is one of the most successful directors to work on ***The Avengers*** and ***The New Avengers*** and went on to a very prominent career in television on both sides of the Atlantic, directing programs as diverse as ***Space: 1999*** and ***Vega$***. His many credits include ***The Professionals, Return of the Saint, Wonder Woman, Hawaii Five-O, B.J. and the Bear, The Love Boat, Simon and Simon, Hart to Hart, V, The Fall Guy, Airwolf, Spenser: For Hire, Magnum P.I., The Return of the Six Million Dollar Man and the Bionic Woman, Highlander, Alfred Hitchcock Presents, Zorro, JAG, Police Academy: The Series***, and ***CI5: The New Professionals***.
Stunt Arranger throughout seasons four, five, and six.
Guest-starred in: "The Grave-Diggers"
Directed (7): "All Done with Mirrors," "Have Guns–Will Haggle," "Gnaws," "Three Handed Game," "Medium Rare," "The Lion and the Unicorn," "Trap"

Bill Bain, b. 18 December 1929 in Wauchope, New South Wales, Australia, **d.** 22 February 1982 in London, England, UK
Bain went on to become a prolific director of British television, directing series such as ***Redcap***, the 1968 BBC ***Sherlock Holmes*** series starring Peter Cushing, ***Manhunt, Armchair Theatre, Callan, Public Eye***, and ***Upstairs, Downstairs***. That last series brought him an Emmy Award in 1975 for Outstanding Directing in a Drama Series for the episode "The Sudden Storm."
Directed (7): "The Undertakers," "November Five," "The Gilded Cage," "Dressed to Kill," "Mandrake," "The Charmers," "What the Butler Saw"

Roy Baker aka **Roy Ward Baker, b.** 19 December 1916 in London, England, UK, **d.** 5 October 2010 in London, England, UK
Baker directed ***The One That Got Away, A Night to Remember, The October Man***, and ***Quatermass and the Pit***. He directed episodes of numerous television shows, including ***The Saint, Gideon's Way, The Baron, The Champions, Department S, Jason King, The Protectors, Minder, The Persuaders!, Return of the Saint***, and ***Danger UXB***.
Directed (8): "The Town of No Return," "Two's a Crowd," "Too Many Christmas Trees," "Silent

Dust," "Room Without a View," "The Girl from Auntie," "The Thirteenth Hole," "Split!"

Don Chaffey, b. 5 August 1917 in Hastings, Sussex, England, UK, **d.** 13 November 1990 in Kawau Island, New Zealand
In film, Chaffey was mainly known for a plethora of fantasy films over the 1960s, 70s and 80s, including ***Jason and the Argonauts, The Three Lives of Thomasina,*** Hammer's ***One Million Years B.C.*** and ***The Viking Queen, Creatures the World Forgot, Pete's Dragon,*** and **C.H.O.M.P.S.** He directed many television shows in Britain throughout the 1960s and 70s and was a favorite director of Patrick McGoohan, who employed him extensively on ***The Prisoner,*** but he worked primarily in American television from the 1980s onwards, including such shows as ***Fantasy Island, CHiPs, Stingray, MacGyver, Vega$, T. J. Hooker, Airwolf,*** and ***Charlie's Angels.***
Directed (5): "Legacy of Death," "Wish You Were Here," "Stay Tuned," "Who Was That Man I Saw You With?," "Requiem"

Charles Crichton, b. 6 August 1910 in Wallasey, Cheshire, England, UK, **d.** 14 September 1999 in South Kensington, London, England, UK
As one of the best remembered directors of his day, Crichton hardly requires my meager introduction here. Suffice to say that he is best known for such classics as ***The Lavender Hill Mob*** and ***A Fish Called Wanda.*** For the latter film, he was nominated for an Academy Award for Best Director as well as an Academy Award for Best Original Screenplay with co-writer John Cleese.
Directed (5): "Death at Bargain Prices," "The Danger Makers," "The Correct Way to Kill," "False Witness," "The Interrogators"

Ernest Day, b. 15 April 1927 in Surrey, England, UK, **d.** 16 November 2006 in Surrey, England, UK
Aside from directing television episodes, Day worked as a second unit director on films such as ***The Spy Who Loved Me, Moonraker,*** and ***Rambo 3.*** Director Robert Day was his brother.
Directed (2): "Angels of Death," "Obsession"

Robert Day, b. 11 September 1922 in Sheen, England, UK, **d.** 17 March 2017 in Bainbridge Island, Seattle, USA
Day made his directorial film debut with ***The Green Man*** in 1956 but went on to direct several 1960s Tarzan films—***Tarzan the Magnificent, Tarzan's Three Challenges, Tarzan and the Valley of Gold, Tarzan and the Great River***—as well as the 1965 Hammer film, ***She.*** Ernest Day was his brother.
Directed (6): "From Venus With Love," "Never, Never Say Die," "Return of the Cybernauts," "The £50,000 Breakfast," "The Positive Negative Man," "Mission...Highly Improbable"

Gordon Flemyng, b. 7 March 1934 in Glasgow, Scotland, UK, **d.** 12 July 1995 in London, England, UK
Aside from his numerous television credits, Flemyng is probably best known for his 1960s ***Doctor Who*** films with Peter Cushing—***Dr. Who and the Daleks*** in 1965 and ***Daleks–Invasion Earth 2150 A.D.*** in 1966. Actor Jason Flemyng is his son.
Directed (2): "The Fear Merchants," "The Winged Avenger"

Cyril Frankel, b. 28 December 1921 in Stoke Newington, London, England, UK, **d.** 7 June 2017 in England, UK
Frankel directed episodes of several British television programs, including ***Randall and Hopkirk (Deceased), Department S,*** and ***UFO.*** He also directed Joan Fontaine in her final film performance in the Hammer film ***The Witches*** in 1966.

Directed (1): "Whoever Shot Poor George Oblique Stroke XR40?"

Robert Fuest, b. 30 September 1927 in Croydon, London, England, UK, **d.** 21 March 2012 in London, England, UK
Artistic director Fuest is easily best known in cinema for his macabre pair of cult films, ***The Abominable Dr. Phibes*** (an ***Avengers*** plot if there ever was one!) and ***Dr. Phibes Rises Again.*** He started out in television as a designer on many television series, including ***The Avengers,*** before leaving to direct television adverts. Later, he was invited back to ***The Avengers*** by Albert Fennell to work on the final season with Linda Thorson. He found fellow director Peter Hammond to be greatly influential when they worked together on the show in the early 1960s.
Directed (9): "Game," "They Keep Killing Steed," "The Rotters," "Take Me to Your Leader," "My Wildest Dream," "Take-Over," "Pandora," "The Midas Touch," "The Tale of the Big Why"

Peter Hammond, b. 15 November 1923 in London, England, UK, **d.** 12 October 2011 in London, England, UK
Though Don Leaver just edges out Hammond for directing the most episodes of ***The Avengers,*** Hammond was a prolific and reliable creative force for the show during its formative early years. Between he and Leaver, they directed the critical first four episodes, establishing the all-important look of the series. Elsewhere in television, he directed episodes of ***Armchair Theatre, Out of the Unknown, Cold Comfort Farm, Rumpole of the Bailey, Tales of the Unexpected, The Return of Sherlock Holmes,*** and ***Inspector Morse.*** Hammond also did some acting in the 1940s and 50s, appearing in the early Hammer film ***X The Unknown*** in 1956 and on television in ***The Buccaneers*** in 1956-57.
Directed (19): "Brought to Book," "Nightmare," "Diamond Cut Diamond," "Hunt the Man Down," "One for the Mortuary," "The Frighteners," "Death on the Slipway," "The Far Distant Dead," "Dragonsfield," "Bullseye," "Death of a Great Dane," "Warlock," "The Golden Eggs," "Conspiracy of Silence," "Brief for Murder," "The Second Sight," "The Golden Fleece," "Don't Look Behind You," "Build a Better Mousetrap"

Richmond Harding, b. 28 September 1923 in Isleworth, London, England, UK, **d.** 21 October 2010 in Salisbury, Wiltshire, England, UK
Harding directed episodes of the following series: ***The World of Tim Frazer*** (which he also produced); the ITV program ***Out of This World; Z Cars, Swizzlewick; Coronation Street; The Flying Swan;*** and ***Emergency–Ward 10.*** He also worked as a third unit director (uncredited) on ***Scott of the Antarctic*** in 1948. He is credited with the suggestion to put Honor Blackman in leather for her portrayal of Cathy Gale. Little other information on his career is available, with his credits ending in 1967, though he lived well into his eighties.
Directed (7): "Mr. Teddy Bear," "The Mauritius Penny," "Traitor in Zebra," "Dead on Course," "Immortal Clay," "The White Dwarf," "Six Hands Across a Table"

Sidney Hayers, b. 24 August 1921 in Edinburgh, Scotland, UK, **d.** 8 February 2000 in Altea, Spain
Like many quality directors, Hayers began his career as a camera operator, focus puller and film editor. He edited several notable films, including ***The One That Got Away*** and ***A Night to Remember*** (both with Roy Ward Baker directing). By the late 1960s, he was well-established in British television, directing such series as ***The Human Jungle, The Persuaders!, Arthur of the Britons, The Zoo Gang, The Professionals,*** and ***The Famous Five.*** By 1980, he was working in America and finding steady employment on such series as ***Galactica 1980, The Fall Guy, The Greatest American Hero, Remington Steele, Philip Marlowe, Private Eye, Manimal, T.J. Hooker, Airwolf, Knight Rider, The A-Team, The Scarecrow and Mrs. King, Dragnet, The New Adam-12, Baywatch,*** and ***Acapulco Heat.*** By the early 1990s, he was back in Europe, directing episodes for the French Tarzan series ***Tarzán***

and the Gerry Anderson series ***Space Precinct***. His last directing credit was for ***CI5: The New Professionals*** in 1999. He died of cancer in Spain in 2000.
Directed (12): "The Cybernauts," "A Surfeit of H_2O," "Man-Eater of Surrey Green," "The Hidden Tiger," "The Superlative Seven," "The Joker," "Death's Door," "Dead Man's Treasure," "The Last of the Cybernauts...?," "Dirtier by the Dozen," "Dead Men Are Dangerous," "Hostage"

James Hill, b. 9 July 1919 in Eldwick, Yorkshire, England, UK, **d.** 7 October 1994 in London, England, UK
Hill was a highly prolific director whose work spanned over five decades. He is likely most famous for his film shorts, ***Giuseppina*** and ***The Home Made Car***, both of which were nominated for Academy Awards with the former winning the Academy Award for Best Documentary (Short Subject). His output was also notably diverse, and he directed a variety of films, including ***Black Beauty*** in 1971, the 1965 Sherlock Holmes film ***A Study in Terror*** starring John Neville, the 1969 science-fiction film ***Captain Nemo and the Underwater City***, again with John Neville, the 1966 wildlife drama ***Born Free***, which became an international hit, and the spy spoof film ***The Man from O.R.G.Y.*** On television, in 1979-81, he produced and directed nearly the entire first series of ***Worzel Gummidge***, as well as its follow-up ***Worzel Gummidge Down Under*** in 1987 and 1989, both with Jon Pertwee playing the lead.
Directed (10): "Castle De'ath," "Quick-Quick Slow Death," "A Touch of Brimstone," "Honey for the Prince," "Epic," "Something Nasty in the Nursery," "The Forget-Me-Knot," "Look – (stop me if you've heard this one) But There Were These Two Fellers...," "To Catch a Rat," "Faces"

John Hough, b. 21 November 1941 in London, England, UK
After working as a second unit director on ***The Baron***, ***The Champions*** and ***The Avengers***, Hough made his directorial debut on "Super Secret Cypher Snatch" in 1968. Later, he directed the 1969 adventure film ***Wolfshead: The Legend of Robin Hood***, which was originally intended to be a television series, and the Hammer film ***Twins of Evil*** in 1971. By the mid-1970s, he was working for Disney and directed three classic films, ***Escape to Witch Mountain***, ***Return from Witch Mountain***, and ***The Watcher in the Woods***—the latter two with screen legend Bette Davis.
Directed (5): "Super Secret Cypher Snatch," "The Morning After," "Fog," "Homicide and Old Lace," "Cat Amongst the Pigeons"

John Krish, b. 4 December 1923 in London, England, UK, **d.** 7 May 2016 in UK
Krish is probably best known for his documentary short film ***I Think They Call Him John*** in 1964 and the thriller ***Out of the Darkness*** in 1985.
Directed (3): "Escape in Time," "The Living Dead," "Something Funny Happened on the Way to the Station"

Don Leaver, b. 27 September 1929 in London, England, UK, **d.** December 13, 2015 in England, UK
Leaver is the all-time directing champion for ***The Avengers***, but it was a case of far more than quantity, as his taut, carefully-timed direction went a long way towards establishing the early style of the show. He was in fact one of only two directors (the other being Bill Bain) to be retained into the film era of the series. He was also a frequently used director on ***Police Surgeon***, so there is a long line of continuity. He went on to a long career in British television and never seemed to suffer for lack of work, frequently working as director and producer on many series. His credits include ***Out of This World***, ***Public Eye***, ***Armchair Mystery Theatre***, ***The Informers***, ***The Gold Robbers***, ***Man at the Top***, ***Armchair Theatre***, ***The Protectors***, ***Zodiac***, ***Special Branch***, ***Operation Patch***, ***Rooms***, ***Hammer House of Horror***, ***Bergerac***, ***Mitch***, ***Prime Suspect***, ***A Touch of Frost***, ***A Fine Romance***, and ***The Bill***.

Directed (20): "Hot Snow," "Square Root of Evil," "Girl on the Trapeze," "Ashes of Roses," "Dance with Death," "The Springers," "The Yellow Needle," "Toy Trap," "Dead of Winter," "A Change of Bait," "The Decapod," "Mission to Montreal," "The Removal Men," "The Sell-Out," "Man with Two Shadows," "The Wringer," "Esprit de Corps," "Dial a Deadly Number," "The House That Jack Built," "How to Succeed....At Murder"

Kim Mills, b. 22 October 1930 in London, England, UK, **d.** 28 August 2006 in London, England, UK
Mills went on to direct episodes of series like ***The Protectors, Mystery and Imagination, The Mind of Mr. J.G. Reeder, The Rivals of Sherlock Holmes, Shadows of Fear, Armchair Theatre, Public Eye,*** and ***Rooms.***
Directed (10): "The Big Thinker," "Box of Tricks," "Man in the Mirror," "Killer Whale," "Death of a Batman," "The Medicine Men," "The Grandeur That Was Rome," "Death à la Carte," "Concerto," "Lobster Quadrille"

John Moxey, aka **John Llewellyn Moxey, b.** 26 February 1925 in Argentina, **d.** 29 April 2019 in University Place, Washington, USA
Soon after ***The Avengers,*** Moxey went to America where he directed a variety of television series like ***Mannix, Kung Fu, Charlie's Angels, The Scarecrow and Mrs. King,*** and ***Magnum P.I.*** He also directed a slew of slightly cheesy television movies in the late 1970s, such as ***The President's Mistress, The Courage and the Passion, Ebony, Ivory and Jade,*** and ***Killjoy*** (starring a young Kim Bassinger).
Directed (1): "Who's Who???"

Leslie Norman, b. 25 February 1911 in Fulham, London, England, UK, **d.** 18 February 1993 in Knebworth, Hertfordshire, England, UK
Norman directed the Hammer film ***X the Unknown*** in 1956 and ***Dunkirk*** with John Mills, Richard Attenborough and Bernard Lee in 1958. On television, he directed episodes of ***The Saint, Department S, The Persuaders!,*** and ***Return of the Saint.***
Directed (2): "Thingumajig," "Bizarre"

Gerry O'Hara, b. 1924 in Boston, Lincolnshire, England, UK, **d.** 9 January 2023
O'Hara directed episodes of ***Man in a Suitcase*** and ***The Professionals,*** as well as films like ***Leopard in the Snow*** (with Keir Dullea). Prior to ***The Avengers,*** he worked extensively as a second unit director on such films as ***Tom Jones*** in 1963.
Directed (2): "The Hour That Never Was," "Small Game for Big Hunters"

Roy Rossotti, b. 1931, **d.** 19 May 2008 in Epsom, Surrey, England, UK.
Rossotti worked as a second unit director on ***Doctor Zhivago*** in 1965.
Directed (1): "The Bird Who Knew Too Much"

Peter Graham Scott, b. 27 October 1923 in East Sheen, Surrey, England, UK, **d.** 5 August 2007 in Windlesham, Surrey, England, UK
Scott worked as an actor, a film editor, a director and a producer over his lengthy career. In cinema, he was responsible for the editing on ***Brighton Rock*** in 1947. He directed the Hammer film ***Captain Clegg*** in 1962 and produced ***Father Came Too!*** in 1964. On television, he directed episodes of ***Danger Man, The Prisoner, Children of the Stones,*** and ***Into the Labyrinth,*** producing the latter two series as well.
Directed (3): "The Master Minds," "The Murder Market," "A Sense of History"

Don Sharp, b. 19 April 1921 in Hobart, Tasmania, Australia, **d.** 14 December 2011 in Cornwall, England, UK

Sharp was one of the more storied directors to work on ***The Avengers*** and is mostly known today for his contributions to Hammer films. He fought in World War II with the RAAF, and after being discharged with the rank of colonel in 1944, he embarked on a career as an actor. After arriving in England in 1948, he acted in films such as ***The Planter's Wife, Appointment in London,*** and ***The Cruel Sea.*** By 1955, he had turned to writing and directing, working on the children's film ***The Adventures of Hal 5*** with future ***Doctor Who*** actor William Russell. By 1961, he was directing television series like ***Ghost Squad*** and ***The Human Jungle.*** His biggest break however came in 1963 when he was asked to direct ***The Kiss of the Vampire*** for Hammer films, and this led to a series of directing jobs for Hammer and other genre-oriented studios; this included ***Rasputin the Mad Monk, Curse of the Fly, The Face of Fu Manchu,*** and ***The Brides of Fu Manchu.*** He also directed the Tony Randall film ***Our Man in Marrakesh*** in 1966. His later career would involve the remake of ***The Thirty Nine Steps*** in 1978 and a return to television (and Hammer) with ***Hammer House of Horror*** and ***Q.E.D.*** in 1980 and 1982 respectively.

Directed (3): "Invasion of the Earthmen," "The Curious Case of the Countless Clues," "Get-A-Way!"

Peter Sykes, b. 17 June 1939 in Melbourne, Victoria, Australia, **d.** 1 March 2006

Australian director Sykes was responsible for horror nightmares such as ***Demons of the Mind*** in 1972 and Hammer Film Productions' penultimate film ***To the Devil A Daughter*** in 1976 with Richard Widmark, Christopher Lee and Honor Blackman. He also directed ***Steptoe and Son Ride Again,*** the second of two films based on the popular television series.

Directed (2): "Noon Doomsday," "Love All"

RELATED MEDIA

"KINKY BOOTS" (1964)

This novelty song—recorded by Honor Blackman and Patrick Macnee for a segment of ***That Was the Week That Was***—was released on Decca Records in February of 1964 and had no significant impact at the time. Later, in 1990, after being promoted by BBC Radio One DJ Simon Mayo, it reached number 5 on the charts in the UK. It was backed with an equally puerile track, "Let's Keep It Friendly." Though admittedly the song does tend to stick in the brain, not in a good way, it proves that the actors should have best stuck to acting. Reportedly, Patrick Macnee had no sense of rhythm at all and had to be tapped on the shoulder in order to know when to sing.

THE DIADEM (1966)

Starring Diana Rigg
Directed by Uwe Beetz

This 20-minute short film was produced in Germany and featured Diana Rigg as an Emma Peel variant who retrieves her stolen golden key from criminals who are intent on taking her piggy bank from a locked strongbox in her home. The film's second part "The Diadem in Color" deals with finding a diadem in a darkened house occupied by spies with stockings over their heads. In the finale, the spies are chucked by Rigg into a moat outside the house. The first seventeen and a half minutes are in black and white, but the final two and a half minutes are in color. It was shot in Germany on 8mm film and features no dialogue. I find it remarkable that Diana Rigg was capable of taking a break from filming ***The Avengers*** in 1966, and indeed that Beetz was able to hire her at all. An even more incomprehensible 7-minute cutdown of the first part of this film exists as "Der Goldene Schlüssel." For reasons unknown, it includes color versions of the same shots that are in black and white in "The Diadem."

DER GOLDENE SCHLÜSSEL (1966)
Starring Diana Rigg
Directed by Uwe Beetz

This 7-minute short starred Diana Rigg as an Emma Peel-type character who flies her own plane and has a dolphin tank in her apartment building. A frogman swims into her home through a series of locks in her basement in order to steal a golden key on a necklace, which magically teleports into the pool for the frogman to find. The dolphins do nothing to stop this. The key opens a strongbox which contains a piggy bank. Two attempts are made to steal this piggy bank, each one unsuccessful, and the film is left with no resolution. The German title translates literally as "The Golden Key." This incomprehensible version of the film was apparently a cutdown of "The Diadem." It is unknown why these shots are in color when they are in black and white in the longer version.

MINIKILLERS (1969)
Starring Diana Rigg, Jose Nieto, Jack Rocha, H. Coscollin, Mme. Million, and El Sali
Written by Michael von Chmielewski and Wolfgang von Chmielewski
Directed by Wolfgang von Chmielewski
Produced by H. G. Lückel and D. Nettemann
Score by Jonny Teupen and M. Rettenbacher

This four-episode series of seven-minute shorts was filmed in Catalonia by a German crew. Shot for the 8mm film market, they star Diana Rigg as (ostensibly) Emma Peel, or some rough facsimile, fighting criminals while on vacation in Costa Brava. There is no dialogue, just music. The title apparently refers to the killer 1960s 'walking dolls' with poisoned tears that are employed by the masterminds. While the titles alone are hilariously cracked and the soundtrack very badly miked (or dubbed), the film series obviously had something of a budget, given that they were able to hire Diana Rigg in addition to a fair-sized yacht and many actors and extras. The series is most notable for a surprisingly adept surrealistic sequence in the second episode that begins with Rigg lounging on the beach. To her surprise, dozens of mannequins pop out of the sand around her along with a giant fishing net that captures both her and the mannequins, dragging the entire collection to a yacht moored in the harbor. The musical score demonstrates a mélange of jazz, flamenco, and disco elements and is nothing if not noteworthy for the alacrity with which it is played.

ESCAPADE (1978)
"I Thought It Was Someone I Knew"
A Quinn Martin Production
Starring Granville Van Dusen and Morgan Fairchild
Written and Produced by Brian Clemens
Directed by Jerry London

This tepid late 1970s *Avengers* 'remake' might give the 1998 *The Avengers* film a run for its money—in terms of its failure. The story follows two American Secret Service agents who try to find another 'runaway' agent by following clues inside stuffed teddy bears. Beset by all the hallmarks of the era, including a relentless disco-flavored musical soundtrack with extra "pooh, pooh, pooh" sounds, *Escapade* never lets up with the boredom. The two leads occasionally produce wit and chemistry, but it's hit-or-miss most of the time, and the reimagining of Mother as a giggling computer named Oz comes across as about five years out of date conceptually. It's genuinely hard to believe that Clemens wrote this. The sad part is that I think it's at least conceivably possible that an American show could be made to capture the class, wit, and fun of the original series, but maybe it wasn't possible back then with the television industry being what it was, or maybe it wasn't possible by Clemens, London, Van Dusen, Fairchild, et. al. In any case, this really isn't worth anyone's time.

THE AVENGERS (1998)
A Jerry Weintraub Production
A Jeremiah Chechik Film
Written by Don MacPherson
Produced by Jerry Weintraub
Directed by Jeremiah Chechik
Editor—Mick Audsley
Production Designer—Stuart Craig
Director of Photography—Roger Pratt, DSC
Executive Producer—Susan Ekins
Music by Joel McNeely
Titles by Imaginary Forces

CAST
John Steed—Ralph Fiennes
Dr. Emma Peel—Uma Thurman
Sir August de Wynter—Sean Connery
Invisible Jones—Patrick Macnee
Mother—Jim Broadbent
Father—Fiona Shaw
Bailey—Eddie Izzard
Alice—Eileen Atkins
Trubshaw—John Wood
Brenda—Carmen Ejogo
Tamara—Keeley Hawes
Donavan—Shaun Ryder
Dr. Darling—Nicholas Woodeson
Butler—Michael Godley
Boodle's Porter—Richard Lumsden
Messenger—Daniel Crowder
World Council of Ministers—Nadim Sawalha, Christopher Godwin, David Webber

My initial reaction to this film was perhaps slightly more charitable than I shall be here, and yet my view of this film is not nearly so harsh as the general *Avengers* fandom may be inclined to intone. Suffice to say that this fan-abrasive, Razzie-winning effort was not well-received, nor is it well-remembered some twenty years later. And while I acknowledge its considerable shortcomings, I feel that some of the criticism lodged at it was slightly unfair and based on expectations that were likely unreasonable. It remains nevertheless a mixed bag with a core failing that cannot be underestimated.

It should be noted from the outset that the lead actors for the film, Ralph Fiennes and Uma Thurman, totally fail to capture the chemistry and personalities of their predecessors, and a considerable amount of that failing lies with screenwriter Don MacPherson. For a start, Fiennes is a fair number of years too young, a tad too casual, and yet paradoxically way too rigid to be Steed. Not once does he manage Patrick Macnee's casual insouciance, his gentle charm, his boyish glee, nor that gentle winking knowingness that is tipped to the audience, letting us know that he's really having loads of fun no matter how serious the moment is. Instead Fiennes' Steed is all stiff upper-lip and buttoned up. He's the suit without the personality.

Uma Thurman's Dr. Peel is equally lacking. Rather than Dame Diana Rigg's stylish flippancy, tempered by a keen intellect and a plethora of skills, Thurman portrays something of a vacuous nineties rebel girl with the ease and seeming invulnerability that is generated by the possession of loads of money. Never once does she manage one of Diana Rigg's wry smiles that betray her amusement at the situations placed before her, completely lacking those winsome expressions that break through her fearless implacability in the face of danger. Rigg's Mrs. Peel was brave because she was enormously capable and self-assured. Thurman's version is comparatively fragile, as if a pale shadow of her predecessor frozen behind glass, and one gets the impression that she merely thinks she's special and indomitable but may in fact fracture at any moment.

In the television series, the original characters came across as best friends who knew they were unstoppable, only occasionally worried about failure, usually laughing their way to victory. The show was absurd—they knew it and the audience knew it, and no one bothered to pretend otherwise. It didn't have to make sense; it was just fun. It was about the relationship of John Steed and Mrs. Peel—two invincible friends. Without that indelible specialness and unique chemistry, the film was doomed to a mere superficial approximation of the series—surreal villains, fencing, bowler hats, Bentleys, and umbrella-fighting.

But it seems clear to me that the production was unable to see or capture that. That may sound unfair—you would expect anyone that sets off on a production of a major motion picture to be at least moderately familiar with the subject if not outright fanboys—but the evidence is interspersed throughout the entire script. Screenwriter MacPherson's misunderstanding of the characters could not be summed up better than with these lines:

Emma: "Rules were made to be broken."
Steed: "Not by me."

These two lines speak volumes about how off base the production was with regard to John Steed and Emma Peel. To suggest that Emma was some kind of rebel, some sort of iconoclast, is about 180 degrees wide of the mark. To suggest that Steed was some kind of stick-in-the-mud rules matron is equally absurd.

Emma was a bit upper-class and lofty, but she was also warm, modern and fun-loving; it was the mixture of these qualities that made her so appealing, but there's nothing about her to suggest that she worked in espionage because she was rebelling against the system. It seems to me that the reasoning behind this extraordinary reinterpretation of the character was to sell the awkward doppelgänger subplot that features a fake Mrs. Peel who is sabotaging Ministry efforts. But if you have to change the personality of a key character wholesale in order to make your narrative work...well, maybe you're on the wrong track. And then to explain Emma's extraordinary talent that they should dive further into the depths of banality with, "My father always wanted a boy..."! Oh dear, not that old cliché! All I can say is: nail in the coffin, this character is dead on arrival.

With reference to Steed, he was well-known for being a rogue, a manipulator, for being a caddish confidence man, legendary for his bluffs. If, on the other hand, that erroneous line was meant to reference his predilection for the trappings of the traditional gentry, then it still missed by a country mile, for those preferences were largely superficial. The real Steed had far more depth than his car, umbrella and bowler.

Another critical error was choosing not to make the film an obvious period piece, for it completely displaces the characters in a way that saps their potential. This mistake had been made before, albeit much more subtly with the consequences far less noticeable. In ***The New Avengers*** in 1976, Steed was updated slightly—he drove Jaguars instead of Bentleys and moved to a country estate with horses. This was forgivable to a large degree. After all, in the 1970s, his style was still vaguely in the realm of believability, especially considering that Macnee was over fifty years old. He could after all be someone's grandfather. On the other hand, by apparently placing Fiennes' Steed in the 1990s and presenting his clothing and style just as it was in the original series, he becomes just a thirty-something hipster choosing to wear his grandfather's clothes.

Having said all that, Fiennes and Thurman are two actors that I have come to admire greatly for their work since. They are most assuredly very capable actors, and their later work speaks for itself—however much their failure here might have cost this film. I will also say in their defense that it is never the fault of the actor when he or she is miscast, and in fairness to everyone involved I'm not sure if anyone could have completely captured the essence of the original characters. That's how unique and special their chemistry was.

Beyond this criticism of the core characters, which I admit is a very substantial requirement for the film's success, I do not think that the typical fan criticism is particularly well justified. Most negative reviews cite the surrealistic elements, such as the teddy bear suits worn by the villains, the weather control technology used, or the mechanical flying bees. It has to be said that none of these set pieces are at odds with the original program at all. If you have a problem with the teddy bear suits, why would you not have a problem with the talking teddy bear in "Mr. Teddy Bear"? If the weather control technology is your concern, then why would you not have a problem with "A Surfeit of H2O"? If you don't like the mechanical flying bees, then why not take issue with "The Cybernauts"?

Incidentally, the latter scene was probably the best sequence in the film overall, despite overly aggressive attempts to update it to modern special effects. Surely, this was the intention. I was orders of magnitude more bothered by the little old lady from the Ministry with a machine gun who stops them in the middle of the road. She stops them at the exact point where a gunman is waiting to ambush them. Why? So, she can shoot the gunman apparently. Why didn't the gunman shoot her before the *Avengers* arrived? Why would she stop them at a point of maximum danger? Why indeed is she standing in the middle of the road with a machine gun in the first place? The whole scene is pointless, conveying information that could have easily been delivered in some other way. It screams of a vain attempt to create surrealism and a fanboy moment by scooping superficial elements from the series.

Fortunately, the teddy bear sequence is the funniest in the film and comes the closest to capturing the spirit of the color Diana Rigg era. It's the old spy film cliché of the SPECTRE-style supervillain about to kill anyone who opts out of their scheme, and it's milked for all it's worth, the tension thrust in our faces many seconds in advance. This tension is comically enhanced by the widened button eyes of the teddy bear suits that cleverly betray the trepidation of their occupants.

Sean Connery is the aforementioned supervillain and he's clearly having a ball not caring about the film or the events therein. His loathing seems to transcend the narrative and strike out towards the film itself. Connery appeared to know he was acting in a likely bomb, but it enhanced his performance. He is above it all and this translates into an onscreen arrogance and nonchalance that we seldom see from the actor. This is fortunate since August de Wynter as a character isn't that much to work with—largely a cookie cutter villain. By contrast, Fiennes and Thurman were working overtime just to muster a tenth of what their predecessors managed, seeming like shallow props for the most part.

The film is graced by the voice of Patrick Macnee as Invisible Jones, who provides a brief distillation of pure nostalgia with his dulcet tones. He declines to fully materialize however, as if uncertain how the whole *Avengers* film pastiche will be received. On one strong note, Mother and Father work well enough as characters, and frankly, as a great fan of Jim Broadbent, I enjoy his version of Mother far more than Patrick Newell's. His performance is probably the best in the movie. Fiona Shaw as Father is also doing a good job, and their dialogue together is a highlight, the closest it comes to the typical wit of *The Avengers*.

Nevertheless, the fact that this is the best thing that can be said about the film—that two minor characters who only appeared in the final season of the original series should be the only part of the film that truly captures its spirit—is proof enough that the film was struggling mightily, scrambling to put together some semblance of the original series and falling short consistently. Is it as bad as many will claim? No, not really. Trust me, get out to the theater more often—there are much worse films coming out every single year! But it is true that the cinematic version of *The Avengers* is a pale alternate-universe shadow of the television series.

BIG FINISH
THE AVENGERS—THE LOST EPISODES (2014-2017)

Adaptations of all twenty-six season one episodes

Regular Cast
Anthony Howell—Dr. Keel
Julian Wadham—John Steed
Lucy Briggs-Owen—Carol Wilson
Dan Starkey—One-Ten

Adapted by: John Dorney
Producer: David Richardson
Executive Producers: Jason Haigh-Ellery and Nicholas Briggs
Music and Sound Design: Toby Hrycek-Robinson

These audio adaptations of Season One of *The Avengers* are really quite enjoyable. Though scripts exist for only fifteen missing episodes of the season, and three episodes exist in their entirety on film, Big Finish has re-created all twenty-six of the Steed and Dr. Keel adventures. Nevertheless, the fact that eight episodes have only synopses and some Tele-snaps or production photographs to work from makes recreations for those stories mere guesswork. Largely, the audios seem faithful, but the atmosphere seems rather 'roomy,' unconvincing and lacking in aural depth. Then again, this is the nature of radio drama, and by and large, the actors and writers do a good job of re-creating the feel of the original series. Indeed, this is the only current way that twenty-three episodes of this particular season can truly be enjoyed. Whether it is the casual fan or the diehard, these productions are well-worth exploring.

DVD AND BLU-RAY REVIEWS

The Avengers—The Complete Series 2, 2009, Optimum Releasing Ltd./StudioCanal (DVD)
The Avengers—The Complete Series 3, 2010, Optimum Releasing Ltd./StudioCanal (DVD)

It should first be noted that these DVDs are Region 2 only and are of superior quality to the DVDs available in Region 1 through A&E Home Video. The source material for these episodes is necessarily inferior to most DVD material today. It is the result of a multi-staged process of recording, each of which produced its own layer of artifacts, which includes videotape dropouts, video off-locks, sound dropouts, and film dirt and sparkle. This inevitably results in an image quality that is substandard (and even challenging) by today's standards. The original video was only 405-lines, which is technically not even up to the DVD standard. Though if the original videotapes were available in playable condition, the result would be razor sharp lines and relatively good quality, the available material was kinescoped (telerecorded) to 16mm film in the 1960s. The nature of telerecording in those days was somewhat inconsistent with contrast, sharpness, and frame alignment varying from week-to-week. Additionally, the exterior sequences were shot on 16mm or 35mm film and then telecined live into the recording of the program. Telecine equipment available in the 1960s was vastly inferior to digitizing techniques available today (high-definition film scanners), and these location sequences typically look terrible compared to the in-studio video recordings. If the original films for these sequences still existed, then they could be scanned in with a high-definition scanner, and the end result would look amazing. Alas, the films are not known to exist.

Despite all this, these episodes look better than they ever have on this latest release. StudioCanal have performed a reasonable amount of correction and cleanup, boosting contrast and removing the most severe artifacts. The sound quality has also been improved over previous releases and for the most part is clear and present without much distortion or hiss. The extras are extensive and include scanned original scripts in PDF format for all episodes starting with "Mr. Teddy Bear." They also include "A Change of Bait" and some extracts from "Hot Snow."

My only notable complaint is the rather irritating menu transitions with the outrageously loud musical sting and the fact that StudioCanal insists on making one watch their corporate logo video prior to the beginning of every episode—this is completely unnecessary as we've already seen it at the beginning of the disc. The Series 2 DVDs also include most of the available Season One episodes, the first act of "Hot Snow," "Girl on the Trapeze," and "The Frighteners." "Tunnel of Fear" is not included as it was recovered several years after this DVD release.

The Avengers—The Complete Series 4, 2015, StudioCanal Limited (Blu-ray)
The Avengers—The Complete Series 5, 2015, StudioCanal Limited (Blu-ray)
The Avengers—The Complete Series 6, 2015, StudioCanal Limited (Blu-ray)

These Blu-rays are a fabulous release and a worthy addition to every fan's collection. Particularly beautiful is the release of season four. Black and white always looks amazing when properly scanned in high-definition, and this release has some of the richest, deepest blacks and the subtlest highlights I've seen on any black and white Blu-ray release. A pleasing natural film grain is visible upon close inspection but never intrudes. While not all artifacts have been cleaned up—some film scratches are evident—they have all been minimized and are never visible when viewed from a comfortable distance. The audio is especially clear and bright without any notable hiss or distortion. My one complaint is that the title sequences look a little less sharp and are dirtier in general than the remainder of the films. Some also show scratches, while others don't. It seems logical to me that they could have simply cleaned up one version of the title sequence thoroughly and then dropped in the credits for each individual episode.

The extras are extensive and include many nuggets of interest to the more serious *Avengers* fan. There are many commentaries with the surviving production crew, including Roy Ward Baker, Brian Clemens, Roger Marshall, Gerry O'Hara, and Don Leaver. Also, see the section on Season One for a list of the available reconstructions for that season.

The release for Series 5 (as they call it) is also very well restored. However, there is some notable inconsistency in contrast and black levels throughout the release. The early episodes appear to have greyish blacks and less contrast overall. However, by the later episodes, the situation seems to reverse and the blacks are very deep, almost overpowering. In between, you will see a few that are nearly perfected balanced, but this is rare. Nevertheless, most viewers will be unlikely to notice or care as the films look better than they ever have before. Perhaps in keeping with the cartoonish colors used throughout the season, the color palette is very rich, vibrant, and saturated. The overall picture quality is amazingly sharp with skin texture and other details visible in closeups.

The extras are extensive for this season as well, including commentaries from Brian Clemens, Peter Wyngarde, Richard Harris, and Cyd Child. And there are more reconstructions for Season One, as well as the independent films "Minikillers" and "The Diadem," starring Diana Rigg.

The release for Series 6 continues in the same vein as Series 5 but has perhaps even better restoration with more consistent film quality and contrast throughout. This is perhaps owing to better film preservation. The colors also generally appear more natural than in the prior release though still vibrant and saturated. Some of the earliest episodes filmed for this season appear to be the least well preserved and the least saturated for reasons that I cannot explain.

The extras are again remarkable and include commentaries from Roy Ward Baker, Brian Clemens, Jeremy Burnham and Veronica Strong, Jennifer Croxton, John Hough, Robert Fuest, and Cyd Child. Plus, there are filmed introductions to several episodes by Linda Thorson. Look out for more Season One reconstructions as well.

The Complete New Avengers, 2012, StudioCanal Limited (DVD)

I've said it before and I'll say it again—StudioCanal, *please* update ***The New Avengers*** with a high-definition release! For quite some time, StudioCanal had misplaced the original camera negatives, and as a result, these DVDs were sourced from analog telecines made in the 1990s. There is a fine veil of distortion over the entire image. Overall, it is soft, even for a DVD. Fine details are invisible, the colors are drab, and the image frequently vignettes out to the edges of the screen. Though film dirt and other artifacts are not overly problematic, every time I look at these episodes I contemplate how beautiful they might look with a high-definition scan from the original negatives. The audio is fairly clear and present without much in the way of hiss or distortion. There are some commentaries with Gareth Hunt and Brian Clemens. The menu system blares the theme music repetitively with every menu selection, and there is no Play All option nor even an option to simply play a single episode.

As far as collecting ***The New Avengers*** into one volume, this release gets the job done, but the series desperately needs to be updated into the 21st century with a high-definition release and more extras.[1]

1 The original 35mm film negatives have since been found, and while Network had been working on a high-definition release, sadly, they went out of business in March 2023 and the project was abandoned. The single episode "The Last of the Cybernauts...??" was released on Blu-ray as part of a Cybernauts collection. However, this is currently the only HD release of ***The New Avengers***, and it's likely to be the last for quite some time.

BIBLIOGRAPHY

(These publications were the primary written sources used in the preparation of this book)

Britton, Barker—***Reading Between Designs: Visual Imagery and the Generation of Meaning in The Avengers, The Prisoner, and Doctor Who***—University of Texas Press, 2003.

Cornell, Day, Topping—***The Avengers Dossier***, 1998, 2013, Virgin Books/Gollancz eBook, London, UK

Richardson, Michael—***Bowler Hats and Kinky Boots: The Unofficial and Unauthorised Guide to the Avengers***, 2014, Telos Publishing Ltd, Kent, England, UK

McGinlay, Hayes, Hayes—***Two Against the Underworld: The Collected Unauthorised Guide to The Avengers Series 1*** (Revised Edition), 2017, Hidden Tiger, UK

Wiseman, Jaz—***The Avengers—Series One Episode Guide – Leonard White's Series One Scrapbook***, 2009, Optimum Releasing

The Avengers: The Honor Blackman Years (Limited Edition Book), 2023—Unstoppable Editions, Essex, England, UK

Hearn, Marcus—***The Avengers—A Celebration: 50 Years of a Television Classic***, 2010, Titan Books, London, UK

Macnee, Rogers—***The Avengers: The Inside Story***—Titan Books, London, England, UK

Leigh, Gary (compiled and edited by)—***The DWB Interview File—The Best of the First 100 Issues—Sydney Newman Interview***

Pixley, Andrew – ***The Avengers Files***, 2004, Reynolds & Hearn Ltd, Richmond, Surrey, UK

Rogers, Dave – ***The Avengers***, 1983, Independent Television Books Ltd, London, UK

Rogers, Dave – ***The Avengers Anew***, 1985, Michael Joseph Ltd, London, UK

Rogers, Dave – ***The Complete Avengers***, 1989, Boxtree Limited, New York, NY, USA

Rogers, Dave—***Ultimate Avengers***, 1995—Titan Books, London, England, UK

Bignell, Franks, Robinson – ***Nothing at the End of the Lane: The Magazine of Doctor Who Research and Restoration***, Issues One and Two Collected, 2008, Kent, England, UK

Molesworth, Richard – ***Wiped! Doctor Who's Missing Episodes***, 2nd Edition, 2013, Telos Publishing, London, UK

Fulton, Roger – ***The Encyclopedia of TV Science Fiction***, 1990, 1997, Boxtree Ltd, London, UK

Cornell, Day, Topping – ***The Guinness Book of Classic British TV***, 2nd Edition, 1996, Guinness Publishing Limited, Middlesex, UK

(Websites referenced)

Johnson, Piers—***The Fashion Guide to The Avengers and the New Avengers***—https://www.dissolute.com.au/the-avengers-tv-series/fashion/

The Internet Movie Cars Database—https://www.imcdb.org/movie_54518-The-Avengers.html

(The reviews in this book are based on what is seen on the television screen or heard in audio form. The sources used were the following DVD/BD and audio releases)

Wiseman, Jaz – ***The Avengers—The Complete Series 2***, 2009, Optimum Releasing Ltd./StudioCanal (DVD)

Wiseman, Jaz – ***The Avengers—The Complete Series 3***, 2010, Optimum Releasing Ltd./StudioCanal (DVD)

Wiseman, Jaz – ***The Avengers—The Complete Series 4***, 2015, StudioCanal Limited (Blu-ray)

Wiseman, Jaz – ***The Avengers—The Complete Series 5***, 2015, StudioCanal Limited (Blu-ray)

Wiseman, Jaz – ***The Avengers—The Complete Series 6***, 2015, StudioCanal Limited (Blu-ray)

The Complete New Avengers, 2012, StudioCanal Limited (DVD)

Big Finish Audios—***The Avengers–The Lost Episodes***—Digital Download (2014-2017)

ABOUT THE AUTHOR

Michael originally worked in technology, first as a systems engineer, then as a web designer and a graphic designer, slowly morphing towards more creative endeavors. He is also an accomplished oil painter and enjoys film photography and studying languages in his spare time.

Quite Quite Fantastic! The Avengers for Modern Viewers was Michael's first book on television; The Grande Marque Edition would be the second. However, in one way or another he has been writing about television since the late 1980s, having written newsletters or maintained websites on the subject throughout the 1990s and early 2000s, one of which inspired this book. More recently, he has written three science fiction novels, including *When Morpheus Overslept*, *Beyond the Empyrean*, and *The Lightning-Struck Tree* (all a part of the ongoing *Along Time's Edge* series) with more on the way.

Michael has lived in both the Atlanta Metro area and Western North Carolina, USA.

EPISODE INDEX

Index Code

A	The Avengers
NA	The New Avengers
###	Episode Number
(First Digit)	Season Number
(Second Digit)	Production Order
(Third Digit)	Transmission Order (using the earliest known UK transmission dates)

Printed in Dunstable, United Kingdom

72796749R00301